STUART FISHER

RIVERS

ESTUARIES, TIDEWAYS, HAVENS, LOCHS, FIRTHS AND KYLES

OF BRITAIN

ADLARD COLES NAUTICAL
LONDON

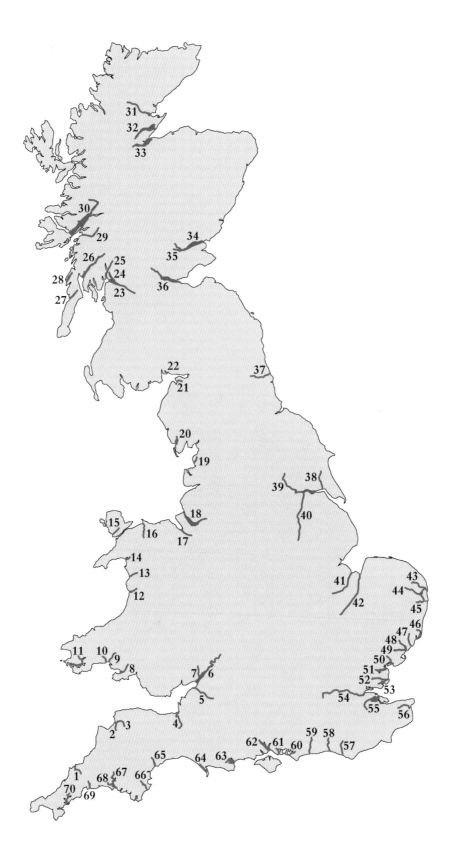

Published by Adlard Coles Nautical
an imprint of Bloomsbury Publishing Plc
50 Bedford Square
London
WC1B 3DP
www.adlardcoles.com

First edition published 2012
Copyright © Stuart Fisher

ISBN 978-1-4081-4656-9

The right of the author to be identified as the author of this work has been asserted by him in accordance with the Copyright, Designs and Patents Act, 1988.

A CIP catalogue record for this book is available from the British Library.

This book is produced using paper that is made from wood grown in managed, sustainable forests. It is natural, renewable and recyclable. The logging and manufacturing processes conform to the environmental regulations of the country of origin.

Printed and bound in India by Replika Press Pvt Ltd

Contents

Acknowledgements

P6 from *Old Friends* by John Betjeman.

P9 from *The Revenge* by Alfred, Lord Tennyson.

P12 from *Troy Town* by Sir Arthur Quiller-Couch.

P15 from *A Trampwoman's Tragedy* by Thomas Hardy.

P18 from *Bristol* by John Betjeman.

P23 from *In Memoriam A H H* by Alfred, Lord Tennyson.

P30 from *Wonderings* by John Masefield reproduced by permission of Lisa Dowdeswell for The Society of Authors as the Literary Representative of the Estate of John Masefield.

P36 from *Egret on the Loughor Estuary* by Caroline Gill reproduced by permission of Caroline Gill.

P38 from *Grongar Hill* by John Dyer.

P42 *The Cleddau* by Andrew Woolnough.

P47 from *The Bells of Aberdovey* by Charles Dibdin.

P49 from *Penmaen Pool* by Gerard Manley Hopkins.

P57 from *The Bard* by Thomas Gray.

P61 from *The Sands of Dee* by Charles Kingsley.

P65 from *Ferry Cross the Mersey* by Gerry Marsden reproduced by permission of Robert Pratt for Gerry Marsden.

P72 from *The Long Drive* by John Masefield reproduced by permission of Lisa Dowdeswell for The Society of Authors as the Literary Representative of the Estate of John Masefield.

P74 from *Valedictory Sonnet to the River Duddon* by William Wordsworth.

P78 from *The Outlaw Murray*, Anon.

P80 from *The Song of the Clyde* by R Y Bell.

P89 from *The Old Soldier of the Gareloch Head* by John Stuart Blackie.

P92 from *The Bloody Sarks* by Ian Hall.

P95 from *Epigram at Inveraray* by Robert Burns.

P99 from *The Lord of the Isles* by Sir Walter Scott.

P101 by John Marsden reproduced by permission of Peter Burns, Birlinn Ltd.

P104 from *The Lord of the Isles* by Sir Walter Scott.

P109 from *The Lord of the Isles* by Sir Walter Scott.

P119 from *Men of Worth* by Archie Fisher.

P123 Anon.

P127 from *The Tay Bridge Disaster* by William Topaz McGonagall.

P132 from *The Lady of the Lake* by Sir Walter Scott.

P134 from *The Lord of the Isles* by Sir Walter Scott.

P142 from *The Fog on the Tyne* by Alan Hull.

P149 from *Come to Britain* by A P Herbert.

P153 from *Rokeby* by Sir Walter Scott.

P158 from *Sirena* by Michael Drayton.

P163 from *Epigram on Rough Roads* by Robert Burns.

P167 from Main Drain pumping station, Anon.

P174 from *Norfolk* by John Betjeman.

P179 from *Singing the Fishing* by Ewan MacColl reproduced by permission of Kerry MacColl for Ewan MacColl Ltd.

P186 by Hugh Bigod.

P190 from *Peter Grimes* by George Crabbe.

P194 from *An Old World Fairway* by Michael Weaver.

P197 from *Felixstowe, or The Last of Her Order* by John Betjeman.

P200 from *Nightmare* by Sir W S Gilbert.

P202 from *River to River* by Martin Newell reproduced by permission of Martin Newell.

P205 from *The Battle of Maldon*, Anon.

P213 from *Punch*.

P236 from *The Dutch in the Medway* by Rudyard Kipling.

P243 from *Murder in the Cathedral* by T S Eliot.

P247 from *Sussex* by Rudyard Kipling.

P251 from *They Died for England* by A F W Eade.

P254 by David King.

P260 Anon.

P268 by James Henry Pye.

P272 from *The Dead Quire* by Thomas Hardy.

P276 from *Moonfleet* by J Meade Falkner.

P280 from *Exeter* by John Betjeman.

P282 Anon.

P286 from *Drake's Drum* by Sir Henry Newbolt.

P293 *The Harbour of Fowey* by Sir Arthur Quiller-Couch.

P297 from *The Love Gift* by John Masefield reproduced by permission of Lisa Dowdeswell for The Society of Authors as the Literary Representative of the Estate of John Masefield.

Every effort has been made to trace authors. A & C Black are happy to correct any error or omission in future editions.

Introduction

Tidal rivers are a unique part of our waterways system, waters which can be overlooked yet can also be very special places. They are where inland rivers finally morph into estuaries, tideways, havens, sea lochs, firths and kyles and then into open ocean, sometimes with aspects of both inland rivers and the sea, sometimes with conditions common to neither, but always memorable places.

They can be very different from each other. Such mighty and historically important rivers as the Thames, Medway, Mersey, Tyne and Clyde are worlds apart from small rivers which wind across flat coastal marshes, empty into rocky sea lochs or feed popular holiday inlets in the West Country. Some, such as the Severn and the Dee, have seen major changes to their natures during recent centuries from major transport links to places too silted up for craft of any size.

A surprise might be the number of superlatives related to these tidal rivers. Time after time we meet Britain's, Europe's or the world's largest, oldest or other prime example of manmade or natural feature. They are often overlooked wildernesses on our doorsteps. Here are the best of human and natural environments, sometimes masquerading as muddy channels. It would be a mistake to ignore them.

Some can drain at their lower ends to leave water which may be too shallow to use and that is frequently lined with banks of silt, which can make landing impossible. However, all that mud is also a haven for birdlife and there is no better way to see it without causing disturbance than from a boat, from huge flocks of waders circling around to individual egrets picking carefully over what morsels are available. Higher reaches can be narrow and tree-lined or edged with reeds, places for more secretive birds to hide. Larger animals can also find refuge from people in what can be, literally, a no-man's-land. Walkers and cyclists discover that visiting this environment can be a chance for them to leave the crowds behind, too, and get off the beaten track, perhaps following great embankments all day with just the sea and the broad sky for company, rarely meeting another person.

Yet other people have been here before and places now unimportant can be steeped in history and in stories which may or may not be fully believable. Kings, queens, Prime Ministers and notable names of lesser pedigree turn up in the most unexpected places.

In the way of adventure playgrounds, the lower ends of tidal rivers bring new challenges for users. Inland boaters have to face and be aware of tides and of ocean waves, which create new safety issues. Sometimes sailing in estuaries can also mean interaction with large craft and industrial or naval complexes. The offshore sailor used to the open ocean can be faced with limited channels and swift currents. Rivers can offer shelter from bad weather or can form traps from which it is hard to escape. Narrowing routes can be restricting for those under sail at the same time as avoiding craft restricted to fairways by their size. Once upstream of tidal water there can be a need for licences or matters of private ownership.

Walkers and cyclists also need to be aware of potential issues and sometimes be as informed about tides as are those on the water. Lack of bridges in remoter areas can be restricting, including over side channels. On the other hand, bridges can often be dramatic, some of our most impressive engineering.

Because of unfamiliar problems, estuaries are often ignored by those whose comfort zones restrict them to inland waters or to the open sea. Here there are challenges to be met but here is also a special environment which can be missed all too easily.

Stuart Fisher

Legend for maps

——— Featured river
——— Other canal or river
■■■ Motorway
——— Other road
——— Railway

▨ Open water or sea

▨ Inter-tidal zone

▢ Built-up area

▨ Woodland

Scale 1:200,000.
North is always at the top.

Photographs

Jim Chapman p270 bottom
Les Chatfield p250 top
Becky Fisher p263 top two
Jim Linwood p275 top
Craig Morley p267 bottom
Angie Muldownie p270 top, p271
David Shapter p195 top left
Iain Simpson p249 bottom left
John Stratford p176 top left
David Striker p188 centre
All other photographs by the author.

Footnote: In Scotland there is a right to use all waters at all times subject to reasonable behaviour, as is normal in most countries. The right to navigate tidal waters in England and Wales is generally undisputed. However, with the exception of a small minority of rivers, most of which require licences, it is claimed by some that there is no right of navigation on some 98 per cent of the non-tidal rivers in England and Wales. Research for a law degree by the Revd Dr Douglas Caffyn suggests that what is being applied is not the law but a series of errors made in the legal textbook *A Treatise of the Law of Waters & of Sewers* of 1830, when water transport was in decline and there was negligible recreational use of rivers, so the mistakes had less significance back then than they do today. Caffyn claims the right of navigation on inland waters in England and Wales has never been lost and has challenged anyone to dispute his findings. Nobody has done so, including DEFRA lawyers who have been reviewing his work since 2004. This book has deliberately restricted its scope to tidal waters, not least while waiting for DEFRA to resolve the legal confusion. For further information see caffynonrivers.co.uk if you are concerned about navigation rights upstream of the waters covered in this book.

By same author
Canals of Britain
(abbreviated CoB in reference panels), 2009
Inshore Britain, 2006

1 River Camel

Where St Petroc and Rick Stein landed

The tide is high and a sleepy Atlantic sends
  Exploring ripple on ripple down the Polzeath shore,
And the gathering dark is full of the thought of friends
  I shall see no more.
John Betjeman

The River Camel rises on Hendraburnick Down, just 5km from Cornwall's north coast. It flows south to Bodmin, following the western edge of Bodmin Moor, before turning northwest and returning to the north coast.

The tidal limit is at Polbrock. The river quickly runs out of momentum and has become placid by the confluence with the River Allen which rises near to the Camel at Camelford and runs parallel all the way. The Camel's banks are lined with sand in which bands of peat can be seen and boats begin to appear on them. There swans and lapwings congregate in flocks.

Wadebridge is the first place where more than a handful of houses are seen together and is based around the 17 arch bridge, of which 13 arches remain visible. The downstream half was built in the 15th century, making use of an island in the river. Before that it was a dangerous ford and there were chapels at each end where travellers could pray before attempting the crossing. Even now there are quite fast rapids beneath the bridge at some stages of the tide although these don't seem to worry the ornamental ducks on the island.

There is a chip shop on the right bank although most of the town is on the left beyond a children's playground. Amongst other facilities are a supermarket and the Bridge on Wool public house. Waterside industry includes boatyards, a builders' yard and a coachworks. Slipways come down to the water by the old quay but the port went into decline with the silting up of the river and the coming of the railway in 1899.

In turn, the railway is no more, having now become the Wadebridge Padstow Path which follows the south bank of the estuary.

The A39 passes high over the estuary on a recent bridge.

The tidal limit at Polbrock.

The bridge at Wadebridge has a tidal rapid beneath.

The estuary below Cant Hill, drained at low water.

The Royal Cornwall Showground, as befits this agricultural centre, overlooks the estuary opposite the confluence with the River Amble at Trewornan, a treelined cleft which is spoilt only by a caravan site located in it.

A windmill dominates the hilltop above Trevelver but the main feature of the upper estuary is the rounded bulk of Cant Hill with Cant Cove and Gentle Jane cutting into its two flanks. The south bank is tame by comparison, its most obvious features being a great heap of rock slab debris and a three arched steel railway viaduct at the foot of Dennis Hill which bears an obelisk to Queen Victoria.

The widest part of the estuary is the pool although it can still have strong tides of over 6km/h. The Camel is the largest inlet in north Cornwall and it is alive with sailing, water skiing and other craft in the summer. Rock Sailing & Water Ski Club is based in an old grain warehouse which is prominent behind the moorings in Porthilly Cove. Strangely, Rock is predominantly sand, just about the only place in the estuary not dominated by rock.

In the summer passenger ferries cross to **Padstow** and have done so since at least the 14th century. They have become an important link in the South West Peninsula Coast Path which follows down both banks of the estuary.

The ferries' route into Padstow is now dictated by the Town Bar and different landing points are used at high and low water. Padstow has an ancient quay and a fishing harbour used by coasters up to 1,300t but only when the tide permits. It was once the most thriving port in north Cornwall, handling fish, wine, slate, ores, timber and Cornish emigrants to America. It was one of the towns to which rioting tin miners headed during hard times. Now it has dinghies, shark angling and powerful sightseeing boats which thunder off down the estuary. Until 1952 it had the largest lifeboat in Britain. The current one is based in an award winning building of 2007. The North Quay has a sobering shipwreck chart. A lobster hatchery is located near the lifeboat station.

Associations with the sea have been long. St Petroc, son of a Welsh king, sailed from Wales with 60 followers to what became Petrocstow in the 6th century, struck water from a rock and founded a monastery, sacked by the Vikings in 981. Padstow has been the ecclesiastical capital of Cornwall. The present St Petroc's church of 1425–50 (with part of the tower from much earlier) has a 15th century font carved from blue Catacleuse stone which outcrops near Trevose Head. It has carved scallop shells on the pulpit to record pilgrims to the shrine of St James in Santiago.

Sir Walter Raleigh presided in the courthouse on the South Quay while Warden of the Stannaries of Cornwall and much of the town remains unchanged with narrow streets. On May Day the 'Obby 'Oss takes to the streets in the oldest dance ceremony in the British Isles, based on pagan origins. Museum exhibits in the town include photographs and documents about the area, tools used in shipping, agriculture and the home, shipwrecks, maritime and lifeboat themes, a collection of minerals and items from the Southern Railway. Chef Rick Stein has nine different restaurants in the town. A tropical bird and butterfly garden has 200 species of tropical birds and a collection of exotic and unusual plants although palms grow quite

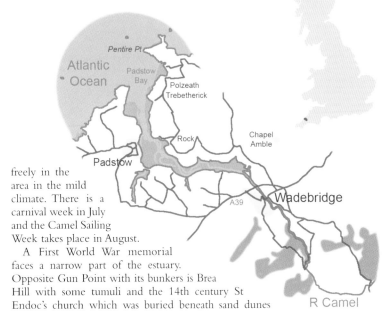

freely in the area in the mild climate. There is a carnival week in July and the Camel Sailing Week takes place in August.

A First World War memorial faces a narrow part of the estuary. Opposite Gun Point with its bunkers is Brea Hill with some tumuli and the 14th century St Endoc's church which was buried beneath sand dunes

7

for hundreds of years and is where John Betjeman is buried.

The Doom Bar led to the decline of Padstow as a shipbuilding and trading port, inconveniencing over 300 vessels which fell foul of it. Fed by the easterly longshore drift which brings sand into the estuary, it changes shape after gales, storms or prolonged periods of northwesterly winds and can create conditions to challenge expert surfers. The sea breaks on the bar at low water and at other stages of the tide large breakers can roll up the Narrows to break in columns of spray at the south end of Harbour Cove if conditions are right.

The coastguard station at Hawker's Cove was formerly the lifeboat station before it became too silted up. There is a 12m daymark on Stepper Point.

If the sea is rough, Daymer Bay is the last safe landing point, kitesurfers permitting. Deposits of glacial till outcrop at Trebetherick and the beach is backed by cliffs. Surfing is banned from the beach.

Ahead lies Pentire Point, composed of knobbly pillow lavas, and the prominent island of Newland. Exit is possible in Hayle Bay at Polzeath but the groundswell is almost always present, the bay faces west and if there is surf anywhere in north Cornwall it will be found here as it traps the waves. The surf is at its biggest around low tide and, although its break is not as fast as some, it can be big. Waves of 2–3m rolling in at the ends of the day are not unusual.

Near to hand are a large car park, the Galleon Café and takeaway, stores, supermarket and toilets with hot showers.

Distance
14km from Polbrock to Padstow Bay

OS 1:50,000 Sheet
200 Newquay & Bodmin

Admiralty Charts
1149 Pendeen to Trevose Head (1:75,000)
1156 Trevose Head to Hartland Pt (1:75,000)
1168 Harbours on N Coast of Cornwall. Approaches to Padstow (1:25,000). River Camel – Padstow to Wadebridge (1:25,000)

Tidal Constants
Wadebridge:
HW Dover −0550,
LW Dover −0220
Padstow:
HW Dover −0550,
LW Dover −0540

Sea Area
Lundy

Rescue
Inshore lifeboat: Rock
All weather lifeboat: Padstow

The Rock Sailing & Water Ski Club clubhouse is a listed building, a former grain warehouse.

Newland, Pentire Point and Hayle Bay at Polzeath.

2 River Torridge

Fighting the Spaniards, fact and fiction

So Lord Howard past away with five ships of war that day,
Till he melted like a cloud in the silent summer heaven;
But Sir Richard bore in hand all his sick men from the land
Very carefully and slow,
Men of Bideford in Devon,
and we laid them on the ballast down below;
Alfred, Lord Tennyson

The River Torridge is home to two major books, *Tarka the Otter* and *Westward Ho!* It is the latter which relates particularly to the estuary although Tarka does swim its length.

The Torridge rises on Welsford Moor and flows southeast then north across Devon to the River Taw. It is tidal from Halfpenny Bridge at Annery Kiln, a toll bridge in the past.

Initially there are stone rapids, drowning out as the tide rises, but these soon give way to mudflats edged by reeds. Numbers of salmon and trout in the river have been much reduced by farm pollution.

The Torrington or Rolle Canal joins beneath powerlines. In use from 1825 to 1871, it brought tub boats down from Torrington, exporting agricultural produce and importing limestone and coal. Restoration can be seen at Sea Lock and its basin.

A wooded reach results in dead trees lying in the shallows on each side of the river but it is wide enough for these not to cause obstruction.

The A386 cuts across a loop of the river at Landcross, scene of the duel between Will Cary and Don Guzman in *Westward Ho!* Mallards and kingfishers are found around the saltmarsh with its sea aster, levées protecting the insides of bends although steep woods constrain the outsides of bends below Hallspill. Otters are still present on the river, as are herons.

A bridge which formerly carried a railway to take clay from Meeth to Bideford quay now has nothing more onerous than a cycle track over it. The River Yeo joins immediately below it, near old limekilns.

The road comes back alongside and a significant cliff

Restoration of the bottom lock on the Torrington Canal.

faces the river above Bideford where the rock has been cut back to accommodate the road.

Bideford is best known for its Grade I listed Long Bridge, carrying the B3233. It also carries the Southwest Coast Path which follows both banks downstream. It had been planned to build the bridge 800m upstream but *Westward Ho!* relates how the materials were moved down each night until an angel told the parson, Sir Richard Gurney, to build it where the materials were left, as a result finding the only firm foundations in the vicinity.

The tidal limit rapid at Annery Kiln bridge.

Fallen trees along the edge of the river at Landcross.

Built in 1286 in timber, it had masonry added around the outside in about 1500. There are two dozen pointed arches, 3.7–7.6m wide. Each was donated by a different village, the size reflecting the size of the sponsoring village. This provides quite a restriction on the flow, resulting in a drop of up to 300mm in the water level at the bridge. In 1968 the two arches at the Bideford end collapsed. Because of chloride attack to the 1925 cantilevered concrete footways it has one of the largest cathodic protection systems of its kind in the country. It takes the local church bell 22 seconds to strike 8 o'clock and a race is held across the bridge each June to try to beat the clock.

This is the start of the Port of Bideford. The town received its charter in 1272 and it was Britain's third largest port by the 16th century. Sir Richard Grenville's *Revenge* was crewed by Bideford men and a brass plate in the church by the bridge records how he died from wounds while fighting 15 Spanish ships in 1591. The church also has a medieval tower and a Norman font which was used to baptize the first Red Indian in England.

In the 17th century there was wool trade with Spain and between 1700 and 1755 it imported more tobacco than London did, trading with the West Indies and North America. Small coasters now export ball clay and import fertilizer and gravel. Fishing vessels also use the quay and the passenger ferry *MV Oldenburg* operates to Lundy. Shipping movements and loads are posted, the public being allowed to use the treelined quay when loading is not taking place.

Charles Kingsley wrote part of *Westward Ho!* in the Royal Hotel, formerly a merchant's house. Another hotel is the Rose of Torridge, Rose Salterne, *Westward Ho!*'s beauty, having that appellation.

Victoria Park has an Armada cannon. The Burton Art Gallery & Museum has ship models (including some by Napoleonic prisoners of war), shells, paintings, ceramics and pewter. Old Ford House has West Country crafts. Bideford was where Susanna Edwards, Mary Trembles and Temperance Lloyd were convicted as witches in 1682, mostly on their own evidence as they seemed to have a death wish.

At the other end of Bideford Bridge is East-the-Water,

The steep wooded bank below Hallspill.

Bideford Bridge, the Long Bridge, undergoes repairs.

home of the 1900 trading schooner *SV Kathleen & May*, the last registered West Country merchant topsail schooner. The three master was retired in 1960 and is now a museum piece. There is also restored railway track with a diesel engine, a buffet carriage, a carriage housing the Railway Carriage Visitor Centre and a replica signal box containing Bideford Railway Museum.

Flood embankment protects the salterns as the 1987 Torridge Bridge carries the A39 high over the estuary. Cliffs overlook the water with wrecks and activity which ranges from rowing to water skiing, water where the depth changes frequently. Herring and blackbacked gulls, egrets and cormorants supervise the mud.

At Westleigh is the William & Mary house of Tapeley with fine 18th century ceilings, porcelain and furniture. It is set in 8ha of the 19th century Georgian Tapeley Park Gardens with Italian terraces, shell house and ice house.

A history of shipbuilding is ongoing at Northam where Appledore Shipbuilders use the 1969 shed which forms Europe's largest covered shipyard, handling craft to 13,000t, bulk carriers, supply vessels and survey ships. Local craftsmen have built replicas of a Roman galley, a Viking longboat, the *Golden Hinde* and the *Nonsuch,* the ship which led to the founding of the Hudson Bay Company in 1668. The area featured in Kipling's Stalky stories.

The Royal Marines use landing craft from Zeta Berth on the opposite shore. In earlier days it was limekilns which were a centre of boating activity.

Appledore has had salmon fishing for over a millennium although bass, cockles, winkles and scallops are more common these days. Some houses in Appledore are from the 16th century but most, often colour-washed, are 19th century. The 1846 quay takes ships to 800t. It was made a free port by Elizabeth I for its part in helping to defeat the Armada. It built 200 Napoleonic War ships in 15 years but shortages of wood in the 19th century resulted in Appledore men going to Prince Edward Island to build

The Kathleen & May *moored at East-the-Water.*

their boats and then sailing them home. The North Devon Maritime Museum in Odun House, formerly the home of shipowners, merchants and mariners, covers naval and merchant marine services, fishing, shipbuilding, Prince Edward Island, rescue, piloting, Vikings, wrecking and local smuggling with tools, models and paintings. A 1948 Appledore salmon boat is a rare survivor, it being usual to burn them when their owners died. There is an Appledore Book Festival in the autumn.

A passenger ferry crosses to Instow with its 17th century quay. A rare 1873 signal box is listed but the level crossing is now used for a cycleway crossing a road, a situation becoming more common these days. Instow attracts artists for the light and cricketers for the North Devon Cricket Club. Instow Sands lead to dunes and wooden leading light towers at the end of the Port of Bideford as the River Taw is joined.

Bideford waterfront. The Rose of Torridge was the discredited heroine of Westward Ho!

The Torridge Bridge takes the A39 clear of Bideford and its medieval crossing.

Distance
11km from Annery
Kiln to the River Taw

OS 1:50,000 Sheets
180 Barnstaple
& Ilfracombe
190 Bude & Clovelly

Admiralty Charts
1160 Harbours in
Somerset & N Devon.
Barnstaple & Bideford
(1:25,000)
1164 Hartland Pt to
Ilfracombe inc Lundy
(1:75,000)

Tidal Constants
Bideford:
HW Dover −0520,
LW Dover −0500
Appledore:
Dover −0520

Sea Area
Lundy

Rescue
Inshore lifeboat:
Appledore
All weather lifeboat:
Appledore

3 River Taw

Sandbanks and services

Fare thee well, Barnstaple steeple, –
Fare thee well, I say,
Never shall I see thee, once agen, a long time ago.
Sir Arthur Quiller-Couch

The River Taw rises on Hangingstone Hill on Dartmoor, near to the sources of the Dart and the Teign, but flows north across Devon and then west to Bideford Bay. It is tidal from the A377's New Bridge although early stone rapids only drown out at the top of the tide. Levées soon

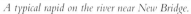

A typical rapid on the river near New Bridge.

The church tower in the woods at Tawstock.

contain the river, moorhens and farmyard geese are on the water and pheasants are on the banks.

Codden Hill provides a long ridge pointing at the river. Topped by a monument, a significant viewpoint, it is 141m high, allowing paragliders to soar above Bishop's Tawton.

An ancient gatehouse is hidden in the trees next to the church tower at Tawstock.

Barnstaple used to have three railway stations but it now has only a single terminus, served by the line from Exeter, these days known as the Tarka Line as this is again *Tarka the Otter* territory. The line has followed the Taw closely since Nymet Rowland and crosses at Little Pill opposite a tower on a hillside.

The A39 crosses on a high 1989 bridge at Lake. High tension powerlines also cross over at Lake with a barely visible angling line reaching down from one cable to the water in the centre of the river. A further railway crossing is on a former railway bridge, now carrying the Tarka Trail for cyclists, Tarka having swum the length of the estuary.

Barnstaple's medieval bridge now carries only local traffic.

Saltmarsh near Penhill Point.

Barnstaple begins with the North Devon Leisure Centre on the south side, offering swimming, squash, badminton and bowls, facing a road with riverside lights ornamented with dolphins, the Imperial Hotel and a decorative clocktower. Herring and blackbacked gulls, mallards, swans, Canada geese and cormorants use the intervening river.

Crossing the river is the Grade I Long Bridge of about 1280, the gift of a London trader. With 16 pointed arches of 5.5–7.9m span, it was partly destroyed in 1437 and again in 1646. As well as the road, it carries the Southwest Coast Path which follows both banks downstream.

Barnstaple is the oldest borough in the UK, having received its charter in 930 from King Athelston and with a mint from 979. A 10th century walled Saxon stronghold, it was captured in 1068 by the Normans. A 1318 church has fine 17th century wall monuments and a twisted wooden spire with a lead coating. Little newer is the 1330 chapel of St Anne, now a museum with pottery, clocks and local life. Barum ware is slipware pottery, the town having made pottery since the 13th century. The Three Tuns inn was a merchant's house of 1450.

The port supplied Armada ships. It is now silted up and little used commercially except for bringing in some sand and gravel at high water. Its trading peaked in the 17th century with links to North America. The old people's rest centre in Queen Anne's Walk was built in 1609 as the Tuscan colonnaded Exchange, a meeting place for shipowners and merchants who placed their bids on the Tome Stone. The Penrose Almshouses also date from this period. Barnstaple changed sides several times during the Civil War. It was the birthplace of John Gay, who wrote *The Beggar's Opera* in 1728, and it was Hardy's Downstaple.

The Pannier Market has farm produce and handicrafts under a roof on iron columns. A wooden canopy covers Butcher's Row, opened in 1855, when all 33 of its shops were occupied by butchers. In 1996 it was judged the Prettiest Floral Town in Europe. It has the Museum of North Devon and the Barnstaple Heritage Centre.

A four day fair in September begins with spiced ale to an Elizabethan recipe, served in silver cups from which all must drink, a white glove being hung in the Guildhall to show that outsiders may trade.

Beyond the Riverfront Café is an austere seven storey civic centre, next to which is the River Yeo, crossed by a modern swing bridge but usually with little water in it. Most of the fast flood comes in the last two hours to high water. At other times the Taw has extensive flats and many dead leads, the channel changing position from day to day as far as Fremington. The A361 crosses on a high bridge from Sticklepath to the industrial estate at Pottington.

From 1874 to 1970 there was a railway line along the north bank towards Ilfracombe while another on the south bank led up the Torridge valley. Now both are gone. A church spire marks Ashford, which was home to R D Blackmore.

Yellow sandbanks contrast oddly with the dark clay banks of the estuary itself. Saltmarsh on the south side to Penhill Point sees creeks cutting in between

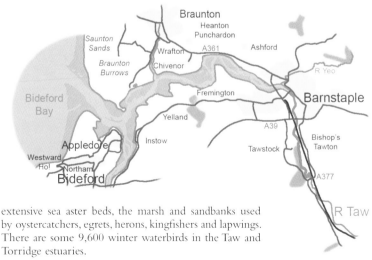

extensive sea aster beds, the marsh and sandbanks used by oystercatchers, egrets, herons, kingfishers and lapwings. There are some 9,600 winter waterbirds in the Taw and Torridge estuaries.

Yellow sandbank near Penhill Point contrasting with the brown mud bank of the estuary.

Distance
18km from New
Bridge to Bideford
Bay.

OS 1:50,000 Sheet
180 Barnstaple
& Ilfracombe

Admiralty Charts
1160 Harbours in
Somerset & N Devon.
Barnstaple & Bideford
(1:25,000)
1164 Hartland Pt to
Ilfracombe inc Lundy
(1:75,000)

Tidal Constants
Barnstaple:
HW Dover −0510,
LW Dover +0500
Fremington:
HW Dover −0510,
LW Dover −0500
Yelland Marsh:
HW Dover −0510,
LW Dover −0440

Sea Area
Lundy

Range
Braunton Burrows
danger area

Rescue
Inshore lifeboat:
Appledore
All weather lifeboat:
Appledore

The castellated restaurant at Heanton Court overlooks the Bassett's Ridge sandbank and water skiing. A limekiln is close to the shore south of Penhill Point, where flows follow the outside of the bend, avoiding the Chivenor Ridge sandbank. The quay at Fremington was very busy in the days when it was served by a railway, the old station now having a lookout tower and the Fremington Quay Heritage Centre. Deposits of glacial till vary the geology.

Wrafton Marsh was reclaimed in 1857 and has become Chivenor Airfield with jets, transport aircraft and helicopters frequently coming and going, this being one of Britain's bases for search and rescue helicopters.

The River Caen separates it from Braunton Marsh, where an embankment of 1814 reclaimed 5.3km^2, and from Horsey Island, no longer quite an island after 1.6km^2 was reclaimed in 1857. Much of the action in *Tarka the Otter* takes place around Braunton Marsh.

Lower Yelland has the Isley Marsh Nature reserve, an upturned boat shelter and the Stone Row historical site. Two piers project on the south side of the estuary. The first served a power station which has now been demolished. The other is the Yelland Oil Jetty, able to take vessels to 2,000t.

At Crow Point, on the end of a spit, a solar powered white steel framework light tower has been in place since 1954. Around it is a firing area, in use when red flags are flying, which is not to be confused with a Tetley's flag behind the tower, intended as a memorial. Royal Marine landing craft operate off the point, coming down the Torridge from Instow. A toll road leads to the point. The American Road was used by the US army to train for the D-Day landings.

Braunton Burrows is one of the largest dune systems in Britain, windblown crushed shell sand up to 30m high. A national nature reserve stabilized with marram grass, the burrows also have round headed club rush, sand toadflax, sea stock and marsh orchids, home to moles, rabbits, hedgehogs, foxes, buzzards, kestrels and magpies.

Opposite is the Skern, draining to leave mudflats and backed by the Northam Burrows Country Park, a national nature reserve. Flows run to 9km/h as the current sweeps between Zulu Bank and Airy Point. Large kites are flown on Westward Ho! beach and the Croyde and Woolacombe surf venues are not too far to the north beyond Saunton Down. Thus, the groundswell gives steep and confused seas over Bideford Bar with surf even on calm days, up to 7m high with storms and perhaps impassable with northwesterly winds.

Further out on the horizon can be seen the island of Lundy.

Yelland Oil Jetty with a storm over Appledore beyond.

Looking across the estuary from Zulu Bank towards Airy Point, Braunton Burrows and Saunton Down.

4 River Parrett

The cake burner and the first admiral

For months we had padded side by side,
    Ay, side by side
Through the Great Forest, Blackmoor wide,
    And where the Parret ran.

Thomas Hardy

The longest tidal headwater of the River Parrett is the River Tone, the roaring river, which rises at Beverton Pond in the Brendon Hills, tidal water on the Parrett itself being stopped at Oath Lock. The Tone used to be tidal from Ham Mills but tides are now stopped at New Bridge, Moredon, by a sluice with a fish ladder on the left which has concrete walls underwater and projecting metalwork at the sides.

It was a barge navigation from 1699 to 1832, excess profits being used to fund a hospital and other public amenities in Taunton. Intended as part of the route from Exeter, it was in bitter competition with the Bridgwater & Taunton Canal.

There are locked slipways both above and below the sluice and a parking area adjacent. At first there are levées but the banks themselves become increasingly steep, muddy and inaccessible, making landing difficult. The water also becomes steadily muddier but the river is still quite narrow and of reasonable depth.

To the south, the 13th century church of SS Peter & Paul with its octagonal tower is prominent on the hill at North Curry. There are occasional windpumps and a surfeit of Environment Agency notices all down the river which the reeds struggle to hide. Lilies are found in the water. Swans, herons, lapwings and swallows are present, the latter well served by insects. Damselflies are found in quantity.

Willows are pollarded with baskets and other products being crafted in willow at Meare Green where there is a Willows & Wetlands Visitor Centre. This is the only place in the country where teasels are still cultivated for the cloth industry.

Windmill Hill lacks a windmill but Stoke St Gregory has another 13th century church with an octagonal tower. Behind Curload are the remains of Slough Court and the village has a pumping station with interesting machinery.

The railway crossing is a late arrival, being built in 1906 and shortening the line from Exeter to Paddington by 32km.

From the 18th century the fields were divided by rhynes, such as Old Rhyne which crosses Curry Moor and joins the Tone at Athelney.

An 1801 monument recalls that the Isle of Athelney was the stronghold which King Alfred used as a base for resistance, fighting the Danes in 878, and it was here that he burned the cakes which he was supposed to be watching for a village woman. There was an austere monastery where Alfred conspired with Gaulois.

At Stanmoor Bridge the River Tone joins the River Parrett. Beyond the King Alfred Inn the A361 crosses Burrow Bridge of 1825, the longest masonry arch in Somerset to carry a road over a river. With a 21m span and 4.3m rise, it is of lias limestone with granite arch voussoirs and piercings. Much more conspicuous, however, is Burrow Mump which is a natural feature and has the unfinished church of St Michael on top.

Flowing north across Somerset to Bridgwater Bay, the Parrett crosses the Somerset Levels which were part of the sea, then fenland and raised mires, and are now extensively drained peat land, the last remaining wetlands in the West

The River Tone near its confluence with the River Parrett. Burrow Mump rises behind with its church.

Country with 520km^2 below high water level. Wildlife includes mallards, kingfishers, egrets, wagtails and perhaps a fox with evidence of many more species through their footprints that are well preserved in the firm mud which lines the edges of the river.

Moorland or Northmoor Green has North Moor to the south and South Moor to the north. A chimney marks a museum of land drainage with an 1830s beam engine with scoop wheel, now restored, the first steam drainage pump in the Levels. Three sets of powerlines cross to the northwest.

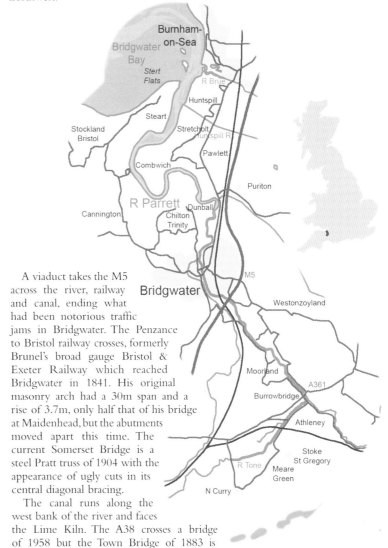

A viaduct takes the M5 across the river, railway and canal, ending what had been notorious traffic jams in Bridgwater. The Penzance to Bristol railway crosses, formerly Brunel's broad gauge Bristol & Exeter Railway which reached Bridgwater in 1841. His original masonry arch had a 30m span and a rise of 3.7m, only half that of his bridge at Maidenhead, but the abutments moved apart this time. The current Somerset Bridge is a steel Pratt truss of 1904 with the appearance of ugly cuts in its central diagonal bracing.

The canal runs along the west bank of the river and faces the Lime Kiln. The A38 crosses a bridge of 1958 but the Town Bridge of 1883 is

The Town Bridge: the heart of Bridgwater.

a wrought iron bridge of graceful but unusual design, replacing an earlier bridge.

Bridgwater takes its name from the Norman Walter de Douai. The Watergate remains from the 13th century castle. The 14th century church of St Mary has a 15th century pulpit and the spire enabled Monmouth to watch the royal troops before the Battle of Sedgemoor at Westonzoyland in 1685. The four day St Matthew's Fair was begun in 1379.

The Blake Museum is in the 1599 birthplace of Sir Robert Blake, a Cromwell land general who was made General at Sea and then the Royal Navy's first admiral. The museum has 19th century West Country ship models and John Chubb paintings and features the Battle of Sedgemoor and subsequent Bloody Assizes. Blake's statute is on Cornhill.

The Bridgwater Arts Centre was the first arts centre to programme activities. Other local entertainments include the indoor Karting World. A less attractive form of entertainment seems to be throwing shopping trolleys and bicycles in the river, there being an excess of both.

The tide rises quickly near high water with a bore which is normally about 500mm but can be 1.2m, largest at Bridgwater, formerly used by barges to assist navigation upstream. Water can be confused downstream, including whirlpools. There is a very high level of suspended solids, especially on spring tides, and the metal content is higher in the summer.

Bridgwater Dock, now a marina. The red and white buoy is a 19th century Bristol Channel mark, standing upside down.

The Quantock Hills rise beyond Pawlett Hams.

Bridgwater traded with the Mediterranean in medieval times and was a busy port until the 18th century. It was intended to rival Bristol as a port and has Georgian houses lining the river quay with a crane at the northern end.

A telescopic railway bridge was built across the river at a 30° skew in 1871. Last opened in 1953, it was later fixed and scheduled as an Ancient Monument. Bridgwater Dock was opened in 1841 with a four storey brick warehouse. A non tidal floating dock, it covers 2,000m² and took ships to 600t via double mitre gates, now blocked off. There were more than 40 scouring culverts but these proved inadequate so Brunel designed a steam drag boat to scrape up silt, used from 1845 until closure of the dock in 1971 and now on display in Bristol's Floating Harbour. A mild steel double leaf bascule bridge of 1907 crosses the entrance. In 1873 it was still Britain's fifth most important coal importing port. Russel Place consists of Georgian style cottages for dock workers with management in the end ones. Now Bridgwater Marina for the canal, it is hoped to restore the river network for cruising.

Concrete mattresses protect the bank beyond the marina. A bridge serves new housing at the northern end of the town.

Blackbacked, herring and blackheaded gulls and cormorants fish the muddy waters. The prevailing westerly winds make known the sewage works before Chilton Trinity by Elms Reach as the estuary steadily widens and banks of mud and even sand become more extensive. For the next 9km the channel meanders between two sets of powerlines radiating out from Hinckley Point nuclear power station. Pillboxes watch the river at intervals.

At Dunball the King's Sedgemoor Drain enters via a clyse or sluice of 1795, rebuilt in 1972 as part of the Parrett Flood Relief Scheme with a freshwater seal to keep out saltwater. It was suggested as the site for a tidal barrage for the Parrett which would keep the river cleaner upstream but result in silting downstream, needing regular dredging. A mark on Cut Point faces Dunball Wharf which takes ships to 2,300t and exports coal and fertilizer, also importing these plus sand, cement, bricks, timber, fishmeal and animal feed. Bibby's Wharf with its silos is unused. Another jetty serves a BP oil depot at Walpole, behind which are a motte and baileys at Puriton.

Skylarks and the wind might be all that are heard in Marchants Reach past Pawlett. Eels and elvers pass unnoticed by most. Views across Pawlett Hams include the Quantock Hills. Bridgwater College's Walled Gardens of Cannington has eight national collections while Cannington Countryside Visitor Centre has golf and croquet.

Combwich, which can flood at high water, has a high mast and conspicuous orange wharf fenders. The Ro-Ro wharf is owned by Hinckley Point power station. Rennie suggested a 120t ship canal from here to Seaton to avoid the transshipment which would be needed for a barge canal. Price later proposed a more modest scheme running only as far as Bridgwater Dock. There are lit navigation lights from here but a wreck lies half buried in the mud opposite Combwich.

Beyond Lobspound Point Stockland Reach runs down from Stretcholt to the confluence with the Huntspill River of 1938–44 which enters via a clyse and also serves as a reservoir for an ordnance factory. The depth is constantly changing in the estuary.

A sewage works is sited beyond Huntspill near where the Dorset and Somerset troops defeated the Danes in 845.

Fenning Island is not an island but may be visited only at high water at weekends. The rivermouth below Combwich and Stert Flats forms 24km² of mudflats, saltings and farmland making up Bridgwater Bay national nature reserve, one of Europe's outstanding wetlands. Shelducks moult in the summer and there are wildfowl and waders including oystercatchers, wigeon and whitefronted geese. The Environment Agency propose not to repair flood defences so that 5km² of farmland on the Steart peninsula is lost to the sea, forming England's largest wetland yet in addition to what is already there. Fishing stakes are in place.

The River Brue enters a rivermouth which is changing faster than most of the coast. Stert Island consists of two islands, on which landing is not allowed from November to March and for which a permit is needed from the warden during the rest of the year.

Ahead is the resort of **Burnham-on-Sea** with a long jetty and a beach which is muddy at low water. Distant views include the isolated 137m Brent Knoll, Steep Holm, less conspicuous Flat Holm and perhaps the Welsh coast.

Distance
32km from Moredon to Stert Point

OS 1:50,000 Sheets
182 Weston-super-Mare
193 Taunton & Lyme Regis

Admiralty Charts
1152 Bristol Channel – Nash Pt to Sand Pt (1:50,000)

Tidal Constants
Bridgwater:
HW Dover −0420,
LW Same as Dover
Burnham:
Dover −0420

Sea Area
Lundy

Rescue
Inshore lifeboat:
Burnham-on-Sea
All weather lifeboat:
Barry Dock

Connection
Bridgwater & Taunton Canal – see CoB p116

Burnham-on-Sea with Brent Knoll standing alone beyond.

5 River Avon

A leading route for explorers and commercial seafarers

Green upon the flooded Avon shone the after–storm–wet–sky
Quick the struggling withy branches let the leaves of autumn fly
And a star shone over Bristol, wonderfully far and high.
John Betjeman

Creeper in autumn colours on a bridge at Temple Meads.

This river offers some unique Victorian engineering.

From its source at Badminton the Avon flows south then northwest to the Severn. At Netham the river divides. Boat traffic takes the feeder to the Floating Harbour and many of Bristol's attractions, the original river channel. The tidal river, the artificial New Cut of 1809, is rarely used, not least because of the large V weir at Netham, requiring approach to be made from downstream. This weir was raised by Brunel to deepen the Floating Harbour. Its shape and the rocks placed below it mean that it can be dangerous and cannot be passed easily even by portable craft.

A bowstring arched concrete road bridge upstream of the weir has grab ropes trailing from it, a minor concession to safety. Although the weir is the official tidal limit, tides above 9.6m can reach Hanham or beyond. Freshets bring sediment. The silt in the river means it is usually murky and it largely drains at low water to leave banks of mud. Fresh easterly to northeasterly winds reduce the flood.

Bristol takes its name from the Saxon Bregstow or Old English brycg-stow, bridge meeting place. It was attacked in 1068 by three of Harold's sons with Irish support but was to become a leading port for seafaring, both exploration and commercial.

Swans, moorhens, mallards and geese use the river, initially edged by reeds and willow trees as it winds past industrial premises. The Paddington to Temple Meads railway passes over Brunel's fine triple arched masonry bridge, one of only two built in Gothic style on the line. The underside of the 30m main arch is festooned with limestone straws which have formed since its construction.

An ornate A38 roundabout bridge crosses the Avon below Arno's Vale. Its newer concrete partner also has coats of arms.

Brunel was chief engineer of the Great Western Railway from 1833, when he was 27, and this was the western end of what was referred to as Brunel's Billiard Table because of its smooth and level ride. The bridge's lines have now been spoiled as it is sandwiched between a pair of steel truss bridges which carry additional tracks.

A retail park occupies the north bank next to the A4320 Bristol Spine Road crossing and the river can be followed on foot from here. Parkland on the north banks leads to a suspension footbridge over the river towards Arno's Vale, where colourwashed houses in a paint catalogue of shades stand along the ridge above the

A gorge in Bedminster hints at what is to come.

A Bristol Harbour Railway train takes passengers on flat wagons beside the river.

river. Colour is added over the river by allowing creeper to grow across a road bridge.

A freight railway line crosses and then Temple Meads station and the line to Taunton are positioned over the river in what is more like a tunnel, many heavy riveted beams supporting the railway and station. It is unusual for the engineer also to be the architect but Brunel was. His old station of 1839/40 now contains the British Empire & Commonwealth Museum and the Exploratory science centre in his engine shed includes an 8.7m functioning acoustic guitar. The 22m span train shed, the world's first to have a roof enclosing the platforms and track, has a mock hammerbeam roof with arches formed by pairs of opposing cantilevers. The new station of 1876 veers away from it on a 300m radius curve. It has a 38m span arched roof and a neo Gothic façade.

Perhaps the most unusual of the bridges on this reach is an arched footbridge where the lower member is also a gentle arch.

Windmill Hill has no windmill but there is a city farm. The A38 roundabout has two bridges over the river, the first a concrete one with coats of arms and the other with ironwork which seems to be mostly decoration, enhanced by the careful paintwork.

By a hospital is a red pole bearing a light marking the barge connection to Bathurst Basin although this connection is now closed. An Avon Weir was proposed below the junction but not built. Beyond brightly coloured advertising for God's Garden is another suspension footbridge which crosses to Bedminster.

With a road on each side, the river cuts a low limestone gorge, an indicator of things to come, this one patched up in places with brickwork. The north bank is joined by foot and cycle ways. The steam powered Bristol Harbour Railway also follows with passengers seated on flat trucks. Blackbacked gulls and floating seaweed suggest a marine environment. Brunel's Underfall Dam flushes silt from the Floating Harbour as it boils up into the river.

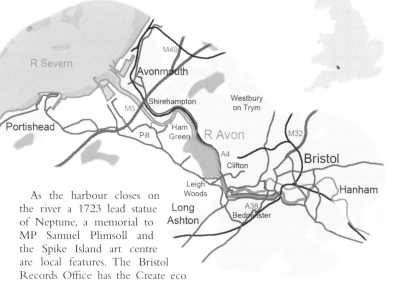

As the harbour closes on the river a 1723 lead statue of Neptune, a memorial to MP Samuel Plimsoll and the Spike Island art centre are local features. The Bristol Records Office has the Create eco

19

The Clifton Suspension Bridge crosses the Avon.

centre. Two early 20th century tobacco warehouses stand on the banks as a freight railway crosses over the Ashton Avenue bridge. A tollhouse with cast iron columns in front was built to control the Bridgwater Turnpike.

The Avon Bridge takes the A3029 Brunel Way across the river before the entrance to the Floating Harbour. The *Great Britain* wedged on exit in 1844, so Brunel altered the Cumberland Basin lock significantly over the next five years. The original wrought iron caisson gates were semi buoyant to reduce the loading. Brunel's wrought iron tubular plate girder swing bridge by the north lock was the precursor to the Royal Albert Bridge at Saltash. There is little commercial traffic now but there are *Balmoral* and *Waverley* wharves, the *Waverley* being the oldest ship plying these waters today, the world's last seagoing paddle steamer, making trips to Penarth, Ilfracombe and Minehead in the summer. The harbour contains iron pyrites, fool's gold, tipped in after being brought back from Canada by Frobisher who was not the last to think he had the real thing.

This was the route used by long lasting Severn trows, with their distinctive D shaped sterns, which used to serve the Bristol Channel ports and go well inland on the canal system. From this seemingly insignificant river came Cabot in 1497 to explore Canada's east coast and in 1620 the *Mayflower* emerged with the first European settlers for the American Colonies.

As the river turns north the left bank becomes North Somerset. On the right bank is Hotwells, named after its intertidal thermal mineral springs, claimed to be good for diabetes. The river flows at up to 9km/h.

The river seems to seek out high land but this is because it is superimposed drainage, the chalk covering having gone, the river carving a gorge in the Carboniferous mountain limestone. The beds dip steeply southwards, leaving steep slabs on which the more agile have placed messages in white paint in various places. At the northern end of the gorge there is old red sandstone. The river flowed from northwest to southeast until it was captured by the Severn, perhaps because of Tertiary downfaulting of the Bristol Channel. The tributaries still flow eastwards and it may have supplied the headwaters of the Kennet.

Ashton Court is in a 3.4km^2 landscaped park with deer and a field system. The University of Bristol botanic gardens cover only 2ha, including the Pulhamite rock garden and Chinese medicinal herb garden, but has 4,500 species.

The iconic Clifton Suspension Bridge was designed by Brunel, who won a design competition in 1834. As competition judge, Telford said it was impossible to build a suspension bridge longer than the 176m main span of his Menai Bridge. He rejected all entries and produced his own design with a shorter span, which was then rejected for being too ugly. Brunel's amended design had a reduced main span. Because of the Bristol Riots and lack of finances it was not completed until 1864, after his death. Indeed, his ghost may have been seen here. The 214m main span was the longest suspension span in the world when built and the deck is 73m above the river. The original chains had been used for the Royal Albert Bridge so the chains from Brunel's dismantled Hungerford Bridge in London were reused here. A competition was run in 2006 to find a modern equivalent. However, if the Clifton Gorge did not have a bridge today any proposal for one would surely be blocked by environmentalists. It is lit at night.

A former railway line on the left bank is well used by cyclists and runners while the right bank carries the A4 with street lights, protected under the bridge by a tunnel and an avalanche roof respectively. Navigation lights beside the river are easy to spot as daymarks, their posts and other infrastructure being painted white.

The village of Leigh Woods is above the cliffs forming the west rim of the 100m deep gorge but the woods themselves reach down to the river. They have been managed since the 13th century and have small leaved limes, ferns, birdsnest orchids, helleborine and various limestone plants. Roundheaded leek, Bristol rock cress and two whitebeam species are not found anywhere else in Britain. Beyond Nightingale Valley is the Avon Gorge Nature Reserve. Stokeleigh Camp, with two banks and ditches, covers 2.4ha and dates from the 2nd–1st century BC. Borough Walls Camp, of the same age, was almost destroyed by quarrying. Ghostly screams have been heard around the gorge after dark.

Clifton is the most elegant part of Bristol, its 18th century Georgian crescents, spa and Regency buildings having been the setting for filming *Berkeley Square*. The 19th century Roman Catholic cathedral building was replaced in 1973 and the Snuff Mill windmill, burnt down in 1777, was restored in 1828 as a house. There are an observatory and a camera obscura. Bristol Zoo Gardens, behind Clifton Down, cover 4.9ha with over 400 species.

Approaching Clifton Down as the gorge widens.

Riverside buildings with a crane at Shirehampton.

The confluence at Pill.

The Avonmouth Bridge takes the M5 high over the river.

Distance
17km from Netham to King Road

OS 1:50,000 Sheet
172 Bristol & Bath

Admiralty Charts
1166 River Severn – Avonmouth to Sharpness & Hock Cliff. Avonmouth to Severn Bridge (1:25,000) 1176 Severn Estuary – Steep Holm to Avonmouth (1:40,000) 1859 Port of Bristol. King Rd (1:10,000). R Avon (1:10,000). City Docks (1:5,000). City Docks to St Anne's Bridge (1:25,000)

Tidal Constants
*Netham Weir:
HW Dover −0340
Cumberland Basin:
HW Dover −0350
Sea Mills:
HW Dover −0400,
LW Dover −0310
Shirehampton:
HW Dover −0400,
LW Dover −0340
Avonmouth:
Dover −0400*

Sea Area
Lundy

Rescue
*Inshore lifeboat:
Weston-super-Mare
All weather lifeboat:
Barry Dock*

A 2nd–1st century BC hill fort has triple banks and ditches and covers 1.2ha.

The Temple Meads to Severn Beach railway emerges from a long tunnel under Clifton Down and Durdham Down to follow the east bank to Avonmouth. Blackheaded gulls and lapwings frequent the moorings at the mouth of the River Trym. The church in Sea Mills is particularly conspicuous in what was the 3rd century Roman settlement of Abona at the end of the road from Bath, sufficiently important for the Avon to be the Abona Fluvius.

Shirehampton Park stands above Horseshoe Bend but the extensive Shirehampton is mostly hidden from the river, just one group of buildings with a crane outcropping in a low cliff and being protected by stone walling. Several small craft are moored in Chapel Pill, just downstream on the other bank.

The river turns again in front of Ham Green with its hospital to reach Pill. Around the mouth of the pill are herons, small craft moorings, the Duke of Cornwall and Portishead Cruising Club. There are 19th century pilots' houses, their much respected cutters having been based here. It was also the departure point for America of Methodists Francis Asbury in 1771 and, in 1784, of Thomas Coke, to become the first American Methodist bishop.

The 400m centre span of the 1.4km long Avonmouth Bridge, carrying the M5, passes high over the Swash Channel. Two sets of powerlines soar over and oil and high pressure gas submarine pipelines cross beneath the river. Trains slow down because of the poor quality of ride for the rest of the line to Severn Beach, the squealing of wheels announcing that they have reached the corner at **Avonmouth**. Conveyors and molasses silos stand on the west bank.

The Avonmouth Docks opened in 1877, replacing Bristol as one of Britain's busiest ports. Two lighthouses on the east side of the river mark the ends of the two entrance jetties. Royal Edward Dock of 1908 has its Number 1 Granary, built at the time, the first of five. Measuring 67 x 22 x 26m high, it was an early reinforced concrete structure designed to the Hennebique system. Foodstuffs, chemicals, crude minerals, scrap and other metals and machinery are exported, forest, iron and steel products, coal, cement, gypsum, ores, fertilizers, sulphuric acid, feedstuffs, cocoa and cereals are imported and vehicles and petroleum products pass both ways, oil tanks being part of the decor. Three wind turbines do not seem such eyesores as they would in a rural setting. A large new container port development is being built with a long seawall out into the estuary.

A reservoir stands on the corner of the Royal Portbury Dock of 1977 on the west bank, reached through the longest entrance lock in Britain, at 366m. It imports vehicles, seen parked along the shoreline, and travelling container cranes handle unit loads.

Depths change frequently in King Road, where flows run to 9km/h, setting towards the bank. The flood gives a westerly eddy close inshore in Portishead Pool. Tides here are the second highest in the world, reaching 13.7m at the spring equinox. On the flood, ships pass and then approach from the north for greater control.

The nearest point of access is **Portishead** but it leaves a bit to be desired. There is no public access to the steamer pier. Larger craft can lock into the marina. Portable craft can land on the beach by the carcass of a wooden ship below the wooded shoreline with the Royal Oak but getting off the beach is rather more testing. Getting a vehicle near on the private roads of the new housing development is even more challenging.

Lighthouses show the entrance to Avonmouth Docks from the River Severn.

The Royal Portbury Dock.

6 River Severn

Britain's longest river

There twice a day the Severn fills;
The salt sea-water passes by,
And hushes half the babbling Wye,
And makes a silence in the hills.

Alfred, Lord Tennyson

Although the Severn is Britain's longest river with the Severn Way Walk from its source to Bristol at 338km, it is far from being the most direct. It rises on Pumlumon Cwmbiga and flows northeast to Welshpool and Shrewsbury before turning south. Even the tidal section meanders as if trying to crumple the remaining river into the space available. From Bristol it becomes the Bristol Channel, Britain's largest estuary. This disguises the fact that it once flowed north with the Dee to the Irish Sea or could even reach it by flowing 19km westwards.

Britain's back door was named after Sabrina, a water nymph who drowned in the river, put more clearly as the Roman Sabrina Fluvius. Later it was to be part of Brindley's Grand Cross scheme.

The river divides round a 4km island on the west side of **Gloucester**, each arm of which has a weir acting as the tidal limit. These weirs prevent the passage of large craft which are, thus, obliged to use the Gloucester & Sharpness Canal instead.

The West Channel has the longer tidal arm. An important feature of the Severn is Britain's largest bore, used for setting the world record for the longest surf ride, met around spring tides and reaching Maisemore weir. This causes the weir to reverse although it can be tidal as far as Upper Lode Lock at Tewkesbury. Despite being a large weir, it has a gentle slope with small rapids below at low water, heading towards low cliffs. Mallards, swans and cormorants use the muddy waters, which are shielded by willows.

The A417 bridge is the sixth at this crossing since 1230, one of its predecessors having collapsed unexpectedly during demolition, killing a worker. A former lock at Maisemore has been abandoned with

bridge and Brunel's Gloucester to Newport railway bridge with its swing span fixed in 1950 after never being opened, is Telford's Over Bridge of 1828, which carried the A40 until 1975. The striking 46m masonry arch was based on the bridge across the Seine at Neuilly, the main soffit having an elliptical curve with a 10.7m rise although the voussoirs rise only 4m by springing 6.7m above the main springing. Seen from underneath, the soffit has an elliptical shape, which helps funnel floodwater. The crown sank 250mm during construction because of inadequate foundations but it remains a scheduled Ancient Monument after carrying traffic for 147 years.

Alney Island and Maisemore Ham lie in the Vale of Leadon, not the only place to claim to be the Garden of England. The southeast side of the Vale of Gloucester is contained by the limestone scarp of the Cotswolds with Churchdown and Robins Wood Hill as outliers. Herring and blackbacked gulls, herons and cuckoos are in evidence. Rafts are tied up and there is the occasional slipway. The river was used traditionally by 4.6m little evidence remaining of its past existence. Water from the remains of the Herefordshire & Gloucestershire Canal arrives over a small step. Beyond a hospital and now sandwiched between the A40

Telford's bridge at Over in the light of dawn.

A boat at Rea not planning on going anywhere.

Framilode with its interesting church.

wide Severn trows although there are only small craft now and not many of them.

The eastern arm joins almost unnoticed at Lower Parting. Upstream flow is only met here for an hour from two hours before Dover high water at spring tides although the suggestion of a new weir here could change that. The river must be treated as a narrow channel for navigation requirements. Although not affected at high water, at low water the level may be up to 1m higher as far as Inward Rocks in spate conditions and flows can be to 11km/h. The prevailing wind against the ebb gives choppy conditions.

Llanthony Secunda Priory, subsidiary to its main priory near Abergavenny, is recorded as having sent Henry VIII 'cheise carp and baked lampreys' at Windsor in 1530. Lady's Well and earthworks follow towards Hempsted.

Stonebench, opposite a large loop round Minsterworth Ham, is a favourite place for watching the bore, which arrives three hours before Dover high water.

Windmill Hill, beyond Elmore, no longer has a windmill. Opposite Elmore Back at Minsterworth there is a slipway next to a prominent stack of roadsigns outside a depot. Here the bore arrives three hours and twenty minutes before Dover high water.

Longney Crib, a widening in the river, sees a change in its character. The muddy banks remain but there are sandbanks in the river which occupy much of the channel at low water. There is a risk of being trapped in a dead lead on a falling tide.

The Crib is a problem for bore surfers as the velocity and wave are lost here as the water spreads out, the wave

Garden Cliff at Strand.

Former wharf buildings at Newnham.

reforming as green waves at the northern end. The bore approaching from downstream is rather different, a tongue of water, the front edge of which can be up to 2.7m high and travelling at 26km/h. It is biggest on the largest spring tides and is reduced by floodwater and opposing winds. More often there is no significant wave in the centre or, if there is, it is less likely to be broken here and this is the safest place to attempt to punch through. The water flows faster at the edges and anything floating near the front of the waves is in danger of being pushed over the edge, even when it is running across dry land. Debris such as tree stumps is also pushed towards the front. Rowing boats have been used traditionally to follow the bore up to Gloucester, returning with the shopping after the tide has turned.

A sheet piled retaining wall has been used to protect a minor road against erosion beyond the Anchor at Epney. A slipway is used for small boats and a hovercraft, suitable for such conditions. Just before the riverside church tower at Upper Framilode the Severn is joined by the River Frome and the remains of the 1779 Stroudwater Navigation which is being restored down to the Gloucester & Sharpness Canal at Saul Junction but not the final reach as the Severn is considered difficult to navigate. The 1730 canal company is the oldest remaining and is still earning money from anglers.

Larks twitter above the levées which hide Wick Court with its moat. Flows run upstream only on springs, for an hour and a half from two and a half hours before Dover high water but they bring up floating wrack to show that it is a marine environment.

Cliff, slipway and moored craft at Newnham.

Old fish traps and a race below Poulton Court.

The railway runs at the foot of cliffs below Etloe.

Garden Cliff at Strand is of red and white layers of Keuper marl, the edge of the Midland plain with the wooded hills of the Forest of Dean rising behind, 110km² of former royal hunting forest. The river divides round Pimlico Sand at low water and is used by shelducks. The bore is inconsistent in its behaviour, often travelling faster in one arm than in the other and it has been known for the second arrival to sweep round the top of the sand and head back downstream on the other side or to reflect off the cliff.

Despite its name, Westbury on Severn stands back from the river and is marked by the church tower of SS Peter & Paul which is separate from the church itself. The church uses shingles made from old cider barrels. Adjacent is Westbury Court, the earliest formal water gardens and the only restored Dutch water garden in Britain. In 1971 this became the National Trust's first garden restoration and has pre 1700 species, a 17th century style parterre and Kip engravings on show.

Broadoak draws attention to itself with a flagstaff outside the White Hart Inn.

Georgian houses and some ropewalks to the river are features of the attractive village of Newnham. A wooded red cliff projects into the current. On top is a church in which a barrel of gunpowder stored inside blew up during a Civil War skirmish. There is an earthwork close by. Commercial boats are beached by a slipway at the foot of the hill.

Seen from Newnham, intimidating quantities of spray are thrown in the air on Portlands Nab and other red and white striped cliffs along the river's edge by approaching bores, even quite small ones. Box Rock is a striking conical structure, with the nearby Box Hole said to be 27m deep.

In the centre of this great river loop is Arlingham with St Augustine's working farm and rooks, lapwings, goldfinches, waders and wildfowl. Hock Cliff is more peaceful than it might have been as there were plans to end the Gloucester & Sharpness Canal here and it was where Brunel proposed a bridge for his Paddington to Milford Haven railway until the Admiralty objected. It faces Awre where the church has a Saxon mortuary chest.

This is where the bore normally first forms as the estuary is much wider past the Noose and Frampton Sands, alongside which is the Vale of Berkeley.

British Waterways'
memorial to the
Purton Hulks.

Kennet barge Harriett and some of the other Purton Hulks.

Frampton Court at **Frampton on Severn** is a Palladian manor of 1733 to which a 1745 Gothic orangery and an octagonal dovecote were added. Rosamund's Green is named after the Fair Rosamund Clifford who met Henry II by the riverside, one of the largest greens in England, surrounded by Georgian and half timbered houses. A Roman villa had a great mosaic and, at Church End, the 14th century canalside St Mary's church has excellent stained glass and monuments and a Romanesque lead font.

The estuary has 85,000 waterfowl including 49,000 dunlins, which the RSPB claimed were threatened with permanent damage by land reclaim, sand extraction, a tidal barrage and sea level rise. Observation towers and hides surround the Slimbridge Wetland Centre set up in 1946 by Sir Peter Scott. This is the headquarters of the Wildfowl Trust with 8km² of pools, mudflats, saltmarsh and grass fields, the world's largest collection of exotic wildfowl, ducks, geese and swans, up to 8,000 including whooper swans, Hawaiian geese which they saved from extinction, Chilean flamingoes and a tropical house with

hummingbirds. Oystercatchers, curlews and bartailed godwits are present all year. The 5,000 whitefronted geese form the largest flock in Britain in the winter, when there are also hundreds of Bewick's swans, teal, widgeon, pintails, shovelers, pochard, peregrine falcons, grey, golden and ringed plovers, turnstones, redshanks, 100 pinkfooted geese and 20,000 common gulls. Whimbrels, greenshanks and ruff are seen on passage.

At low water the channel runs west from Frampton to Poulton Court with its moat. Wooden frameworks for salmon baskets stretch out into the river at intervals. Small sand rapids form with broken water, white water hardly seeming the appropriate term for these chocolate coloured waves. The railway runs along the west bank at the foot of gorse covered cliffs below Etloe.

On the opposite side of Waveridge Sands it is the canal which runs along the bank. Its embankment was shored up with 81 sunken wood, steel and concrete vessels, 30 still visible. Some of these Purton Hulks are now considered of historical value and they have each been supplied by the Friends of Purton with a small

The huge bottom lock on the Gloucester & Sharpness Canal.

plaque giving its details, an excellent, informal, open air exhibition. One was an IRA gun runner until caught in 1921 by the Royal Navy.

In 1876 the river finally got its Severn Railway Bridge, not for passengers but to bring Welsh and Forest of Dean coal to the port at Sharpness. It was one of the longest railway bridges in the UK with 21 wrought iron bowstring trusses 38 to 99m long on cast iron piers, a 12 arch masonry viaduct at the northwest end and a swing span over the canal. A flight of three Spitfires on delivery from Birmingham to Bristol were flown under it during the Second World War. On a later occasion one of the pilots attempted to repeat the stunt alone, finding to her horror at the last moment that the tide was now in. In 1960 the petrol barges *Wastdale H* and *Arkendale H* collided with it in fog, the resulting explosion killing five of the six crew and bringing down two spans. The rest of the bridge was demolished in 1969 and sold to Chile as a road bridge. The piles, abutments and boats are still there at what is the limit of Gloucester Harbour.

The old north entrance of the Gloucester & Sharpness Canal at Sharpness has been closed off although the sluices can open automatically without warning. The active entrance is able to take 7,000t ships. The tides are 12.5m on normal springs although 15.2m has been exceeded. The massive gates are essential although the attractive lockmaster's house is less expected. Most lockings take place approaching high water as low water level is normally close to bedrock. Silos are prominent, the docks importing grain, animal feed, fertilizer, timber, cement, coal, aggregates and scrap metal, also exporting grain and scrap metal. This is a major centre for British Waterways' freight income. Occasionally a narrowboat makes the run to or from the Avon but it is not without risk. Boats coming upriver may turn below the lock and approach slowly in reverse, stemming the flood. Wrecks draw attention to the problems of this piece of water.

Flows outwards are from three hours before Dover high water to 9km/h and inwards from six hours before Dover high water to 11km/h. Flows are in the channels at low water but across the sands at high water.

Across Saniger Sands is Naas House and **Lydney** Harbour, the latter developed from 1810 by the Severn & Wye Tramroad Company and able to take ships to 400t. The River Lyd has been disused since mining finished but could become a marina. Houses are red and brown, built from old red sandstone.

Strong flows create an eddy off the harbour and small eddies and swirls become features of the estuary to beyond the bridges. Salmon baskets are used and a 2.7m sturgeon netted here in 1937 was the largest fish caught in a British river, weighing 230kg.

The estuary below Sharpness is buoyed and has leading lines for vessels to negotiate the channels between sandbanks. Marks show the mouth of Berkeley Pill, which had been proposed as the canal terminal.

A monument on Nibley Knoll on the distant Cotswolds recalls William Tyndale, a local who translated the *Bible* into English, being burned at the stake for his injury to the Christian faith. Rather closer at Berkeley is the tower of the church of St Mary the Virgin, Norman on a Saxon site, the tower being separate from the church itself. A resident was the Witch of Berkeley who was popular and had a good standard of life after selling her soul to the Devil. However, he claimed her from her coffin in the church in 1065, impaling her on the spikes growing out of the back of his horse and riding away with her. Screams and horse neighing are heard over a wide area.

Earl Godwin slaughtered the nuns in the adjacent 11th century convent, which was then used as the site of Berkeley Castle in 1153. This Norman fortification is one of England's oldest inhabited castles, with a motte and bailey but no moat although the surrounding meadows could be flooded. Elizabeth I was a frequent visitor.

A less respected monarch was Edward II, whose liking for young men disgusted Queen Isabella and his council. He was locked in a cell for five months with the smell and disease risk of dead animals rotting in a well between the walls before being murdered in 1327 by two jailors with a red hot poker. His screams are also said to echo round the countryside. A breach in the ramparts results from the actions of Cromwell during the Civil War.

A museum in the chantry features Edward Jenner, who was born in the village and experimented on local children, discovering vaccination in 1796, leading to the worldwide eradication of smallpox in 1980 by inoculating with the milder cowpox. Bacterial action results in Double Gloucester cheese, made locally.

Beyond Black Rock and Bull Rock, the latter with a 15m steel mast light beacon, is Berkeley power station. Used from 1962 to 1989, this 280MW plant was the world's first commercial nuclear power station and also the first to be closed.

Frameworks carry Conigre leading lights, followed near Hayward Rock by Fishinghouse leading lights on a GRP tower and a steel mast. The flow ebbs to 9km/h past Lydney Sand with Aylburton Warth and Cone Pill on the right bank shielded by Guscar Rocks and Hills Flats protected by rock platform as the left bank changes from Gloucestershire to South Gloucestershire.

A large triangular tidal reservoir has been built off Oldbury power station. Submerged at half tide, it is 6m underwater at high tide but entry is prohibited. Cooling water surges out near a pair of lattice masts. Canada geese might be found on the ledges used for the reservoir's low retaining walls. The Ledges starboard buoy is moored off its northern corner, settling on the rock platform at lower water and keeping a circle free of weed. The main channel changes to the right of the estuary between Shepardine Sands and Oldbury Sands, avoiding Count Rock, Narlwood Rocks, High Heron Rock and Cloudsmoor Rocks to head for Pillhouse Rocks and run down the west bank as Slime Road to Beachley. Opened in 1968, Oldbury nuclear power station was the first in Britain to have a concrete pressure vessel, and was in use until 2008.

While the right side has Sedbury Cliffs at the end of Offa's Dyke and its long distance path, the left bank has the extensive marsh of Littleton Warth, broken only by Oldbury Pill, Pillhead Gout and Littleton Pill with its

Ledges buoy aground off Oldbury power station's tidal reservoir.

The first Severn Bridge carrying the M48.

The former ferry terminal at Old Passage.

The Second Severn Crossing passes over the English Stones.

sailing club plus occasional salmon weirs along the edge of Oldbury Lake. Ebbs run to 9km/h.

At Beachley with the Army Apprentices College, the Hen & Chickens support the Lyde Rock light on a 12m black framework and deflect the flow back to the centre of the channel. Off Aust Cliff there is severe disturbance, whirlpools, surf waves, overfalls and tidal rips over Aust Rock and the isolated rock areas of Leary Rock, Upper Bench and Great Ulverstone as the water flows over these obstacles at high water but in the channels at low water.

This narrowing was used in 1966 for the Severn Bridge, one of the longest suspension bridges in the world with a 990m main span and 300m side spans. The 120m towers keep the streamlined deck 37m above the water and the bridge pioneered the use of triangular hangers to reduce vibration. It used less than half the weight of steel of the two year older Forth Road Bridge, of similar span. However, severe corrosion in the main cables and extensive internal reinforcement following the box girder bridge collapses of the 1970s has resulted in weight restrictions and the downgrading of the road to the M48 with the main traffic between England and Wales removed. The Welsh border and Monmouthshire arrive with the River Wye at Beachley Point.

The red cliff at Aust has a band of white false Cotham marble along the top where beds have broken up and been recemented, retaining important dinosaur fossils, so constant in thickness that it is hard to believe it is a natural feature. The motorway Severn View services at Aust have joined the 8,000m² St Augustine's vineyard. In 602 St Augustine summoned the Celtic bishops, who had agreed in advance that they would cooperate only if he rose from his throne and treated them as equals when they entered. He did not and future hostilities resulted.

The flow out is from three hours twenty minutes before Dover high water and in from four hours twenty minutes after Dover high water to 11km/h although this may be affected by spates. There is virtually no slack. As the flow reverses it may be ebbing on one side of the channel and flooding on the other and turbulent with it. Even millpond conditions elsewhere can reveal great swirls and areas of standing waves.

The following powerlines are the longest overhead cable crossing in Britain, reaching 1.6km between the main pylons.

Road traffic was carried between the wooden pier at Old Passage (now derelict) and one at Beachley by three car ferries until the Severn Bridge was built.

The beacon on Chapel Rock off Beachley Point is set against a masonry wall containing an arch. Redcliffe Beacon is next to a sailing club while a small lighthouse stands on Charston Rock, its reflector surrounded with flexible strands which keep off such birds as pigeons. These are happy to commute across and even butterflies cross the wider parts further downstream.

Aust Warth and Northwick Oaze form more marshy shoreline past a shooting range to Redwick and New Passage. The railway originally ran to New Passage where it finished on a 500m timber jetty (the remains of which are still visible at low tide and some masonry of which is built into the sea wall) for the 3km steam ferry crossing to Black Rock. Opened in 1863 as a broad gauge line for passengers only, it reduced the journey between Bristol and Cardiff from 151km to 61km.

On the Welsh side Caldicot Level is edged by Mathern Oaze, cut by Mathern Pill and St Pierre Pill and with the metal towers of Redcliffe leading lights. Charston Sands lead to Charston Rock, which covers but bears a white, round, light tower with a black stripe. Black Rock (which is actually red and white) had a 220m railway jetty, of which pile stumps remain, and a masonry arch takes a footpath across the former cutting. Lady Bench with its light beacon is an area of rock off Portskewett.

Beneath the northern end of the English Stones

from Redwick to Sudbrook runs the Severn Tunnel, the longest in Britain for over a century at 7km. Built between 1873 and 1886, it used 76,000,000 bricks and was a notable engineering feat. The tunnel passes through gently dipping Triassic marls and sandstones for 2.4km and is then downthrown against coal measures before returning to the marls for the last 1.6km at the west end. There were many problems with inflow of water during construction and the flow broke through near the east portal, clay having to be tipped on the bed of the river at low tide to seal the leak. The Big Spring of Sudbrook proved the worst point of leakage. In 1929/30 the tunnel was grouted with 8,000t of cement, grout appearing on the surface and out of connecting fissures, many of which had obviously developed since the tunnel's construction. The largest pumping station supplied 70l/s of water from the tunnel to a brewery and a paper mill at Sudbrook.

The railway emerges from its western portal at Sudbrook to meet the Gloucester to Newport line at Severn Tunnel Junction, the railway and two sets of powerlines being the major features on a shore which is generally flat after the ivy covered rocks and the remains of a fort and church at Sudbrook.

The M4 is now taken across the Second Severn Crossing of 1998, very much longer than its predecessor at 5.2km but less dramatic as most of it is on columns with just a 460m span in the centre cable-stayed from 150m high H frames, the total length including approach viaducts of 25 and 27 spans built from glued concrete segments. The Severn Bridges Visitor Centre explains all. Off great rock pavement, boulders and weed of the English Stones is the most difficult part of the Severn for large vessels which have to negotiate the Shoots where the spring flow rate is 15km/h and where a southwesterly wind against the ebb can create great difficulties. Over half of the channel is obstructed at low water by the English Stones, interrupted by the Salmon Pool and English Lake, with only the relatively narrow Shoots as a navigation channel before the smaller Gruggy rock platform. The area is deceptive. In the Civil War a Royalist boatman left a party of Roundheads to drown after disembarking them at what he claimed was the Welsh shore. Flows out start three hours and twenty minutes before Dover high water and in from four hours after Dover high water to 15km/h. In 1933 it was proposed as the line for the Severn Barrage, a possibility still being discussed. A family who had their farm compulsorily purchased for the motorway approach to the Severn Bridge had it happen again on their replacement farm when the Second Severn Crossing was built.

Protecting the shoreline against the prevailing wind and waves between New Passage and Severn Beach, where there are no saltings, is the Binn Wall. Dating from the early 17th century or even earlier, it was rebuilt in 1818 after storm damage as a 3.0–5.2m high earth bank with 1.1m of stone pitching on the seaward face. A natural bank of gravel at its northern end proved a temptation over the years. J L McAdam, surveyor of the Bristol turnpike, was fined by the Wall Commissioners in 1823 for using it in road construction and the Bristol & South Wales Union Railway also had to be warned off. Following overtopping, it was further widened and raised in 1979 with sheet piling and interlocking concrete blocks. The wall is uncompromising although there is a slipway by the end of the B4064 at Severn Beach.

Although still muddy, this is no longer a river but an arm of the sea. From here the Welsh Grounds, sand and mudflats, which dry up to 6km from the Welsh coast or most of the way to the English coast, widen out and continue until beyond Newport. Sand is firm on falling tides but can form quicksand on the flood. Gravel Banks dry for up to 2km from the shoreline at low tide. The scale of the estuary is brought out by aircraft flying silently down the middle.

Distance
62km from Maisemore to Severn Beach

OS 1:50,000 Sheets
*162 Gloucester
& Forest of Dean
172 Bristol & Bath*

Admiralty Charts
*1166 R Severn
– Avonmouth to
Sharpness & Hock
Cliff. Avonmouth
to Severn Bridge
(1:25,000). Severn
Bridge to Sharpness
(1:25,000). Sharpness
to Hock Cliff
(1:25,000). Sharpness
Docks (1:10,000)*

Tidal Constants
Llanthony:
HW Dover −0150
Minsterworth:
HW Dover −0220
Epney:
HW Dover −0230
Wellhouse Rock:
*HW Dover −0310,
LW Dover −0050*
Sharpness Dock:
*HW Dover −0310,
LW Dover −0100*
Berkeley:
*HW Dover −0320,
LW Dover −0130*
White House:
*HW Dover −0340,
LW Dover −0230*
Narlwood Rocks:
*HW Dover −0340,
LW Dover −0250*
Beachley:
*HW Dover −0350,
LW Dover −0330*

Sea Area
Lundy

Range
Redwick rifle range

Rescue
*Inshore lifeboat:
Weston-super-Mare
All weather lifeboat:
Barry Dock*

Connection
*Gloucester &
Sharpness Canal – see
CoB p119*

7 River Wye

Essential for affluent gentlemen

And yet, when western skies were clear,
The distance hard, and rain was near,
A blueness shewed against the sky,
The Welsh Black Mountains, beyond Wye.
John Masefield

In 1695 the Wye Navigation Act allowed 'the free and open Navigation upon the Rivers Wye and Lugg, and the Streams falling into them', the only such catchment in England and Wales. The Wye Tour became essential for affluent gentlemen and is still probably the most popular touring river in the country for small boats. The river retains a right of public navigation. Below Bigsweir it is also tidal.

The graceful arch of Bigsweir Bridge.

The valley is becoming much steeper by Llandogo.

The River Wye, Gwy in Welsh, rises on Pumlumon Fawr, 4km from the source of the River Severn, which it eventually joins after picking a more direct route southeast across Wales. In fact, at one time it may have been one of the headwaters of the River Kennet via the Avon until captured by the Severn.

Sometimes the tide reaches to Redbrook, which is why Offa's Dyke joins there. The dyke, started in 785, is Britain's longest Ancient Monument and was intended to separate Mercia from Wales but allow the Welsh to keep control of the river rather than using the river as the border. The 168km Offa's Dyke Path of 1971 does not follow the dyke exactly but is closer to it down the estuary than it is further north. These days, however, the river does act as the national boundary with the English county of Gloucestershire on the east bank and the Welsh county of Monmouthshire on the west.

Bigsweir Bridge of 1824 has a 50m span with particularly well made cast iron arch segments carried on circular stone piers. Two masonry flood arches were added in the middle of the 19th century. A notice by the public footpath along the bank attempts to ban boating and there is a prominent private notice beside each layby upstream on the A466. The boater can come up with the tide, perhaps from Brockweir, although most include the estuary as part of a longer tour, Hereford being a favourite starting point.

It is one of Britain's most beautiful rivers, especially the tidal stretch, despite the mud as the tide ebbs, and was described enthusiastically by Francis Kilvert it in his *Diaries*. The narrow wooded valley is particularly attractive in the autumn and is all AONB and SSSI to Chepstow. The Forest of Dean & Wye Valley Country Park includes many of the woods around the estuary.

The valley was formerly followed by a railway but now there is only the road. When the river runs above the normal level there are swirls and boils, accompanied by plenty of floating debris.

Buzzards, geese, swans, kingfishers, mink, otters and dragonflies may be seen and there are salmon, brown trout, grayling and sea lampreys.

A meander formerly took the river out below St Briavels Castle. All down the estuary there are low water weirs, often steps built by anglers but some larger, which are difficult to inspect because of the mud. Thus, it pays to get the timing right so that they are covered as far as possible. The first is Bigs Weir, shot left of the island when this and the rapid are exposed.

Beyond Cuckoo Wood is the village of Llandogo. St Oudoceus wanted to build a monastery and a knight offered to him as much land as could be circled in a day by a hunted deer. Such offers usually ended up being rather more generous than the landowner had intended but in this case the dogs and deer did not come up to scratch and only surrounded enough land for a church.

Llandogo adjoins Cleddon with the Cleddon Bog Nature Reserve and the Cleddon Shoot which falls over 150m in 800m. Ridingstream Weir is a small rapid at low water. Elvers are netted in March and exported to Spain and for stocking European rivers.

At the foot of Bargain Wood is Coed-Ithel Weir, a small rapid at low water with a channel in the centre. Below St Briavels Common is the Jubilee Plantation of 1979 by the National Committee of Wales. Above Coed Beddick is the Botany Bay Scout camp.

Although access points are often opposed on the river there is a jetty on the east bank above the bridge at Brockweir. The hamlet below Triangle had shipbuilding and seven cider houses in the 1830s, resulting in so much lawlessness that a Moravian church was built.

Brock Weir is a small rocky rapid, the tide rising from five hours before Dover high water.

The steep and gloomy Caswell Wood has bat boxes and owls. Tall stone columns remain from the railway which crossed to a tunnel under part of the wood. The road edges the river past the Moon & Sixpence. The Victorian Old Station visitor centre at Tintern Parva has a Wye Valley Railway exhibition, GWR carriages and a model steam railway. Other attractions in the village are Gregory Farm horse rescue centre, Parva Farm Vineyard (possibly used by Cistercian monks five centuries ago) and Abbey Mill craft centre with mill buildings, a water wheel and a trout pond. St Michael's church used to flood with high tides. Lyn Weir had a lock and is followed by Ash or Abbey Tintern Weir.

Tintern Abbey is one of Britain's most beautiful historic sites. It was founded by Walter de Clare, Lord of Chepstow, perhaps as a penance for killing his wife but failing to get himself killed on a crusade. Built from 1131 by French Cistercian monks, it was rebuilt in 1270 by Roger Bigod III, the Earl of Norfolk, maybe as a penance after confrontations with Henry III. It later provided a refuge for Edward II. Following the Dissolution in 1537 it was left with no roof but with majestic arches, fine doorways, intricate stonework and a 21m traceried west window.

The river flows below wooded banks beyond Brockweir.

The windows are the finest Gothic windows in Britain and Turner was moved to paint the abbey, the best preserved medieval abbey in Wales. Wordsworth wrote about it and Francis Kilvert described it. A storey remains of the monks' domestic quarters with dining room and the Great Drain which connected the kitchens, toilets and infirmary with the river. In the 18th century some workmen moved stone slabs and found intact bodies which then crumbled to dust. As they discussed the discovery in the abbey in the evening there was a violent thunderstorm.

The monks brought ironmaking here. After they left, Britain's first brass was made here in 1568 and the village later added a wireworks. An old tramway bridge remains.

The name is derived from Dinas Teryn, Teryn being King of Morgannwy, killed in about 600 in a battle with the Saxons.

The old red sandstone gives way to mountain limestone with mixed woodland, especially oaks, and bluebells in the spring with reeds along the river. It is rare to have meanders in deep gorges but as the covering rocks were removed the line was imposed on the lower rock with incised meanders following rejuvenation. From here to Chepstow the cliffs become steadily more dramatic and such delights as Big Green Meanie attract rock climbers. The Devil's Pulpit above Shorn Cliff is a leaning rock column from which the Devil baited monks building the abbey.

Plum, Stow and Wall Weirs follow down to Livox Quarry, where the railway line is still in use as an industrial line although it leads into a tunnel and away from the river at Dennel Hill. On the inside of the meander Livox Farm is sited on a peneplain 60m above the river, where there are herons, chaffinches, robins and great tits.

Hook or Battings Weir is on Prior's Reach below a fort site. Above Trough Weir is Wynd Cliff with the 200m Eagles Nest viewpoint. Wyndcliff Wood has lime coppice, whitebeam, yew and such rock climbs as Questor. The 365 Steps, less if they are counted, were laid out in 1828 for the Duke of Beaufort. Around Lover's Leap Valentine Morris and landscape architect William Knowles set out ten viewpoints including the Grotto, Druid's Temple and Chinese Seat. Morris ran up gambling debts and ants attacked his plantation in Antigua, as a result of which he ran into debt and left

Tintern Abbey's striking ruins.

Below the Devil's Pulpit.

Limestone cliffs overshadow Prior's Reach.

Chepstow in tears while sorrowful crowds lined the road and muffled church bells rang.

Above Walter's Weir are the dramatic Piercefield Cliffs and then Chepstow Racecourse, Wales' premier horse racecourse in a picturesque setting, also used for a large Sunday market.

A dark oak and beech wood fringed with wrack leads up to two more fort sites, Apostles Rocks and a path which passes through the Giant's Cave. Opposite are the remains of a church and then the river turns sharply through 180° at the foot of cliffs at Wintour's Leap and Broadrock with climbers on high pitches almost straight up from the river. Sir John Wintour was a Royalist, surprised by Roundheads both here and at the lower Sedbury Cliffs, on one occasion getting to boats on horseback. The venue could have been confused as the cliff height here is not something to be jumped with or without a horse.

Intoxicated, Thomas Moxley fell off the cliff, again not the full height it would seem as he only broke a leg before being rescued by fishermen from the flooding tide, not that it helped him much because, after a full recovery, he was hung two years later in Monmouth for horse theft.

One poacher always walked stiff legged so that it looked no different when he was carrying a gun down his trousers. He denied the accusation of his shooting pheasants with the unanswerable claim that 'The only bird I shot was a rabbit and I knocked that down with a stick.'

On the inside of the tight bend in the river is an unusual large lagoon on the downstream side of the loop. Longhope Reach has Chit Weir and was crossed by the Roman road from Lydney to Caerleon.

Chepstow is the gateway to Wales and it was on top of the river cliffs at the end of the reach that Chepstow Castle was built as the first Norman stone castle in Britain in 1067, a new build rather than the upgrade of a wooden one. Initially called Estrighoiel from the Welsh ystraigyl, bend, it has three separate enclosures. The Lower Ward is 13th century with the Great Hall. The Middle Ward has the ruins of the 1067 square Great Tower and the original 12m high Norman keep. The Upper Ward leads to the Barbican watchtower by William FitzOsbern, whose son Robert rebelled against the king and was imprisoned for life. Consequently, the castle passed to the de Clares, of whom Gilbert Strongbow had an extra finger on his right hand, could place his hands on his knees while standing upright and fully justified his name. The castle was used for advances into Gwent and was remodelled in the

13th century. There is a 1225 gatehouse, state apartments and a deep cellar which allowed resupply by ship from Bristol during sieges, successfully resisting a siege by Owain Glyndwr. It was a prison for Edward II, Edward IV, Jeremy Taylor who wrote *Holy Living & Dying* and, for 20 years, for Sir Henry Marten, a signatory of Charles I's death warrant although his imprisonment seemed fairly relaxed, being allowed to go out for meals and to have friends to visit. It was besieged and captured three times in the Civil War. In 1648 it was taken for the Royalists by Sir Nicholas Kemeys, Cromwell's cannons damaged it badly, a Roundhead swam across the river and set the castle's escape boats free and surrender was refused, Kemeys and many others being killed. It was in disrepair from the late 17th century. It has jackdaws and was used for filming *Robin of Sherwood*.

Tutshill, at the end of the Wye Valley Walk, is approached over an elegant five span cast iron bridge of 1816 by Rennie. One of the earliest iron bridges in the country, the radial grid pattern in the spandrels produces a unique curved spacial pattern when seen from the water.

Chepstow was an important port and market. It was the port from which the Chartist leaders of the Newport Riots were transported to Tasmania in 1840. The Saxon cheap and Old English ceap both translate to market. Pigs

The Lover's Leap cliffs in the distance.

The bottom end of the Piercefield Cliffs.

Climbers tackle pitches at Broadrock.

Chepstow Castle has a commanding position overlooking the river.

were noted in the street in 1804 and leeches and opium could both be bought in the market later than this. The fortified Town Gate on the main street is 16th century. Almshouses were provided by a wine importer in 1717. A churchyard has the grave of Elizabeth Webb who died in 1758 at the age of 46, having had 28 children. An 18th century merchant's house is home to Chepstow Museum, covering local history, the wine trade, shipbuilding, salmon fishing and traps (including a boathouse with salmon fishing boats and equipment) and William Williams who won a VC at Gallipoli, being killed while trying to position landing craft under fire. The town was the birthplace of J K Rowling.

Tides here are exceptional, a 21m tide having been recorded, and the banks get muddier as the water ebbs. A sailing club has a jetty which floats on the top half of the tide, users being invited to make a donation to funds via the adjacent Boat Inn, something for which many sailors must have contributed with gratitude. The moorings in front of limestone cliffs otherwise are stunning.

Two bridges cross, the first being a recent one to take the A48 across instead of using Rennie's bridge. The other was a light arched tubular suspension bridge, built in 1852 by Brunel to carry the South Wales Railway which now follows the bank, a precursor to his Royal Albert Bridge at Saltash. In 1962 it had to be replaced after a plate buckled, the new bridge being a more utilitarian truss.

The 13th century Port Wall was largely rebuilt in the early 1500s but some sections are intact, including behind the works of steel fabricators Mabey Bridge, whose products have included railway rolling stock and bridges, not least the Wye and Severn Bridges.

The limestone gives way to Keuper marl at Sedbury and the banks are much lower from here, except at Bulwark where there is an isolated section of cliff surrounded by housing estates, following a quarry and a fort site.

Powerlines cross at the final bend at Beachley, where gated slips serve the Army Apprentices College. Bugles and helicopters give military atmosphere with jets flying over providing additional sound effects.

Rennie's elegant bridge of 1816, one of the first iron bridges in the country.

Few town centre moorings can provide such a dramatic backdrop as Chepstow.

Ahead is the cable stayed cantilever Wye Bridge carrying the M48. It is a major structure with a 230m main span but has always been upstaged by the Severn Bridge, to which it is joined by a 10 span steel viaduct. From here it is seen at its best.

There are herring and blackheaded gulls, also mud which can be so soft that it will not support a mallard.

Powerlines cross high above the two rivers and Hunger Pill. Chapel Rock, off Beachley Point, has a black metal framework carrying a sector light, sited within a ruin.

A new A48 bridge accompanies the bridge which replaced Brunel's tubular railway bridge.

The Wye Bridge carrying the M48 with the Second Severn Crossing beyond.

Distance
23km from Bigs Weir to the River Severn

OS 1:50,000 Sheets
162 Gloucester & Forest of Dean
172 Bristol & Bath

Admiralty Charts
1166 R Severn – Avonmouth to Sharpness & Hock Cliff. Avonmouth to Severn Bridge (1:25,000). Severn Bridge to Sharpness (1:25,000)

Tidal Constants
Tintern: Dover –0320
Chepstow: Dover –0340
Beachley: HW Dover –0350, LW Dover –0330

Sea Area
Lundy

Rescue
Inshore lifeboat: Weston-super-Mare
All weather lifeboat: Barry Dock

35

8 River Loughor

Bridges two by two

Will you be waiting for me in the afternoon,
when gentle waves springclean your cockled shore?
Still waters stroke the windswept sands each June:
ten thousand birds have waded here before.
Caroline Gill

To Welsh speakers it is the Afon Llwchwr and to the Romans it was the Leuca Fluvius. The River Loughor rises on the Black Mountain near Carreg Cennen Castle above Trapp, just 800m from the Afon Cennen, and flows southwest across Carmarthenshire. The estuary forms the boundary with Swansea on its east bank. Improved under an 1815 Act to carry coal traffic, the estuary is now all SSSI.

Two bridges cross the river at its tidal limit, a road and a railway bridge, as at each crossing point. The first carries the Central Wales railway line from Shrewsbury to Llanelli, originally built as a horsedrawn tramway and then to become the Llanelli Railway.

Passing over the river and the railway where **Pontarddulais** meets Hendy is the A48.

Access is difficult at this point and it would be better to come up the river from Llangennech or Loughor although Solman's Restaurant and public houses offer refreshment near the bridge.

The river is less appetizing than some with an odour of effluent. Low tide cobble rapids appear at first as the river winds past an earthworks and a motte and the Afon Gwili joins. Kingfishers, moorhens, mallards and swans use the river.

The M4 crosses and then a long brick viaduct carries the Llanelli to Tairgwaith freight railway line. Both structures have stone debris in the river beneath them, accompanied by lengths of reinforcing steel and other metalwork. Another motte stands between them.

The character changes after these two bridges, the river cutting a wide valley in the soft shales but the water mostly shallow.

The Afon Morlais joins opposite Morfa Mawr, marshes fronting much of the estuary. Lapwings, oystercatchers,

A low water stone rapid below Hendy.

The brick viaduct near Waungron now carries only freight.

Pysgodlyn provides a backdrop with the Brecon Beacons beyond.

The trestle railway viaduct across the estuary at Loughor.

Pen-clawdd with the Gower rising behind.

herons, cormorants, egrets and blackbacked gulls hang about the mudflats, fish sunbathe in the shallows and anglers line up along the edges of the estuary. Opposite Llangannech are the remains of a chapel while powerlines pass over to give a fix on location.

The mud is gradually replaced by sand around Yspitty, where there is redevelopment and new housing. The east bank has Loughor with the Loughor Boating Club which offers an economical park and launch facility for visitors.

estuary in front of Pen-clawdd. The B4295 meets high water at Dalton's Point.

There are mussel banks at Salthouse Point, off Crofty. The sandy bed is covered with cockle shells but there is conflict between cockle fishermen and environmentalists interested in oystercatchers having the shellfish. Stakes in the sand show where fishing nets are placed in season.

Depths (or lack of them) are subject to frequent change and there are the remains of an old training wall in the

Distance
12km from Hendy to Crofty

OS 1:50,000 Sheet
159 Swansea & Gower

Admiralty Charts
1076 Linney Head to Oxwich Pt (1:75,000)
1167 Burry Inlet (1:25,000)

Tidal Constants
Burry Port:
*HW Dover −0500,
LW Dover −0450*

Sea Area
Lundy

Rescue
Inshore lifeboat:
Burry Port
All weather lifeboat:
Tenby

Rhossili Down dominates the end of the Gower.

There is an inshore rescue boat station sharing the slipway and an offshore lifeboat anchored on the sand at the top of the tide. Jets and jetskis attempt to outdo each other for noise creation.

The final bridging point, yet again, has a road and a railway. The A484 is followed by a timber trestle viaduct carrying the Paddington to Fishguard railway. The east bank at this point has also been used to site two castles, the Roman Leucarum fort and Loughor Castle, now in disrepair. This site is on the north bank of the Afon Llan which joins here, isolating the Gower with the help of extensive marsh.

A maypole of wires, illuminated at night by purple light, is an interesting feature covering the first roundabout west on the A484 on the north side of the estuary although what it does for drivers' concentrations is open to question. Better hidden on this road is the world's largest span corrugated steel railway tunnel, 16m wide and 52m long.

Levées follow the shore. Beyond a sewage works and a caravan site is the Millennium Coastal Park, claimed to be one of Britain's most visited attractions. Behind it is the Wildfowl & Wetlands Centre with ducks, geese, curlews, redshanks, pintails, wigeon, teal, peregrine falcons and short eared owls in 80ha of saltmarsh, ponds, lakes and reedbeds to Penrhyn Gwyn.

There is rather more marsh on the south side of the

estuary although this drains extensively to leave the extensive sweep of Llanrhidian Sands covering tens of square kilometres down to Whiteford Burrows.

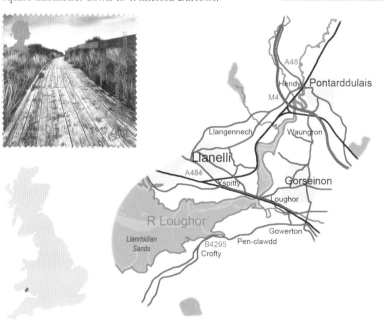

9 Afon Tywi

The mysteries of Merlin

Deep are his Feet in Towy's Flood,
His sides are cloath'd with waving Wood
And antient towers crown his brow,
That cast an awful Look below;

John Dyer

Rising in a bog between Crug Gynon and Crug yr Wyn on the Ceredigion/Powys border, the Tywi flows southwest across Carmarthenshire to Carmarthen Bay. It is tidal from Bryn Myrddin. Upstream of this is Merlin's Hill, where the magician was kept in enchanted bonds by Vivien and where might be heard his groans for allowing a woman to learn his spells.

Approach needs to be made from downstream and there are some conspicuous angling notices

A low water stone rapid above Wenallt.

Carmarthen Castle being repaired next to County Hall. The river has a high quayside.

Carmarthen Castle gatehouse.

banning the public even from using gateways. There is salmon and trout angling both by coracle and from the bank, there being successive flights of steps down from the B4300 above Wenallt.

Initially the river passes through alluvial meadows with gravel rapids at intervals.

The Afon Gwili joins from Abergwili, which has the Bishop's Palace and a museum with Stone Age and Carmarthen Roman finds.

The river has buzzards, Muscovy ducks, domestic geese, kingfishers, cormorants, herons and mallards as it passes round some large meanders. The A40 crosses the river twice, an awkward line which keeps it clear of Carmarthen.

Carmarthen is the gateway to west Wales. It was the Roman Moridunum Demetarium with a 2nd century amphitheatre overlooking the meanders. Reputedly, it was one of three forts required as a wedding gift by Helen when she married Macsen Wledig, alias Romano-British emperor Magnus Maximus, who had dreamed of her and then found her in Arfon and married her. In the 5th century it was the birthplace of Merlin, the Welsh Caerfyrddin meaning Merlin's castle. Many of Merlin's prophecies were written as poems from the 9th century and recorded in the *Llyfr Du Caerfyrddin*, the black book of Carmarthen, about 1200. It was claimed that the town would fall if Merlin's oak did so but a 19th century trader, annoyed at disturbance caused by people gathering under it at all hours, poisoned it without any apparent demise of the town. The distinctive County Hall, with its high pinnacled slate roof, has been built next to Carmarthen Castle, constructed with a motte and bailey about 1109, restored by Edward I and extended in the 14th century. The residence of Welsh princes and sited on a bluff, the remains include towers and a solid gatehouse.

It is difficult to find parking for more than four hours but the road along the top of the high quayside has a limited number of free and unrestricted places for early arrivals, with steep steps leading down to the river.

A modern cable stayed footbridge, S shaped in plan, leads from the station to a roundabout with a red dragon sculpture in wire. The town has the highest concentration of Welsh speakers and hosts one of the best livestock markets in Wales.

The station was built on the line which formerly ran to Llandeilo and up the Gwili valley but is now a terminus, awkwardly placed as it sits off the main line, meaning that trains have to reverse direction if they visit this important town.

A historic house contains a museum by the river while aerials and a monument crown the hill above the college as the A40 makes its return crossing.

The Fishguard to Paddington railway was built by Brunel in 1854 across the river at a skew angle with a bridge which rolled back along the rails to leave a 15m gap for ships. In 1910 it was replaced by a substantial Scherzer rolling lift bascule bridge. The line now follows the water closely to Kidwelly.

A leisure centre, schools and a college are the river's final neighbours as it leaves Carmarthen.

Powerlines cross and the river turns to run along the foot of a rocky hillside covered with trees and with the remains of Castell Moel. This returns the river to the railway, where it has scoured the embankment and it has been necessary to install a large amount of concrete mattress to protect the railway.

More sets of powerlines cross near Towy Castle Farm

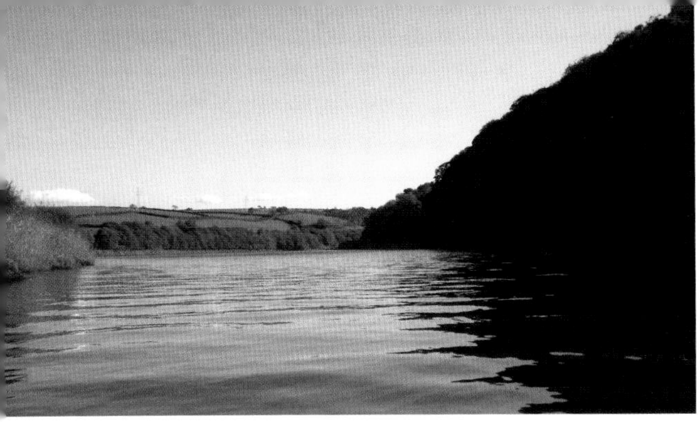

The high wooded hillside at Cwrthyr.

and shallows become more extensive, especially a shelf of clay which runs diagonally towards Morfa Bach with its moorings and sailing club. When it is just submerged, lapwings and blackbacked and herring gulls standing on it give a clue to its location.

The estuary is wide and shallow with constantly moving sandbanks, flooding to over 9km/h, by the time it reaches Ferryside. The fishing village hosts the River Towy Yacht Club and has a jetty and sandy beach, reached from the road over a level crossing by the station. Conditions can be choppy at high water with southerly winds.

Distance
21km from Bryn Myrddin to Ferryside

OS 1:50,000 Sheet
159 Swansea & Gower

Admiralty Charts
1076 Linney Head to Oxwich Pt (1:75,000). Afon Tywi (1:75,000)

Tidal Constants
Carmarthen:
HW Dover −0500
Ferryside:
HW Dover −0500,
LW Dover −0350

Sea Area
Lundy

Rescue
Inshore lifeboat:
Burry Port
All weather lifeboat:
Tenby

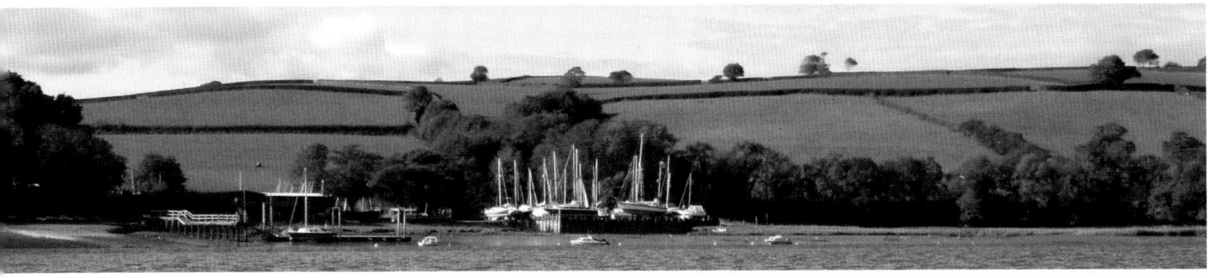

Morfa Bach's sailing club.

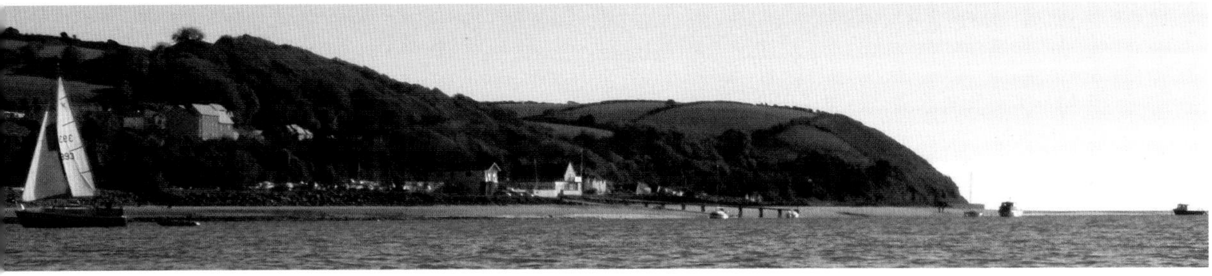

Ferryside receives some shelter from its cliffs.

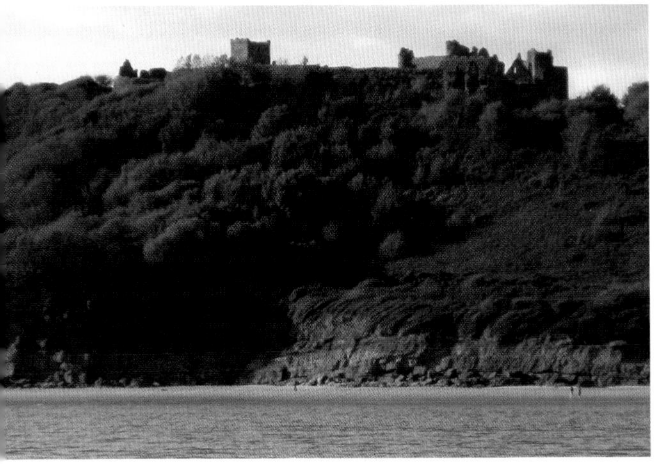

Llansteffan Castle is one of the finest ruins in Wales.

The River Towy Boat Club is at Llansteffan, a fishing village and conservation area which features in stories by Dylan Thomas. Guarding the estuary is the Norman Llansteffan Castle, one of the finest ruins in Wales. It has 12th century bailey and ringwork, massive defences from the 13th century and a 15th century gatehouse. Belows is St Anthony's Well.

Cockle and mussel beds are farmed, there are net stakes in the sand and sea anglers set their tripods along the shore. Between Ferryside and St Ishmael, where the Gwendraeth joins, the railway is forced against the cliff and runs along the seawall. Hang gliders and jets provide assorted aerial traffic over the estuary.

Wharley Point stands 109m high, the gatepost beyond which the Afon Taf joins.

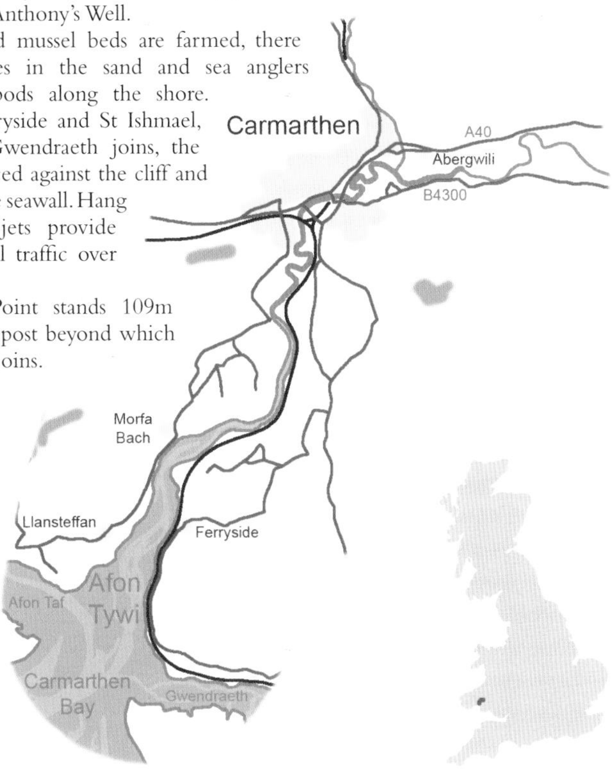

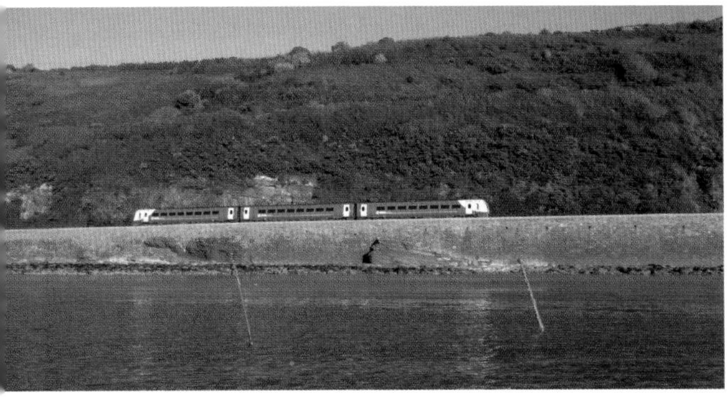

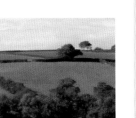

The railway pushed onto a seawall below Ferryside. Salmon net stakes stand in the foreground.

10 Afon Taf

Under Sir John's Hill

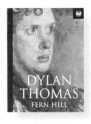
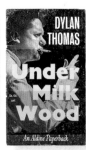

Getting on and off the Afon Taf is difficult anywhere except Laugharne and even there it can be very muddy once the mouth of the River Coran drains. The Afon Taf rises near Crymych and flows southeast to Carmarthen Bay.

There is a fast flood to Backe, where there is an earthwork on the bank with the A477 on its other side, soon to

The well proportioned stone bridge at St Clears.

Dylan Thomas' boathouse at Laugharne.

cross on a heavily reinforced stone bridge. Moorhens, kingfishers and kestrels hunt along the river as it sweeps past meadows.

The long straggling village of **St Clears**, birthplace of Thomas Charles who founded the British & Foreign Bible Society, has a motte and bailey site by the Afon Cynin. The confluence is at the end of the village, just below where the A4066 crosses on a well proportioned stone bridge, a simple flat arch with pierced spandrels.

The river is lined with reeds. After two sets of powerlines it passes another motte and bailey site at Trefenty.

By Whitehill Down the feel has become more of estuary. The Afon Cywyn joins with the remains of an old church on each of its banks. A bird hide looks across to the saltmarsh SSSI opposite the confluence with views of mallards, swans, herons, cormorants, herring and blackbacked gulls, oystercatchers, curlews and sandpipers. Levées have been built on one side of the river. Facing is more marsh with sea aster and a wooded hillside, behind which are a fort site and St Martin's church with 500 year old yews, an Oberammergau carving of St Martin of Tours giving his cloak to a beggar, the grave of Dylan Thomas and a replica of the Westminster Abbey plaque to Thomas.

On the west bank in the Laugharne conservation area is one of the most popular tourist attractions in Wales, the boathouse home of Dylan Thomas from 1949 to his death in 1953 and now a museum to him. Bought for his family by Margaret Taylor, wife of historian A J P Taylor, it is now a museum containing original writing and furnishings. He wrote in the Shack, a shed along the path. Thomas' popularity was not universal, however, especially at the time. His best known work, the first radio play, *Under Milk Wood*, seemed to use Laugharne as the setting for Llaregyb. Reversing the name did not throw people off the scent, many locals having apparently been used unwillingly, sometimes with unendearing traits.

There is an 18th century barn in the centre of Laugharne. The largest building on the shore is the ruined Laugharne Castle, built in the 12th century by Rhys ap Gruffydd, visited by Henry II in 1172 (from which King Street got its name), frequently attacked in the 12th and 13th Centuries, including being badly damaged in 1215 during Llywelyn the Great's uprising, and bombarded by Cromwell, after which only two of the 13th century towers remained. Turner painted the castle, of which the outer bailey has gone. The gatehouse and other work are mostly the Tudor mansion conversion of Sir John Perrott, approved by Elizabeth I in 1584. With Georgian and Victorian gardens, it was the home of Richard Hughes, author of *A High Wind in Jamaica*, who lent the gazebo to Thomas, where he wrote his *Portrait of the Artist as a Young Dog*. Thomas drank in Brown's Hotel and the Cross House Inn, the latter now torn between promoting the writer and Sky Sports.

Cockles were the former source of wealth of the village so the Portreeve, elected every six months to preside over the Corporation of Laugharne, wears a chain of gold cockleshells. Every three years the bounds of this village of small cottages and Georgian houses are beaten. The town hall housed a jail and Bell House had a bell to summon the ferry across the river. An ancient village cross is built on a 13th or 14th century base in Grist Square and funeral processions formerly processed three times around it.

The west side of the village was guarded by Roche Castle, now a ruin, and by Sir John's Hill, prominent out

Laugharne Castle from the River Coran.

Wharley Point, where the Taf meets the Tywi.

Distance
12km from Backe to
the Afon Tywi

OS 1:50,000 Sheets
158 Tenby
& Pembroke
159 Swansea
& Gower

Admiralty Charts
1076 Linney Head
to Oxwich Pt
(1:75,000)

Tidal Constants
Ferryside:
HW Dover −0500,
LW Dover −0350

Sea Area
Lundy

Range
Pendine artillery range

Rescue
Inshore lifeboat:
Burry Port
All weather lifeboat:
Tenby

of the windows of Thomas' boathouse and used in various guises, under its own name, as Fern Hill and perhaps as Milk Wood.

Marsh backs extensive low tide sand on the south side of the final reach of the estuary. There is also marsh on the north side from Black Scar but it is replaced by steep hillside from wooded Craig Ddu with SSSI from there to Wharley Point where it meets the Afon Tywi. The depths past the sand dunes of the Laugharne Burrows SSSI change frequently and there are likely to be breaking waves off Ginst Point in any weather conditions. Flows run to 9km/h with the Pendine's Proof & Experimental Establishment range an additional complication in the final part of the estuary. Towers stand at the end of Pendine Sands, one of the longest beaches in Wales. Leading to a mini resort, the 13km beach was used for speed record attempts, Sir Malcolm Campbell making 235km/h in *Bluebird* in 1924 and Parry Thomas being killed here three years later in another attempt. Today all is quiet when the range is not in use.

11 Milford Haven

Oil importing capital in a national park

Past Angle with its lifeboat
Towards oil refineries
Where tankers large and small
Unload at jetties.

Past the power station
Supplier of electricity
To the dockyard at Pembroke Dock
From where ferries went out to sea.

Under the Cleddau toll bridge
And as it is so high
The views they cannot be missed
From the highway through the sky.

It flows on through the country
To Picton where it divides,
The Eastern and Western go their way
To where the sources hide.
Andrew Woolnough

The Eastern Cleddau rises at Crymych, less than 2km from the source of the Afon Taf. However, it is the Western Cleddau which is the longer tidal arm. It rises 2km from Cardigan Bay but flows south across Pembrokeshire to the Bristol Channel.

The tidal limit is at the A487 bridge in Haverfordwest. On the east bank is a car park which could not be more convenient were it not for the two hour limit. Facilities close at hand include a large Morrisons supermarket, a Chinese restaurant, the Fishguard Arms and the Old Bridge Café & Restaurant by the fine medieval stone bridge in the centre of the town. Although the banks are built up, there are kingfishers as well as mallards and swans. Some of the modern Waterside Market is actually built over the water.

Haverfordwest was probably Viking in origin and name. A market town, it was also a thriving port, taking ships to 200t and with pirates in the 16th century. It traded in wool, hides and corn and the mayor may still call himself the Admiral of the Port of Haverfordwest.

Haverfordwest Castle was built about 1100 on an outcrop. It was attacked in 1219 by Llewelyn the Great, who torched the town, in 1405 by Owain Glyndwr and in 1648 by Cromwell, who ordered that it be flattened.

The old stone bridge in the centre of Haverfordwest.

Haverfordwest Castle, seen from the Western Cleddau.

It formed part of the Landsker Line between the Welsh speaking north and the Norman-English south. It has been a prison, then a police headquarters and now holds the Castle & Museum, featuring Pembrokeshire artists and the Pembrokeshire Yeomanry and having the Pembrokeshire Records Office.

St Mary's church of the 13th and 15th Centuries is one of the most interesting in Wales with a fine oak roof, mayoral bench ends from the priory and carvings of an ape playing a harp and a pig playing a crwth. There are Georgian buildings in the town and Goat House by John Nash, who was from Pembrokeshire. Also from here was General Sir Thomas Picton, who was killed at Waterloo.

Despite riverside development, some old wharf buildings remain. There is a weir with a fish ladder in the centre. It has a vertical step, is closed in at the ends and is

The weir and fish ladder exposed in Haverfordwest.

The remains of Haverfordwest Priory.

dangerous with the river in spate. At other times there is a route across a muddy brick apron on the left to a flight of steps which avoid the problem.

Before the next bridges there are the remains on the right bank of the 1200 Augustinian priory by Robert of Hwlffordd. The first bridge carries the A4076 and the other carries the Clarbeston Road to Milford Haven railway, which Brunel built with a 9.1m lifting span. Beyond are the remains of the Gasworks Quay by gas pipeline facilities, next to which portable craft are launched to avoid the weir and parking restrictions upstream.

Merlin's Brook joins from amongst the reeds as the town is left behind. The area has a plateau landscape and the estuary is a ria, drowned by postglacial sea level rise. A Special Area of Conservation with numerous SSSIs, it has up to 25,000 birds including buzzards, magpies, blackheaded, blackbacked and herring gulls, cormorants, egrets, herons, Canada geese, shelducks, teal, wigeon, curlews, redshanks, spoonbills, ruffs, green sandpipers, dunlins and ospreys plus otters.

Powerlines cross near the tumulus at Uzmaston and an oil pipeline passes underneath. A rocky hillside with trees and gorse marks the start of the Pembrokeshire Coast national park, Britain's only coastal national park, with some of the best riverside scenery in Britain. Soft mud appears as the tide ebbs and there is just the occasional house as the channel widens towards Boulston.

Little Milford retains mine winding gear. In the 19th century the Hook area produced a quarter of all Welsh anthracite, some from bell pits which had been started in the 17th and 18th Centuries. Mining finished in 1949 although there are the remains of railway and tramway links.

From Hook Reach mudholes can behave like quicksand, the safest places to walk being stream beds, gravel, mussel beds or the bladder wrack and sea aster which are now appearing. Air does not just bubble up with the tide—it can gush up at ferocious rates.

Millin Pill joins after Underwood and the Eastern Cleddau joins at Picton Point to form the Daugleddau. The fort site on the point should not be confused with the 13th century Norman Picton Castle to the northeast, later converted to a country house on a reach which was used as an RAF flying boat base. Salmon are caught here by compass fishing using a net between two poles and there are also sea trout.

Earthworks were constructed at Landshipping. Landshipping Quay, a mooring area for sailing boats, retains the line of a tramway. Thin seams of coal can be seen in the bank. In 1800 a mine here was the first in Pembrokeshire to install a steam engine. Garden Pit Colliery flooded in 1845, drowning 45 men, and all the local mines had closed by 1867.

Sprinkle Pill also exported coal although this was superseded by limestone quarrying. There are mussel beds off the inlet and Sam's Wood has wild service trees. From here to the Carew River is a no planing zone so it is a peaceful area as well as one of beauty, edged with hillsides of woods.

Behind Blacktar Point is Black Tar, which loaded culm and balls of anthracite and clay mix which burned more slowly. Opencast pits were also used for smuggling and to hide from pressgangs. At the head of Llangwm Pill is Llangwm, established in the 16th century by Flemish weavers fleeing religious persecution. The name may be derived from lang heim, a long way from home. It had mining and fishing for herrings and oysters. There was a matriarchal society, the fisherwomen walking 19km to Tenby with baskets of fish to sell, carried on their heads. Strangers were kept away from the village by stoning them. The public house was closed by the teetotal landowner in the 19th century

after a haymaker was stabbed following a drinking session. The position was reversed in 1953 when the bakehouse was converted to a pub. A slip and moorings make the inlet more welcoming today.

Coedcamlas Farm was the home of author Dick Francis. Beggars Reach runs from Port Lion past the best of the trees, Benton Wood, and was named as it was used by those who could not afford to fish in the better and more expensive reaches. A submarine oil pipeline crosses and heather grows around Garron Pill.

Castle Reach funnels the wind and has fierce tides where boils surface, the river's highest spawning ground for herrings. The oaks of Lawrenny Wood hide Lawrenny with its Norman church but the white 13th century Benton Castle by Bishop Beck of St David's, with its peacocks and welk pots, is seen over the trees.

Lawrenny Quay, at the mouth of the Creswell and Carew Rivers, has a yacht club and water skiing is allowed from Jenkins Point to the Cleddau Bridge. In the 19th century bark was collected from the stunted oak woods for a factory to make naphtha, used for explosives.

A submarine power cable

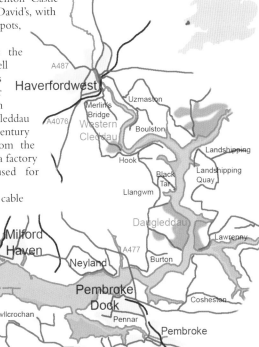

Downstream of the railway bridge is a popular launch point.

Gorse, trees and rock line the bank near Uzmaston.

crosses after Mill Bay and powerlines pass high overhead, marking the end of the national park here.

Cosheston Pill joins between Cosheston Point and, on the other bank, Waterloo and Pembroke Ferry. Pontoons are part of a disused fish farm. *Warrior* was moored here as a refuelling jetty until restored and moved to Portsmouth. Burton Point has the remains of a NATO jetty.

Burton Ferry and its counterpart have been superseded by the Cleddau Bridge, carrying the A477 37m overhead. Its length of 820m makes it one of the longest simply supported spans in Europe, not without problems. In 1970 a bolt was removed from a buckled plate during construction until after an inspection had taken place but the bridge collapsed, killing four people. This, together with other collapses at Loddon Bridge and on the Yarra in Australia, led to the Merrison rules which rethought box girder bridge design and construction. Skeletons dug up during construction of the bridge may have been plague victim sailors from the 1650s.

There can be confused water under the bridge from an hour before to an hour after local high water on spring tides. There are strong eddies on the outgoing flow to Hobbs Point, especially on springs.

The estuary widens to become what Welsh speakers call the Aberdaugleddyf and what Old Norse called Mel-fjorthr, the sandy fjord. Milford Haven is one of the world's finest natural harbours and was praised by Defoe and Nelson and featured by Shakespeare. The only industrial area in southwest Wales, it imported wine, fruit, spices, salt and hardwood and exported coal, salt herrings, cattle, hides and, perhaps, the stones for Stonehenge about 2550 BC.

Westfield Pill joins from the north between Barnlake Point and Neyland, the original town of Milford Haven until 1859. In 1856 Brunel had made it the terminal for his broad gauge South Wales Railway to serve Irish

Benton Castle shows above the trees of Benton Wood.

The Cleddau Bridge and Neyland from the old NATO pier.

44

Pembroke Dock with its Irish ferry terminal.

packets and transatlantic services but it could not take the bigger ships of the 20th century and the terminal was moved to Fishguard in 1906. Meanwhile, it had handled the *Great Eastern*, the world's biggest ship at the time, displacing 19,000t, after which Great Eastern Terrace is named. Brunel's statue faces the water, these days the home of Neyland Yacht Haven and small craft moorings.

Pembroke Dock was a 19th century planned town with a grid layout and Georgian houses, beginning at Hobbs Point, where Countryside Council for Wales divers recovered four large sacks of angling debris, including 130 weights. A submarine oil pipeline crosses. It was the town where poets Roland Mathias and Raymond Garlick founded the *Anglo-Welsh Review* literary magazine. Central to the town's existence was the Naval Dockyard, opened in 1814 as the world's most advanced and closed in 1926 with 75% unemployment in the town. It sent many soldiers to the Crimea and was defended by two Martello Towers from 1851. Up to 4,000 men built over 250 ships including the *Duke of Wellington* in 1852, the largest ever three deck man of war, and seven royal yachts. The *Great Western* had her annual maintenance in the drydock. Sheds remain from the Second World War Sunderland and Catalina flying boat base and there were fuel storage tanks so the port was subjected to heavy incendiary bombing in 1940/1. A Ro-Ro ferry service was started to Rosslare in 1979 and construction of Pembroke Port was begun a decade later in part of the old Naval Dockyard.

A jetty at Carr Spit helps keep craft away from Carrs Rock and the spit deflects current north. Flows run out on the south side of Pembroke Reach to 7km/h and in on the north side to 4km/h, increasing to 6km/h with a westerly wind, with an eddy on the north side on the ebb.

By 1974 Milford Haven was Britain's busiest port, handling 59,000,000t/year including 99% of Britain's oil, the first refinery having opened in 1960. Business has now eased to 38,000,000t/year at what is Britain's fourth most active port but it remains the busiest oil port, handling 97% of British fuel.

Large vessels have restricted movement and strong winds are more frequent than in most other British ports, perhaps indicated by a leaning red light column, but there is little fog. Navigation is not permitted within 100m of a petroleum berth or a tanker moored to one.

Llanstadwell is fronted by Hazelbeach, a Martello Tower and the Neyland Yacht Club. Although the Gulf refinery has closed above Wear Point it has jetties to handle tankers to 165,000t for the LNG terminal of SemLogistics and Dragon.

Opposite, Pennar Mouth drains the Pembroke River, Pennar Gut and Crow Pool. The adjacent former oil-fired 2GW West Pennar Power Station was built on reclaimed land at Pwllcrochan Flats. There was a skirmish in the Pwllcrochan churchyard when Easington militia attacked Cromwell's troops who were landing stores in preparation for an attack on Pembroke Castle. The church, with its octagonal steeple on a square tower, was closed in 1982 as families were moved away from the refinery danger area.

The Chevron oil refinery begins with flare stacks. It would be interesting to know how much energy they burn as waste gas compared with the energy generated by the three wind turbines behind the north shore. There were major explosions at the refinery in 1992 and 1994. The terminal can handle tankers to 275,000t. Jetties up to 1km long with up to 2.2km of berthing crossheads on each side of the haven make quite an impact on navigation, especially as it can be hard to identify lights at night because of tanker deck lights, but small craft are offered inshore routes with columns painted as a pair of orange slalom gates near the northern end of each jetty.

Fort Popton of 1864 houses Texaco's archives. The national park returns at Bullwell Bay but the industry has not finished. BP's Ocean Terminal, to pump oil from Popton Point to the former Llandarcy refinery, has berthed the 327,000t *Universe Kuwait*.

At Newton Noyes on the north shore the Royal Navy Armaments Depot remains a prohibited area although the pier is disused. A swing bridge crosses Castle Pill.

Milford Haven is where Henry Tudor landed in 1485

Oil refinery terminal by Wear Point.

Oil tanks and terminal on the south side of Milford Haven with an inshore route under the jetties.

before the Battle of Bosworth and the setting up of the Tudor dynasty. The town was founded by Quaker whalers fleeing religious persecution in Nantucket during the War of Independence in 1793. They supplied sperm whale oil to London for lighting and chose a grid layout for the town. It was built on land owned by Sir William Hamilton and was visited in 1802 by his wife, Emma, accompanied by Nelson. The Royal Navy's lease expired at the height of the Napoleonic Wars and Charles Grenville increased the charges for the site they were using so they moved to a new site at Pembroke Dock. St Katherine's church is associated with Nelson.

The Fish Quay is an important fishing area, formerly with one of the biggest British fishing fleets but now used mainly for offloading Spanish boats for dispatch by road. The Milford Haven Heritage & Maritime Museum is in a former whale oil store, a seal hospital in an old oil tank, the Kaleidoscope Discovery Centre, the Rath Water Gardens, a helipad, Milford Marina and moorings. The 1991 Cutty Sark Tall Ships Race was hosted here.

Beyond Hubberston Point at Hakin, perhaps named after the Norse King Hakkon, is Gelliswick Bay with the Pembrokeshire Yacht Club, swimmer warning buoys from April to September and the vandalized Victorian Hubberston Fort.

The Total oil refinery access jetty has under it red maerl, thousand year old coral from calcified seaweed.

In front, Esso's Herbrandston Terminal was decommissioned in 1983 but has been rebuilt as the South Hook LNG terminal. The largest construction project in Europe, it has containers like giant Thermos flasks, is importing 20% of Britain's LNG and is mostly in the national park, returning here. Renovating the jetty and fitting cathodic protection was also one of the largest jobs of its kind within the UK, the jetty now being able to handle 265,000m^3 LNG tankers from Qatar.

The large inlet of Angle Bay has mudflats and rocky ledges with oarweed and oystercatchers. It used to be good for shellfish and seaweed was collected for laver bread.

Behind Angle Point and sited in an anticline is Angle, Norse for corner. It is medieval with a fishermen's chapel. The 16th century Old Point House pub has a fire which has been alight for three centuries and produces the best chips in Pembrokeshire, according to the gulls which steal them from the garden. Three women inherited the manor and each built a castle, including the Hall and a fortified tower. A windmill stands to the south of the bay.

Water skiing takes place from the lifeboat station to West Pill at the foot of North Hill with its medieval strip fields, bluebells, dovecote and aerial. Lobster pots are laid out in Chapel Bay and there is a disused Victorian fort.

Off South Hook Point is another fort, circular with underground water tanks. In use from 1859 to 1867, it had a garrison of 168 but now acts as a hording for flapping environmental protest banners. There is another fort on each side of Sandyhaven Pill.

Thorn Island has a fort which had a hundred artillerymen present from 1852 to 1859, one of seven in Milford Haven. Now a hotel which has hosted the world hopscotch championships, it has issued a proposal for cablecar access.

There is a roadhead at West Angle Bay which has rocky ledges and rockpools but safe bathing, with swimmer warning buoys out between April and September. It has the remains of a raised beach. There was brickmaking where the old red sandstone returned to Carboniferous limestone.

East Blockhouse Point has the remains of a Tudor blockhouse built for Henry VIII in 1539. Masts of a radar station, gun emplacements and a sea level Second World War searchlight battery have been more recent defences but the site has not been used since 1979. It receives a heavy swell in westerly to southwesterly gales. Flows out are from four and a half hours before Dover high water and in from an hour and a half after Dover high water to 3km/h.

On the far side of the haven is St Ann's Head with its lighthouse and radar.

Distance
30km from Haverfordwest to West Angle Bay

OS 1:50,000 Sheets
157 St David's & Haverfordwest
158 Tenby & Pembroke

Admiralty Charts
1076 Linney Head to Oxwich Pt (1:75,000)
1478 St Govan's Head to St David's Head (1:75,000)
2878 Approaches to Milford Haven (1:25,000)
3273 Entrance to Milford Haven (1:12,500)
3274 Milford Haven – St Ann's Head to Newton Noyes Pier (1:12,500)
3275 Milford Haven – Milford Docks to Picton Point (1:12,500). Pembroke Reach (1:5,000). R Cleddau (1:12,500, 1:50,000).

Tidal Constants
Haverfordwest:
HW Dover –0440
Black Tar:
HW Dover –0450,
LW Dover –0500
Neyland:
HW Dover –0450,
LW Dover –0500
Milford Haven:
Dover –0500
Dale Roads:
HW Dover –0500,
LW Dover –0510

Sea Area
Lundy

Rescue
Inshore lifeboat: Angle
All weather lifeboat: Angle

The vandalized Victorian Hubberston Fort and South Hook LNG terminal.

Thorn Island with its fort. St Ann's Head is visible beyond.

12 River Dovey

Ancient legends with a hint of truth

Pretty maidens come again
Join us in a merry strain,
To all who live on land or main
Say the Bells of Aberdovey
Charles Dibdin

Rising on Aran Fawddwy, the River Dovey flows southwest to Cardigan Bay, forming the boundary of the Snowdonia national park from **Machynlleth** and, initially, separating Gwynedd from Powys. It is tidal from

River, railway and road are forced together at Glandyfi.

In the quiet reaches above Dovey Junction.

Derwenlas but permissible access is not available in the upper reaches and running up from Aberdovey may be the best option.

The water is clear, at first with slate flake rapids at low water, later moving to gravel rapids. There are salmon, sewin, river trout, bass and flatfish in the river.

The Romans sited a fort near the river at Pennal, at the foot of hills rising up to 633m Tarrenhendre. The railway has been following the south bank and continues to do so until it reaches the coast but, at Dovey Junction, the Cambrian Coast line branches off and crosses the river on a bridge which includes a navigation span, to follow the north bank to the coast. One of the most scenic lines in Britain, it was built between 1863 and 1867, 50km of railway exposed to coastal conditions.

The river is SSSI here and is national nature reserve all the rest of the way to the coast. Birds include wagtails, mallards, farmyard and Canada geese, swans and oystercatchers and there are hawker dragonflies.

The Nant y Gog joins just after the railway and the left bank becomes Ceredigion on an earlier line of the tributary. The Einion River joins after the railway and this and the A487 are squeezed between the Dovey and the foot of the hills at Glandyfi. This tributary flows down from Eglwys Fach with its waterwheel after passing the iron smelting Dyfi Furnace, in use for half a century until 1810, using fuel from the local woods, now one of the best preserved charcoal blast furnaces.

There is a hide by the Domen Las site on the edge of the Ynys Hir nature reserve, not an island but with saltmarsh, mudflats, reedbeds, pools and oak woods. There are kites, redstarts, wood warblers, pied flycatchers, winter wildfowl, 67 breeding species of bird including lapwings, redshanks, blackcaps and treecreepers and there are also 31 species of butterfly. On the estuary there are herons and blackbacked and common gulls.

Foel Goch at 475m and 521m Moel-y-Llyn are peaks on the south side as the high land pulls back to leave an increasingly flat shoreline. However, the north side becomes steep to the water's edge, forcing the railway to tunnel through headlands. Carn March Arthur is said to have the imprint of the feet of King Arthur's horse where he took off to leap the estuary. Tyddynbiddell Hill is only 279m high but its closeness to the estuary results in striking scenery. The channel shifts but a boatyard is sited at Aber-Tafol where the channel is forced against a point.

The Afon Cletwr joins after a 2km straight run across flat ground from the direction of wind turbines and of Tre Taliesin, the burial place of the 6th century bard Taliesin. His mother, the witch Ceridwen, made a herb potion which was to give her ugly elder son all knowledge after boiling it for a year. Three drops of it were consumed by Gwynion Bach after they splashed on his finger while stirring the brew. A chase ensued as the witch and the thief changed from hare/greyhound to fish/otter to bird/hawk and finally to grain which she ate as a hen. The wise Taliesin was later born.

Traeth Maelgwyn leads back to Cors Fochno, one of the finest lowland raised peat bogs in existence. Declared a Ramsar wetland site, it has good winter birds. The Afon Leri runs into the estuary through a tidal cut which is now straight for over 4km, Aberlerry showing where it once meandered into the sea.

On the outskirts of Aberdovey is the Outward

Machynlleth

Derwenlas

Glandyfi

Aberdovey

Eglwys
Fach

Aberdovey
Bar

R Dovey

Cardigan
Bay

Fochno

The north side of the estuary is mountainous, unlike the marshy south side.

Bound Sea School, which ran the first Outward Bound course in 1941 and provides members for mountain rescue teams and lifeboat crews.

Aberdovey was a fishing port in the 16th century and built 45 ships in the middle of the 19th century. It was proposed as an Irish ferry terminal but became an Edwardian resort. It has won many floral awards. The maritime museum in old warehouses has model ships, early RNLI equipment, navigation instruments, sailors' tools and ropework.

Dovey Yacht Club played a central role in the development of the GP 14, the black bell on its sail being a Bell of Aberdovey. There are many moored boats off the town, together with water skiing and jet skis.

The north bank continues as a low sandy coastline. Facing it is Cerrigypenrhyn spit and Twyni Bâch with the Dyfi National Nature Reserve. Its dunes have marsh and bee orchids, marsh helleborine, rest harrow and birdsfoot trefoil, home for shelducks, ringed plovers, linnets, reed buntings, skylarks, meadow pipits and stonechats and such butterflies as the large skipper, grayling, wall brown and small heath.

Buoys have to be moved as the bar moves. There can be a heavy sea over the bar with southwesterly winds against the ebb. Outgoing flows run from two hours forty minutes before Dover high water to 11km/h and they are ingoing from four and a half hours after Dover high water to 6km/h.

Cantref Gwaelod was the domain of Gwyddno Garnhir, Lord of Ceredigion, and was said to stretch from Cardigan to Bardsey off the coast, protected by embankments and sluices. One night in 440 the keeper, Seithenyn, got drunk and left the sluices open or perhaps the guardian or priestess of the fairy well allowed it to overflow. The result was the same. Everyone drowned. The Bells of Aberdovey can still be heard from beneath the sea when danger threatens. The fact that there are 7,000 year old fossil trees in Cardigan Bay helps support the legend.

Distance
14km from Derwenlas to Cardigan Bay

OS 1:50,000 Sheet
135 Aberystwyth & Machynlleth

Admiralty Charts
1484 Plans in Cardigan Bay. Aberdovey (1:25,000) 1972 Cardigan Bay – Central Part (1:75,000)

Tidal Constants
Aberdovey:
HW Dover −0250, LW Dover −0210

Sea Area
Irish Sea

Rescue
Inshore lifeboat: Aberdovey All weather lifeboat: Barmouth

Tree covered slopes on the north side of the estuary towards Aberdovey.

The pier at Aberdovey.

13 Afon Mawddach

Wales' best sea loch

The Mawddach, how she trips! though throttled
If floodtide teeming thrills her full,
And mazy sands all water-wattled
Waylay her at ebb, past Penmaen Pool.
Gerard Manley Hopkins

The Afon Mawddach rises on Dolhendre and flows southwest across Gwynedd to Barmouth Bay. It is tidal from the old bridge at Llanelltyd although a notice on the *downstream* side attempts to ban canoeing and swimming. Many small craft launch at Penmaenpool, which is more welcoming.

Above the bridge at Llanelltyd are the ruins of Cymmer Abbey, founded in 1198 by the Cistercians, with great arched windows, intricate columns and an unusual tower. A settlement site and a tumulus indicate old inhabitation of the area. The Clogau gold mine has produced gold for royal wedding rings and a golf course caters for other interests.

There are gravel rapids when not drowned out by the tide. The river is used by mallards, dippers, kingfishers and wagtails and by salmon and sewin. A replacement bridge suits the needs of current traffic on the A470.

The sides of the valley are wooded with the Precipice Walk and New Precipice Walk among the trees. John Ruskin said the only walk to beat Barmouth to Dolgellau was Dolgellau to Barmouth and Wordsworth extolled the views.

The Afon Wnion quickly joins after a couple of meanders.

Penmaenpool is a hive of activity, despite the fact that the toll bridge over the river is only open for limited hours during the daytime. Above the bridge are a car park, toilets and a signal box which has been turned into an observatory. In 1966, 15 people including four children were drowned when an overloaded ferry from Barmouth collided with the bridge while turning on a strong flood tide for the King George III Inn landing.

The Ruabon to Morfa Mawddach railway used to follow the southern shore of the estuary but has now been replaced by the popular Penmaenpool–Morfa Mawddach Walk and cycleway. Railway signals remain in place by the busy inn. Herring gulls, waders, ducks, geese and a wide selection of winter birds add to the activity on the water for birdwatchers. There was boatbuilding and in the 19th century there was a gold rush with trial pits on the hill to the south.

The Afon Cwym-mynach joins and the estuary steadily widens. This is claimed to be one of Britain's loveliest estuaries and Wales' closest equivalent to a Scottish sea loch although the sand is a bit too golden and the cycleway and footpath along the edge a bit too heavily used.

The Afon Cwm-llechen flows down almost from the summit of 750m Diffwys to the north, passing St David's gold mine (a goldfield abandoned early in the 20th century), the remains of an ore crushing mill and a tramway bridge, to join the Mawddach at Bontddu. Another river joins opposite from high on 893m Cadair Idris, the chair of the giant Idris, which Francis Kilvert found desolate.

Blackbacked and common gulls, cormorants, herons, oystercatchers and Canada geese are present and dead leaves drift along the sandy bottom. Boathouses are tucked into odd corners and there are secluded sandy beaches, not that sand is in short supply. The Afon

The old bridge at Llanelltyd is the tidal limit.

One of the rapids with Cadair Idris rising beyond.

Dwynant flows down through woods and past gorse and heather from the side of 588m Craig y Grut to join the Mawddach at Cutiau. Opposite, another stream flows down from 546m Braich Ddu over waterfalls and through Arthog with its outdoor centre to flow into the estuary by the prominent wooded hillock of Fegla Fach.

The Snowdonia national park stops short of Barmouth as the boundary tries to follow the winding channel, which may turn upstream at times and have downstream leads which peter out. H W Tilman lived here although he rarely brought his boats to Barmouth. His journeys by Bristol Channel pilot cutter to Greenland and the Southern Ocean for climbing are recalled by the 3 Peaks Race from Barmouth to Fort William with runs up Snowdon, Scafell Pike and Ben Nevis.

A stream falls past the Merioneth Paradoxides trilobite sculpture in stainless steel and a limekiln into a small inlet above Barmouth Bridge. At one time the inlet sheltered up to 150 ships, including some undertaking transatlantic crossings.

Dabs and flounders find the conditions suitable and mussels coat rocks by the bridge. The 730m bridge, built in 1867 for the Cambrian Coast railway, has rock foundations only at the

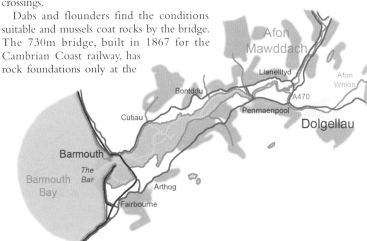

Heather and gorse cover the hillside above Maes-y-garnedd.

northern end. A pair of 12m fixed spans adjoin a 41m swing span on a central pivot, replacing an unusual span which tilted and pulled back over the track. There is then a 36m span and 113 5.5m spans on timber trestles, many with glassfibre sleeves to resist marine borer attack.

There is a strong eddy at the northern end on the ebb although the lifeboat launches through a tunnel under the end of the bridge. On the hillside above is Dinas Oleu, the first acquisition of the National Trust in 1895.

The resort of **Barmouth** has a 13th century church with a fine east window and some inscribed stones from the 5th century. Ty Crwn is a small round lock-up for drunk sailors. Ty Gwyn is a Tudor tower house, believed to have been used by those plotting the overthrow of Richard III, now housing a Tudor exhibition with guns, cannons and medieval shipwreck treasure. The 18th century fishing harbour was said to have an approach like Gibraltar and 318 ships were built here in the century from 1750. Alleyways lead up the escarpment to Penygraig. There is a lifeboat museum and the headquarters of Merioneth Yacht Club on the quayside. These days assorted pleasure craft play a central role. The Mawddach Wool Race takes place to Dolgellau in July and the following month sees the regatta.

Penmaenpool with its toll bridge and the signal box which is now an observatory.

The King George III at Penmaenpool. The signals remain in place on the former railway line.

A passenger ferry operates across to Penrhyn Point, the end of a spit with a flagstaff and the Fairbourne & Barmouth Steam Railway. Built in 1890 by the McDougall flour family to carry materials to build Fairbourne, trains were horsedrawn and the railway's 686mm gauge is the smallest in Wales. The engines, half size replicas of other engines, are still being built.

Ynys y Brawd is joined to the mainland by a barrage and shows a light on a stone groyne. The flow is outgoing from two hours fifty minutes before Dover high water to 11km/h with a strong eddy at the island end and ingoing from four hours twenty minutes after Dover high water. The end of a stone patch is marked by Y Parc, a red tripod light beacon. In Barmouth Bay the bar changes considerably and so buoys need to be moved. There is surf, especially on ebb tides in winter, but in summer the bay has users from jet skis to lion's mane jellyfish.

Wooded mountainside at Rhuddallt.

The disused quarry on Bryn Brith above Arthog and the small but prominent Fegla Fach.

Looking across the estuary from Coes-faen towards Cadair Idris.

Barmouth Bridge stretches out across the estuary.

Distance
13km from Llanelltyd to Barmouth Bay

OS 1:50,000 Sheet
124 Porthmadog & Dolgellau

Admiralty Charts
1484 Plans in Cardigan Bay. Barmouth (1:25,000)
1971 Cardigan Bay – Northern Part
1972 Cardigan Bay – Central Part (1:75,000)

Tidal Constants
Barmouth:
HW Dover –0250,
LW Dover –0140

Sea Area
Irish Sea

Rescue
Inshore lifeboat: Barmouth
All weather lifeboat: Barmouth

51

14 Afon Dwyryd

A fantastic railway and a fantasy village

Llyn Conglog on Moel Druman is the source of the Afon Geodol, later to become the Afon Dwyryd, meaning two fords, as it flows southwest across Gwynedd. It is tidal from the bridge at Maentwrog but launching here is difficult. Small craft may be able to launch across the fast A487 at Bryn Mawr, otherwise it will be necessary to come up from Penrhyndeudraeth or Porthmadog.

At first the river has a slate stone bed with some minor rapids, the home of mallards, kingfishers and dippers. There are levées as the river leaves Maentwrog with its church spire clad in slate and surrounded by ancient yews. Pryderi was buried at Maentwrog after being killed in single combat by Gwydion, who was helped by greater strength, skill and magic. Above is the fine ancient oakwood of Coed Maentwrog.

Conspicuous on the hillside above Tan-y-bwlch is Plas Tan-y-Bwlch of 1748. A 19th century owner of the house, William Edward Oakley, planted firs in the shape of his initials amongst the oaks on the south side of the valley. It is now the Snowdonia National Park Study Centre, surrounded by rhododendrons, azaleas, rosebay willowherb and pied flycatchers. Course participants are given £5 vouchers if they arrive by public transport.

One form of public transport is the train, running high

The old bridge at Maentwrog is the tidal limit.

Maentwrog and its slated spire church.

above the centre through Coed Llyn y Garnedd, which also brought up seawater to fill the bathing pool. This is the Ffestiniog Railway, the best of the Welsh narrow gauge lines, the world's oldest passenger-carrying 597mm gauge line and the most scenic, run by the world's oldest independent railway company. Founded in 1832, it was built to transport slate from Blaenau Ffestiniog to Porthmadog for export. Until the 1860s horses pulled the empty wagons up a route which often features sheer drops from the tracks but rode back in carriages as trains ran down by gravity. Footpaths and nature trails follow through the woods, where the trains are often hidden by the trees. Trains now carry only passengers, pulled by diesel or steam locomotives, including the unique Double-Fairlie locomotives like two steam engines back to back.

The Rhaedr Du joins below a power station, bringing water down from Llyn Trawsfynydd, which serves the much larger Trawsfynydd nuclear power station. Above the confluence are the trees of Coed Felinrhyd with 623m Meol Ysgyfarnogod rising beyond.

Reeds grow beside the river as the bed becomes sandy and dead tree leaves lie on the bottom. Herons, fish and flatfish feed here. At Bryn Mawr the A487 comes alongside although there is a nature reserve in the adjacent woods.

Before the railway was built, slate was brought to Bryn-Dwyryd for shipping, the stone quay still being in excellent condition, surrounded by heather and gorse.

By **Penrhyndeudraeth** the north bank has ceased to be within the Snowdonia national park. There was an explosives factory here but it was also home to pacificist Bertrand Russell for 15 years. Richard Owen was a quarryman born in 1831 who died in the workhouse here in 1909 as the poet and writer Glaslyn the Bard.

A road toll bridge and the Cambrian Coast railway cross the river together, followed by powerlines. There are SSSIs on both sides and extensive marshland. Ynys Gifftan rises to 39m in front of Glastraeth marsh, which runs for over 2km to the confluence with the Afon y Glyn at Llanfihangel-y-traethau.

The star of the estuary is Portmeirion, built between 1925 and 1972 by Sir Clough Williams-Ellis to show that

A Ffestiniog Railway train leaves Plas Halt.

Plas Tan-y-Bwlch overlooks the river but is below the railway.

a beautiful site could be developed without spoiling it and without advertising. The name is derived from Portofino and Meirionydd, the former inspiring the Italianate styling with domes, campaniles, pastel-washed cottages (many rescued from other parts of the country), its own lighthouse and even a sailing boat which is actually part of the seawall. Castelldeudraeth is a Victorian sham although the motte remains from the castle of Gruffydd ap Cynon, Prince of Gwynedd, built in 1130 but knocked down late in the 19th century by two landscape gardeners in order not to attract visitors. Those days are long gone and there is now an entry fee to the village, which is closed to the public in the evenings. Noël Coward wrote *Blithe Spirit* here but it is better known as the setting for the cult TV series *The Prisoner*, for which there is a museum in No 6. Viewers who remember the title sequence of the sphere chasing No 6 across the sands will appreciate that the estuary can be short of water. On the other hand, in the 19th century Yr Hwntw Mawr, a big man living here while building the Cob, robbed a farm, killed a girl who surprised him and tried to escape across the estuary on foot but was caught and hanged.

Helped by the mild climate, the 70ha of Y Gwyllt's woodland gardens, subtropical woodland, cypresses,

eucalyptuses, Himalayan flowering trees and magnolias contribute to some of the finest wild gardens in Wales. Flowers also feature on Portmeirion's distinctive pottery.

From Trwynypenrhyn with its caves the views open up to the north to 552m Moel-ddu. Oystercatchers, herring gulls, waders and ospreys are seen around the estuary. The sand is not densely packed and releases significant amounts of air when pressed down. The extensive Traeth Bach leads back to Morfa Harlech which

The distinctive Pen y Foel with its wood.

Bryn-Dwyryd was the quay for slate before the railway came.

is 5.5m wide at the top, 27m wide at the base and built on rush matting to allow the reclamation of 2.8km² of mudflats which turned out to serve as indifferent farmland. The Cob carries the former main road and the Ffestiniog Railway to its terminus at Madock's harbour of 1808, from where Blaenau Ffestiniog slate was exported to the USA and Europe. Retired engines are on show in the railway museum by the harbour. A major development came in 2009 with a railway connection through the streets to the restored Welsh Highland Railway to give a 64km line to Caernarfon, the UK's longest heritage line.

The gateway to the Lleyn, Porthmadog was a schooner building centre. A maritime museum, in the ketch *Garlandstone* before it went to Morwellham, is now on the quay. A mill used for grinding corn for ships' biscuits is now a pottery and there is a car museum.

Borth-y-Gest, below 262m Moel-y-Gest with its hilltop fort, is the Victorian village from which Prince Madog, son of Owain Gwynedd, was said to have sailed to America in the 12th century. It adjoins Garreg Wen, where young harpist David Owen composed *Dafydd y Garreg Wen* on his deathbed in 1741 and then dreamed he heard it being played to two doves in an evergreen country. When his coffin was being carried to Ynyscynhaern cemetery, where his grave can still be seen, it was followed by two doves.

Pont Briwet, a toll bridge and railway bridge.

Distance
13km from Maentwrog
to Tremadog Bay

OS 1:50,000 Sheet
124 Porthmadog
& Dolgellau

Admiralty Charts
1512 Plans on Lleyn
Peninsula. Approaches
to Porthmadog
(1:25,000)
1971 Cardigan Bay
– Northern Part

Tidal Constants
Criccieth:
HW Dover −0300,
LW Dover −0150

Sea Area
Irish Sea

Rescue
Inshore lifeboat:
Criccieth
All weather lifeboat:
Pwllheli

is reclaimed and is a national nature reserve with a large rabbit warren. Harlech Castle can be seen to the south.

Beyond Harlech Point the Dwyryd joins the Afon Glaslyn, the Roman Tisobis Fluvius.

Porthmadog was named Portmadoc after founder William Madocks. The spelling was changed in the 20th century to reduce the English overtones and make it sound as if named after Prince Madog. In 1808–11 Madocks built the Cob. At 1.3km long and 6.4m high it

The north side of the estuary ends at Ynys Cyngar, not an island, across a golf course from Morfa Bychan with Criccieth Castle visible in the distance.

Flows in the estuary are strong, outgoing from three hours before Dover high water and ingoing from four hours twenty minutes after Dover high water. The bar in Tremadog Bay changes position and depth constantly and the sea breaks when there are winds of over force 4 from the south to southwest.

The fantasy village of Portmeirion. The boat is of stone, part of the seawall.

15 Afon Cefni

It was easier for the Vikings

While much of the Afon Cefni consists of straight cuts, this was not always the case, as suggested by the remains of a meandering watercourse to its northwest. However, neither was that likely to have been its state before 1760, until which time ships, not least those of the Vikings, could reach as far inland as Llangefni.

The Cefni rises at Capel Coch and flows southwest across Anglesey to Malltraeth Bay and is tidal from the small bridge just below the A5, near the former coalmining village of Pentre Berw. In its heavily modified form it has a non tidal channel outside the levée on each side and is accompanied by cycleways over the bridge and beside the river. Otherwise it is totally isolated for the first 4km as it cuts across Malltraeth Marsh, the only landmark being a set of overhead powerlines.

In places there are reeds or sedges along the banks but often there are only embankments grazed by sheep, occasionally some gorse. Birdlife is more varied, with grebes, moorhens, swans, mallards, buzzards, lapwings,

The bridge at the tidal limit carries a cycleway.

The river is in fairly straight cut across Malltraeth Marsh.

cormorants, egrets, herons, oystercatchers, wagtails and blackheaded and herring gulls.

The roads return at Pont Maquis and a lane follows the north side of the river but is separated from it by the drainage channel. The river becomes steadily shallower as it approaches Malltraeth. Glan-traeth used to have a zoo and a standing stone near it must be indicative of some other long forgotten activity.

A viaduct carries the Euston to Holyhead railway over,

the main transport link between London and Ireland. A pair of engines pulling a single wagon with white containers will be moving nuclear material from Wylfa power station.

Malltraeth was sacked by the Vikings. In the 18th and 19th Centuries it was a shipbuilding port, although there is no harbour as such, and it was the centre of Anglesey's coalmining industry, supplying Parys Mountain. Telford built the Cob in 1815, reclaiming farmland and creating

The main railway link between London and Ireland.

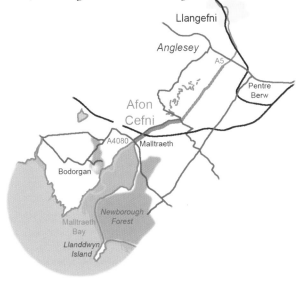

The Afon Cefni passes through Malltraeth Cob as a rapid. The non-tidal flanking drains pass through sluices.

Most of the time there is only a shallow channel on the west side of the estuary.

Malltraeth Pool. The A4080 passes over one end, crossing the Afon Cefni with low tide rapids below it and passing over the two adjacent drainage channels with sluices at the downstream end. From 1947 to 1979 Malltraeth was the home of bird artist Charles Tunnicliffe, who wrote about the area in his *Shorelands Summer Diary*.

The river now opens up into a wide estuary, the flow down the west side and the rest being Malltraeth Sands, usually dry and reaching across to mudflats, salt and brackish marsh, lagoons and then Newborough Forest with the high peaks of Snowdonia rising beyond to give a jagged skyline. This is national nature reserve with a nature trail, pheasants, razorbills, redshanks, greenshanks, sandpipers and other waders. Boats moor in the shallow water down to Bodorgan, the most attractive part of the estuary.

Dinas-lwyd is a conspicuous outcrop as the river discharges into Malltraeth Bay. To the south is Llanddwyn Island, not normally an island, while to the west is Pen-y-parc with its promontory fort. Further up the coast is Valley Airfield, ensuring plenty of activity as training jets and helicopters come and go.

Newborough Forest is backed by the peaks of Snowdonia.

Dinas-lwyd marks the start of Malltraeth Bay.

Distance
11km from Pentre Berw to Malltraeth Bay

OS 1:50,000 Sheets
114 Anglesey
115 Snowdon

Admiralty Charts
1464 Menai Strait (1:25,000)
1970 Caernarfon Bay (1:75,000)

Tidal Constants
Llanddwyn Island:
HW Dover −0100,
LW Dover −0120

Sea Area
Irish Sea

Rescue
Inshore lifeboat:
Trearddur Bay
All weather lifeboat:
Porthdinllaen

Malltraeth Sands are uncovered for much of the tidal cycle.

16 Afon Conwy

Europe's most complete town walls

On a rock, whose haughty brow
Frowns o'er old Conway's foaming flood,
Robed in the sable garb of woe,
With haggard eyes the Poet stood;
Thomas Gray

The name means the glorious river. Rising on Migneint, it flows north to Conwy Bay. It is tidal from Tan-lan but there have long been disputes about access and notices purport to ban canoes even down on the tidal section.

The river was a freshwater pearl fishery and the only UK spawning area for smelt. The water is peaty and there are low water grade 1 rapids to Trefriw.

The peak of Grinllwm, cloaked in Coed y Gwmannog, rises above the river.

Trefriw is at the confluence with the Afon Crafnant.

Coed Gwydir blocks both sun and wind from the west.

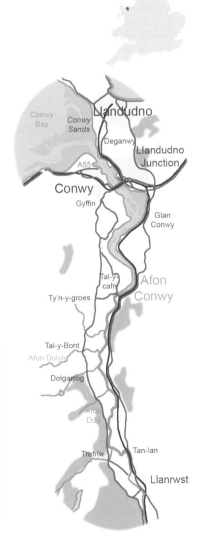

The pipe bridge at Dolgarrog is an important foot crossing.

Upstream is a great rounded bulk of wooded hill and some wind turbines are visible. There are sheep on the levées, reeds often line the river and there are pied wagtails, swans, mallards, herons, cormorants, swallows and waders.

The Afon Crafnant joins just before Trefriw which built ships to 40t with the quay which was used until 1975. The church of St Mary was founded by Llywelyn the Great in the 13th century. The Victorian Trefriw Wells Spa used water piped from wells. Also Victorian, Trefriw Woollen Mills, making bedspreads and tweeds, were located to use

Limestone outcrop below Hafodty.

two hydroelectric turbines, no longer there, and to use the water for washing the wool. The village also claims to possess the world's biggest garden maze.

The Snowdonia national park boundary follows just to the west of the river. The river valley itself, which tends to be exposed to wind, is on the join between Snowdonia's Ordovician volcanic rocks and the Silurian shales and mudstones of the Denbighshire hills.

Above Coed Gwydir is a disused mine while the Romans discovered chalybeate wells and established baths below this wood.

At the foot of 389m Mwdwl is the site to which Edward I moved Maenan Abbey from Conwy, now demolished although a hotel still carries the name. A fort site stands in the trees above it. Following the right bank closely is the Blaenau Ffestiniog to Llandudno Junction railway which could be upgraded to take slate waste from Blaenau Ffestiniog to the West Midlands and Greater Manchester as road base.

A pipe bridge across the Conwy is a useful facility for local pedestrians but a footbridge across the Afon Ddu, which joins directly above it, has a notice saying that it may only be used by anglers. The bridge has long been used as a launch point for small craft, not least the Conwy Ascent canoe marathon which comes up from Conwy Morfa with the tide, but new owners of the aluminium works site have been expected to lock the gate, preventing vehicle access to the lane leading down to the bridge. Aluminium works at Dolgarrog, built in 1907 to benefit from hydroelectric power, have now been demolished. The town lies at the foot of 976m Foel Grach, one of Snowdonia's top 14 peaks. The Afon Porth-llwyd joins past the works, bringing down water from Llyn Eigiau Reservoir where the dam failed in 1925, drowning 16 people.

Powerlines cross and the river divides round some islands. By Coed yr Arw a rock ledge forms a rapid once the water drops a metre from high water. There are

Rapids near Tyn-y-groes.

occasional small navigation marks but prominent yellow buoys give limits for 'watersports' although they seem to apply only to fast and noisy watersports such as water- and jet-skiing. Reedbeds and saltmarsh are designated SSSI. A steep channel beside a low water island has the remains of an old bridge and a sump formed by a mine adit.

The Afon Dulyn joins at Tal-y-Bont and then more powerlines cross before the river forces the railway and road against the foot of a prominent limestone cliff.

After the confluence with the Afon Roe, which flows down from 610m Tal-y-Fan, the Caerhun estate has a church on a low mound, the remains of the Canovium Roman fort of 78 at the lowest fording point on the river, where there may also have been a Roman quay.

Boats along the shore at Bodnant.

Llansanffraid Glan Conwy faces the estuary.

Pines make a change from all the deciduous trees and there are Canada geese, egrets, kingfishers, lapwings, common and blackbacked gulls and oystercatchers. At low water there is a grade 2 rapid to follow with a cave in the cliff. Seaweed begins to appear.

At Tal-y-cafn there has been a ferry crossing since at least the 14th century. A bridge now takes the B5279 over while stakes remain in the river from an earlier bridge. Above the bridge is a slipway with a notice stating that it is only for the use of local residents. A motte below the bridge shows it was a point considered worth guarding.

Benarth Hall is built on a prominent wooded hill.

Conway Castle approached by distinctive bridges.

Deganwy with the remains of Deganwy Castle.

The feel of the valley changes from river to estuary as mud banks begin to appear. Levée constrains the left bank and some large boats are grounded below Bodnant. Bodnant Garden, begun in 1875, is amongst the world's most spectacular gardens, 40ha being laid out early in the 20th century by the 2nd Lord Aberconwy. There are national collections of rhododendrons, magnolias and eucryphias, camellias, daffodils, azaleas, roses, hydrangeas, clematis, water lilies, a 55m laburnum tunnel, Britain's largest sequoia, five Italianate gardens, formal lawns, a wild garden, a rock garden, a wooded valley and an old mill.

Powerlines pass over for the last time. Beyond Iolyn Park above Gorse Hill the Groes Inn achieved the distinction in 1573 of being the first licensed house in Wales. The historic Cymryd site is on a small headland below it.

The right bank has a neolithic burial chamber and a windsock, its orange contrasting with the white houses of Llansanffraid Glan Conwy, which takes its name from St Brigid and the valley. It was she who, during a 5th century fish famine, threw rushes into the river and a few days later they turned into shoals of sparlings or brwyniad, meaning rush-like. Felin Isaf is a 17th century watermill with machinery mostly from about 1730.

The river formerly flowed to Penrhyn Bay, probably being diverted to its present course by icesheets. The Cob was built to reclaim land, not entirely successfully as lagoons remain, perversely acting as a bird sanctuary and used by a bird shooting club. The Conwy nature reserve has herring gulls, ducks, geese, waders and good winter birds. In 1992 the RSPB said the Conwy was threatened with permanent damage by recreational use and a barrage. Much tunnel spoil had been tipped here, which could be why the silt in the river gives way to strata of harder clay scoured by the flow.

Resisting the flow rather better is the high wooded hill with Benarth Hall sited on top. Round the west and north sides of the hill flows the tributary Afon Gyffin, which used to have another watermill.

Not surprisingly, **Conwy**'s most conspicuous building is Conwy Castle at the water's edge, one of the best preserved of Edward I's iron ring of castles. Built in 1283–7 of Denbigh grit, it has eight huge towers, shaped to suit the rock on the site. The 38m long Great Hall, now roofless, is bow shaped with a barbican at each end. The castle has a museum of Edward I and his Welsh castles, including a scale model.

Three bridges squeeze across the river next to the castle. The first is Stephenson's 1848 Tubular Bridge carrying the Euston to Holyhead railway. It was built with two rectangular tubes each weighing 1,300t with one end on rollers and ornamentation in the form of towers with turrets and battlements. In 1899 the length was reduced from 122m to 94m but it had already advanced the science of bridge building. Next to it is the earlier castellated Conwy Suspension Bridge of 1826, the most successful of Telford's Gothic bridges. Of 100m span, it was one of the first suspension bridges with two lanes and with a cable of wrought iron bars. It now carries only pedestrians. The final bridge is the 1958 Conwy Arch, 94m span with long wing walls and pilasters like cutwaters on the downstream side only. It has an asymmetric shape because there were plans to demolish Telford's bridge and build the other carriageway of the new bridge on its site but a worldwide protest resulted in the job only being half done and the

suspension bridge being reprieved, if rather hidden by its neighbours.

Removing the bottleneck would only have transferred it to the town. Conwy is Britain's best preserved fortified town with some of the most complete town walls in Europe, 1.2km long including 22 towers and three original gateways. Local buses ease through the archways with perhaps 50mm of clearance on their mirrors on each side so there is no way that the town could handle modern road freight traffic.

The medieval, Jacobean, Georgian and Victorian town has over 200 listed buildings. St Mary & All Saints' church was founded in 1190 although most of it is from 1300 on a new site, the Cistercian Aberconwy Abbey, a tombstone of which inspired Wordsworth's *We Are Seven*. Aberconwy House, also of 1300, is the only surviving medieval merchant's house in the town, one of the oldest houses in Wales. Built of stone and timber, it still has only limited electric lighting. Plas Mawr, rebuilt in 1576, is the best preserved Elizabethan town house in Britain, with 1665 furniture, a haunted room, notable plasterwork and a 17th century garden. Char Bazaar Teapot Museum covers three centuries and Seion Chapel is Grade II.

Pleasure craft and fishing vessels are moored off the Town Quay, which has the smallest house in Britain. The 19th century two storey building is 1.8m wide, 2.5m deep and 3.1m high, belonging to a 1.88m fisherman until 1900, when it was condemned for human habitation although it is still earning revenue from those who pay to see the inside. Mussels from the estuary are cleaned in a building by the quay.

The traffic problem was solved in 1991 when the A55 North Wales Expressway was routed through an immersed tube tunnel placed in a trench dredged across the estuary, the first immersed tube tunnel in Britain, the engineering made more complex by the fact that it curves in both plan and elevation.

On the east bank **Llandudno Junction** merges into Deganwy, the name a corruption of Dinas Conwy. The 7th century Deganwy Castle, built on a rugged hill above the town, has been destroyed many times, including by lightning. A tower stands further back on high ground. The railway has a couple of hand powered cranes and a level crossing leading to a slipway down the shingle beach.

Conwy Marina is sited in a basin which has been used to manufacture sections of Mulberry Harbour and also the immersed tube tunnel. Between the plutonic volcanic crag of Conwy Mountain and the extensive Conwy Sands in Conwy Bay is Conwy Morfa with its golf course, sand dunes and Butterfly Jungle, 590m^2 of tropical garden and fish pool with over 300 butterflies, other insects and tropical birds, although it had military targets during the Second World War.

Flows run to 11km/h but the channel changes constantly and the buoys have to be moved. Amongst mussel banks the fairway turns from northwest to west at an 11m black metal column with a sector light. In the distance can be seen the west side of **Llandudno**, the Great Ormes Head, Puffin Island and Anglesey.

A mermaid was once washed up in the bay. She asked the local fishermen to help her back to the sea but they refused. Before she died she cursed them and said they would always be poor. This was given as the reason for the fish famine which St Brigid addressed during the 5th century..

Distance
19km from Tan-lan to Conwy Bay

OS 1:50,000 Sheet
115 Snowdon

Admiralty Charts
1463 Conwy Bay & Approaches (1:25,000). Conwy (1:10,000) 1977 Holyhead to Gt Ormes Head (1:75,000) 1978 Gt Ormes Head to Liverpool (1:75,000)

Tidal Constants
Conwy: HW Dover −0300, LW Same as Dover

Sea Area
Irish Sea

Rescue
Inshore lifeboat: Conwy All weather lifeboat: Llandudno

17 River Dee

Formerly northern England's major port

They rowed her in across the rolling foam,
  The cruel crawling foam,
  The cruel hungry foam,
 To her grave beside the sea:
But still the boatmen hear her call the cattle home
  Across the sands of Dee.

Charles Kingsley

Chester was founded in 79 by the Roman 20th Legion, who named their Deva fortress after the River Dee although the Old English name came from ceaster, a Roman fort. The Roman amphitheatre, holding 7,000, was the largest in stone in Britain, half of it having been excavated, and it had a shrine to Nemesis. The Romans' legacy ranges from the cheese rolling contest and a Roman bath house below Spud-U-Like to the Roman and medieval red sandstone walls which run for 3km around the city, the most complete Roman fortress walls in Europe. In what is the English city with more ghosts than any other, the footsteps of a Roman sentry are heard passing through the walls of the George & Dragon Inn and returning 20 minutes later at the site of a Roman cemetery.

There were Viking raids in the Dark Ages but Æthelflæd drove them back and had extended the walls by the 10th century.

Grosvenor Park has a miniature railway while Grosvenor Museum features Chester silver, art, natural history and the Romans.

The Saxon minster became the Benedictine abbey in 1092, replaced with Gothic construction in 1260–1537 and made Chester Cathedral four years later. The inside was restored in 1868–76 by Sir George Gilbert Scott but the west front is still 16th century. St Werburgh's tomb is inside, the 1380 carved choirstalls are the best in the UK, it has the most complete monastic cloisters in England and there is fine stained glass, the marked score of Handel's *Messiah*, first rehearsed here in 1742, and a 19th century cobweb picture. A weakness in the central tower resulted in construction of the separate Addleshaw Tower or Chester Space Rocket to hold the 13 bells in the 1960s. This is the most popular free attraction in the UK. St John's church, founded in 1075, is one of the region's first Norman churches although now in a Victorian exterior. There is a 14th century anchorite's cell. The 14/15th century church of St Mary is an excellent example of Perpendicular styling.

Katie's Tea Rooms are the largest in England, contained in a 1,000 year old building with beams, wattle and daub. There has been a covered market since 1139, developing into the Rows, two tiered 13th century galleries in magpie style. The Three Arches of about 1200 is Britain's oldest shopfront. Stanley Palace is one of the city's finest timber buildings while Bishop Lloyd's timber framed town house from the early 17th century has ornately carved biblical scenes and fantastic animals. The Bear & Billet of 1664 was one of the last timber framed houses in Britain for three centuries.

Chester was noted for its archers so the term 'more than one yew bow in Chester' was consideration for those who had lost lovers or partners at Agincourt, Crécy or Poitiers. Welshmen were an ongoing problem. Henry IV banned them after sunset and they were only allowed to have knives for meat. The Pepper Gate has been kept

locked since a medieval mayor's daughter hit a ball away in a game, sent her English noble fiancé to search for it and escaped through the gate to a waiting Welsh knight.

Charles I watched his army being defeated at Rowton Moor in 1645 from what has become the King Charles Tower in the walls, now with a Civil War exhibition. The city was besieged for two years until starved out. To get the Wishing Steps to produce the required results it is necessary to walk the walls, then run up, down and up again without drawing breath.

Queen's School of 1883 is on the site of a gaol where public executions took place from 1809 to 1866. More cheerful is the Victorian

The Bear & Billet, Three Kings Tea Room and Olde Edgar.

Chester's Salmon Leap fish pass where the Environment Agency showed that small boats do not disturb fish.

Chester weir's opening boat gate. Beyond are the city walls.

Old Dee Bridge in the centre of Chester.

Diamond Jubilee Eastgate clock of 1897, the world's most photographed after Big Ben.

The Victorian style town hall of 1869 with its 49m sandstone clocktower has the Chester Tapestry inside. Chester Toy & Doll Museum has the biggest collection of Matchbox toys in Europe, there is a Broadcasting Museum, Chester Visitor Centre is in a Grade II building and the Dewa Roman Experience has a galley and street. There are town criers at noon in the summer and the filming of *Hollyoaks* brought the city to a wider audience.

The Dee rises at Dduallt and flows northeast to Liverpool Bay. It is normally tidal from Chester weir but high tides can reach Farndon. Above the weir is a Victorian bandstand and the Groves, which has had a rowing regatta from 1733, the oldest in the world. The 52m long weir is the oldest mill dam in Britain, built in 1071 by Hugh Lupus, the 1st Earl of Chester and cruel nephew of William the Conqueror. The mills were destroyed by floods in medieval times and by fire in 1895. The weir was raised in the 20th century. The 1,800km^2 catchment to here delivers an average natural runoff of 37m^3/s to the weir. A minimum compensation flow of 4.2m^3/s is taken down the Salmon Leap fish pass on the left, which has been used for canoe slaloms and by the Environment Agency to show that salmon are not affected by small boats. On the right is an unusual weir gate which can be opened to allow larger craft through but only when the water is high enough. The stream is outgoing from twenty minutes after Dover high water and ingoing from an hour and a half before Dover high water.

A rock rapid makes the river below the weir impassable by any craft at low water. It is crossed by the Old Dee Bridge built in the 14th century by Henry de Snellston, its seven red sandstone spans from 7 to 15m on the line of a Roman road crossing. In 973 King Edgar was rowed on the river by subservient kings. The mayor is still the Admiral of the Dee, a title first given to the Black Prince in 1354, and the Duke of Westminster is Sergeant of the Dee.

The castle was built in 1070 by William the Conqueror and rebuilt in 1788–1822 as one of the best examples of Greek Revival style outside London. It includes the Cheshire Military Museum including an Ypres trench. The Agricola Tower is the oldest remaining part of the castle, dating from the 12th century with fragments of 13th century wall painting and the medieval vaulted St Mary de Castro chapel on the first floor, protected by the castle walls.

Willows, Himalayan balsam and giant hogweed are some of the river's screening plants. The river has moorings and there can be scum on the water but it is used by herons, cormorants, mallards and moorhens. A large car park next to the river is unusual in allowing overnight parking, appreciated by visitors with campervans.

Next to it is the Grosvenor Bridge taking the A483 over the river. There was a 25 year delay to the opening of

Grosvenor Bridge, the world's fourth longest in masonry.

Rennie's bridge in 1832, when its 61m span and 13m rise made it the world's longest single span in stone. It is still the world's fourth longest.

The Roodee is on the site of the Roman port, some of the Roman harbour walls still being visible. The Water Tower protected the harbour from 1322, built on the bank although it is now 200m away and accompanied by the Water Tower Gardens with their triple maze. By the Middle Ages it was the most important port in the north of England but the river was silting badly by the 15th century, forcing trade to the village of Livpul. The Roodee became the horse racecourse in 1539, the oldest in the country.

The banks remain muddy, rising steeply past horse chestnut trees on the outside of the bend towards quality housing on the top of the hill above.

The Holyhead to Euston railway crosses over. A cast iron span collapsed in 1847, killing five, the subsequent inquiry leading to the development of wrought iron then steel plate girders after Robert Stephenson had tried to blame the accident on derailment, refuted by witnesses.

Powerlines twice cross a sharp bend in the river. Between them the river is joined by the short Dee Branch of the Shropshire Union Canal.

The river has been canalized from here to avoid flooding and has high banks as seaweed floats up with the tide. A sewage works is marked by a green dome as it faces across to a golf course.

A turn at Lache takes the river from the English county of Cheshire to the Welsh county of Flint. Just before another turn in front of an industrial estate at Saltney it is joined by the remains of Sir John Glynne's Canal from Bretton. Lapwings investigate the silt. The river runs dead straight for 9km. A footbridge crosses and cyclists follow both banks.

Beyond Hawarden Airport fendered piles and a berth have been installed at the edge of the river. Airbus A380 wings are manufactured here and shipped out by specially designed motor barge to Mostyn for onward transport to Toulouse.

Activity increases again at Sandycroft near where

The end of Sir John Glynne's Canal.

Dredging near Hawarden Airport.

powerlines cross the river. A shooting school on the north bank is approached from Sealand Manor.

In 946 a statue of the Virgin Mary fell off the roodloft in St Deiniol's in **Hawarden**, killing the wife of the castle governor. The statue was tried by jury, condemned to death by drowning and thrown in the river. Fortunately, it floated, eventually washing ashore in Chester.

Pillboxes appear at intervals, as do abandoned wooden hulls.

The A494 bridge crosses between Garden City and **Queensferry**, the main traffic route between northern England and north Wales. The fixed steel bridge replaces the large rolling bascule bridge next to it, not wide enough for current requirements but still looking smart.

The bascule bridge at Queensferry.

Hawarden Bridge no longer opens.

Derelict jetty and wreck at Shotton.

Local residents at Wepre.

The channel is marked with plastic cans on poles. A timber training wall acts as an approach guide to Hawarden swing bridge of 1889, carrying the Wallasey to Shrewsbury railway. The name was taken from Gladstone's home village and was opened by his wife. The swinging section, a record 87m long, was fixed in 1971.

Shotton steelworks provide an industrial backdrop as cattle from the fields opposite stand nonchalantly in the river at Wepre, accompanied by blackbacked gulls, egrets and Canada geese. Fishing boats are moored around the Old Quay House at **Connah's Quay**, named after an 18th century innkeeper. The stream is outgoing from an hour and ten minutes after Dover high water and ingoing from fifty minutes before Dover high water. Small slipways are present in places on the south bank while boulder groynes form reefs on the north shore.

Shotton Wharf exports steel although a tidal dock is disused. Four sets of powerlines form a web across the river in front of the striking cable stayed bridge carrying the A548, a dual carriageway at this point but to narrow down to a town street in Flint. A row of blast furnaces on the south bank lead the eye away from a dry ski slope.

Training walls edge the channel with metal framework light towers at the ends and tide gauges. The north bank seems to contain quite a bit of slag. Thereafter it has marsh and interesting saltings. This is thought to have been the route taken by the Mersey from Runcorn in preglacial times and the Dee estuary is still silting up. It mostly drains at low water and can be rough when the water is shallow. There are frequent changes of channel. A 500mm bore can develop on spring tides at the start of the flood with initial flow to 15km/h.

A tidal barrage has been proposed but would be opposed by bird enthusiasts, who have a hide on the south bank and who have already claimed that the birds are at risk of permanent damage from land reclaim, recreation, oil and gas development and sea level rise. Waterfowl include 30,000 oystercatchers, 21,000 knots, 18,000 dunlins, 9,000 pintails, 8,000 redshanks, 5,000 teal, 5,000 shelducks, 2,000 grey plovers and 1,000 godwits.

The chimney of a papermill precedes Pentre Ffwrndan where the Romans had lead mines. Behind Flint Sands are the considerable remains of **Flint** Castle, the first of Edward I's chain of Welsh castles, its keep separate from its moat. This is where Shakespeare has Bolingbroke trapping Richard II although he should probably have used Conwy Castle. The moat is now mown lawn and sea aster marsh stretches to seaward, contrasted with the time of the castle's construction when it could have been replenished by ship. Next to it is an inshore lifeboat station, one which would seem to lack the requisite water for much of the time, surely a candidate for a hovercraft.

The empty estuary with mud and sand to the horizon contrasts with the approach channel in the Middle Ages.

Distance
19km from Chester to Flint

OS 1:50,000 Sheet
117 Chester & Wrexham

Admiralty Charts
1978 Gt Ormes Head to Liverpool (1:75,000)

Tidal Constants
Chester:
HW Dover +0120,
LW Dover +0520
Connah's Quay:
HW Dover +0200,
LW Dover +0400

Sea Area
Irish Sea

Rescue
Inshore lifeboat: Flint
All weather lifeboat: Hoylake
Hovercraft: New Brighton

The cable stayed bridge at Connah's Quay.

Flint Castle, the first of Edward I's chain of castles.

18 River Mersey

Owning half the world's shipping lines

People... they rush everywhere...
Each... with their own secret care...

So, ferry 'cross the Mersey,
And always take me there,
The place I love.
Gerry Marsden

The weir at the tidal limit in Warrington.

The River Tame rises at Standedge, flowing westwards before becoming the River Mersey on its journey to Liverpool Bay. Tides are stopped by the large Howley Weir beside Victoria Park in Warrington. The river was used by Mersey flats, having been made navigable before 1697, and there is a disused lock across the neck of the tight turn in the river below the weir.

The ingoing flow runs for an hour and forty minutes here at the start of Port of Liverpool control. The water is dirty and the banks steep and muddy, shaded with beeches and poplars as the river passes both business and retail parks.

Warrington takes its name from the Old English *wering*, village at a weir, or Celtic *werid*, ford. The Romans called it Veratinum, ford town, as they had a crossing here and a settlement at Wilderspool. They made iron, bronze and pottery, possibly siting Britain's first glass furnace here. The town was originally south of the river on the Latchford bank but was moved to the north by the Saxons and renamed Walintune by the Normans.

From 1757 to 1786 Warrington Academy was one of the principal seats of learning for dissenters denied access to Oxford and Cambridge. Students included Jean Paul Marat and Joseph Priestly, who discovered oxygen after attending chemistry lectures. In the 17th and 18th Centuries the town made sailcloth, pins and clocks, a clockmaker making the first spinning frame for Richard Arkwright in 1769. Warrington Museum & Art Gallery

Eel nets between the West Coast Main Line bridges.

There have been six Warrington Bridges since 1305. The latest, from 1915, is one of a pair forming a roundabout across the river for the A49 and its adjoining roads. The rise is only one tenth of the 44m span because of the height constraints, the arches springing from below high water level. It has eight parabolic reinforced concrete ribs and was the first British bridge to be built with reinforced concrete hinges. Construction was in two halves to reduce traffic disruption.

Before opening, it was load tested with tramcars and steamrollers, having settled 80mm during construction. Arpley Bridge carries a freight railway line and the following truss carries a road into an area with restaurants.

features Roman items, 18th and 19th century glass, ceramics, paintings, geology and wildlife.

Warrington's transporter bridge.

Fiddler's Ferry with its power station and the Ferry Tavern.

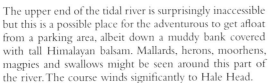

Club racing at Fiddler's Ferry.

Britannia arms on the Runcorn–Widnes railway bridge.

The upper end of the tidal river is surprisingly inaccessible but this is a possible place for the adventurous to get afloat from a parking area, albeit down a muddy bank covered with tall Himalayan balsam. Mallards, herons, moorhens, magpies and swallows might be seen around this part of the river. The course winds significantly to Hale Head.

At the end of a straight reach the river bends to the right opposite a disused and overgrown link which ran to Walton Lock and up to the Manchester Ship Canal, a surprising line which required craft to make two successive 150° turns. The canal runs parallel to the river as far as Eastham and the Trans Pennine Trail for equestrians follows to Hale Bank.

Walton Arches take the West Coast Main Line over with bridges at two levels, eel nets perhaps strung out between them. The railway has obliterated the junction with the Runcorn & Latchford Canal, the derelict course of which remains for 4km to Norton Marsh. Levées confine the river although there is plenty of marshland outside the banks.

Crossing the river is the disused transporter bridge of 1914 which served Joseph Crosfield's first soapworks at Bank Quay. The 103m long gantry has a 61m clear span passing 23m above the river at high water.

Bank Quay reach is crossed by a recent footbridge to new housing and turns to pass between a sewage works and a landscaped refuse tip, around which is Moore Nature Reserve. There are reeds along the banks and shallows begin here, to become extensive further down the estuary. Lapwings are numerous and there are Canada geese and blackheaded, blackbacked and herring gulls.

A small turbine fan marks the mouth of the Sankey Brook which flows down from Sankey Bridges. This was formerly used by ships to reach the St Helens Canal, arguably the first of the industrial canals, later extended along the right bank to Widnes to avoid some of the shallows.

The Penketh reach leads to Fiddler's Ferry with the Ferry Tavern and a sailing club with a rare slipway. Behind is the large power station, start of a couple of sets of powerlines over the river and also the source of the waste ash sent to Cuerdley Marsh lagoons which form a

The arch of the road bridge and the railway bridge between Runcorn and Widnes.

large triangle on the north side of the river. Smaller but equally distinctive on the south side are the tower of the Daresbury nuclear laboratory and a massive 1892 water tower which is a key feature of Liverpool's water supply from Lake Vyrnwy. An Eddie Stobart warehouse has been built next to the Manchester Ship Canal, which comes right alongside the river at Randles Sluices, allowing large ships to glide through the marsh landscape although the largest no longer do so.

From here the river moves from Warrington to Halton. Hempstones Point is at the edge of Wigg Island, occupied by Astmoor Salt Marsh. It is proposed to take the cable stayed Mersey Gateway bridge across to meet modern traffic requirements.

Runcorn takes its name from the Old English *rum cofa*, spacious bay. Across Runcorn Sands is **Widnes**, from

A substantial variant of the derrick crane below Runcorn.

Chemical plant at Weston Point on the Weaver Navigation and Manchester Ship Canal. The Bridgewater Canal now ends above.

The ridge of Helsby Hill rises above Frodsham, the M56 and the marshes of Frodsham Score.

the Old English *wid ness*, broad headland. The St Helens Canal joins the river at Spike Island, the world's first dock, canal and railway interchange complex, its name coming from the slang for lodging houses. An alkali works in 1847 established the chemical industry here, explained in Catalyst, the museum of the chemical industry.

Two bridges cross the Runcorn Gap. The A533 is taken over the 330m span bowstring Runcorn–Widnes Silver Jubilee Bridge, a steel arch with a reinforced concrete deck which has 23m clearance over the river. Replacing another transporter bridge, it was the third largest bridge of its kind in the world when built in 1961 and is the largest bridge under local authority control.

It was not built as a suspension bridge as wind tunnel tests showed there was a risk of oscillation from the adjacent railway bridge. This 1868 structure has three 93m lattice girder main spans carrying the Lime Street to Euston railway and needing 59 arches for the Widnes approach in order to obtain the required height. The piers are in battlemented Victorian Gothic revival style with Britannia crests.

Flows are ingoing for two and a half hours here and the ebb is swift to leave a largely empty channel with depths and positions which change frequently. There are vertical mud cliffs which are exposed below high water. Tide height is increased by a southwesterly wind and decreased by a northeasterly wind. Even though it is a tidal navigation, an Act of 1805 theoretically allows tolls to be collected.

The estuary was the Seteia Aestuarium to the Romans and is SSSI to environmentalists. The RSPB claimed there was a risk of permanent damage to birds from pollution, sand extraction and a barrage. The former was addressed by the Mersey Estuary Pollution Alleviation Scheme with 28km of sewers up to 2.4m in diameter, intercepting

26 outfalls and taking their effluent to Liverpool Wastewater Treatment Works in Sandon Dock. While the water remains opaque, beaches such as New Brighton are significantly cleaner. There are 64,000 winter wildfowl including 24,000 dunlins, 11,000 teal, 5,900 pintails, 3,800 redshanks and 3,400 shelducks. There are cormorants, curlews, godwits and, below the surface, lesser octopus, lumpfish, plaice, dabs, whiting, cod and sea trout.

Although surrounded by human activity and industry, much of the Mersey estuary remains inaccessible to most people and so forms a relative oasis. It is mostly too shallow for sailing craft and much of the southern side is closed off by the Manchester Ship Canal. Thus, it is possible to observe the bird life with its industrial backdrop but be isolated from potential conflicts.

Beyond the prominent Tesco presence on the north bank Ditton Brook joins under a graceful modern arched bridge. It leads past a chemical works site to Hale Bank and a country park.

Standing in front of the docks on the Manchester Ship Canal is a massive derrick crane, dark and sinister. The Bridgewater Canal now ends on top of Runcorn Hill with its housing although it originally descended to the River Mersey. The chemical works begin in earnest, brightly illuminated at night. Around the estuary excessive pumping from boreholes has drawn in saltwater contamination. Seldom Seen Rocks are off Weston Point. Weaver Sluices allow the River Weaver to discharge across the Manchester Ship Canal into the River Mersey.

Frodsham Score fronts Frodsham Marsh, an area susceptible to fog. The shoreline is of hard layered clay behind Frodsham Deposit Grounds, used for dumping silt dredged from the Manchester Ship Canal. **Frodsham** was once a major port on the River Weaver. An aerial at Frodsham stands at one end of a line of red cliffs which

Birds pass the refinery infrastructure at Stanlow Point. Note the superstructures of shipping moored on the Manchester Ship Canal.

extend to the 141m high sandstone **Helsby** Hill, at the foot of which the Runcorn to Birkenhead railway and the M56 run parallel to the shore.

Helsby Marsh and Ince Marshes extend as Ince Banks which it is proposed to reclaim although they are presently the preserve of wildfowl and waders, Canada geese, eiders, oystercatchers and many others. The lower land to the southwest now allows clear views through to the Welsh hills. Ince comes from ynys, the Welsh for island. At Ince a partly ruined manor house of about 1500 used to belong to the Abbots of Chester. These days it is lost in the development, starting with the power station. On the canal are Ince Powergen Berth, Ince Tying-up Berth, Ince Oil Berth and Ince Coaster Berth for petroleum products. The bridges of larger tankers show above the marshes as they move slowly along the canal or discharge their cargoes.

Stanlow Banks are also proposed for reclaim. The River Gowy empties past the raised Stanlow Point and Stanlow Abbey remains accessible only from the River Mersey. Dominating the scene is the Stanlow oil refinery, started by Shell in 1924 with a mass of chimneys, flares, tanks and lights. The quantity and intensity of the lights are such that this would be an interesting trip to undertake at night although the shallows are hard enough to see even in daylight. On the canal are Stanlow Oil Docks for three tankers for petroleum spirit and also Stanlow Chemical Berth.

The refinery ends at **Ellesmere Port** which was built by Telford in 1833 and was the finest canal port in England. It is located at the end of the Shropshire Union Canal which was every bit as important in its day as the Manchester Ship Canal was to become. The name comes from Ellesmere in Shropshire which was intended to be served by canal via Trevor. Sandwiched between the ship canal and the M53 Mid Wirral Motorway, but not accessible from the estuary, is the Ellesmere Port boat museum, opened in 1976 with 30 canal craft, painted boatware, tools, plans, documents, a working steam engine and four cottages from the 1840s to the 1950s. It is

Britain's premier canal museum with the world's largest collection of floating historic craft.

A paper works stands high on Mount Manisty, a large heap of spoil named after the engineer who deposited it while constructing the Manchester Ship Canal. More oil storage depots are found each side of the hill and another car factory. There is a Ro-Ro ferry and container terminal. Along the shore the banks grade quickly from silt which is almost liquid to sand which is scooped into pools by the tide.

Cheshire gives way to the Wirral and Ellesmere Port becomes Poole Hall Bay Embankment. Until now the large vessels have been kept the other side of a wall. Eastham Locks mark the end of the Manchester Ship Canal, the largest of our canals, built 1887–94. The large lock is 183m x 24m. About eight vessels per day pass through each way although most do not go beyond Stanlow. The largest shipping movements take place around high water with the middle lock in use up to four hours each side of high water. Behind is the Queen Elizabeth II Dock for bulk petroleum and liquid chemical vessels up to 40,000 dwt. At this point the shipping channel is narrow and buoyed.

Eastham Woods Country Park is marked by a half timbered building by the shore. Eastham Ferry was operated to Liverpool from the early 1800s to 1929 but a much older service was Job's Ferry, operated by monks 800 years ago for King John.

A chemical works at Bromborough (from the Old English Bruna's fort) is a reminder that it was here that the Lever Brothers established their soap works, from which have come many of the best known washing powder brands, including Sunlight, after which the 53ha Port Sunlight was named. The Port Sunlight Heritage Centre displays the enlightened model garden village built in 1888 by William Hesketh Lever for his workers. It includes the Lady Lever Art Gallery, created by the 1st Viscount Leverhulme in 1913, with English 18th century and pre-Raphaelite paintings, furniture, Wedgwood and oriental porcelains.

The high vertical wall of Mersey Wharf fronts

Glistening silt slopes down to the water at the approach to Bromborough Pool.

The twin towers of the Royal Liver Building beyond the red Albert Dock, Echo Arena and BT Conference Centre in Liverpool.

Bromborough Pool, formerly Bromborough Dock, from which a stream discharges down a flight of steps. It was opened in 1990 for vessels to 6,000t. The southwest corner of the wall is a favourite place for throwing vehicles off the edge, resulting in a heap of twisted metalwork, foul ground best avoided.

A disused lighthouse on the north shore marks Hale Head, surrounded by the drying Score Bank. Dungeon Banks lead to Eastham Sands. A section of the Trans Pennine Trail follows the shore to Liverpool.

Near Hale skylarks sing above oilseed rape fields. At the top of the hill is the tower of Hale church, opposite which is the History Tree, a tall tree trunk carved in the form of a man wearing a ruff. The churchyard contains the grave of the Child of Hale, 2.82m John Middleton, who lived from 1578 to 1623 and who was sent by landowner Sir Gilbert Ireland to wrestle the court champion of James I, won by dislocating his thumb, and retired to Hale with his £20 prize money. It was claimed that he was attacked by a bull but threw it over a hedge. An existing handprint suggests his actual height was nearer 2.4m.

There are ruins of Hale Hall, designed by John Nash. Behind the housing estates of **Speke** is Ford's Halewood car factory.

Halton gives way to Liverpool at the start of John Lennon Airport. Apart from the aircraft, its conspicuous features are the control tower overlooking the river and a runway light gantry running out into the estuary at the end of the main runway.

The black and white Tudor Speke Hall has everything except location, being surrounded on three sides by runways and taxiways. Built in 1530 near the river, it is one of the best preserved timber framed houses in Britain with Jacobean plasterwork, carved furniture, tapestries, William Morris decoration, Victorian interiors and kitchen, Roman Catholic family priestholes and eavesdropper and spyholes. A Victorian garden contains 16th century Adam and Eve yew trees, a maze, a grassy moat, an Elizabethan stone bridge and woodland.

Garston Rocks stand off **Garston** Docks with their piles of scrap metal but there is a safe approach from downstream through the Garston Channel, which is fully buoyed. Mersey Channel Collision Regulations apply. There is another extensive area of rock on the Devil's Bank off Otterspool, a section of coast with attractive older housing and a landscaped promenade area. Included are the Festival Gardens at Dingle, converted from a wasteland to a site for the National Garden Festival with such delights as the Yellow Submarine.

At New Ferry an area of mown grass fronts a housing estate. New Ferry to the Festival Gardens is the preferred site for a 1.9km long Mersey barrage which would generate 700MW but drown out 40% of the mudflats for the birds. It would have a lock at each bank. Energy is already delivered to the Sloyne in the form of the Tranmere Oil Terminal which receives tankers to 320,000t.

At low tide there is firmer ground and less of a slope at Rock Ferry.

The river feeds down into the Narrows where the traffic becomes busier and the currents faster. This section of the estuary may be a glacial channel, deepened in places for Manchester Ship Canal traffic, the former route to Shotton having been filled with glacial drift. Flow through the Narrows was probably southwards until after the Pleistocene glaciation. The end of the Wirral is sinking at 9mm/year and this could cause a major threat to Liverpool shipping if a new channel develops.

Formerly with a shipbuilding area on the shore, Liverpool's Afro Caribbean area of Toxteth has been remembered more recently for its riots in 1981. It leads to the southern docks which are now used for recreational boats and include a marina. Yellow Duckmarine, based on rebuilt DUKWs, allow the public to see the docks from the water.

Liverpool takes its name from the Old English lifer, sludge, although sand is now revealed along the seafront at low water. It received its charter from King John in 1207 and grew from the fishing village of Livpul to the second city of the British Empire, adding the UK's Capital of Pop and the 2008 European Capital of Culture to its accolades. Its affluence resulted from the Liverpool Triangle. Ships took salt and textiles to west Africa, carried slaves from there to the West Indies and brought sugar, molasses and spices back on the home leg.

There are 250 monuments and 2,500 listed buildings including the largest collection of Grade II buildings outside London. The Royal Liverpool Philharmonic is Europe's third oldest orchestra. Only London has more museums, galleries and theatres. The city includes Europe's oldest African and Chinese communities.

The world's oldest independent shipping company, the Bibby Line, was founded here in 1817 and the first transatlantic steamship, the *Savannah*, arrived two years later. Liverpool built the *Royal William* which made the first transatlantic crossing with passengers in 1838. The first transatlantic liner, Samuel Cunard's *Britannia* paddle steamer, crossed from Liverpool in 1840. Brunel's *SS Great Britain* made her maiden voyage from here in 1845 and his *Great Eastern* ended up on the Mersey as a floating funfair until broken up in 1888. Liverpool owned half the world's shipping lines and by 1930 Liverpudlians owned 40% of British shipping. In the century to 1930, 9,000,000 emigrants left from here, Europe's

main departure port for America. Bonfires on Good Friday for the burning of Judas Escariot are a custom which may have been imported by sailors from Iberia or Latin America.

Two cathedrals rise on the skyline. The Anglican cathedral by Giles Gilbert Scott in red sandstone Gothic with its 101m tower was completed in 1978 after 74 years, the largest British cathedral and the fifth largest in the world. It is 194m long, has the highest vaulting in the world at 53m, the highest Gothic arches at 33m and the world's highest and heaviest peal of bells. The Roman Catholic Metropolitan Cathedral of Christ the King, the work of Sir Frederick Gibberd, built 1960–7, has been irreverently nicknamed the Mersey Funnel or Paddy's Wigwam because of its unique design, a 59m diameter crown of thorns with 13 chapels leading off, flying buttresses and a wedge shaped belltower.

Recent buildings on the waterfront are the matching oval BT Conference Centre and Echo Arena. The granite Albert Dock of 1846 by Jesse Hartley has stone and brick warehouses which form the largest group of Grade I buildings in the UK. Claimed to be Britain's top heritage attraction, they have the Beatles Story, featuring the world's greatest pop group, brought up in the city. They also have the Fingerprints of Elvis exhibition and the Tate Northern, the largest gallery of modern art outside London, plus many places to eat, drink and shop. The Merseyside Maritime Museum includes slavery, emigration, the Battle of the Atlantic, shipbuilding, pilotage, merchant shipping, sugar, the *Titanic* and the *Lusitania*. The Albert Warehouse has ship models, marine paintings, navigation, emigration and the marine environment generally. There is an International Slavery Museum and HM Customs & Excise have a museum. Among the moored craft is the *Planet*, the former Mersey Bar and Channel lightvessel. There is a Rennie footbridge and the Liverpool Link brings the Leeds & Liverpool Canal to its new terminus. A pumphouse with a 40m chimney is now a public house pumping beer for its customers.

The Three Graces are the Port of Liverpool Building, the Cunard Building and the Royal Liver Building, the latter thought to have been the largest reinforced concrete building in the world when completed in 1908, at 92m x 54m x 51m to the main roof. It has the largest clock in Britain, started as George V was crowned, and has the 5.5m Liver Birds on top of its 90m towers, actually poor sculptures of St John the Evangelist's eagles. The Museum of Liverpool has now joined them.

Liverpool Landing Stage is a 350m long floating structure from which leave fast ferries to Douglas and Dublin. On the Pier Head is a *Titanic* memorial, the ship's owners being the White Star Line with their headquarters in Albion House. The Western Approaches Museum is in the Fortress, 4,600m^2 of office basement which controlled the Battle of the Atlantic and sent 1,300 convoys from here, perhaps because so many of the ships were Liverpool owned.

Road tunnels pass under the Mersey. The 3.4km Queensway Tunnel of 1934 to Birkenhead was the world's longest underwater tunnel for decades. The later Kingsway Tunnel to **Wallasey** was cut in a band of Bunter sandstone almost free of pebbles.

The Mersey River Festival in June is the largest free maritime festival in Europe and there is an annual Cross-Mersey Swim. Elizabeth Gaskell's *Mary Barton* and Dickens' *Uncommercial Traveller* used the setting. Like Tyneside, Merseyside is the setting for many romantic novels. It was used for filming *The Virgin of Liverpool, Between the Lines, 51st State, The Hunt for Red October, My Kingdom, In the Name of the Father, Letter to Brezhnev, Backbeat* and *Priest*, being the most filmed city outside London. Its musicians have had 56 number one hits, more than any other city. Local artists include Alan Bleasdale, Clive Barker, Beryl Bainbridge, Linda Grant,

A Manx cat at the Pierhead in front of the Royal Liver Building.

Nicholas Hawthorne, Adrian Henri, Roger McGough, Jimmy McGovern, Nicholas Monsarrat, Brian Patten and Willy Russel. Eleanor Rathbone was the first woman councillor fighting for better pay and conditions for Liverpool workers, votes for women and, as an MP, the family allowance. Both Littlewood's and Vernon's football pools began here. In 1841 the world's first public health engineer, Dr William Henry Duncan, was appointed.

The triangular run these days is undertaken by the Mersey ferries from Liverpool Landing Stage via Seacombe and Birkenhead. It was started in 1282 by the monks of Birkenhead Priory.

Cammell Laird are based at the Princess Dry Dock. They built America's first iron paddle steamer, the *John Randolph*, which was shipped in pieces for reassembly. Other craft they have built include battleships, destroyers, aircraft carriers, submarines and tankers.

Much of Birkenhead's marine activity takes place around the West and East Float, the estuary of the Birket. The Alfred Dock can be used as a lock if Alfred Lock is not long enough. Two tugs were built in 1851 from the timbers of the first Chinese junk in Europe. Six years later the American navy sailed with half of the Atlantic telegraph cable, made here, and the following year Livingstone sailed in the river steamer *Ma Robert*, also built here for him. These days Ro-Ro ferries operate from the Twelve Quays to Belfast and Dublin.

The East Float has the Historic Warships Museum, including the Falklands frigate *HMS Plymouth* which was hit four times but took the final surrender of the Argentinians. *HMS Onyx*, the only non nuclear submarine, landed SAS and SBS members. *HMS Bronington* of 1953, commanded by the Prince of Wales, was the Royal Navy's last wooden boat. *U534* is one of the last four U boats, failing to surrender when the Germans gave the order and being sunk by the RAF although the crew escaped.

The Edgerton bascule bridge has models and information on the docks. The Giant Grasshopper is the steam pump

for the 1886 tunnel, Europe's first underwater railway tunnel. The first tramway in Europe had been opened in 1860 and still has historical trams running.

Birkenhead takes its name from the Old English *bircan*, birch. It has a domed townhall and a Norman Priory of 1150, the oldest building on Merseyside. A brighter local product was the vivid Della Robbia ware pottery.

The east side of the river has continuous enclosed docks through Vauxhall, Sandhills and **Bootle** (the Old English *bothl* being a large dwelling house) to Crosby. In 1824 there were 60 docks. The first enclosed commercial wet dock in the world had been started in 1710 and was in use from 1715. The Seaforth container depot, flanked by half a dozen wind turbines, was set up in 1973 with the world's first computer controlled operation, despite the bitter opposition of the trades unions.

An amber isophase light on the Port Radar Station indicates a large vessel is inbound. Tugs join ships here for the estuary. Buoys are moved as the channel changes and ships have to deal with flows to 9km/h.

Ferries allowed New Brighton to develop as a resort with a coastal promenade in the 1830s. The Wirral Show, one of the largest free shows in the country, is where Sibelius' music was first heard in public in England. The town has a domed Roman Catholic church, a Floral Pavilion, a New Palace and had, from 1898 until its demolition in 1921, the New Brighton Tower, the tallest structure in Britain. The pier has gone and the beach also disappeared after the building of Seaforth Docks, exposing Perch Rock. Training walls have restored the sand, probably courtesy of the Brazil Bank in Liverpool Bay, and personal watercraft are allowed to use the beach facing onto the river and some moorings. Lion's mane jellyfish also share the water. Off Fort Perch, built in 1827, is the disused white granite tower Rock Lighthouse.

Mersey ferries Snowdrop and Royal Iris at the Seacombe terminal. Behind is the ventilation system for the Kingsway Tunnel.

The Perch Rock lighthouse with the adjacent fort.

Distance
42km from Howley to New Brighton

OS 1:50,000 Sheets
108 Liverpool
109 Manchester
117 Chester
& Wrexham

Admiralty Charts
1951 Approaches to Liverpool (1:25,000)
1978 Gt Ormes Head to Liverpool (1:75,000)
3478 Manchester Ship Canal & Upper R Mersey (1:25,000). Ellesmere Port & Stanlow Oil Docks (1:10,000). Runcorn & Weston Pt Docks (1:10,000)
3490 Port of Liverpool (1:15,000)

Tidal Constants
Fiddler's Ferry:
HW Dover +0120,
LW Dover +0530
Widnes:
HW Dover +0050,
LW Dover +0420
Hale Head:
Dover +0400
Eastham:
HW Dover +0020,
LW Dover +0040
Liverpool:
Dover +0020
New Brighton:
Dover +0010

Sea Area
Irish Sea

Rescue
Inshore lifeboat:
New Brighton
All weather lifeboat:
Hoylake
Hovercraft:
New Brighton

Connection
St Helens Canal – see CoB p196

19 River Lune

The red rose and the healthy river

Lamps burned in the bedrooms, the world was awaking,
Near Lancaster city we passed the first man.
Ere we left him behind us the morning was breaking,
And soon all about us the day's work began.

John Masefield

The River Lune is formed at Wath at the confluence of the Sandwath Beck and Weasdale Beck.

The 15km River Lune Millennium Park runs from Caton to Lancester and has an assortment of carvings, sculptures and signs.

Most of the weir which forms the tidal limit is a high vertical structure with a moat running around the bottom and overlooked by a building on a single pillar. Down the middle of the weir is a fish ladder in three steps. When the tide is in these may be possible to descend but at low tide the bottom step is about a metre high with a 10m towback and a further rapid to follow. It looks lethal.

The run down into central Lancaster passes a tower block which appears to be built on a rock outcrop.

A small shop in a back street on the other bank stocks Lancashire clogs. Despite the advances of modern technology it seems that the local shepherds still find them the most practical and dry footwear and the shop also supplies clog dancers all over the country.

Lancaster is the red rose city, centre for the Lancastrians in the Wars of the Roses. It takes its name from lune, Celtic for healthy, and ceaster, Old English for fort. The market square is where Charles II was proclaimed king in 1651. In the 19th century local palaeontologist Sir Richard Owen planned London's Natural History Museum and invented the word 'dinosaur' but claimed Darwin's natural selection theories did not fully explain evolution.

The Romans built a bath house in Lancaster. The 15th century Perpendicular Benedictine Priory church of St Mary includes a Saxon wall and doorway on the site of a Roman fort and contains 13th century carved choirstalls, some of the earliest and finest in England, in addition to fine needlework and Abyssinian Coptic crosses. A Saxon church of about 600 was replaced with a 1380–1430 model, the memorial chapel of which has the colours of the King's Own Royal Lancaster Regiment.

Beyond a large plate girder bridge is the Norman Lancaster Castle. The massive gatehouse is 15th century but most of the castle was restored in the 18th and 19th Centuries. Its two storey square keep dates from the late 11th or early 12th century and was heightened from its original form. There remains part of a bailey curtain with a round and two square towers. In 1800 it was extensively rebuilt as a prison and still partly used for this purpose, past residents including the ten Demdyke witches of 1612 and Quaker founder George Fox, its implements including a clamp last used for branding criminals in 1811. The 11th century Hadrian's Tower has a cat o' nine tails last used in 1915. The Turret or John of Gaunt's Chair has a view to the Isle of Man and was used to signal the approach of the Armada. The county court is still here and there is also a heraldry display with over 600 shields. There are the remains of a Roman fort by the river.

Less dramatic buildings include the Baroque Music Room of the 1730s with ornate plasterwork, the Judges' Lodgings town house with Gillow furniture and a museum of childhood. Lancaster City Museum with Roman

The Millennium Bridge snakes across the river.

Plover Scar lighthouse.

Distance
13km from Skerton to Plover Scar

OS 1:50,000 Sheets
97 Kendal & Morecambe
102 Preston & Blackpool

Admiralty Charts
1552 Ports in Morecambe Bay. R Lune & Approaches to Heysham (1:25,000). Glasson (1:12,500) 2010 Morecambe Bay & Approaches (1:50,000)

Tidal Constants
Lancaster:
HW Dover +0100
Glasson Dock:
HW Dover +0040,
LW Dover +0240

Sea Area
Irish Sea

Rescue
Inshore lifeboat:
Fleetwood
All weather lifeboat:
Fleetwood
Hovercraft:
Morecambe

material found locally is in the 1783 Georgian former town hall, together with the Museum of the King's Own Royal Lancaster Regiment. The Cottage Museum is in an artisan's house of about 1820. St Peter's Roman Catholic church of 1859, in Geometrical style, was one of Paley's finest, with ten bells, notable architecture and stained glass and one of the finest organs of its type. It became a cathedral in 1924. The Lancaster Maritime Museum in the 1764 custom house has a set of 37 sheets of plans of 1880, covering the Lancaster Canal at 1:1,584, a 1920s fisherman's cottage and **Morecambe** Bay fishing, shrimping, cockling and mussel collecting.

Bonded warehouses line the river and small fishing boats anchor alongside. A modern railway bridge sits on noticeably older piers as it passes high over the river.

The striking cable stayed Millennium Bridge now crosses the river.

Lancaster is soon left behind and the long haul down the estuary begins. At Oxcliffe Hill the Golden Ball stands alone, overlooking the river and advertising bar snacks and beer from the wood. Also known as Snatchems, it has had associations with pressgangs and smugglers and is said to be haunted with cold spots in the kitchen and pans leaping off the table. The line of the river is given by two sets of overhead powerlines which can be seen to rise at the point of crossing. Attempts have been made to scour a deeper channel by tipping lines of stones along each side of the river. At low tide these form rapids where the river contemptuously passes out over one line and back in again further on. Colloway Marsh on the right is

popular with estuarine birdlife while trees at Ashton Hall are slanted by the prevailing wind.

At Glasson a jetty is used for loading scrap iron onto coastal freighters while also visible are the masts of smaller boats which passed through the lock gates to the harbour with an arm linking to the Lancaster Canal. The estuary is made more pleasant for being lined with sand rather than mud.

The road to the hamlet of Sunderland gets covered by the tide. At the beginning of the 19th century it was a port for the West Indies, which could explain Sambo's Grave.

At high tide the end of the River Lune is marked by the lighthouse at Plover Scar although tides do go out for a long way and there is a further 6km to Point of Lune at low tide. At Plover Scar there is a notice advising of the Wyre Lune Sanctuary and that birds are not to be shot, adding, in smaller letters, south of the lighthouse. To the north, **Heysham** nuclear power station dominates the skyline while Fleetwood can be seen away to the southwest.

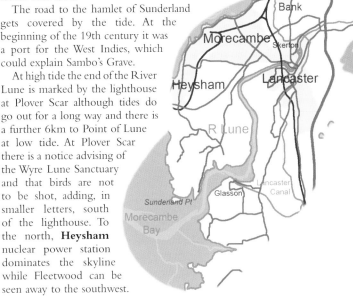

20 River Duddon

One of Lakeland's most active rivers

I thought of Thee, my partner and my guide,
  As being pass'd away.—Vain sympathies!
  For, backward, Duddon! as I cast my eyes,
I see what was, and is, and will abide;
Still glides the Stream, and shall for ever glide;
William Wordsworth

The River Duddon rises on Long Scar below Pike of Brisco, descends from Wrynose Pass and flows south to the Irish Sea. It is in one of the few Lakeland valleys not to contain a lake.

At Duddon Bridge a band of Coniston limestone and the remains of a 19th century blast furnace stand in the woods to the west of the river, sited to benefit from nearby charcoal and iron mines as well as the river and the limestone.

The bridge carries the A595 and marks the boundary of the Lake District National Park for the right bank although it continues on the left to Greety Gate. Despite another weir and a couple more rapids, the character of the river now changes. A levée on the right bank runs all the way to Millom and there is a section on the left bank between Greety Gate and Foxfield.

The River Lickle joins and the river opens out to sandy shallows exposed to the prevailing headwind. The estuary is crossed by a set of powerlines and the Carnforth to Whitehaven railway, once envisaged as the main line to Scotland before a more direct inland route was developed.

Beyond Foxfield the estuary widens and the low tide channel meanders to and fro across it. A fast current can develop at the bottom of the tide with calving walls of sand.

Angerton Marsh and Millom Marsh are saltmarsh which inspired Wordsworth and many other writers. Huge numbers of wading birds gather on the mudflats

Duddon Bridge at low tide summer levels.

Warning notice at Foxfield.

and Duddon Sands and a typical day might show oystercatchers, plovers, curlews, redbreasted mergansers and cormorants. Footpaths cross the estuary which is effectively drained at low tide but it floods quickly and can catch out those without local knowledge, especially as the channel tends to change its position.

This is one of the few places in England where high mountains, moorlands and fells come down close to sea, estuaries and bays and it is worth looking back to see the panorama of the Lakeland peaks from which the river has emerged.

Landmarks further down the coast come in the form of aerials above Millom Park and Dalton-in-Furness and slate tips between Grizebeck and Kirkby-in-Furness and near Askam in Furness.

An isolated peninsula of rock with sheep grazing on top contrasts with the otherwise low lying land with sand dunes down towards **Askam in Furness**.

Millom Castle dates from the 14th century while the 12th century church of the Holy Trinity has fine windows. Millom's church spire is another conspicuous landmark.

Borwick Rails Harbour used to ship iron ore. Now it imports iron in the form of ships for breaking. Ironically, **Millom** was once a shipbuilding centre although it is in sight of Barrow-in-Furness which continues the tradition.

Millom also quarried haematite iron ore until 1968. In the 19th century the mine had 11 shafts and was the busiest in Britain. Now it is just a large lake behind Hodbarrow Point, marked with the remains of lighthouses. Tracks lead through the mine area to Millom where the folk museum has a full scale drift of the Hodbarrow Iron Ore Mine as well as replicas of a miner's cottage kitchen and blacksmith's forge and a display of agricultural relics.

Completing the story of former endeavours is the skeleton of a wooden ship embedded in the sand at the point where one of Lakeland's most active rivers meets the energy of the Irish Sea.

Distance
10km from Duddon Bridge to Hodbarrow Point

OS 1:50,000 Sheet
96 Barrow-in-Furness & South Lakeland

Admiralty Charts
1320 Fleetwood to Douglas (1:100,000)
1346 Solway Firth & Approaches (1:100,000)

Tidal Constants
Duddon Bar:
Dover +0020

Sea Area
Irish Sea

Rescue
Inshore lifeboat:
Barrow
All weather lifeboat:
Barrow
Hovercraft:
Morecambe

Black Combe seen across the Duddon estuary.

21 River Wampool

Old columns in sandy shallows

The B5307 bridge with a large log visible underneath.

Sandbanks near Angerton.

The Angerton–Whitrigg bridge, close to quicksand.

The River Wampool is not the typical Cumbrian river falling off the fells in a series of rapids and lakes. Instead, it meanders its way across the coastal plain to the north of the Lake District, flowing northwest to the Solway Firth. It issues from a pond at Hawkesdale Pasture as the Gill Beck, not taking on the name of River Wampool until West Curthwaite, where it is joined by the Chalk Beck.

The tidal limit is at the Laythes. Depth is reasonable at first but gets shallower towards the estuary at low tide so it is worth small craft taking the tide into account and leaving before the top end of the tide.

The water is dark but clear, meandering through farmland. The only conflicts with the rural view are a couple of circular arcs of hangars on the disused airfield at Powhill, the river flowing towards them and then away as it twists and turns although the high banks obscure views to all but the black and white cows which peer over fences with slight surprise. Vegetation is profuse, including arrowhead in the water and stinging nettles on the banks which attract red admirals in summer. The birds are mostly inland at first, skylarks and lapwings somewhere overhead, mallards on the water, swifts skimming down to drink on the wing and wagtails hopping along the banks. Oystercatchers are the first signs of the proximity of the sea.

Kirkbride, the largest village in the area and the site of a Roman fort, is passed unseen although the bell on the end of a chapel at Angerton is glimpsed once.

The bridge carrying the B5307 is followed quickly by the two sections of embankment which formerly approached the bridge over the river, carrying the Carlisle to Silloth railway. A couple of bends later the river appears to be about to go under a high brick arch but at the last minute it veers away and passes the other side of a wood. The bridge actually carries a minor road over the dismantled railway line.

The road, which is never too far from the right bank over the rest of its course, has achieved increased importance as part of the Cumbria Cycleway which proves popular with those on two wheels. From here to Anthorn the right bank is a steadily expanding marsh as far as the road, the Solway Commons.

Angerton is where John Bull began the revival of the open canoe under sail in Britain.

The final bridge across the river to Whitrigg looks a substantial metal structure but at low water it can be seen that most of the sections do not reach the ground, the bridge being supported on four slim piers. This is a reflection of the change in nature of the bed. So far it has been sand or clean clay but now there are carved sandbanks and the river is getting both wider and shallower. The bed is very soft sandy silt, not able to take the weight of a person standing on it although it may bear a person on the move. Notices on the bank warn of quicksand. This gives a potentially dangerous situation for anyone who runs out of water and needs to portage.

From Bank House to Angerton House there has been a great deal of debris tipped into the river, mostly metal of all sorts on the left bank, farm machinery, kitchen implements, lawn mowers, cars, coils of wire and an array of other waste. The most charitable interpretation is that it is an ill-conceived attempt at bank stabilization. Otherwise it is just an eyesore.

Another railway route is crossed, the former line from the Cumbrian iron ore mines to the smelting furnaces of Strathclyde, last used in 1921. It is distinguished by several lines of piers in the channel which are cut off above bed

Columns of the former railway bridge downstream of Angerton.

level, above or below the surface depending on the water level. The final obstacle of this nature is a group of posts in the water at a point overlooked by some gorse bushes.

Moving on towards Longcroft, the river is bounded on both sides by the grazing land of Newton Marsh. Cormorants and shelducks are found on the water. A small bore comes in on spring tides and the level rises very rapidly, taking only a few minutes to rise from low water to high water level.

The village of Anthorn is the only place where the road comes right alongside the river. The western extremity of the village is gathered around an old farm and terminates at a much older cross. Across the river estuary towards Newtonholme runs a public footpath.

Dominating all and the whole upper end of the Solway Firth are a forest of radio masts on a former airfield. These used to be part of the communications link with our submarine fleet but have been superseded by satellites. Even so, they have not been dismantled and are brightly lit at night. The thirteen masts form a six pointed star, all linked with interconnecting wires. Around the perimeter are brick buildings at intervals.

The River Wampool discharges into Moricambe, as does the River Waver, the enlarged estuary of the two rivers emptying into the southern side of the Solway Firth. At low water it largely drains, channels being shallow and their positions moving frequently amongst the sandbanks. The whole area is popular with birds, including curlews which frequent the foreshore.

On the southeast side of Moricambe is **Newton Arlosh**, founded by the monks of Holme Cultram after the flooding of Skinburness in 1303. Newton Marsh gives protection against attacks by the sea and the 14th century church was built to resist attack by border raiders, having 1.5m thick walls, a tower with no external door and windows in the form of narrow slits.

The road follows the north bank of Moricambe as far as Longdyke Scar, after which the portage to the road is significantly longer. Across the Solway Firth lie the Scottish hills, particularly Criffel, dominating the firth.

Distance
13km from the
Laythes to Cardurnock

OS 1:50,000 Sheet
85 Carlisle &
Solway Firth

Admiralty Charts
1346 Solway Firth
& Approaches
(1:100,000)

Tidal Constants
Annan Waterfoot:
HW Dover +0110,
LW Dover +0300

Sea Area
Irish Sea

Rescue
Inshore lifeboat:
Silloth
All weather lifeboat:
Workington

The village of Anthorn is dwarfed by the forest of radio masts.

The River Wampool shoreline near Longdyke Scar, looking towards the Lake District peaks.

22 Lochar Water

Birds, Burns and banking

To Andrew Murray of Cockpool–
   That Man 's ma deir cousin to me;
Desire him cum and mak me aid
   With all the power that he may be.
Anon

A narrow twisting section at Upper Locharwoods.

Eastpark observation tower near the river.

Rising on Watchman Moor as Park Burn, Lochar Water flows south across Dumfries & Galloway to the Nith Estuary national scenic area and the Solway Firth.

Road access is always limited. The final bridge is where the B725 crosses at Bankend although the road is not wide enough to leave a vehicle. The best place to park is on the B725 at the southern end of the village.

Upper Locharwoods is at the end of the Black Grain Plantation, part of Mabie Forest. From here the river becomes tidal but with quite fast flow over some clay rapids when the tide permits. The banks are lined with reeds and the river meanders excessively so that much of the wind is kept off and, even on the exposed reaches, it never comes from any direction for very long. Added to this, the river is now turning in a generally easterly direction so the prevailing wind is following.

In doing so, the river moves away from Ward Law, which has a Roman fort on top and another fort site in a circle of trees. Beyond Shearington is the major fort in the area, Caerlaverock Castle, named after the lark's nest. One of the finest medieval castles in Scotland, it is Britain's only castle with a triangular bailey. Built in the 1290s, it was subject to many sieges, including by Edward I. After sequences of being ruined and rebuilt in the 14th century, a mansion with fine carved panels was added in the 1630s by Robert Maxwell, the 1st Earl of Nithsdale.

Initially, herons, swans and mallards are the birds most likely to be seen on the water and larks are to be heard. Trees lean into the muddy water from time to time and there are occasional blockages, primarily reeds so it is not hard to force a passage. Water lilies are found in some reaches. A rowing boat at Locharwoods is lowered from a lift on the bank.

Beyond Eastpark a levée follows the south bank for

Criffel rises on the far side of the Nith estuary.

a couple of kilometres, less obvious than the life rings positioned at its foot. Beyond this bank is a pyramid shaped observation tower. The Wildfowl & Wetlands Trust's Caerlaverock Wetlands Centre is sited beside 5.7km² of merse, saltmarsh where birdlife is ideally viewed from October to April. It is one of the best places in Britain to see whooper swans. There are pinkfooted and greylag geese, other wildfowl and waders. Winter flocks of barnacle geese can exceed 12,000. There is a notable goose migration in April. The RSPB have said that the 130,000 wildfowl in the Solway Firth are threatened by climate change. Four legged wildlife includes badgers and natterjack toads.

It is never a good sign when swans in the middle of the river start walking. Beyond Nether Locharwoods the river widens and becomes shallow for much of the time. There is some braiding as the water carves between low banks of silt, later sandbanks. Groynes to prevent erosion can stretch most of the way across the river with low posts, concrete lumps and rocks which tend to get spread about in the shallows. Views can be extensive at times, back to Criffel on the far side of the River Nith, on to a wooded hill near Ecclefechan and to the mountains of the Lake District in England. Oystercatchers and curlews inhabit the widening estuary.

The last vehicle access point is a track beside the Brow Well by the Raffles Burn, occupied by the kingfisher.

Lochar Water widens between sandbanks below Powhillon.

The well, which has iron impregnated mineral water, was visited by Robert Burns, seeking a cure for his final illness. The well looks most unattractive and a notice warns that its water is not potable. Sea bathing was another aspect of the cure he was seeking. From here Burns sent his publisher a final song, *Fairest Maid on Devon Banks*, and an uncharacteristic plea for £5 to stave off a legal action by a creditor, possible incarceration in a debtors' prison exacerbating his illness as it had done his father. He walked to Clarencefield, where he visited what is now the Farmer's Arms. He had no money but the landlord appreciated who he was and served him. Burns died a couple of days later.

Standing back from the estuary is the unassuming hamlet of Ruthwell. It has the Savings Bank Museum in recognition of the fact that the Revd Henry Duncan set up the first savings bank here in 1810. It became the Trustee Savings Bank, now absorbed into Lloyds TSB. William Paterson, a co-founder of the Bank of England in 1694, had come from Lochmaben, 15km north.

Distance
10km from
Shearington to the
Solway Firth

OS 1:50,000 Sheets
84 Dumfries &
Castle Douglas
85 Carlisle &
Solway Firth

Admiralty Charts
1346 Solway Firth
& Approaches
(1:100,000)

Tidal Constants
Silloth:
HW Dover +0050,
LW Dover +0100

Sea Area
Irish Sea

Rescue
Inshore lifeboat:
Silloth
All weather lifeboat:
Workington

A makeshift groyne runs most of the way across at Cockpool.

Brow Well beside the Raffles Burn, sought by the dying Burns.

Duncan also rediscovered the 5.5m late 7th century Anglian stone Ruthwell Cross with runic and Latin inscriptions. One of the best in Europe, it has verses from *The Dream of the Rood* and is a rare example of Anglo-Saxon poetry. It is in Ruthwell church.

Over the final kilometre to the Solway Firth the Lochar Water widens to be over a kilometre wide, the flow being mostly confined to shallow channels between extensive areas of muddy sand, some of it quicksand. When the tide does come in it can arrive as a bore, the full width of the estuary covering in a couple of minutes as a sheet of water sweeps across. This is a windswept area to be treated with caution.

At low water the channel reaches across Blackshaw Bank for at least 13km, nearly to the English shore, on which the most conspicuous features are the aerials at Cardurnock.

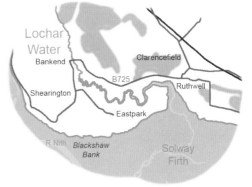

The bore sweeps into the estuary.

23 River Clyde

From heavy industry to culture

I sing of a river I'm happy beside,
The song that I sing is the song of the Clyde,
Of all Scottish rivers it's dearest to me,
It flows from Leadhills all the way to the sea.
It borders the orchards of Lanark so fair,
Meanders through meadows with sheep grazing there,
But from Glasgow to Greenock, in towns on each side,
The hammers' ding-dong is the song of the Clyde.
R Y Bell

At Dalmarnock the Clyde still has inland river proportions.

The cleansing river rises on Gana Hill and flows as the Crow Burn then Daer Water, becoming the Clyde and flowing northwest across South Lanarkshire and Glasgow to the Firth of Clyde. Earlier it may have been part of a drainage line to the Firth of Forth from Strachur on Loch Fyne or even including Glen Aray. The Clota Fluvius to the Romans, it remained shoaled and shallow until 1770, when stone jetties were built out from the shore to increase scouring. Between 1884 and 1890, 1,000,000m³ of material was dredged per year, giving a minimum depth of 7.3m at low water below Glasgow Harbour. It has long been Scotland's most important commercial river.

Glasgow is the largest city in Scotland, founded in 543 by St Mungo. Glas is green and the rest of the name

St Andrew's suspension footbridge.

is from the Gaelic cu, dear place, or Welsh cau, hollow. A royal burgh from 1454, Defoe thought it the cleanest, best built and most beautiful city in Britain after London. In the 19th century it was the second city in the Empire, the finest Victorian city in Britain, built on Victorian prosperity, Scotland's main industrial centre. With the Industrial Revolution came the slums but these have now been cleared largely and the heavy industry replaced by the arts, recognized when it became the 1990 European City of Culture. This is the UK's second biggest retail centre after London.

The river is tidal from Dalmarnock Bridge of 1891, the A749 being carried on its five 17m plate girder spans. The surroundings are industrial premises but there is a sculpture by the end of the bridge and the river is shielded by alders and willows, giant hogweed and Himalayan balsam to hide the city and make it surprisingly secluded here.

The three arched Dalmarnock Railway Bridge of 1897, widened in 1923, carries the Dalmuir–Lanark line, accompanied by the piers of the 1861 bridge. A small boatyard has a slip on the south bank. A waterworks of 1807 had water taken under the river in cast iron mains carried in flexible wooden frameworks which Watt designed after studying the tail of a lobster. In 1894 Dalmarnock became the site of Scotland's first large sewage works, greatly improving the health of the city. The M74 has been completed close to the river through the **Rutherglen**, connecting the southern motorway network more directly to the M8 in the centre of Glasgow.

Low rise masonry arches faced with granite form the 1896 Rutherglen Bridge carrying the B763 by Shawfield greyhound stadium and Richmond Park. Glasgow has 70 parks, the most in Europe for its size. Water screened by rosebay willowherb, poplars and lifebelt posts is used by herons, mallards, swans and cormorants.

The four span prestressed concrete Polmadie footbridge of 1955 crosses to Glasgow Green, 52ha of Glasgow's oldest park, where Prince Charlie reviewed his troops in 1745 after his retreat from Derby. Oatlands tower blocks look uninspiring but the aroma of fresh coffee beans drifts across and lifts the mood. Glasgow Rowing Club's boathouse is also on this reach. The red sandstone People's Palace & Winter Gardens of 1898 features industry and politics.

The King's Bridge of 1933, carrying the A74, is a good example of its period. The four 21m spans have the reinforced concrete deck on steel plate girders, supported on arched piers, a design feature to be repeated further down the river. Based on the Doge's Palace in Venice is the 19th century Victorian Templeton carpet factory, now a business centre.

St Andrew's suspension footbridge of 1854 is an ornate structure with cast iron Corinthian columns and two tiers of wrought iron chain links, the parapets having been replaced with Warren girders in the 1950s. A 44m monument of 1806 is to Nelson. Past the Gorbals the river is shared with geese, the Glasgow Humane Society with its rescue boats and the Clyde Amateur Rowing Club. George Geddes II was Humane Society officer from 1889 to 1932, having saved 56 lives by 1917. Glasgow Police Museum presents the UK's oldest police force. St Andrew's in the Square is a beautiful 18th century church restored as a theatre. Four diminishing square towers with Gothic and Renaissance details form the 50m Merchant's Steeple, the remains of the Merchants' House of 1659 which were to be built into the Fish Market building of 1872.

Rosnea
Kilcreggan
Firth of Clyde
Gourock

TEMPLETON CARPET FACTORY
GLASGOW 1990
EUROPEAN CITY OF CULTURE

The Pipe Bridge includes a weir with three lifting gates, normally closed to prevent scour and silting downstream. At high water a gate can be lifted to allow small boats through, provided advanced notice has been given. Gates with combination padlocks allow small craft to be portaged past the barrier. Glasgow College of Nautical Studies is situated below the weir with a selection of unusual structures such as a framework bearing a commercial ship lifeboat ready for launching in the middle of the river.

Several of the city's major bridges cross this reach leading alongside the Broomielaw. The 1872 Albert Bridge with its wrought iron elliptical arches carries the A728 and is supported on cast iron cylinders which go down to 26m below high water. It replaced Robert Stevenson's elegant five span bridge of 1835, which could have been restored if the claims of dredging damage had not been overstated.

The first railway crossing of the Clyde in Glasgow in 1870 served St Enoch's station, which had the largest glazed arch span in Scotland at 62m but was closed in 1966. The title now goes to the high level part of Queen Street station of 1879, 140m long with a 52m span. The Clyde Viaduct of 1898 was built around and under the earlier bridge, its heavy steel lattice arches and turreted red sandstone piers supported on 30m columns, carrying a freight railway.

The Victoria Bridge of 1854, carrying the A8, is the oldest across the river here, its five arches skewed at 61°. The central arch has a 24m span and 3.2m rise, faced in Dublin granite, one of the finest of its kind in Scotland.

Glasgow Central Mosque joins the Mercat Cross, a 1929 replica of the medieval original. The 38m Tolbooth Steeple is the sole remnant of the tolbooth of 1626, one of only three crowned steeples in Scotland, its former prison described by Scott in *Rob Roy* and its hangings by Margaret Thomson Davis in *The Glasgow Belle*. Tron steeple is the only remaining part of St Mary's church of 1637, burned down in 1793 by drunken members of Glasgow Hellfire Club. The Sharmanka Kinetic Gallery & Theatre has Eduard Bersudsky's mechanized sculptures, described as Heath Robinson meets Hieronymous

Bosch. David Hamilton's 1805 listed Hutcheson's Hall in neo Classical style has a Scottish town house steeple, notable staircase of 1876, statues of the Hutchesons from a 1641 building and portraits of Glasgow dignitaries. Robert Adam's 1794 Trades Hall of Glasgow is Glasgow's oldest secular building still used for its original purpose, its mahogany panelled rooms with Baroque electroliers and its reception room with oak fireplaces and an Adamesque ceiling. Strathclyde University, founded in 1796, has sculpture inspired by the standing stones of Callanish. William Young's Glasgow City Chambers of 1888 are Victorian in Italian Renaissance style, having paired classical marble columns with pediments, turrets, cupolas, magnificent staircases, mosaics, stained glass, gilding and a banqueting hall decorated by the 19th century Impressionists the Glasgow Boys. George Square has the most statues in Scotland,

The Pipe Bridge: the barrage can be opened for small boats.

including Queen Victoria, Prince Albert, Scott, Burns, Gladstone, Peel, James Watt and Sir John Moore. St Andrew's Roman Catholic cathedral is Gothic with an 1816 college chapel front. The Gallery of Modern Art dates from 1996.

Just a century older is the Clockwork Orange, the Subway, passing under the river. The 1.22m gauge line is Scotland's only underground but was the third in the world. Initially it was hauled by an endless cable, the driver using a gripper device to hold onto it when a train was ready to move. There was no access route to the line so carriages had to be lifted in and out by crane. The river flooded the workings ten times during construction.

The Lighthouse of 1895 has Scotland's Centre for Architecture, Design & the City with the Rennie Mackintosh Centre for this leading Art Nouveau designer who worked from 1868 to 1928.

Perhaps the most elegant of Glasgow's bridges is the Portland Street suspension footbridge of 1853 with its 130m main span suspended from Greek style towers by four chains of 3m eye bar links.

The four storey Iron Building is Gardner's Warehouse, probably the UK's oldest surviving cast iron fronted commercial building, state of the art when built in 1856.

McBrayne's Royal Route to Oban via the Crinan Canal began from Jamaica Street Bridge and was named after Queen Victoria's use of it 1847.

The A77 is taken over two bridges. The first is Glasgow or Jamaica Street Bridge. It was the widest in Britain when built in 1835, its seven arches in Aberdeen granite probably Telford's finest. It was replaced in 1772 by a bridge by John Adam but this was undermined by dredging and it was rebuilt again in 1899 in Telford's original style. The George V Bridge of 1928 was designed to complement it, carrying the other carriageway. The three span reinforced concrete structure with Dalbeattie

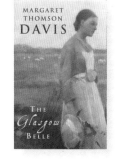

granite facing has a 51m central span, giving 5.6m clearance. Between the two have been two Caledonian Railway bridges carrying the West Coast Main Line from its Glasgow Central terminus, a tapering station with tracks in echelon and a

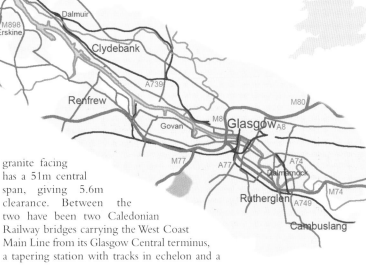

Portland Street suspension footbridge, Jamaica Street bridge and the Caledonian Railway viaduct beyond in central Glasgow.

The double finback Tradeston bridge with the M8 beyond.

roof of Warren girders to spans of 110m. The 1875 viaduct was demolished in 1967, its 4.6m diameter cast iron shafts founded on bedrock 26m below high water. Its 1905 replacement has a central 59m span, carrying ten tracks, edged with lattice parapets.

Ten storeys high and three bays wide is the 1902 Hatrack. Crossing the river is the 110m double finback Tradeston foot and cycle bridge of 2009 with a cumbersome top heavy appearance.

The M8 crosses over the 1970 Kingston Bridge, actually two five lane bridges, one of Europe's busiest sections of road. The cantilevered prestressed concrete box girders give a 140m main span with a minimum clearance of 18m. The quay wall moved in the 1980s and refurbishment

A dome for the Harbour Tunnel, a skewed arch bridge and the Finneston crane.

Bell's Bridge, BBC Scotland, Glasgow Science Centre and Glasgow Science Tower.

in 1996 involved jacking each 25,000t box clear of its bearings.

This is the start of the large craft navigable channel, improved to Port Glasgow in 1771. Over the next century the channel was deepened from 1.2m to 6.7m.

Scotland Street School Museum was designed in 1904 by Mackintosh. Henry Wood Hall, home of the Royal National Scottish Orchestra, was Trinity church with its Victorian Gothic spire.

Most distinctive of the bridges here is the Clyde Arc or Finneston Bridge of 2006, supported by a single arch which crosses not only the river but also the road on a diagonal. Domes mark the ends of the 220m Harbour Tunnel of 1895, the first in Scotland to be dug with a tunnelling shield. The two 4.9m diameter vehicle tunnels were closed in 1943 and the pedestrian one between them in 1980. Vehicles had to be lifted in and out at the ends for crossings. Bell's Bridge of 1988 is a 130m cable stayed footbridge with an 88m swinging span. There is also the 2002 130m Millennium Bridge, a footbridge opening with a pair of 17m bascules. After the City Inn, Stobcross Quay has a 190m 150t Titan crane, the Finneston Crane.

This is an important redevelopment area. The Clyde Auditorium or Armadillo has 3,000 seats and a titanium sheeted exterior by Sir Norman Foster. Also here is the Scottish Exhibition & Conference Centre and the Glasgow Science Centre, a four storey building including a planetarium, the Scottish Power Space Theatre and Scotland's only Imax theatre, Scotland's leading Millennium project. Experimental photovoltaic cells are to be floated as giant solar lilypads to provide power. The least imaginative of the new buildings belongs to BBC Scotland although they present the Scottish TV news with the Clyde Arc and Kingston Bridge as a live backdrop. Plantation Quay has the 100m Glasgow Science Tower, the tallest building in Scotland, which rotates but has had trouble with its pivot.

Beyond the *PS Waverley* berth, Princes Dock, formerly the Cessnock Dock, was partly used in 1988 as a National Garden Festival site. An accumulator operated hydraulic cranes, lifts and pumps and has been preserved. The southern end has an octagonal chimney with eight sculpted wind panels inspired by Athens' Tower of the Winds. This is now a seaplane berth. Seaplanes operate to and from the river between the Millennium Footbridge and King George V Dock. A helipad on the north bank of the river is near a corbelled Italian campanile tower which disguises a water tower. The Riverside Museum trams, ship models and exhibits generally of land and sea opened

in 2011. With it at Yorkhill Basin is the three masted barque *SV Glenlee* of 1896, restored after vandals sank her in Seville, is one of the last Clyde-built tall ships. The 1901 Kelvingrove Art Gallery & Museum in red Victorian sandstone is the UK's most visited museum outside London with Britain's finest collection of British and European paintings including Rembrandt, Mackintosh

BAE Systems work on warships at Govan (top and bottom).

An urban fox drinks from the tidal river.

the opposite winds have the converse effect. The strongest flows are for the first hour after the tide turns but there may be no flood with heavy rain.

Fairfields Basin built Blue Ribband ships from 1864, particularly the Empress liners for the Canadian Pacific Line. It became Govan Shipyard, building destroyers for the Royal Navy. BAE Systems still use it for naval craft.

The Clyde Tunnel of 1964 takes the A739 under the river. At 800m long it is the longest and most advanced of its kind in Scotland. In water bearing glacial deposits, boulder clay, silt, sand and esker gravel over Lower Carboniferous shale and sandstone, the twin dual carriageway bores have cast iron linings and tension piles to prevent the reinforced concrete approaches from floating.

Victoria Park includes Fossil Grove, an area of 330,000,000 year old stumps and roots of extinct trees, discovered in 1887.

Clydeholme Shipyard built the first British oceangoing diesel vessel, the *Jutlandia*, in 1911. The yard was used by Swan Hunter until closed in 1965. Today it has a Titan crane picking over heaps of scrap metal. Commercial wharves begin here but foxes come down to the river to drink and eye up the blackbacked gulls. King George V Dock is the longest in Clydeport at 760m, handling steel, timber, minerals, bulk cargo and Ro-Ro traffic.

A Titan crane stand sentinel over a scrap quay.

Art Nouveau furniture and the earliest complete suit of armour in Britain, a 15th century suit from Milan, the Milanese being considered the leading makers of armour. Damaged in Second World War bombing is the 19th century Kelvin Way Bridge with a red sandstone arch over the River Kelvin, pairs of bronze sculptures being positioned on the abutments. The Royal Infirmary and Western Infirmary are both near the Kelvin. The Subway passes back beneath the Clyde.

Flows run out from two hours ten minutes after Dover high water and in from three hours forty minutes before Dover high water. Flows are weak but heavy rain, snowmelt and winds from the north to the east increase the rate and duration of the ebb while dry conditions and

Clydebuilt, the Scottish Maritime Museum at Braehead, features shipbuilding and engineering, the Blitz, tobacco and Singer sewing machines. One of the oldest of the Clyde-built vessels remaining is the *MV Kyles*, on view. During the Second World War 2,000 ships were built here.

Regeneration at Braehead includes Braehead Shopping Centre, Sainsbury's, a skating and curling rink and Xscape, the UK's biggest real indoor snow slope and with the UK's largest freestanding climbing walls. Across the river are views of the great outdoors with the Kilpatrick Hills. The south bank changes from Glasgow to Renfrewshire and the north bank to West Dunbartonshire. The **Renfrew** Ferry carries passengers by the Ferry Inn.

The MV Kyles at the Scottish Maritime Museum.

Sculpture at the front of the Scottish Maritime Museum.

largest when built, had a clocktower with 7.9m diameter faces, visible from the river. Clydebank College faces the river.

Lapwings and magpies frequent Newshot Island, now a peninsula past which seaweed floats. Effluent boils up in the river from a sewage works where the Duntocher Burn joins at Dalmuir. Powerlines cross high over Mountblow.

Another inlet shelters behind a peninsula above disused ferry slipways. Over everything is the 1971 cable stayed Erskine Bridge carrying the A898. Its 300m main span is supported by 38m steel towers on slender 53m concrete

Shipbuilding continues at Clydebank.

Aircraft fly over Rothesay Dock with 1.9km of quays, petroleum tanks and facilities for bulk cargoes. Just 2km from the end of Glasgow Airport main runway, aircraft are low here and the echo back off the dock wall can sound like a second aircraft hard on the heels of the first.

At the confluence with the River Cart, where flows are stronger on the ebb, the south bank has open fields for the first time. The north side was commercial. A 49m high Titan crane with 85m cantilever was built for John Brown's shipyard in 1907. Shipbuilding shops served the former UIE Shipbuilding yard where some of the world's finest ships, such as the *Aquitania*, *Queen Mary* and *Queen Elizabeth II*, were built for the Cunard Line. The sinking of their *Lusitania*, built in 1906, was a major factor in the USA's becoming involved in the First World War. Their *Hood* battle cruiser was completed in 1920 but sunk in 1941 by the *Bismarck* with the loss of 1,416 lives. The river was dredged to 11m to let them out. **Clydebank**, rebuilt after the Second World War, built the *Queen Elizabeth II* in 1967 as its last liner before moving over to North Sea oil rigs until 2001. Clydebank Museum is in the townhall. Until pulled down in 1961 the Singer works, the world's

piers, the only Scottish bridge with single cables over central piers. It has aerodynamic box girders with the unusually light weight of 690kg/m^2 and was a precursor for the French Millau Viaduct. It is now toll free, like all other Scottish bridges. Although it gives 55m clearance over the river it has been hit by an oil rig being moved downstream. A patch across the centre of the underside has the appearance of a heavy duty sticking plaster. The last bridge on the Clyde, this is where fog is most likely to be found. There is a tide gauge near the bridge.

St Patrick was born at Old Kilpatrick and taken to Ireland by raiders. Alternatively, his piety offended the Devil who ordered all Scottish witches to oppose him so he found a boat and left for Ireland. They pursued him to the Clyde but, not being able to follow, threw a boulder at him, the site of Dumbarton Castle. There is a holy well dedicated to him. A church of 1812 is on the site of a church of about 800.

The inner Clyde has 21,000 winter waterfowl including 4,100 eiders, 2,300 redshanks, 440 goldeneyes, 170 scaup

Titan crane and adjacent passenger lift at Clydebank.

and oystercatchers which the RSPB said were at risk of permanent damage from marina development and land reclaim.

A Roman fort is on the line of the Antonine Wall, built in 142 from Bo'ness to Bowling and abandoned in 214. The wall has a stone base with turf and clay above, 4.3m wide and up to 3.7m high with a 3.7m ditch on the north side.

The Erskine Hospital appears more like a stately home and looks down on the estuary from its position in Big Wood.

Bowling Harbour is at the end of the Forth & Clyde Canal and has a number of decaying wrecks around the perimeter. Some of them could have already been there in

The pioneering Erskine Bridge passes high over the river.

The hospital at Erskine.

An old pier at Bowling with a tree left by the river.

1934 when the kilted Seumus Adam and Alastair Dunnet, the future editor of the *Scotsman*, set out to paddle to Skye, as told in their *Quest by Canoe*. Bowling is also thought to have been the home port of the *Vital Spark*. A monument and Dunglass Castle stand by the former Dunglass oil terminal. They face saltings.

The Lang Dykestone training wall runs along the south side of the fairway for 3km, marked by nine masonry towers, the wall itself only showing at low water spring tides. From Milton Island the north side also has some beacons including the Dumbuck Beacon ruin off a disused quarry, Petty Roy Beacon off some targets and the Leven Perch at the confluence with the River Leven. Terns fish the waters. Views to peaks in the north are extensive even from the water.

Dumbarton is from Dun Briton, the fort of the Britons, Dumbarton Castle. This was built on a steep 72m dolerite plug in the 5th century, believed to have been the longest continually fortified site in Britain. The capital of Strathclyde and of the North Britons, it controlled the route up the Vale of Leven and the lowest fording point of the Clyde at Dumbuck. A sundial given by Mary, Queen of Scots recalls that this is where she left for France in 1548 at the age of six to marry the Dauphin. After her flight to England in 1568 the garrison held out until 1571. The castle retains its 12th century gateway, Wallace Tower, where William Wallace was imprisoned by the English in 1305, and its dungeon and modern barracks.

Dumbarton was the port for Glasgow until the Clyde was dredged in the 19th century. It had shipyards using local iron. Craft built included the *Cutty Sark*, the *TSS King Edward*, which was the world's first commercial turbine passenger steamer, and early hovercraft. Dennys built the 100m long by 2.5m deep Ship Model Experimental Tank in 1883, the world's first purpose built test tank, used for commercials hulls including the *Canberra* and now owned by the Scottish Maritime Museum. Outside is the engine of the *Leven* of 1824, the oldest marine engine in existence. Distilling is another business in the town.

Dumbarton Bridge over the River Leven had a pier and two of its five masonry arches collapse soon after

Dumbarton Castle guards the Clyde and the mouth of the Leven.

completion in 1765. Smeaton advised using the debris as foundations for a rebuild and it is still carrying traffic today.

The remains of extensive old ponds, which were used for seasoning timber, run along the coast from Langbank to Woodhall. After Renfrewshire changes to Inverclyde Finlaystone Point is overlooked by Finlaystone House which had connections with both John Knox and Robert Burns. With a clan display and doll museum, it is set in 4ha of grounds with notable snowdrops and a granite path in a grass maze.

Broadstone Castle was joined by the former Broadfield psychiatric hospital at the start of **Port Glasgow**, originally the fishing village of Newark. The turreted Newark Castle was built in the 15th century by George Maxwell and extended in the 16th century by Patrick Maxwell, who also murdered two of his neighbours and beat his wife of 44 years, the mother of his 16 children. A further happening of note locally was the funeral procession along the shore of a girl who had died of tuberculosis, interrupted by a mermaid who rose to give public health advice in poetry.

The town began Glasgow's prosperity in the 17th century by importing tobacco, sugar and cotton from America, continuing to do so until the 18th century deepening of the Clyde, after which it went over to shipbuilding. There are slipways and a jetty. Steamboat Quay has a 1962 replica of the *Comet*, built in the same yard as the original.

Cockle Bank and Mussel Patches, visited by herring gulls, curlews and guillemots, stand off the former Scott-Lithgow shipyards with the Kingston Basin and gas holders. The Firth of Clyde Dry Dock of 1964 is 305m long with a 46 x 13 x 3.4m gate. The following year a notch was let into the head of the dock to allow it to take the 85,000t *Queen Elizabeth*, the largest liner afloat. Great Harbour, its outer wall running between Maurice Clark Point and Garvel Point, has a molasses jetty and receives tankers. Cranes stand along the docks.

The Firth of Clyde officially begins here and it is from here that a tidal barrage has been proposed to cross the Clyde to Ardmore. The coast is continuously built up from Port Glasgow through Greenock to Gourock. The 610m long James Watt Dock of 1886 with Ro-Ro facilities adjoins Victoria Harbour, the 19th century HM Customs & Excise Museum & Exhibition, a college and a leisure centre.

Greenock is industrial with a pair of Titan cranes. In the 17th century it shipped herrings to France and the Baltic, being the leading herring port on the west coast of Scotland. The pirate Captain Kidd was born here in 1645 and James Watt was born here in 1736, there being a statue of him in the Watt Library, built in 1835 by his son, also James. There is a 75m tower on the Classical municipal buildings of 1886. The area was heavily bombed in 1941.

During the Second World War, Tail of the Bank was an assembly point for Atlantic convoys and it has also been used for reviews.

Flows begin outwards an hour and twenty minutes after Dover high water and in at four hours forty minutes before Dover high water.

The McLean Museum & Art Gallery features James Watt, ship and engine models and other maritime material.

Clydeport's Greenock Ocean Terminal is prominent with container ships moored in front of travelling cranes. There is a tide gauge and a control tower with a high forward raked glass face. A leading line covers the Hole, a 70m depression surrounded by water which is otherwise mostly little over 20m deep.

The River Channel becomes the Firth of Clyde Channel at Whiteforeland Point. Between Fort Matilda and the coastguard station is a sailing club dividing two slipways, one being their own. Behind is Lyle Hill with an anchor and Cross of Lorraine memorial to the Free French killed in the Second World War Battle of the Atlantic.

Between Ironotter Point and Kempock Point is Gourock Bay with a slip in the southeast corner, sailing vessels moored around the isolated remains of a pier towards the centre of the bay and the Dunoon vehicle ferry terminal on the southwest side.

The Gourock Waltz was something from the dance floor, not the windswept water. The bay has notable sunsets and did provide shelter from a storm for the *Vital Spark*, despite the fact that it had grown to a shipwreck of epic proportions as Para Handy expanded the tale on his train journey into Glasgow. On the other hand, Dougie, the mate, in disparaging remarks about yachting, suggested taking one's pyjamas and fruit juice to join the yacht at **Gourock**

Clydeport container terminal at Greenock.

Distance
41km from
Dalmarnock to
Gourock Bay

OS 1:50,000 Sheets
63 Firth of Clyde
64 Glasgow

Admiralty Charts
1994 Approaches to R
Clyde (1:15,000). Gt
Harbour (1:5,000)
2000 Gareloch
(1:12,500). Rhu
Narrows (1:6,250)
2007 R Clyde
(1:15,000)
2131 Firth of Clyde
& L Fyne (1:75,000)

Tidal Constants
Glasgow:
HW Dover +0140,
LW Dover +0200
Renfrew:
HW Dover +0140,
LW Dover +0200
Bowling:
HW Dover +0130,
LW Dover +0200
Port Glasgow:
HW Dover +0120,
LW Dover +0130
Greenock:
Dover +0120
Helensburgh:
Dover +0120

Sea Area
Malin

Rescue
Inshore lifeboat:
Helensburgh
All weather lifeboat:
Troon

Connection
Forth & Clyde Canal
– see CoB p288

Claimed to be the flywheel of the Comet *at Helensburgh but perhaps off an earlier terrestrial use for the engine as the flywheel would have been too big for the boat.*

Robert the Bruce died in Cardross in 1329. Extending the village up is Geilston, where the 17th century Geilston Garden has a small country house with a walled garden in a wooded glen. A target site is on the shore at the start of Ardmore Bay.

The 31m high wooded Hill of Ardmore is almost an island, a low neck separating Ardmore Bay from North Bay. Gorse bushes surround the peninsula, around which is a path popular with dog walkers, yet seals and blackheaded gulls are not deterred. It is the start of the Firth of Clyde and, before Craigendoran, of the Dockyard Port of Gareloch.

Dilapidated piers at Craigendoran are near the end of the Highland Boundary Fault which runs from here across Scotland to Stonehaven. The village merges into **Helensburgh**, named after Lady Helen, wife of Sir James Colquhoun who bought the village of Milligs in 1776 and advertised for weavers. He was unsuccessful so he converted it to a superior residential town with a grid layout, its promotion being helped by the arrival of the railway in 1858. A monument in Hermitage Park, a lawn area facing the front, is reputedly the flywheel of the *Comet*, launched in 1812 by the first provost, Henry Bell, who ran a regular service to Glasgow from his wife's Baths Inn for those taking seawater cures. This was the world's first steam vessel in public service, 13 years before the first public steam railway engine.

Helensburgh Pier, a 240m wooden structure with a slipway, is used by excursion steamers and has passenger services to Gourock and Kilcreggan in the summer. The width of the firth at this point allows extensive views to the south. Near the pier is the Henry Bell Obelisk. The town was the birthplace of John Logie Baird, the inventor of television, and was associated with Prime Minister Andrew Bonar Law. It was the base for Robin Lloyd-Jones and the *Argonauts of the Western Isles*.

A seawall protects the coast, leading past moorings to the **Rhu** Narrows at the mouth of the Gare Loch, closed during the movement of nuclear submarines. Streams are weak but affected by wind, snowmelt and heavy rain.

A wall of fir trees surrounds Culwatty Bay and a building with significant aerials. Degaussing ranges are located off Rosneath Point and a pillbox adds to the sinister mood. The Ardmore Channel is a defined Narrow Channel for users. A light beacon marks Rosneath Patch.

A 130m lattice radio mast tops Gallow Hill, the rest of which is totally rural with a cornfield sweeping down to Meikleross Bay. At the west end of Portkil Bay an underwater spit reaches out from Portkil Point. Road access is reached at **Kilcreggan**, where the pier is visited by steamers as part of the Clyde's appeal to holidaymakers from Glasgow and further afield.

on a Saturday, only to find she had dragged her moorings and damaged a boat belonging to a Lloyd's surveyor.

The Argyll & Bute shore has a shoreline footpath at Ardoch but, after West Dunbartonshire gives way to Argyll & Bute, the only bridge under the Glasgow Central to Fort William railway leads to a road where there is no suitable parking. There is a road allowing access at Cardross, a large timberyard being sited on the west side of Cardross Bay.

The view from Kidstone Park.

24 Gare Loch

Base for nuclear submarines

And here we often met,
When with lightsome foot we sped,
O'er the green and grassy knolls
At the Gareloch Head.
John Stuart Blackie

Hotels both burned down in the 1990s, allegedly arson following declining business as work at the Faslane naval base declined.

Amenities in **Garelochhead** include a play area, football pitches and to

ilets. A cuckoo calls from the surrounding woods

The loch from Whistlefield with Garelochhead in the foreground and Faslane on the left in the distance.

Gare Loch cuts southeast to join the Firth of Clyde. It is synonymous with the Faslane naval base and, as such, movements are restricted for security reasons. It all forms part of the Clyde Dockyard Port of Gareloch & Loch Long and is deemed to be a Narrow Channel for the purposes of the International Regulations for Preventing Collisions at Sea with various rules including restrictions on the use of whistles. There are additional restrictions when nuclear submarines are being moved and they frequently exercise surfaced or submerged in Gare Loch. Three vertical green lights and pennant 9 give warning of ship movements which may last an hour, when the area has to be cleared by other boats. Restrictions are imposed by polite MoD police in fast inflatables.

In the depressed times after the First World War the loch was used for mooring mothballed ships. Hurricane Jack's hiring out of one for a wedding party in the Para Handy stories resulted in his sacking from the ideal job of being a caretaker on the *Jean & Mary*.

The head of Gare Loch is only 1km from Loch Long and Loch Goil but the intervening ridge is some 200m high.

Streams are imperceptible except at the Rhu Narrows near the southern end of the loch. The head of the loch drains, leaving an area of sharp stones, mussels and barnacles. The Route 81 Project slip is located at the head of the loch but most people need to launch from one of the roads which follow the shore closely except at the naval base. A high seawall needs to be negotiated but there are steps down. The Dahlandui and Garelochhead

in the spring and oystercatchers frequent the shore. A church with a spire breaks the roofline and there is an old ornamental iron drinking fountain.

Sailing and windsurfing take place past the moorings at the head of the loch. Surveillance can begin unexpectedly soon with a seal following closely.

The Clyde submarine base occupies the facilities used by the Home Fleet at the end of the Second World War, starting at Rowmore. Submarines bottom off Rowmore Point.

Protected by a massive floating boom is the shiplift. This structure with its reinforced concrete deck resting on 822 tubular piles 50m long by 600mm to 1m in diameter is at the heart of the maintenance facility for the Vanguard submarine fleet. Added in 2009 was a 200m long floating jetty built in Greenock, able to withstand a 10,000 year earthquake and other such inconveniences while handling nuclear powered Astute class hunter killer submarines.

Faslane Bay is a Protected & Restricted Area. The west side of the restricted area is defined by a sector light at Rowmore although it

Rowmore is the start of the naval installations.

The shiplift is protected by a massive floating boom.

is not visible from water level and even large ships can only see it with difficulty during daylight. Trouble should be avoided by going to the most northerly jetty, taking a bearing of 176°T and establishing a transit on the west side of the loch. The far end of the restricted area is defined by a pair of special marks in transit 550m southeast of the drydock at the southern end of the base but these are far from clear, either. When shipping movements are taking place it may be permissible for small boats to use the edge of the loch outside the line of black and yellow barges moored down the west side.

Opposite the main gate of the base is a chapel site and also a peace camp. The sound of gunfire issues from a range somewhere in the complex.

A patch of woodland containing a motte on the east side comes at the return of the east shore to civilian rule. Shandon boasts the Shandon School of Equitation, including an indoor school, but boaters will be more interested in Blairvadach Outdoor Education Centre with its sailing courses.

The rounded ridge on the west side is partly planted with Garelochhead Forest and has been taken over to an

The Faslane facilities, ending with a floating drydock. The Strone rises to Beinn a' Mhanaich and a further ridge to Beinn Tharsuinn.

Garelochhead Forest on the ridge above Clynder with one of the moored barges in the foreground.

The Rhu Point Light Beacon stands only 200m from the southwest side of the loch.

extent by a colourful display of yellow gorse. Behind the low seawall at Clynder are a picnic area and toilets. Para Handy claimed the older midges here and elsewhere on the Gare Loch showed the younger ones how to get the right grip on their prey. Stroul Bay is used by seaplanes and has moorings below a hilltop aerial, giving way to a substantial works constructed on Limekiln Point at Rosneath.

The Royal Northern & Clyde Yacht Club, founded in 1824, has a jetty at **Rhu**, from the Gaelic rudha, a promontory. It comes before the spit causing the Rhu Narrows where velocities can increase to 9km/h. The spit, terminated by Rhu Point Light Beacon, helps restrict approach to the loch for naval defence purposes. Closure of Rhu Narrows is indicated by a red over two green lights or a red flag with a white diagonal.

Beyond the seawall is a church with a flat roofed tower and eight small spires. The churchyard has a statue to Henry Bell.

Rosneath Bay includes **Rosneath** POL jetty and is backed by a forest walk and caravan site, ending with Castle Point Light.

It faces across to Rhu Marina, inshore rescue boat station, Royal Corps of Transport jetty, landing craft and wreck. A seaplane operates from the marina to add to the interest and eider ducks nest on the pontoons.

The more refined air of Helensburgh begins to emerge at Glenarn Gardens, a woodland garden with a burn, daffodils, primulas, bluebells, rhododendrons, magnolias and embothriums and at Woodcote garden with azalias, roses and paintings. Kidstone Park at Cairndhu Point, dating from the late 19th century, has a bandstand, play equipment, toilets and picnic benches. It also has a large car park, avoiding later problems with parking restrictions on the A814. This was found the most convenient place to run two submarine cables across the loch. Again, the beach is of stones, mussels and barnacles.

The view across the River Clyde towards Greenock, past a large green dolphin marking the channel, is panoramic.

Ardencaple Castle was built to the northwest of Helensburgh. On the north side of the town is Hill House of 1903, considered to be Charles Rennie Mackintosh's finest domestic architecture. Original and idiosyncratic, it was designed for publisher Walter W Blackie as a family residence, has a harled exterior and makes comprehensive use of coloured glass in the interior. Mackintosh also designed the furniture and the building now contains a display about him.

Behind the 3km seawall on the front is McLaren Naval & Maritime Books, an excellent secondhand and antiquarian nautical bookshop.

Distance
10km from Garelochhead to Helensburgh

OS 1:50,000 Sheets
56 Loch Lomond & Inveraray
63 Firth of Clyde

Admiralty Charts
1994 Approaches to R Clyde (1:15,000). 2000 Gareloch (1:12,500). Rhu Narrows (1:6,250). Faslane Base (1:6,250) 2131 Firth of Clyde & L Fyne (1:75,000)

Tidal Constants
Garelochhead:
Dover +0120
Shandon:
Dover +0110
Rhu Pier:
Dover +0110
Helensburgh:
Dover +0120

Sea Area
Malin

Rescue
Inshore lifeboat:
Helensburgh
All weather lifeboat:
Troon

Kidstone Park, the most westerly end of Helensburgh.

25 Loch Long

Straight enough for a torpedo range

The Campbell and the Cameron, MacDonald o' Glencoe
Ranked alang wi' Gregorach and marched o'er the snow
Far o'er the loch frae Arklet Glen and doon the past Parlan
By Loch Long whose shores are held by the thieves o' MacFarlane
Ian Hall

Arrochar, overlooked by Cruach Tairbeirt, the dry valley, Ben Reoch and Tullich Hill, from the mouth of Loin Water.

There are other lochs longer than Loch Long but few are straighter. It is almost possible to travel the 20km from Succoth to Ardentinny in a straight line.

At its head it is fed by Loin Water which rises at the foot of Ben Vane, meaning middle hill, and flows into the loch by the A83 bridge. There is parking on the abandoned section of road on the southwest side of the bridge.

Loch Long is a sea loch, heading southwest through Argyll & Bute to the Firth of Clyde on a line which funnels the prevailing headwind, the loch being subject to squalls. Tidal flows outwards begin an hour and twenty minutes after Dover high water and inwards from four hours forty minutes before Dover high water, increasing to 2km/h at the mouth.

The loch forms part of the Clyde Dockyard Port of Gareloch & Loch Long and is considered to be a Narrow Channel as defined by the Collision Regulations. No craft is allowed within 150m of naval areas. Submarines exercise on the surface and submerged. Upper Loch Long was a torpedo range with targets, buoys, submarine cables and beacons at regular intervals down both sides of the loch until the end of the range 1km before Cnap Point.

The right bank is the Cowal Peninsula. Ardgartan Forest forms part of the Argyll Forest Park which surrounds the head of the loch and takes in most of the

The old Admiralty Torpedo Testing Station pier below Beinn Narnain.

92

west bank, including moorland, conifer plantations and surviving oakwood plus Argyll's Bowling Green. Peaks making up the latter include Beinn Narnain, 926m high with a summit only 3km from the sea, and the Cobber or Ben Arthur, named from the shape of its summit and with lots of bare rock to keep climbers occupied.

Arrochar, one of the places Para Handy called home, is where his crew had a particularly bad attack of midges which he claimed considered paraffin a treat, far from being repelled by it. The village is surrounded by the Arrochar Alps, between which there is a 2km dry valley running eastwards to Tarbet on Loch Lomond. The gap is used by the A83 and the Crianlarich to Glasgow railway

The Arrochar at the Glenmallan ammunition jetty.

Hoses on the end of a jetty at the Finnart Ocean Oil Terminal.

which continues down the east bank to Portincaple. It is paralleled by powerlines and the A814 with a switchback surface giving speed control without the suspension damage caused by traffic humps on so many roads. Concrete walls shore up this road at frequent intervals.

The dry valley was also used in 1263 by part of the fleet of King Haakon of Norway which diverted up Loch Long, the boats being dragged 3km overland to freshwater Loch Lomond to attack further inland.

An aerial on the right hillside is located above the former Admiralty Torpedo Testing Station as it stands beside the old military road which is now the A83. It was an early reinforced concrete jetty from 1915, similar to Suishnish jetty on Raasay. Public access is not allowed.

Swallows and gannets hunt above the water, the latter looking down through the clear depths onto cod, congers, dabs, flounders, mackerel, plaice and rays. The rocks are covered with barnacles, mussels and assorted wracks while oaks, alders, rowans, birches and other deciduous trees screen the banks, attractive to wagtails, herons and ravens.

A caravan site is located at Ardgartan on the alluvium brought down by Croe Water. The A83 follows Glen Croe to the Rest & Be Thankful Pass which replaced General Cope's road of 1745, still used each year for a car hillclimb. Opposite is Ardmay House Hotel where the owner claims to be the only hotelier blending and exporting his own brand of Scotch. He also has bar curling with ice table and miniature curling stones.

Glenmallan jetty has a 150m prohibited area, serviced by ammunition ships supplying the Glen Douglas Munitions Depot. These ships accelerate quickly and throw up metre high washes which can break heavily or cause clapotis at the edges of the loch.

Both shores rise steeply as far as Cnap Point, marked by a prominent white cone with orange stripes down it. The mountains gradually decline in height but Beinn Reithe at 653m, for example, has its peak only 1.7km from the water.

The A814 moves away at the Finnart Ocean Terminal, leaving 8km with no lochside roads. The oil terminal has three piers for tankers up to 300,000t. At the centre of the terminal is a traditional stone house with pipelines crossing the lawns and passing the windows with an air of unreality.

Opposite Portincaple is Meall Daraich and the Carraig nan Ròn light column on which an oystercatcher has been found nesting. The column marks the northeastern side of the end of Loch Goil. On the edge of Loch Goil is the 14th century Carrick Castle, built by the Argylls. In 1651 it was fortified in case it was

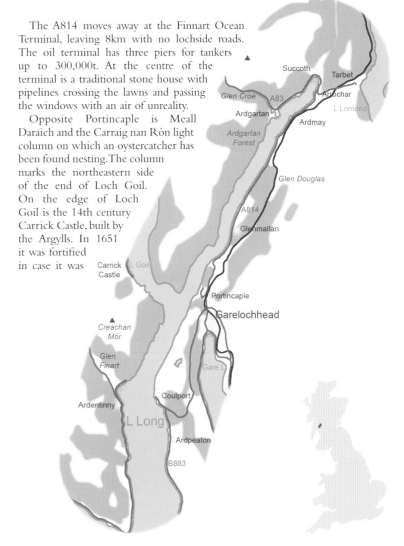

Looking north from the mouth of Loch Long towards Ardentinny, Glen Finart and Creachan Mór with the loch leading right.

besieged by Commonwealth troops. However, it was burned by the Earl of Atholl's troops in 1685 and now stands roofless but with the walls intact.

Powerlines cross high above Loch Long at a point just 1.5km from the head of Gare Loch, so close that the two lochs almost cross.

A massive structure at Port an Lochain is the Coulport Trident submarine explosives handling jetty. Built in the Hunterston construction yard, it is 200m x 80m x 47m high and is moored in over 80m of water after being towed up the Clyde. It is the world's biggest floating concrete dock at 85,000t. Technically, it is extremely advanced, having compensation for the rolling motion of a ship, responding to tidal rise and fall and being able to remove and replace nuclear reactors safely. It has been designed to withstand 300km/h winds, 0.2g earthquake forces and collision by 100,000t tankers bound for the Finnart Ocean Terminal. It is not visible from inland and is protected by line after line of security fencing, vast amounts of razor wire and batteries of video cameras and watchtowers. This makes the water side rather tame by comparison, with a 150m exclusion zone and a restricted area which keeps other craft to the west side of the loch, and security which is ensured by police launches staffed by extremely polite policemen whose job would be easier if markers of some kind or leading lines were to be placed at the requisite distance offshore to offer guidance on the location of the edge of the restricted area. Three

vertical green lights and pennant 9 give warning of ship movements when the area has to be cleared by other boats. When nuclear submarines are present the approach becomes less polite. Robin Lloyd-Jones was chased by marines with sub machine guns in an inflatable after he paddled too close to one, described in *Argonauts of the Western Isles*.

Engineer John Kibble of Coulport designed himself a conservatory in 1865, a striking dome 13m high and 45m in diameter with a dozen fluted columns, influenced by the design of the Crystal Palace at a time when glass with slim iron bars was not usually used as a construction material. It was later moved to Glasgow where it can be seen at Kibble Palace.

Between Shepherd's Point beacon and Ravenrock Point light structure is Finart Bay at the end of Glen Finart. Ardentinny Hotel has been a prominent landmark since the early 1700s.

On the east shore a measured distance may be marked for vessels wishing to conduct speed measurements.

The lochside roads now begin again, Coulport being sited at the end of the B883. The Firth of Clyde lies in front with Cloch Point opposite and the houses of Gourock stacked up but this does not mean a return to mass civilization. Mink live amongst the shoreline rocks at Ardpeaton.

A possible landing is at Gairletter Point where there is a caravan site and inlet to a boathouse beside the road.

Distance
23km from Succoth to Gairletter

OS 1:50,000 Sheet
56 Loch Lomond & Inveraray

Admiralty Charts
2131 Firth of Clyde & L Fyne (1:75,000)
3746 L Long & L Goil (1:25,000).
Upper L Long (1:25,000).
Approaches to Finnart (1:12,500)

Tidal Constants
Arrochar:
Dover +0110
Lochgoilhead:
Dover +0110
Coulport:
Dover +0110

Sea Area
Malin

Rescue
Inshore lifeboat:
Helensburgh
All weather lifeboat:
Troon

The Trident submarine explosives handling jetty at Coulport, the world's biggest floating dock.

26 Loch Fyne

Puffers and seafood

There's naething here but Highland pride,
And Highland scab and hunger:
If providence has sent me here,
'Twas surely in an anger.
Robert Burns

The military bridge across the River Fyne at the loch head.

A low fall under the old military road bridge above the present A83 bridge is the tidal limit. Water leaving Beinn Bhalgairean flows southwest as the Allt an Tàillir, then the River Fyne. Fyne Ales Brewery is by the bridge with a power station further back, the flattened valley floor wedged between 676m Clachan Hill and 811m Binnein an Fhìdhleir. Alders, raspberries, blackberries and midges surround the bridge.

Gravel rapids lead down to Loch Fyne, which has acquired a reputation for its seafood and begins with an oyster bar.

Streams in the loch are mostly weak although stronger off salient points. It is a submarine exercise area, surfaced submarines sometimes towing sonar on wires so that it is necessary to cross at least 1.5km behind. The loch can be sheltered and is mostly forested, especially by oaks and fir trees. Mountain ringlet butterflies are found at high level around the head of the loch and Natterer's bats are found down the west shore.

The A83 follows both banks as it rounds the head of the loch, a cross above it on the west bank. In the eastern direction at Cairndow it departs up Glen Kinglas which

is, effectively, an air gap despite the presence of Kinglas Water. Cairndow was noted as a place where both Julian and

Gregorian New Years were celebrated after the calendar changed. It was also where the *Vital Spark's* crew were unable to sell an 8kg German cannon for £1. Ardkinglas House was designed in 1907 by Sir Robert Lorimer for Sir Andrew Noble. Ardkinglas Woodland Gardens has a noted pinetum and the Grand Fir, the tallest tree in Britain at 57m. Overshadowing it are 719m Beinn an t-Seilich and 732m Stob an Eas. A large area of loch in front of the house is covered in floats for growing mussels. Unconstrained are cormorants and pieces of wrack which float with the tide.

Gleann Beag or Hell's Glen divides Ston an Eas from 610m Cruach nam Mult, a ridge easing down from 565m Cruach nan Capull through 484m Creag Dhubh. Across the loch is Dunderave Point, from dun a rudha, promontory fort. Dunderave Castle was built in 1598 by the Macnaughtons. An unfortunate mistake in the 18th century resulted in a Macnaughton marrying the wrong one of two sisters and eloping to Antrim with the other, when the castle passed to the Campbells of Ardkinglas. It was restored in 1911 by Lorimer and was featured by Neil Munro in *Castle Doom*. There is a fortified mound in front with assorted animal sculptures and a TV satellite dish by the water.

St Catherines has a jetty from where a passenger ferry can operate to Inveraray. The clear water is occupied by moon jellyfish, oystercatchers, common gulls, herons and wetsuited divers.

The A83 makes another detour around the head of Loch Shira where the River Shira discharges. Conspicuous on Dun Còrr-bhile is Dun na Cuaiche, serving as fort, watchtower and folly. On the other side it overlooks

Ardkinglas House and Glen Kinglas.

Dunderave Castle on Dunderave Point.

Aray Bridge over the River Aray by Inveraray Castle.

the River Aray, which joins Loch Shira under Aray Bridge of 1776. The two 20m masonry spans are separated by an oculus for aesthetics but the steep bridge struggles to handle A83 traffic with a single lane.

Inveraray Castle, facing the bridge, has been the seat of the Inveraray Campbells since the 15th century. It was rebuilt in 1844–94 in Scots baronial style with turreted conical towers, state dining room and drawing room with beautiful ceilings, wall panelling, tapestries and porcelain and an armoury with 1,300 weapons. A cross and standing stone are positioned in the castle grounds.

The Campbells were on the Government side during the 1745 uprising. Already with the Glencoe massacre to their name, the Campbell chief, the 3rd Duke, Archibald, held the unfair trial in 1752 of James Stewart for the murder of Colin Campbell at Appin, described in *The Trial of James of the Glens.* Of the 15 member jury 11 were named Campbell.

Inveraray was the oldest royal burgh in Argyllshire, awarded its title in 1848 by Charles I while he was imprisoned in Carisbrooke Castle and retained until 1975. The architecturally noted white buildings are from a 1746 Georgian planned village for the Duke of Argyll, replacing an older village which was cleared in 1810. The Old Town House was the customs house of 1753. Inveraray Jail is a popular attraction these days. Inveraray Museum is joined by the Combined Operations Museum, this being HMS Quebec where 250,000 men were trained during the

Puffer Eilean Eisdeal *and schooner* Arctic Penguin *at Inveraray.*

Glenbranter Forest rises behind Strachur Bay.

Second World War. There is an Argyll war memorial on the lochside.

A 500 year old Celtic cross in Main Street may be from Iona. The Presbyterian church of 1794–1806 by Robert Milne had a central dividing wall so that services could be held simultaneously in English and Gaelic, the Gaelic part now being the church hall. All Saints' Episcopalian church of 1923 has a 38m great belltower, the finest peal in Scotland and the world's third heaviest peal of ten bells.

In the 19th century there were 250–400 boats landing 15,000–20,000 barrels of Loch Fyne herrings a year here. Para Handy had claimed they were so thick that it was impossible to get the anchor down at times. Now there are two boats permanently at the pier. The *Arctic Penguin* of 1911 is a three masted iron schooner with a maritime heritage centre covering Clydeside and the Queens, the Highland clearances and the *Vital Spark*. This latter name on puffers seems to becoming almost as common as *Thomas the Tank Engine* on railway engines. The one moored here, despite the name, is the *Eilean Eisdeal*, formerly the *VIC 72*, one of the last puffers to be built in 1944, a couple of decades after local author Neil Munro wrote the last of his Para Handy stories.

Beyond Newtown Bay and An Otir is Newtown at the foot of a hill studded with cairns. Among the pines is the 24ha Argyll Wildlife Park with the snowy wallaby as well as badgers, wildcats, deer, owls and over a hundred species of wildfowl. Am Buachaille stands at 323m above a

Bàrr an Eich seen from Kenmore.

Eilean Aoghainn with Stob Odhar beyond.

Seals resting on the southern extension of Eilean Aoghainn.

Minard Castle faces the loch.

Distance
40km from
Achandunan to
Otter Ferry.

OS 1:50,000 Sheets
55 Lochgilphead
& Loch Awe
56 Loch Lomond
& Inveraray

Admiralty Charts
2131 Firth of Clyde
& L Fyne (1:75,000)
2381 Lower L Fyne
(1:25,000)
2382 Upper L Fyne
(1:25,000)

Tidal Constants
Inveraray:
HW Dover +0130,
LW Dover +0150
Lochgilphead:
HW Dover +0120,
LW Dover +0130

Sea Area
Malin

Rescue
Inshore lifeboat:
Tighnabruaich
All weather lifeboat:
Campbeltown

caravan site and Lùib Iomaire Mhóir as the Douglas Water joins past a chambered cairn. Creag an h-Iolaire suggests the presence of eagles.

A cup and ring marked rock is found in the trees at Ardnagowan.

Strachur has a dun and the smiddy has been restored as a blacksmith and farrier museum. A circular enclosure may be an early Celtic site. The Strachur Estate bridge of about 1783 has a 7.9m masonry arch with a pair of 900mm diameter blind oculi. Little newer is the 1792 church which uses sculpted stones from the chapel at Balliemeanoch. The village sits in a wind gap, the River Cur dropping to the far side of the village and then flowing away southwards. Strachur would not give the *Vital Spark*'s crew 10 shillings for their German cannon. Above Strachur Bay is the 481m nipple of Cruach nan Capull.

Amongst a small group of houses isolated in the trees at Kenmore Point is a monument. Wagtails investigate the rocky shore where limpets and sea anemones thrive. Beyond Pennymore Point and 359m Dùn Leacainn is Furnace at the mouth of the Leacann Water. In 1754 the trees on the forested hills attracted Lancashire ironmasters who used the timber for smelting. Granite quarries here have paved half of Glasgow but left a block which looks like a castle. There was also a gunpowder factory which blew up in 1883. It was where the crew of the *Vital Spark* attended a ball, helped by knowing the doorman and speaking Gaelic, Para Handy giving the Tar a black eye in an altercation and not missing him from the four man crew until off Lochgair the next day.

Sandhole, above Whitebridge Bay, suggests varied geology but there is another disused quarry at the foot of 420m Beinn Ghlas beyond Blackstone Bay.

Crarae Glen Gardens, started in 1912 by Sir Archibald and Lady Campbell of Succoth, is one of the west coast's great gardens, like a Himalayan gorge with rare trees, one of the best rhododendron collections in Scotland and the national collection of southern beech. Crarae was another village which celebrated both New Years. It was at a ball here that Macphail, the *Vital Spark*'s engineer, had obtained his hat, where the crew were unable to sell the German cannon for a shilling or even to abandon it on the quay and where their attempt to take in paying lodgers was not too successful. There are a chambered cairn and cemetery by Crarae Point.

Across the loch is a chapel site overlooking Kilbride Island. The Strathlachlan River flows into Lachlan Bay past a chapel and the ruin of Castle Lachlan. Some of the castle dates from the 12th century. The keep is 15th century and there are sections of wall up to 14m high. This stronghold of the MacLachlans of MacLachlan was attacked in 1746 after Culloden by the Hanoverian navy while occupied by a widow and her children. All around is Strathlachlan Forest.

The red squirrel was reintroduced to Minard in 1847, spreading from here through the southwest Highlands and north towards Dalmally and Glen Dochart.

Achagoyle Bay and Brainport Bay lead to the Minard Narrows. A 7m black and white striped round tower with a black framework top marks Sgeir an Eirionnaich, Paddy rock. Another mark fixes An Oitir as it reaches out to Eilean Aoghainn, which may have had a castle before Castle Lachlan. It is accompanied by the smaller Fraoch Eilean and sometimes by seals and gannets. The 19th–century Minard Castle replaces a 16th century version between Minard Bay and Union Bay.

A chapel site on the point beyond Creagan Dubh does not have an obvious congregation within sight but platforms in the hillside above must have been cut by someone. Above is 436m Cruach Chuilceachan.

Loch Gair receives some shelter from Ardcastle Wood. Cairns and a square white tower at Pointhouse mark the other side of the mouth. Bootlace weed, sea urchins and blackbacked gulls might be met.

The Largiemore Burn enters at Largiemore with a pier along the shore.

Glas Eilean helps to shelter Port Ann, which belongs to the Crown.

The Narrows flow to 4km/h, ebbing from an hour after Dover high water and flooding from five hours before Dover high water. The fast flow is caused by the Oitir or spit reaching over halfway across the loch from Otter Ferry with a mark at the end. Additional protection took the form of a motte at Ballimore. Dun Dubh would have undertaken a similar function above a cave near Silver Craigs.

From here lower Loch Fyne continues on a larger scale to the Sound of Bute.

The mark at the end of the spit.

27 West Loch Tarbert

Lateral thinking won Kintyre for Magnus Barefoot

They held unwonted way;–
Up Tarbat's western lake they bore,
Then dragged their bark the isthmus o'er,
As far as Kilmaconnel's shore,
*   Upon the eastern bay.*
Sir Walter Scott

The head of West Loch Tarbert and the isthmus sailed over by King Magnus Barefoot.

Lichened oaks interspersed with fir trees surround the loch as it widens out with thrift on the rocks above water level and festoons of wrack and wolf mussels below, oysters and moon jellyfish, for which this is a breeding area. The birdlife includes oystercatchers, cormorants, cuckoos, sandpipers and hooded crows which seize mallard chicks as their mother tries to frighten them off.

Eilean da Ghallagain exhibits small scale folding of its igneous rock. A pair of islets to the southwest, one topped by a metal post, form a popular hauling out area for seals.

Beyond Eilean Eòghainn, Eileann Ceann na Creige has been linked to the shore to allow it to be used as a car ferry terminal to Port Askaig and to Port Ellen on Islay, a terminal marked by a beacon. Between the terminal and Whitehouse the peninsula of Eilean Araich More with its dun has become a resting place for another wreck.

Dunmore on the west side has another fort site and a mausoleum but the most prominent feature in summer is

The quay and a wrecked fishing boat at West Tarbert.

West Loch Tarbert runs southwest from **Tarbert**, nearly joining up with East Loch Tarbert and separating Knapdale from the Kintyre peninsula. As with a number of other sea lochs in Argyll & Bute, it faces directly into the prevailing headwind.

In the ongoing disputes between the Vikings and the Scots, King Edgar agreed with King Magnus Barefoot that the Scots would have the mainland and the Vikings the islands, islands being defined as anything which Magnus could travel round in his longboat. Magnus sailed round the Kintyre peninsula in 1098 and had his boat dragged 1.4km across the isthmus to complete the circumnavigation and claim Kintyre, something Edgar had certainly not intended, the Vikings retaining Kintyre until 1263.

There is a parking area by the head of the loch, overlooked by an aerial.

Flows are barely perceptible in the loch but the head has a very flat bed so it may be necessary to walk some distance over hard mud with worm casts to reach water deep enough to float a boat.

The West Loch Hotel at West Tarbert precedes a quay which handles fishing boats, one of which lies wrecked in the shallows just to the north of the quay.

There are standing stones both sides of the loch and the Abhainn na Cuile enters on the west side. A modern cottage looks notably out of place.

a display of redhot pokers in the garden of a house standing on the shore. Another house has its own harbour built out of gabions, thoughtfully used as a perch by a heron.

Rock outcrops tend to be small but important in navigational terms. Sgeir Mhein off Rubha Mhein is marked by a red light while a green light is located off Corran Point, opposite which is the large drying islet of Achadh-chaorann Bay. Corran Point is at the foot of the distinctively shaped 142m Dùn

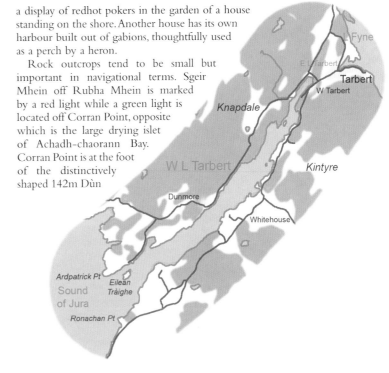

Seals on an islet after Eilean da Ghallagain.

The bungalow and flagpole at Dunmore give a Nordic feel to the shoreline. Dùn Skeig is already clearly visible in the distance.

Looking inland up the loch.

Distance
15km from Stonfield to Eilean Tràighe

OS 1:50,000 Sheet
62 North Kintyre & Tarbert

Admiralty Charts
2131 Firth of Clyde & L Fyne (1:75,000)
2168 Approaches to Sound of Jura (1:75,000)
2475 Sound of Gigha (1:25,000)
2476 Lochs & Harbours in Sound of Jura & Approaches. W L Tarbert (1:25,000)

Tidal Constants
Sound of Gigha:
HW Dover +0340,
LW Dover +0420

Sea Area
Malin

Rescue
Inshore lifeboat:
Campbeltown
All weather lifeboat:
Islay

Skeig hill which forms the southwestern end of the loch and which is an obvious site for a vitrified fort and duns. Vegetation includes rhododendrons and yellow irises and provides an environment amenable to vipers. A jetty faces Ferry House but there is no longer a ferry service to disturb the fish basking in the shallows. Birdlife includes eider ducks and blackbacked gulls.

Eilean Tràighe and several smaller islets complicate the mouth of the loch which ends between Ardpatrick Point and Ronachan Point. The ebb starts six hours before Dover high water at up to 2km/h and the flood at Dover high water at up to 1km/h.

At the mouth the view changes from the relatively narrow loch to the striking view across the Sound of Gigha to Gigha Island and, beyond it, across the Sound of Jura to Islay and Jura. The contrast with the creeklike atmosphere of the head of the loch could hardly be greater.

There is a convenient parking area on the A83 to the south of Ronachan Bay.

West Loch Tarbert and Dùn Skeig seen from the Sound of Gigha.

28 Loch Sween

Probably Scotland's oldest inhabited castle

Who is he provides this fleet,
At Castle Sween of many hills?
A vigorous man who fears no blast,
His masts up raised, seeking his right.
John Marsden

shallows. Deer browse amongst the rhododendrons and oaks but wildcats remain higher up or, at least, hidden.

Flows are imperceptible in the wider part of the loch but quicker in the narrows and nowhere is narrower than at Scotnish where a wooden hoist stands on a small jetty, the narrows ending at a picnic area.

Wooden sailing vessel moored at Scotnish where rhododendrons bloom along the hillside.

Despite being in Argyll & Bute, heading southwest across Knapdale, Loch Sween takes its name from the Suibhne family of Ulster.

Trident shaped, it is a sea loch, heading directly into the prevailing wind. The longest arm is the most northerly of the three, Caol Scotnish. It is easy for portable craft to launch onto it but parking is a problem, the only practical proposition being the passing places on the single track B8025, a practice which is frowned upon despite the light traffic. A swan disapproves of sharing the water.

Near the head of the loch are a well and cross, hidden in the alders, oaks and other trees surrounding the water which resembles a pond here. The water is clear despite the bed of mud and shells. Yellow irises grow around the head of the loch, thrift finds a foothold on the rock outcrops and wracks act as reminders that it is all tidal.

Caol Scotnish is narrow and dotted with islets but sailing boats do get up this far to moor in this sheltered, idyllic setting. Oystercatchers and herons frequent the

Caol Scotnish widens out into Loch a'Bhealaich which gives access to Tayvallich, the largest village in the area, formerly a herring and lobster fishing centre and now providing moorings for sailing craft.

This, in turn, passes the high wooded hill fronted by Sròn Bheith to join with the other two arms of Loch Sween. Between these other two is Port Lunna with a marine farm while the far branch leads up to Achnamara with its outdoor centre. The centre did much pioneering work on helicopter rescue of sea kayak paddlers with regular practical sessions on the loch involving helicopters.

Cala Islet and Eilean Loain are barely distinguishable from the west side of the loch, the tree covering on Eilean Loain blending with the trees on the mainland although the tree cover reduces steadily towards the coast. The shoreline is rocky but low, ideal for cormorants.

Thrift lines the banks in the sheltered headwaters of Caol Scotnish.

Sròn Bheith separates Loch a'Bhealaich from the main body of Loch Sween.

Head of Loch Sween and Eilean Loain from above Taynish.

Taynish Woods are a fine example of undisturbed coastal oakwoods.

On the east side there is an old cross in the woods near Daltote Cottage.

A round building with a conical roof draws attention to the channel which leads in behind the north end of Taynish Island. This island and the Ulva Islands virtually block the mouth of Linne Mhuirich. Although there are at least four routes into the linne, two drain at low tide and the others are less than obvious. Equally inconspicuous is the entrance to Ceann an t-Sailein, an inlet which, doubtless, formerly joined with Loch na Cille to give the Island of Danna its name but which is now closed off by a very short isthmus carrying the road.

On the east side are another cross, a cairn and a dun, followed by the masterpiece, Castle Sween. Probably the oldest stone castle on the Scottish mainland, it dates from the start of the Norman influence on castle building while the Vikings were still dominant. The lower rectangular keep dates from the later 12th century,

Looking down Loch Sween past Taynish Island towards the Sound of Jura.

Castle Sween, surrounded by a sea of caravans and, often, by water skiers.

Seen from the mouth of Loch Sween, Castle Sween's position on the right shore of the loch is much more prominent.

the two storey tower in one corner is 13th century, the 15th century Macmillan's Tower was added by Alexander Macmillan, the keeper until 1481, and there is a 16th century round tower in the other corner. The walls are 2.2m thick and 12m high with no openings except a sea gate on the west side, now ruined. It may have been besieged by Robert the Bruce early in the 13th century but was ruined by Sir Alexander Macdonald in 1647 with the forces of the Marquess of Montrose and the Highland clansmen supporting the Royalists. It has been further spoiled by a caravan site all around it, powerboats and water skiers operating from here to add to the commotion of low flying jets.

Danna has calcareous rocks with rich flora. Rhizostoma jellyfish swim in the water, eider ducks fly past and seals haul out on the outcrops of Sgeir Bun an Locha within sight of the powerboats.

Gradually the view opens out from the parallel sides of Loch Sween to take in the panorama of the MacCormaig Isles, the Sound of Jura, Jura itself and, beyond, the higher peaks of Mull, a breathtaking contrast to the intimacy of the head of the loch.

The ebb at the mouth of Loch Sween starts six hours before Dover high water and the flood starts two hours after Dover high water at up to 3km/h. Strong southwesterly winds may reverse the ebb.

Danna is only approachable through a locked gate and the minor road on the east side of the loch is some way up the hillside. It is possible to take out at the head of the B8025 at Keillmore where there is a parking area.

Loch Sween opens out into the Sound of Jura with the MacCormaig Isles and, beyond them, the Paps of Jura.

Distance
17km from Arichonah to the Sound of Jura

OS 1:50,000 Sheets
55 Lochgilphead & Loch Awe
61 Jura & Colonsay
62 North Kintyre & Tarbert

Admiralty Charts
2168 Approaches to Sound of Jura (1:75,000)
2169 Approaches to Firth of Lorn (1:75,000)
2396 Sound of Jura – Southern Part (1:25,000)
2397 Sound of Jura – Northern Part (1:25,000). L Sween (1:25,000)

Tidal Constants
Carsaig Bay: Dover −0610

Sea Area
Malin

Rescue
Inshore lifeboat: Campbeltown
All weather lifeboat: Islay

29 Loch Etive

Remote with a sting in the tail

To where Dunstaffnage hears the raging
Of Connal with his rocks engaging.
Sir Walter Scott

From Stob na Bròige the peaty water flows southwest as the River Coupall, River Etive and then Loch Etive through Argyll & Bute to the Firth of Lorn. The water becomes tidal as it enters the loch at Kinlochetive, a point

The dramatic view northwards from the head of Loch Etive.

An indication of the savage power unleashed when water floods down off Ben Starav.

which can be reached down Glen Etive by vehicle using a 20km single track road but not from below as there is no road for 15km, making it a wonderfully remote piece of water with dramatic scenery. Unfortunately, midges have no problems getting here. Another possible encounter might be with the Fàchan of Glen Etive, a monster with one eye, one arm from his chest and one leg, striking the pose used by Celtic seers when casting spells. A further resident was Deidre NicCruithnigh or Deidre of the Sorrows who was invited back to Ireland by former fiancé King Conacher of Ulster but was killed by him.

The derelict pier at the head of the loch has been renovated and is being used to ship out timber from Glenetive Forest.

Winds are erratic or blow along the loch. Flows are negligible to the Bonawe Narrows although the scenery is dramatic and the shoreline steep to as far as this point. The Allt a' Bhiorain also joins the head of the loch past 590m Meall nan Gobhar as it starts a ridge which rises up to 839m Beinn Trilleachan with the Trilleachan Slabs at 40°, much enjoyed by rock climbers. Facing across the loch is 1,078m Ben Starav with its golden eagles. Each has steep sides which sweep down to the water. Ben Starav has notable dry clefts of boulders where spates have gouged out channels. Looking back up the glen shows more stark peaks.

Oak, birch and hazel trees, bracken and bluebells cover the lower flanks, inhabited by deer, tree pipits, redstarts and warblers, with herons, seals and wrack in the loch itself.

Each side of 800m Stob an Duine Ruaidh a significant stream enters, the Allt Coire na Làrach after Rubha Doire Làrach and the Allt Ghiusachan at Inverghiusachan Point.

A pier, moorings and boathouses serve a couple of cottages at Barrs in the most remote part of the loch, also used by swans. Some pillow lava edges Rubha Bharr. Beyond the point is Bàgh na Dalach, into which the Allt Easach and Abhain Dalach discharge.

The wider River Kinglass enters Ardmaddy Bay

Beinn Trilleachan rises beside the head of the loch.

A pair of remote cottages at Barrs.

Woods alongside the loch towards Barrs.

beyond the relative plateau of 439m Monadh Liath and the River Liver joins Inverliver Bay. A further tributary on this side is the River Noe into Port an Dòbhrain, backed by the highest mountain in the area, the 1,126m Ben Cruachan, conical hill.

By comparison, the Cadderlie Burn flowing from 578m Meall Dearg to Camas na Cùirte is less extreme. The peaks on the west side step back up to 714m with Beinn Mheadhonach although 555m Beinn Duirinnis is more dramatic for being closer. Heather grows beside the loch.

Both sides of the loch have been used for quarrying. Industry now includes mussel floats around Rubh' Aird an Droighinn. Bonawe Quarries export crushed granite and, formerly, top quality setts, including those for Glasgow's King George V Bridge and for the entrance to the original Mersey Tunnel.

Dun Mor can be found as a mound at the mouth of the River Awe. The river, partly obstructed by tree debris, produces a spit. With Eilean Duirinnis, now a peninsula, the loch is forced through the Bonawe Narrows. Named from the Gaelic Bun Atha, mouth of the Awe, the gap was formerly the only crossing point for the loch. The ferry has gone, leaving an awkward break in the B845 and only high powerlines across the water.

Inverawe Smokery is on one bank of the Awe, facing across to Bonawe Furnace, the most complete charcoal fuelled ironworks in Britain, an Ancient Monument. The furnace was operated from 1753 to 1876 by Furness ironmasters who used local oak and birch for charcoal and shipped ore from Ulverston to use with local limestone, exporting pig iron to Cumbria and making cannon balls for use in the Napoleonic wars. The furnace employed 600 people. Its bellows were powered by a breast shot waterwheel fed from the River Awe and it had an early tramway with tracks of slate. Kelly's Pier of 1753 is named after Alexander Kelly, who leased the furnace. A drystone structure 120m long and 6.1m wide, the pier was used by the Newland Company of Furness to unload the iron

The loch cuts between Ben Cruachan and Beinn Duirinnis.

Pillow lava rolls into the loch.

The heart of the Bonawe Furnace complex.

ore and there are the remains of a timber extension for steamships.

Flows begin out through the narrows from three hours before Dover high water at up to 3km/h and in from three hours and fifty minutes after Dover high water at up to 5km/h.

There are tidal ponds at the back of Airds Bay, where there are cormorants, mallards, herring and blackbacked gulls and oystercatchers. The River Nant enters through Taynuilt, where the houses are of granite from Inverawe Quarry. Station buildings house the West Highland Brewery and Shore Cottage won the 1989 Egon Ronay Tearoom of the Year award for Lily McNaught, who moved here after her author husband, Noel, drowned in a kayak in the Severn estuary. In 1308 Robert the Bruce routed the men of Lorn here. A windfarm shows on the skyline near Loch Nant.

For centuries there was a 3.7m granite pillar near Airds Bay House to St Nessog. Furnace workmen moved it to Taynuilt in 1805 and set it up as the first monument in Britain to Nelson, positioned even before his funeral took place.

Airds Point is steep to but faces the mouth of the River Esragan which has deposited debris to fill in its side of the loch. Fish cages and mussel floats are anchored along the side of the loch in the clear water. A jetty and moorings lead to the mouth of the Allt Nathais.

A jetty serves Ardchattan Priory & Gardens. The priory of St Catan, a follower of St Columba, was established in 1231 by Duncan MacDougall, the Lord of Lorn, for the Valliscaulian monks from Burgundy, vegetarians who also ate fish from their pond and from the loch, as they still do. Robert the Bruce held a Parliament here in 1308, the last in Gaelic. A strange devouring toad monument was set up to priors Duncan, Dougall and family in 1502. A 16th century prior had a nun from Kilmaronaig as a girlfriend. When the order made a surprise visit he hid her under the floorboards. Unfortunately the visitor was hosted in this room and stayed a long time. It is claimed that the nun is still there. The priory was taken over by the Bishops of Argyll in 1617. Marriage associations with the prior meant that Colkitto the Younger left it unharassed in 1644 but it was burned by Cromwell a decade later. Red Colin Campbell is buried here. There are ruins and 1.2ha gardens which have existed since the 13th century.

Near St Baodan's church is a well which grants penny wishes at the foot of the 350m rounded bulk of Na Maoilean.

The railway follows the shoreline to Connel, squeezing

round Dùn Chathach at Rubha nan Càrn. There is a pier at the back of the bay sheltered by Rubh' a' Chàirn Bhig. Facing Linne na Craige or Stonefield Bay and taking some shelter from the Abbot's Isles are Achnacloich Gardens with a castellated house set amongst oaks and larches.

The low Moss of Achnacree extends across much of the loch from the foot of 308m Beinn Lora, dotted with cairns and chambered cairns and with lochans including Lochan nan Rath and Lochan na Beithe. Peat cutting takes place.

From the Kilmaronaig Narrows the water gets serious, an indication of what is to come. The southern half of the narrows are obstructed by islets and flows run to 11km/h, out from three hours and twenty minutes before Dover high water and in from three hours and forty minutes after Dover high water, an eddy forming on the southwest side on the ebb and a race and eddy on the southeast side with the flood. Kelp waves as the water boils.

The velocity eases for a while in Connel Sound. Black Crofts face Dunfiunary with a house and round tower. The church in Connel has stained glass showing the bridge and the Falls of Lora. Just upstream is an old jetty which offers little practical help.

Connel Bridge of 1903 is of particular value as a marker of the falls. The bridge was the second longest cantilever railway bridge in Europe, second only to the Forth Bridge. The flows were too strong for the piers to be in the water so they are 160m apart and lean inwards. There is a clear 152m span including a large 71m suspended span, giving 15m clearance over the water. The bridge uses 2,600t of steel. Road traffic was added in 1914 and the railway closed in 1966.

The Falls of Lora are formed by a ledge just upstream

Highland cattle by Linne na Craige.

from the bridge, starting near the north bank and reaching more than halfway across the sound. At low water springs there is a 1.5m fall over the ledge. Most of the water passes on the south side. On the ebb there is a chute on the north side used by white water kayaks. This meets the main flow from the south side below the bridge to form a line of standing waves and boils which continue for 1km beyond Ledaig Point. On the flood there is a wide area of broken water over the ledge. Flows are officially up to 11km/h but some claim they exceed 15km/h. There is no slack water. It goes out from three hours and twenty minutes before Dover high water and in from three hours and twenty minutes after Dover high water. However, times can vary by as much as an hour and a half, more often early if there is a westerly wind and

Off Kilmaronaig the ebb is already moving fast. The pictures were taken at spring tides but in calm conditions.

low pressure and later with the opposite conditions. The advice is to pass within an hour of the turn of the tide and to be aware that stopping on the east side of the bridge to inspect is not easy. Once ashore, however, there are good viewpoints from the A85 to the west of the bridge and from the A828 on the bridge itself.

The shoreline at North Connel is occupied by Connel Airfield with gliding at the Connel Flying Club. The tide drops to leave a wide shingle area at Ledaig Point, the southern end of Ardmucknish Bay.

Camas Bruaich Ruaidhe or Salmore Bay has moorings and a fish farm but most of the moorings are in Dunstaffnage Bay where there is a marina with a slip and there is shelter from Eilean Mòr and the rocks which make up Eilean Beag. At the back of the bay are the large premises of the Scottish Association for Marine Science.

A jetty stands by Dunstaffnage Castle. The capital of the kingdom of Dalriada was here or hereabouts and the Stone of Destiny, now in Westminster, was brought from Tara and built into the castle wall until 843. The present building was started in the 13th century by the MacDougalls, the Lords of Lorn and was used by

Alexander III as a base to drive the Vikings out of the Hebrides. It was captured by Robert the Bruce from Alexander MacDougall, the Lord of Lorn, in 1309. It was the residence of the Lord of the Isles in 1455 but would have passed in 1470 to Colin, the 1st Earl of Argyll, who married one of the three daughters of Sir John Stewart, the 3rd Lord of Lorn. To secure the succession Sir John married the mother of his illegitimate son, Dugald. He was stabbed at the altar by Allan Macdougall but the priest managed to complete the service before he died so Dugald took Lorn but eventually the Stewarts were left with Appin. The Captains of Dunstaffnage are descendents of the 14th century hereditary constables of the castle appointed by the Argylls. Old Colkitto was brought here and hanged from the mast of his own galley. The castle was garrisoned during the Jacobite uprisings and was a prison for Flora MacDonald for ten days in 1746. The quadrangular walls are up to 2.7m thick, the castle retaining the great curtain wall and the 17th century tower house over the 13th century entrance. The adjacent ruined chapel of St Maelruba of about 1250 has beautiful architectural detailing and many Campbell graves.

Distance
19km from Gualachulain to Ardmucknish Bay

OS 1:50,000 Sheets
49 Oban & East Mull
50 Glen Orchy & Loch Etive

Admiralty Charts
2388 L Etive & Approaches (1:25,000). Dunstaffnage Bay to Connel Bridge (1:7,500)

Tidal Constants
Bonawe:
HW Dover –0320,
LW Dover –0300
Connel:
Dover –0510
Dunstaffnage Bay:
Dover –0520

Sea Area
Malin

Rescue
Inshore lifeboat:
Campbeltown
All weather lifeboat:
Oban

The Falls of Lora at Connel Bridge during the ebb. The rock shelf is clearly visible above the bridge.

The flood over the Falls of Lora seen from Connel Bridge. The broken water is over the central rock shelf.

30 Loch Linnhe

Following the great slip

Full many a shrill triumphant note
Saline and Scallastle bade float
Their misty shores around;
And Morvern's echoes answer'd well,
And Duart heard the distant swell
Come down the darksome Sound.
Sir Walter Scott

The Dubh Lighe rises on Streap Comhlaidh and flows south to Loch Eil, which runs east to Loch Linnhe, lying along the line of Glen Albyn as it slides southwest across the Highlands to the Firth of Lorn. The tidal limit and start of Loch Eil at Kinlocheil are at the foot of 503m Meall nam Maigheach although there are more dramatic peaks ranged to the west of the loch. Flows are imperceptible until beyond Fassfern. The wind normally blows along the loch and produces a short sea and increasing rainfall with southwesterly gales.

Alders, sedges and blackbacked gulls stand at the head of the loch while patches of wrack and common seals float with the tide.

The West Highland line follows to Fort William, a stunning route from Mallaig in its own right but with added interest for railway enthusiasts with the Jacobite steam train service. It has further impetus from the fact that Harry Potter's Hogwarts Express was filmed on the line. The A830, built in 1812 by Telford, is the current Road to the Isles.

Beinn an t-Sneachda at 625m shelters the loch from the north. Small rivers join, the Fionn Lighe at the head of the loch, the Garvan River at Garvan, the Dubh Uisge at Duisky and the An t-Sùileag at Fassfern. The ridge from Stob Coire a' Chearcaill running down through 609m Bràigh Bhlàigh on the south side and Druim Fada, long ridge, peaking at 744m Stob a' Ghrianain on the north side create conditions which often result in mist until Fort William. There are oakwoods on the north side and birches on the colder south side. Herring gulls and cormorants are present and the loch is used for mussel floats.

Achdalieu Lodge is the base for Outward Bound's Loch Eil Centre. A sea of caravans overlook the start of the Annat Narrows, where there can be a race. Flows start outwards at three hours fifty minutes before Dover high water and inwards from two and a half hours after Dover high water at up to 9km/h. Underwater experiments take

The Jacobite passes the end of the Caledonian Canal.

place with diving from barges moored in the Narrows and also in the Corran Narrows.

A long pier, 58m tower and travelling cranes beyond Annat Point serve the Scottish Pulp & Paper Mills on the shore of the loch. There is a monument at Corpach and Treasures of the Earth, Europe's finest collection of gemstones, crystals, minerals, nuggets and fossils in simulated mines, caves and caverns. The 6m white cylindrical tower with dark conical roof is Corpach Light, marking Sea Lock at the start of the Caledonian Canal which gives boats an inland route northeast across Scotland. This uses Glen Albyn, Glen Mór or the Great Glen, where northern

Corpach Sea Lock on the Caledonian Canal.

Ben Nevis, head in the clouds as usual.

The Cona Glen and Glen Scaddle lead into Inverscaddle Bay.

The Corran ferry passes the sector light at the Corran Narrows.

Scotland has moved 100km northeast along a wrench fault which has then been scoured by glacier. Without this shift Loch Eil would discharge by Colonsay and Fort William would be opposite Fortrose. Loch Linnhe is a former pre glacial river which ran through the North Channel and Irish Sea with the Sound of Mull rift valley as a tributary. It is deep enough to be used as a submarine exercise area. Wind is funnelled along the loch and rainfall is increased. More often than not the peaks are shrouded in cloud, mist, rain or some other meteorological form.

Flows off Corpach are to 5km/h but then currents are weak. Herons, swans, shelducks and black guillemots take no notice as jets thunder over.

There is a sharp change of direction at Rubha Dearg island to face southwest into the prevailing wind blowing up Loch Linnhe. Beyond Caol a peninsula separates the River Lochy at Inverlochy from Am Breun Chamas sands with the long island of An Caol running parallel. Otters and roe deer might be seen. The River Nevis also joins from the south of the red and grey granite Ben Nevis, the

highest mountain in Britain at 1,344m. The first ascent was in 1771 but 150,000 people now climb it each year. At times there have been a weather observatory and a hotel at the summit. Being 7km from the water makes its presence very obvious down Loch Eil although the summit is usually lost in cloud. The name means poisonous or terrible in Gaelic but there is an annual race to the top, taking from an hour and twenty five minutes. On a clear day Ireland can be seen from the top but it contributes to the high rainfall in the area. A Model T Ford, unicycles, a wheelchair, a bed, a piano, an organ and a barrel of beer have all been taken to the summit. Two prominent penstocks running down the front of the mountain bring Loch Treig water to the aluminium smelter at its base.

From the jetty at Camusnagaul a passenger ferry operates across to Fort William.

Fort William was founded in the 1650s by General Monck with a fort in 1690 for William III to control the Highlanders. It was attacked by the Jacobites in 1715 and 1745, being dismantled in 1855. This was the main

The Ballachulish Bridge crosses the mouth of Loch Leven.

Sgorr Dhearg guards the end of Glen Duror.

emigration port for Highlanders in the 19th century. Now it is a tourist centre, the capital of Lochaber, and full of hikers with rucksacks. A heliport and Underwater Centre Pier are more functional. There is a mountain rescue post and attempts to close the hospital have been resisted. The West Highland Museum features the Jacobites, bagpipes recovered from Culloden, Celtic relics, arms, clans, tartans, archaeology, wildlife and an unusual 18th century portrait which looks like a blur until reflected in a polished cylinder, when it reveals a portrait of Prince Charlie. There is also a Scottish Crafts & Whisky Centre.

The shores of Loch Linne run straight at first. Material has been washed into the loch at Stronchreggan by the Abhainn Sron a' Chreagain but the River Kiachnish has made little impact on the east shore.

The River Scaddle empties into Inverscaddle Bay and gives views towards the peaks round the Cona Glen. The bay has Eilean nan Gall in the centre but drains at low water. It has the rare floating seaweed Ascophyllum mackayii which has no roots and is unanchored, resting on the mud in mats when the tide is out.

The *Stirling Castle* ran aground in 1828, fatally injuring Colonel Alexander MacDonnell who had opposed the building of the Caledonian Canal as use of Loch Oich would have imposed upon his privacy.

Flows through the Corran Narrows are fast, officially to 9km/h although some say to 22km/h on the flood which starts an hour after Dover high water. The flow out begins five hours and twenty minutes before Dover high water. There are sudden swirls and it can be rough with wind against tide, overfalls across the whole width if the winds are strong. Eddies form on both sides of the loch after passing through the Narrows on both ebb and flood tides. An Camas Aiseig has a southeasterly flow for eleven hours and northwesterly for just an hour and a half with overfalls on the ingoing stream. The eddy

na Gucaig stand on the sides of the loch, Corran Point is a low obstruction to the line of the loch, marked by the white lighthouse with its sector light. A church is one of 32 similar ones designed by Telford to commemorate Waterloo.

The Abhainn Righ flows down from Glenrigh Forest past a forest trail and a shoreside caravan site at Bunree. The water is clear but there are midges. Flows begin southwest five hours before Dover high water and northeast an hour and ten minutes after Dover high water at up to 4km/h in the centre of the channel off Rubha Cuil-cheanna, the end of Loch Leven. At Onich there is the Clach-a-Charra site. The Ballachulish Bridge can be seen crossing the loch with a backdrop of Glencoe peaks.

From Rubh' a' Bhaid Bheithe both sides of Loch Linnhe show precipitous mountains with steep valleys. Disused quarries are the toenails of 1,024m Sgorr Dhearg. Oystercatchers are present.

James Stewart, James of the Glens, was hung for the shooting at the wood of Lettermore in 1752 of Colin Campbell, the Red Fox. This followed an unfair trial at Inveraray, a story kept alive by Robert Louis Stevenson's *Kidnapped*, which uses the manhunt after the shooting as a central theme. It is thought that many Highlanders know who did it, possibly his son, and that the information is still passed down in secret.

A pier precedes Kentallan Bay which appears sheltered except from the north but can produce violent squalls in various directions with westerly gales. It was during an excursion from here that Sunny Jim managed to fill the *Vital Spark*'s milk can with beer and was obliged to play his melodeon for the whole of a ball after the booked pipers became inebriated.

Above is Glenduror Forest. Ardshiel was exiled and his

at Rubha Dearg is 1km/h from four hours after Dover high water but increases to 3km/h in An Camas Aiseig from three hours and forty minutes after Dover high water. A further complication is the short but frequent vehicle ferry crossings
Although 598m Beinn na Cille and 616m Beinn

Map labels: Glen Dubh Lighe, Gleann Suileag, Kinlocheil, A830, Fassfern, Glen Mor, Caledonian Canal, L Eil, Corpach, R Lochy, S Garvan, Duisky, Caol, Glen Garvan, Camusnagaul, Inverlochy, Stronchreggan, R Nevis, Fort William, Glen Scaddle, Cona Glen, R Kiachnish, R Scaddle, Inverscaddle Bay, Ardgour, Beinn na Gucaig, Glen Gour, Corran Narrows, Glenrigh Forest, Sallachan, Onich, Sallachan Pt, L Leven, Glen Tarbert, R Tarbert, Inversanda Bay, L Linnhe, Glenduror Forest, Kentallen, Kilmalieu, Rubha Mòr, Cuil Bay, Glen Duror, Salachan Glen, B8043, Camasnacroise, L a' Choire, Kingairloch, Shuna Island, Portnacroish, Glensanda, Appin, Port Appin, Elnaig, Eriska, An Sleaghach, L Crean, Lynn of Lorn, Bernera Island, Lismore, Duart Pt, Eilean Musdile, Firth of Lorn

Shuna with Mull in the distance.

Castle Stalker in Loch Laich.

Stewart estate from Ballachulish to Kentallan forfeited to George II after the 1745 rebellion.

Crom Roinn is part of a low shoreline which initially has a parklike feel towards Rubha nam Mòine and remains low to Rubha Mòr, the outer point of Cuil Bay, which has been declared the best beach in Scotland in one survey. The River Duror enters at the back of the bay.

The Salachan Burn enters opposite Eilean Balnagowan, an island with some sheltered inlets which have been declared a bird sanctuary and where porpoises might be seen. Here the coast moves from the Highland region to Argyll & Bute.

Flows through the Sound of Shuna run southwest from five hours and forty minutes before Dover high water and northeast from forty minutes after Dover high water at up to 2km/h. The shelter by the Knap encourages its use as moorings and by black guillemots and there is also a fish farm near the ruins of the small square Castle Shuna. The flat topped island is a single farm.

In the centre of Loch Laich, which largely drains, is Castle Stalker, as in animal stalking. From about 1500 it was the seat of the Stewarts of Appin before becoming the 16th century hunting lodge of James IV. Ownership then alternated between the Stewarts and Campbells, the castle becoming ruined but now having been restored. In *Monty Python & the Holy Grail* it was Castle Argh!

Reefs are marked to the north of Port Appin.

Port Appin, terminal for the passenger ferry to Lismore.

Portnacroish was the scene of a 1468 battle between the Stewarts and MacDougalls. It was also the sequel to the only decent thing to happen during the Glencoe massacre. A Campbell had spared a woman and child, killing a dog to get his sword bloody. He met the child 40 years later, by which time he was the innkeeper at Portnacroish, and the two embraced.

Eilean nan Caorach with its limekilns, Inn Island and Sgeir Bhuidhe with its 8m white tower produces the Appin Narrows, flowing southwest as at the Sound of Shuna and northeast from half an hour after Dover high water at up to 5km/h. Restless kelp waves with the flow.

It was from Port Appin, sheltering behind a tall outcrop, that Mary MacArthur contributed to the *Oban Times* and

West Highland Times for over 70 years from 1926. There is a wildlife museum and jetties. A passenger ferry serves Lismore. The 40km² island of Dalradian limestone is very fertile, hence its Gaelic name of Ieis Mor, great garden. Most houses are towards the northern end.

At the far end of the outcrop is a natural arch overlooking Rubha Clach Tholl. Off this point are Appin Rocks across which both streams set strongly.

The channel widens out into the Lynn of Lorn in front of Airds Bay. Lorn was the Celtic kingdom of 500, established by Lorn, Angus and Fergus Mor.

Loch Creran empties swiftly past Dearg Sgeir, Glas Eilean and the much larger Eriska, which is only an island when there is water in An Doirlinne. A 5.5m iron

A natural arch by Appin Rocks.

Mountains around Loch Creran lie to the east.

Branra Rock marked to the northwest of Eilean Dubh.

cage marks Branra Rock, which has an artificial reef on its west side. Eilean Dubh in the centre of the channel has heather on top and bootlace weed and anemones in the surrounding shallows. Flows run southwest from five hours and twenty minutes after Dover high water and northeast from forty minutes before Dover high water at up to 2km/h.

From any distance the Kingairloch shore looks like a wall of mountains. In fact, they are not cliffs but the peaks do rise quickly from behind the frequent stone beaches, most of which are inaccessible from landward.

Meall Dearg Choire nam Muc is a mere 734m but less than 4km from Camas Mhic a' Phì.

Flows are rather easier at up to 4km/h past Sallachan

Approaching Inversanda Bay with Tòrr an Fhamhair.

Glen Tarbert runs to Inversanda Bay.

Sgeirean nan Torran.

Point, marked by a red painted octagonal beacon with a ball on top and a boulder beach which reaches round into Camas Shallachain, another bay with a clockwise eddy during the ebb. Entering to the west of the aerial past Sallachan is the River Gour which drains the Ardgour mountains through Loch nan Gabhar with a fort site on its bank.

The peaks now close in with 508m Beinn Leamhain only a kilometre from the shore, rising beyond to 650m Sgorr Mhic Eacharna and 885m Garbh Bheinn, popular with climbers.

At Inversanda Bay the River Tarbert discharges into a sheltered inlet.

The 509m Meall a' Bhràghaid starts the Kingairloch proper, the first 6km with no road, just rocks covered with barnacles and limpets. Predatory flyers include buzzards. The Sgeirean nan Torran are only small islets but prove useful landmarks halfway down this section of remote shore.

Rubha na h-Earba introduces Camas Chìl Mhalieu and an eddy which works on the flood for 6km to beyond the mouth of Loch a' Choire. The B8043 follows the shore at the back of the eddy to Rubha na h-Airde Uinnsinn,

Camas na Croise with the mouth of Loch a' Choire.

Europe's largest granite quarry, Glensanda, in the rain.

Stranded moon jellyfish at Eignaig.

after which the coast is largely remote from roads to the Sound of Mull.

Camas na Croise receives the Glengalmadale River which descends between 591m Meall nan Each and 651m Beinn na Cille. Loch a' Choire with its large fish farm not only receives water from the Abhainn Coinnich but also violent squalls which rush down off the mountains. A couple of aerials are located by the road as it turns inland past the prominent 739m Beinn Mheadhoin.

The ebb begins five hours before Dover high water and the flood an hour and twenty minutes after Dover high water at up to 1km/h, taking with it moon and lion's mane jellyfish and Atlantic grey seals.

Between 569m Sgurr Bhuic and 474m Meall na h-Easaiche, a pair of streams dropping down Dearg Uillt have blasted through the bank of stones which form the shoreline. It is possible to sit at the bottom and look up the lines of these kilometre long streams falling down straight courses at 50% gradient.

Round the corner the red granite is being removed fast from Glensanda Harbour where a jetty with a moving conveyor loads crushed granite onto 150,000t bulk carriers. This is Aggregate Industries' 1980s superquarry, the first in Britain and the largest granite quarry in Europe. It has a visual impact greater than had been anticipated by the planning authorities. Each of the buttresses left on the front face is larger than the cube of the nearby castle, built in the 15th century by Ewen MacLean.

There is an hour and a half stand at high water with flows to 2km/h. In the Lynn of Morvern the ebb begins five hours before high water at Dover to 2km/h but the flood starts an hour and twenty minutes after Dover high water to 6km/h, setting towards Sgeir nan Tom to the north of Lismore. Winds are unpredictable but usually parallel to the coast.

The wall of peaks continues, 253m Tom Allt na Mèinne, 290m Meall nan Clach, Meall a' Chaorainn at 481m and 513m An Sleaghach. Below them is Eignaig, less a village than three buildings, at least one of which is now no more than a couple of walls hiding in the bracken. Curlews are the main signs of life unless a school of porpoises should happen to be about.

The main water activity takes place off Rubha a'Mhòthair. On springs, overfalls reach from 200m east of the point nearly to Rubha Croinn on Bernera Island from the start of the ebb for three to four hours, the edge of the overfalls being sharply defined at the northern end. The ebb flow causes eddies and further interest was added by using this as an explosives dumping ground in the past.

Rubha an Ridire with its 200m basaltic cliffs is another interesting spot with strong tidal streams and eddies, races and heavy overfalls dangerous to small vessels with opposing winds. Flows from Loch Linnhe and the Sound of Mull meet here or divide according to the state of the tide. Flows begin northwest from an hour and twenty minutes after Dover high water to 6km/h and southeast from five hours forty minutes before high water at Dover to 4km/h. A southwesterly wind can funnel along the sound from the Salen gap while a northeasterly wind goes in the opposite direction.

Just beyond the point is Eilean Rubha an Ridire, an island coated with wrack at sea level and screaming with terns above. It has two wrecks on it, the northern one 60m north of the point a historic vessel with a 75m exclusion zone around it.

With suitable visibility the views are breathtaking, landmarks including the lighthouse on Eilean Musdile. A light marks the Glas Eileanan or grey rocks in the middle of the sound with flows to 3km/h as car ferries pass from Oban to Castlebay, Lochboisdale, Arinagour and Scarinish. There can be overfalls off Scallastle Point with Sgeir Mhic Chomhain and Sgeir nan Gobhar and to Loch Don.

Mull means mass of hill. The volcanic island covers 910km^2 and is the third largest of the Hebrides.

Looking from Eignaig across to Lismore.

Flows begin southeast five hours and forty minutes before Dover high water and northwest an hour and twenty minutes after Dover high water at up to 5km/h.

Java Point is the start of Craignure Bay, where terns and hooded crows might be seen. The bay has an eddy with flows in either direction. At the back of the bay is Craignure and the island's main ferry terminal with a regular vehicle service from the 140m Craignure Jetty to Oban. In *Kidnapped* Stevenson records that the ferry to Lochaline, as used by David Balfour, formerly ran from here.

The 1983 260mm gauge steam and diesel Mull Rail, claimed to be the only passenger-carrying miniature railway on a Scottish island, runs for 2km. There is a radar tower and a monument on Rubh' a' Ghuirmein.

At the western end of Duart Bay is Camas Mòr, beside which is Torosay Castle of 1856, a Victorian baronial mansion by David Bryce. Visited by Winston Churchill, Lily Langtree, Dame Nellie Melba and the public hordes, it has notable Edwardian furniture and pictures. The 5ha of Italian terraced, woodland, water, rock and Japanese gardens by Sir David Lorimer include an Italian statue walk. The 19 statues were brought from a derelict Paduan villa, most of the cost of getting them here being the journey from the docks in Glasgow. Other attractions include the Isle of Mull Weavers.

Duart Castle on Mull.

There are red deer around Camas Mòr, which is separated from the rest of Duart Bay by the Eilean Trianach peninsula. A 150m diameter exclusion zone north of Duart Point protects a Spanish Armada wreck, allegedly with treasure still aboard. There can be a race but it can also be calm, especially in the wind shadow with a southerly wind.

Duart Point comes from dubh aird, dark headland, on which is Duart Castle, the home of Clan Maclean since they ousted the MacDonalds as Lords of the Isles in about 1250. It was the chief of a chain of castles to Mingary which could pass messages quickly by beacon. The keep dates from 1390. Spanish officers of the *Almirante de Florencia* Armada galleon explosion at Tobermory were kept in the dungeon, contained in 3.7m thick walls. Some of the buildings were reconstructed in 1633 by Sir Lachlan Maclean. It was captured by the first Duke of Argyll in 1674, was garrisoned during the Jacobite uprisings and was later fired, falling into decay. In 1912 it was bought back and restored, now with 100 rooms, by Sir Fitzroy Maclean. Today it contains displays on the Macleans and on Scouting, Lord Maclean having been Chief Scout in the 1960s. It was used for filming *The Tweenies*. A Millennium Wood has been planted with trees and shrubs native to Argyll.

The southerly stream flows for seven hours and twenty minutes, not as strong as the northerly stream which runs to 6km/h. There can be steep overfalls.

Landmarks are slightly confusing as a 9m granite tower like a castle is a memorial to novelist William Black and bears a sector light.

Unusually, cruise liners are a significant part of the shipping, although car ferries remain the main users, passing between Lady's Rock with its 12m high red metal framework light beacon and Eilean Musdile at the end of Lismore. The lady in question was the wife of Lachlan Maclean of Duart. A former Campbell, she failed to provide him with an heir and twice tried to poison him. In 1523 he wanted to marry the daughter of Maclean of Treshnish instead so he chained her to the covering rock. She was rescued by men from Tayvallich, who were rewarded by her father, the 2nd Earl of Argyll, with a mill on Loch Sween. It was claimed that Lachlan Maclean saw his wife at a funeral and escaped but was murdered by his brother in law in Edinburgh.

The William Black memorial tower resembles a castle.

Distance
73km from Kinlocheil to Eilean Dubh

OS 1:50,000 Sheets
40 Mallaig & Glenfinnan
41 Ben Nevis, Fort William & Glen Coe
49 Oban & East Mull

Admiralty Charts
1791 Caledonian Canal. Corpach to Ft Augustus (1:75,000)
2171 Sound of Mull & Approaches (1:75,000)
2372 L Linnhe – Corran Narrows, Ft William & Corpach. Corran Narrows (1:10,000). Ft William & Corpach (1:6,250)
2379 L Linnhe –Central Part (1:25,000)
2380 L Linnhe – Northern Part (1:25,000)
2387 Firth of Lorn – Northern Part (1:25,000)
2389 L Linnhe – Southern Part (1:25,000). Glensanda Harbour (1:7,500)
2390 Sound of Mull (1:25,000)

Tidal Constants
Loch Eil Head:
Dover −0440
Corpach:
HW Dover −0510, LW Dover −0500
Corran:
HW Dover −0510, LW Dover −0520
Port Appin:
HW Dover −0520, LW Dover −0540
Craignure:
HW Dover −0500, LW Dover −0510

Sea Area
Malin

Rescue
Inshore lifeboat: Loch Ness, Campbeltown
All weather lifeboat: Oban

Connection
Caledonian Canal – see CoB p296

31 Kyle of Sutherland

Pioneering Highland bridges

Rain falling in Benmore Forest flows southeast by way of Dubh Loch Mór, the River Oykel, Loch Ailsh and the Kyle of Sutherland down to the Dornoch Firth. Good tides reach Innis nan Damh where a Bailey bridge takes a minor road over the River Oykel in an area subject to flooding but with boulder banks and gravel rapids when the peaty water is at a lower level. Although it is a marshy area it has alders, gorse, broom, cow parsley, bluebells, white clover and bird's foot trefoil. Bracken appears as the banks steepen and an anglers' hut is passed. Midges are present but larger flying wildlife includes

Local residents with fine sets of horns.

Alders line the River Oykel near Ochtow.

Carbisdale Castle, now a youth hostel.

The distinctive Oykell Viaduct.

116

The bowstring girder bridge at Bonar Bridge, built to carry the A9.

wagtails, swallows, oystercatchers, common gulls, cuckoos, pheasants, pochard and herons.

Caisteal nan Corr's remains are passed near Ocktow. The River Cassley joins at Invercassley and the river becomes more estuarial in nature with lower banks, a wider valley and a change of name. Sedges line the water and there are islands with mallards and blackheaded gulls. A monument at the A837/A839 junction is not obvious from the water, unlike the wind turbine farm on the hillside above. There are forest walks behind Altass but clear cutting of timber on the south side of the river, along with two Càrn Mór brochs.

Beyond Shin Forest the River Shin joins below the power station at Invershin. Power station operations can result in unexpected currents in the kyle with flows upstream both above and below the confluence.

Foxgloves, thrift and lichens colour the banks and there are swans on the water. Antiquities include a standing stone, cairns, settlements and the remains of Invershin Castle. The prominent Carbisdale Castle was built in 1914 for the Dowager Duchess of Sutherland, now a youth hostel surrounded by forest walks and north of a 1650 battle site.

Seals off Wester Fern Point.

is another forest walk below a settlement site, a chambered cairn and other cairns in the vicinity of the powerline crossing. Sea and brown trout and salmon use the kyle.

The original bridge at **Bonar Bridge** was a graceful iron lattice arch built by Telford in 1812, the longest ever prefabricated span at the time, inspiring at least ten others in the next 18 years but destroyed by a flood in 1892. The current structure is a segmental steel tied arch of 1973 with rather minimalist appearance, a 104m span with 20m rise. When built it carried the A9,

The Inverness to Wick railway crosses the 1867 Oykell or Shin Viaduct, a 70m main span which is an outstanding example of an early wrought iron lattice girder, unusual for having the tracks above the tall lattice. Joseph Mitchell's bridge also has five high masonry arches and separates Invershin and Culrain stations which are request stops 600m apart. In 2000 a walkway was added to the bridge, its open lattice floor inducing vertigo for walkers who look down and its steps being a problem for cyclists.

Invershin House is a public house with restricted opening.

An aerial above Balblair Wood marks where the kyle widens significantly except where it has been constricted by material washed down to the mouths of the River Carron and Wester and Easter Fearn Burns. The first of these constrictions is beyond Drumliah where there

which came up each side of the kyle to reach the crossing. The A9 now takes a more direct route and it

Looking back towards Bonar Bridge from above Easter Fearn.

Pines and gorse below Creich Mains.

Distance
35km from Innis nan
Damh to the Dornoch
Bridge

OS 1:50,000 Sheets
16 Lairg & Loch Shin
20 Beinn Dearg
& Loch Broom
21 Dornoch & Alness

Admiralty Charts
223 Dunrobin Pt to
Buckie (1:75,000)

Tidal Constants
Meikle Ferry:
HW Dover +0100,
LW Dover +0110

Sea Area
Cromarty

Rescue
Inshore lifeboat:
Kessock
All weather lifeboat:
Invergordon

is the A836 which crosses in front of the Bridge Hotel. A garden at the east end has plaques relating to all three of the bridges which have been sited here.

At the west end is a parking area with an obviously modern stone circle. Rather than being a simple folly, each boulder is of different rock, forming a geological exhibit of rocks from all over the north of Scotland, a table in the centre identifying them all like a viewpoint key.

Behind Càrn Mór and Swordale, oak and birch woods hide Loch Migdale. Ardgay, on the southwest shore, has birches and larches. There is a hatchery at the mouth of the Allt Eiteachan. Further upstream at Kincardine is the sculptured Eitag Stone, at the site of a 19th century cattle market.

After Little Creich with its cross and church remains, the north shore of the kyle reaches its most attractive, a steeply rising rocky hillside with pines and gorse, beds of wrack in front. The shallow waters are dotted with branch debris but off Wester Fearn Point there may be numerous seals resting on the sandbanks. Terns dive in the shallows. Dùn Creich has a strategic position on a wooded hill, beyond which the kyle widens again, the south shore guarded by the broch of Dùn Alascaig. There are chambered cairns on both shores, lack of development having allowed so many of these antiquities to survive.

Spinningdale takes its name from a mill built in 1790 by a philanthropist to bring prosperity to the area although it burnt down in 1806. The shell remains.

This reach is dominated by the dark bulk of Struie Hill on the south side, topped by an aerial and Dounie Wood. From here, the shoreline becomes much indented between points. The Allt Muigh-bhlàraidh joins between Rubha nan Sgarbh and Ardmore Point, Balblair Distillery on its bank above Ardmore near Edderton. Behind Newton Point is Ospisdale with its Ospis Stone, a 3m Pictish stone with a fish symbol recalling a battle against the Vikings and named after a Norse chieftain. A narrow exit leads from Loch Ospisdale with Skibo Castle, built in 1898 by Andrew Carnegie, and from Loch Evelix, fed by the River Evelix. The spire of Edderton's 1793 church stands at the back of Cambuscurrie Bay.

The piers at Meikle Ferry and at Ferry Point on the end of the long Ness of Portnaculter show the original route across. The A9 now goes over the Dornoch Bridge, 893m long with 21 spans. Built by the cast and push method, it was the longest bridge of its kind in Europe when built.

The Dornoch Firth takes its name from the Gaelic dornach, a fist sized stone, although that does not seem appropriate here. Low sedimentary rocks are covered with Cuthill Sands, backed by dunes and Cuthill Links. There are moon jellyfish and this is another area for seals.

A significant current can result from spates or snow thaw in the three major rivers upstream. Normal flows run out from two hours and twenty minutes after Dover high water and in from three and a half hours before Dover high water.

The Dornoch Bridge now carries the A9.

32 Cromarty Firth

Rigs at rest

Leave the fishing trade lads, there's money to be made,
The handline and the Shetland yawl are from a bygone day,
Come to Aberdeen lads, there's sights ye've never seen,
Be a mudman on a pipeline or a fitter at Nigg Brae.

Archie Fisher

The Black Isle is neither black nor an island but a peninsula between the Cromarty, Beauly and Moray Firths. Snow is less likely than elsewhere in Scotland so there is less chance that it will be white in winter and it offers fertile farming country used for wintering animals. Under its Gaelic name of Ardmeanach it was given by Mary, Queen of Scots to her husband, Darnley.

The Cromarty Firth is the final section of a water journey which begins on Meallan Mhic Iamhair and flows east through Loch na Mòine Mòire, Loch an Fhairlaid, the Abhainn Dubh, Loch Crann, Loch a' Chroisg, the River Bran, Loch Achanalt, Loch a' Chuilinn, Loch Luichart, Loch Achonachie and the River Conon.

The former Highland Railway from Inverness to Wick passes over a bridge of 1862 with five 22m span segmental arches by Joseph Mitchell. Founded on rock, it crosses at the tidal limit at an oblique 45° and is unusual in that the ribs are not perpendicular to the piers and the wingwalls are curved in both plan and elevation.

Apparently a kelpie had its lair here. There were also king otters, which were larger and lighter in colour than the normal models. Catching one and setting it free permitted the granting of a wish although killing it and wearing the pelt gave protection from bullets and swords. Licking the liver of a freshly killed black otter gave the power of healing burns by licking. It must have taken quite a bit of trial and error to discover all this. These days there are red deer with more mundane characteristics.

Conon Bridge village was the home of General Sir Hector MacDonald or Fighting Mac although there is no evidence that he had any of this special protection.

Parking is available at the entrance to a former factory at the southeast corner of the A862 bridge, some of it reserved for anglers who fish for salmon and sea trout.

An ashlar masonry toll house with a two storey octagonal tower, located near the northern end of the bridges, was designed in 1829 by Telford. Little remains of Telford's original bridge of 1809. There are the remains of a chambered cairn on the other side of Maryburgh.

The channels of peaty water divide round islands of alder. Beyond the A835 bridge an archipelago of marshy islands with buttercups, broom, bog cotton and cow parsley becomes more

The unusual railway bridge at Conon Bridge.

sandy with dog roses and thrift. Mallards, terns and midges are present.

The skyline to the north is dominated by 1,046m Ben Wyvis but the foreground has a dome with Loch

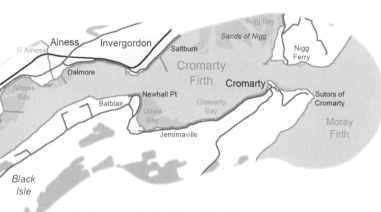

Ussie on top. At the Dingwall end is a tower monument to Sir Hector MacDonald. **Dingwall**, the administrative centre of Ross & Cromarty, was the Viking's thing-vollir, their justice field or parliament. It was captured from Duncan by the Vikings with the help of Macbeth, who ruled Ross-shire from Dingwall Castle before seizing the Scottish throne. The castle was ruined by 1700 although parts of the tower remain. Dingwall Museum includes military material, a reconstructed kitchen and a smiddy. Inverpeffer in Gaelic, Dingwall is at the mouth of the River Peffery. This was extended by the 2km Dingwall Canal in 1817 through what is now a rifle

Wooded reach near Maryburgh.

Sir Hector MacDonald's monument at Dingwall.

range danger area opposite Alcaig but it suffered silting and was disused from 1884.

Behind Alcaig at Ryefield are the remains of the Ferintosh distillery, run by the Forbes but burnt down by the Jacobites in 1689. The following year it became Scotland's first legal distillery. In compensation for the damage, the Forbes were exempted from duty on their

The Cromarty Bridge takes the A9 directly across the firth.

whisky from 1695 until 1785, when reimposition of duty pushed up the price of whisky.

The Cromarty Firth was formerly the Roman Portus Salutis, the harbour of safety, then the Viking Sykkersand, the safe sand. One of the largest natural harbours in Europe, it is surrounded by low sedimentary rocks.

On the shoreline are the remains of a church at Urquhart and a chapel at Mountgerald. The Cromarty Bridge carries the A9 straight across the firth on 67 piers. There is just 3m clearance so port control begins on the downstream side.

The southern side rises fairly steeply with slopes covered in grass with gorse, bluebells, orchids, larks and swallows. On the clear water are oystercatchers, shelducks and cormorants while seals and dolphins hunt offshore. The human activity is mostly on the northern side, from Cnoc an Teampuill and Foulis Castle at Ardullie.

At Evanton the River Sgitheach and the River Glass enter. The airfield is disused but flying activity ranges from jets closing on the bombing range at Tain to kites which have been reintroduced here. The Highland Deephaven jetty at the end of the Highland Deephaven causeway is used for loading submarine pipeline, the first of the oil industry activity within the firth.

Beyond Alness Bay, where Ardroy Sand drains, Alness Point shelters the buttressed Alness storehouse and hangars before the River Averon or Alness enters. The river passes through **Alness**, noted for its flower displays. An earth and rubble embankment pier with a ruined 5m concrete and brick light tower protects the east side. At its root is Dalmore distillery, in operation since 1839 and producing a malt which is the world's most expensive whisky.

Along the shore road are to be found the Symbol Stone and a golf course. **Invergordon** had its name changed from Inverbreakie by Sir William Gordon of Embo, who bought it in the 18th century and laid out the town plans, which now include arts and karting centres. Invergordon was an anchorage for the Royal Navy Home Fleet in both World Wars and remained a naval and seaplane base until 1956. In 1931 it was the scene of the Invergordon mutiny by 12,000 sailors after the Government cut their pay by 25% and reduced their benefits in the wake of the Wall Street crash, some strikers being jailed or dismissed. These days it is the North Sea oil industry for which this is a support centre. Invergordon Service and Supply Bases have two storage tanks. Semi submersible and jack up rigs are likely to be moored anywhere within the firth. Their anchors and other equipment may be found up to 900m away from them.

West Harbour has a ferry terminal taking cruise and Ro-Ro ships. Teanich distillery is marked by its two towers. The Saltburn Pier has a conveyor which served the aluminium smelter until 1981.

There is a former storehouse at Ferryton Point on the south shore. In fact, it was Balblair which was the ferry point for Invergordon until the Cromarty Bridge was built, a pier and moorings preceding Newhall Point.

Flows here run to 5km/h at the surface, where they may be continuously outwards. However, subsurface flows may be more conventional with ebb and flood. Snow melt and heavy rain will increase the outgoing flow and decrease the ingoing flow.

Udale Bay drains completely at low water, leaving mostly sand with a few mussel beds and clumps of bootlace weed as a national nature reserve. At the back of the bay are the remains of St Michael's chapel with four-century old tombs of the Holms of Ferryton. Newhall Burn enters at the southern corner before Jemimaville, which faces across the water towards Barbaraville.

Nigg Bay mostly drains to leave another national nature reserve with bartailed godwits and knots between October and March. The Cromarty Firth has 26,000 winter waterfowl including 8,300 wigeon, 1,700 redshanks and 170 scaup, which the RSPB claimed were

There are usually rigs moored in the firth.

The Nigg fabrication yard.

under major threat from pollution and cockling. The Sands of Nigg have three significant channels at low water, Delny Dock with a 100m diameter exclusion zone round a military wreck, Big Audle and the Pot. Nigg Oil Terminal has storage tanks, handles crude oil, is at the end of a pipeline from the Beatrice Field and takes tankers to 160,000t. Adjacent is an oil rig fabrication yard from the 1970s on reclaimed land with cranes, large buildings and a 27m grey framework light tower. A graving dock is next to Nigg Ferry, which was used by pilgrims going to the shrine of St Duthus at Tain, by Robert the Bruce and by James IV. There is a 4m light structure. Signs for the King's Ferry show the standard two cars inside a ship only this time that is correct. This is the smallest car ferry in Britain, taking just two vehicles at a time.

At the east end of Cromarty Bay is the village of **Cromarty**, fronted by the Royal Hotel overlooking moorings. The use of its name in the shipping forecast is not an indication of its importance so much as an attempt to get names which are distinctive and unlikely to be confused with others when listening at sea in poor conditions.

It replaces a village which was taken by the sea and was a burgh of barony and administration centre for the Black Isle. In the 17th century it was a fish and grain centre, followed by much 18th century industry including fishermen's cottages until the herring industry failed. The village was at its most important from 1770 to 1830, Smeaton beginning the harbour in 1781 with two piers and a detached breakwater, still with fishing boats. A 13m lighthouse was built in 1846 by Alan Stevenson to run on sperm whale oil, its revolving light with the innovations of a stronger bronze lantern and inclined astragals giving a better beam with a 23km range. The lighthouse and its cottage are now an Aberdeen University research station for bottlenose dolphins, harbour seals and seabirds.

With its narrow vennels or alleyways and Georgian cottages it is said to be one of the best preserved 18th century villages and one of the three best coastal towns in Scotland. There was formerly a brewery. A hemp works using St Petersburg hemp had the biggest buildings of their type in the UK. The 18th century Cromarty Courthouse covers seven centuries and uses Scotland's first computer controlled animated figures in a court sequence.

Hugh Miller's cottage is the only thatched cottage in the village and is where he was born in 1802, the cottage having been built in 1711 by his grandparents, the last fishertown cottage of its era. It is now refurnished in 19th century style with fossils and geological samples. He was a pioneering fossil collector, geologist, stonemason, antiquarian, writer, folklorist and church reformer, editing the *Witness* newspaper from here. He discovered many new fossils, including the flying fish Ptericthyodes milleri. There is a monument to him and a stone with an inscription by him to commemorate emigrants.

The village had more than its fair share of original thinkers. Thomas Urquhart, the first person to translate Rabelais, was knighted in 1641 and invented his own language in 1653 although, obviously, it did not catch on.

A 17th century boundary dispute between Sandy Woods and a neighbour resulted in him having himself buried outside the cemetery close to the road in order

Cromarty as a sea mist rolls in off the Moray Firth.

to be able to put his side of the story first on the Day of Judgement.

Shipowner John Reid was rejected by Helen Stuart in 1740 but managed to capture a mermaid by the Dropping Cave, releasing her in exchange for three wishes, a better deal than with king otters. These were that neither he nor his friends would drown, that Helen Stuart would relent and a third which was not revealed. At least the first two came true.

Cromarty House was built on the site of Cromarty Castle in 1770, approached through a tunnel so the owner did not have to think about servants. One of the Urquharts had 36 children and thought he was dead so his bed was hoisted to the battlements every night to make it easier for him to be taken to heaven.

Miller suggested that the narrow entrance to the firth was cut by the River Conon during the Tertiary period when there was a thick layer of old red sandstone and Mesozoic strata. The Sutors Stacks, the shoemakers, rise up to a bold headland on each side. The north side was protected by the 12th century Dunskeath Castle, the Gaelic fort of dread, with an earthwork near North Sutor.

Blackbacked gulls float over kelp while bracken climbs up the hillside. World War gun emplacements are found at the Sutors Stacks.

Flows out into the Moray Firth begin an hour and twenty minutes after Dover high water and in from four hours before Dover high water at up to 3km/h.

An inaccessible cove below the Sutors Stacks.

Distance
32km from Conon Bridge to the Moray Firth

OS 1:50,000 Sheets
21 Dornoch & Alness
26 Inverness
& Loch Ness

Admiralty Charts
223 Dunrobin Pt to Buckie (1:75,000)
1077 Approaches to Cromarty Firth & Inverness Firth (1:20,000)
1889 Cromarty Firth – Cromarty Bank to Invergordon (1:15,000)
1890 Cromarty Firth – Invergordon to Dingwall (1:15,000)

Tidal Constants
Dingwall:
HW Dover +0100
Invergordon:
HW Dover +0050,
LW Dover +0040
Cromarty:
Dover +0040

Sea Area
Cromarty

Range
Dingwall rifle range

Rescue
Inshore lifeboat:
Kessock
All weather lifeboat:
Invergordon

Wartime fortifications guard the Cromarty Firth.

33 Beauly Firth

From a beautiful place to the Riviera of the North

Rising on Sgurr a' Bhealaich Dheirg, water flowing northeast to the Moray Firth follows the Allt Cam-bàn, the River Affric, Loch Affric, Loch Beinn a' Mheadhoin, the River Glass, the River Bran, the River Beauly and the Beauly Firth. The River Beauly is tidal from the A862 bridge at Balblair. Limited riverbank parking is available from a track at the southwest corner of the bridge in an area with a gravel pit, memorial and fort site.

The Lovat Bridge was originally built by Telford for the Great North Road, the A9, with some difficulty because of logs which kept hitting the arch centring during floods whilst construction was taking place. There are five segmental arches in red sandstone, of progressive size, the largest 18m arch in the centre and the smallest at the ends hidden by vegetation. The bridge was repaired in 1829 after flood damage and two spans were rebuilt in 1894 after an arch collapsed in a flood. There are large abutments and semi hexagonal piers which extend up to act as pedestrian refuges but overall lines are graceful with a double string course and archivolts accentuated over the arch rings.

Pheasants squawk in the woods as anglers fish for salmon. A cable passes low across the river with powerlines rather higher.

The Inverness to Wick railway crosses on what appears to be a single span although there are more over the shallows to the left, hidden by trees. The dormitory town of **Beauly** has only recently acquired a station, well used but with a platform so short that only one door of a train can be used. The town has the Made in Scotland craft centre and houses the Beauly Firth & Glens Trust.

The river divides round a large island of alders with mallards and herons by the water. Buttercups, broom and dog roses are progressively replaced with plantains, sedges, reedmace and other reeds.

Almost the last building in Beauly is the priory of 1230, ruined after the Reformation but with notable windows and arcading and a fine 16th century monument to Sir Kenneth Mackenzie. It was visited in 1564 by Mary, Queen of Scots and the name of beau lieu, beautiful place, may have been given by her or by the town's French founders. It has been a burial place for the Frasers of Lovat and there is a large Boer War memorial of 1905.

The Beaulieu Firth or Basin is an area of low sedimentary rocks with

Telford's Lovat Bridge was built for the Great North Road.

Seals at the head of the firth.

sandbanks reaching out as much as 6km, over half the length of the firth. A SSSI, it is a Canada goose migration moult ground and has 49,000 winter wildfowl including 2,800 redshanks, 2,100 bartailed godwits, 2,000 redbreasted mergansers, 1,000 goosanders and common gulls, which the RSPB claimed were at risk of major threats from pollution and land reclaim.

A long pier runs out into the shallow water at Milton and gives protection to Redcastle. The shores of the firth are generally lightly populated but a caravan park at Craigrory faces across the water to another one at Mains of Bunchrew.

A 4m green framework light tower at Clachnaharry marks the end of the 1822 Caledonian Canal. Sea Lock is used for four hours each side of local high water (three hours before Dover high water to five hours after Dover high water) although this reduces to two hours each side of local high water at spring tides as the bed dries for 300m. Most use of the canal is by

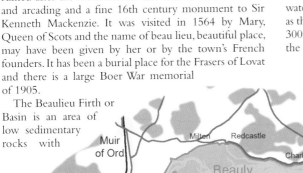

The original light at the end of the Caledonian Canal.

Ord Hill is topped by a fort site.

Gorse, dog roses, thrift and lichen on conglomerate near the mouth of Munlochy Bay.

pleasure craft but some surprisingly large commercial vessels also take this short cut across Scotland. In 1954 it took the prototype Watson class lifeboat *William Taylor*, conducting sea trials on its scenic journey from Littlehampton to being stationed at Coverack.

Construction of the end of the canal proved difficult. Telford and Jessop built twin embankments on the mud, surcharged them with stone and left them for six months, during which time they sank 3.4m. They then excavated the lock chamber at the end and built it with an inverted arch. The Clachnaharry swing bridge, taking the railway across the canal at a 65° skew, was not without its problems for Joseph Mitchell in 1862. The two 38m hogbacked girders are pivoted on the east side of the canal with a 15m counterbalance arm, painted white to reduce thermal expansion.

The water now comes under Inverness Harbour Trust control until Chanonry Point.

On the north shore Kessock Road is faced by Charlestown and North Kessock with its two disused slips, the larger in front of the North Kessock Hotel. Another local business is a targe manufacturer. The Black Isle Wildlife & Country Park has been established here. There are only two or three dolphin populations in the UK and the dolphin and seal centre benefits from the only known resident dolphin population in the North Sea, the world's most northerly colony of bottlenose dolphins, of which 130 specimens have been identified individually. Underwater microphones are used. Porpoises, seals and sea trout are also here, perhaps because the turbulence stirs up food. CCTV is trained on kite nests.

An inshore lifeboat station with a 4.6m sector light beacon is located next to the bridge.

At South Kessock the River Ness joins with flows to 9km/h. Entry to Inverness Harbour is usually in the two hours to local high water, namely an hour before Dover high water to an hour after Dover high water. **Inverness** takes its name from the Gaelic inbhir nis, the mouth of the noisy river. A city which is the largest community in the north of Scotland, it is the capital of the Highlands and one of the oldest settlements in Scotland, in existence in the 6th century. The original inhabitants were Picts who wore only woad although they would often have been blue quite naturally with that dress code. David I created it a royal burgh. It was occupied by Prince Charlie during the 1745 uprising and ransacked by Cumberland the following year after Culloden in consequence. From 1817 it was the centre of the Highland sheep and wool trade, helped by improved transport in the form of the railway from 1855. The harbour, which had been started in 1249, was moved downstream after the railway bridge was built in 1862. Telford's Thornbush Quay of 1817, built with masonry underwater to save money, was improved in 1899 and 1908 and Shore Street Quay was added in 1883. Longman Quay is an addition of 1985 on reclaimed land.

The Kessock Bridge is the most southerly of the 20th century bridges taking the A9 across estuaries. Based on the Rees bridge over the Rhine near Düsseldorf, it was the longest cable stayed bridge in Europe when built in 1982 and the first of its kind in Britain. The main span is 183m and it gives 29m clearance below its continuous steel deck. The 75m towers can cause great turbulence. There were two earthquakes in Inverness in the 20th century and so there are a pair of 390t hydraulic buffers at the north abutment to allow for movement in the Great Glen fault. A submarine gas pipeline crosses below the bridge to the Black Isle

Flows beneath the bridge are turbulent and there can be a race and whirlpools. They begin outwards an hour and a half after Dover high water to 9km/h, 11km/h with heavy rain or snowmelt. There is a slack from five hours forty minutes after Dover high water. Flows inwards begin four and a half hours before Dover high water to

7km/h and there is another slack from an hour before Dover high water. The route now turns northeast into the Moray Firth, the inner part of which is also known as the Inverness Firth. Flows run out along the northwest shore to 4km/h and in to 2km/h.

Craigton Point is low but Ord Hill rises beyond it to 191m, wooded with archaeological trails and an Iron Age dun on the top. Beyond Kilmuir is the ruin of St Mary's church, almost on the shore.

The steep Craigiehowe shows conglomerate along the shoreline, enhanced with gorse, foxgloves, thrift and heather. Oystercatchers pick amongst the wrack. The hill with its cave protects the entrance to Munlochy Bay, which drains almost completely to leave mud which has been designated a bird sanctuary. The other side of the entrance has Wood Hill with the remains of Ormond Castle at its northeast end.

Telford's harbour dries at the back of Avoch Bay. The fishing village is built with gables facing the sea so that boats can be protected between them in stormy weather. There is an Avoch Heritage Centre in this village where the residents claim to be descended from Spaniards shipwrecked in an Armada vessel. An interesting feature is the modern bus shelter which appears to be roofed with an upturned boat. The railway which used to run from Muir of Ord along the coast here to Fortrose has long gone but the shore from Avoch to Rosemarkie claims to be the Riviera of the North.

Fortrose has another drying harbour by Telford, this one built in 1817, formerly for fishing but now used for sailing. The ruined cathedral was one of Scotland's finest medieval buildings, constructed from Black Isle red sandstone with 14th century details, a vaulted roof, an octagonal belfry, inlaid marble memorials to the Seaforth Mackenzies and a separate chapter house. It is said to have been destroyed by Cromwell as a source of stone for a new castle in Inverness. A significant well is sited on Broomhill. There is a Boniface Fair in the village.

Chanonry Ness is a low spit running out to Chanonry Point. On the end is a memorial to the Brahan Seer, Kenneth Mackenzie, who apparently didn't foresee his own demise and was burnt in a barrel of tar in the 16th or 17th century by the Countess of Seaforth for his predictions about the Mackenzies, especially that her husband was philandering in Paris. A correct prediction was the extinction of the Seaforths in the 19th century with the last earl seeing all his sons die before him.

The 13m white tower lighthouse of 1846 by Alan Stevenson had a revolving light with the innovation of a stronger bronze lantern and inclined astragals to give a better beam.

This is the leading place in Britain to see dolphins from the land, also minke whales and harbour porpoises.

On the Drummossie Muir shore a bank of large angular rocks protects the shore road in front of the Longman industrial estate and leads down to a shoreline of mud heavily embedded with mussels which increase to a substantial bank of mussel shells by the Longman Point light beacon. At Longman Point there are herring and blackbacked gulls and cormorants.

On the east side of the bridge and nearly as prominent is the Inverness Caledonian Thistle football stadium.

Gradually the scenery opens up with extensive views back along the line of Glen Mor and, later, up Munlochy Bay to a skyline of the dramatic peaks of Wester Ross. Closer at hand, the Inverness to Aberdeen railway line and the A96 follow the shore while the Inverness to Perth railway line loops round and heads south. A train heading south in 2000 passed through the approaches to Culloden viaduct and probably triggered an embankment collapse after two days of heavy rain.

It is a coast of extensive drying banks with low grassland and occasional tree clumps. The coast may be gentle but 4km away is Culloden Muir, part of the

The lighthouse at Chanonry Point.

The Kessock Bridge and the Longman Point light beacon.

Culloden Muir where the Jacobite dream ended.

The distinctive silhouette of Alturlie Point.

Castle Stuart stands back from the shoreline.

Looking back from Fisherton with Ord Hill prominent.

largest fort, 640m long on a 17ha site housing 1,600 infantry. It never saw action and remains one of the finest late artillery fortifications in Europe. Land approach is through two tunnels and over a timber bridge across a ditch, all covered by at least two walls of cannons. The site is protected by 1.6km of ramparts. It contains the museums of the Queen's Own Highlanders with predecessors the Seaforth Highlanders, the Queen's Own Cameron Highlanders and the Lovat Scouts, medals and uniforms, the Seafield Collection of arms gathered by Sir James Grant in the 18th century for a regiment of foot and militia, an Armstrong gun of 1865 with early rifling and typical barracks rooms of 1868, 1813 and 1780, the

Fort George, one of the finest late artillery fortifications.

Distance
29km from Lovat Bridge to Rosemarkie Bay

OS 1:50,000 Sheets
26 Inverness & Loch Ness
27 Nairn & Forres

Admiralty Charts
223 Dunrobin Pt to Buckie (1:75,000)
1077 Approaches to Cromarty Firth & Inverness Firth (1:20,000)
1078 Inverness Firth (1:20,000). Inverness (1:5,000)
1791 Caledonian Canal. Fort Augustus to Inverness (1:75,000)

Tidal Constants
Inverness:
HW Dover +0100,
LW Dover +0050
Fortrose:
Dover +0100

Sea Area
Cromarty

Range
Fort George firing range

Rescue
Inshore lifeboat:
Kessock
All weather lifeboat:
Invergordon

Connection
Caledonian Canal – see CoB p296

larger Drummossie Muir, on the ridge above Smithton, Culloden and Balloch, the battlefield which carries more significance than any other for many Scots. This was the site of the last land battle in Britain when, in 1746, as had been prophesied by Brahan Seer at the site two centuries earlier, the Duke of Cumberland took 40 minutes to beat Bonnie Prince Charlie's army, ending the Jacobite rebellion which had intended to place a Stuart on the throne. Charles Stuart lost 1,200 men to Cumberland's 310. Nearly three centuries on, many Scots still sympathize with the cause.

Sewage works buildings on the shore include a prominent white sphere and, if the wind is from the southeast, there is a less than pleasant odour. Beyond the works is a chambered cairn as the railway and A96 move inland past a ring cairn. There is also a cairn on Alturlie Point, dominated by a ridge with a sand and gravel pit and some pines which keep their heads down from the weather. There are houses on the point but the most conspicuous structure is a bird hide on stilts, like an overgrown privy, and guyed down, a lifebelt adorning its front. Would the birdwatchers not be less conspicuous looking out of one of the less prominent buildings?

Beyond the point the bay runs back between a chambered cairn and a motte while Castle Stuart stands in good repair beside the B9039, an old military road.

Fisherton is largely hidden on top of a steep bank. Bird feeders are scattered amongst the gorse and the pebble shoreline is littered with gun cartridge cases. Also unseen are Dalcross, Inverness Airport and its associated industrial estate although helicopters and other aircraft take off and land with regularity. Flocks of lapwings circle overhead.

Ardersier is one of the best known names in the North Sea oil industry yet appears as an unspoilt village, extending to Cromal Mount where the line of a dismantled railway follows the shore. The clue was given by the odd tower or crane jib in the distance, the McDermott Base platform construction yard being 4km away at Whiteness Head until closed in 2002.

The water tower on the bank has a fairy story appearance, built to look like a tall house with two high chimneys.

The OS map shows the beach to the south of the B9006 to be a danger area from the firing ranges here. The range booking office think this is overcautious and the road remains open to public traffic.

Fort George was built in 1748–69 for George II, following the Jacobite rebellion and the Battle of Culloden, to prevent any future uprising. It is Britain's

Each section of wall was covered by a lookout point.

oldest featuring Private James Anderson of the 42nd Royal Highlanders. The fort is still used as a barracks and military depot for the Black Watch, including a chapel of 1767. More recent features are a helicopter landing site, a water tower and firing ranges. The latter affect the inshore area, especially towards Whiteness Head. Firing normally stops while boats are passing.

Chanonry Point and Ardersier Point have grown towards each other from opposite sides of the firth and are the best example in Britain of this feature with four or five successively higher levels of beach being visible. There can be a race through the gap, which is at right angles to the main trend of the firth and, indeed, of Glen Mor, with turbulence and eddies. Flows run out from an hour after Dover high water to 6km/h with a slack from five hours and twenty minutes before Dover high water. Flows start inwards at four hours before Dover high water to 5km/h and there is another slack from two hours and twenty minutes before Dover high water.

Those multiple layers of beach are used for a golf course with a cross facing out over Rosemarkie Bay to the greater Moray Firth.

34 Firth of Tay

From the former capital to the city of discovery

Beautiful railway bridge of the silvery Tay,
The longest of the present day.
That has ever crossed o'er a tidal river stream
Most gigantic to be seen.
Near by Dundee and the Magdalen Green.
William Topaz McGonagall

Flowing east across Perth & Kinross to the North Sea, the River Tay cuts between the Sidlaw and Ochil Hills. A major salmon angling river, it is the longest and fastest flowing river in Scotland.

It is tidal from Scone, just below the confluence with the River Almond. A horse race course loops round beside the river where a ford formerly crossed a shallow rapid to the site of a Roman camp next to what they called the Tava Fluvius. Scone Park was long the centre of Scottish rule. **Scone** had been the capital of Pictavia in the 6th century. Kenneth MacAlpine beat the Picts and united the Scots here in 838. He brought with him the Stone of Destiny, a 660mm block of red sandstone. It could have been Jacob's pillow at Bethel, brought to Scotland by Joseph of Arimathea, perhaps given to a Celtic king who married the daughter of a Pharaoh. St Columba is said to have rested his head on it as he died on Iona. It may have been the Irish coronation stone and is supposed to give a thunderous groan if sat on by anyone other than the rightful heir to the throne. The prophesy was that the Scots would rule where it was. Edward I took it to Westminster Abbey in 1296 as part of the Coronation Chair in an attempt to unite Scotland and England although it was another four centuries before James VI of Scotland became James I of England. It has remained in Westminster except for a brief excursion in 1951 when it was stolen and left on the high altar of Arbroath Abbey, scene of the 1320 independence Declaration of Arbroath. Moot Hill's elaborately decorated chapel is where all 42 Scottish kings and Charles II were crowned.

The 16th century castellated pink stone Scone Palace was the home of abbots and royalty before coronations and was described in *Macbeth*. After the Calvinist sermon by John Knox in 1559 it was ransacked and burned by the mob but was rebuilt in 1580, used by Prince Charlie, enlarged in 1804 and was the home of the Earls of Mansfield. The asymmetrical Georgian House is by William Atkinson. Defoe claimed the Long Gallery was the longest in Scotland. It was used by Victoria and Albert in 1842 to practise curling. There is French furniture including Marie Antoinette's writing table, one of the finest collections of porcelain in the country, ivories, 16th century needlework including bed hangings made by Mary, Queen of Scots, clocks and a Reynold's portrait of the first earl. The grounds have a pinetum, rhododendrons and azaleas, a maze in green and copper beech in the form of a five pointed tartan Murray star, a lime avenue, an adventure playground, peacocks, highland cattle and veteran agricultural machinery.

In 1437 James I was warned by an old woman that if he crossed the water he would not return alive. He was stabbed in Blackfriars monastery by the Earl of Atholl's supporters and his wife fled with the 6 year old James II to make Edinburgh the new capital.

Scone was the centre of the Culdees church. There is a friar's den on the Catmoor Burn. A visitor centre at Quarrymill gives information.

Back from the west bank is Dewar's distillery, carpenter John Dewar having undertaken a career change in Perth

in 1846. Muirton stands back from the river so that the bank is natural rather than being built up. The North Inch is the site of the 1396 Battle of the Clans where 30 each of Clan Chattan and Clan Kay fought to the death, during which the Black Chanter fell from Heaven and is now in the Clan Macpherson Museum in Newtonmore. The site

Perth Bridge and the church where the Reformation started.

was used by Prince Charlie to drill his troops. Now it is a golf course accompanied by a museum and the Bell's Sports Centre, one of the best in the country and with the largest solid dome at 67m diameter.

The surprisingly short waterfront in **Perth** begins with a bridge carrying the A85. An eight arch bridge lost six of its arches to a flood in 1621, apparently as a result of the city's iniquity, and was replaced by a ferry, not easy with low tide rapids here. Perth Bridge of 1771 has seven pink Perth sandstone arches over the river and two more over land, the largest at 23m, making the whole structure 272m long, the longest in Scotland and the longest for Smeaton. It was widened in 1869 by cantilevering out the footways. The water is deepest in the arch to the right of centre. The depths of flooding since 1814 are marked on the north side of the west abutment.

Perth, the Fair City, takes its name from the Welsh for a copse. It developed on linen manufacture. It was a royal burgh from 1210 and was attacked seven times including by Edward I, Wallace, Robert the Bruce and Edward III. The strange Gowrie Conspiracy took place in 1600, James IV allegedly abducted at the house of the Earls of Gowrie, the earl and his brother (in whose Huntingtower Castle the king had earlier been imprisoned for a year) being killed by the king's supporters, a mystery which has never been cleared up. In 1651 the Roundheads took the city.

Much of the city was rebuilt in the 18th and 19th Centuries, including, in 1893, the 14th century house of Catherine Glover, the central character in Scott's *The Fair Maid of Perth*, later to become a Bizet opera. John Buchan, later Lord Tweedsmuir, was born in Perth.

The Black Watch Museum in Balhousie Castle features the regiment since 1739 while the Museum & Art Gallery takes a wider look at the city. It is a city divided by vennels, from the French venelle, alley.

The city was earlier called St Johnston or St John's Town after the 1243 kirk. After being exiled, John Knox preached a sermon in the kirk on idolatry in 1559, starting the Reformation and leading to the ransacking of local friaries and churches across Scotland. Later, Montrose used it as an arsenal. For two centuries it was divided into three separate churches but it was reunited and the medieval

Friarton Viaduct carries the M90 across the Tay.

Kinnoull Hill's cliffs above the river.

fabric restored in 1926 as a memorial to the First World War dead. It has a 15th century choir, fine stained glass, valuable pewter and a font with some of the best 16th century English silverwork.

Since 1960 the A93 has been carried over the Queen's Bridge, the first long span prestressed structure in Scotland. The 48m main span was designed to suit the former four span Victoria Bridge on this line.

The Royal George and the Capital Asset are waterfront watering holes. There is a ship's figurehead of a Highlander at the entrance to the Salutation Hotel, where Prince Charlie stayed.

The river divides round the 1.7km Friarton or Moncreiffe Island. Crossing the island and both arms is the Tay Viaduct of 1864 carrying the Perth to Dundee railway, 396m long with 10 masonry arches across the island, a further 14 iron spans on masonry piers over the river arms. The western arm is the larger and there was an opening span at the west end of the viaduct but it has now been fixed.

The 1832 Round House was a water tower in Roman temple style with a domed 660m^3 cast iron storage tank and a 34m boilerhouse chimney with a classical vase pot, the water being drawn under the river from filter beds on the island and then fed to the city by gravity. It now houses the Fergusson Gallery.

The South Inch on the west bank was used for cricket games between English guards and their Napoleonic prisoners but the Scots did not take the game seriously. The prison is still in use. The Scottish game is golf, played at King James V Golf Club on the island, the course being reached from the railway footbridge.

The harbour was built in 1883 by Robert and Alan Stevenson, who removed fords to increase the spring tide depth from 3.6m to 4.9m. It has a four hour stand at low water and is still used commercially to handle agricultural and timber products, sand and chemicals.

The channel on the east side of the island is more direct but narrower as it slips between alders, willows,

giant hogweed, dog roses and cow parsley with common and blackheaded gulls on the water. Above are Branklyn Gardens, said to be the finest hectare of private garden in the country. By John and Dorothy Renton, it has notable rhododendrons, alpines and herbaceous and peat gardens, including the blue Himalayan poppy and the national collection of Mylnefield lilies.

The two channels rejoin and turn eastwards to pass under the M90 Friarton Viaduct of 1978 with spans up to 174m long, 30m above the floor of the valley, nine spans of box girders on concrete piers. At the end it turns in front of the dramatic wooded Kinnoull Hill with its cliffs and its 19th century Kinnoull Tower folly by the Earl of Kinnoull, based on Rhine castles.

The river becomes more open, edged with sedges, buttercups and forget-me-nots and used by herons, swans, geese, mallards and dinghy sailors. Kinfauns has Fairways Heavy Horse Centre opposite a sewage works on Sleepless Inch. Kinfauns Castle and a tower stand on the hillside above the river. Polytunnels appear increasingly along the Carse of Gowrie, named after the 6th century King Gabran of Argyll. The mild climate makes this one of the world's leading berry growing areas along the north side of the river.

The banks become steadily lined more thickly with reeds, often with deciduous trees behind. The fairway is occasionally marked with buoys and lights.

Fairly complete is the 16th century fortified mansion of Elcho Castle with many round and square towers, still with iron grills over the windows.

Balhepburn Island has now merged into the southern shore. The A90 and railway turn away before Inchyra, where there is a pier with another at Cairnie beyond the powerlines. There was a Roman camp at St Madoes and they had a pontoon bridge across the Tay towards the mouth of the Earn. There was also a Roman fortress on the south side beyond Carpow Bank.

The estuary now widens towards a maximum of 5km just before Dundee but is shallow with increasing mudbanks. Flows to 6km/h make it the fastest flowing estuary in Britain, resulting in confused water with wind against tide. From the northern shore along the Carse of Gowrie, mud banks reach out for up to 3km. This is the shore with the wildlife, edged by a screen of fine reedbeds, the reeds being exported for thatching.

Wonder Bank, Abernethy Bank, Mugdrum Island with its wind turbine and Kerewhip Bank push the flows through North and South Deeps. The firth is the best place in Britain for winter eiders with 20,000 of them, plus shelducks. Unfortunately, it also attracts shooters.

The two sides of the estuary are completely different. The southern side has the deep water channel with surprisingly large ships using it, the fairway being sufficiently narrow for vessels having not to be obstructed.

At the foot of Ormiston Hill is **Newburgh**, named in 1266 by Edward III, a royal burgh. There are 18th century merchants' houses, piers and the Hard and the Shore, useful features where Little Bank, Crombie Point, Peesweep Bank and McInne's Bank are far from solid. The Laing Museum features geology, archaeology and Victorian emigration. The 12th century Lindores Abbey has several royal graves. It was a base for the Inquisition in Scotland and frequently sent heretics to the stake. The abbey's symbol of a bear is cut into the hillside.

The name of Port Allen suggests somewhere rather more than a couple of houses at the end of a lane but there

The banks partially covered with the Braes of the Carse rising beyond the Carse of Gowrie on the north side of the firth.

can be a few small craft in the port. At low tide there are rocks set in silt. Clays, dropped as rock flour from icebergs during the last Ice Age when this was below sea level, have been the basis of a brickworks at Errol.

As below the water, the adjacent land is much less steep on the north side with about 5km of farmland rising to little more than 10m before the Braes of the Carse suddenly climb with Pole Hill at 288m. Behind them are the Sidlaw Hills with King's Seat at 377m and Auchterhouse Hill at 426m.

A narrow screen of trees also fronts much of the Carse of Gowrie shore, hiding Errol Park and Errol.

Here, the peaty water running over mud is decidedly brown. Sure as Death Bank merges into Carthagena Bank and then the massive Dog Bank, edged by saltmarsh. The

Coat of arms on the sea wall at Dundee.

Norman's Law on the south side of the firth.

mudflats are good for waders. Now and again there are rock breakwaters, the longest reaching out nearly 1km.

Approaching Grange, an Errol Airfield is now used by Paragon Skydiving and the rectangular canopies floating down are a frequent sight. In the corner is the quaintly named Seaside, technically correct but a long way from the sandy beaches and rockpools conjured up by such a name. One of the few buildings which does stand out prominently is Castle Huntly, now a young offenders institution.

The railway from Perth to Dundee has been gradually closing on the coast and now runs along the shore at Kingoodie, a village with an old sea cliff and a pier. A quarry supplied the sandstone from which much of old Dundee was built but the prominent buildings today are five tower blocks at **Invergowrie**.

Invergowrie Bay is noted for its winter birdwatching, anything from greylag geese to oystercatchers. It also has two mid tide rocks, the Cows of Gowrie, which are said to approach land at 25mm/year. When they come to land the Judgement Day will be near at hand, it is said. It seems more likely that the land will reach the rocks as development pushes the shore out.

On land, Perthshire & Kinross gives way to the city of Dundee and Dundee Port Authority takes control on the water. At first the city is held back by the airport. The 3km straight shore is edged with broken reinforced concrete but the A85 comes alongside and is edged

by a stone seawall, at one point incorporating a sculpted coat of arms which can only be seen from close up on the water. At low water there are the sands of My Lord's Bank and gaps in the seawall let sets of steps give access at intervals.

On the south side of the estuary a line of trees hide the site of the 14th century Ballinbreich Castle and then the Ochils rise steeply but with rounded green summits, 285m Norman's Law being the highest. This is an old red sandstone area and the firth follows the former peak of the Ochil-Sidlaw anticline.

Ballinbreich Castle was on just enough of a bend in the coast to give views over Durward's Scalp to the minor Flisk Point and Balmerino, Eppie's Taes Bank keeping boats of any size to the south side of the estuary.

The Cistercian Balmerino Abbey was founded in 1299 by Alexander III and his mother, Queen Ermyngarde, who is buried beneath the high altar, as a subsidiary of Melrose Abbey. It was damaged in 1547 by English raiders under Sir Thomas Wyndham and wrecked by John Knox and the Reformers. In the grounds is a propped Spanish chestnut tree of about 1560, thought to be the first in Scotland.

From Balmerino the bank outside Jock's Hole and Naughton Bank pushes larger craft into the centre of the channel and away from Wormit Bay with its scallops.

Running north from Wormit is the Tay Bridge, originally built in 1878 as the longest railway bridge over water in the

The Tay Bridge reaches out across the firth.

world at 3.3km, carrying the North British Railway Waverley to Aberdeen line. It is still the longest solely railway bridge in Europe, having been overtaken by the Storebelt and Øresund road/rail crossings in Denmark. It was built of wrought iron as steel was too new and an untried material. Construction was poor but, more importantly, as was usual at the time, Thomas Bouch made no allowance for wind loading. It was thought that anything able to support its own weight and that of anything crossing would be sufficiently robust to withstand the weather. A storm 18 months after it was opened took down all 13 navigation spans, an engine, six coaches and 75 people with brittle failure of the cast iron. Engineers had a radical rethink and wind loadings have subsequently been incorporated into design calculations. A new bridge was built 18m upstream by W H Barlow, using the same spacing for the 86 spans so that the non navigation spans could be reused. The old piles remain to above water level, acting as fenders for the 1887 bridge and a reminder of the disaster.

Dundee is named from the Gaelic for Daig's fort, now Scotland's fourth city or the Biggest Village in Scotland, built around the 174m volcanic/andesite plug of Dundee Law. On a lower hill is the Mills Observatory, the only full time British public observatory, with a 250mm telescope, a resident astronomer and a planetarium.

There was a Celtic settlement before the Romans invaded in the 1st century, much of the city being destroyed in successive attacks by the English and the Scots. It is one of Scotland's oldest burghs, created a royal burgh in 1190 by William the Lion. Wallace was educated here and, in 1288, began his anti English action by killing the son of the English Constable of Dundee. Religious reformer George Wishart was a native. Admiral Adam Duncan was born here in 1731, defeating the Dutch at the 1797 Battle of Camperdown. Another celebrated resident was William Topaz McGonagall, the world's worst poet, whose one statue is in Johannesburg and whose poetry actually sounded better when read by himself.

Dundee has been known for jute, jam and journalism. The jute industry was prominent in the 19th century, whale oil being used to soften jute for spinning. The Camperdown works were then the world's largest jute mill with Cox's Italianate stack of 1866 the tallest remaining chimney in Scotland at 86m. The jam industry was based on local fruit but expanded to include such products as marmalade and fruit Dundee cake. When Mary, Queen of Scots was ill she wanted something for 'ma malade'. Two of the most enduring periodicals have been the *Beano* and *Dandy* comics.

The oldest building in Dundee is the 1495 St Mary's Tower church steeple. An orchard given by Mary, Queen of Scots to the Franciscan Greyfriars monastery in 1564 had huge blind arcading built in 1601 and became the Howff cemetery, the name coming from the meeting place for the Nine Trades' Guild of Dundee until 1778. St Andrew's church of 1772 by Samuel Bell was paid for by the traders' guild, whose emblems are on the stained glass windows. The congregation took soup together after services, to which the Revd John Glas objected, leaving to set up the adjacent Glasite church in 1777. St Peter's Free Church of Scotland of 1834 drew people to the Revd Robert M McCheyne, to whom there is a monument with a mural alongside illustrating the history of Dundee. The neo Gothic St Paul's Cathedral of 1853 by Sir George Gilbert Scott on the site of Dundee Castle is noted for its stained glass and Italian reredos above the high altar.

The University of Dundee was founded in 1881 and has botanic gardens. The City Museum has the world's oldest astrolabe, from 1555, and the Natural History Museum has the skeleton of the Tay Whale.

The city was a major whaling centre in the 18th century, helped by having one of the best deep natural harbours on the east coast. There were 14ha of docks including work by Smeaton in 1770 and by Telford in 1815–34 although some docks have been filled in to build the Tay Road Bridge. By the Riverside Drive Retail Park, the Discovery Quay public house is at the heart of the City of Discovery. A ramp leads up in front of the Olympia Leisure Centre where the five water slides loop over the quayside but the rapid river, wave and spa pools remain hidden. Discovery Point is Scotland's premier visitor centre with some notable old ships. The frigate *HMS Unicorn* of 1824 is the oldest British built ship afloat, 46m long with 46 guns which were never fired in warfare. She was used as a powder hulk at Woolwich then an RNVR training ship in Dundee for a century, being decommissioned in 1968. Scotland's only wooden warship and one of only four afloat in the world, she is now a Royal Navy museum. Scott's *RRS Discovery* of 1901 was built in Dundee, like Shackleton's *Terra Nova*, and was one of the last wooden three masters built in Britain but the first for scientific research, based on a whaling ship design, spending two winters in the Antarctic ice. The North Carr lightship of 1933 played an unwitting part in the War in 1939 when the Luftwaffe used her as a guide in their first air raid on mainland Scotland.

Woodhaven has moorings off Pluck the Crow Point. **Newport-on-Tay** has stone Regency and Victorian houses at what was a ferry port for Dundee for 800 years until the road bridge was built in 1966. Carrying the A92, it was the longest road bridge across a river in Britain, its 2.2km long concrete deck on steel box girders supported on 42 piers, the deck rising from 10m above sea level at the Dundee end to 38m at Newport. Ships go out through the southern navigation span and in through the northern one, no use of the two spans either side of the navigation spans being permitted.

Streams are strongest in the centre of the river, heavy rain and snowmelt increasing the outgoing flow but reducing the ingoing flow. The current weakens or even becomes slack three hours and ten minutes after Dover high water.

Camperdown Dock leads into Victoria Docks, used only for small craft. There are 1.4km of riverside wharves, handling general cargo and offshore oil business including crude oil. A pair of wind turbines stand on the hillside beyond.

Claypotts Castle was built in 1569–88 for the Strachans but later became home for Bonnie Dundee, John Graham of Claverhouse. It is a four storey rectangular tower house with round towers on opposite corners and a huge arched fireplace. Entrance is by a small door covered by a gunport.

Shackleton's RRS Discovery.

The slim profile of the Tay Road Bridge with the North Sea beyond.

Graham had a brownie who did tasks at night for a nightly bowl of cream but he left because of the wasteful way the maid prepared vegetables, beating her with a kale stalk and cursing the house and its residents as he left.

From Greenside Scalp the southern shore runs straight to three lighthouses. The 23m white tower of the Tayport High Light is a sector light. Beyond gorse bushes is the old grey light tower, off which is a spoil ground.

Tayport was a ferry port for Dundee although the harbour dries. Above is the 17th century tower of Ferry-Port-en-Craig church with a list. The Larick Beacon pile lighthouse remains still provide daytime warning of Larick Scalp, the start of Abertay Sands which run east for 10km at low water although the coast turns south after 4km at high water.

The ferry served Broughty Ferry with its piers. Home to the jute merchants, it was said to have been the richest square mile in Europe. Guarding the north side of the entrance is the tall square Broughty Castle, restored in 1860. The site was used from 1547 to 1945, held by the English against a combined Scottish and French force and taken by Cromwell. It is now a museum of whaling, local seafaring, seashore wildlife, arms and armour.

Larick Beacon at Larick Scalp.

Broughty Castle guarded the mouth of the Tay.

Distance
42km from Scone Park to Tayport

OS 1:50,000 Sheets
*53 Blairgowrie & Forest of Alyth
54 Dundee & Montrose
58 Perth & Alloa
59 St Andrews*

Admiralty Charts
*1481 R Tay
(1:25,000,
1:100,000). Dundee
Docks (1:12,500)*

Tidal Constants
Perth:
*HW Dover +0440,
LW Dover −0440*
Newburgh:
*HW Dover +0430,
LW Dover +0530*
Dundee:
*HW Dover +0350,
LW Dover +0340*

Sea Area
Forth

Rescue
*Inshore lifeboat:
Broughty Ferry
All weather lifeboat:
Broughty Ferry*

35 River Earn

Shallow with a final tidal rapid

But, for the place—say, couldst thou learn
Nought of the friendly clans of Earn?
Sir Walter Scott

The River Earn flows east from Loch Earn to the River Tay, becoming tidal from near Craigend.

The stepped gash in the side of Moncreiffe Hill marks the line of the M90. The appearance of mud on the banks

The bridge at Bridge of Earn.

Low tide rapids at Bridge of Earn.

132

The River Earn flows quietly into the Tay.

The church at Easter Rhynd is invisible under ivy.

Distance
*14km from Craigend
to the Firth of Tay*

OS 1:50,000 Sheet
58 Perth & Alloa

Admiralty Charts
*1481 R Tay
(1:100,000)*

Tidal Constants
Newburgh:
*HW Dover +0430,
LW Dover +0530*

Sea Area
Forth

Rescue
Inshore lifeboat:
Broughty Ferry
All weather lifeboat:
Broughty Ferry

just before the river's second railway bridge indicates that the water has become tidal but even this does not prevent the running of a final grade 2 rapid if the tide is down a little.

Bridge of Earn is passed on the right bank between the A912 and M90 bridges but he village is not seen from the river. Sand gradually replaces the mud on the bed but the river remains shallow and the lining of trees continues.

The river gives one very large last meander and passes the old church at Easter Rhynd, completely smothered in ivy although 1930s graves in the churchyard are in excellent condition.

The Earn submits and flows quietly into the Tay just beyond an open ferry crossing point.

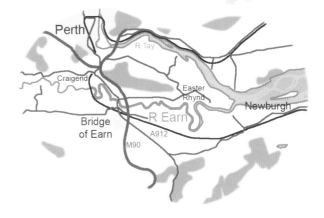

36 River Forth

Old Stirling's towers arose in light,
And, twined in links of silver bright,
*   Her winding river lay.*
Ah, gentle planet! other sight
Shall greet thee next returning night,
Of broken arms and banners tore,
And marshes dark with human gore,
And piles of slaughtered men and horse,
And Forth that floats their frequent corse,
And many a wounded wretch to plain
Beneath thy silver light in vain!
Sir Walter Scott

The Wallace Monument is visible from a wide area.

William Wallace defeated the English in 1297 at the Battle of Stirling Bridge by attacking when he had half of the much larger English army on each side of the river. The wooden bridge, then the lowest on the river, was destroyed in the action. The current Auld Brig from 1415 is one of Scotland's finest surviving medieval bridges. In coursed Ballengeich stone with rounded arch spans to 17m, it was blown up in 1745 to keep the Stuart army out, the four southern spans being rebuilt four years later. It was crossed by every Scottish king from James I and by Charles II but not by David Balfour and Alan Breck in Stevenson's *Kidnapped* after they changed their minds about the wisdom of doing so. Its cobbled deck now carries only pedestrians and cyclists.

The bridge is officially the tidal limit for the Forth but currents sweep up through it with no intention of stopping. Flows out are from five hours and twenty minutes after Dover high water and in from an hour after Dover high water with mudbanks increasing steadily downstream. The river flows east to the North Sea, cutting between the Ochil Hills and Campsie Fells.

The A9 passes over the adjacent William IV Bridge of 1832 by Robert Stevenson, its five segmental greenstone arches to 20m. Beyond a disused quay a pair of three span viaducts take the Perth to Larbert railway over. The first is an open Pratt truss of the Caledonian Railway from about 1900, the other a lattice girder of about 1880 for the North British Railway. The line to Alloa was closed to passenger traffic but has been reopened.

The river winds excessively, the meanders adding some 14km to its length. Mown lawns between the bridges give way to rugby pitches beyond. The river is lined with alders and willows, reeds, sedges, giant hogweed, buttercups, cow parsley and forget-me-nots and used by magpies, blackheaded gulls, herons and, as far as Alloa, whooper swans, with salmon, trout and sea trout.

A bend at Ladysneuk turns the river away from a cliff

The Auld Brig at Stirling, scene of major events.

Stirling Castle overlooks the town.

JAMES III 1460-1488 · JAMES V 1513-1542 · MARY ...1567 · JAMES VI 1567-1...

at the foot of a hill which bears the National Wallace Monument, a striking and distinctive 67m tower of 1869 by J T Rochead which is visible over a wide area. It has 246 steps, a stone crown and medieval weapons including Wallace's 1.63m sword. It is sited at the point from which Wallace drove the English into the marshes and has views over seven battlefields. Beyond is the University of Stirling.

A footbridge at Cambuskenneth gives 4m clearance over the river.

Further meandering brings the river near the centre of **Stirling**, the name from striveling, the place of strife. At the top of the town is a 760m volcanic neck and the material it has protected from glacial scouring, a prime example of a crag and tail. Stirling was occupied by the Middle Stone Age, was used in the Bronze Age and has Iron Age defensive work remaining. It was made a royal burgh by Alexander I with the royal household resident and was the Scottish capital. Stirling Castle was built before 1125 with an irregular enclosure. It passed between the Scots and English in the 13th and 14th Centuries but was Scottish from 1342, the seat of the Stewart kings. The Duke of Albany, Earl of Lennox and Walter and Alexander Stuart were executed here in 1425. James II stabbed the 8th Earl of Douglas here while under royal safe conduct. John Damien, the Abbot of Tungland, tried to impress James IV by flying from the battlements. It was where Mary, Queen of Scots spent much of her childhood, often revisiting it as queen. In 1820 political martyrs Baird and Hardie were executed here. It is perhaps Scotland's grandest castle. Much of the stonework was done by French masons. The Great Hall of 1503 may be Scotland's finest secular building, the hammerbeam roof having used about 350 oak trees. It was built to hold Parliament but was used as barracks in the 19th century. The Royal Palace of James V of about 1540 is one of the best surviving examples of French Renaissance architecture in Europe and the best in Scotland. Mary, Queen of Scots married Darnley here secretly in 1565. She was crowned in the Chapel Royal and James VI was baptized here in 1566. There is a medieval kitchen, 16–18th century fortifications, a gatehouse and the Regimental Museum of the Argyll & Sutherland Highlanders. Prince Charlie failed to take it in 1745 although the town had surrendered.

A statue of Bruce in the town commemorates **Bannockburn** when Edward II was beaten to create the Scottish nation. The 16th century town defences were by Mary of Guise, the Scottish Regent. It ceased to be a royal town after James VI went to England in 1603.

Argyll's Lodging of 1630 by William Alexander, the 1st Earl of Stirling, is the best and most complete Scottish example of a 17th century aristocratic town house. It was bought in 1866 by Archibald Campbell, the 1st Marquis of Argyll, who extended it. It later became a military hospital, then a youth hostel, and is now furnished as in the 1680s.

Mar's Wark is the uncompleted remains of a Renaissance palace by the Earl of Mar, the hereditary governor of Stirling Castle and Regent of Scotland, about 1570. It was occupied by James III and Princess Anne in 1589 while they were waiting for completion of work on rooms in the castle but later became the workhouse.

The 1414 Church of the Holy Rude has an unusual open timber roof. Much of it remains from 1460. It is where the infant James VI was crowned in 1567 with a sermon by John Knox. It is the only Scottish church to have had a coronation and still be in use. Cowane's House of 1649 was built as almshouses but has also been a hospital, Queen Mary's Palace and a guildhall. It was given by philanthropist John Cowane, the town's greatest benefactor, his image slightly tarnished by the illegitimate son he left with Alice, his servant. His statue is next to one of the oldest bowling greens in Scotland.

The Mercat cross, at the medieval market, was restored in 1891 and is guarded by cannons. The Tolbooth

Cambuskenneth Abbey ruins in a bend of the river.

was built in 1705 by Sir William Bruce, with steeple, clocktower, guilded weathervane and one of the few remaining ogee shaped Dutch pavilion roofs. It is haunted and now houses an arts centre. The Smith Art Gallery & Museum, Old Town Jail, Darnley's House and the detention barracks are all features of the town. Stirling Festival is the second largest in Scotland.

In the lower part of the town is the striking 2009

The Ochil Hills bound the river to the north.

Forthside footbridge, a 114m long three span inverted Fink truss with the stanchions leaning out progressively at 5° intervals.

The Augustinian Cambuskenneth Abbey was founded in 1147 by David I and was one of the richest abbeys in Scotland, as a result of which it was frequently pillaged during David II's reign. Robert the Bruce's Parliament had met here in 1326 and it was the burial place of James III and Queen Margaret. A western doorway and a 14th century Italianate belltower which was struck by lightning in 1361 are most of what remains. The Earl of Mar, an abbot who later married and turned Protestant, took many of the stones for his house in Stirling.

The A91 has been extended down the length of one meander to cross at Upper Taylorton with 4.2m clearance over the river. Reaches running northwards have the Ochil Hills to give a dramatic backdrop. Coalmines have been sunk by the river at Manorneuk and Headtown.

Between them the Bannock Burn joins quietly from the direction of the battlefield. All powerlines over the river are on high pylons and two sets across reaches of the river in this area also converge on the battlefield.

The river widens steadily with mud banks, the position of the channel changing frequently. Boats appear by the river and at Fallin there are limekilns with another mine

Waterside industry at Alloa.

The Clackmannanshire and Kincardine bridges.

behind. Oystercatchers, blackbacked gulls and wrack are parts of an increasingly maritime environment. The River Devon joins unobtrusively below Cambus, facing across to a disused crane and pier further down the reach.

Pillars run out into the river beyond Tullibody Inch, the remains of an old railway bridge and the section of line down the adjoining meander having been removed. The active industry of Alloa faces the larger Alloa Inch. Alloa was made a burgh of barony in 1497 and bought the coal exporting rights. Brewing, glassworks with the last brick glass cone in Scotland and spinning have all been important industries, John Thomas Paton donating the townhall. The leisure centre had the second flume in Scotland. Rather older are the Alloa Museum, the Mercat cross and Tobias Bauchop's house of 1695, the oldest remaining town house in the district.

The harbour has been closed and the wet dock filled although the pier remains. Flows begin outwards four hours and forty minutes after Dover high water and in from twenty minutes before Dover high water to 6km/h.

A 17th century tower remains from St Mungo's church with its fine 18th century monuments. More important is the 14th century Alloa Tower, at 24m the largest surviving tower house in Scotland. Said to have been built by Bruce, it is the ancestral home of the Earls of Mar & Kellie. Mary, Queen of Scots spent some of her time here as a child and it is supposedly where she was reconciled with Darnley. It was claimed that her son died at birth, the son of the earl being substituted as James VI. There are oak beams, an 18th century Italian style sweeping staircase, medieval dungeons and portraits and silver on loan from the present earl. Defoe claimed the 16ha gardens were the finest in Scotland.

Beyond a cairn and the Cross Slab is another 14th century tower by the Bruces, the Clackmannan Tower, much altered in the 15th century and now a ruin. The Black Devon winds round it to join the Forth.

The Pineapple, across the Forth, was a 1761 garden retreat folly for the 4th Earl of Dunmore, a former governor of Virginia where a sailor would announce his return by placing a pineapple on the gatepost. With excellent masonry, it was restored in 1974 and is now a wildlife oasis with a crab apple orchard, woodland and pond with great crested newts.

Bonded warehouses survive at Kennetpans from an 18th century distillery which was one of the largest in Scotland. Running across the river from the site of the **Kincardine** power station, closed in 2002, to the Pow Burn is the 2008 Clackmannanshire Bridge. Of prestressed concrete box girder, it is the world's second longest incrementally launched concrete bridge, carrying the A876 for 1.188km on 26 spans at 40° skew to avoid salt flats used by migratory birds, with SPA, SSSI and Ramsar sites. It is twice the length it would need to be if it took the most direct route. The spans cross two fault lines. Unusually, single round columns are used for minimum visual impact, these standing on single piles with no pilecaps. A quarter of the prestressing tendons can

Culross, a prime Scottish royal burgh.

be removed at any one time under normal traffic loading for future replacement.

The area is good for wildfowl and waders which roost in the ash settling ponds of the power station. Somehow, its brooding bulk seems more genuine and in keeping with the bridges than the three frivolously coloured tower blocks in the centre of the town. The town has a 17th century Mercat cross and Ferry and Town Piers. Sir James Dewar, inventor of the vacuum flask, was the son of the local innkeeper.

The Kincardine Bridge, carrying the A985, was the longest road bridge in Scotland and the longest swing bridge in Europe when built in 1936, a total length of 822m including twin 46m swinging spans on a central pivot. It took 13 minutes to open and close again but it operated so smoothly that it only required a 1.5kW motor and it was said that a penny would stand on edge while it was turning. There is 9m clearance under the spans but wires trail down into the water. It has not opened since 1988 as ships up to 2,000t no longer trade with Alloa, as they did when the bridge was built. Getting the jack up barge under to build the new bridge left very little clearance on one of the few days in the year when this was possible. Any problems in this manoeuvre would have delayed the new bridge by at least six months. At neap tides flows go out from four hours and forty minutes after Dover high water and in from twenty minutes before Dover high water. At spring tides the corresponding figures are five hours and forty minutes before Dover high water and ten minutes after Dover high water to 7km/h. Each side of the constriction in the shorelines there is a Leaky Tide where the flow reverses temporarily after the normal tide has turned. The water boils broodily.

Longannet power station at 2.3MW was completed in 1971 as Europe's largest power station with a 300m x 150m main building on land reclaimed with Kincardine power station waste ash behind a seawall, crossed by a conveyor and a cooling water intake. The twin to Cockenzie, it was sited to be fed by conveyor from the Fifeshire coalfield's Hirst seam. It was Scotland's leading polluter. Waders roost in the ash settling ponds and there are herring gulls.

The inner estuary of the River Forth generally runs about 3km wide and reflects many of Scotland's notable activities from different eras. There is an anchorage in Grangemouth Roads, where seals are present.

An outfall channel runs in front of Blair Castle and Dunimarle Castle, the latter with paintings, glass, books and Empire furniture, some of which belonged to Napoleon. West church has remains partly from the 12th century although the graveyard is still in use. There was also digging for slate.

The picturesque Culross with its crowstepped gable cottages is the most complete 16/17th century Scottish royal burgh, even an electricity substation being hidden in an old house. It was based on iron mining, salt panning and linen manufacture, marine trade with the Low Countries resulting in red pantiles being brought back.

The Hammermen of Culross had a monopoly on iron baking girdles but later ventures into quarrying and shoemaking were less successful.

The first Scottish coalminers were the monks of the Cistercian abbey built in 1217 by Malcolm, the Earl of Fife, extended in the 16th century, becoming a parish church in 1633, being restored in 1823 and 1905 and now mostly in ruins although the choir is still used. The abbey is haunted by a friendly Cistercian monk. The coalmining had reached a depth of 73m by 1575 with drainage and ventilation by Sir George Bruce. James VI visited in 1617, being taken along a mineshaft 1.6km under the sea, to come up on a small island. Finding himself surrounded by water, he panicked and shouted 'Treason!' The undersea workings were destroyed by a storm in 1625. Experiments had been undertaken in an attempt to extract tar and varnish from the coal.

Chapel ruins from the 16th century are on the birthplace of St Kentigern or Mungo. Culross Palace, built in 1597 and extended in 1611, was the unique Jacobean merchant's house of Sir George Bruce, with crowstepped gables, red pantiles, Baltic pine, Dutch floor tiles and glass, murals painted on the walls and ceilings, 17/18th century furniture, Scottish and Staffordshire pottery, herbs, vegetables, fruit trees and Dumpy hens, all early 17th century species. Abbey House, where Scott was to visit Sir Robert Preston in 1830, may have been by Inigo Jones for Lord Kinloss, Bruce's elder brother and Master of the Rolls.

The 1626 Town House was the legal and commercial centre of the village with a tower added in 1783, the council chambers having a Georgian interior. The old courtroom has debtors' cells. Another 17th century building is the Study with a fine painted ceiling to the study at the top of the tower, where Bishop Leighton of Dunblane composed his sermons. Also of note is the Mercat cross and the House of the Evil Eye, named after its windows. An important event of the cultural calendar is an annual dinner to McGonagall.

Off Low Valleyfield are the large Preston Island settling ponds which intrude into Torry Bay. A strong southwest wind against the ingoing flow can cause a heavy sea and dangerous conditions off Craigmore Rocks. At neap tides flows run out from five hours and forty minutes after Dover high water and in from fifty minutes before Dover high water. At spring tides the corresponding times are out from four hours and fifty minutes after Dover high water and in from forty minutes before Dover high water at up to 4km/h, affected by easterly winds, strong rain and snowmelt.

The Bluther Burn runs into the back of Torry Bay at Low Torry and there is a standing stone near Torryburn. Church remains face out from the edge of the bay. The bay drains, spread with reefs down the east side, is good for waders and has the Torry light beacon, a 12m green structure. Off the bay are the Bo'ness ship anchorages. Gradually the water becomes cleaner.

This is the start of the Dockyard Port of Rosyth with a restricted area past Crombie Pier to Ironmill Bay.

The Grangemouth petrochemical complex was the first place to receive North Sea oil.

The picturesque dormitory town of Charlestown was built from 1756 by Charles, the 5th Earl of Elgin, and has a village green, rare in Scotland. He used coal, limestone and salt on his estate to develop saltpans and a bank of limekilns. An 1820 wagonway had an inclined plane and a large three arched bridge, a passenger service being added in 1894. The pier and harbour shelter a sailing centre but the industrial legacy is 3m of oily mud. Further out, Charlestown Roads are a warship anchorage.

Limekilns is another delightful village with a yacht harbour, having lost its kilns. Drystone piers shelter Bruce Haven. The oldest building is the 14th century King's Cellar, used by monks and then kings as a wine cellar, school, library, chapel, ballroom, air raid shelter and, finally, masonic lodge. The village was described in *Kidnapped*, David Balfour and Alan Breck being rowed across the river from here by a serving maid.

On the shore are the remains of Rosyth church, after 1630 used only for burials, including those of foreign seamen. A 19th century vault was used to store corpses for three months, after which they were unlikely to be stolen for medical school dissection in Edinburgh.

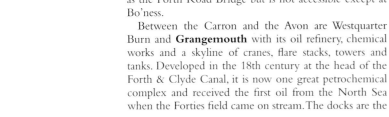

The **Rosyth** naval base is more compact than Devonport. HMS Cochrane from 1909 to 1917 for Dreadnoughts, it later supported nuclear submarines, protected by restricted areas, sometimes as far as the Oxcars. Commercial traffic has been added, handling timber, general cargo and cruise liners. Behind St Margaret's Hope it has spread across an area with Rosyth Castle and a dovecote. There is some silting here.

Mudflats begin in earnest on the south side at Powfoulis and Skinflats, the best place on the Forth for watching wildfowl and waders. Bird species include curlews, lapwings, herons and shelducks.

On the water, the smell of fresh sawdust may be carried on the breeze, an aroma which does not agree with the messages the eyes are receiving. The River Carron enters on the south side.

The A904 now runs parallel to the south shore as far as the Forth Road Bridge but is not accessible except at Bo'ness.

Between the Carron and the Avon are Westquarter Burn and **Grangemouth** with its oil refinery, chemical works and a skyline of cranes, flare stacks, towers and tanks. Developed in the 18th century at the head of the Forth & Clyde Canal, it is now one great petrochemical complex and received the first oil from the North Sea when the Forties field came on stream. The docks are the second largest in Scotland with tankers, liquid chemical vessels and LPG carriers entering and leaving. There is a lattice structure to the entrance lock. Levels change quickly in the fast flow. The mudflats are being reclaimed and a sewage works on the bank of the Avon is lost in the forest of other structures.

Earlier construction was the Antonine Wall, completed in 143 with a 4.2–4.9m turf rampart, a 3.7m deep x 12m wide ditch and military road alongside, defining the northwest limit of the Roman Empire. Kinneil means wall's end. There is a fortlet, as there were at 3.2km intervals along the wall. The line was abandoned in about 163.

Kinneil has been a colliery, seaport and whaler base, Tidings Hill being the point from which the returning whalers were spotted. Two fossilized trees have also been found here. In the church ruins, witches were supposed to have danced to the devil's tunes.

In 1936, demolition was begun of the mostly 16th century Kinneil House but 16/17th century wall paintings were uncovered so the house was restored with these fine paintings and the decorated ceilings. The White Lady is the ghost of Lady Lilbourne who jumped from a window to her death in the Gil Burn. Kestrels nest in the buildings. As well as old church and village remains there is a museum with Bo'ness pottery in 17th century stables and James Watt's cottage, Watt having discovered steam power in an outhouse in the early 1770s with water from the Gil Burn.

The Bo'ness and Kinneil Railway is Scotland's largest railway collection with 6km of line, steam hauled trains, historic steam and diesel locomotives, rolling stock and relocated buildings. A Swedish engine is the largest in Scotland.

A Roman camp site was located at **Bo'ness**, short for Borrowstouness from the Old English Beamweard's farm headland. The harbour is now closed and largely silted up. A crude oil submarine pipeline crosses to Torryburn. The ebb here runs as at Kincardine Bridge but the flood is from fifty minutes before Dover high water to forty minutes after Dover high water to 4km/h. The flood is short and sharp on springs but more nearly equal to the ebb on neaps.

The estuary now becomes part of the Dockyard Port of Rosyth although most of the naval interest is on the north shore.

The Upper Forth Boat Club have their moorings at Bridgeness, overlooked by a church with a fine crown and by a building which could be a silo disguised as a castle but is probably a castle disguised as a silo. Bridgeness Tower was a windmill, marking the actual eastern end of the Antonine Wall. There is another Roman fort site to accompany the location of Carriden House.

The silted-up harbour at Bo'ness, overlooked by the ornate church spires of the town.

Blackness Castle, planned as a ship.

Lion's mane jellyfish float about over banks of mussels, oblivious of the gas pipeline passing beneath to Charlestown. On the hill to the south is Champany where Mary, Queen of Scots held picnics in la campagne.

The Scots wanted to build a castle at Blackness but the English king refused, suggesting a ship be built instead. The Scots duly built their ship out of stone. Bar the bows facing out to sea, the undiscerning Englishman might still mistake it for a castle. The 14th century craft was strengthened for artillery in the 16th century and acted as a royal castle, a prison for Covenanters in the Civil War and an armament depot, being used into the 20th century. It was a location for filming Zeffirelli's *Hamlet* and also for *The Bruces*. Submarine cables now cross to Charlestown.

The Black Burn at the start of Wester Shore Wood marks the change from Falkirk to West Lothian. A tower on the hill locates the House of Binnes, mostly built in 1615–85 for General Tam Dalyell and his father, occupied for 350 years with magnificent Italian style plaster ceilings, furniture and portraits. It marked the transition period from fortified strongholds to gracious mansions. Tam commanded the king's army in the Civil War and later reorganized the Russian forces for the Czar. When Charles I was executed Tam refused to shave or cut his hair until the monarchy was restored. After 1660 he commanded Charles II's forces in Scotland with severity against the Covenanters and formed the Royal Scots Greys here in 1681. His boots were claimed to have the property of bringing to the boil any water poured in although it is questionable how many people would then have wanted to use that water.

Some 4km² of the water off Abercorn Point is a reserved area for a Royal Navy anchorage. The fluke of an anchor projecting from the water in the shallows seems large enough to be the kind of thing the Royal Navy might have mislaid. Great crested grebes get their heads down for a closer look.

The point is marked by a wall running round the hilltop. Abercorn church is a 12th century building on the site of a 7th century monastery around the 5th century church of St Serf. On display are 8th century Anglican crosses and hogback monuments.

A tower like a lighthouse draws attention to Scotland's finest stately home, Hopetoun House, designed for the 1st Earl of Hopetoun, an ancestor of the 4th Marquis of Linlithgow, who handed it to the nation while remaining resident. The oldest part was by Sir William Bruce from 1702 with some of the best carving, wainscotting and ceiling painting in Scotland. In 1721 it was enlarged by William Adam with a grand facade, curving colonnades and state apartments, the interior being completed by his sons from 1752 to 1767 with rich silk wall coverings and paintings by Rembrandt, Reubens, Van Dyck, Canaletto, Titian and Gainsborough. An 18th century strongroom has iron doors and shutters. Food from the kitchen travelled by steam heated railway and was reheated in the serving room before being delivered to the State Dining Room. An observatory tops the house. The red deer park and grounds were influenced by Versailles and there are a flock of Hebridean or St Kilda sheep, black with four horns each on the rams. Behind is the Stanleyhill Tower ruin.

Flows run out from three hours after Dover high water and in from an hour and forty minutes before Dover high water to 3km/h for four hours each way. A white light tower with a red band marks Beamer Rock,

an inconvenient obstacle in the centre of the shipping channel, dividing the Forth Deep Water Channel from the Main Channel. It can cause a race and eddies to Inch Garvie on the ebb although this is only 400m long on the flood. West Lothian gives way to the city of **Edinburgh** at Port Edgar Marina, formerly a Royal Navy establishment and now with the Port Edgar Sailing School. It has strong flows across the entrance with weak eddies off the breakwater heads on both flows.

The Forth Road Bridge carries the A90 46m clear of the water. The first long span British bridge of modern times, it was one of the longest suspension bridges in the world, the longest span in Europe when built in 1964 and the first bridge with a main span of over 1km not built by Americans. Two 156m towers support its 2.5km total length, using 39,000t of steel with 31,000km of suspension wire, the first British bridge to use cable spinning. The piers have 100m exclusion zones round them. Traffic loadings have reached twice the design loading allowed at the time of construction so a complex strengthening exercise has been undertaken, jacking a piston of 300t of strengthening steel up the centre of each tower column to relieve 6,000t of load on each of the existing columns, lifting the entire bridge while still in use and leaving it 40mm higher than before. Even so, the bridge is due to close in 2019 because of cable corrosion. A second bridge is planned just to the west. Flows underneath run to 5km/h.

The ferry between North Queensferry and Queensferry was begun in the 11th century by St Margaret, wife of King Malcolm Canmore. **Queensferry** is named after her. She regularly crossed between Edinburgh and Dunfermline in the 11th century. Many of the current buildings are 17th century. Plewlands town house in Queensferry dates from 1647 and other 17th century buildings include a church, the tolbooth and the Hawes Inn where Robert Louis Stevenson began writing *Kidnapped*. Sir Walter Scott also featured it. Hawes Pier car ferry crossing point had been improved by Rennie in 1808–17 with a central breakwater to assist sailing vessels. It is now used by the *Maid of the Forth* trip vessel to take several loads of tourists each day out to Inchcolm. There is an old lighthouse and the Queensferry Museum, which features the bridges, the burgh and the natural history. The August Ferry Fair's Burry Man collects money

The Forth Road Bridge.

139

The Forth Bridge, a totally unique structure and the flagship of 19th century Scottish engineering. The train gives the scale.

for charity with two attendants, his covering of burrs perhaps having developed in hard times as a scapegoat to be driven out, taking bad luck away from the fishermen. Times were not always hard, however. Defoe reported that there were so many herrings in the 18th century that they could be caught by hand. There is an inshore lifeboat located near the notable clocktower.

The Forth Bridge, carrying the Aberdeen to Waverley railway above the river with 44m clearance, is the world's most distinctive bridge. It was built in 1883–90 when confidence in Scottish engineering was at a low ebb in the aftermath of the Tay Bridge disaster. A two span suspension bridge design by Sir Thomas Bouch was abandoned after his Tay Bridge collapse although the base of one of his piers carries a 10m round black lighthouse. Benjamin Baker's design was the world's first major structure to be built entirely of steel and its lack of decoration upset traditionalists. Unlike the Tay Bridge the design allowed for conservative wind loadings which were twice what would be considered necessary today. Using enormous steel tubes reinforced at joints with rings like bamboo, it was built as balanced cantilevers and was the world's largest cantilevered bridge. The maximum height from the bed of the river is 138m and the total length 2.5km although thermal expansion changes its length by a metre. The two main spans are each 521m. It contains 54,000t of steel, held together with 6,500,000 rivets. It was the first construction project to use site lighting. There were 60 fatalities amongst the 4,600 workforce, many of them blamed on Hawes Inn whisky. The bridge is known for the continuous painting of its 59ha surface which takes 32m^3 of red paint and results in each point being repainted every three years. A new formulation of zinc, epoxy and polyurethane from the oil industry should result in greater protection. These days it is again floodlit and was used for filming *The Thirty Nine Steps*.

All that steel results in an 11° magnetic anomaly below the bridge. Flows run eastwards from three hours and forty minutes after Dover high water and westwards from two hours and twenty minutes before Dover high water for six hours at up to 11km/h. The Forth Deep Water Channel passes under the northern span, where there can be turbulence. The water is exposed to easterly winds where they are constricted at the head of the Firth of Forth, the Roman Bodotria Aesturium. The flows stir up food which attracts terns, cormorants, porpoises and whales.

Picturesque North Queensferry has moorings protected by the Railway Pier and Town Pier, Battery Point and Carlingnose Point, the latter with rare herb rich calcareous grassland supporting dropwort, field gentian, bloody cranesbill, harebell, common meadow rue, bell heather, migrant birds, fulmars and butterflies. There is a Forth Bridge Visitor Centre Museum and a Duelling Stone which marks the site of one of the last duels in Scotland, where Mr Westal killed Captain Gurley with a pistol in 1824 after a gambling argument.

Set in an old quarry is Deep Sea World, Scotland's national aquarium with the world's longest underwater safari, the UK's biggest aquarium at 4,500m^3 and the biggest private exhibition. As well as Europe's largest collection of sand tiger sharks there are wolf fish, conger eels, rays, turbot, piranhas, clownfish, octopus, seahorses, lobsters, crabs, frogs, seals, corals and the skull of a sperm whale stranded in the estuary. The firth then widens out into Inverkeithing Bay.

Just below the bridge is Inch Garvie, a 12m high rocky isle. A castle was founded on the island in 1491 by John Dundas. It was captured in 1651 by Cromwell. The castle was dismantled and the stones used for ballast in the bridge caissons. Various remains of wartime fortifications from the 20th century also litter the island, having served

as a prison, acted as an infectious quarantine hospital and being retained for defence of the bridge during the Second World War. Off it is a spoil ground.

At Long Craig there is an excellent example of a Rennie pier, protecting Whitehouse Bay from westerly winds. Beyond Whitehouse Point is Peatdraught Bay with a beach of shell sand. BP's Hound Point Marine Terminal has catwalks and dolphins with a submarine pipe to Whitehouse Point where a couple of firefighting tugs are moored. The terminal handles crude oil from the Forties field. Both the terminal and any tankers have 100m exclusion zones round them.

The hound in question was the favourite of Sir Roger de Mowbray. Both he and the dog were killed in the Crusades but the dog's spirit returned and it can be heard on stormy nights or when the death of a Laird of Barnbougle is close.

Pines and heather cloak the foot of 118m Mons Hill, around which Dalmeny Park is located, a cairn being hidden in the woods. The rocky Buchans intrude into Drum Sands with their many seabirds. This is the first expanse of sand, as distinct from mud, but when the Ordnance Survey issued the first edition of their maps with colours to mark shore material they had them brown, like the rest. This did not go down well with those promoting tourism and the OS had to issue an erratum. These days there is a pollution warning and some areas of sand seem remarkably fine and sticky in texture. Sewage pollution discourages swimming at the rivermouth and the local mussels are no longer safe to eat.

The 13th century Barnbougle Castle is right on the shoreline. It was used as a study by the 5th Earl of Rosebery after he retired as Prime Minister. It was the 4th earl who replaced it in 1815 with Dalmeny House, in Tudor and Gothic style copied from other Scottish houses. This has 16th century Scottish furniture and paintings, 18th century British prints and French furniture, a Rothschild collection of porcelain, British portraits, Goya tapestries intended for Spanish royal palaces, Napoleonic items and Louis XIV carpet planned for the Louvre. The 5th earl had three ambitions as a young man, to breed the winning Derby racehorse, to marry the richest woman in the world and to be Prime Minister. He achieved all three.

Beyond Snab Point is Eagle Rock, carved by a Roman to show an imperial eagle or possibly Mercury. The course of the River Almond varies its channel as it reaches across the sands.

Cramond has evidence of occupation from about 8500 BC, the oldest known mainland site in Scotland. It was the 3rd century Caer Almond Roman fort by Severus, built as a supply depot for the Antonine Wall. There were iron mills and a fort which housed the 2nd and 10th legions under Lollius Urbicus, a medieval

Barnbougle Castle, surprising close to the water.

The more recent Dalmeny House.

tower having been added later. It could have been the starting point for the first circumnavigation of Great Britain, undertaken by the Romans in the 2nd century. A Roman bath house found in 1975 had nine medieval skeletons in its drains. There has been a church since the 6th century although much of the village dates from the 17th century. Whitewashed cottages reach along the riverbank past moorings to a slipway. The village now has parking, toilets and other facilities around a pleasant harbour area.

A causeway with concrete piles runs out to the 8ha Cramond Island which is uninhabited and needs permission to land on it. A line of islands stretch across the firth, beginning with Inchmickery with its bird sanctuary and Second World War fortification designs in battleship profile, the Cow & Calves and Oxcars with its lighthouse.

The firth has 72,000 winter wildfowl including 8,900 knots, 8,900 pinkfooted geese, 4,100 redshanks and 2,800 bartailed godwits which the RSPB claimed were under major threat from marina development and land reclaim.

The view downstream brings in all the islands, North Berwick Law, the Pentland Hills, Arthur's Seat and the massive gas holders of Leith. Overhead, planes descend to Edinburgh Airport at Turnhouse.

Distance
66km from Stirling to Cramond Island

OS 1:50,000 Sheets
57 Stirling &
the Trossachs
58 Perth & Alloa
65 Falkirk
& Linlithgow
66 Edinburgh

Admiralty Charts
728 Rosyth
(1:5,000)
736 Firth of Forth
– Granton &
Burntisland to Rosyth
(1:15,000)
737 R Forth –
Rosyth to Kincardine
(1:17,500). Crombie
Jetty (1:7,500)
741 Plans in the
Firth of Forth & R
Forth. Kincardine to
Stirling (1:20,000).
Grangemouth & R
Carron (1:10,000)

Tidal Constants
Stirling:
HW Dover +0500,
LW Dover −0410
Alloa:
HW Dover +0430,
LW Dover +0400
Kincardine:
HW Dover +0410,
LW Dover +0310
Grangemouth:
HW Dover +0410,
LW Dover +0310
Rosyth:
HW Dover +0350,
LW Dover +0340
Leith: Dover +0340

Sea Area
Forth

Rescue
Inshore lifeboat:
Queensferry
All weather lifeboat:
Anstruther

Cramond at the mouth of the River Almond.

37 River Tyne

The history of heavy engineering on one river

A museum in Wylam is set in the 1781 stone cottage birthplace of George Stephenson, the Father of the Railways. The house was occupied by five families, the upper storey being reached by a ladder. In 1814 he designed *Blutcher*, the first flanged wheel adhesion engine, in 1825 he designed *Locomotion* which pulled the world's first passenger train from Stockton to Darlington (for which he was the engineer) and in 1829 added the world's most famous engine, *Rocket*, as well as building the Liverpool to Manchester and other railways and inventing a mining safety lamp. Wylam Railway Museum in the old schoolhouse also features the pioneers, who included William Hedley, Timothy Hackworth and Nicholas Wood, all from the village, Hedley giving his name to *Puffing Billy*. Wylam Ironworks operated from 1835 and a road bridge over the river began life carrying a wagonway in 1836. The 1835 Tudor style station is one of the world's oldest still in regular use. Wylam Wagonway followed the left bank and took coal from Wylam Colliery to Lemington, the railway which replaced it closing in 1968.

Tyne comes from the British Celtic for to flow. Flow from here changes from precipitation discharge to tidal flow. The bridge is at the river's tidal limit but is not as friendly as implied by the Boathouse public house with its brewery. There is a weir under the bridge with alternate arches having higher and lower steps, up to 500mm to 1m high, dangerous in spate with a long towback which has drowned. Despite being tidal, there is an uncomfortable rapid on river left to grade 3, extending over several hundred metres at grade 2 at low tide, the last rapid on the river. Seals have come up this far.

The right bank becomes Tyne & Wear and Northumberland is left completely before Ryton. Once clear of the rapids, the river settles down to a calm reach before the busy section to come although wooden piles worn to points show plenty of past use here. Sycamores, willows, ashes, hawthorn and gorse grow along the banks yet there are three golf courses between Clara Vale and **Ryton**, where a hill topped by a church and motte pushes the railway back against the river bank. With the wind in the right direction the scent of the sea begins to be detected although swallows still swoop over the river. Tyne Rowing Club is located near the Newburn Hotel with long steps down to the river and also a slipway for launching small craft. An old pumping station has been rebuilt as the Big Lamp microbrewery and children's play area.

The former wagonway bridge at Wylam and the tidal rapid, grade 3 at the top.

A rural reach to Ryton.

In 1068 Copsi, ally of William I, was killed in **Newburn** by Oswulf, Earl of Northumbria.

Beyond Newburn with Newburn Hall Motor Museum the landscape becomes industrial with an electricity substation. The Newburn Riverside is a loop of the Tyne with a brick cone centrepiece on a restored industrial site and coal workings, an example for Stella.

An octagonal brick tower, presumably a water tower, stands on top of the hill at **Blaydon** above the Black Bull and a stream leading down from the restored 18th century Path Head watermill. Teasels are the last plant life of note for a while as a car breaking yard stands on the river bank at Blaydon Haughs and assorted vehicle debris is strewn down to the river. The Geordie anthem *Blaydon Races* dates from when this was a popular day out for the Newcastle public.

A bridge takes the A1 over, followed by the disused Scotswood railway bridge, and then the A695 crosses from Blaydon to Scotswood on a bowspring girder bridge which looks like a cheap imitation of the more famous bridge in the city centre. Mud banks make landing difficult at low water but a slip at Derwenthaugh Marina can be used. Jetskis are amongst the river's users. Next to the Holiday Inn is the confluence with the River Derwent.

Beyond the confluence is the Metro Centre, Europe's largest shopping complex with 350 shops, over 50 eating places, Metroland (Europe's only indoor theme park), the 11 screen UCI cinema, 20 lane GX Superbowl, Europe's most spectacular Christmas decorations, free parking for 12,000 cars and its own bus and railway stations. Covering 2.1km^2, it is built on 40 years of power station waste ash. Visitors have topped 150,000 per day. Sunday trading is part of the story, surprising as the Church Commissioners for England still retain a 10% interest in the venture. This was one of the first Enterprise Zones in the UK, the venue opened in 1986, served by 1,000 buses and 90 trains per day. Bill Bryson decided it was not the worst place in Britain, an accolade he eventually bestowed on Milton Keynes.

Perhaps Nimrod surveillance aircraft might be seen passing over.

Whickham, from the Old English *quic ham*, estate with a hawthorn or other quickset hedge, inspired the *Lads of Whickham* hornpipe.

The Elswick Reach runs past the now built up southern edge of **Newcastle upon Tyne**. There are frequent tide gauges, the river ebbing to 2km/h and flooding to 1km/h. Some arches painted on the river

wall at Elswick face across to Dunston and the confluence with the River Team in the 43m deep channel cut by the River Wear before the Ice Age. At the end are the massive braced timber Dunston Staithes of 1890 built for loading coal, the 520m long structure now Grade II and used in 1988 by Wayne Sleep to perform 158 ballet grands jetés in two minutes.

Unusually for a city venue, the river runs in a deep cutting between Newcastle and Gateshead. As a result, the next straight has the highest concentration of important historical bridges in Britain, all visible in line, the most stunning way to arrive in this city.

The first of these is the Redheugh Bridge of 1870 built as a double Warren cable stayed cantilever bridge with cast iron tubular booms which served as water and gas mains. In 1901 it was rebuilt as an unusual four span bridge with Pennsylvania trusses. It has now been established with Phoenix cobble and a mosaic of pebbles, ceramics and stainless steel.

The King Edward VII bridge of 1906 carries the East Coast Main Line 34m above the river and allowed through running rather than reversing direction in Newcastle as previously, feeding into Stephenson's Newcastle Central station which has been in use since 1850. The first major station roof to use long span curved iron ribs as well as being curved in plan, it won John Dobson an 1858 Paris Exhibition medal. Next to it is the Life Science Centre with a strange mix of everything from DNA to white knuckle rides.

The Queen Elizabeth II Metro bridge was completed in 1978.

Chatham Quay is part of Newcastle Harbour. It was the first English coal port, in the 19th century, becoming a shipbuilding and engineering centre, then producing heavy armaments and munitions, the river being dredged all the way to the sea. It was synonymous with coal, using 6.1m long but very wide Tyne keels. The city retains a large urban herring gull colony.

On the north side, parts of the city walls remain. Built between 1265 and the 14th century, they are 4.3–7.6m high and 2.1–3.0m thick. Below them are the Hanging Gardens of Hannover Street. On the **Gateshead** side is the Riverside Sculpture Park with sculptures including the Blacksmith's Needle, Cone, River God, Rolling Moon and Relief Sculpture which features the bottom 50km of the

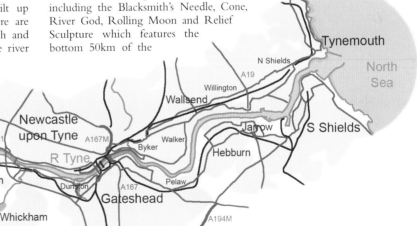

King Edward VII, Queen Elizabeth II, High Level, Newcastle Swing and Tyne Bridges, a view which cannot be matched in Britain.

river. Gateshead was the goat's headland from the Old English gat.

The 412m High Level Bridge of 1849 was one of the last two links in the East Coast Main Line, giving clearance for sailing ships. By Robert Stephenson, it was the world's first double deck bridge and was years ahead of its time in segregating road from rail traffic, carried 37m above the river. The piling involved one of the first uses of Nasmyth's steam hammer and it used cast iron columns and cast iron arch ribs, tied together with wrought iron chains at road deck level with the road hung on wrought iron tension rods. It featured in *Get Carter*. A railway bridge east of the station is of an interesting cast iron segmental pattern.

The Roman Pons Aelius may have been at the original end of Hadrian's Wall with a river fort here. The site at the north end of this bridge was chosen by Robert Curthose, eldest son of William the Conqueror, to build his new castle in wood in 1080. Henry II had it rebuilt in stone in the decade to 1178, including a three storey square keep which remains one of the best examples of Norman military architecture, together with 19th century roof and battlements by Dobson, great hall, garrison rooms and queen's chambers.

Beyond the castle is St Nicholas' cathedral, given that status in 1882 but built on a Norman church site of 1091 and including some remains of 1175. Although one of the smallest cathedrals in Britain, it is one of the most lavishly decorated, particularly the 62m lantern tower of 1470 which is the earliest and most delicate and ornate of the four in Britain. It has a pre Reformation font and 15th

century circular stained glass in a side chapel, having been extended in the 18–20th Centuries. A notorious burial in 1782 was that of press gang leader Captain Bover, perhaps the original bovver boy.

Between the castle and the river is Bessie Surtees' house, actually a pair of 16/17th century merchants' houses with a rare Jacobean timbered finish, carved dark oak panelling, elaborate plaster ceilings and a blue window marking where the beautiful daughter of a banker eloped in 1772 with John Scott of lower social standing. They married in Scotland, the families later relented and he became Lord Eldon, Lord Chancellor of England. Eldon Square is Newcastle's main city centre shopping area replacing the 19th century classical heart demolished in the 1960s.

The Pons Aelius was replaced by a medieval bridge with houses, swept away in the 1771 flood. The line was again used in 1876 by Sir William George Armstrong who had engineering works at Elswick and built the low level Newcastle Swing Bridge. On roller bearings on a central support, it is 86m long and weighs 1,200t. Operated by hydraulic pressure, it was the largest of its type in Britain and takes three minutes to swing. The Guildhall stands at its end.

Most spectacular of the bridges is the Tyne Bridge of 1928. Inspired by New York's Hell Gate Bridge, it was built as the lowest bridge on the Tyne and had the world's longest single span at 162m, the arches rising to 52m. It was used as the model for Sydney Harbour Bridge and served the same purpose in *Shallow Grave*. It is crossed by the Great North Run, the world's biggest half marathon. It normally carries the A167 which becomes the A167M

The advanced High Level Bridge with the castle and cathedral crown at its north end.

at the north end beyond Dean Street bridge arch, carrying the East Coast Main Line, the 24m x 24m elliptical span of 1848 being part of a 740m viaduct.

The river is narrow, ebbing to 6km/h and flooding to 5km/h. More than any other major river, there is a sense of being totally surrounded with high banks and multiple bridges, features of interest close at hand in all directions.

Newsweek voted Newcastle one of the world's eight most creative cities and the *Times* voted it the next capital of England for its vibrancy, humour and sense of identity. It has the highest concentration of Grade I buildings outside Bath. Plans include being the world's first carbon neutral city, including tidal power and the planting of new forests. Its cultural legacy ranges from the Playford dance Newcastle and the *Newcastle Hornpipe* via the High Level Ranters to Gateshead's Mark Knopfler and the Lighthouse Family. Daniel Defoe lived here in the early 1700s. Gateshead was also home to Joseph Swan who invented the carbon filament bulb. Moseley Street was claimed to be the first in the country to be lit by electricity in 1891, just as it had been the first to be lit by gas 80 years earlier.

Newcastle Quayside has a Sunday market and a lot happens at any time. Redevelopment includes the Hilton Newcastle Gateshead Hotel. The former Fife steelworks is now an American style nightclub, the first of a number of Baja Beach Clubs, while the adjacent marine police station has become a restaurant with a difference. The Copthorne Hotel and the Newcastle Quayside are by the river.

Newcastle Trinity House, in 14th century listed buildings, was established several decades before the London equivalent. The Trinity Maritime Centre has models of ships and the quayside in 1772.

The Tall Ships Race visited the Tyne in 1986, 1993 and 2005.

The Grade I St Mary's church with Norman origins was badly damaged by fire in 1970. Restored, it has been deconsecrated and is now an information centre.

The *Turbinia*, now in the Discovery Museum, was built here as the first steamboat in England and the fastest ship of her day.

Opened in 2004 was the Sage Gateshead music centre by Sir Norman Foster with its billowing glass ballrooms. Seating 2,000 in three halls, it has practice rooms, a music school and a music library and is home to the Northern Sinfonia chamber orchestra, a regional orchestra and Folkworks. Its £44,000,000 Lottery grant was the largest awarded outside London.

This follows in the wake of the icon of the age, the Gateshead Millennium Bridge of 2001, also known as the Blinking Eye, now the lowest downstream bridge on the river. It has two parallel arches connected by suspension rods. The main arch is 45m high and spans 130m. The other carries a footway and cycleway. When closed,

there is 4.5m clearance over the water. The whole structure rotates 40° in 4 minutes to give 25m clearance for shipping, the delicate lines being spoiled only by the late addition of heavy piling beneath to keep large boats in the centre of the channel. To start the bridge opening requires 1,000t of thrust but this reduces to nothing when the 850t structure is in its fully up position. The bridge was fabricated in AMEC's yard 10km downstream and brought up by the 120m high 3,200t *Asian Hercules II*, one of the world's largest floating cranes. Engineers drove down to Wallsend to give the all clear and met the crane coming up the river with the bridge, the captain having already made the decision himself. There was a 3mm tolerance on the span's fit. The only one of its kind and illuminated at night in 93 computer controlled colours, 30,000 people queued to cross it on opening day. In terms of the number of visitors attracted and the increase in land values in its vicinity, it had paid for itself by the spring of 2003.

At its end stood the derelict Baltic Flour Mills of the 1940s, now converted to the Baltic Centre for Contemporary Art, the biggest contemporary visual arts centre outside London with 3,000m^2 of galleries and including a 20 screen cinema and library. Across the river and still in use is the Cooperative Wholesale Society's warehouse of 1901. Eight storeys and 38m x 27m, it is an early example of a reinforced concrete structure using Hennibique principles.

The Premier Travel Inn sits amongst new housing and the Ouse Burn enters, plans for a tidal barrage intending to turn it into a canal environment. The 280m x 33m high Ouseburn railway viaduct of 1839 and another at Willington were the earliest laminated timber arch railway bridges in Britain although another planned to span the Tyne was never built. The Ouseburn viaduct was replaced by an iron bridge in 1869.

St Peter's Reach runs between East Gateshead, with the Gateshead International Stadium noted for producing Steve Cram and many others, and Byker, a former colliery area now with much residential housing. The shoreline is still industrial with Redland Aggregates and the silos on Spillers' grain berth. St Peter's Marina boasts the Bascule Bar & Bistro while, opposite, on the Felling Shore, is the Elephant on the Tyne with trots of moorings and a kayak modified as a submarine. Bare rockfaces are exposed on the shoreline, surrounded by cow parsley and bracken. International Paint, catering for the boat industry, have a factory beyond.

Ribs of a wooden boat lie up against the bank protection work at St Anthony's Point. Across St Anthony's Reach is the Bill Quay Community Farm with Old Spot and Saddleback pigs, Jacob's sheep and English longhorn

Gateshead Millennium Bridge, Baltic Centre for Contemporary Art and Sage Gateshead music centre.

The submarine kayak at the Elephant on the Tyne.

St Anthony's Point across from Bill Quay and Pelaw Main.

cattle, a surprising location next to the landscaped site of Pelaw Main colliery.

On the other side of Bill Reach the heavy industry begins in earnest on the Walker shore with the Offshore Technology Park. Travelling cranes serve Shepherd Offshore and others now working exclusively for the offshore industry. The song *Byker Hill & Walker Shore* recalls the colliery days here and there is also a *Byker Hill* traditional tune. American Timothy Dexter sucessfully sold coal to Newcastle when he believed a hoax that there was a huge market, sending ships of Virginia coal which arrived during a coal strike.

Herring and blackbacked gulls haunt the waters that would have supplied more fish in the past. An anti aircraft gun on the corner at **Hebburn** was one used for an area once worth defending more than today. In the 19th century Tyneside built 40% of the world's shipping. The decline has been over a long period. In 1936, 67% of the insured men of **Jarrow** were unemployed, leading to the Jarrow March to London. The *Mauretania* was launched in 1907 and as recently as 1981 the latest *Ark Royal* was launched. Now such names as Swan Hunter and Cammell Laird no longer build ships. Ships come in for modification and repair but that is all. Some of the cranes are kept busy with offshore work. AMEC's Hadrian's Yard refitted the 300,000t Nigerian *Bonga* gas platform, 300m x 75m x 32m high, the biggest vessel ever to enter the Tyne. Also here is the Offshore Energy Centre, opened to showcase British fabrication expertise.

Wallsend takes its name from the fact that it was at the eastern end of Hadrian's Wall. Its fort was named Segedunum, strong fort. Built in the 120s to billet 600 soldiers, it is exactly the same size as Chesters and has England's only working Roman bath house. It is the most extensively excavated Roman fort in Europe and has revealed a granary, barracks, workshops, stables and a hospital, the site in use for nearly three centuries. It has the most complete Roman fort plan in Britain, overlooked by a modern 35m observation tower, and has

Newcastle Offshore Technology Park at Walker.

a reconstructed section of wall. It has been voted one of the world's top ten museums.

Sting was one of the local residents.

On the other side of Long Reach is the site of Hebburn Colliery, power now being produced by an aerogenerator.

Willington Gut was crossed by the other wooden railway viaduct, longer but lower than Ouseburn and on the route now used by the Metro. Beyond Willington Quay is the last Tyne crossing as the Tyne Tunnel of 1967 and 2011 takes the A19 under, the eralier bore considered to be one of the least safe in Europe because of its lack of escape routes.

Flows on the ebb run to 5km/h and on the flood to 3km/h. Howden Jetty on the front of Howden Pans is used by Tilcon for aggregates next to the tidal Northumberland Dock. Shell have an oil depot opposite, powerlines passing high over the river beyond them next to the River Don. On the east side of this is the Tyne Car Terminal, used for exporting Nissans, the modern frontage to Jarrow Slake, noted for its waders.

Hebburn Riverside Park has a sculpture trail but the noted sculpture the Spirit of Jarrow recalls the 1936 march, as did Alan Price's song.

Bede's World is at Gyrwe, to use the spelling of the Anglo-Saxon tribe, a 4ha Anglo-Saxon farm with half timbered building, sunken grubenhaus and monastic workshop, all built with traditional tools and methods, and rare breeds of cattle, wild boar, sheep, geese, crops and a museum. The Venerable Bede was medieval Europe's greatest scholar. His *De Temporum Ratione* of 725 promoted the use of the AD method of calculating dates in England and in 731 he wrote the *Ecclesiastical History of the English People*. There are displays of excavated glass, pottery, sculpture and metalwork. St Paul's church was founded in 681 by Benedict Biscop, was destroyed about 870 by the Vikings, who also visited Jarrow in 794, and had a monastery built over it in 1075. The complete Saxon chancel of 681 remains, containing the world's only Saxon coloured glass window, made before 850 and found at Jarrow and Monkwearmouth. It also contains Bede's oak chair or what is left of it as girls placed splinters from it under their pillows to dream of their future husbands, brides sat on it after wedding ceremonies to ensure fertility and expectant mothers soaked chips from it and drank the water to ensure easy childbirth. The initials carved into it have no obvious significance.

The widest part of the river is a nominated swinging area between the Tyne Tanker Berth and the Tyne Bulk Terminal where grain silos are served by conveyor.

Off Whitehill Point the peak ebb flow eases to 4km/h opposite Riverside Quay with its transit sheds and container terminal, the largest quay on the river.

Tyne Dock was infilled with material from the second Tyne tunnel. Catherine Cookson, Britain's most popular author, was born near Tyne Dock in 1906 and set many of her books in Jarrow and the Mill Dam area of South Shields, Mill Dam resulting from the infilling of a tributary in 1819 to make work for ex Napoleonic War soldiers. Particularly relevant are her autobiographical *Our Kate*, *The Fifteen Streets* and *Tilly Trotter*. Also born in South Shields in 1894 was author Elinor Brent-Dyer, who wrote the *Chalet School* series of novels, and the town has produced Dame Flora Robson and Ridley Scott and was home to New Zealand Prime Minister Sir William Fox.

Shields Harbour Reach begins with the International Ferry Terminal at Royal Quays on the west side with car ferries to Bergen, Stavanger, Gothenburg, Amsterdam, Hamburg and Haugesund, 600,000 passengers per year using Tyne Commission Quay. Royal Quays Marina is located in the former Edward Albert Dock. The Wet 'n' Wild Waterpark, including eight flumes, a Lazy River and Calamity Canyon, is Europe's biggest indoor water park.

There is also a discount shopping outlet here.

A clock tower is prominent at the start of Shields Harbour Reach on its east side. There is a memorial to 3,000 merchant seamen lost in the Second World War after sailing from South Shields. There is also a statue of Dolly Peel, a smuggler and fishwife who rescued men from the pressgangs by hiding them under her petticoats. When her

Work on the Nigerian Bonga *gas platform.*

husband was taken she went with him, disguised as a man, to work in the ship's surgery. Buildings of note include the listed Customs House of the 1860s which has been extended and presents theatre, cinema and music. The Old Town Hall is an Ancient Monument, built in 1768 with a grand staircase, Italian marble, stained glass, oak panelling and elaborate ceiling cornices. It is cobbled in front with red and grey setts in the pattern of the Union Flag. St Hilda's church of 1790 is on a site used since the 7th century and has a 24 light chandelier and a model of the *Original* lifeboat of 1790, designed by parish clerk William Wouldhave. Local businessmen and thousands of others had watched the loss of the *Adventure* and her crew 300m from the shore and put up a two guinea prize for a lifeboat design. Wouldhave had also watched the incident and based his design on an orange segment shaped water scoop used by a woman at a well which, he noted, always self righted. He was only offered half the prize money. The world's first lifeboat service began here the following year.

A mural covering the whole of the end of a building overlooks the departure point for the passenger ferry across to North Shields where there is the Landing Lights beacon by Martin Richman below what was the world's largest ship repair yard, redeveloped as housing, the docks forming basement parking below 11 storey tower blocks. Market Dock has the Spirit of South Shields and Irene Brown's Fleet sculptures.

The Sea Cadets' TS Collingwood and the Beacon public house are surrounded by generally newer buildings along the river front, **South Shields** being a shipbuilding and shipping town which was badly bombed during the Second World War. At Lawe Top there is a museum with weapons, armour, coins, jewellery and tombstones. The Arbeia Roman fort with its reconstructed gateway was used in the building and garrisoning of Hadrian's Wall by the 5th Cohort of Gaul and to supply the legions in Scotland. The foundations of eight granaries remain, one from the Antonine period and the others built under Severus. An area of 1.6ha dates from 160, in 208 it was enlarged to 22 stone granaries and in 220 it was converted to a normal garrison and may have been used until the 5th century. The site has been used for 5,000 years and

Spirit of South Shields statue.

The Scarp separates the riverside buildings at North Shields from the rest of the town.

The ancient sector light at South Shields.

Distance
32km from Wylam to the North Sea

OS 1:50,000 Sheet
88 Newcastle upon Tyne

Admiralty Charts
152 R Tyne to R Tees (1:75,000)
156 Farne Islands to R Tyne (1:75,000)
1191 R Tyne to Flamborough Head.
Approaches to R Tyne (1:75,000)
1934 R Tyne (1:7,500). Willington Quay to Dunston (1:12,500)
1935 Approaches to Blyth, R Tyne & Sunderland (1:30,000)

Tidal Constants
Newcastle-upon-Tyne: *HW Dover +0430, LW Dover +0440*
N Shields: *Dover +0430*
Entrance: *HW Dover +0440, LW Dover +0420*

Sea Area
Tyne

Rescue
Inshore lifeboat: Tynemouth
All weather lifeboat: Tynemouth

this is the most extensively excavated supply base in the Roman Empire, one of the best preserved Roman forts.

Towards the river is Conversation Piece, 22 bronze Wobbly Men style figures by Juan Munoz.

Flows reach 5km/h at the bottom of the Shields Harbour Reach, where dolphins and harbour porpoises might be seen.

North Shields, like South Shields, is named after the fishermen's shielings or huts, from the Middle English schele. The Fish Quay offers excellent fish and chips. Adjacent to Western Quay, also used by fishing boats, a statue commemorates Stan Laurel, a resident before going to the USA. The Scarp rises steeply from the waterside in a town which has both a large urban herring gull colony and pigeon lofts. Two lighthouses in transit with the harbour entrance are disused. A wave trap in front of the lifeboat station and below Clifford's Fort uses No 1 Groyne, a wall of spaced timbers, to let only some of each wave pass through.

There is another wave trap on the south side in front of the pilot jetty. Between the two are the Narrows where the ebb runs to 5km/h while the flood can be 6km/h. The ebb is unchanged through the wider Entrance Reach but the flood is only to 4km/h. The dredged fairway runs from the centre of the entrance, closer to the green buoys than to the red Herd Sand buoy. The main sector light for the rivermouth is an ancient looking structure on columns on Herd Groyne.

Eider ducks frequent Entrance Reach and the Coast to Coast cycle route finishes down its north shore.

The South Pier is the longer at 1.6km. Built 1855–95, it contains 3,000,000t of stone and was designed by James Walker. Waves can break over it. With a large swell meeting the ebb, waves can break up to 800m inside the breakwaters and a race can form across the ends of the piers.

A monument with cannons from the *Royal Sovereign* on the north side commemorates locally born Admiral Collingwood who took over after Nelson's demise at Trafalgar. All Royal Navy vessels salute the statue on entering the Tyne. Close by is the Spanish Battery, where there is parking.

The Black Middens surf break can sometimes be one of the best in Britain with a left barrel over a boulder reef on the bottom half of the flood, powerful but rarely working. The flood starts half an hour after Dover high water to 2km/h and the ebb runs from six hours before Dover high water, being substantially longer when the Tyne is in spate. It was less enjoyable in 1864 after the steamer *Stanley* and schooner *Friendship* were lost here with 24 lives, metres from safety in a severe storm. This resulted in the formation of the first volunteer Life Brigade, one of only three surviving and located high above the rivermouth. The Watch House Museum, the setting for Robert Westall's ghost story *The Watch House*, was their home and covers local wrecks and rescues. Behind, **Tynemouth** Metro station has a curio fair and Britain's only urban bothy.

On the headland above Prior's Haven are the substantial remains of a Benedictine priory founded in 1090 for monks from St Albans on a 7th century monastic site. It was frequently attacked by the Danes between 800 and 1000. St Oswin in 651, St Henry of Coquet in 1127, St Osred and several kings are buried within it. An Anglican monastery was destroyed in the 9th century. A monk stole a pig's head from the kitchen of Seaton Delaval manor. The lord of the manor caught him and beat him so that he died the following year. The other monks refused absolution until he gave a grant of land to the monastery and a cross inscribed with his sin, a fragment of which is now in the Newcastle Museum of Antiquities. When an easterly wind blows, a hooded monk might be seen looking out to sea. Two presbytery walls still stand full height, there is a 14th century gatehouse and barbican and there are splendid roof bosses in the chantry chapel which was fortified and to which a Gate Tower was added by Robert de Mowbray during the border wars at the time of Richard II. After the Dissolution Henry VIII retained it as Tynemouth Castle. Underground chambers beneath the gun battery from the two World Wars were mostly dismantled in 1956.

The area featured in the work of American artist Winslow Homer.

An aerial overlooks the 930m North Pier made from blocks weighing up to 40t. Each breakwater ends with a lighthouse. There is a strong set across the entrance and there can be heavy seas in the entrance with a northeasterly wind against the outgoing flow.

Tynemouth with Collingwood's statue on the left and the priory and coastguard base on the headland.

38 River Hull

A river that did not impress the Vikings

Some of you find that Mentone is dull–
Come over and try a wet Sunday in Hull.
A P Herbert

Flowing south across Holderness to the River Humber, the River Hull is tidal from Struncheon Hill weir and lock at Hempholme, above which the Beverley & Barmston Drain diverges but runs parallel as a non tidal river almost to the Humber. The Driffield Canal, which uses the canalized river, continues to Aike, being most accessible to liftable craft at Wilfholme Landing.

In 1817 there was an attempt to run a passenger service between Driffield and Hull but this was unsuccessful and the river remains quiet and the water clear this far inland although an algal scum floats down.

It is possible to see considerable distances over the flat land of Arram and Leven Carrs, where some of the land is below sea level. Reedbeds occupy marshy areas inside the levées, marsh marigolds adding colour. There may be mallards, swans, moorhens, larks, lapwings and even the occasional seal, having worked up through the mud of the lower river.

A small rapid on the left leads water in and out of the Leven Canal, now with a sluice across the end and used for angling.

On the other side of Arram is the large Leconfield Airfield, also disused although jets roar across at low level from elsewhere.

From the A1035 crossing at Hull Bridge and the Crown & Anchor there are the Hull Bridge Boat Club moorings alongside Swine Moor with an assortment of craft from a diminutive speedboat to a houseboat. Geese and horses watch from the embankments.

Further moorings run down the east side of **Beverley**, barges having structural work done on them through to sunken wrecks. There was a trawler shipyard here and craft built included the Humber keel *Sobriety* in 1915,

Assorted craft moored by the Crown & Anchor at Hull Bridge.

now based in Goole. Beyond a swing bridge is the lock at the end of the Beverley Beck, home to the Humber keel *Comrade*.

Beverley, from the Old English bever lecc, beaver clearing in the woods or beaver stream, was a wool town and the capital of the East Riding of Yorkshire, almost surrounded by the common land of Beverley Pastures. The skyline includes the top of the towers of the Humber Bridge and also Beverley Minster. The Minster Church of St John was founded in the 8th century and rebuilt in 1220–1420 with towers from 1390, some of the finest Gothic architecture in Europe, a place of pilgrimage for those seeking the miracles of John of York, who gave up the archbishopric to live as a recluse, dying in 721. The minster had a frithstool or sanctuary chair carved from a single stone from Dunbar which

A seal beside the River Hull at Arram.

Work on craft at Beverley.

... while others have seen better days.

gave 30 days' sanctuary to fugitives while their cases were discussed. William the Conqueror's Toustain ignored this and led in his soldiers but was struck by lightning which turned his head round and reduced his limbs to lumps, after which the immunity rule was given more respect.

Some more of the finest English Gothic architecture is found in St Mary's church of 1120–1525, a central tower, a ceiling decorated with panels of the English kings down to Henry VI, carved misericords and a carving of Alice's white rabbit. Many of the town's houses are Georgian.

The river returns to open country beyond Weel as it passes Weel and Stone Carrs although powerlines are seen more frequently. The banks, which have been low and clean, now become increasingly silty with teasels after Wawne. Flows can reach 15km/h. Glasshouses are built to the west of the river between Thearne and Dunswell as the East Riding of Yorkshire gives way to Kingston upon Hull.

The built-up area begins at Kingswood where the modern twin Ennerdale drawbridges carry the A1033 dual carriageway over the river. Bridges over the river lift or swing to allow through working boats which can be large for the size of the river. These bridges include the pair of Stoneferry drawbridges carrying the A1165, Wilmington swing railway bridge and rolling bascule bridges.

A prominent wind turbine on the bank marks a chemical works and the start of the industrial part of Hull with a car scrapyard and old brick warehouses by the river. Sheet piled edges become continuous. At low water there are high silt banks and gentle rapids. The former Clarence Flour Mills are notably large. The Beverley & Barmston Drain does not join until a little over a kilometre from the Humber.

Twin lifting bridges at Stoneferry.

One of Hull's bascule bridges.

Kingston upon Hull takes its name from the Old English royal estate. Unusually, the city name is abbreviated to the name of the river on which it sits. Originally it was called Wyke from the Danish vik, creek, a reflection on the small size of the river.

It was used by the Cistercian monks of Meaux Abbey as the principal wool exporting port and they straightened the lower reach to assist. These days wool is imported from Australia and New Zealand. The city was laid out in 1293 for Edward I, who provided its charter six years later. It was fortified in the 14th century, becoming important for Greenland whaling in the 16th century and developing Baltic trade. It was the third most important centre for shipbuilding, including the *Bounty* and England's first steam packet; it was recently the UK's largest deepwater fishing port and was the third largest port with 11km of docks although these are mostly along the Humber rather than upon the Hull. It was much damaged during the Blitz.

The Scott Street Lift Bridge is permanently raised but the A165 uses the North Street rolling bascule bridge and Drypool Bridge is another bascule model. The 18th century Georgian Pease Warehouse has now been converted to flats and the Premier Inn is a more recent tall building.

Churches include the Charterhouse chapel with rare Georgian church architecture and the 1820s St Charles Borromeo Roman Catholic church. St Mary the Virgin's church, from the 14th century, has a 15th century nave and chancel and a tower from 1697, rebuilt in the 19th century in neo Gothic, the east window retaining some medieval glass. Holy Trinity is claimed to be the largest parish church in England, the first major building in brick, dating from 1285 although restored in 1869 and 1907. It has the 1366 tomb of William de la Pole, Hull's first mayor in 1331, England's most prominent merchant and ancestor of the Earls of Suffolk, his statue standing by the Victoria Pier.

A bronze wall panel recalls that Robinson Crusoe began his voyage here and a statue of local Amy Johnson marks her solo flight to Australia in 1930. Wilberforce has a 27m statue. Wilberforce House, his birthplace in 1759, has an exhibition of slavery, tools, a slave ship interior, Hull silver, toys and Victorian military uniforms in a Jacobean building with Georgian and Victorian features, 17th century oak panelled rooms where Charles I dined in 1639 and an 18th century staircase with rococo plaster ceilings. The Streetlife Museum has cars, coaches and

The Arctic Corsair, *Britain's last sidewinder trawler.*

151

an 1871 tram from Ryde Pier, the world's oldest tram. The Maritime Museum in former dock offices shows models, paintings, whaling, fishing, shipbuilding, the best collection of scrimshaw in Britain and coverage of Hull and the Humber. Trinity House, established here in the 14th century, has Captain Cook's gun and silver plate. Humberside marine paintings from the 16th century are included in the Ferens Art Gallery. The Hull & East Riding Museum has the 12m long Hasholme Iron Age plank boat of 1000–800 BC from North Ferriby and exhibits on Bronze Age warriors, Roman mosaics, geology, archaeology and natural history. Maister House, rebuilt in 1743 after a fire, is a rare example of a merchant's house with a notable hall and staircase, stucco and delicate ironwork. Hands on History is located in the grammar school of 1583. Another statue is of George Smith, killed in 1904 in the Russian Outrage when the Russians fired on Hull trawlers on the Dogger Bank, mistaking them for Japanese with whom they were at war. Moored on the River Hull in the city as a fishing museum is the *Arctic Corsair*, Britain's last remaining sidewinder trawler.

The city has a Fish Pavement Trail with 41 species including an electric eel outside a substation and a shark outside a bank. There are also 35 public houses in the Kingston upon Hull Ale Trail. The Sailmakers Arms is in a former chandlery. The Olde Black Boy of 1337 is haunted and was involved with smuggling, the slave trade, cock fighting, pressgangs and undesirable activities generally. The Olde Corn Exchange public house was the Excise Coffee House of 1788. The King's Ale House has nautical decoration while the Mission, in a former Seamen's Mission, has a seamen's chapel with pulpit and stained glass. The listed Empress Hotel was the Old Dock Tavern until 1879. Also listed is the George Hotel with Hull's smallest window. The 18th century Olde White Harte, not to be confused with the listed White Hart Hotel, was the home of Hull's governor, Sir John Hotham, who barred Charles I from the town in 1642, probably precipitating the Civil War. The Grade II Mint bar was a bank of about 1870 while the similarly listed Kingston Hotel of 1882 has

a back bar built in 1795 from Canadian pine. The city has been used in filming *Only Fools and Horses*.

The original town moat joining the Hull and the Humber was converted in 1778 to form the first purpose built enclosed dock outside London, the 560 x 78m Hull Town Dock, later to become the Queen's Dock, now the Queen's Gardens after being filled in. Humber Dock became Princes Dock, now with the Princes Quay shopping centre built over much of it on stilts. The Old Harbour was the original, used by vessels up to 500t, commercial vessels sometimes reaching it by reversing up. The Ellerman Wilson Line, founded here, was the world's largest steamship company.

The A63 crosses Myton Bridge by the 1980 tidal barrier, pairs of vertical yellow lights flashing when the river is closed. A decision was taken against canalizing the river and it continues to ebb for eight hours and flood for four and a half with potentially dangerous currents. A signal sounds when there is fog.

The final bridge is the 30m span Millennium swing footbridge by the site of Henry VIII's South Block House, a large citadel. The dominating feature of Sammy's Point these days is the Deep, a tetrahedral aquarium angled out over the confluence with an observation point, the deepest tank and the deepest viewing tunnel in Europe and the world's only underwater lift, the building fronted by a shark sculpture. For both entertainment and research, it has a coral atoll, coral wall, Pacific, North Sea and polar environments, seven shark species, conger eels and rays.

The Minerva Hotel of 1831 was built on reclaimed land. Public toilets in front are some of the best kept in the country. The Cask & Cutter has nautical decoration. Minerva Pier was the location in 1999 for the controversial Two Sisters sculpture, a 6m cylinder of chalk which was lowered into the Humber and was supposed to dissolve in three months. The £50,000 object was gone in 30 days.

Beyond the pier is Hull Marina, converted from the Railway Docks in 1983, hosting 330 craft and the 1927 Spurn lightship, built in Goole. An 1846 cast iron swing bridge near the entrance has now been fixed. The former maritime heart of the city has moved away to more distant locations.

Distance
23km from Aike to the River Humber

OS 1:50,000 Sheet
107 Kingston upon Hull

Admiralty Charts
109 R Humber & Rs Ouse & Trent (1:50,000) 3497 R Humber – Immingham to Humber Bridge (1:25,000). Hull Docks – Western Part (1:10,000)

Tidal Constants
Struncheon Hill Lock:
HW Dover −0150, LW Dover −0140
Beverley:
HW Dover −0250
Kingston upon Hull: HW Dover −0450, LW Dover −0440

Sea Area
Humber

Rescue
Inshore lifeboat: Cleethorpes
All weather lifeboat: Humber

Connection
Driffield Canal – see CoB p268

Hull Barrage and the Deep.

38 River Ouse (Humber)

King of the swingers

Where is that banner now?—its pride
Lies 'whelmed in Ouse's sullen tide!
Sir Walter Scott

The Yorkshire Ouse has been used commercially since at least Roman times. Rising in the Yorkshire Dales as the River Swale, it flows southeast to the Humber. It is tidal from the lock at Acaster Malbis, reached from the B1222 on the Naburn side by following directions which include a bar and restaurant that closed in 1997. The final weir is large and rugged but can drown out. Like the two parallel locks, it is Grade II. The locks were built in 1757 and 1888 and refurbished in 1998 by RJB Mining because of local mining subsidence. There are unusual ground paddles and lattice swing bridges across the lock chambers, mechanized by placing the motors inside the hand winches to retain appearances. Indeed, almost every crossing of the river features a swing bridge. The lock is used from three hours before local high water until four and a half hours after it.

It is a river which carries quite a lot of tidal flotsam, especially sections of tree large enough to impede cruisers.

Between Bell Hall and a disused airfield

The final weir on the Ouse at Naburn.

A lattice swing bridge of 1872 takes the B1222 high over the river at Cawood by the Ferry Inn, recalling the former route across. A fire beacon is recent but the gateway remains from the Saxon castle which became the 14th century palace for the Archbishops of York. This was where Wolsey was arrested and sent south and it was visited by Henry III, Edward I, Queen Margaret, Queen Isabella, Henry VIII and Catherine Howard.

Powerlines cross beyond Kelfield and there are more moats here and around Ricall, which follows. In 1066 Harold Hardrada left his ships here in a last Viking attack on Britain, fatal for him, which weakened Harold of England ahead of the Battle of Hastings.

Before **Barlby** the river doubles back in front of the A63, now using the route of the East Coast Main Line which has been diverted west to avoid the Selby coalfield and the swing bridge over the river. Railway construction on this scale had not been undertaken for many years and it was necessary to dig out the 19th century contract documents for guidance.

Large mills greet arrival in **Selby**,

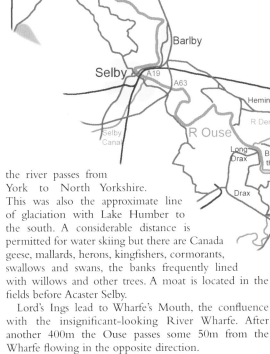

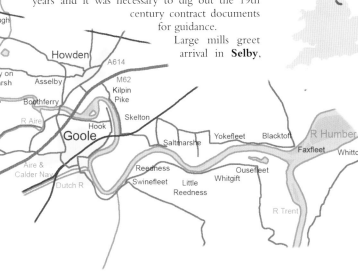

the river passes from York to North Yorkshire. This was also the approximate line of glaciation with Lake Humber to the south. A considerable distance is permitted for water skiing but there are Canada geese, mallards, herons, kingfishers, cormorants, swallows and swans, the banks frequently lined with willows and other trees. A moat is located in the fields before Acaster Selby.

Lord's Ings lead to Wharfe's Mouth, the confluence with the insignificant-looking River Wharfe. After another 400m the Ouse passes some 50m from the Wharfe flowing in the opposite direction.

Naburn's lock chambers are crossed by lattice swing bridges.

Cawood's bridge being swung.

not least the Rank Hovis flour mill, but trees growing out of the high staithes in front show that they have not been used for some decades. The river turns sharply in front of the Westmill Foods mill which is heavily buttressed.

Selby was probably founded by the Danes, an early Christian centre and market town based on one of Britain's richest coal seams. It was Britain's largest inland port and one of the furthest inland. Selby Abbey was founded in 1069 by Monk Benedict of Auxerre with approval from William the Conqueror. The Benedictine abbey was rebuilt about 1100 and survived the Dissolution but was attacked by Cromwell and also suffered a fire in 1906. One of the best churches in England, the limestone building has three towers and a 14th century window by an ancestor of Washington with family arms which were to develop into the American flag. The 12th century Abbots Staithe is Grade II, one of the oldest buildings on the inland waterways, and probably imported stone, lead and iron for the abbey. The town has many Georgian houses and a 1790 market cross. It may have been where Henry I was born in 1068 and it was in the centre of an area where several Civil War battles were fought.

Flows to 17km/h are some of the fiercest in the country, at times enhanced by an eagre. Taken with the corner, this is not an ideal place for two swing bridges. The A19 crosses the swing Selby Toll Bridge, rebuilt in 1970 with a dated look to comply with a 1790 Act. The 1792 bridge had one of the first uses anywhere of ball bearings, reputedly cannon balls. Rubbish piles up against the piers,

especially with fast spring flows, and the bridge is often damaged by shipping. The adjacent railway bridge of 1891 replaces one of 1839. These days it carries only the Leeds to Hull railway but also carried the East Coast Main Line until the coalfield diversion. The five span bridge has a 40m swing span on 24 steel rollers, the piers taken down 24m to sandstone bedrock. The station on the south bank of the river has interesting cast iron Vierendeel platform awning supports.

The Selby Canal's bottom lock faces the river on the right. The opposite bank is used by the Trans Pennine Trail for horse riders, having followed the general line of the river since Naburn. Selby is left past the chemical plant and under the A63 on the modern Ouse Swing Bridge.

Hemingbrough has a particularly tall and slender church spire, accentuated by the flat landscape. Powerlines are also conspicuous, especially those on high pylons to take them clear of shipping. They converge on Drax power station, the second largest coal fired station in Europe and the UK's largest at 3.9GW, supplying 7% of Britain's electricity, and also with the first biomass processing facility of its kind in the country. Below Drax Abbey Farm, a reminder of the adjacent priory site, there is a discharge point for the power station cooling water, jets of water falling the height of the tall bank.

Barmby Barrage brings in the River Derwent, the border with the East Riding of Yorkshire and the start of navigation lights. There used to be a ferry between Long Drax and Barmby on the Marsh and, later, a railway

Some serious buttressing on Westmill Foods works in Selby.

Formerly the East Coast Main Line with the A19 beyond.

Entrance lock for the Selby Canal.

crossing a swing bridge. These have now gone, as has a Roman building sited near the river. Moorhens and skylarks remain.

The Ouse runs between the wooded Asselby Island, no longer an island, and Fort Hill to reach the confluence with the River Aire, the junction pointing upstream to suggest the flood flows are much stronger than the ebbs. Boothferry no longer has a ferry but the A614 is carried on the

1932 Boothferry Bridge. A viaduct carries the M62 over the river, the only bridge on the tidal river not to have a section which swings open.

Howden, a village with medieval and Georgian houses, has the 13th century minster of Saints Peter & Paul. Nave columns remain from 1267 although the choir collapsed in 1696. There is a windmill beyond the motorway. The river widens round Howden Dyke Island and there are shallows. Howdendyke has a fertilizer works and a sugar factory. A 190m jetty can take vessels up to 3,000t, the river being used by seagoing commercial vessels from here. A fire beacon stands on the bank at Kilpin Pike. Opposite, the hulls of wrecked wooden barges are spread along the Hook bank.

The final bridge across the river is the Skelton or Goole Bridge which carries the Hull to Doncaster railway, the finest bridge of its kind in the British Isles. Built in 1869, it was the second largest swing bridge in the world with six sets of three wrought iron hogback plate girders on cast iron cylinders up to 27m long and a 77m long swing span of 650t on 36 rollers. It takes a minute to swing and is hit frequently, not least in the late 1980s when it was closed for nine months after being hit by a Swedish freighter. Although the Humber port limit is just below the bridge there are more shallows in the river, as the Sandhall Reach name hints.

Goole takes its name from the Middle English gole, a sluice or drain. The docks were established after the Aire & Calder Navigation arrived in 1826, handling coal and textile export and developing trade with the Baltic and Europe. Boats to 4,500t are handled, a high intensity white light showing when vessels are locking out and the area has to be kept clear. Large ships use the locks from two and a half hours before local high water for four hours but barges and small craft may use them at any time. A black flag or a fixed white signal light shows from local high water for 45 minutes.

The town skyline behind Goole Bight includes a windmill and St John's church of 1845, built with Aire & Calder Navigation assistance. The small 1885 Grade II water tower has a 140m³ cast iron tank on a fluted brick shaft. It was superseded in 1927 by a reinforced concrete water tower with a 3,400m³ tank on a ring of columns around a central tower, the largest in Europe when built.

The Ouse Swing Bridge carrying the A63 at the end of Selby.

Drax power station is the second largest in Europe.

The A614 bridge at Boothferry with the M62 beyond.

156

Wrecks on the shore above Hook.

Goole Museum has many Reuben Chappell shipping and maritime pictures and the converted 1915 Humber lightship *Audrey*.

In order to ensure proper dredging the Aire & Calder Company took over the 16km downstream. As well as the Aire & Calder Navigation the Ouse is joined by the tidal Dutch River, which runs alongside it. Flows are fast through Goole Reach, which is increasingly edged by reeds.

There are a couple of windmills off Swinefleet Reach, which is joined by the Swinefleet Warping Drain. Cotness Roads, Whitgift Roads and the Blacktoft Channel make long sweeping curves eastwards past Saltmarshe, Reedness, Whitgift, Yokefleet and Blacktoft, small riverside

communities. Little Reedness has a church with a tower which appears to lean significantly. A lighthouse near Ousefleet is built midway along Whitgift Roads for no apparent reason. Opposite is another windmill while there is another moat behind it and a final set of powerlines across. Blacktoft Sands have been designated a nature reserve with tidal reed swamps, saltmarsh, mudflats, brackish lagoons, blackheaded gulls, oystercatchers, marsh harriers, avocets, shelducks, bearded tits breeding, birds on passage and a hide to watch them.

Floods can exceed 11km/h. Between Trent Falls and Faxfleet is the Apex Light which marks the end of a training wall. Here the Ouse joins the Trent to become the Whitton Channel of the River Humber.

Distance
59km from Acaster
Malbis to the River
Humber

OS 1:50,000 Sheets
105 York & Selby
106 Market Weighton
112 Scunthorpe
& Gainsborough

Admiralty Charts
109 R Humber &
Rs Ouse & Trent.
Whitton Ness to
Goole & Keadby
(1:50,000). Goole
(1:5,000)

Tidal Constants
Naburn:
HW Dover −0050
Selby:
HW Dover −0220
Barmby:
HW Dover −0240
Goole:
HW Dover −0340,
LW Dover −0120
Blacktoft:
HW Dover −0410,
LW Dover −0200

Sea Area
Humber

Rescue
Inshore lifeboat:
Cleethorpes
All weather lifeboat:
Humber

Aground on a sandbank above Goole.

A container ship passes Little Reedness.

40 River Trent

The powerhouse of England

All thy sands, silver Trent,
Down to the Humber,
The sighs that I have spent
Never can number.
Michael Drayton

The lethal Cromwell weir.

A converted windmill at Carlton on Trent.

Marnham Boat Club and High Marnham power station.

Britain's third longest river, the Trent, flows southeast from Knypersley Reservoir and then northwest to the Humber.

It is tidal from Cromwell Lock, which can only be approached along a gated road. The lock was enlarged in 1906 and is a long portage for small craft coming down the river. The large weir is of dangerous design and, not surprisingly, has caused a number of fatalities, not least 10 soldiers of 131 Independent Parachute Squadron on a night exercise in 1975. A short portage is possible theoretically on the right but it would involve crossing the high sided Slough Dyke which leads into a tempting tunnel on river right but this feeds into the towback area of the weir and could be equally dangerous to anyone swept through accidentally.

There were no such problems when the Danes used it to invade up to Nottingham or for the Romans, for whom this was the Trisantona Fluvius. It was part of Brindley's Grand Cross water scheme and had a passenger service between Nottingham and Gainsborough in the 19th century. There is a towpath to Gainsborough but there are times when it changes bank where there are no longer connecting ferries. Villages are set back from the high banks because of the flood risk and it meanders but remains a commercial waterway for gravel and for transporting large power station loads. Pleasure craft tend to use it to link up parts of the canal system rather than for cruising in its own right.

Kilometre posts give distances as far as Gainsborough and there are posts with navigation marks. These are cut from brush material so that the starboard markers on the left bank look like miniature Christmas trees.

There was a Roman bridge at Cromwell but timbers found have been dated to the 8th century. Cromwell's current contribution to history is the Vina Cooke Museum of Dolls & Bygone Childhood with a thousand dolls in the 17th century former rectory.

Cormorants, mallards, herons, great crested grebes, oystercatchers, sandpipers, curlews, larks and wagtails are seen in limited numbers and there are migrants in the winter.

Collingham Wharf loads gravel. The Jolly Bargeman had a full time ostler for the barge horses until it became a private house in 1929. Initially the shoreline is of gravel or steeper banks may have tipped stones. Later these are to give way to high silt banks with a vengeance. Sometimes these are reinforced with bundles of fascines.

The East Coast Main Line and the A1 traffic roar away at Carlton on Trent, where there used to be a ferry across at Carlton Wharf. A former windmill is now a tower house with fine views over the river. Around Carlton Rack anglers have not just cut steps down the banks. They have staircases of great stone slabs.

Sunken barges are used as bank reinforcement around the gravel loading staithe at Besthorpe Wharf. Canada geese stand on the bank amongst the celandines in the spring.

Another windmill faces Spring Head at **Sutton on Trent** where Sutton Wharf had the Meering Ferry. Beyond Smithy Marsh more gravel pits are served by Girton Gravel Wharf. A submerged wall is located on the inside of a righthand bend. Occasional submerged islands are clearly marked by large warning notices.

A water skiing area is equally clearly indicated for Marnham Boat Club, based below the red cooling towers of the disused High Marnham power station. South Clifton Wharf also has lost its ferry across to

Disused railway viaduct at Fledborough.

High Marnham. Simple spans of Fledborough Viaduct across the river join brick arch viaducts on each side, part of the Chesterfield to Lincoln railway. It was closed in 1980 after a derailment although freight trains from the west can still reach it.

The right bank changes from Nottinghamshire to Lincolnshire. More angling staircases have been built at what is a gathering place for swans near North Clifton and where a red sand cliff provides a nesting venue for martins. The Romans sited a vexillation fortress here and rooks have a community of their own. Vexation is caused where craft regularly run aground on an anti erosion wall. Two bridges cross, a smart truss which carries only a pipe and the simple Newton on Trent or Dunham toll bridge, the only road crossing between Newark and Gainsborough.

Dunham Rack leads to Laughterton Marsh, from where there used to be a ferry to Church Laneham with its Norman church.

Once again there is water skiing in front of the 2GW Cottam power station. The cooling water from the power stations all down this river must raise its temperature and make it more pleasant for users. There are two islands with willows. Redland's Trent quarries produce coarse sand for concrete. Despite the activity, pheasants and woodpeckers might be heard.

After the river doubles back on itself it is joined by the Fossdyke Navigation at Torksey lock. This was built by the Romans and used by the Vikings to attack Lincoln,

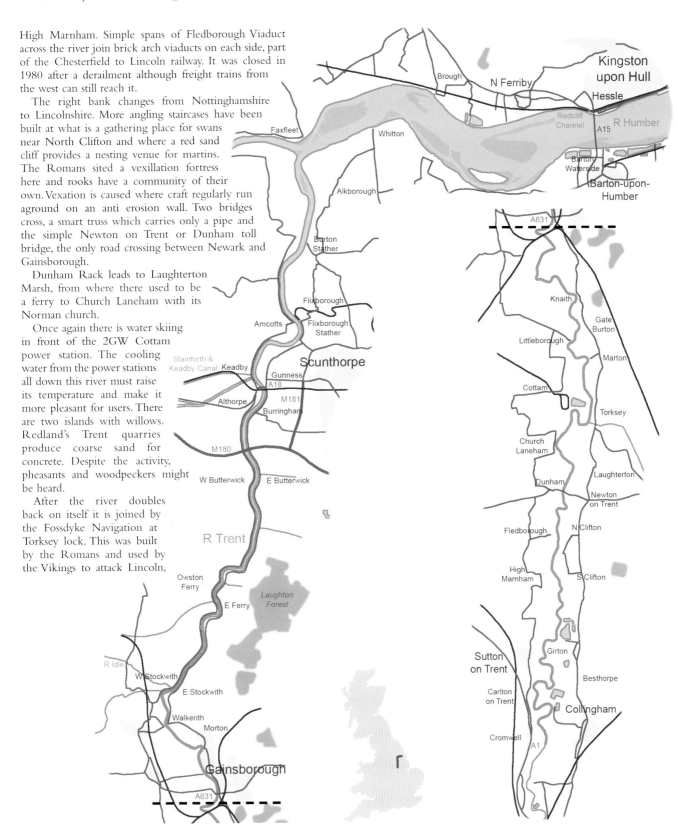

Massed swans near North Clifton.

A striking pipe bridge in front of Dunham toll bridge.

The remains of Torksey Castle.

the lock being a more recent construction. At one time much of the Trent's water flowed east through the Lincoln Gap.

Torksey Castle is the remains of a castellated 16th century Elizabethan manor which was burned by the Royalists during the Civil War. Torksey potteries were formerly on the bank in the village. The abandoned Torksey Viaduct of 1849 was an early box girder bridge. This time the remaining track is from the east. An oil terminal was set up to supply Lincolnshire airbases.

Coots and moorhens frequent the increasing reed coverage beside the river. Powerlines pass both sides of the remains of the 1799 Marton Mill at Trent Port. The Romans had a fort site at Marton. There is a ford at Littleborough, their Segelocum, occasionally uncovering on the line of their road from Lincoln to Tadcaster. It was the route used by Harold's army on their way to Hastings in 1066. A subsequent ferry no longer exists although a Norman church with herringbone masonry survives.

The Burton Château folly is a lodge of Gate Burton hall and is the earliest known work of John Platt, built in 1747 when he was 19 for a Gainsborough lawyer's weekend retreat. Next to woods on a ridge overlooking the river, it seems to be particularly well located.

Knaith Hall has a similar location overlooking Out and Upper Ings. The Romans had a pottery kiln here. A bridge over the river in the 12th century was short-lived. In the trees was a nunnery until 1539, also a chapel.

The 2GW West Burton power station is built at the site of West Burton village. New works have been built along the riverbank but seals come up this far.

The Grimsby to Sheffield railway passes over, followed by the A631 over the masonry bridge of 1791 with three semi elliptical arches to 21m and toll houses at the east end that were used until 1932.

The Trent Port public house, Dog Island which is not an island, oil wells and the old Watson shipyard are all that occupy the left bank. **Gainsborough**, from the Old English Gegn's stronghold, occupies almost exclusively the right bank where the land is higher. A market town, it is one of Britain's furthest inland ports and this is where coastal shipping starts. The wharf timbering has been extensively renewed and the river here has been suggested for a tidal lock.

A 2000 walkway has been set up along the right bank as part of Gainsborough Riverside, which has also seen the conversion of wharves to domestic accommodation and there is a Lidl store. The port with its difficult tidal waters was used as the basis for St Ogg's in *The Mill on the Floss*. The medieval timbered Old Hall manor house of about 1460 replaces an earlier one wrecked by the Lancastrians during the Wars of the Roses. It is where Richard III stayed in 1483 on his way back from his second coronation in York, Henry VIII met Catherine Parr and the Separatists worshipped secretly 40 years before sailing to America via

Distant power station at West Burton.

Amsterdam in 1607 as the Pilgrim Fathers. It has a notable Great Hall and a fine medieval kitchen.

An earlier castle here is where Danish invader Sweyn is said to have died in torment at the hand of the ghost of St Edmund who had been killed by the Danes in 874 and was now back with a spear. Sweyn's son, Cnut, was declared king here and it is claimed to be where he failed to prevent the tide rising, not little waves up the beach but a 1.8m eagre. Had he survived such an onslaught it would seem odd to hear such timid versions of the tale for other locations. The eagre may exceed 1.5m between Keadby and Gainsborough, usually on tides above 7.6m at Hull but sometimes on smaller spring tides although the effect has been reduced by flood prevention work. It is not only the water itself which is dangerous to small craft but because large commercial craft may be following it up for the cheap, fast ride. Floods can exceed 11km/h. The ebb runs for nine hours and forty minutes or even over ten hours so that the flood has to come in fast in the remaining time to restore the level.

The town was fought over frequently in the Civil War. The Georgian All Saints church has a Perpendicular tower and there are several Victorian churches. At Morton there is a hospital and a windmill before the river moves into willow lined countryside like that of the fens.

Walkerith had a ferry across the river, as did East Stockwith until the 1950s, facing West Stockwith at the end of the Chesterfield Canal and the River Idle, surprisingly with no connection between the two without having to go out onto the Trent. Locks are only opened near high water. During high flows hand operated winches each side of the lock are used to assist sailing vessels off the Trent and onto the Chesterfield Canal. Floodwalls are of concrete here. The Cuckoo Way footpath follows the canal from the village. There is a Miniature World museum with dolls and models and the White Hart on the bank.

The left bank now becomes North Lincolnshire between Heckdyke and Gunthorpe. Three windmills are all private residences, one near the end of the Warping Drain, used for flooding the flat agricultural fields with silt.

East Ferry faces the Dutch style houses of Owston Ferry. A drain is fed in from the direction of Laughton Forest and the River Eau opposite North Ewster, something which now happens with increasing frequency.

East Butterwick, a finger village built along the right levée where another drain enters, was connected by ferry to West Butterwick, which ends with another windmill. The M180

The well-sited Château folly near Gate Burton.

Wharf buildings in Gainsborough are being restored.

The rolling bascule King George V Bridge at Gunness.

Grove Wharf near Flixborough.

Distance
100km from
Cromwell to Hessle

OS 1:50,000 Sheets
106 Market Weighton
107 Kingston
upon Hull
112 Scunthorpe
& Gainsborough
121 Lincoln &
Newark-on-Trent

Admiralty Charts
109 R Humber
& Rs Ouse &
Trent (1:50,000).
Humber Bridge to
Goole & Keadby
(1:50,000). Keadby
to Gainsborough
(1:100,000)

Tidal Constants
Cromwell Lock:
HW Same as Dover
Torksey:
HW Dover −0120
Gainsborough:
HW Dover −0230
Owston Ferry:
HW Dover −0310
Keadby:
HW Dover −0330,
LW Dover −0100
Burton Stather:
HW Dover −0400,
LW Dover −0140
Brough:
HW Dover −0420,
LW Dover −0350
Humber Bridge:
HW Dover −0440,
LW Dover −0420

Sea Area
Humber

Rescue
Inshore lifeboat:
Cleethorpes
All weather lifeboat:
Humber

Connections
Fossdyke Navigation
– see CoB p280
Chesterfield Canal
– see CoB p274
Aire & Calder
Navigation – see CoB
p248

crosses with a high proportion of lorry traffic and then Burringham is another finger village which had a ferry across to Althorpe.

Powerlines cross with increasing regularity. Totally unique, however, is the King George V Bridge of 1916, the largest bridge built by the Great Central Railway. The five span structure is 167m long and has a 50m 4,000t Scherzer rolling bascule span which was fixed in 1960, carrying the A18 as well as the Doncaster to Grimsby railway. With three lines of lattice girders, it was one of the first of its type in Britain and was the heaviest in Europe, replacing an 1866 swing railway bridge 60m upstream.

Gunness Wharves, immediately downstream, have use by commercial shipping on a scale not seen upstream and navigation lights begin. The Trent is joined by the Three Rivers, which flow side by side and straight for the last 3km, and by the Stainforth & Keadby Canal. On the other side of Keadby another Warping Drain joins.

Grove Wharf and Neap House Wharves have more shipping while wind turbines stand on the ridge to the east. Opposite Amcotts, Flixborough Wharf was built in 1938 in anticipation of the Second World War, when a hit on the bridge would have disrupted **Scunthorpe**'s steel production. Instead, the big bang came at Flixborough Stather industrial estate in 1974 when leaking cyclohexane at the Nypro UK works exploded, killing 28 and flattening the site.

King's Ferry Wharf was built at Burton Stather in 1969 by Victor Waddington, the region's champion of moving freight by inland waterway.

The Cliff brings a steep hillside with gorse next to the river, untypical of this river, before diverging to Alkborough.

The Trent becomes the Humber at Trent Ness, Trent End, Apex or Trent Falls, where it is joined by the Ouse. Trent Falls suggests something more serious than the small race which develops. Apex Light marks the end of a training wall which covers opposite Faxfleet Ness. The Humber, Abus Fluvius to the Romans, had more cutting power when the sea level was lower. It drains 260,000km^2 and has a 6.1m tidal range, second only to the Severn in Britain. The main route begins with the Whitton Channel and is subject to very rapid changes above Hull so the light floats and light buoys are moved as necessary.

The sediment movement also affects banks. Whitton Sand, the Humber Wildfowl Refuge, is becoming a permanent island for pinkfooted geese and landing is prohibited from 1st September to 20th February. The Humber has 120,000 winter waterfowl including 31,000 knots, 4,100 curlews, 5,200 redshanks, 27,000 golden plovers, 24,000 lapwings, shelducks and blackheaded gulls. The RSPB said they were at risk of permanent damage from pollution, port expansion, cockling and sea level rise.

Whitton Channel passes the Devil's Causeway and Whitton to Whitton Ness. Crossing to the northern or East Riding of Yorkshire shore involves intersecting the route of the Ermine Street crossing, the Roman road from York to Lincoln, the Romans having their Petuaria fort at Brough. These days Brough has its aerodrome and the British Aerospace works and hangars.

Brough Roads become the Redcliff Channel after Oyster Ness which runs inside Redcliff Middle Sand and Redcliff Sand, real sand not mud, for once. Disused quarries behind the ness give way after a fire beacon to **North Ferriby** where the 1000–800 BC Hasholme Iron Age plank boat was found.

The 30m chalk Lincoln Ridge runs from Sewerby to the Lincolnshire fens but, during glaciation, was breached between **Hessle** and **Barton** where the Little Eastern Glacier on the east met Lake Humber on the west. Hessle Whelps are a steep sea which forms through this gap when a westerly wind opposes the flood and can be dangerous to small craft. There can also be eddies. The *Lincoln Castle* floating restaurant was the Humber ferry until 1978, running across the estuary to Barton Waterside.

The constriction allowed the Humber Bridge to be built in 1981, carrying the A15 although most traffic still uses the M62 route. With a 1.41km main span and a total length of 2.22km, it was the world's longest single span suspension bridge. The 156m piers were the first to use hollow reinforced concrete piers in a major suspension bridge and the 44,000km of suspension wire give the deck 30m clearance above the water, perhaps indicated by the tiny windmill beside and almost under the Hessle end of the bridge. From here the estuary steadily widens out past Hull to Spurn Head.

The Humber Bridge beyond a sandbank, seen from the Redcliff Channel.

41 River Nene

The short cut to where the sea was

I'm now arriv'd – thanks to the Gods! –
Through pathways rough and muddy,
A certain sign that makin roads
Is no this people's study:
Altho' I'm no wi' Scripture cram'd,
I'm sure the Bible says
That heedless sinners shall be damn'd
Unless they mend their ways.
Robert Burns

Few rivers have changed as much in recent centuries as the Nene. It still rises above West Haddon, the name coming from the nine wells at its source, and it still flows northeast to the Wash. Downstream of Peterborough it used to flow via Ramsey and March to the Wash at Wisbech. Most of that route still exists although it is little more than a ditch at Yaxley, from Outwell it goes to the River Great Ouse at Denver Sluice and the Wash is now some 17km north of Wisbech. Powered craft tend to use the King's Dyke and **Whittlesey** Dyke to reach March from Peterborough.

The biggest change came in 1728 with an artificial cut from Peterborough, the 20km to Guyhirn being almost straight. The river was tidal from Woodston Staunch above Peterborough until 1937 when Dog-in-a-Doublet Sluice was built at North Side, a fish pass being added in 1998. Three huge guillotine gates stand across the river, a tiny Environment Agency notice just in front advising of their presence. A pair of staircase locks to the Thorney River have been converted to a sluice.

The Dog-in-a-Doublet public house is now closed. The name came from a leather jerkin made by the publican's wife for the decoy man's terrier after it lost all its fur to skin disease.

High water is two hours and ten minutes before Dover high water but flows outward begin three hours before Dover high water and inward from five hours and twenty minutes after Dover high water. Levels vary from day to day. Until the mid 19th century lighters carried materials to form temporary staunches to deal with shallows. The water remains shallow, landings are few and difficult and the channel lies along the line of the prevailing wind, levées helping to make it a wind tunnel. Pillboxes occasionally defend the line.

Formerly under Lake Fenland, these peat fens are artificially drained land reclaimed from marshland to give rich alluvial farmland. There is hardly a building or road near the river beyond the B1040 crossing until Guyhirn but there are cormorants, herons, swans, mallards, shelducks, moorhens, oystercatchers, lapwings and larks.

Running parallel on the south side between Peterborough and Guyhirn is Morton's Leam. Cut in 1478–90 by Bishop John Morton of Ely, it is 12m wide and 1.2m deep, the first large straight cut in the fens to improve the gradient, bypassing part of the Old Course of the River Nene. Between the two channels is another Wash, much of it RSPB reserve with blacktailed godwits, redshanks and wildfowl.

Passing Bassenhally Moor, Popley's Gull is a kink in what is otherwise an

The Dog-in-a-Doublet Sluice at North Side.

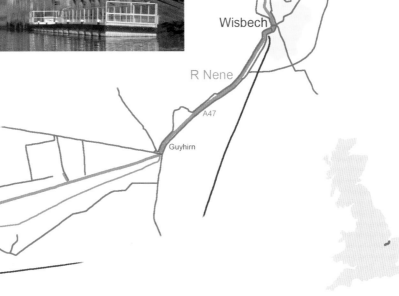

From Popley's Gull the cut runs straight for another 10km.

Eel nets at the side of the river.

unbroken straight cut of 16km. An aerial where the New Wryde Drain joins marks the point where Peterborough is left, the river now being entirely in Cambridgeshire. Eel nets may be pegged along the side of the river. The Meridian is crossed at the start of Adventurers' Land, named after those who put up the venture capital for the drainage scheme. Also crossed is the line of a buried Roman causeway and, at Guyhirn, a former railway line with its piers remaining and the busy A47, which is to follow most of the way to Wisbech. Morton's Leam is joined just above the road bridge, bringing with it the Nene Way footpath which is to follow to Guy's Head. Seals may come up this far.

From here it looks more like a river and less a drainage channel. The peat is left behind and it becomes silt fen.

Elgood's brewery at Wisbech.

The Rose Tavern and other traditional riverside buildings in Wisbech are now protected by a utilitarian wall.

A pontoon is moored for those who need to land. There are buttercups and cow parsley and a barn owl may hunt over the reeds. The agriculture turns increasingly to orchards although the conspicuous trees are a screen of poplars at Cold Harbour Corner where there is a chimney facing across to another chimney and an aerial by Primrose Farm. At Bevis Hall control passes from the Environment Agency to the Port of Wisbech.

Wisbech, on the Wash coast until medieval times, was a market town and capital of the fens, named after the River Wissey which formerly flowed here. The Georgian building which has housed Elgood's brewery since 1795 stands on the bank in a 1.6ha Georgian garden with a yard of ale maze. They were pioneers in producing low alcohol bitter, using shallow open copper cooling vessels for hopped wort, unique in England although much used in Belgium. The odour of malt drifts across the river.

The waterfront has Dutch styling with the North Brinks as one of the best Georgian streets in Britain. Peckover House was the town house of a Georgian Quaker banking family in 1722, with fine rococo wood panelled rooms, carved mantlepieces and plaster, in an 8,000m² walled Victorian garden with 300 year old orange trees, maidenhair and tulip trees with a thatched barn. It must have influenced Octavia Hill, who was born in the town in 1838 and was to be a London housing reformer and cofounder of the National Trust. A 21m statue commemorates another local reformer, Thomas Clarkson, a slavery abolishionist. He is also featured, along with the port of Wisbech, the original manuscript of *Great Expectations* and transcripts of Burns' *On a Suicide* and *On Rough Roads*, in the Wisbech & Fenland Museum of 1846, one of the oldest purpose built museums in the country.

A Norman castle is incorporated into a Regency House. The church of SS Peter & Paul has Norman work and a monument to 18th century sculptor Joseph Nollekens and hosts the annual Rose Fair. Until about 1860 small Whirling Cakes were sold locally in memory of a woman baking cakes in the 17th century but carried away over the church by the Devil in a whirlwind. Current celebrations include Apple Day.

The town was used for filming *David Copperfield*, *Micawber* and *Martin Chuzzlewit* and it was Walbeach in Dorothy L Sayers' *The Nine Tailors*. In the 11th century the 2.13m tall but lazy Tom Hickathrift carried out many feats, including killing the Wisbech giant who was terrorizing the area. There are plenty of hostelries facing the river including the Rose Tavern, Red Lion, Hare & Hounds Hotel and White Lion Hotel.

A concrete riverwall faced with garish red brick was added on each side in 2010. It is to be hoped that it will become mellower with time. Flows out begin three and a half hours before Dover high water, ten minutes after local high water, and flows in begin five hours and twenty

minutes after Dover high water for three hours. Flows are fast, especially at the bottom of the tide, tides being reduced by strong southerly winds. There can be a race under the Town Bridge carrying the A1101. The old line of the River Nene from Outwell became the Wisbech Canal but this was only fed from the Nene at high water and was abandoned. A barrage has been considered to the north of Wisbech, maybe even north of Sutton Bridge. This would have solved the problems of the Wisbech Canal but it has been lost for too long.

Below the double bridge the river turns away from a windmill and past a street with such premises as the Tasty China and a warehouse converted to residential use. Wisbech Yacht Harbour has pontoon moorings in the river upstream of 800m of quays which take ships to 2,000t, handling timber, grain and fertilizer. There are navigation lights on poles along the bank from here.

Blackbacked and herring gulls are found on the river as it moves out into open country. The right bank becomes Norfolk but as recently as the 16th century this was the coastline, wrack floating up as a reminder. An aerial marks a sewage works at Ferry Corner, the ferry also being long gone.

High pylons carry three sets of powerlines across above Foul Anchor with another set beyond. The river passes into Lincolnshire just before being joined by the North Level Main Drain. Vermuyden's original sluice of 1649 is now isolated on the east side of the current

Wisbech warehouse gets a new lease of life.

Sutton Bridge's Cross Keys Bridge, the Nene's last crossing point.

Hovercraft at the mouth of the river.

line of the Nene. Telford built a sluice on the west side. George Stephenson added another in 1859 but it bulged seven years later and the walls had to be rebuilt with a footbridge added as a strut between them. A fourth sluice was added upstream in 1871 to be safe. At the far side of Tydd St Mary's Marsh the South Holland Main Drain joins through a sluice.

St Matthew's church at **Sutton Bridge** is the only flint church in Lincolnshire. The Grade II Cross Keys Bridge is the last on the river, the third on the site since 1825. When built in 1897 it also carried a railway but that has gone and it now takes only the A17. The 51m span is swung by hydraulic power, being the first bridge to have the control cabin on top and turning with the bridge.

Flows outward begin four and a half hours before Dover high water, ten minutes before local high water, and flows inward from four hours twenty minutes after Dover high water. Flows can exceed 7km/h. Control passes from the Port of Wisbech to the Port of Sutton Bridge. Docks built in 1881 collapsed a month later. A new port with 350m of quay serves Europe, Scandinavia and the Baltic. Behind is a golf course. Hole 9 is the approximate place where King John is supposed to have lost his jewellery with the rest of his baggage train after signing *Magna Carta*.

The Nene Outfall Cut or Wisbech Cut was designed by Rennie and built in 1827–30 by Telford, who diverted the old channel and scoured out the required depth in a few months. Users now include small workboats and even hovercraft, well suited to the Wash which drains large areas at low water.

At Guy's Head a pair of 12m brick daymark towers by Rennie have stood beside the river like entrance pillars since 1831. They are called lighthouses although not lit and are becoming increasingly hard to see as trees grow up around them. Ornithologist Peter Scott lived in the east one, which inspired Paul Gallico's *The Snow Goose*, and there is now a Peter Scott Walk. Lutton Leam joins from the west side through Scottish Sluice.

Flows out begin five hours before Dover high water and in from three hours twenty minutes after Dover high water. Depths and lines change frequently in the Wash despite a training wall. A sperm whale stranded on the sand and mud was the first to be subject to an attempt at refloating. Birdwatching and bird shooting are local activities, upstaged by the RAF Holbeach bombing range to the west. Across Breast Sand is a 10m high trial sandbank reservoir, now growing grass on its sides.

Daymark at Guy's Head, formerly occupied by Peter Scott.

42 New Bedford River

The tidal bypass

These Fens have ofttimes been by Water drown'd
Science a remedy in water found
The power of Steam she said shall be employ'd
And the Destroyer by Itself destroy'd

Anon

The River Great Ouse or Bedford Ouse rises at Greatworth and flows northeast to the Wash. It can be tidal from Brownshill Staunch although the range is limited and, even then, only at spring tides. The guillotine gates allow the lock to be reversed, tied open in times of flood. Significant changes in level can be handled, however, and there are levées from here. Two barges are moored below the lock as a floating landing stage for boat crews. A large gravel conveyor high over the river makes the lock easy to locate.

In 1947 a serious breach of the south bank flooded many square kilometres of Ouse Fen, the hole being sealed by building a dam around army amphibious vehicles. Formerly there were osier beds. Willows and reeds line the banks and there are marsh marigolds now. Birds range from terns to swans and cormorants while bream and roach live in the water.

The spire draws attention to St Mary's church at Bluntisham which has an unusual three sided apse from the 14th century. The Queen Anne rectory, now Bluntisham House with a doorway from Slepe Hall in St Ives, is where Dorothy L Sayers was raised.

Bandy, the precursor to ice hockey, was invented at Bury Fen, a site used for major ice skating contests.

Also beginning here in 1836 were builders merchants Jewsons, who had limekilns at the entrance to what is now Westview Marina and the Quiet Waters Boat Haven.

Piers from the former St Ives–Ely railway stand on each side of the river and the Roman Car Dyke also is crossed. A Romano-Gallic bronze statue, possibly of Emperor Commodus, was found in 1826 and is now in the British Museum.

Earith, meaning muddy landing place, has a high street with fine early 19th century houses. The Crown, Riverview Hotel and Bridge End Stores advertise themselves to boaters.

Blue dragonflies hover around the reeds. Of greater interest are grey seals which come up this far and are enjoyed by all except anglers.

The Old Bedford River leads off to the left before the river arrives at the Hermitage, a most interesting spot. Although the Great Ouse is tidal upstream, Hermitage Lock has its gates fitted so it is non tidal downstream. Instead, the tidal flow is taken by the New Bedford River or Hundred Foot Drain which ebbs for ten and a half hours and floods for two hours, resulting in some fast flows, like a bore without a front wave, perhaps peaking at nearly 10km/h on springs. As a result, hire craft are not allowed to use it. Many would not do so anyway as the River Great Ouse, Old West River, Ely Ouse or Ten Mile River downstream of the lock is prettier despite being 16km longer and much slower. However, the New Bedford is a unique channel. Like other fenland tidal channels, it requires the user to have done some prior research on tide times.

It is an artificial cut which runs almost straight across the fens. The work was carried out about 1650 for the Duke of Bedford, who hoped to recover the losses made by his father on the Old Bedford River which runs parallel some 200m to 1km away. Cornelius Vermuyden

Brownshill Staunch, the tidal limit, with a gravel conveyor.

and his Dutch navvies were drainage experts who turned the fens into some of the richest agricultural land in Britain, for their pains being hated by the local inhabitants who had earned their livelihoods by fishing and wildfowling although the work has done much to prevent subsequent flooding. The unique feature is that the two rivers each have a high outer bank and a low inner one so that the whole of the area between them, the Hundred Foot Washes, can contain floodwater or storm surges from the Wash and is regularly drowned out in the winter. Embanking of the channels and 5m shrinkage of the peat since the 17th century have left the rivers above the surrounding fenland. In addition to the three major channels, including the River Delph which runs between the Old and New Bedford Rivers, there are various other channels all running parallel and forming the main method of draining the fens.

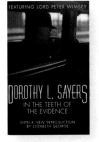

The New Bedford River is tidal only below Mepal on neaps. The river is weed free and muddy, which leaves it free of swans but with high silty banks which make exit difficult as the level drops, the river depth varying from 300mm to 1m. It is an extremely peaceful river except from September to January on Mondays to Saturdays when duck shooting is taking place.

The southwest end of the Hundred Foot Washes contains a large but unseen earthwork, the Bulwark. Perhaps built by the Romans, it was modified in Cromwellian times.

The Washes themselves are the largest area of regularly flooded grazing marshland in Britain and one of the world's finest wetlands. They form a textbook example of conservation farming with cattle grazing selected areas but not others, no spraying or fertilizing, progressive cropping of osier beds and willow holts to give a range of habitats and a permanent grassland in summer accompanied by a rich flora with an enormous range of insects, animals and birds.

Reeds, thistles, docks and purple loosestrife are prominent amongst the plants and 44% of British aquatic plant species are present. Vegetation ranges from common reed sweet grass, reed canary grass and tufted hair grass through meadow rue, yellowcress, bittersweet and large bracket fungi to such rarities as sulphur water dropwort, slender spikerush, mousetail, whorled water milfoil, tasteless water pepper and fringed water lily.

Animal life includes foxes, rabbits, stoats, weasels, voles, harvest mice, otters and mink.

The Hermitage. The tidal New Bedford River goes under the A1123 while the lock leads to the non tidal lower River Great Ouse.

The higher outer bank of the New Bedford River.

It is the birdlife, however, which makes the Washes of international importance and Britain's most significant inland site for waterfowl. Of prime importance are the 3,000 Bewick's swans which overwinter here from November until March, a leading European site and the largest British concentration of them, and the blacktailed godwit for which this is the main British nesting site. Also present in the winter are great crested grebe, whitefronted goose, water rail, kingfisher, fieldfare, redwing, over 40,000 wigeon and the largest British concentration of whooper swans. Ruff joust in the spring and in the summer there are garganey, shelduck, lapwing, redshank, reed warbler, goldfinch, redpoll and several hundred pairs of yellow wagtails. Little grebe, heron, mallard, teal, gadwall, pintail, shoveler, tufted duck, pochard, goosander, redbreasted

merganser, snipe, little owl, shorteared owl and numerous rarer species may be seen at any time, the result of the farming methods employed and the influence of the Wildfowl Trust, RSPB and Cambridge & Isle of Ely Naturalists' Trust who own over half of the Washes.

Despite the generally straight line, the river does bend to and fro and visibility is often not as far as might be expected.

At Sutton Gault the bridge has fenders at different heights to allow for different states of flooding rather than for the limited tidal variation. The public house sign adjacent is beautifully simple, no words, no background, just a thin metal rectangle with a slim metal anchor swinging freely inside it.

A bypass bridge separates the hidden riverside Gault Hole from the village of Mepal. Next to the Three Pickerels is a house which has been designed to fit into a triangular site, one end, the front and the back being visible simultaneously and the pitched roof, which changes size halfway along, undoubtedly having been a nightmare to design.

Conspicuous landmarks are now lacking until approaching Oxlode where a single dark box on top of the embankment on the right is a bird hide with opening window slots overlooking the Purls Bridge nature reserve. Most of the hides are on the far side of the Hundred Foot Washes.

Near the Grunty Fen Drain pumping station a system has been rigged up for collecting driftwood from the river and a large stack of firewood results on the bank.

Lying 3km beyond the village is the girder bridge which carries the railway line between Ely and Peterborough. This is the most conspicuous feature visible on the river because of the distance over which it can be seen, although jets usually make their presence more obviously noticed as they fly over.

After the railway bridge is the Hundred Foot Pumping Station which lifts water from the Main Drain to the New Bedford River. Its history is perhaps typical of developments in drainage of the fens as a whole. In 1756 a windmill was built to pump water from the drainage channel to the main river. In 1830 a 60kW steam engine driving a 12m diameter scoop wheel was installed, the wheel being increased to 15m diameter in 1882. In 1914 the steam engine was replaced with a 300kW model able to pump $3.3m^3/s$ and this was joined by a 170kW oil engine in 1926, able to handle an additional $1.7m^3/s$. In 1951 the steam engine was replaced by a 400kW oil engine.

The river crosses from Cambridgeshire to Norfolk along the line of the A1101 although the road itself runs along the side and does not cross until Suspension Bridge where there is no longer a suspension bridge.

Something else which used to cross near here was the Old Croft River which drained the Lark and Cam via Wisbech to the Wash. Now it feeds only a few ditches into the Middle Leading Drain, a shadow of its former self. The joke is completed by the Croft Hills down its east bank which are totally below sea level and must be

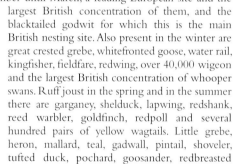

The Three Pickerels at Mepal.

168

The river stretches away from Mepal.

The prominent railway bridge.

the only range of dry land hills in the world where the height of the loftiest peak is negative.

The following footbridge across the river is puzzling because its method of support is far from obvious, not least because the lattice girder sides are covered with lengths of wood. It serves the Welney Wildfowl Refuge, claimed to be the best viewpoint for the Hundred Foot Washes. The bridge allows people to look out without being noticed although viewing is generally done from the public hides or the heated observatory for members. The 3km² site is flooded in winter with many birds around a series of lakes running parallel to the river. In summer there are a wide variety of wild flowers. Gulls are also seen more often now.

Powerlines cross and then sluices on the left mark the confluence with the River Delph which has followed the northwest side of the Hundred Foot Washes but switches across at this point. A little further on, the New Bedford River crosses the line of the Roman road from Brampton to Water Newton.

At one time the River Great Ouse reached the Wash at Wisbech. It may have been diverted to the Roman Littleport to King's Lynn canal following the floods of 1236.

Denver Sluice, beyond the Jenyns Arms, is the key to the fens drainage. It was built in 1652 by Vermuyden to hold back flood tides but allow river water out at low water. It burst in 1713 when a river flood met a tidal surge. It was rebuilt in 1750 by Labelye and again by Rennie in 1834, this time with gates facing both ways, since modified to guillotine gates. The Cut-off Channel and River Great Ouse join above the sluices with the New and Old Bedford Rivers and Well

Creek joining below and the River Great Ouse and Relief Channel leaving, the latter through additional guillotine gates, the most complex arrangement of major channels in Britain. Unlike the Gloucester & Sharpness Canal, which bypasses a difficult stretch of the River Severn and then returns boats beyond it, the Relief Channel of 2003 abandons boats in the middle of nowhere and

169

The Main Drain reaches the Hundred Foot Pumping Station.

Looking across the Hundred Foot Washes.

The Welney Wildfowl Refuge's mysterious footbridge.

does not allow them back onto the River Great Ouse. It takes much of the water, however, meaning that the only navigation route to the sea is silting badly and sandbanks are forming and moving about. Muddy banks are exposed and landings difficult, willow mattresses being used to prevent unwanted scour.

The New Bedford River is the only channel to flow without obstruction into the River Great Ouse. Flows inward run for three to three and a half hours with high water four hours and ten minutes before Dover high water. It crosses peat fen formerly under Lake Fenland, now rich alluvial farmland, and is followed by the Fen Rivers Way to King's Lynn.

To the east is the restored Denver corn windmill, home of inventor Captain Manby in 1765. Along the banks are reeds, cow parsley and buttercups with oystercatchers.

The Old Bedford River and Well Creek join in quick succession at Salters Lode.

The A1122 crosses at **Downham Market**, a Saxon fen island town. Noted for its black and white clock, it is where Nelson went to school. Grouped around the crossing are the towering Heygates Mill, the original Sue Ryder outlet centre and Hermitage Hall Collectors' World with its Dickens' Victorian Christmas and Dame Barbara Cartland rooms.

The muddy water can have fierce eddies. The geology changes from peat to silt fen. Reedmace appears and an owl box is sited on the bank. Blackheaded gulls are here and swallows nest under the bridge at Stowbridge.

Control of the river passes from the Environment Agency to King's Lynn Port Authority. Crabb's Abbey occupies the west bank.

A conspicuous line of poplar trees mark the abutments of a former railway crossing at Wiggenhall St Mary Magdalen, this bend having been considered for a barrage to be used for scouring out the river when discharged. Scour might also have affected the lefthand upstream pier of the road bridge by the Cock public house, appearing to have settled significantly. The church has 15th century glass in the north aisle and notable Jacobean panels. Priory cottages date from the 17th century.

On the other hand, the church at Wiggenhall St Peter stands roofless on the bank of the river. The church at Wiggenhall St Germans has richly carved pews and stands by the Crown & Anchor.

The new St Germans pumping station serves the Middle Level Main Drain and protects 700km^2 of low land, being followed quickly by Mill Basin and Smeeth Lode joining the 5km Eau Brink Cut. Sets of piers stand in the river but only larks break the tranquility.

Two sets of powerlines run from a power station and a muddy slipway descends the bank as the Relief Channel joins through a sluice. A large industrial building occupies much of the bank as far as the A47 crossing, followed by a spare set of piers and the final bridge. Boats are moored in the river as the River Nar confluence is approached.

Bishop's Lynn took its name from the Welsh llyn, lake. It received its charter in 1204 but was renamed **King's Lynn** after Henry VIII seized the manor during the Dissolution. A Civil War bombardment by Cromwell killed 80 following a five week siege because the town sided with the king, one of the few places in East Anglia to do so. The Black Death killed a further 7,000. The medieval street pattern remains. Originally built on three islands, the town suffered badly in the 1953 and 1978 floods.

There are 620m of river quays. In the 14th century this was England's third port and it still takes ships to 2,000t. Beyond Mill Fleet are silos and a loading gantry. Hampton Court is a 14th century house and warehouse. St Margaret's House of 1475 has the last Hanseatic warehouse in Britain. The large 16th century warehouse containing the Green Quay Wash Discovery Centre is near Bradley's Restaurant & Wine Bar. Behind

The River Delph enters the New Bedford River through sluice gates.

is St Margaret's church of 1101, one of the largest town churches in the country, with a Georgian nave of 1741 after a storm brought down the earlier spire. It has two of England's largest brasses from the 14th century, a 17th century moon clock which gives the next high water, a fine 18th century rococo organ case and columns which are 'slarntendicular', one word to illuminate the architecture, dialect and sense of humour of this part of Norfolk.

Thoresby College is Tudor. The 1421 Trinity Guildhall, one of two in the town, is in chequered flint and became the town hall with Jacobean porch, Victorian council chamber and Tales of the Old Gaol House in the adjacent 1784 building with its original cells, some of the finest civic regalia in existence including the gold and enamel King John cup of about 1340 and the *Red Register*, one of the oldest paper books in existence. There is also a Victorian Town House Museum of Lynn Life. The medieval Clifton House has a five storey watchtower. Facing Pur Fleet is the 1683 Palladian Custom House with a lantern on top and a statue of Charles II over the door.

A house with a diamond brick in the wall is where the heart of Shady Meg Read was supposed to have hit it on bursting from her body when burned for witchcraft in 1590 and was even said to have bounced on into the river. Alternatively, it may have been that of a maid accused of murdering her mistress in 1531 and lowered into a cauldron of boiling water. Witch Mary Taylor was burned for murdering the landlady of the Queen's Arms, her assistant, George Smith, being hanged. Mary Smith was hanged in 1616 for selling her soul to the Devil to get rid of the other cheese sellers from the market.

More positively, Fanny Burney, the first major female English novelist, was born here in 1752. Five years later George Vancouver was born, sailing with Cook, becoming a commander, charting Hawaii and southwest Australia, acquiring Western Australia and beginning negotiations with the Spanish for British Columbia. John Smith, the Father of Virginia, was apprenticed here and John Mason founded New Hampshire and became Governor of Newfoundland.

Greyfriars Tower and garden featured in the BBC's *Restoration* and *David Copperfield* and *Martin Chuzzlewit* were filmed here.

A pedestrian ferry crosses to West Lynn.

St George's Guildhall of 1406 in chequered flint is the largest complete 15th century guildhall surviving in England, housing King's Lynn Arts Centre. Shakespeare's company performed here. The Corn Market Hall of 1854 with its classical facade is now a concert hall.

St Nicholas' chapel is the largest surviving parochial chapel in England, noted for the carved angels in its 15th century roof. True's Yard has a Fishing Heritage Museum in restored 1850s and 1920s fishermen's cottages, the last remaining such yard in King's Lynn.

An owl box below Downham Market.

The New Bedford River rejoins the River Great Ouse at Denver Sluice.

Stowbridge with swallows nesting under the bridge and Dutch building styles.

Wiggenhall St Peter church, now roofless.

172

The Relief Channel returns to the River Great Ouse.

The final reach down to the A47 at King's Lynn.

A 16th century pilot house has a round tower. Alexandra Dock and Bentinck Dock serve Europe and the Baltic, handling timber, fertilizer and grain. Fisher Fleet became home for smacks and seine netters with fishing vessels bringing in shrimps, cockles and mussels from the Wash. Blubberhouses Creek sent ships to Spain in the whaling days. Sea trout, eels and flounders are found in the river, as are blackbacked and herring gulls, great crested grebes and avocets.

A final set of powerlines pass high over the river next to the sewage works and the diverted Babingley River now enters the Great Ouse here. The Marsh Cut was straightened in 1852 and the Lynn Channel is now directed by training walls which cover at half tide. Flows start out three and a half hours before Dover high water and in from four hours and twenty minutes after Dover high water, sometimes in excess of 4km/h, although tides are influenced by the wind and big spring tides often arrive late. Large vessels use the channel only at high water. Beyond Vinegar Middle lie the sand and mud banks of Bull Dog Sand while the bed often changes further out in the Wash.

Traditional wharf buildings at King's Lynn.

The Custom House at King's Lynn.

Distance
73km from Brownhill Staunch to the Wash

OS 1:50,000 Sheets
*131 Boston
& Spalding
132 North West
Norfolk
143 Ely & Wisbech
154 Bury
St Edmunds*

Admiralty Charts
*1200 Wash Ports
(1:37,500). Lynn
Cut (1:37,500).
King's Lynn
(1:10,000)*

Tidal Constants
King's Lynn:
*HW Dover −0430,
LW Dover −0240*
West Stones:
*HW Dover −0440,
LW Dover −0400*

Sea Area
Humber

Rescue
*Inshore lifeboat:
Hunstanton
All weather lifeboat:
Wells
Hovercraft:
Hunstanton*

173

43 River Bure

Mills and marshes

There after supper lit by lantern light
  Warm in the cabin I could lie secure
And hear against the polished sides at night
  The lap lap lapping of the weedy Bure,
A whispering and watery Norfolk sound
Telling of all the moonlit reeds around.

John Betjeman

One of the most important of the Broads rivers, the River Bure rises at Melton Constable and flows southeast across Norfolk to Breydon Water. On the way it connects many of the broads and provides the only link to the southern broads.

The broads were 12–14th century peat diggings, shown

Wroxham Broad at the head of the tidal River Bure.

Passing the entrance to Salhouse Broad.

A converted windmill betwen Hoveton and Horning.

by underwater peat ridges along parish boundaries. They form Britain's only lowland wetland national park.

Wroxham Broad is one of the larger ones, 1.2km x 400m, covering 45ha and used for sailing. Upstream, **Wroxham** is a major Broads boating centre while **Hoveton** has Roy's, the largest village store in the world.

The River Bure is tidal from Wroxham Broad but is far from typical of tidal rivers. It is heavily tree lined as far as the River Ant. Ashes, alders, willows and birches pour down the banks to merge with reedmace, reeds and then marsh marigolds so that the banks themselves are rarely visible. The water is heavily used by cruisers but is equally busy with swans, herons, Canada geese, mallards, great crested grebes, coots, moorhens and blackheaded gulls. Far from being upset by all the activity, anglers seem more friendly than is often the case.

Almost opposite Wroxham Broad is Hoveton Great Broad. This covers 42ha and was used as a short cut by wherries to miss out some of the river bends but is now private and used as a nature reserve with swallowtail butterflies, Norfolk hawker dragonflies and nesting terns. A nature trail on railway sleepers laid over 3m deep mud can only be reached by boat.

Beyond Salhouse Little Broad is Salhouse Broad, which is open to boats. Opposite Sedge Fen and Hoveton Marshes is Decoy Broad, which is private. Indeed, there are often small channels disappearing into the greenery, sometimes with private notices by them or even padlocked gates across them.

A windmill has been converted to a private house with commanding views on one corner. Presumably it was not surrounded by trees at the time it was built.

Hoveton Little Broad or Blackhouse Broad allows navigation during Easter week and from Whitsun until the end of October but does not permit landing.

One of the largest villages on the river is Horning with Lower Street, facing across to Woodbastwick Fens & Marshes, which are private. It has the appearance of containing many second houses or retirement homes for those able to afford them, often with channels or docks off the river for moorings. Some houses are reed thatched and everywhere is kept very smart, Horning being claimed to be the prettiest Broads village. At Horning there is a Mississippi style paddle steamer moored near the Swan Inn, followed by the Staithe 'n' Willow and the New Inn, the oldest one in Horning and with the only day boat basin in the Broads. The Old Ferry Inn by the passenger ferry was the abbey mead store and it has the ghost of a beautiful girl in a green cloak who passes through the bar and goes into the river or may be seen on the bank nearer the abbey, possibly raped and murdered by drunken monks from the abbey. It was a venue used by Arthur Ransome. The Ferry Marina and Wood Dyke complete the village's inlets.

A kilometre boardwalk down Cockshoot Dyke leads to Cockshoot Broad, which is private and dammed. The broad was badly silted and ecologically dead but a metre of mud was pumped out in 1982 and it now has clear water with hornwort, bladderwort and other species. In the spring the bittern might be heard booming.

The Bure Marshes are a nature reserve. Next to them, Ranworth Dam blocks Ranworth Broad, closed to boats, with four wherries abandoned at the entrance. There is a boarded nature trail and a floating thatched conservation centre to view tufted ducks, shelducks, swallows, house martins and more. Malthouse Broad may be used, however.

St Helen's church at Ranworth has been called the cathedral of the Broads. Its 15th century painted rood screen is one of the best in Britain with illustration of saints, lions, dogs, swans and ducks. Its tower has 97 steps.

Horning Hall accompanies the chapel of the abbey hospice. It was the fatal capsize of a dayboat here in 2003 which led to the Broads Authority Act of 2009 to control boating on the Broads more closely.

A channel bypasses a meander round Ward Marsh, a cut which is particularly busy with boat traffic. At the western end is the confluence with the River Ant. The eastern end of the loop is still in use as it leads to Fleet Dyke and South Walsham Broad. The scenery now is more obviously marshland. High water here is an hour and a half after Dover.

The Benedictine St Benet's Abbey was built near the Bure's north bank in 816, being rebuilt in 1020 by Cnut with a carved gatehouse, fishponds and perimeter wall enclosing 14ha. In 1066 the Saxon monks supported King Harold and held out against a four month siege by the Normans until they were let in by the monk Ethelwold in return for being made abbot. The Normans allowed him to be ordained then hung him, his ghost sometimes being seen suspended from the eastern end of the abbey. The abbot was also bishop of Norwich. In 1537 the bishopric lands were surrendered to Henry VIII but the monastery lands were retained and still provide income to the bishop of Norwich, who continues to hold the title of abbot of St Benet's. A service is held here on the first Sunday in August by the bishop, who arrives by wherry in his regalia, when the Norfolk Broads are blessed. The abbey faces a modern cross further down the bank. Astonishingly, a Georgian windmill was built in the middle of the site in the 18th century with the western arch of the abbey inside the mill and forming a structural part of it.

At Thurne Mouth the River Thurne joins on the outside of a bend which is so extreme that it looks more like a layout prepared by man than by nature. Just up from the confluence are two windmills, including the white Thurne windpump of 1820. The Weavers' Way footpath also arrives and follows the Bure.

Two more mills stand at the edge of Upton Marshes. Beyond Upton Dyke is Clippesby Mill.

Horizon Craft, Bridge Craft and Anchor Craft are suddenly met together with the Bridge Stores at **Acle** Bridge, a venue with a complex history. It was an execution site with bodies hung in the bridge arches and left to decompose, where they obstructed navigation. In 1768 Edmund Mallett was hung for the capital offence of horse stealing. He had been trying to support four wives and their children, none of whom knew of the existence of the others.

In about 1930 the concrete Acle Bridge or Wey Bridge was constructed to carry the A1064. A man who murdered his wife had his own throat slit by her brother. A year later the brother's throat was cut by the skeleton ghost. The appearance of blood on the bridge each April 7th made the story additionally macabre.

The Bridge Inn and restaurant has a circular room in the garden with a huge conical thatched roof and a wherry weathervane. Another windmill stands northeast of the bridge.

The water and banks steadily become more muddy from here. Acle Dyke leads to Acle with its thatched church. Muck Fleet, with a dam across the end, feeds in next to another windmill and there is a further windmill at Stokesby, which also has a Ferry Inn.

A stern wheeler moored outside the Swan Inn at Horning.

Apparently a regular perch for a heron.

The A47 and Thorpe–Great Yarmouth railway each bend round the river, their only bend between Acle and Yarmouth. There are two windmills near the bend, the second being the 1883 Stracey Arms wind drainage pump, a restored four storey mill with boat cap, all supported on 12m piles. It contains an exhibition of Broads windpumps, a staithe serving both the mill and a shop. A couple

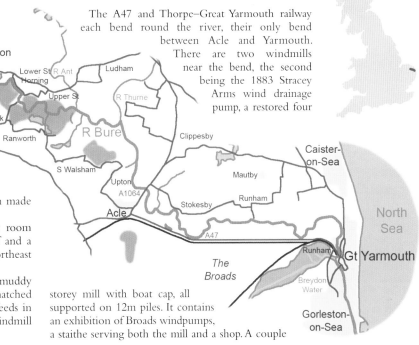

Part of the waterfront in Horning.

A desirable little retreat at Upper Street on the Bure Marshes.

The wherry Albion, *now based in Ludham as a trip boat.*

St Benet's Abbey with a windmill built inside. The other arch of the abbey is a structural member across the inside of the mill.

of derelict mills follow beyond Runham. Two more with sails are met at Mautby Marsh Farm and near Three Mile House. In addition, the turbines of a wind farm stand over towards the coast.

As the tidal silt becomes more conspicuous, so do such marine plants as sea aster and wrack with egrets, oystercatchers and blackbacked and herring gulls. One of the channel marker posts has a pair of boots nailed to it for no obvious reason.

Beyond North Denes aerodrome and heliport serving

The restored Stracey Arms mill.

Landscape with reeds, derelict mills and diggers.

Mautby Marsh Farm's mill.

The mill near Three Mile House.

the North Sea platforms the river eases into the back of Great Yarmouth, accompanied by a high stepped concrete wall as it passes Yarmouth Marina and Johnny's Diner. Currents accelerate past marine industry premises towards another Runham.

Built from 1261 to 1400, the town walls are one of the most complete sets in England, including the substantial 13th century brick North West Tower on the east bank which guards the White Swan and the northwestern approach to Yarmouth. Large craft are prevented from coming up the river by low bridges. Amongst these are a set of arches which carried railway lines but now nothing more than a cycle track, the corroded holes in the metal suggesting they are suspect even for that purpose.

The River Bure joins the River Yare at the east end of Breydon Water, which can be rough with high winds and may have a race at the confluence, the start of the fast run through Yarmouth.

Distance
37km from Wroxham Broad to the River Yare

OS 1:50,000 Sheets
133 North East Norfolk
134 Norwich & the Broads

Admiralty Charts
1534 Approaches to Gt Yarmouth (1:25,000)
1543 Winterton Ness to Orford Ness (1:75,000)

Tidal Constants
Gorleston:
HW Dover −0220,
LW Dover −0210

Sea Area
Thames

Rescue
Inshore lifeboat:
Gt Yarmouth & Gorleston
All weather lifeboat:
Gt Yarmouth & Gorleston

The 13th century North West Tower in Runham.

44 River Yare

Ancient centres of population separated by the marshes

O it was a fine and a pleasant day.
Out of Yarmouth harbour I was faring
As a cabinboy on a sailing lugger.
For to go and hunt the shoals of herring
Ewan MacColl

At the confluence of the River Wensum with the River Yare, the Yare upstream is marked as a narrow dyke. It is clear that the Wensum is the major river, if not the longer, and it has the longer tidal channel and the greater interest as it provides the reason for the location of Norwich, capital of Norfolk and, at one time, England's third city with a financial basis of wool and cloth.

The Wensum rises at Wellingham and is tidal from the A147 Norwich inner ring road, the westbound carriageway of which is carried over the wrought iron spans of St Crispin's Bridge. This 17m span former railway bridge has latticed spandrels and patterned open balustrades in cast iron.

To start this high up on the river requires a portable boat, a working knowledge of getting from each car park to the river and whether there is access and banks which are low enough. Most boats will find it easier to approach from downstream. Even then, shallow draught is required. High water is two and a half hours after Dover.

For most boats the upper limit is the New Mills water powered air compressor station with sluices beneath a building right across the river. The mills, which are being restored, are less than 200m down from the bypass.

Looking downstream from here gives the best view from the river of the castle, built from 1067 in the centre of the loop formed by the river. Its keep of Caen stone was constructed as a royal palace. One of the largest keeps in the country on the country's largest motte, its Norman architecture was second only to the Tower of London and it was the most ambitious secular building in Europe of its time. A cube with decoration on the outside, it was refaced in Bath stone in 1839. It was the county jail for 650 years until 1887 and was used for public executions until 1849 when extra spectator trains were run from London for the hanging of James Rush for the Stanfield Hall murder, death masks being stored in the dungeons. When 20,000 farmers rebelled against enclosures in 1549 they were suppressed by the Earl of Warwick and their leader,

New Mills water powered air compressor station blocks the River Wensum in Norwich.

Cotman, the only city with its own art school. The ghost of a lady in a black Victorian dress has been seen. The Royal Norfolk Regimental Museum is linked to the castle by the prisoners' tunnel and a replica First World War communications trench. The 1.6ha Castle Green Park now has under it the Mall Norwich for shoppers, Norwich being one of the country's top ten shopping destinations. Nearby is Henry's where landlord John Aggas was stabbed in 1787 after stopping a drinking session by son-in-law Timothy Hardy and friends, who had broken in after being turned out earlier, Hardy being tortured to death. Also in the vicinity is the Murderers, where a prostitute was stabbed by her client in a dispute over the fee.

The narrow St Miles Bridge of 1804 is the last remaining one of its kind in East Anglia, originally carrying much traffic from Bullard's Anchor brewery next to it but now only cyclists and pedestrians. It is narrow and its 11m span is carried on four cast iron sectional ribs. It has the city arms on parapets which were reached by the 1912 flood and has a hose spout on the west side.

Norwich, given its charter in 1194 by Richard I, contains a compact jumble of medieval buildings with Georgian and new housing. The Ribs of Beef faces the Mischief. Elm Hill Quay faces a slipway. The Inspire Hands-on Science Centre occupies the medieval St Michael's church. The Roman Catholic cathedral of St John the Baptist, begun 1884, has fine Gothic revival architecture with unique stained glass which was funded by Henry Howard, 15th Duke of Norfolk. The sunken Plantation Garden is in Victorian style with a folly. The Art Deco

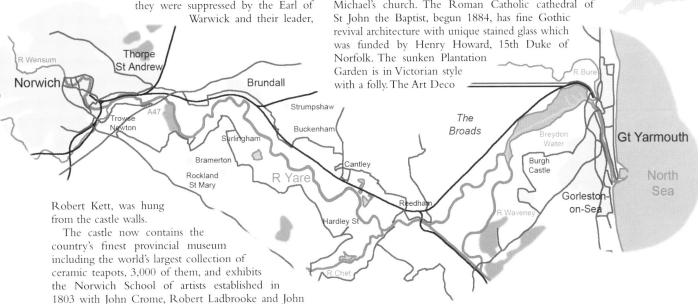

Robert Kett, was hung from the castle walls.

The castle now contains the country's finest provincial museum including the world's largest collection of ceramic teapots, 3,000 of them, and exhibits the Norwich School of artists established in 1803 with John Crome, Robert Ladbrooke and John

Bullard's Anchor Brewery and St Miles Bridge of 1804.

Norwich Theatre Royal seats 1,300 while a medieval merchant's house hosts a cinema and the 18th century Assembly House venue is well used. The Perpendicular church of St Peter Mancroft, rebuilt in 1455 on 1075 Norman foundations, has a Perpendicular font of 1463, Flemish tapestry from 1573, medieval glass in the east window and a memorial to physician Sir Thomas Browne who promoted cremation but was buried himself.

The market place is used every day except Sunday, has been used since 1025 and is the grandest in England. A 62m square tower tops the 1938 City Hall. The flint Guildhall from 1407 was much restored in the 19th century and contains a regalia collection second only to London's, a Liberty Bell presented in 1894 by Norwich, Connecticut, and a Spanish admiral's sword given by Nelson in 1797 after Cape St Vincent. The Maddermarket contains a replica Elizabethan Shakespeare theatre and has the ghost of a black robed priest who comes to celebrate mass.

Strangers were Dutch religious refugees, brought in during the 14th century to help Worsted cloth production, more here than anywhere else, but the Strangers' Hall Museum of Domestic Life in a town house from 1320 has rooms from Tudor to Victorian, the Lord Mayor's coach and C S Rolls' car from 1898, a Panhard-Levassor. The Bridewell Museum of trades and industries has a 1920s pharmacy and a 1930s pawnbroker in a prison used from 1583 to 1828 for women and beggars. The Victorian Mustard Shop includes a museum of Colman's mustard, an essential feature of Norwich.

Another bridge with a hose spout is Blackfriars, named after the 13th century timber original built by the monastery's Dominican monks. The current bridge has a 14m masonry span of 1784 by Sir John Soane with cantilevered footways and ornate cast iron railings added later.

St Peter Hungate Church Museum of Christian artifacts occupies a church rebuilt in 1430–60 with a hammerbeam roof and Norwich painted glass. St Clement's church has the 1575 grave of Protestant archbishop Matthew Parker, whose fanaticism and continued prying into other people's affairs earned him the nickname Nosey Parker.

The house at 19 Magdalen Street is haunted by a woman murdered in the bedroom. In the 1970s it had repeated problems with a typewriter operating itself.

Although the river formed a major part of the city's defences, a 6m high wall was added in the 14th century, running from the most northerly point on the river loop, where it can still be seen, round the west side of the city for 3.6km. The largest of its kind in the country, it had ten fortified gateways with towers between. Inside are 1,500 historic buildings and the most complete medieval street pattern in England. There are more pre-Reformation churches than in any other city in Europe, including over 30 flint churches from the Middle Ages.

On the river are swans, blackheaded and blackbacked gulls and blue dragonflies, marsh marigolds add colour and there are willow trees, one of which stands against the prominent 15m round Cow Tower at the northeast corner of the river loop, part of the 14th century defences.

The 13th century Bishop Bridge by the Red Lion is the last remaining medieval bridge in Norwich. In red brick and flint, it has three arches of 4.6–7.6m, stone ribs, cutwaters at both ends of the piers and refuges in the parapets, on which are the city arms. It was owned by the priory until 1393. A fortified Ethelbert gate tower at the west end rested on two of the arches until 1790 but had to be removed as it was distressing the bridge. It is shallow underneath and hire craft are not permitted upstream. A wherry mast was erected near a boatyard which used to build them, there having been 200 trading to Yarmouth.

Beyond parkland containing the Great Hospital of 1249, Pull's Ferry, named after an 18th century boatman, has a 15th century house with an arch. Now over dry land, it was a watergate which guarded a canal dug to take materials to the cathedral, lasting for three centuries. The 1096 Benedictine cathedral occupies the largest close in England. One of the finest complete Norman buildings in Europe, in Caen stone, it has the largest 13th century monastic cloisters in England, repaired after they were burned in 1272 by citizens rioting against the tax imposed on the annual fair by cathedral monks. The 14th century roof bosses are unique. The 96m spire is

The Cow Tower. The medieval fortifications made good use of the river.

Bishop Bridge is the only medieval bridge remaining over the River Wensum.

The 15th century arch at Pull's Ferry guarded a canal leading to the cathedral.

the second highest in England, blown down in a storm in 1362 but rebuilt in 1480, on top of Britain's highest Norman tower. It has flying buttresses, a Saxon bishop's throne from the 8th century, the grave of founding bishop Herbert de Losinga and also that of nurse Edith Cavell, executed by the Germans for helping prisoners of war to escape from Brussels in 1916. The cathedral featured in P D James' *Devices & Desires*. The Erpingham Gate, carved with many figures, was given in 1420 by Sir Thomas Erpingham, who commanded the English archers at Agincourt. In 1349 the Black Death killed 2,000 people, a third of the city's population, the bodies being left in Tombland. Tragedy struck again in 1381 when the mayor was killed during the Peasants' Revolt, put down by military bishop Henry le Despenser, who gave the cathedral's screen behind the altar.

New housing beside old wharf buildings in Norwich.

Foundry Bridge with TS Lord Nelson *and* Thai on the River.

The boat used as the ferryman's hut at Reedham Ferry.

The River Yare proves popular by Whitlingham Broad. The award-winning centre building with its boat-shaped cabins lies beyond.

The Adam & Eve, the oldest public house in Norwich, was built in 1249 as a brewery for the cathedral builders. It has the ghost of Sam, Lord Sheffield, who was taken there to die.

A statue near King Edward VI School records one of their more prominent pupils, Nelson. A church contains Norwich Puppet Theatre, one of only three in the UK.

Between the Compleat Angler and the Nelson is Foundry Bridge of 1886. A single 17m wrought iron span with decorated balustrades, it was built in the adjacent railway yard and launched sideways from the former bridge.

The east side of the river loop has moorings for pleasure craft. It can be reached by 500t coasters but has not been used commercially since 1989. Two significantly large vessels moored here are the Sea Cadets' *TS Lord Nelson* and Thai on the River, a huge wooden restaurant on a barge. Various other eateries and the Queen of Iceni public house are located around a corner. Restored wharf buildings and new housing in sympathetic style come with the Novi Sad Friendship Bridge for pedestrians.

Dragon Hall is a 1427 merchant's centre for the sale of cloth, with a gold painted carved dragon and a crownpost roof, the only medieval merchant's trading hall surviving in western Europe.

The 14th century cell of St Julian has been rebuilt in St Julian's church following wartime bombing. Her *Revelations of Divine Love* is the first book known to have been written in English by a woman. Another woman writer from Norwich is chef Delia Smith, also known for her support of Norwich City Football Club. Their ground is beyond Carrow Bridge, carrying the A147. Their nickname of the Canaries comes from the Dutch refugees who liked the birds and produced a distinct breed with good colour and song.

Prison reformer Elizabeth Fry was born here in 1780. With a different view of prison was 24 year old William Sheward who, in 1836, killed his 38 year old wife in a domestic dispute, cut up her body and disposed of the parts. He remarried in 1862 and had three children but handed himself in to the police with remorse seven years later, to be hung for his crime. Local weaving apprentice Samuel Lincoln was an ancestor of American president Abraham Lincoln.

The city has February Spring and October Autumn Literary Festivals, a Leap Dance Festival in May, the largest CamRA festival outside London in October and the Norfolk & Norwich Festival, the oldest single city music festival in England. Local businesses include the headquarters of Her Majesty's Stationery Office and Aviva, better known by their former name of the Norwich Union insurance company. Norwich was the first place to have postcodes.

The river turns east again past industrial premises, perhaps with the odour of mint if the wind is from the south, to recall that railway contractor Samuel Morton Peto served as MP for Norwich. Red flags fly next to Trowse Swing Bridge of 1987, carrying the Liverpool Street–Thorpe railway. This is the third swing bridge at the site but the first for British Rail where the overhead powerlines swing with the track. The bridge pivots on the south bank, its 6m tail carrying 200t of kentledge to balance the 20m nose, lifting 300mm on jacks before turning. Electrical contacts are independent of the supply to the rest of the 25kV powerlines.

Two sets of powerlines cross above a boatyard and the confluence with the River Yare. On the south side of the river is the newest broad, Whitlingham, landscaped from former sand pits. The white dome of the centre building covers boat shaped cabins beneath. It has a 1.5km rowing course and a range of other watersports. Most appreciated is its beach of sand from the excavations, used by people able to walk there from the city. It has not been stocked for anglers as fish could lower the water quality.

The tidal range is still small. The Wherryman's Way follows the river from Norwich to Yarmouth.

Taking the original line of the river rather than the New Cut involves passing the church at **Thorpe St Andrew**, approached through a lytch gate bearing a sundial and forming part of an earlier church which stands as a ruin in the churchyard.

The King's Head, Buck and Boat & Bottle all crowd this reach, along with the first of the marinas which set the public afloat during the summer. The main navigation is rejoined by a rowing club and the land is hilly and wooded at first although it becomes progressively more open and flat.

The A47 crosses at Whitlingham Marsh. Conveniently spaced public houses cater for the tourist traffic, the Woods End at Bramerton, the Ferry Inn at Surlingham and the Coldham Hall at **Brundall**.

Reeds become a more regular riverside feature, complete with reed buntings, great crested grebes and greylag geese.

The Yare is a main route through the southern Broads and Surlingham Broad and Rockland Broad are signposted to the right of the river. Between these two is Strumpshaw Fen with its hides while Strumpshaw Hall Steam Museum has steam road and railway vehicles. Other channels lead to villages or are private or nature reserves. Buckenham Marshes also have a hide to view one of Britain's largest flocks of bean goose. Another form of signposting is a continuous series of speed limits. Boat washes have shaped the earth banks and rotting tree stumps have also been sculpted into weird shapes. Steel and wood piling is gradually being introduced to protect the banks from erosion.

The valley becomes lined with marshes, crossed by a network of drains. Windmills were once used to pump the water clear but most of the mills now stand derelict with just their brick shells remaining.

The Red House at Cantley is completely overshadowed by the silos of the huge sugar beet factory, the first in the UK. Until 1962 the beet was delivered by motorized wherry. The public front was renovated in 2010, including installing a public slipway.

Hardley Mill was restored in 2009 as the only working drainage mill in south Norfolk and opened with a windmill exhibition.

An obelisk at Hardley Cross next to the confluence with the River Chet marks the boundary of the

The mill at Berney, seen through a gap in the walls of the Roman Burgh Castle.

The A47 crosses the northeastern end of Breydon Water on a lifting bridge.

The lifting bridge in Great Yarmouth.

jurisdictions of the Norwich and Yarmouth navigation authorities.

The Ferry Inn at Reedham is where the road crosses the river via a small chain guided ferry capable of carrying two cars at a time. The ferryman has a hut on the south bank in the form of an upended boat, reminiscent of a sentry box.

An adjacent windmill has been converted into a futuristic dwelling with a greenhouse like structure built around the outside part way up the body of the mill. Reedham is generally a most attractive village with a number of delightful cottages lining the river between the Lord Nelson and the Ship. East of the village, the railway crosses on a swing bridge.

The New Cut, dating from 1832, runs southeast to the River Waveney while the Yare turns northeast past reedbeds which supply thatch for the village.

Shelducks and oystercatchers may be seen and even common seals may come ashore and rest up beside the river in Reedham Marshes.

One of the mills in the marshes has arms but from there can be seen the fully restored Berney mill. The seven storey Berney Arms Mill is 21m high with a rotating boat cap, four white sails and a fantail on a tarred brick body. Built in 1870, it was used until 1880 to grind cement clinker made from the chalky mud of the river and was later used with an unusually large 7.3m scoop wheel to drain the meadows, being used until 1984. The highest remaining Norfolk marshmill and an Ancient Monument, it is probably the finest mill in the country. It is unique in having its own railway station but no road access, most people coming by boat. It claims to offer the best food and wine in the Norfolk Broads.

The Roman Burgh Castle is visible as the River Yare and the River Waveney enter Breydon Water. The lake is a nature reserve and its most characteristic residents are cormorants standing on top of the poles lining the navigation channel with their wings outstretched in a vertical cruciform, faces to the wind, in order to dry their feathers. The lake would probably be of more interest to wildlife were it not for its sloping concrete sides. A windpump behind the southern levée is typical of those used by kestrels as nesting sites.

A pier and the Yarmouth bypass bridge at the east end of Breydon Water are the only warning of the dramatic change that takes place on turning the corner.

Suddenly the countryside becomes city in a few metres. The River Bure leads in from the rest of the Broads.

A notice forbids hire craft to go any further and this should apply to anyone unsure of being safe in the fast currents and not interrupting the movements of the many commercial ships in the narrow and busy final 5km to the sea.

This final run through **Great Yarmouth**, named after the river, is filled with industrial activity and interest, ancient and modern. Just beyond the bascule bridge, on the right, is a magnificent thatched warehouse with a wherry weathervane. The Elizabethan House Museum just downstream on the other bank was built by a wealthy Tudor merchant in 1596. It has a 17th century circular Flemish window showing a herring buss, 16th century panelled rooms, Elizabethan plastered ceilings, a Tudor bedroom, a Victorian kitchen, contemporary furniture, town regalia, a display of Victorian toys and games, Lowestoft porcelain, 18th and 19th century drinking glasses and displays of 19th century domestic life. It was said to have been used for plotting against Charles I by owner John Carter, a friend of Cromwell. The daughter of a later owner fell in love with a young man who was sent to sea to get rid of him, where he was drowned. The daughter saw his ghost and drowned herself. The ghosts of the pair were seen floating beside the ship and the guilty crew member confessed, the father dying of a broken heart. The nearby flint Tolhouse Museum dating from the 13th century is one of the oldest municipal buildings in England and served as a courthouse and jail until the 19th century. The cells may be seen in the dungeons and other rooms contain a history of Yarmouth. The Heighning Chamber was used for fixing wholesale rates for herring and the corporation's cut until 1835.

The Rows were heavily bombed in both World Wars but the Old Merchant's House, a 17th century town house with splendid plaster ceilings, local original architectural and domestic fittings and 17th and 19th century ironwork, and other 17th century buildings have survived. The customs house dates from 1720 and the Maritime Museum for East Anglia is in a shipwrecked sailors' home of 1861, featuring herring fishing and fishing gear, lifesaving, shipbuilding, sailors' arts and crafts, Nelson, Norfolk wherries, Norfolk's inland waterways, ship models, paintings, photographs, tools and the Second World War. St Nicholas' church is the largest parish church in England although not the only one to make the claim. Great Yarmouth Museum Exhibition Galleries have their place and the Anna Sewell House Museum is the birthplace of the author of *Black Beauty*, her grandfather having founded the river steamer service to Norwich. Daniel Defoe wrote enthusiastically about the quayside. The filming of *Keeping up Appearances* recorded some of the town more recently and there will be something somewhere on the Norfolk Giant, Robert Hales, who died in 1863 aged 43, 2.34m high and weighing 203kg. Yarmouth was the first place in eastern England to suffer an air raid in 1915.

The 44m Norfolk Pillar with its 217 steps is topped by Britannia, some think oddly, facing away from the sea. It was built in 1819 to honour Nelson, who landed here after the Battle of the Nile in 1798 and sailed to and from the Battle of Copenhagen in 1891.

It was near the monument that Dickens set Peggoty's hut in *David Copperfield*. More drama on the beach

in 1900 resulted in Herbert Bennett being hanged for murdering his estranged wife with a bootlace, much evidence pointing to his guilt. Eleven years later another woman was strangled on the beach with a bootlace.

Just south of Nelson's monument and an aerial is a power station.

Yarmouth has been one of the largest herring ports in the world. In medieval times it was famous for smoked red herrings because shoals of herrings congregated off the coast each autumn. It grew rich on herrings in the Middle Ages. This led to successive arguments with the Cinque Ports and then the Dutch over herring rights and reached the point where the Cinque Ports attacked the Yarmouth fleet while escorting the king to Flanders in 1297, resulting in the burning of 29 ships and the killing of 200 men. The Yarmouth Free Herring Fair every autumn was one of the greatest medieval trade fairs. Thomas Nashe wrote about the Yarmouth fishing in *Lenten Stuff* in 1597. In the 19th century the coming of the railways meant that many more people could buy the Yarmouth bloater, invented in 1836. The herring peaked in 1913 with over 1,100 drifters operating out of the port but use of the drifters as wartime minesweepers and overfishing of stocks in peacetime have destroyed the industry. The town hall has a golden drifter weathervane. Fish found today include dab, sole, cod, whiting, bass and spined weaver.

However, instead of bewailing its loss, Yarmouth has turned to other industry. Since the 1960s it has become a base for first the offshore gas industry and then the oil industry. A run down to the South Denes passes rig supply vessels, small fishing boats, a lightship, the Yarmouth lifeboat and continuous industry with names familiar throughout the offshore world. One of the less likely names was a steel fabrication yard under the name Turmeric. The name originally belonged to two girls running an ailing domestic business. A potential steelman bought the whole firm as being quicker than registering a new name. The yard turned out some sizeable structures for the North Sea.

The Gallon Can, Ferryboat Inn and Quay Largo may offer services required but this is not a wise place to stop.

The final turn east out into the North Sea involves passing the jetty bearing the coastguard station, a jetty which can obscure large vessels turning into the rivermouth until the last moment.

The geography of the area has changed significantly over the years. The spit used to reach to Gunton but in Roman times it was an island. The present river mouth was cut in the 16th century and has been maintained since then. The harbour has been extended seawards with a new port area north of the river entrance. The seabed off Yarmouth is subject to frequent change.

The river is ingoing from five hours forty minutes after Dover high water at up to 4km/h and outgoing from half an hour before Dover high water at up to 11km/h although the ebb can be continuous for eighteen hours with heavy rain and wind can also have an effect. There is a slack period an hour and a half after local high water and two hours after local low water. Flows begin south six hours after Dover high water and north from twenty minutes before Dover high water at up to 5km/h.

On the horizon a large platform of the Hewett gas field may be seen, one of the reason's for Yarmouth's continuing prosperity.

The lighthouse in Gorleston, adjoining an amusement arcade.

The harbourmouth at Great Yarmouth, overlooked by the coastguard station.

Distance
50km from Norwich to Yarmouth Roads

OS 1:50,000 Sheets
134 Norwich & the Broads

Admiralty Charts
1534 Approaches to Gt Yarmouth (1:25,000). Gt Yarmouth Outer Harbour (1:7,500). Gt Yarmouth Haven (1:7,500)
1535 Approaches to Lowestoft (1:25,000)
1543 Winterton Ness to Orford Ness (1:75,000)

Tidal Constants
Gorleston:
HW Dover −0220,
LW Dover −0210

Sea Area
Thames

Rescue
Inshore lifeboat: Gt Yarmouth & Gorleston
All weather lifeboat: Gt Yarmouth & Gorleston

45 River Waveney

Water, reeds and sky

Were I in my castle
Upon the River Waveney,
I wouldne give a button
For the King of Cockney.
Hugh Bigod

Ellingham Mill has a very steep sluice. Launching is difficult, either down a steep bank and off a high abutment or else a longer portage down the left bank to launch where the bank is a little easier before it runs into private property. The water is tidal from here although there is little indication of this for a long way. There are water lilies with purple loosestrife and ash trees along the banks. Even the cormorants with the swallows are becoming more common inland. Fields of cattle show no knowledge of estuarine conditions.

New Dyke runs parallel with the right bank of the river for over 3km, making occasional connections.

The disused Geldeston or Shipmeadow Lock with its oval sides is the head of Broads National Park control, Bliss noting in his 1934 *Canoeing* that the navigation authority upstream were brewers Watney, Combe & Reid. Beside the lock is the candlelit Locks Inn which is only open during the boating season as there is no road access. Access downstream to the lock is blocked by a fallen tree so approach needs to be made from below the lock island. There is a wide channel by passing the lock but it is obstructed by low hanging chains across the river. They are so heavy that they act more like solid bars when attempting to pass.

Overlooking Geldeston Marshes, above which kestrels hunt, is Shipmeadow where the 18th century workhouse has become a poultry farm.

Powered craft can reach this point. There are various speed limits, initially 5km/h although boat hirers with the throttle open can get far higher speeds.

After Geldeston Dyke, allowing access to Geldeston, the banks become more wooded until the powerlines at the start of Barsham Marshes opposite Dunburgh. At the end of the marshes is Roos Hall, one of the most haunted houses in England. The Devil's footmarks are found inside a wardrobe, there are ghosts in a guest room and in the garden and a coach and horses arrives with a headless groom on Christmas Eve.

Boathouses and small properties flank the river as it approaches the market town of **Beccles**. This was a seaport in Saxon times with a noted herring fishery in

Hired craft ignoring the speed limit at Geldeston.

Boathouses and summerhouses at Beccles.

St Michael's church and its separate bell tower at Beccles.

The attractive waterfront at Beccles.

the 11th century, a fact which would seem most unlikely from today's inland river environment. These days it is a holiday and boating centre. There were four great fires in the 16th and 17th centuries, the town now having a mixture of Tudor, Queen Anne, Georgian and Victorian housing. Dominant on the ridge above the river is St Michael's church where Nelson's parents were married in 1749 and his father was the rector. Its 30m stone bell tower stands separate from the church to prevent it from slipping down the bank and was sold in 1972 for 1p to the town council, who then spent a further £68,000 restoring it, the penny being embedded in a plaque. There are clocks on three sides but not facing the river as it is said the town's residents would not even give their Norfolk neighbours the time. Behind it is the Grade I Sir John Leman school of 1632 containing the Beccles & District Museum with a 19th century printing press, agricultural costumes and implements, cultural and domestic items and wherry building tools. There is a William Clowes Printing Museum. Other buildings of note are the 18th century octagonal town hall and the Waveney Antiques Centre with dealers in books, furniture, clocks and silver. Waveney Enterprises is a company where special needs workers make assorted craft items. Two of the more resourceful members of the community in the 18th century were John and Mary Key of the appropriately named Smugglers Lane who stored contraband under the bed of their daughter who had been rubbed with mustard and turpentine to simulate the potentially fatal scarlet fever, to the effect that customs officials were less than keen to carry out a thorough search. Also unenthusiastic was local resident Adrian Bell, the author and reluctant compiler of the first *Times* crossword.

The Loaves & Fishes public house begins an attractive waterfront. Towards the far end of the town a low arched bridge keeps some boats on the downstream side. High water here is four hours after Yarmouth Bar.

Beyond the A146 bridge the river heads out between Gillingham and Beccles Marshes in a reach which is used for sailing regattas. The lack of room to manoeuvre seems to engender slick tacking.

Together with the marshes are stands of carr, Alder and Stanley Carrs following the left bank, after which the former Beccles to Great Yarmouth railway has left a brick pier standing in the middle of the river.

Long Dam Level, Six Mile Corner, Short Reach,

Castle Marsh, Seven Mile Carr and Short Dam Level all seem to merge together without obvious distinguishing features. There may be mink or blackbacked or herring gulls in places and there may be Aldeby Hall Staithe and Worlingham Staithe, even the disused Castle Mill, but they all withdraw into the typical Broads riverscape where the pleasure is in travelling for the sake of it with few distractions or interruptions.

The river originally flowed on eastwards through Oulton Broad and Lake Lothing but from Carlton Share Mill it turns north, in due course northwest in its new route to the sea.

An oasis in the marshes is where the Burgh St Peter ferry crossed to Peto's Marsh. The Waveney Inn, Mariners Stores and marina accompany the River Centre. Standing back from the river beyond the staithe area is a most unusual 13/14th century thatched church with a brick and stone tower which is stepped like an Inca pyramid.

Oulton Dyke joins from the right. Reedmace is more frequent but there is no shortage of reeds which are harvested in the winter in sheaves for thatching, the stubble being burned back to encourage new growth. The hand harvesting leaves a line of reeds at the water's edge,

187

Sailing regatta in progress alongside Gillingham Marshes.

Burgh St Peter's odd stepped church tower.

those growing just away from dry land. The Lowestoft to Norwich railway follows, initially on the right bank. Burgh, Blundeston, Somerleyton and Wheatacre Marshes front sections of river where water skiing is permitted.

Standing back from the river is Black Mill, now little more than an ivy clad chimney and a derelict hut.

At Somerleyton the railway crosses one of a pair of swing bridges, the other being at Reedham. These were the first swing railway bridges and are each 42m long with double tracks. Repairs to the bearings in 2010 needed handmade parts.

Somerleyton Staithe marks Somerleyton, a mid 19th century village with ornamental cottages built by railway engineer and developer Samuel Morton Peto. The village is best known for Somerleyton Hall and Park.

By now streams have become strong and tidal flows are a major factor in progress. The Landspring Beck arrives unobtrusively. On the other bank is Herringfleet Mill, built about 1820, the last surviving smock drainage mill in the Broads and the last full size working mill in the county. It has four sails and a braced tailpole with hand winch, octagonal with tarred weatherboarding and a boat cap, clinker built in three dimensional curves and tapers. The external 4.9m x 230mm scoop wheel lifts water 3m to the river. It is still operated sometimes.

The Herringfleet Hills arrive suddenly on the right. Rearing to a height of 20m, they seem relative mountains in this flat area, some of which is below sea level. The Suffolk boundary leaves over them, the river fully in Norfolk at last.

Another brick pier in the centre shows where the Beccles to Great Yarmouth railway crossed back over the

The pioneering Somerleyton swing railway bridge.

188

river. A signal box on the disused line has been converted to a house with its own moorings. Behind its railings is a replica of the *Rocket*.

The New Cut of 1832 leaves, forming the Island.

St Olaves takes its name from the patron saint of Norway. Its most conspicuous feature is the cast iron tied arch bowstring bridge of 24m clear span and 4.6m rise above the deck, a classic of its type and unique in East Anglia. The A143 crosses over it before leaving the river for the last time. Some boats may be limited by the bridge height, high water being two and a half hours after Yarmouth Bar.

The priory remains are rather older, the undercroft and brick vaulting ceiling dating from the early 14th century. There is reputed to be a secret passage to the Bell Inn, the oldest public house in Broadlands, haunted by the Grey Lady. Undoubtedly, here is a fine street of 17th century houses.

Old signal box at Haddiscoe with Rocket *replica and mooring.*

Remains of the Roman Burgh Castle, the final reach of the River Waveney as it enters Breydon Water and the Berney Arms Mill.

In front of St Olaves an insignificant channel cuts into the reeds, the outlet from Fritton Decoy. Now the centre of Fritton Lake Country Park, it takes its name from the fact that it was much used for catching ducks. This may be the source of the flocks of feral Egyptian geese on this part of the river. The village features in Arthur Ransome's *Coot Club*. Just by the decoy outlet is a working trestle windpump.

The river curves back in a loop, almost meeting the New Cut again. There is another mill on the edge of Fritton Marshes, almost below the powerlines. In this area it is common for overhead wires to be lifted well clear of shipping on high pylons but the ones here are unusual in that they are rectangular and have no arms, unlike the more usual tapered structures. A further mill on the Island has no arms, either. Water skiing is again permitted on part of this reach.

After skirting Fritton Marshes, the river passes the Scots pines of Waveney Forest, a major feature in a landscape generally flat and devoid of trees. The Pettingills Mill near Seven Mile House has ivy on top while the one beyond it on the right bank has no top at all. A further mill stands on the edge of **Belton** Marshes.

Trees do not reappear until Burgh Castle, a scrappy hamlet of caravans, ship repairers and the Fisherman's Bar and stores at Burgh Staithe.

Past Langley Marshes, Burgh Castle Reach comes under Great Yarmouth Port Authority Control. Burgh Castle is still in a remarkably good state of repair with three of the four walls of this trapezoidal fort, built in 297 by the Romans, still intact with their projecting bastions, later used to enclose the bailey of a 2ha Norman castle. The ITV Sherlock Holmes *Sign of Four* episode was filmed here. Garionnonum was one of a line of forts built up the east coast to resist the Saxons who were less subdued here than in the south.

On the right is a final church with a round tower, a speciality of the area.

The Waveney joins the River Yare in Breydon Water, a former sea estuary with a buoyed fairway.

The OS map says there is mud and sand along the shore but there is little sign of the sand. Wildfowl and waders in migration such as curlew, whimbrel, bartailed and blacktailed godwits, green and wood sandpipers and ruff find 7.7km^2 of mudflats, saltmarsh and pasture. In winter there are bean, Brent, whitefronted and pinkfooted geese, wigeon, shelduck, pintail, shoveler, scaup, goldeneye, Bewick's swan, marsh and hen harriers, short eared and snow and Lapland buntings. There are common species such as blackheaded gull and oystercatcher and even such species as avocet and egret are appearing.

The nearest parking is at the Church Farm Country Inn where the picture window gives a fine view over the end of Breydon Water and its marshes.

Distance
37km from Ellingham to Breydon Water

OS 1:50,000 Sheets
134 Norwich & the Broads

Admiralty Charts
1535 Approaches to Lowestoft (1:25,000)

Tidal Constants
Gorleston:
HW Dover −0220, LW Dover −0210

Sea Area
Thames

Rescue
Inshore lifeboat:
South Broads
All weather lifeboat:
Gt Yarmouth & Gorleston

46 River Alde

Mysterious activity on Europe's largest vegetated shingle spit

With ceaseless motion comes and goes the tide,
Flowing, it fills the channel vast and wide;
Then back to sea, with strong majestic sweep
It rolls, in ebb yet terrible and deep;
Here Samphire-banks and Saltwort bound the flood,
There stakes and sea-weeds withering on the mud;
And higher up, a ridge of all things base,
Which some strong tide has roll'd upon the place.
George Crabbe

Snape Maltings are rather more than the concert venue for which most people know them. The 19th century Victorian maltings, by Newson Garrett, were some of the largest of their kind and have become the main venue for Aldeburgh Festival, begun in 1948 by Benjamin Britten, Eric Crozier and Peter Pears but moved here after it outgrew Aldeburgh, now the largest music festival in England. In 1969 the maltings burned down but were restored the following year with the addition of a concert hall, one of the finest in Europe. Snape Mill House, a former windmill, is where Britten lived and wrote *Peter Grimes*, based on Crabbe's poem, *The Borough*.

The complex includes antique, art and other shops, the Plough & Sail, residential building and Moore and Hepworth sculptures yet the storage of barley has not been forgotten. There is extensive parking adjacent to the quay, where east coast barges are moored against the high wall. The B1069 crosses on the river's last bridge with tidal sluices just upstream. Small craft might find it easier to launch upstream of the bridge but without parking or with difficulty down the steep reedy bank below the maltings. There is a ramp down from the quay but it is often obstructed by a trip boat.

In 1862 a 15m Saxon boat was excavated and the location may have been used by the Romans. George Ewart Evans talks in *Ask the Fellows who Cut the Hay* of

East coast sailing barges moored alongside the maltings at Snape.

shipping grain from Blaxhall to London and Newcastle and the part played by the Crown in Snape in bringing in contraband.

Rising at Dennington, the Alde flows southeast then southwest across Suffolk to the North Sea. From the bridge it lies entirely within the Suffolk Coast & Hills AONB. The water flows to 7km/h and the marsh paths cover at high water. In many respects it is remarkably similar to the River Blyth, to the north. The channel meanders between expanses of silt which change to lagoons of silt as soon as the ebb begins. Withies mark the navigable route. Birdlife includes curlews, redshanks, oystercatchers, lapwings, shelducks, egrets, herons, cormorants and blackbacked gulls.

Ikencliff, with its picnic site, edges Cliff Reach and has the sweep of Tunstall Forest behind. Iken was a fishing village, catching salmon, sea trout and herring. The Anchorage has St Botolph's thatched church, which burned down the year before the Snape Maltings fire. Botwulf had used the site for a monastery in 654, when it was an island. The low marshland means that church towers are important navigation aids while the river is mostly embanked from here.

Long Reach is also the widest as it passes Iken Marshes. Short Reach curves round Aldeburgh Marshes and has some gravel for those who need a hard landing. Westrow Reach has small craft moorings before a complete change of direction and character at the start of Europe's longest vegetated shingle spit.

Aldeburgh, which may take its name from the Anglo-Saxon aldburgh, old fort, or Old English Alda's fort, mostly dates from the early 19th century, having lost its 16th century buildings to the sea. It fared better than Slaughden, now little more than a sailing club. Amongst the buildings lost here was the beachman's dwelling where George Crabbe was born in 1754. His poem The Borough was inspired by the area. In the 16th century Aldeburgh was one of the leading east coast ports, men from the district serving with Drake, whose Greyhound and Pelican were built locally.

Home Reach, with its shellfish beds, is just 50m from the sea. Indeed, the river broke through the spit for a few hours in 1953. Thus, the Martello tower is on both the shore and the river bank, this being the most northerly of the Napoleonic defences of the 1800s and unique in having a quatraform shape, much larger than all the other Martello towers.

Material in the spit, where there is an almost total absence of sand, moves southwards. Most of the spit is bird reserve or for military use and access on foot is only allowed from Orford Quay. It has saltmarsh, mudflats, brackish lagoons, grazing marsh and many rare species of plant.

At the end of Sudbourne Marshes, Blackstrakes Reach takes the river round Lantern Marshes, on which are a number of high masts. It was an electronic intelligence centre where the USAF experimented with over the horizon radar for detecting ballistic missiles. This not only failed to work properly but also interfered with ships' radios. A secret military site from 1913 until 1993, it was used by the Royal Flying Corps, RAF and Atomic Weapons Research Establishment for the first radar experiments and for atomic weapons testing during the Cold War. It is now a transmission station for the BBC's World Service. Perhaps the submarine power cable which crosses the river packs more power than might be expected for the few buildings, large though some of them area, the pagoda buildings having been used for atomic work.

From here the river becomes the River Ore and is controlled by Orford Town Trust.

Across King's Marshes can be seen Orford Ness lighthouse. The site was first protected in 1634 after 32 ships were lost in one February night, to be attacked twice in the early 1700s by the French, who stole fittings and the keeper's bedding. The current 30m tower was built in 1792, the most powerful on the east coast and the first to be controlled remotely from Harwich.

A visitor centre serves those who cross the river from Orford. Moorings front Orford, Orford Sailing Club ensuring there is always plenty of activity on the water and the Lady Florence trip boat operates between here and Iken. Huts selling fresh seafood are reminiscent of those at Walberswick on the Blyth. The Jolly Sailor was

East coast sailing barge moored at Ikencliff.

a smugglers' inn, built with timbers from ships wrecked in the 17th century. There are two smokehouses for cheese, chicken and fish, Orford Butleys being smoked herrings. Local oysters are also sold. There are many brick and timber cottages in the village and baskets are sold from a house which also has the Dunwich Underwater Exploration Exhibition.

Two towers dominate the village. One is that of St Bartholomew's church, built in the 14th century with wool profits although it is partly Norman. It is used for some of the Aldeburgh Festival performances, including some Britten premiers, and still has stocks if anyone

Iken church at the start of Long Reach.

Moorings at Aldeburgh.

Orford Castle with the River Ore beyond.

The first Martello tower of the line round the coast.

gets too riotous. Ruth Rendell also used Orford and Aldeburgh as the setting for *No Night is Too Long*.

The other tower is that of the three storey keep of the Norman Orford Castle, built 1173 for Henry II. Its unique 30m high polygonal keep is cylindrical inside, has three rectangular towers and is one of the best in Britain, ashlar over septaria with spiral staircase, dungeons, cannons and Caen stone battlements. At the time, Orford was a prosperous port at the end of the spit. The castle was granted to the Earl of Norfolk in 1280. It was taken by the French after King John's death and had several changes of hands subsequently. It had rectangular towers to cover the defenders, the last part of the outer wall collapsing in 1841. Even during the Second World War it was used as a lookout point.

The most unusual resident was the Wild Man of Orford, caught by fishermen in the 13th century. Bald and naked but hairy with a long beard, he would not talk, even when hung up by his heels and tortured. He was imprisoned in the castle for several months, eating only fish, but, when taken to the sea to swim with nets beneath him, managed to escape, which could explain why his ghost is said to remain.

A pillbox provides more recent defence for the village. For many years the spit paused at Stonyditch Point,

Some of the masts on Lantern Marshes.

Havergate Island with craft anchored in the Gull, to its right.

where there is no landing because of a nature reserve. An 1813 plan was to close off the Gull with lock gates and cut through the spit to make Orford commercial again.

Havergate Island is 3km long and up to 700m wide, covering 1.2km², formed in the middle of the 16th century. It was drained but flooded again by artillery during the Second World War. Since 1947 it has been an RSPB nature reserve with hides and huts. Landing is not permitted to prevent bird disturbance but large groups of bird enthusiasts wander about with tripods and long lenses over their shoulders. The lagoons are maintained at a level to appeal to avocets, for which this has been Britain's biggest breeding colony since 1947 with 100 pairs. There are also breeding terns, waders in the spring and autumn and bitterns, Canada geese, marsh and hen harriers, short eared owls and herring gulls.

Most boat traffic uses the Narrows but the Gull winds to the north of the island, leaving between Chantry Point and Cuckold's Point on the island, picking up the Butley River before the Lower Gull returns between Dove Point and Flybury Point. Boyton Marshes are another bird sanctuary. From here a water ski area runs inside the spit and the Suffolk Coast & Heaths Path follows the north bank. Outside is Orford Beach, an inaccessible, steep, shingle bank.

Another pillbox stands below the Hollesley Bay Colony, a young offender institution. Brendan Behan wrote *Borstal Boy* after a stay in 1958 and described swimming at Shingle Street.

Barthorp's Creek emerges after winding round Oxley Marshes. Opposite is North Weir Point, facing Hollesley Bay, with a few additional gravel islands at low water. In the 19th century the spit was over 2km longer but this was lost in a single storm, leaving the current 16km long structure. There is a bar with a minimum depth of 300m. Flows run out at up to 11km/h from an hour and twenty minutes after Dover high water and in from five hours before Dover high water, an hour after local high and low water respectively. The entrance can be dangerous with strong onshore winds, especially against the ebb. Flows in the bay are parallel to the coast, stronger northeastwards from fifty minutes after Dover high water than southwest from five hours ten minutes before Dover high water.

Marks are often moved to reflect changes in the channel. Amber may be found on the gravel beach at Shingle Street where there is parking, sometimes in appropriately deep gravel. Never revealed was the reason why the village had to be evacuated on one occasion during the Second World War although suspicion lies with the military experimental site on the spit.

Distance
24km from Snape to Hollesley Bay

OS 1:50,000 Sheets
156 Saxmundham
169 Ipswich
& the Naze

Admiralty Charts
1543 Winterton
Ness to Orford Ness
(1:75,000)
2052 Orford Ness to
Naze (1:50,000)
2693 Appproaches to
Felixstowe, Harwich &
Ipswich with Rs Stour,
Orwell & Deben
(1:25,000)
2695 Plans on E
Coast of England.
Rs Ore & Alde
(1:25,000)

Tidal Constants
Snape:
HW Dover +0240
Iken Cliff:
HW Dover +0220,
LW Dover +0240
Slaughden:
HW Dover +0140,
LW Dover +0200
Orford Quay:
HW Dover +0120,
LW Dover +0140
Ore Bar:
HW Dover + 0030,
LW Same as Dover

Sea Area
Thames

Rescue
Inshore lifeboat:
Aldburgh
All weather lifeboat:
Aldburgh

Orford Haven, towards the southern end of the spit.

47 River Deben

Finding Anglo-Saxon boats and German aircraft

Who will come a-sailing,
Who will come with me,
Down the sunny Deben
To the distant sea?
Michael Weaver

Assorted craft rest on the mud at Melton.

The River Deben rises at Kenton and flows southeast across Suffolk to the North Sea. It becomes tidal at a weir between Ufford and Bromeswell, at which point it is narrow and shallow, accompanied by watercress and reeds and with a gravel bed, soon to be replaced by silt. The only obvious activity is from swans and on the Lowestoft to Ipswich railway, which crosses as the river widens.

The highest point of easy public access is Wilford Bridge, carrying the A1152. A stepped embankment leads down from a rough parking area by the bridge, a graceful concrete skewed arch with brickwork above.

From here the river is all within the Suffolk Coast & Hills AONB although the reason is not obvious at first. The river widens again with large boats moored or sunk at Melton and a silt lagoon on the east side. Lapwings, oystercatchers, herring and blackbacked gulls and cormorants use the water. A domed building and a water tower are conspicuous on the right.

Above is Sutton Hoo with a group of tumuli. In 1939 the owner had seen ghosts and asked an archaeologist to investigate. The discovery of large iron rivets led to the unearthing of the imprint of the largest and most complete English boat of the first millennium although the wood had not survived. Measuring 27 x 4.5m, it was a clinker built longboat containing what is thought to be the burial site of Rædwald, one of the earliest known English kings, who reigned from about 610 to 625. In the boat was the richest treasure ever discovered in Britain, including one of only four Anglo-Saxon helmets found in Britain, a 320mm helmet of about 600 in iron tinned with bronze panels. Exquisite jewellery was also unearthed. The finds are displayed in the British Museum while the National Trust have an exhibition on site with a replica of the burial chamber. The mounds have produced other important finds, including a second ship burial.

The ferry across the river was supposedly used in 1800 by Margaret Catchpole and Will Laud to escape after she broke out of Ipswich jail in the Revd Richard Cobbold's semi biographical novel.

Opposite Ferry Cliff is Tidemill Yacht Harbour and there are moorings through Woodbridge. The 3ha pond was for the weatherboarded tide mill, resplendent in white. Built in 1170, it was rebuilt in 1793 and used until 1957, when the 560mm square oak shaft broke. It carries a 6.1m diameter wheel driving four millstones. The Grade I building was restored in 1982 and can be used

Woodbridge tide mill in excellent repair.

Moorings off Ramsholt.

The hidden beach at Ramsholt.

Felixstowe Ferry jetty, mostly used by youngsters catching crabs.

on the bottom four hours of the tide. Inside are models and displays.

Woodbridge, from the Anglo-Saxon Woden burh, Woden's town, is largely Georgian although it had shipbuilding and rope and sailmaking from Elizabethan times, Edward III and Drake using Woodbridge ships. The 15th century St Mary's church has a tower with buttresses that change shape with height. It also has the tomb of Thomas Seckford, the Master of the Court of Requests of Elizabeth I, who commissioned many of Woodbridge's buildings. The oldest building in town is the King's Head, a monastery in the 13th century, where monks brewed beer, some of whom are still present as spirits. The 1575 Elizabethan Shire Hall with Dutch gables houses the Suffolk Punch Heavy Horse Museum, cataloguing the world's oldest breed of working heavy horse. Woodbridge Museum has replicas of the Sutton Hoo treasures and material on resident Edward Fitzgerald, who undertook a free translation of *The Rubá'iyát of Omar Khayyám* and was visited by Carlyle and Tennyson. Fitzgerald, Crabbe, Bernard Barton and landscape painter Thomas Churchyard were known as the Wits of Woodbridge. A less welcome visit brought the Zeppelin bombing raid of 1915.

Woodbridge used to export butter but the port is no longer used commercially. On the other hand, Deben Yacht Club members make good use of the river, which now widens further with low banks past mudflats and saltings. Flows out are from an hour and fifty minutes after Dover high water and in from three hours forty minutes before Dover high water.

Troublesome Reach leads down to Kyson Point at the end of Martlesham Creek, facing across to Haddon Hall. Methersgate has another hall and a quay while the Hams brown cliff is unusual for the area, before the Tips. Egrets,

teal, wigeon, shelducks, curlews and turnstones frequent the marshes.

Waldringfield has a sailing centre, members of which have included Carl Giles, perhaps drawing on his local experiences for his annual RNLI Christmas card design.

Kirton Creek is one of the larger inlets.

All Saints' church at Ramsholt has a Norman round tower. It is also unusual for having a mud free beach, making it a popular place to launch small boats. King's Fleet enters Sea Reach.

Felixstowe Ferry Sailing Club is surrounded by moorings and accompanied by a slipway and a narrow jetty for a passenger ferry across the estuary, mostly obstructed by a line of youngsters feeding scraps of

195

Bawdsey Manor was where radar originated.

bacon to the crabs and occasionally landing one. In the 19th century the crossing used steam powered chain ferries. The ferry forms an essential link in the Suffolk Coast & Heaths Path with a visitor centre on the east side.

Beyond the red Bawdsey Cliff is Bawdsey Manor, begun in 1886 by Sir Cuthbert Quilter, a folly in Gothic, Tudor, Victorian, Flemish and oriental styles, set in 60ha of grounds. It was here that radar was invented, important for the outcome of the Battle of Britain. The Germans got wind that something was going on and sent the *Graf Zeppelin* to investigate.

A Martello tower stands on the other side of Woodbridge Haven. The channel is narrow, sometimes as little as 100mm deep and not helped by jet skis racing about. The channel and bar move, meaning that buoys often have to be repositioned. The entrance can be dangerous, particularly with wind against tide. Flows out begin forty minutes after Dover high water and in from five hours fifty minutes before Dover high water at up to 7km/h. The east side of the haven has several islands of gravel, close to being a spit at low water. Beyond these, flows are parallel to the coast to 4km/h, stronger northeastwards than southwestwards.

Distance
17km from Ufford to
Woodbridge Haven

OS 1:50,000 Sheets
156 Saxmundham
169 Ipswich
& the Naze

Admiralty Charts
2052 Orford Ness to
Naze (1:50,000)
2693 Appproaches to
Felixstowe, Harwich &
Ipswich with Rs Stour,
Orwell & Deben
(1:25,000)

Tidal Constants
Woodbridge:
HW Dover +0120,
LW Dover +0050
Woodbridge Haven:
HW Dover +0040,
LW Dover +0020

Sea Area
Thames

Rescue
Inshore lifeboat:
Harwich
All weather lifeboat:
Harwich

A Martello tower guarding Woodbridge Haven.

48 River Orwell

Europe's largest container terminal

With one consuming roar along the shingle
The long wave claws and rakes the pebbles down
To where its backwash and the next wave mingle,
A mounting arch of water weedy-brown
Against the tide the off-shore breezes blow.
Oh wind and water, this is Felixstowe.
John Betjeman

Rising at Mendlesham Green, the River Gipping flows southwards across Suffolk to be joined by the River Stour in Harwich Harbour, having undergone a personality change to become the River Orwell in the estuary stage beyond Ipswich.

Ipswich was a Saxon settlement which became a medieval port and had its heyday in Victorian times. A Scandinavian attack in 991 by Olaf was bought off with a heavy tax which was to lead to the Danegelds of following years. The Danes stormed Ipswich again in 1010 and were beaten off in 1068. Use of the term 'Orwellian' for sinister authoritarianism comes indirectly from the river, George Orwell being picked as a pen name by Eric Blair, whose parents lived near the river.

The weir at the head of the tidal section has a slope and then a vertical drop, a shoot with the tide in but impossible with the tide out, when gravel shallows lead to another small drop before passing between forbidding sloping concrete walls past a cycle and skateboard park and towards the A137 bridge. Beyond are old flourmills. Sometimes heard are the restored 14th century bells of St Lawrence, the oldest ring in the country. Not taking itself too seriously, Ipswich has a bronze statue of Giles' Grandma cartoon character.

The New Cut bypasses Ipswich dock, metamorphosed into a marina with much smart new building around it. It usually has a lightship in residence, the Steamboat Tavern and various moored fishing boats. A velocity control structure is a giant venturi with gate rising from the river bed but passage is possible by small craft even with the gate raised. Beyond it lies the dock entrance and the former Tolly Cobbold brewery.

There is a grain loading wharf on the left and a container terminal on the right. This commercial atmosphere continues on the left with a power station cooling water intake, a sewage works and a vehicle storage area. On the right, however, leisure activities come to the fore. The Orwell Yacht Club precedes the confluence

with the Belstead Brook and Fox's Marina on the other bank.

Arching high over the river is the graceful 1.3km long Orwell Bridge of 1982, taking the A14 to Felixstowe docks. The bridge piers are protected with small concrete tripods, interlocking parallel to the channel but tipped at random upstream and downstream. There was a history of bearing problems when the bridge was first built.

Light aircraft buzz around from Woodbridge airfield. Beyond the bridge the valley widens out with gentle

Restored wharf buildings in the centre of Ipswich.

wooded slopes down to the water. It is now all AONB and the Stour & Orwell Walk follows the estuary. Parks become popular. Freston Park has the prominent six storey 1550s Freston Tower, perhaps an eyecatcher, a lookout tower or one of the earliest follies, maybe to tie in with Elizabeth I's 1561 visit to Ipswich. Orwell Park at Nacton and Woolverstone Park both house schools.

In the summer the Orwell is popular with yachts, windsurfers and east coast sailing barges. There

is a marina at Woolverstone and Pin Mill Sailing Club at Chelmondiston has an annual barge sailing match at the beginning of July. Suffolk Yacht Harbour is between Levington and Trimley St Martin.

From Collimer Point, where flows run to 2km/h, there are earth levées.

Approaching Harwich Harbour the scenery changes again. The container

A skateboard park next to the river in Ipswich.

Ipswich Docks now a smart marina with flour mill apartments.

From the business of brewing to business offices.

Haven Authority. Flows are outgoing at Fagbury Point to 3km/h and ingoing to 2km/h, perhaps faster than when Fagbury Cliff, behind the container terminal, was the riverbank.

Felixstowe, Old English for Filica's meeting place, is now the meeting place for containers. Trinity Container Terminal with its many travelling cranes is the busiest container terminal in Europe, handling 40% of Britain's containers as well as timber and oil. Northwesterly to northeasterly winds increase the water level while southwesterly to southeasterly winds reduce it. Barometric pressure can also alter the water level by a metre from what is predicted.

The water becomes more choppy and the remains of several wrecks are passed approaching Shotley Point, dominated by a green water tower and by a mast in the grounds of HMS Ganges, used as a training establishment until 1977 and then used for police training. The name is from a ship formerly used there. Beyond the marina and museum a seawall runs round the point where there are moorings over Shotley Flat and Bloody Point. Flows are outgoing from an hour and twenty minutes after Dover high water to 5km/h and ingoing from four hours forty minutes before Dover high water to 2km/h.

Harwich takes its name from the Old English herewic, army camp, showing its strategic importance over many centuries. King Alfred fought the Danish fleet in 885 and Edward III gathered his fleet here in 1340 for Sluys. Christopher Jones, the master of the *Mayflower*, was a resident and it was from here that he began his voyage, the boat eventually being broken up in Ipswich. Drake, Frobisher, Hawkins and Nelson all sailed from here and it was here that Charles II became the first recreational

The Orwell Bridge soars across the estuary.

A large ship passes Collimer Point and the marina facing it.

cranes of Felixstowe stand with their jibs pointing to the sky while Harwich presents a more familiar skyline.

Tidal mudflats edging Trimley Marshes are wintering quarters for large flocks of waders, particularly Brent geese, and are used by herring and blackbacked gulls, curlews and sanderlings. The flooded former farmland is a nature reserve with a visitor centre.

Ipswich Port Authority hands control to Harwich

yachtsman. A mail packet service ran to Hellevoetsluis from 1661 until 1836, when the trade was lost to Dover. The royal dockyard was begun in the 17th century and it was the headquarters of the King's Navy when Samuel Pepys was its secretary and an MP.

Passenger ferries run across Harwich Harbour to Shotley Gate and Felixstowe while Ro-Ro vehicle ferries operate to Turku and Cuxhaven and car imports are

Felixstowe handles 40% of Britain's container traffic.

Leading lights and colourful beach huts at Harwich.

handled by Navyard. Ha'penny Pier has a visitor centre featuring Harwich and the *Mayflower* in what was built in 1854 as the ticket office for the first continental ferries. There are both deep water and inshore lifeboats, the old lifeboat house now being Harwich Lifeboat Museum with the last Clacton offshore lifeboat, an 11m Oakley.

Lights of 1665 were replaced by 'misleading lights' in 1817, superseded in 1863 after several ships ran aground. The 27m tall nonagonal High Light is now a radio museum while the 14m decagonal wooden Low Light contains Harwich Maritime Museum. In the event of the French appearing, the lower light was to be blown up and quickly replaced by a replica in the wrong place. The replacement light, like a pagoda, is an Ancient Monument and was painted by Turner.

A 1667 crane is the only surviving double treadmill crane in the UK, used in the royal dockyard until 1927 and now moved to the Green. An Ancient Monument in oak and weatherboarded, its two wheels are each 4.9m in diameter and 1.2m wide on a common 360mm square axle. The jib projects 5.4m and swings through 180° but it has no brake so a piece of wood had to be jammed in place instead.

The 55m diameter redoubt fort of 1808 had accommodation for 300 soldiers. It was for protection against Napoleon and had 11 guns but was also armed in both World Wars. It has a museum of local finds, a 12t cannon, 6m deep dry moat and cells within its 900mm thick walls around a 26m parade ground.

St Nicholas church of 1822, built on the site of an 1177 church, has a 17th century tile collection. The Guildhall was rebuilt in 1769 and the Electric Palace of 1911 was one of the first purpose built cinemas. Tolly Cobbold's brewery was founded here in 1723 but merged with Tollemache in Ipswich in 1746. The Essex Way footpath follows the shore.

Posts in the shallows foul the bay leading to a breakwater with fortifications at Blackman's Head. This keeps out some of the sea, being built to replace where

Beacon Cliff was excavated for cement production, causing Landguard spit to extend. A small craft channel tries to keep recreational boats apart from the stream of ferries and freight vessels heading in and out of the harbour.

On the inside of the spit but close to the fairway is Landguard Fort, built in the 16th century, used against the Dutch in 1667, the last invasion of England, and rebuilt in 1744. Felixstowe Museum is sited here. Also on Landguard Point are a tall radar scanner, a pillbox and flocks of migrant and coastal birds.

Harwich's man powered crane.

Distance
18km from Ipswich to the North Sea

OS 1:50,000 Sheets
169 Ipswich
& the Naze

Admiralty Charts
1491 Harwich &
Felixstowe (1:10,000)
2052 Orford Ness to
Naze (1:50,000)
2693 Apppproaches to
Felixstowe, Harwich &
Ipswich with Rs Stour,
Orwell & Deben
(1:25,000). Ipswich
(1:10,000)

Tidal Constants
Ipswich:
HW Dover +0110,
LW Dover +0040
Pin Mill:
Dover + 0100
Harwich:
HW Dover +0050,
LW Dover +0030

Sea Area
Thames

Rescue
Inshore lifeboat:
Harwich
All weather lifeboat:
Harwich

49 River Stour

The Iron Lady, the witchfinder and the crooked paymaster

For you dream you are crossing the Channel, and tossing about in a steamer from Harwich –
Which is something between a large bathing machine and a very small second-class carriage –
Sir W S Gilbert

At low water most of the Stour estuary is silt covered in green weed with a narrow channel meandering across it. At high water some of it seems little deeper.

The River Stour rises at Wratting Common and flows east to the River Orwell, mostly acting as the Suffolk/Essex border, even as it twists down the estuary. It was canalized from Sudbury in 1713. The northern arm at Cattawade is one of the oldest statutory navigations in the UK. A barrage and sluices have been built at Cattawade to keep out the salt water, obviating the need for Brantham lock. The sluices close automatically at high water but there is an adjacent slipway and local services include a sandwich van beside the A137.

Navigation is controlled by the Harwich Haven Authority. Ramblers have the Stour & Orwell Walk along the north shore, all AONB, while the railway follows the south shore from Manningtree to Harwich. Ornithologists have 36,000 waterbirds including 15,000 dunlin, 1,900 grey plovers, 1,400 blacktailed godwits, oystercatchers, terns, blackbacked and blackheaded gulls, curlews, egrets, cormorants, Canada geese and swans. In 1992 the RSPB said they faced the threat of permanent damage from marina developments, land reclaim and dredging.

Cattawade poet Thomas Tusser wrote his *A Hundreth Good Pointes of Husbandrie* in 1557. A chemist who worked in the local Xylonite factory and had her own way with words was Margaret Thatcher.

The Liverpool Street–Thorpe railway passes over both arms of the estuary and through the industrial estate on a viaduct which is the river's last crossing.

Manningtree is claimed to be the smallest town in Britain at 9ha. It has been a market and sailing town since 1238. The Stour Sailing Club and slip are by the Crown Hotel although often facing extensive mud. In July there is a regatta for gun punts, which have not been developed as Norfolk punts have.

The town has many Georgian buildings and the Swan Basin and fountain, part of a spa. Lofts were all linked to allow smugglers to escape. There were large maltings and Castle House has paintings and drawings by Sir Alfred Munnings, president of the Royal Academy in the 1940s.

The most notorious resident was Matthew Hopkins, an unsuccessful lawyer, who became Witchfinder General and probably had about 400 women put to death in 14 months in 1645/6, accounting for a third of all English people killed for witchcraft over two centuries. Some were hanged on the green. It was said that he failed his own test by not drowning so he was hanged, his ghost returning to his office in the Thorn Hotel. However, such an outcome would have been too convenient and wishful thinking by too many people so his death by tuberculosis in 1647 may have been more likely.

From Manningtree the docks of Harwich and Felixstowe can be seen the full length of the estuary.

Mistley Place Park Environmental & Animal Rescue Centre has over 1,000 animals and birds, mostly rescued, in 10ha of woodland, pasture and lakeside and with a hedge maze.

In 1732 Richard Rigby inherited Mistley. He had made a fortune as a politician, stealing nearly £500,000 as Paymaster of the Forces, and planned to build a spa town but was accused of embezzlement and the spa was not built. The pair of identical Mistley Towers with their Tuscan columns were built in 1776 by Robert Adam as the ends of a neoclassical church for the spa. The rest of the church was demolished in 1870. During the construction a dog was buried alive to chase off ghosts and its own ghost has since been seen.

With a southerly wind, Mistley's most obvious business is its malthouse. Baltic Wharf's history probably goes back much further as there was a Roman road here from

Mistley's twin towers.

The Royal Hospital School is prominent at Holbrook.

Ferries and a jack up platform at Parkeston.

A lightship regenerated as Radio Sunshine off Shotley Gate.

River Stour

Distance
16km from Cattawade
to the River Orwell

OS 1:50,000 Sheets
168 Colchester
169 Ipswich
& the Naze

Admiralty Charts
1491 Harwich &
Felixstowe (1:10,000)
1594 R Stour
– Erwarton Ness
to Manningtree
(1:10,000)
2052 Orford Ness to
Naze (1:50,000)
2693 Approaches to
Felixstowe, Harwich &
Ipswich with Rs Stour,
Orwell & Deben
(1:25,000)

Tidal Constants
Mistley:
HW Dover +0110,
LW Dover + 0030
Wrabness:
HW Dover +0100,
LW Dover +0030
Harwich:
HW Dover +0050,
LW Dover +0030

Sea Area
Thames

Rescue
Inshore lifeboat:
Harwich
All weather lifeboat:
Harwich

Colchester. The village was used for filming the BBC's *Brothers in Trouble*.

Flows are outgoing from an hour and fifty minutes after Dover high water and ingoing from two hours twenty minutes before Dover high water. Moon jellyfish go with the flow.

There are nature reserves at the back of Jacques Bay but it is Holbrook Bay which has the conspicuous feature, the Royal Hospital School, its central stone tower with white pinnacle acting as a daymark. It was founded in Greenwich in 1712 for the sons of seamen and lifeboatmen but moved here in 1933. Sailing is one of the school's sport options.

Wrabness has beach huts and some rare sand plus a church with a separate belfry. The Stour Estuary Nature Reserve has hides, woods, mudflats and saltmarsh with ducks, geese, waders, nightingales and woodpeckers around Copperas Bay to Parkeston Quay. Copperas Bay takes its name from the ferrous sulphate which was collected for ink, dyeing and tanning.

A wooded bank 2–6m high runs from Harkstead Point to Erwarton Ness, which is low and rounded.

Mudflats and marsh around Erwarton Bay are backed by a 4–5m earth bank topped by trees.

Parkeston was named after Charles Parkes, the first chairman of the Great Eastern Railway. After a dispute with Harwich a new terminal was established for the Netherlands from 1874, now called Harwich International Port. Ro-Ro vehicle ferries go to Gothenburg, Esbjerg, Hamburg and Hook of Holland and passenger ferries to Esbjerg, Cuxhaven, Ijmuiden and Hook of Holland. There are high speed ferries, cruise liners, tankers, car transporters and

container and grain ships. The tanks of a refinery stand at the back of the port and there may even be the odd jack up rig moored alongside.

Bathside Bay has wrecks and produces septaria, a soft clay which sets to stone in seawater and can then be used for building.

Boats moored around Shotley Gate include several lightships, mostly with their locations displayed although one has been redecorated and fitted with masts as Radio Sunshine. There are piers, a radio tower and a Martello tower but the site remains HMS Ganges to many, a former naval training centre for boys which was named after the training ship moored here for years. There is an HMS Ganges Association museum to tell the story next to the passenger ferry terminal from **Harwich** and the marina at Shotley Point.

Flows are outgoing from an hour and twenty minutes after Dover high water to 4km/h and ingoing from four hours forty minutes before Dover high water to 2km/h.

Ahead are all the container ships and cranes in the port of **Felixstowe**, laid out in one line.

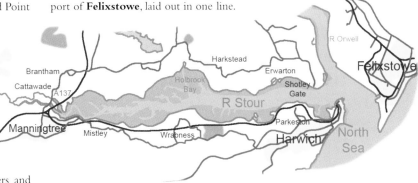

50 River Colne

Famous for oysters since Roman times

Here the Saxon Sea comes hacking
While the River Colne expands
Mersea Flats and Cocum Hills
Gazing south to Maplin Sands
Where the biggest river spills
Martin Newell

Tidal flows are stopped above the East Bridge by sluices although Thames barges could formerly reach East Mills. Mill buildings have been converted to residential use and face across the river to parkland and the centre of Colchester.

Colchester is one of Britain's oldest recorded towns, dating from the Iron Age with a settlement in the 7th century BC. It was the capital of Cunobelin or Cymbeline of the Catuvellauni, the king of southeast England, until 42 AD, and the site of his mint. The Romans established their first British capital here, Camulodunum, in 49 although it was captured and burnt to the ground by Boudicca and the Iceni in 60. The Romans rebuilt it in the 2nd century and nearly 2km of their 3rd century city walls remain, enclosing 44ha and their street layout, which they used as a retirement town. The city name may be from the fortress on the Colne or it may be named after King Coel of East Anglia who built up the town around 219 and who was claimed to have been the father of the Emperor Constantine. It is said he was the one in the nursery rhyme so his pipe would have to have been a musical one as smoking pipes had nothing to put in them for many centuries. The Hole in the Wall public house fills a gap in the Roman wall.

The Roman Temple of Claudius, built 50–60, was one of the oldest recorded buildings in Britain and was the site used by William the Conqueror for his castle in 1080. With a keep 46m x 34m, it was the Normans' largest, similar to the White Tower in London but 50% larger. Its prison was used by Witchfinder General Matthew Hopkins in the 17th century to torture suspected witches, including Rebecca West who was accused of killing a child by witchcraft and confessed to marrying the Devil. James Parnell, the first Quaker martyr, was imprisoned here in 1656 and made to climb a rope for his food even though he was an invalid, falling to his death. In the 1680s the height was reduced from four storeys to two. The Colchester & Essex Museum has Roman antiquities and medieval, Saxon and Norman material.

The 15th century Siege House was converted by Colchester's Parliamentarians prior to an attack by the Royalists. Red rings mark places where it was peppered by lead shot.

In the 1570s, 600 Flemish weavers were invited to come to the town to escape religious persecution in the Netherlands. Their cloth spinning was to help the town's revival.

The town surrendered during the Civil War after an 11 week siege but Sir Charles Lucas and Sir George Lisle were later executed in 1648. For many years the grass would not grow where they were shot and a memorial in the Victorian Castle Park now marks the event. The site of a Parliamentary fort of about 1648 is now occupied by St Andrew's church.

The first Augustinian priory in England, St Botolph's, was built in the 12th century with a notable arcade at the west end. Some of the nave remains despite serious damage by Roundhead fire in 1648. Adjacent is the two storey flint gatehouse of the Benedictine abbey of St John, complete with octagonal turrets and battlements. Colchester has been a garrison town since Napoleonic times.

In 665, 5,000 residents died in the plague. Another 17th century death was the murder of Alice Mellor, whose ghost in the Red Lion caused such severe haunting of a room that it was sealed until rediscovered in 1972. Sir William Gull, born in Colchester, was medical advisor to Queen Victoria but was also suspected of being Jack the Ripper.

A 1718 Georgian town house has the Hollytrees toy and costume museum while another Georgian town house has the Minories Art Gallery and Firstsite arts centre with Constable paintings. The Natural History Museum is in All Saints' church. A rose show and carnival take place in July. The city was used for filming *The Fourth Protocol* and Jane Taylor wrote *Twinkle, Twinkle, Little Star* here.

Mills have become residential by the tidal limit in Colchester.

A lightship now houses Colchester's Sea Cadets.

An oyster smack by the new jetty in Rowhedge.

Rising near Steeple Bumpstead, the River Colne flows southeast to the North Sea. Even below the ancient bridge carrying the A137 it is narrow and weedy, home to mallards and moorhens. At low water its bed is a steep V of silt, the mud continuing past Wivenhoe.

The St Botolphs–Colchester railway crosses as much new housing comes into view, recognized by a small spire on each block. The remains of brick piers for another bridge are found near Hythe station. The Hythe may have been a Roman harbour. The barge *Exact* was built lopsided to get under a bridge as an exact fit after another got trapped under the bridge on a rising tide. The lowest bridge over the river is followed by larger craft moored to King Edward Quay, including a lightship which serves as a Sea Cadet base. From here to Wivenhoe can be floodlit from the west bank.

Matching tower blocks in Wivenhoe Park mark the University of Essex, established in 1964. By now the river has become more open with swans, egrets, cormorants, blackheaded gulls and swallows, some spilling over from Hythe Lagoons, no doubt.

The Colchester to Clacton railway runs along the east bank until turning away at Wivenhoe although another branch formerly followed the river closely to Brightlingsea. On the other side of the tracks, Wivenhoe Woods contain 16ha of ancient sweet chestnut trees.

Rowhedge is a Victorian brick town, recalled in Pamela Evans' *The Tideway Girls*. In the early 20th century it promoted ocean yacht racing and has a history of boatbuilding from smacks to lifeboats. In front of the village sign is a new floating walkway, replacing a fixed one which used to run down to the river by the Anchor and the Olde Albion, the former advertised on the road by an old Austin van. Because of the heavy silt deposition it is worth knowing about a relatively clean slipway hidden amongst recent housing at the southern end of the front. A wreck is half buried in the silt between the slip and the confluence with the Roman River.

The front at **Wivenhoe** is rather easier to find from the water than by land. The weatherboarded or plastered buildings of the Victorian town have been joined by the redevelopment of Cook's Quay where a fence makes landing difficult. The church has fine brasses to Sir George Beaumont and Elizabeth de Vere. Garrison House, with some of the finest pargeting in Essex, took its name after some of Cromwell's troops stayed. A 1750s plan to turn it into a spa with a boat service from London was not a success. Furthermore, an earthquake in 1884 damaged over 200 buildings. By the Rose & Crown is the Nottage Maritime Institute, founded in 1894 with funding from the will of a landowning captain and moved to the quay in 1947, where nautical courses are offered. In addition to smuggling, the town's nautical interests have included boatbuilding since Elizabethan times with fast yachts in the 19th century, Second World War wooden minesweepers and even Mulberry Harbour sections. The venue was used for filming the BBC's *Plotlands*. There are moorings through the town, Wivenhoe Sailing Club has a slip and there is a Thames barge race.

Below the port is the Colne Tidal Barrier, normally open but showing three vertical red lights when passage is prevented. Commercial traffic is not normally allowed above here these days. Flows are outgoing from an hour and forty minutes after Dover high water and ingoing from four hours twenty minutes before Dover high water. Buoys mark the fairway from here and may be moved as the channel migrates.

Fingringhoe Ballast Quay has been in use since 1708 and is still very active with aggregates being shipped to London.

Alresford Creek had a ford and Roman villas on each side.

Herons, pheasants and curlews frequent the marshes which are increasingly marine with sea aster and wrack.

The Anchor in Rowhedge.

Fingringhoe Wick Nature Reserve was established in 1951 with 51ha of sandy beach, reedbeds, saltmarsh, former gravel pits, heathland, woodland, hides, an observation tower, a visitor centre and 200 species of bird including Brent geese, dunlins and breeding nightingales. On the shore is a dilapidated jetty, a wreck and, astonishingly, a banner telling boaters to go away and come back by road.

Around Aldboro Point the east side has banks of hard clay, picked over by oystercatchers. The Colne has been famous for oysters since Roman times and these may have been amongst the attractions of the river for the Romans. In the autumn the mayor and corporation of Colchester hold an Oyster Feast to commemorate the granting of oyster fishing rights to the town by Richard I. They arrive by boat, propose the loyal toast and consume gingerbread and gin, the mayor making the first oyster dredge of the season. Gingerbread may have been an offering to a sea god. Colchester natives are considered the best oysters. Boats must not ground on the oyster beds in the channel.

A further hazard is the Fingringhoe ranges danger area on the west side beyond Geedon Saltings, red flags or lights being shown when they are in use. Geedon Creek drains the area of the ranges and divides round Rat Island, a wildlife sanctuary with the biggest colony of blackheaded gulls in Essex.

The front at Wivenhoe, easier to find by river than by road.

Fingringhoe Wick Nature Reserve finds boats unacceptable.

The Pyefleet Channel follows, separating Mersea Island from the mainland with the wreck of the *SS Lowlands* near the shore.

On the east side, Bateman's Tower stands like a stubby pencil point before Westmarsh Point at the end of Brightlingsea Creek. **Brightlingsea** was an associate Cinque Port, the only one north of the Thames, and is now a yachting centre.

By St Osyth Stone Point is the 1810 Martello Tower 1, used by the Royal Navy as HMS Helder during the Second World War and now as the East Essex Aviation Society & Museum with aircraft parts recovered locally, including a P51D Mustang and Tempests. Beyond here, Ray Creek discharges past Point Clear from inside Sandy Point.

Facing across Brightlingsea Reach is the Mersea Stone on the end of Mersea Island, beyond which is another nature reserve.

Flows run outward to 3km/h and inward to 2km/h.

Distance
13km from Colchester
to Mersea Island

OS 1:50,000 Sheets
168 Colchester

Admiralty Charts
3741 Rs Colne
& Blackwater
(1:25,000).
Brightlingsea
(1:12,500). R
Colne (1:12,500).
Colchester Quays
(1:12,500)

Tidal Constants
Colchester:
HW Dover +0120
Wivenhoe:
HW Dover +0110
Brightlingsea:
Dover +0110

Sea Area
Thames

Range
Fingringhoe rifle range

Rescue
Inshore lifeboat:
West Mersea
All weather lifeboat:
Walton & Frinton

An east coast barge anchored off the yachting tower at Brightlingsea.

51 River Blackwater

Home of the east coast sailing barges

If that thou be willing thy people to redeem,
To yield to the seamen at their own choice
Tribute for a truce, and so take peace of us,
Then will we with the tax to ship betake us
To sail on the sea – and hold truce with you.
Brithnoth made answer – his buckler he grasped,
Brandished his slender spear – and spoke.
'Hearest thou, sea-robber, what this people say?
For tribute they're ready to give you their spears,
The edge poison-bitter, and the ancient sword.'

Anon

The head of tidal water at Beeleigh Falls is a complicated junction. The Chelmer & Blackwater Navigation crosses the top of the weir referred to as the falls. On the west side it is the canalized River Chelmer. On the east side it is artificial cut. The Blackwater, which rises at Sewards End as the River Pant and flows southeast towards the North Sea, crosses the navigation and discharges down the weir. Below, it meets up with a couple of bypass channels. Boats using the navigation look down as they pass between Beeleigh Lock and Beeleigh Flood Lock, the latter usually open, but there is no navigation connect to the estuary at this point. To the north is Langford with its Saxon church and Museum of Power in a steam pumping station.

There is a gravel rapid below the falls but this quickly gives way to the silt which is an extensive feature of the estuary. Initially reeds block out views beyond the banks but kingfishers, lapwings and waders search the mud and cormorants and egrets perch higher up.

Cormorants and egrets watch the river ebbing.

Beeleigh Abbey looks peaceful enough on August 11th.

Looking down from Beeleigh Falls at low water.

Unseen on the left bank is a golf course while the right bank hides the 12th century Beeleigh Abbey, where wailing heard on August 11th is that of Sir John Gate awaiting execution. Beyond it is a mound, passed by the A414 after it crosses the river.

Next to the Welcome is Fullbridge, which leads to one of the steepest hills in Essex. The 10th century Saxon port of **Maldon** takes its name from the Old English mael dun, hill marked by a cross or other monument. The ancient hill town, chartered in 1171, has St Mary's Norman church and the 13th century church of All Saints with the only triangular tower in Britain and some big people. The

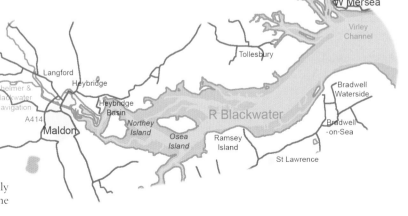

An east coast barge moored below the bridge in the centre of Maldon.

graves include that of Lawrence Washington, ancestor of George, and Edward Bright, who died at the age of 29 in 1750, the biggest man in England at 279kg and needing a crane to lower him down. There is a 1928 Washington window presented by the people of Maldon, Massachusetts, and outside is a statue of the 2.13m Bryhtnoth, Earldorman of Essex.

The 15th century Moot Hall has a medieval Plantagenet spiral brick staircase, 18th century court room and five bells. From before the days of public libraries, Dr Plume's library of 1704 has 7,000 books and panelled walls. Maeldune Heritage Centre in the Plume Building accompanies Maldon Millennium Garden in 10th century style with monastic and wild herbs. The seven 13m long Maldon Embroidery panels cover a millennium of the town's history from the Battle of Maldon. A Georgian Oakwood House is home to the Hayletts Gallery.

Large boats, old flourmills and weatherboarded houses are met below the bridge, as are swans, geese and mallards. Flows out begin an hour and forty minutes after Dover high water and in from four hours twenty minutes before Dover high water. Heybridge Creek is followed by numerous moorings and the Hythe, a yachting centre and the biggest collection of Thames sailing barges still afloat, described in *Down Tops'l* and still raced. The 19th century stackies carried complete haystacks up to 3.7m above the decks and were wide and shallow, able to get into surprisingly small inlets. Indeed, it was claimed they could go anywhere after a heavy dew.

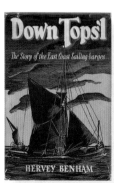

Maldon Yacht Club and Maldon Little Ship Club, the Queen's Head and the Jolly Sailor, Maldon District Museum, the RNLI Rowing Race and Maldon Mud Race, the latter with memorable black organic silt, cater for a wide range of tastes. The estuary was used in the BBC's *Lovejoy*.

Maldon sea salt has been produced since Saxon times, the current works built in 1882, a surprising location because of the level of silt in the water.

Byrhtnoth led the defenders at the Battle of Maldon.

Maldon is the leading home for the east coast sailing barges.

Promenade Park with its esplanade is Edwardian although it looks much more recent with a funfair, large children's play area, marine boating lake, slipway, Second World War memorial tree avenue and a prominent statue of Byrhtnoth.

Beyond on the south bank is the site of the 991 Battle of Maldon with Byrhtnoth leading the defenders. The Vikings, under Olaf Tryggvason with 93 ships, camped on Northney and took a fortnight to kill all the Saxons, recorded in *The Battle of Maldon*, the first English epic poem, an extract of which opens this chapter.

Gravel pits lead to Herrings Point. Opposite is Northney Island, 1.3km² of nature reserve with breeding and wintering birds, oystercatchers, curlews, blackbacked gulls, terns, waders, Brent geese and shorteared owls. The 18th century seawall was damaged in 1874 and 1897. Although there are many trees it is heavily divided with numerous channels between small islands and is 60% covered at high water. A Grade 1 SSSI, it requires a permit for landing. Before the Norman Conquest it was called Uvesia and Stone Age flint scrapers have been found. A more recent artifact is the rudder from the barge *Gillman*.

Heybridge Basin with Sea Lock is at the end of the Chelmer & Blackwater Navigation, built to here to avoid the tolls in Maldon. Small craft moorings surround the former smugglers' village of Heybridge.

Collier's Reach is the main channel to the north of the island. Before the last glaciation the land was higher and this was the mouth of the Thames.

A causeway runs out from Decoy Point to Osea Island, 1.2km² with wildfowl and the site of Roman saltpans. In 1903 it was set up by Fred Charrington of the brewing family as an Edwardian temperance and anti narcotics retreat after watching a domestic dispute in an east London public house. The scheme was undermined by the fact that boatmen made most of their money by smuggling out whisky and gin. During the First World War it was used as a base for fast torpedo boats and minelayers. Boatbuilders

Iain Oughtred and Fabian Bush used it as a base in the 1980s for producing Acorn Skiffs. The owners, Caius College, don't allow landing above high water except by approved members of the yachting centre.

Flows run out from an hour and twenty minutes after Dover high water with a fast ebb and in from four hours forty minutes before Dover high water.

The Stumble, to the north of the island, almost dries and Goldhanger Creek has oyster beds, marked with buoys and withies, where boats must not ground.

The main channel passes south of the island, to be joined by Lawling Creek. Stansgate Point was the site of Stansgate Abbey. Tony Benn's family are local landowners. Ramsey Island is not an island but the Stone manages some sand in place of the mud. Stone Sailing Club is joined by powerboats and water skiing in St Lawrence Bay.

There are occasional sunbathers and swimmers but the embankments of concrete slabs, fringed by saltings with wrack and silt mean that local knowledge is needed to find reasonable locations. Behind Thirstlet Creek the embankments are of stone bonded with bitumen, steep, precise and uncompromising. A pillbox protects Tollesbury Wick Marshes.

Pewet Island nature reserve protects the moorings in Bradwell Creek. Bradwell Waterside has the Green Man smugglers' public house, Bradwell Centre for Outdoor Learning and a slip beside Bradwell Quay Yacht Club.

Visible the whole length of the estuary are the two blocks of Bradwell nuclear power station of 1962, one of the first full scale Magnox reactors in Britain, with a visitor centre. Standing off it is a large intake jetty.

Flows run out to 4km/h and in to 3km/h.

Beyond Shinglehead Point the northern shoreline breaks up into a series of creeks and islands, Great Cob Island, Cobmarsh Island and Mersea Island with South Channel, North Channel, Virley Channel, Mersea Quarters and Besom Fleet forming entrances to an extensive area of salt and freshwater marsh with complex muddy channels.

Distance
17km from Langford to Bradwell Waterside

OS 1:50,000 Sheets
168 Colchester

Admiralty Charts
3741 Rs Colne & Blackwater (1:25,000). Bradwell (1:12,500). Maldon (1:12,500)

Tidal Constants
Maldon:
HW Dover +0150
Osea Island:
HW Dover +0140,
LW Dover +0110
Bradwell-on-Sea:
Dover +0110

Sea Area
Thames

Rescue
Inshore lifeboat:
West Mersea
All weather lifeboat:
Walton & Frinton

52 River Crouch

The Cowes of the east coast

The River Crouch flows eastwards across Essex to the North Sea from a pond at Stockwell Hall, Little Burstead. There are concrete railway sleepers and other debris beneath the railway bridge below Wickford, the tidal limit. From a housing estate a path leads down to the river through Shotgate Thicket, a wood which acts as a wildlife reserve owned by Essex Wildlife Trust.

Here the banks are steep and muddy, overlooked by a sewage works, and muddy water is the general order. High water is about half an hour after Burnham-on-Crouch.

At first it is narrow but already there are signs of the saltmarshes to come and large dragonflies flit about.

The tide floods through the tide lock gates at Battlesbridge.

The old tide mill turned restaurant at Battlesbridge.

Sea aster on the saltings above Hullbridge.

There are only three road crossings, the new and old A130 and, after a collection of riverside shacks, a minor road at Battlesbridge. Battlesbridge is one of the gems of the river, located where tidal doors were built to allow vessels to proceed upstream. This river was an invasion route for marauding Danes although it is unlikely they got up much beyond this in their boats. The doors are now tied open and a powerful flow of water sluices through.

Adjacent is a mill with tidal mill wheel. Just upstream is an old wharf building and an adjacent building with a conical roof topped with an oasthouse cowling. There are five buildings dating from the 17th and 18th centuries in the vicinity. Below the road bridge is a magnificent granary building which is now Battlesbridge Antiques Centre, the largest antiques outlet in Essex with 70 dealers plus places of refreshment. Trading barges regularly reached the mill and can still do so.

A small inlet towards Gorse's Farm has a jetty which is now becoming overgrown and there are a couple of wrecks in this area, one before the inlet and another below Oldtree Point as sailing boats begin to be encountered.

The marshes start in earnest down Spitty's Reach, reeds giving way to sea aster, one of the first plants to move onto the mudflats, its fleshy leaves providing a cover of greenery for wildlife.

The caravan site at the head of Long Reach is sited above moorings for dinghies and powerboats while jet skis come up through Short Reach, further noise being added by youths on motorbikes on the levées which are almost continuous features of this river right down to the sea and beyond.

Fenn Creek drains **South Woodham Ferrers** which stands back from the river. Named after de Ferrers, a Norman knight with William the Conqueror, it had a saltmaking industry until the 18th century. From the 1890s it became a commuter town for London but much of the development nearest the river is since 1981 when it became a brick paved, pedestrianized, new town around its white weatherboarded clocktower, its jumbled up Toytown houses each appearing too neat to be real.

Hullbridge, on the south side, consists of chalets and moorings, the Anchor and other public houses, much less pretentious and seeming to have more of an aim to life.

The notable exception on the north bank is the Marsh Farm Countryside Park, 1.3km^2 of reclaimed marshland with commercial cattle and milking displays, sheep and pigs, pet animals, free range chickens and rare breeds based around traditional Essex farm buildings. The farm is very informatively laid out for visitors and has two picnic areas (one indoors) and a nature conservation zone at the east end with warblers on the dykes and migrant birds including Brent geese in the winter. There are leaflets, displays, souvenirs, a tea room, an adventure play area and riverside walks.

From Brandy Hole, Brandy Hole Reach runs down past an area of marsh of about 1km^2 which floods, reclaimed by the river after the sea wall breached.

The area around Clementsgreen Creek, which drains the east side of South Woodham Ferrers, is much used by water skiers.

Stow Creek, its channel marked by withies as it runs down from Fambridge Yacht Haven, is the start of another area of innundation, this time on the north side of Longpole Reach. The seawall broke down in 1897 and it was never restored.

North Fambridge and South Fambridge face each

other across the river. The public house on the south side is accompanied by a public telephone and fresh lobsters can be bought from the lobster ponds but the attractive 15th century Ferry Boat Inn on the north bank has greater interest for being haunted by the ghost of an old ferryman. It was also the base for the slightly disreputable Flexible Yacht Club, exposed in Mike Peyton's *Floating Assets*.

On the higher ground to the south is Ashingdon where the church was built by Cnut to celebrate his victory over the Saxons. Further along at Canewdon there is a church with a 15th century tower on Beacon Hill. This hill was Cnut's command post before his Danish army beat the English under Edmund Ironside at the Battle of **Ashingdon** in 1016 which gave him the country north of the Thames.

The hill overlooks Shortpole Reach, Landsend Point, Raypits Reach and Easter Reach, alongside Bridgemarsh Island which is cut off by Bridgemarsh Creek linked to Althorne Creek. In fact, it is more marsh than island. Despite being over 3km long there is little more to show than breached levées at high water.

Althorne Creek gives access to Bridgemarsh Marina

Two Royal Navy minesweepers on a courtesy visit are surrounded by a forest of pleasure boat masts at Lion Wharf.

Traditional buildings along the front at Burnham-on-Crouch, the river's last vehicle access point.

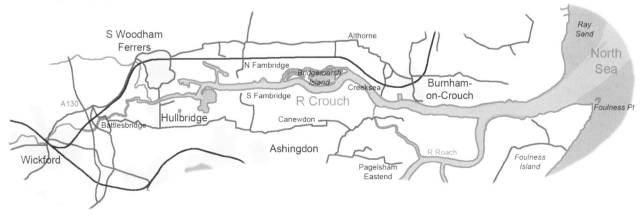

opposite Black Point. The next 2km form Cliff Reach, the cliff itself being all of 10m high, twice the height of the bank at any other point on the river. The reach ends at Creeksea, Anglo-Saxon for place at the creek, one of the locations where Cnut is said to have tried unsuccessfully to turn back the tide to prove he was only human.

Opposite is the start of Wallasea Island, no longer a true island as the road giving access now divides Lion Creek from Paglesham Creek. There is a forest of masts as the river now has rows of moorings continuously to beyond Burnham-on-Crouch, through which a passenger ferry picks its line across from Wallasea Island to Baltic Wharf, on its way passing the Burnham Yacht Harbour excavated on the north bank and wrecks littered along both banks.

Burnham-on-Crouch is one of England's leading yachting centres with the Royal Burnham Yacht Club and the Royal Corinthian Yacht Club. Burnham Week is at the end of August, the longest running annual yacht regatta on the British mainland, and there is a carnival at the end of September. The only thing which prevents the Cowes of the East Coast or Pearl of the East Coast from becoming a greater tourist trap is that it is a fair way from anywhere else and not on the road to anywhere. The elegant quayside with its Star Inn, Olde White Harte Hotel and Anchor is pedestrianized but it is possible to park here out of season near the weatherboarded customs house, useful because this is the last vehicle access point to the river, steps leading up with access through heavy tidal doors in the wall.

The town takes its name from the Old English burna ham, stream village. There is an elegant Georgian High Street with an octagonal Victorian clocktower. The town's oyster beds are disused and it was a centre for cockles and whelks. A museum looks at local and maritime history and agricultural features of Dengie Hundred. There is also a swimming pool. The stream here runs up to 9km/h with a 3m tidal range. Burnham-on-Crouch is left past the sewage works and the Ringwood Bar.

Wallasea Island had 330m of its north flood defences breached in 2006 to create 1.2km² of marshland in a scheme to turn farmland from the 16th to the 19th century to the largest manmade saltmarsh in the UK with seven islands likely to appeal to oystercatchers, avocets, little terns, grey plovers, dunlins and curlews and be a breeding ground for bass, herring and mullet. It is also supposed to dampen storm waves although it seems rather far inland for that purpose.

A long wide reach runs past this site down to Wallasea Ness where Brankfleet, the final reach of the River Roach, enters on the right.

The Crouch and Roach between them have 22,000 waders and wildfowl, including 5,600 Brent geese and 2,100 golden plovers. Despite the present happy coexistence with all the boating activity, the RSPB claimed the area to be in immediate danger of permanent damage by recreation.

The north bank of the River Crouch has pillboxes at intervals, some of which are bricked up. These derelict fortifications face Foulness Island on which landing is not permitted. The island's name derives from the Old English fulga naess, meaning wild birds promontory, indicating that it has only become an island in recent times although the birds have long been present.

Foulness is known for its different forms of flight. For some years it was under discussion and public enquiry as one of the proposed sites for London's third airport although successive Governments failed to reach a decision. Direct rail and motorway links to London were proposed for the site which would have covered the island and involved much reclamation from the Maplin Sands, not unprecedented as much of Foulness itself has been inned from the sea over the years. The final form of flight is brought about by the Ministry of Defence who purchased the island in 1915. Foulness is a military firing range and the public are not admitted to the island, excepting the couple of hundred civilians who live there and farm the soil which Arthur Young, in 1814, described as being the richest in the country. The water running 12km northeast from Foulness Point is a prohibited area for shipping, no great loss for larger vessels because of the shallowness of the water. However, small boats may go into this area when the ranges are not active. Firing usually takes place during working hours, leaving weekends free. This range is unusual in that live shells are fired onto the sands to be collected at low tide for examination. The towers and buildings have a discarded look, an appearance belied by a new radar scanner on top of one. Indeed, one of the facilities on the island is a wind tunnel which is able to simulate the effect of nuclear blast on vehicles.

The River Crouch discharges into the North Sea between Holliwell Point and Foulness Point. To the north lies Ray Sand and Dengie Flat, a 3km width of muddy tussocks which provide spring and autumn feeding for Brent geese, teal and shelducks, joined in the winter by many other species, even the heron.

Although it is not permitted to take a vehicle beyond East Wick it is possible to reach south of Holliwell Farm or near Holliwell Point with permission or in an emergency.

Distance
28km from Wickford
to the North Sea

OS 1:50,000 Sheets
167 Chelmsford
168 Colchester
178 Thames Estuary

Admiralty Charts
1975 Thames Estuary
– Northern Part
(1:50,000)
3750 Rs Crouch &
Roach (1:25,000).
Burnham-on-Crouch
(1:10,000)

Tidal Constants
Battlesbridge:
HW Dover +0200
Hullbridge:
HW Dover +0150,
LW Dover +0200
North Fambridge:
HW Dover +0150,
LW Dover +0200
Burnham-on-
Crouch:
Dover +0120
Holliwell Point:
HW Dover +0120,
LW Dover +0130

Sea Area
Thames

Range
Foulness Island
danger area

Rescue
Inshore lifeboat:
Burnham-on-
Crouch
All weather lifeboat:
Sheerness
Hovercraft:
Southend-on-Sea

Looking south across the saltings at Holliwell Point towards Foulness Island shrouded in autumn haze.

53 River Roach

Black silt but the lowest rainfall in Britain

Saltings and withy groynes near Mucking Hall.

Fleethall Creek is the longest tidal arm of the River Roach, becoming tidal 600m from Southend Municipal Airport on the edge of **Rochford**, fairly active with small airliners and private aircraft. It flows eastwards across the Essex marshes to join the River Crouch.

The estuary drains extensively and has a fast current. Stambridge Mill is now disused. The adjacent building is a former tide mill which was powered by water stored in ponds next to what is now a cricket pitch.

There are moorings for a selection of pleasure craft. Groynes of withies help stabilize the silt against the swift flow. The low tide mudflats make the river a popular destination for wildfowl. The River Crouch Marshes are an internationally important bird area, especially for the Brent goose. The RSPB said they were threatened by recreation, grazing, mud loss and saltmarsh erosion.

The levées which are present here are to continue for the full length of the river. Concrete slab revetment protects the levée on the south bank. The silt is brown on top but it is not loadbearing and is black and glutinous beneath the surface.

Before Great Stambridge Hall is a church with a tower topped by a diminutive spire in white board. Closer to the river is a large battery farm. There used to be a wharf at Mucking Hall with its moat. Most of the creeks and inlets are now inaccessible to anything too large to penetrate the many leads off this quiet river to reach pools where herons or cormorants fish.

A pillbox tops the levée near Barton Hall but the majority of the flat landscape lies hidden beyond the banks which are either of mud or else faced with slabs. Climbing them gives views of cornfields, often edged with drainage channels. There was a quay near Roper's Farm, from where Barling is marked by its church spire,

beyond which lies Great Wakering, the driest place in Britain with a mere 430mm per year of rain.

After Blackedge Point the river enters the Paglesham Reach which is an extensive mooring for sailing boats. Potton Creek or the Violet, a popular mooring for fishing boats, leads south at Barling Ness and separates off Potton Island on which landing is forbidden as it belongs to the Ministry of Defence.

At water level there are banks of compacted mud and clay, etched by the water and covered with a fine coating of green weed. Patches of wrack float in the water where there are stones and gravel and occasional bands of shells are exposed in the clay. It is an unusual shoreline, suitable for rabbits to run free.

The main intrusions into the skyline are the clump of trees at Paglesham Eastend with the inevitable flock of rooks circling around them and the tower of the church at Paglesham Churchend visible behind. There are now fewer trees, the elms being

211

Cornfield on Barling Marsh separated from the River Roach by a drainage channel and the levée.

Moorings at Paglesham Eastend.

Distance
14km from Rochford
to the River Crouch

OS 1:50,000 Sheets
168 Colchester
178 Thames Estuary

Admiralty Charts
3750 Rs Crouch &
Roach (1:25,000)

Tidal Constants
Rochford:
Dover +0130
Burnham-on-
Crouch:
Dover + 0120

Sea Area
Thames

Ranges
Potton and Foulness
Islands danger areas

Rescue
Inshore lifeboat:
Burnham-on-
Crouch
All weather lifeboat:
Sheerness
Hovercraft:
Southend-on-Sea

lost to Dutch elm disease. Amongst the trees remaining is the Plough & Sail, the public house where then Prime Minister Ted Heath met members of the Defenders of Essex just before the cancellation of the project to build the third London airport on Maplin Sands.

The old boatyard is the dominant feature of the shoreline, surrounded by moored pleasure craft and the wooden skeletons of former piers projecting out into the soft mud. Earlier, there was a barge and smack building business in a weatherboarded shed outside the seawall. One barge left on the slipway before breakfast had launched herself when the men returned, so quietly that she had not even been noticed by the nearby oyster dredgers. Oysters are dredged from the riverbed mud but need to be properly cleaned. The boatyard is the lowest point on the river which can be reached by road although there is a charge for using the slipway.

There is a sunken barge on the north side of the channel and oyster beds just above. Paglesham Pool marks the start of Wallasea Island to which attention is drawn by a prominent pillbox at the confluence.

Wallasea Island is no longer an island, Paglesham

Pool having been crossed with an embankment near its north end.

Opposite Potton Point is a spread of mudflats alongside Devil's Reach which is popular with wildfowl. Seabirds find this a little more sheltered than the Maplin Sands. Canada geese, blackheaded and blackbacked gulls and cormorants are amongst the commoner species although large numbers of other birds overwinter here.

Yoke Fleet enters at Potton Point, beyond which is Foulness Island, again forbidden for landing as it belongs to the MoD. On Foulness a dilapidated selection of lattice pylons, gantries and old buildings lie scattered at random across the horizon in military fashion, quietly rusting.

Horseshoe Corner leads past Whitehouse Hole where the river turns north for its final run through Quay Reach and Brankfleet.

Pleasure and fishing boats are moored here with access apparently being made from Foulness Island.

Oystercatchers rush past in flocks while herring gulls announce their presence with their familiar cries rather than with speed. Terns drop like stones to the water to take small fish. Shelducks flap around with pretended broken wings, trying to attract the boater away from their broods of growing ducklings.

In the 19th century it was described as 'an idyllic paradise of wild life, with swans reflected in the still blue waters of the fleets; as the sea lavender bursts into flower, a purple glow would steal over the marshes, and creek and pool were royally fringed with sea aster.' The sea aster is still one of the first plants to move onto the reclaimed mudflats.

This is a particularly active reach for sailing craft, showing how pleasure craft can share the water without problems.

From Crow Corner the east bank curves gently into the River Crouch at Nase Point but the west side ends abruptly at Wallasea Ness and its low tide extension, Brankfleet Spit, again popular with waders.

The nearest public road is up the Crouch at Burnham-on-Crouch although continuing to Lion Wharf has the convenience of being on the south bank.

Wrack coats the bank looking south from near the River Crouch at Brankfleet.

54 River Thames

Britain's best known river

Filthy river, filthy river,
Foul from London to the Nore
What art thou but one vast gutter,
One tremedous common shore.
Punch

Although the River Thames rises at Thames Head near Kemble and flows eastwards to the North Sea, the River Churn is a rather longer tributary so the source should really be near Cowley. Using volume as the ruling criterion would make Swindon sewage works the source. However, this is not the reason for the name, coming from the British Celtic for dark river. In the upper reaches it is also known as the Isis, the Tame and Isis meeting below Dorcester to form what the Romans called the Tamesis Fluvius. More books have been written about the Thames than about any other river in Britain, possibly in the world.

Formerly tidal from Staines, the tidal limit is now at Teddington Weir. The river flows in a drowned valley, the tertiary beds of the London Basin syncline having artesian conditions although the head used to be some 30m higher. The London clay deposited in its valley has been a valuable source of material for brick manufacture.

Teddington takes its name from the Saxon Tuda's farm. Teddington Weir of 1811 is the longest on the river with an average flow of $81\text{m}^3/\text{s}$ although it can reach $350\text{m}^3/\text{s}$ in the winter. Ice damaged the weir in 1827 and there were further breaches later in the century. A long suspended footbridge crosses the river above the locks. The barge lock is 198 x 7.6m, the largest on the river, the 54m lock is for launches, the 15m coffin lock for skiffs is the smallest in Britain and there are rollers, all reconstructed in 1931. When the old London Bridge was rebuilt the water level dropped 760mm here but there was still enough for a tug to pass through in 1906 during a flood without having to open the gates. The 1947 flood recorded $714\text{m}^3/\text{s}$ but water was pumped to flow upstream during the 1976 drought.

Water has not been the only problem. In the early 19th century there were repeated attacks on the lock house so guns and a bayonet were supplied. In 1969 it was the venue for Monty Python's fish slapping dance.

Until the 19th century the best salmon in England came from the Thames but pollution increased until by 1957 there were no fish between Richmond and Gravesend. Cleaning up has restored it to being one of the cleanest metropolitan estuaries in Europe. There are dace and roach to Battersea, the estuary is the largest nursery ground for sole in England and Wales and in the spring Teddington is reached by elvers, flounder fry and even seals.

It can take water over three weeks to travel from here to Southend, despite the fast flow rates. Levels are higher with strong and continued northwesterly and westerly winds, especially with storm surges, while easterly to south southeasterly winds have the opposite effect. Currents set towards the outsides of bends and there may be eddies on the insides. Over half the property in England and Wales at risk of flooding lies around the tidal Thames. Driftwood can be a problem and there are passive collector boats for flotsam.

At first the estuary is almost entirely recreational but this gradually changes to having mostly industrial use lower down. In the 18th and 19th centuries over 2,000 ships were built on the tidal Thames. A triangle of red discs or lights shows when a bridge arch is closed, a white light or bundle of straw when a bridge arch is restricted and an orange light when it may be used. Oil and gas jetties and their vessels have 60m exclusion zones round them. The biggest washes are put up not by commercial ships but by commuter boats which rush around the centre of the city at high speed. With 30,000 shops, 6,000 restaurants and 3,800 public houses the capital has vast numbers of residents and visitors moving about, some by river.

Next to the weir are Teddington Television Studios, having produced many comedy films and programmes including *This is Your Life*, *Opportunity Knocks* and *Pop Idol*. The Landmark Arts Centre is also here, as is Haymarket Media Group, Britain's largest independent publishers. The Anglers public house backs onto the river with a 'No fishing' notice while the Tide End Cottage faces Ferry Lane and an area which can be used for unloading small craft although it can flood at high water. The Thames Path continues to the Thames Barrier, on both banks most of the way.

There are moorings below the weir and the British Motor Yacht Club have their base. A plaque recalls the 100 Little Ships assembled here in the Second World War by Toughs with headquarters in the Tide End for Operation Dynamo to help rescue British and French troops from Dunkirk beaches. Their boatyard closed in 1999.

Coots, mallards, wagtails, magpies and blackbacked gulls share a river which is lined with willows and other trees initially. Flocks of feral parakeets roam the woods on this part of the river.

St Alban's church is based on Clermont-Ferrand cathedral after the vicar and churchwarden paid a visit in 1889 and wanted one like it. Choristers have included Noël Coward.

The Boundary Stone of 1909 marks where Environment Agency control passes to the Port of London Authority.

Strawberry Hill was Horace Walpole's Gothic revival fantasy castle, spawning the Strawberry Hill Gothic style, where he wrote the first Gothic novel, *The Castle of Otranto*.

Former gravel pits have become Ham Local Nature Reserve, home of Thames Young Mariners, an active watersports centre. At dawn on Easter Monday this is the start of the final leg of the staged section of the Devizes to Westminster canoe race, Britain's best known canoeing competition. A water skiing area adds further activity at Cross Deep, off Swan Island or Chillingworth Ait.

Pope's Grotto is a set of tunnels under the A310 to connect his former house with his riverside gardens, the tunnels lined with geological specimens. Fielding wrote *Tom Jones* locally. The site is totally upstaged by the large St James School for Boys, built prominently on a bend of the river by a tea merchant in 1844 to look like a tea caddy.

Twickenham, from the Old English twicce hamm, river fork enclosure, alludes to the $8,000\text{m}^2$ Eel Pie Island with a nature reserve at each end. In the centre were 18th century gardens and an 1830 hotel where Edwardian tea dances were held. In the 1960s it became a hippie commune and then a jazz and rock venue where The Rolling Stones, The Who, Pink Floyd, Eric Clapton, David Bowie, Rod Stewart, John Mayall, The Yardbirds and Genesis were amongst those who would become better known. The hotel burned down in 1971 and Eel Pie Marine followed in 1996. The island featured in

Richmond Hill viewpoint protected by Act of Parliament.

Richmond Canoe Club, a hive of activity.

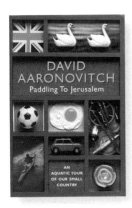

The Palladian Marble Hill House of about 1724 was built in 27ha of grounds by George II, while still Prince of Wales, for his mistress, Henrietta Howard, the Countess of Suffolk. It was later used by George IV for his illegal wife, Mrs Fitzherbert. Decor is based on Wilton carpets, handpainted Chinese wallpaper and 18th century furniture and paintings. The park by Alexander Pope includes Britain's largest black walnut tree and Britain's first weeping willow trees, grown from a twig taken from a basket holding a present of figs sent from Turkey, from which all weeping willows in England are said to be descended. It was used for filming *Shakespeare in Love*.

Richmond Park is the largest royal park at over 10km^2 with 600 red and fallow deer, introduced to this royal hunting ground in 1637.

Building the towpath led to riots and bloodshed by objectors. There were further problems in 1898 when Joseph Glover threatened to use Glover's Island or Petersham Ait for a soap company advertising hoarding but it was bought by a local resident and given to the council. Uniquely, the view from the hill is protected by a 1902 Act of Parliament and it has been painted by Turner and Reynolds, a local, and used in *The Heart of Midlothian* and for filming *The Hours*. The view encouraged William Byrd II to call his settlement in Virginia Richmond. Prominently positioned on top of the hill is the Grade II Royal Star & Garter Home of 1916 for disabled servicemen although a move is planned to somewhere cheaper to run.

Richmond Theatre was used for filming *Neverland* and Richmond Ice Rink has artists on ice. Moorhens and herons on the river are joined by members of the galleried Richmond Canoe Club, which attracts immigrant paddlers, especially Irish and South Africans, and has produced many superlative performances although these did not include the coaching of David Aaronovich, described in his *Paddling to Jerusalem*. The Great River Race for traditional boats runs from here to Greenwich.

The river has Corporation Island and there is a tunnel under Richmond Ait. By Richmond Landing Stage is Richmond Bridge of 1777, replacing a horse ferry. This particularly fine bridge by James Paine and Kenton Course carries the A305 and has five stone arches and stone balustrades, being widened in 1929. Turner painted it in 1876. Van Gogh threw in the ear ring of Ursula Loyer, the daughter of his landlady, because she would not return his affections.

Local hostelries include the White Cross and the Slug & Lettuce in a listed pumphouse.

A gateway led to the Richmond Palace of 1125, built for Henry I. Edward I and II

Nicholas Nickleby and it was here that Trevor Bayliss invented the clockwork radio. The Snapper Bridge, named after antiques dealer Michael Snapper, dates from 1998 after British Gas drilled through the post tensioning cable of a 1957 post tensioned reinforced concrete bridge of pioneering design.

In Orleans Gardens the 1730 Octagon Room of Orleans House was built to entertain Queen Caroline to dinner but is now an art gallery by James Gibbs for Louis Philippe. St Mary's church was by John James in 1714 although it has a 14th century tower. Its graves include those of Alexander Pope, actress Peg Woffington, *Times* founder John Walter and pioneering plant physiologist Stephen Hales. Artist Sir Geoffrey Kneller was a local resident and tea merchant Thomas Twining lived in the vicarage, the 1726 Dial House from the sundial above the door. The CND Ban the Bomb logo was designed here by Gerald Holton. York House of 1633 has become the council offices with flowers and classical white Italian sea nymph statues in a pool by the river.

The Baroque Ham House of 1610 was built for Sir Thomas Vavasour and passed to the Duke and Duchess of Lauderdale. It was enlarged in 1670, the CABAL Cabinet met here and it is where James II was ordered to retire on the arrival of William of Orange. The Stuart building is one of Europe's most complete survivals of 17th century fashion, furniture and paintings. It is also one of Britain's most haunted houses. An icehouse and dairy with cast iron cows' legs join the earliest known purpose built still house, a private pharmacy. The formal gardens with lavender parterres survived the 18th century English Landscape Movement and there is a statue of Father Thames. *The Young Victoria, Never Let Me Go, Monty Python, Sense & Sensibility, Spiceworld* and *John Carter of Mars* were filmed here.

Petersham church, partly Norman, retains its box pews. It is where the Duke and Duchess of Lauderdale were married, as was Prince Rupert in 1664, and has the grave of local explorer George Vancouver.

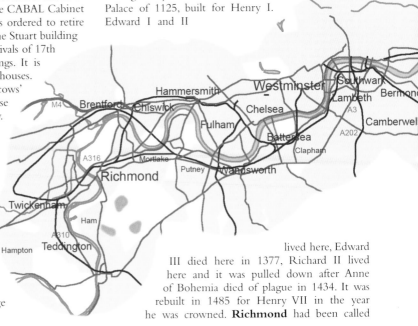

lived here, Edward III died here in 1377, Richard II lived here and it was pulled down after Anne of Bohemia died of plague in 1434. It was rebuilt in 1485 for Henry VII in the year he was crowned. **Richmond** had been called

Richmond half tide lock with the sluices lifted.

Sheen but it was renamed by the Earl of Richmond in Yorkshire, who died here in 1509. Wolsey downsized here after Henry VIII relieved him of Hampton Court. Mary I and Philip of Spain honeymooned here. Elizabeth I objected to the navigation within sight of her palace, had the world's first flushing WC here, was a prisoner of Mary here and died here in 1603. Charles I was another resident while avoiding the plague. Maids of Honour Row was built in 1724 for the attendants of George II's wife. Other residents of the area have included Rolling Stones members, the Mills acting family, explorer Sir Richard Burton who introduced pyjamas and the *Kama Sutra*, writers George Eliot and the Woolfs, and the Attenborough brothers. Richmond Green was the jousting square and the scene of the first recorded tied cricket match.

Actor Edmund Keane was buried at the church after Westminster Abbey had refused him because of his drunkenness.

The waterfront at Isleworth.

Richmond Railway Bridge by J W Jacombe-Hood takes the Waterloo to Twickenham railway over to St Margarets, where Dickens wrote *Oliver Twist* in 1838. A tunnel passes under the river. It stands next to Twickenham Bridge of 1933 by Alfred Dryland. Carrying the A316, it was the first large three pinned reinforced concrete bridge.

Removal of the old London Bridge and excessive abstraction above Teddington Weir left the river too shallow so Richmond Half Tide Lock was added in 1894, a Grade II structure. Three 3.7m high weir gates are normally lifted for the top four hours of the tide, a pair of amber lights indicating that they are open. At other times three red discs or lights are shown over each gate and it is necessary to use the lock on the right or the rollers on the left. The decorative iron Richmond Footbridge passes over the top. Flows run out to sea for around eight hours and in from three and a half to five hours at up to 7km/h.

Birdlife on the river by Syon House.

The Old Deer Park occupies the right bank with a golf course and Kew Observatory of 1769, an obelisk by the towpath to align for true north. From here to Fulham Railway Bridge rowers cross in unconventional places and often do not follow the usual rule of the road.

Sheen Gulls lead to the confluence with the River Crane. There had been a plan in the 18th century to build a London Canal from Boulter's Lock at Maidenhead to Isleworth because of the state of the Thames. A weir had been built in the 16th century by the Duke of Somerset. Isleworth Ait forms a 4ha nature

conspicuous since Teddington but they pass over Syon Reach, crossing the winding river for at least the fifth time as they make their descents. Otherwise it is a peaceful reach with herring gulls and cormorants, flanked by buttercups, ragwort and cow parsley. The fort style mansion of Syon House, built in 1547 on the site of a Roman village and then a medieval Bridgettine convent, has been less peaceful and Syon Abbey, England's largest abbey church, was one of the first religious houses to be closed after the Dissolution. Henry VIII's coffin spent a night here and his corpse was savaged by dogs, as had been foretold. It was a prison for Katherine Howard until her execution, Lady Jane Grey was here when she accepted the crown, Charles I came here as a prisoner to see his children and it was loaned to Pocahontas

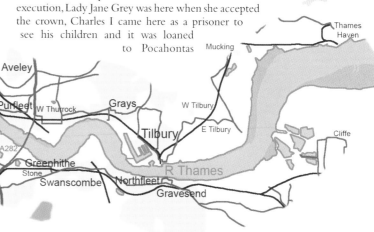

reserve and screens the White Swan at **Isleworth**, Thistleworth in Elizabethan times. Georgian houses surround the 15th century Tudor London Apprentice, a rowing holiday destination for apprentices. Residents included Turner. All Saints' church has a 15th century tower and 18th century nave walls. Plague victims were buried behind the church after being brought by barge. After a Second World War fire a new church was built inside.

Aircraft on final approach to Heathrow have been

in 1616. It was the London home of the Duke of Northumberland, who had the interior remodelled by Robert Adams in 1762, one of his finest interiors, whose family still live here. The spectacular 1826 Great Conservatory dome, the world's first in glass and metal,

215

covers 900m² with free flying birds inside and inspired the Crystal Palace. The 81ha Syon Park by Capability Brown is where Prince Rupert defeated the Parliamentarians in the 1642 2nd Battle of Brentford, driving the defenders into the river and damaging fishing nets. An ammunition barge blew up here the next day, was mistaken for gunfire and overturned the potential Turnham truce to end the Civil War. An early wrought iron footbridge over an ornamental lake is to a 1790 design by James Wyatt, a similar one being built later in the duke's estate at Alnwick. The park has been designated a SSSI with over 200 specimens of rare trees. It has the London Butterfly House, the British Heritage Motor Museum and a garden centre which is one of the largest in London. It was used for filming *The Madness of King George* and *Gosford Park*.

Opposite, behind an uncompromising sloping concrete embankment with grab chains, are the 1.3km² Royal Botanic Gardens. Edith Holden, author of *The Country Diary of an Edwardian Lady*, drowned here while trying to reach horse chestnut buds. Julius Caesar crossed in 54, beating Cassivellaunus.

The dock was used until 1964, had large railway yards and was the birthplace of the Bantam tug. It is now a marina with housing replacing the railway tracks.

Edmund Ironside routed the Danes in 1016 but was then speared by Earl Edric hiding below his latrine.

The Grand Union Canal joins along the course of the River Brent. At **Brentford** cruising boaters replace their South of England Circuit with the London Circuit to Limehouse. The current sets north towards Soaphouse Creek and Goat Creek. Rivermen handled unpowered lighters with just an oar. One novice coming up the river failed to make the entrance to the canal, getting it on a later time past as he was carried up, down and up again with successive tides. Hog Hole separates Lot's Ait, which grew osiers and repaired barges until 1980, from Brentford Aits where trees were planted to screen Brentford gasworks.

St George's church has become a Musical Museum with organs, pianos, musical boxes and the world's largest collection of music rolls. A 61m tower marks an 1867 Victorian waterworks housing the Kew Bridge Steam Museum with steam beam engines which were used until 1944. The nine principal beam engines form the world's largest collection of steam pumping engines and include the Grand Junction 2.29m engine which is the world's largest working beam engine, built in Hayle in 1846. There are also a forge, traction engines and a steam railway. The Grades I and II buildings have some unusual roof details. A pumping station for the London Ring Main has also been sited here.

Georgian houses overlook the cricket at Kew Green and St Anne's church has the graves of Gainsborough and Zoffany.

Kew Bridge, also known as the King Edward VII Bridge, carries the A205 South Circular. On an earlier bridge here George III was informed that he was king. The bridge was built in 1903 by Sir John Wolfe-Barry and C A Brereton. Perhaps its most difficult load to pass underneath was a barge carrying Concorde to retirement, needing to wait for the spring tide to drop sufficiently to give clearance while still retaining sufficient depth under the hull. No road designated as motorway crosses the tidal Thames. This is the nearest it gets, 500m from the end of the M4 at Chiswick Flyover.

Strand-on-the-Green was a fishing village, the cottages

Palm House, Kew Gardens

Pagoda, Kew Gardens

Sackler Crossing, Kew Gardens

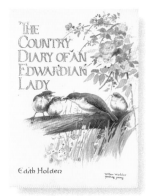

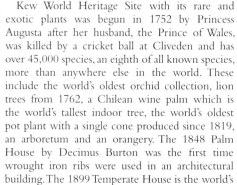

Kew World Heritage Site with its rare and exotic plants was begun in 1752 by Princess Augusta after her husband, the Prince of Wales, was killed by a cricket ball at Cliveden and has over 45,000 species, an eighth of all known species, more than anywhere else in the world. These include the world's oldest orchid collection, lion trees from 1762, a Chilean wine palm which is the world's tallest indoor tree, the world's oldest pot plant with a single cone produced since 1819, an arboretum and an orangery. The 1848 Palm House by Decimus Burton was the first time wrought iron ribs were used in an architectural building. The 1899 Temperate House is the world's largest surviving Victorian glass structure. The Princess of Wales Conservatory of 1987 has ten climate zones. A treetop walkway was added in 2008, 200m long and 18m above the ground. The 69m flagstaff is the world's tallest. An explorer train serves those who prefer to stay on the ground. The 50m high octagonal Pagoda with 253 steps, completed by Sir William Chambers in 1762 when it was the tallest and most accurate Chinese building in Europe, had 80 gold plated decorative dragons which were pawned by Prince Rupert to pay his debts. Queen Charlotte's Cottage is on the site, as is Kew Palace of 1631, a red brick Elizabethan building in Dutch style and the smallest royal palace. It was the home of George III from 1800 to 1818 when there were problems with flooding and was where his wife died in 1881, in which year Queen Victoria's parents were married here.

Construction of Brentford Dock in 1859 unearthed Stone, Bronze and Iron Age weapons and Roman coins.

Thomas Hawksley's tower at Kew Bridge Steam Museum.

used by fishermen until the 1770s. Georgian houses present a fine river terrace. Zoffany was resident from 1780 to 1810 and used local fishermen as Apostles in his *Last Supper* but he used the Kew churchwarden as Judas so the painting went to Brentford instead. His house has been occupied by TV writer Carla Lane. Dylan Thomas visited, Nancy Mitford wrote *The Pursuit of Love* here and John Guillermin, John Bird, Donald Pleasance, Ernst Blofeld and Eamonn Andrews were residents. The waterfront was used in filming *Help!*

The Maids of Honour teashop has cakes made to a secret Henry VIII recipe. The 1480s City Barge was used by the Lord Mayor of London's barge in the 18th century. Oliver's Ait is near Kew Pier and may be where Oliver Cromwell was a regular who escaped through a tunnel as the Royalists approached the 17th century Bulls Head during the 2nd Battle of Brentford. There is a Café Rouge. A dugout canoe excavated may have been used as a ferry.

Kew Railway Bridge of 1869 by W R Galbraith has wrought iron lattice girder trusses with decorative cast iron caps on cast iron cylindrical piers and carries the District Line.

Chiswick, from the Old English cese-wic, cheese farm, hosts 6ha of the Public Records Office, the national archives including the *Domesday Book*, *Magna Carta*, Shakespeare's will, the *Titanic* papers and much more.

Mortlake Reach sets north and passes between Chiswick Quay Marina and the large Mortlake Crematorium site.

The A316 crosses back over Chiswick Bridge of 1933 by Alfred Dryland. It has the longest concrete arch on the Thames with a 46m centre span, the reinforced concrete faced with Portland stone. The current now sets southwards. The 6.4km University Boat Race, started at Henley in 1829, used to finish at the Ship but now stops at the Pile Stone. The Head of the River Races use the course in the opposite direction, 420 eights setting off at five minute intervals in the world's biggest rowing event.

Duke's Meadows and golf course face onto the river at Mortlake, painted by Turner and having produced a 6th century BC continental Iron Age dagger. Flemish weavers worked in England's first tapestry factory, operating from 1619 to 1703 before becoming a brewery with hops and coal arriving by barge. Watney's Stag Brewery, the largest in London, now produces Budweiser, Mortlake having brewed beer since the 15th century. The Depot restaurant is in former stables and St Mary's church has a 16th century Tudor tower with bells which were rung whenever Elizabeth I passed on the river. Graves include sanitary reformer Edwin Chadwick, PM Henry Addington and Dr John Dee, who was the first to speak of the British Isles and British Empire, a scientist and astrologer to Elizabeth I. Explorer Sir Richard Burton is buried under a tent shaped tomb at the adjacent Roman Catholic church of St Mary Magdalen.

Barnes Railway Bridge, carrying the Hounslow to Clapham Junction railway, was built in 1849 by Joseph Locke and J E Errington on three cast iron arches. Three wrought iron bowstring trusses were added in 1895 using complementary lines to produce an unusual but attractive effect, a footway also being taken across at mid level to hold Boat Race spectators.

Small Profits Drawdock has a refreshingly frank name at Barnes, site of the granaries for Mortlake manor. Locals included Gustav Holst, Henry Fielding, who lived in an Elizabethan house with a Georgian facade, and Royal Ballet founder Ninette de Valois. Barnes church has a 16th century tower which was consecrated by Archbishop Langton on his way back from the signing of *Magna Carta*. A bandstand is surrounded by sports grounds, including the grounds of Fulham Rugby League Club. Corney Reach is exposed to the wind, often resulting in rough conditions as it runs past the disused Leg of Mutton Reservoir, now a nature reserve.

Chiswick House of 1725 by Lord Burlington is one of the best British examples of 18th century Palladian architecture and has a William Kent interior. Foreign Secretary Charles James Fox and PM George Canning both died in the same room in the house. It is situated in 32ha of Italianate gardens and a park with an ornamental bridge, temples, statues, obelisks and an amphitheatre which hosts theatre and opera, said to be the first English

The Chiswick waterfront by Kew Railway Bridge.

landscape garden. This has been both a mental institution and a zoo during its history. Adjacent is Hogarth's House, his Queen Anne country residence from 1749 to 1764, his mulberry tree still in the garden. A museum has his paintings and engravings, including *The Harlot's Progress*, *The Election* and *Marriage à la Mode*. Rousseau lived in Chiswick. Hogarth, Whistler, Henry Joy, who sounded the Charge of the Light Brigade, and cab driver Frederick Hitch, who won a VC at the Battle of Rorke's Drift, are buried at St Nicholas' church.

Chiswick Eyot has willows which were grown originally for the materials to make fish baskets. Fuller's Griffin Brewery is London's oldest brewery, from the 16th century, hops and malt having been brought by barge. In front is Bedford House which was occupied by the Redgrave acting family. Chiswick Reach sets northwards towards the 17th century Dove, Rutland Arms and Blue Anchor. Swans are on the water.

Vanity Fair opens here and features Walpole House, which was home to Charles II's mistress Barbara Villiers, Irish politician Daniel O'Connell, John Thorneycroft, actor Sir Herbert Beerbohn Tree and fashion designer Jasper Conran at various times. Sir Alan Herbert, who lived in **Hammersmith** Terrace, used the area in *The House by the River* and *The Water Gipsies*, in which the 17th century Dove, which boasts Britain's smallest bar, became The Pigeon. Another drinker here was James Thomson, who wrote *Rule Britannia*'s words. Megaphone inventor Sir Samuel Morland was a local. A museum to Arts & Crafts Movement founder William Morris is in Kelmscott House, Upper Mill, the house he occupied from 1878 to his death in 1896. The first electric telegraph had been set up in the back garden in 1816. Edward VII lived here. The Amateur Rowing Association are based here and St Paul's Preparatory School is where the Normandy Invasion was planned.

Thorneycrofts moved to Southampton in 1904 as their destroyers were getting too large for the bridges on the river. Hammersmith Bridge of 1827 had carried 12,000 spectators during the 1870 Boat Race. Its piers and abutments were retained when rebuilt by Bazalgette in 1887 but it is the lowest on the Tideway with only 3.7m clearance at high water below its 128m main span. The most decorative of the London Thames bridges, it carries the A306 and has twice been bombed by terrorists. The original bridge was the subject of Walter Greaves' *Hammersmith Bridge on Boat Race Day*. The area has been used for filming *Sliding Doors*.

Combined sewers discharge to the river more than

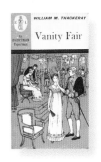

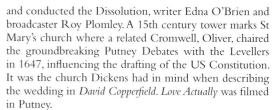

once a week on average. This is being addressed with a Thames Tunnel to run from here to Crossness, below the river to Limehouse. It will be the deepest tunnel in the UK, as much as 75m down, and will be up to 7.2m in diameter, for completion by 2020.

The flow sets north towards the Riverside Studios, which were the world's most advanced in 1954 and have been used for filming *Dr*

Hammersmith Bridge offers the least clearance on the Tideway.

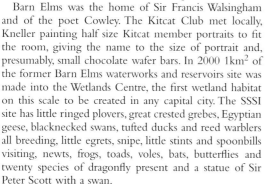

Who, Dixon of Dock Green, Hancock's Half Hour, Opportunity Knocks, Z Cars, Play School and many others, now an arts centre. Neighbours at Chancellors Wharf were record company Poly Gram.

Queen Caroline lived in the 17th century Brandenburgh House while George IV was trying to divorce her, the watermen holding a large demonstration in support of her. She died here in 1821 after being barred from his coronation, the house then being demolished.

Harrod's Depository of 1914 not only stored goods for those returning from the Empire but also had temporary flats they could occupy while looking for permanent accommodation. There were soap and candle factories behind them. Thames Wharf was Duckham's oil depot, its canteen becoming the River Café in 1987, quickly taking the *Times* Italian Restaurant of the Year Award. Chef Jamie Oliver was found here. Richard Rogers, husband of owner Ruth, has his architectural headquarters behind.

Barn Elms was the home of Sir Francis Walsingham and of the poet Cowley. The Kitcat Club met locally, Kneller painting half size Kitcat member portraits to fit the room, giving the name to the size of portrait and, presumably, small chocolate wafer bars. In 2000 1km² of the former Barn Elms waterworks and reservoirs site was made into the Wetlands Centre, the first wetland habitat on this scale to be created in any capital city. The SSSI site has little ringed plovers, great crested grebes, Egyptian geese, blacknecked swans, tufted ducks and reed warblers all breeding, little egrets, snipe, little stints and spoonbills visiting, newts, frogs, toads, voles, bats, butterflies and twenty species of dragonfly present and a statue of Sir Peter Scott with a swan.

Fulham was famous for its market gardens and gave its name to loaded dice. The loaded river sets south here. Fulham Football Club's stadium is named after Craven Cottage which burnt down in 1888. Fulham Palace was the residence of the Bishops of London from 1141 to 1973. The brick quadrangle dates from the 16th century and it had England's largest moat, dug in the 10th century by the Danes and filled with river water. The gardens had Europe's first tamarisk tree and England's first acacia, magnolia and maple. It is now a museum and café.

Putney, from the Old English Puttan-hyth, Putta's wharf, was an island. The University Stone has been the start of the Boat Race since 1845, the Putney Embankment of 1888 being lined by boathouses. It is also a boardsailing area. Gibbon was born at Putney and residents included Thomas Cromwell, who was Henry VIII's Chancellor

and conducted the Dissolution, writer Edna O'Brien and broadcaster Roy Plomley. A 15th century tower marks St Mary's church where a related Cromwell, Oliver, chaired the groundbreaking Putney Debates with the Levellers in 1647, influencing the drafting of the US Constitution. It was the church Dickens had in mind when describing the wedding in *David Copperfield. Love Actually* was filmed in Putney.

The towpath ends at Putney Bridge where five arches of white granite, designed by Bazalgette in 1886, carry the A219 over. It has churches at both ends. Ten bishops are buried in All Saints, Fulham, with its 1440 tower which featured in filming of *The Omen*. Feminist Mary Wollstonecraft had thrown herself off an earlier bridge after being abandoned by her lover but was recovered unconscious by boatmen. Putney Railway Bridge was added three years later by W H Thomas and W Jacomb to take the District Line over.

The river has one of the largest smelt populations in the UK, coming up in the early spring to spawn on the gravels of the **Wandsworth** Reach. This sets towards the south and Wandsworth Park of 1903. Across the river is Hurlingham House, the 18th century home of Dr Cadogan. The Hurlingham Club was set up for pigeon shooting but later introduced horse polo to England, the name being retained for the sport although it no longer takes place here. Hurlingham Business Park is sited on the former polo grounds of 1875. Businesses which have moved on include the Shell oil terminal, Calor Gas depot, gasworks and Blue Circle cement wharf.

In the 1760s there was a cornmill at the mouth of the River Wandle. The Ram Brewery was sited next to it from 1581 to 2006, when converted to housing. The Ship Inn of 1876 nearly closed in 1981 but was the Pub of the Year a decade later. Its sign is the ship used by Allan Young of the brewery to explore the Northwest Passage in the 1870s.

A refuse transfer station opened in 1984 was the most advanced in Europe, sending 4,000t of refuse per week by barge to Mucking Marshes.

Wandsworth Bridge of 1940 by Sir Pierson Frank carries the A217 and has a very heavy appearance. Most bridges from here have high intensity white lights to show when a large vessel is about to navigate an arch, isophase lights at 15 flashes per minute for a single vessel or 90 very quick flashes per minute for more than one vessel.

Battersea Reach was painted by Monet and Turner. Whistler used it in his *Chelsea Reaches*. Price's candle factory of 1830 used palm oil from Sri Lanka, landed by barge. Molasses House was the site of a sugar wharf. Now there is landing at Battersea Heliport.

B Baker and T H Bertram built the Battersea Railway Bridge in 1863 with both broad and standard gauge tracks, using it for the Clapham Junction–Olympia line.

Old Battersea House of 1899 has the ghost of an elderly lady.

Chelsea Harbour Marina is on the site of a railway goods yard. Residents have included Michael Caine, Tom Stoppard, Elton John and Robbie Williams. The 76m Belvedere Tower with its rising and falling tide ball stands at the end of Chelsea Creek, the Kensington Canal from 1820. It was painted several times by James McNeil Whistler, not to universal acclaim. Ruskin's comments about *Black & Gold; the Falling Rocket* resulted in a libel case which Whistler won but he was awarded only a farthing in damages, suggesting that the judge was inclined to agree with Ruskin.

St Mary's church of 1777 stands on the riverbank on a Saxon church site, some stonework surviving from 1379, surrounded by modern tower blocks. Poet William Blake was married here in 1827. Turner sketched from a chair in the vestry. American traitor Benedict Arnold is buried in the crypt. A passage which passes under the river to Cremorne Pier is now blocked. The wrought iron Cremorne Gates are at the entrance to Cremorne Pleasure Gardens, in use from 1840. They had gas lamps, fireworks and balloon flights. Genevieve Young, the Female Blondin, crossed the river on a tightrope in 1864. However, the gardens became notorious and were closed in 1877.

It is not just the fishing village which has gone. Lots Road Power Station, built in 1904 as the largest ever, to serve the District Line, with one of the earliest steel framed buildings in the London area, closed in 2002 after the longest working life of any power station in the world. The Montevectro building is on a site occupied by mills from 1794, including the Hovis flour mill of 1887–1994, supplied with grain by barge until the late 1980s. The Morgan Crucible works were also here.

The current sets south, allowing houseboats to moor against Cheyne Walk, a smart area with 18th century Georgian houses behind wrought iron fences. Mrs Gaskell was born here, Turner, Belloc, Steer, Dante Gabriel Rossetti, Augustus John, Whistler, the Folletts, Mick Jagger, Marianne Faithfull and the Brunels lived here and George Eliot died here. Keith Richards' house was used in filming *Performance*. Northern Ireland Secretary Willie Whitelaw held secret talks here with IRA officials Gerry Adams and Martin McGuinness in 1972. The King's Head & Eight Bells was formed in 1580 by merging two inns, Henry VIII being a frequent customer.

The Chelsea, Albert and Victoria Embankments were built from 1847 to 1874 to cover the interceptor sewers built by Bazalgette after the Great Stink and the 1853 cholera outbreak. They reclaimed 21ha and changed the character of the river, providing riverside roads and walkways through some of the most important parts of London.

Bazalgette added the iron Battersea Bridge in 1890, carrying the A3220. Its predecessor had been painted by Turner and Whistler, whose statue is at the northern end. Battersea was named after the Old English Beaudric eg, meaning Beaudric's marsh or island.

Chelsea was another island, its Old English name of cealc-hyth being a chalk wharf or landing place. A 6th century BC Iron Age dagger was found in the river, as was a 1st century Celtic bronze shield with red glass studs. Chelsea may have been the capital of Mercia in the 6th to 9th centuries. It was Sir Thomas More's 1523 Tudor Beaufort House which did most to make Chelsea fashionable although he was executed in 1535 for refusing to take the Oath of Supremacy. Henry VIII acquired the local Chelsea Manor the following year. He married Jane Seymour here secretly in 1536 and gave it to Catherine Parr as a wedding gift. Anne of Cleves died here and Elizabeth I visited as a teenager. Parr lived here and secretly married Admiral Thomas Seymour but, in 1548, she caught him with Princess Elizabeth in his arms. Parr died that year but Seymour was then arrested for piracy and treason, for which he was executed. Sir Hans Sloane was a later resident, his art collection forming the basis of the British Museum.

The Norman Chelsea Old Church of St Mary has Sir Thomas More's private chapel of 1528, rebuilt in 1958 after serious Second World War damage, a More monument, a window to Blake's wedding in 1782, a Curtis window with a map of his garden, chained books donated in the 18th century by Sir Hans Sloane, monuments, brasses, a fine carved pulpit and a museum in the tower.

T S Eliot and Henry James were local writers and Ian Fleming began his James Bond series by writing *Casino Royale* here. Carlyle's Queen Anne house of 1708 is where he lived from 1834 to 1881 and where he wrote *The French Revolution* and *Frederick the Great*. Set in a Victorian walled garden, it became a memorial museum to the Sage of Chelsea.

The first English porcelain factory was at either Chelsea or Bow. Chelsea was influenced by Sèvres and Miessen although forgeries are more common than genuine products.

Chelsea became the centre of the Swinging 60s in London. A more mundane importance these days is hosting a pumping station on the London Ring Main.

The Albert Bridge takes the A3031 over but with a 2t weight limit. Built in 1873 by Rowland M Ordish, it has cast iron towers and an unusual combination of cable stayed and suspension support. It was closed and propped in the 1970s because of defects. Part of its present loading is 3,000 lightbulbs which result in a striking appearance at night. Troops are still instructed to break step when crossing. It was used for filming *Sliding Doors*. At the

Wandsworth Bridge with some of the many new buildings.

St Mary's church at Battersea hemmed in by modern buildings.

northern end is David Wynne's stunning statue of a boy holding onto the fin of a leaping dolphin, sculpture at its best.

The swampy Battersea Fields were used for growing cabbages and the first asparagus in Britain. In 1829 they were the venue for a duel fought between the PM, the Duke of Wellington, and Lord Winchilsea, when both aimed to miss. Spoil from the Royal Victoria Docks was used in 1858 to convert them to the 80ha Battersea Park for recreation for the lower orders with tennis, hockey, a boating lake with angling, a children's zoo, a deer park, a Hepworth statue, Moore's Three Standing Figures of 1948 and, in 1864, the first football match played to FA rules. The site was used for the Festival of Britain in 1951 and it has seen the annual start of the London to Brighton veteran car run. The Peace Pagoda by the river was donated in 1985 by Japanese Buddhists forty years after Hiroshima. White posts mark a measured half mile.

Chelsea Physic Garden is one of Europe's oldest botanical gardens, founded in 1673 by the Worshipful Society of Apothecaries. Its 1.6ha include one of the oldest rock gardens in Europe, using stone from the Tower of London and lava from Iceland. It had England's first greenhouse in 1681. The first English cedar tree was

Albert Bridge has its cables lit by lightbulbs at night.

Boy with a Dolphin statue by the Embankment at Chelsea.

Battersea Park's pagoda.

planted here two years later, it grew the first cotton seeds sent to America in 1732 and it has the largest olive tree in England at 9m. Head gardener Philip Miller, who served owner Dr Hans Sloane for 50 years, wrote the *Dictionary of Gardening.* In the 1850s Dr Ward designed the cases used to send tea plants from China to India and rubber plants from Brazil to Malaysia.

The National Army Museum covers military activity since Agincourt, both British and Indian, and has uniforms, guns, aircraft and a Centurion tank.

Oscar Wilde lived in Tite Street, where he wrote *Lady Windermere's Fan, A Woman of No Importance* and *The Importance of Being Earnest* in the 1890s.

Under pressure from Nell Gwyn, Charles II had Wren produce the Royal Hospital Chelsea from 1682 to 1692 for retired soldiers, the Chelsea Pensioners whose red uniforms are based on those used by the Duke of Marlborough's forces in the 18th century. In 1852 two people were crushed when the Duke of Wellington lay here in state for seven days. The hospital overlooks Ranelagh Gardens where Handel's *Water Music* was first played publicly and where the Chelsea Flower Show has been held in May since 1913.

Thin lipped grey mullet come up to Chelsea Reach in the summer and it is the biggest nursery for bass fry in the southern North Sea.

Ernest James Buckton and Harry John Fereday replaced the 1858 Chelsea Bridge in 1937 with the first British self anchoring suspension bridge with one of the first uses of high tensile steel wire. Carrying the A3216, it has a 107m main span. Close to it is Grosvenor Bridge. In 1860 the Victoria Bridge was the first railway bridge over the Thames in the London area, carrying standard and broad gauge tracks. By the time of its rebuild in 1967 it had become three bridges but for ease of reconstruction it became ten separate bridges, each carrying one line on a welded steel box arch. Between the two crossings the Adrenaline Club have the world's tallest bungee tower at 91m, positioned at Grosvenor Dock, the end of the former Grosvenor Canal to Victoria station and by the mouth of the Westbourne.

Battersea gasholders include the last of its kind with 18m tall cast iron guide columns and of the waterless kind with the piston in a 90m high cylinder holding 190,000m³ of gas.

Battersea Power Station, built in 1933 and disused since 1983, is Grade II and due to be modified for other purposes. Like an upturned table, the Art Deco structure by Sir Giles Gilbert Scott has four fluted chimneys 102m high and was Europe's largest building in brick. Three tunnels pass under the river and were used for the Pimlico District Heating Scheme in 1951, an early combined heat and power scheme on the north of the river. A fire here in 1964 caused blackouts which delayed the launch of BBC2. This had been the scene of an assassination attempt on Charles II in 1671 when he came to swim in the river. Turner painted the sunset here. Behind the power station is Battersea Dogs & Cats Home for strays.

Rubble from St Katharine's Dock was used to reinforce marshland at Pimlico. The 3.2ha Dolphin Square was Europe's largest block of flats, 1,250 of them, when built in 1937, residents having included the Princess Royal and many MPs. Bram Stoker died at St George's Square and Lady Diana Spencer was photographed in a translucent dress while working here at a kindergarten.

Elm Quay has a 1988 statue of Old Father Thames by Stephen Duncan. Nine Elms became the site of the Covent Garden Flower Market in 1973, a return nearer to home for what was the market garden for **Westminster** Abbey convent. Nine Elms Reach sets north at what was the prehistoric tidal limit at the confluence with the Tyburn.

Vauxhall Bridge of 1906 by Sir Maurice Fitzmaurice carries the A202 and replaced an unstable cast iron toll bridge with five steel arches, between which are statues representing the arts and sciences. Architecture holds a model of St Paul's cathedral. Oak posts remain from a Bronze Age bridge from 1500 BC. Faulkes Hall was built about 1200 for Faulkes de Breauté, whose griffin motif has become the logo for Vauxhall cars, founded here in 1857. Pleasure gardens, opened in 1660, had

music, fountains, fireworks, lights and balloon flights but were closed in 1859 as they had become sleazy and the owners were bankrupt. They inspired Copenhagen's Tivoli Gardens and led to all Russian railway stations being called vokzals. In 1977 the Vauxhall City Farm was established here, including alpacas. Neptune's Fountain was located at the altar of the 1864 church of St Peter. The Vauxhall Cross MI6 building, Spooksville or a selection of other nicknames, was built next to the River Effra in 1993. It featured in the filming of *The World is Not Enough* in 1999 and was undamaged by an IRA rocket attack the following year. Vauxhall had a Civil War fort. A more recent way to keep watch is by London Balloon with tethered flights to 120m.

Gasholders include one from 1879 which was the largest ever built at the time but then nearly doubled to 31m to hold 170,000m³ of gas. They mark the Oval cricket ground, used for the first Test against Australia in 1880 and also the FA Cup Finals from 1870 to 1899. Doulton pottery was made locally from 1815 to 1956. The Victoria Line passes under the river.

A 15m exclusion zone extends out from the embankment from the bridge to Lacks Dock. The Albert Embankment runs from here to Tower Bridge, each lamp standard with dolphins at the base. Cumberland Sailing Society met at Vauxhall and were the only one in the world promoting sailing between 1775 and 1815, in 1830 becoming the Royal Thames Yacht Club. Residents of Peninsula Heights have included Jeffrey Archer, Stanley Baker and Richard Harris.

Typhoid vaccine was developed at the Royal Army Medical College, now Chelsea College of Art & Design. From 1816 to 1890 Millbank Prison was the largest in Britain. Sidney Smith replaced it in 1897 with the neo Classical Tate Gallery, now Tate Britain, donated by sugar magnate Henry Tate along with his own paintings and containing the greatest collection of British art since 1500, including Reynolds, Constable, Gainsborough and Blake. Turner's works are in the Clore Gallery of 1987.

In 1963 the 32 storey 118m Millbank Tower was the tallest reinforced concrete office building, clad in stainless steel and glass and including the Speaker's Stable car park. The Millbank Tendency referred to its use by New Labour between 1995 and 2002 after they took it over from Vickers. The site had once had a mill on the bank of the Tyburn.

Lambeth Reach sets to the southeast. It has the offices of the International Maritime Organization and the Fire Float Fire Brigade. Debris from the Great Fire was found here 900mm above the Roman level.

Lambeth Bridge is painted the same red as the colour used for the benches in the House of Lords. The five span reinforced concrete bridge of 1932 by Sir George Humphries has the A3203 on top. Underneath, it can have a standing wave at the start of what can be one of the roughest reaches on the Tideway. Horseferry refers to the fact that it was the only ferry carrying horses and carriage across the Thames in London, not without capsizes, as experienced by both Archbishop Laud and Oliver Cromwell in the 17th century. In 1688 it was the route taken by Mary of Modena and her baby, the Old Pretender, when fleeing abroad from the Glorious Revolution which deposed James II. The end of the bridge is now watched by MI5's headquarters in Thames House, bristling with aerials. The bridge has pineapples on its pillars.

St Mary-at-Lambeth church has the graves of Captain Bligh of the *Bounty* and the Tradescants, whose collections form the basis of the Museum of Garden History housed in the church. They imported rare plants such as pineapples, yuccas, lilacs and honeysuckle and some even more rare items such as phœnix tail feathers and dragon and griffin eggs, of relevance to setting up the Ashmolean Museum. Garden tools also feature in the

museum, to which statues on Lambeth Bridge draw attention.

Lambeth Palace has been the residence of the Archbishops of Canterbury since 1197, despite being bombed. The crypt of 1220, where Anne Boleyn was forced by Cranmer to admit to adultery before her execution, has Purbeck marble pillars. There is a much restored chapel from about 1230, the guardroom has a 14th century roof and portraits of many Archbishops, the Lollards' Tower

Battersea Power Station, waiting for a new lease of life.

where John Wycliffe's followers were imprisoned is from about 1450, the notable Tudor red brick Morton's Tower gateway is from 1495 and the 28m long Great Hall with hammerbeam roof and library of about 1,500 books and manuscripts is from 1660. During the Civil War Royalist poet Richard Lovelace was another prisoner. Cranmer compiled the *Book of Common Prayer* in the Cranmer Tower in 1552, in the same century as Cardinal Pole, the last Roman Catholic archbishop, planted what is now Britain's oldest fig tree.

Westminster Boating Base is a fairly demanding location for youngsters to pursue watersports. It is located in Victoria Tower Gardens which have a Gothic revival drinking fountain, a statue of Emmeline Pankhurst and Rodin's 1895 sculpture *The Burghers of Calais*. The 101m Victoria Tower, built as the world's biggest tower, itself houses the parliamentary archives since the 11th century.

Tia was rescued by Battersea Dogs & Cats Home

Lambeth Bridge and Lambeth Palace.

221

It was near here in 1688 that James II dropped into the Thames the Great Seal of England, not yet found.

An 8th century Benedictine abbey was built on Thorney Island between two arms of the Tyburn, serving as the foundation for Westminster Abbey, rebuilt in 1065 by Edward the Confessor. All but the nave was rebuilt again in 1245 by Henry III in French Geometric Decorated style influenced by Rheims, with flying buttresses and, unusually, two

documents in the basement destroyed most of it in 1834 but a neo Gothic replacement by Sir Charles Barry and Augustus Pugin was built in 1846–60 using stone brought from North Yorkshire by narrowboat and Trent sloop and positioned so that it could not be surrounded on foot. A 70m security exclusion zone extends down the west side of the river from 200m north of Lambeth Bridge to Westminster bridge. St Stephen's Hall was the original chamber. Westminster Hall, founded in 1097 by William Rufus, has a 1399 hammerbeam roof by Richard II, one of the widest spans in Europe at 21m and the first Norman hall in England. Guy Fawkes and friends tried to blow up Parliament in 1605. In 1941 it was hit by 14 bombs so it was rebuilt in Gothic style by Sir Giles Gilbert Scott by 1950 with seats for 437 of the 635 members.

Housing the world's first and mother of parliaments, the Houses of Parliament cover 3.2ha with 1,100 rooms, 3km of passages and 100 staircases. The terrace is a later addition. Statues outside include Oliver Cromwell, Churchill, Disraeli, Canning, Peel, Smuts and Richard the Lionheart.

A 1.2m crack in the 14t Big Ben bell of 1858 is the cause of its distinctive boing, recorded live for BBC news bulletins, its chime copied from Great St Mary's church in Cambridge. The name was given by a heckler during a three hour debate on the topic. The clockface is 7m in diameter and the clock is adjusted by adding or removing a 1d piece. It features in Virginia Woolf's *Mrs Dalloway*. If Parliament is sitting a light is shown at the top of the 98m Clock Tower or the Union Flag is flown.

The Italianate St Thomas' Hospital was moved from Southwark to the east bank in 1871, based on a French hospital visited by Florence Nightingale and using land recovered by the building of the Albert Embankment. It is founded on piles on Roman pavement 6.1m below the present ground level. It is dedicated to the apostle St Thomas and to St Thomas à Becket and includes a Florence Nightingale museum.

Despite opposition and attempted sabotage by ferrymen, Westminster Bridge was built in 1750, financed by £5 lottery tickets. The river could still be forded on foot in 1846. Removal of the old London Bridge resulted in serious scouring and the bridge was rebuilt in 1862 to carry the A302 on a seven arch cast iron structure with ornate Gothic detailing by Thomas Page and Sir Charles Barry to match the Houses of Parliament. It was one of the first structures to use Robert Mallet's buckled plates for the decking. Balancing Lambeth Bridge, it is painted in House of Commons bench green.

Houses of Parliament with Battersea Power Station beyond.

cloisters. All English monarchs since 1066 except Edward V and Edward VIII have been crowned here. The Coronation Chair contains the Stone of Destiny, brought from Scone by Edward I. Over 3,000 statesmen, warriors, scientists, musicians and poets are buried here. Present are Edward III's shield and 2.1m sword. The 11th century Pax chapel housed the first royal treasury with the 17th century abbey plate. The chapel of Henry V, added in 1519, is the finest Tudor Gothic architecture in the country, inside the best Early English architecture, with complex fan vaulting. There are banners of the Order of the Bath and a parrot of 1702, England's oldest stuffed bird. In 816 St Peter appeared to local fishermen and promised good catches if they gave a tenth to the abbey clergy. In the early evening the ghost of a murdered monk chats to visitors, there is a ghost of John Bradshaw who signed Charles I's death warrant and there is the ghost of a wounded and muddy First World War Unknown Soldier.

The 900 year old abbey gardens are probably the oldest in London, the Benedictine physic garden, and have Britain's oldest living fruit trees. The Chapter House of 1253 is one of the largest in England, decayed, restored in 1865 and bombed in 1941 but with some of the finest medieval English sculpture. St Margaret's is the Protestant church of the House of Commons. Milton, Pepys and Churchill were married here and Caxton buried here. The east window shows Henry VIII and Catherine of Aragon beside a crucifix while John Piper's abstract windows replace those damaged during the Second World War.

The moated Jewel Tower of 1365, for Edward III's valuables, is one of two remaining parts of the original Palace of Westminster, now the Parliament exhibition. The royal palace of 1078 to 1512 has housed Parliament, the speaking place, since 1265. Fire caused when burning

Wordsworth's sonnet about the bridge was eloquent but many arriving here are breathless for other reasons. The London Marathon for runners ends on top of the bridge while the Devizes to Westminster Race for canoeists ends at the bridge, the 1979 record of fifteen and a half hours still standing.

The river is busier downstream of the bridge. Boudicca's chariot statue with its knives on the wheels stands above Westminster Pier. Portcullis House of 2001 in the Metropolitan Police's former New Scotland Yard is a reminder of other Whitehall offices in the vicinity, including the Treasury, Ministry of Defence and Downing Street.

The Victoria Embankment of 1870 was the first electrically lit street in London, containing a 2.5m sewer, a subway and the District Line. It covered the muddy bank, improved the navigation and carries the A3211, shaded by plane trees. There is a 2005 Battle of Britain memorial, a plaque to Bazalgette, who designed the project, and statues of Robert Burns and Sir James Outram. Two paddle steamers moored as restaurants are the *Tattersall Castle*, a 1934 Humber ferry, and the *Hispaniola*.

The east end of the bridge is guarded by an 1837 lion on the orders of George VI, formerly painted red to promote the Red Lion brewery. It is made of Coade

The lion outside County Hall.

Westminster Bridge, County Hall and the London Eye.

stone, an 18th century long lasting artificial stone made in Lambeth, for which the formula has now been lost. The six storey County Hall, built in 1908 by Ralph Knott, was the headquarters of the London County Council, then the Greater London Council, until closed down by Margaret Thatcher. In Edwardian Baroque style, it is faced in Portland stone. It now contains a hotel and the London Aquarium, Europe's largest aquarium with 30,000 fish, 365 species, including Britain's only zebra shark. It also houses the Saatchi Gallery including works by Tracey Emin and Damien Hirst.

The London Eye is the world's largest observation wheel, 141m high, weighing 2,100t and carrying 32 capsules to represent the 32 London boroughs. This 2000 Ferris wheel turns at two revolutions per hour, carrying up to 15,000 passengers per day and allowing them to see up to 40km. It is the UK's top paid for attraction.

The 17th century beach was used for growing willows and asparagus. It was used as the venue for the Dome of Discovery in the 1951 Festival of Britain and has been the Jubilee Gardens since 1977.

When built in 1962, the Shell building was the tallest building in London at 103m and the largest office block in Europe, covering 3ha, its 26 storeys faced in Portland stone. The 1930s Shell-Mex building, on the 1880s site of the world's largest hotel, has the world's largest clockface, Big Benzine.

Waterloo station of 1848 was rebuilt in 1900 with the Eurostar terminal added in 1990. Although Eurostar moved to St Pancras in 2008, Waterloo remains the largest British station, covering 12ha with 24 platforms extending a total of 6.2km.

Hungerford Railway Bridge is a combined foot and rail crossing. Sir J Hawkshaw used the bases of Brunel's original suspension footbridge, 206m long and proving Telford wrong on the unltimate length possible, when he rebuilt it in 1864, the chains already having gone to be reused on the Clifton Bridge in Bristol. The Golden Jubilee footbridges were added on each side of it in 2003. The railway bridge served the new Charing Cross station with its Art Deco facade, the original footbridge being criticized for linking the West End with the worst part of Lambeth. Charles Dickens worked in a boot polish factory as a boy, used in *David Copperfield*.

King's Reach, named after George V, sets north, away from the South Bank complex. The Royal Festival Hall is on the site of the Red Lion Brewery, which used river water. The hall is the only building remaining from the Festival of Britain, when the Royal Engineers built a Bailey Bridge across the river to carry pedestrians but had to recover it after it fell into the water. In Modernist style with glazing and a roof of green copper, the hall can seat 3,000 and was the first post war Grade I building. The 1967 Queen Elizabeth Hall and Purcell Room and 1968 Hayward Gallery have since been added. This was the site of the 76m Skylon, a vertical structure supported entirely on wires. A 19th century Shot Tower survived until 1962,

used for making shot for cartridges by allowing lead to solidify as it fell.

Cleopatra's Needle, at 21m high, is the tallest obelisk in the UK and the 11th tallest in the world. The 186t pink granite column, by Thotmes III in Heliopolis in 1475 BC, was given to Britain in 1819. It was collected in 1878 in a wrought iron cylinder which was lost in the Bay of Biscay, along with six lives. It was later found and eventually erected with a pair of sphinxes at its base, now with 1917 bomb damage to them. The needle had nothing to do with Cleopatra. Its partner has had a less traumatic life and is sited in New York's Central Park. Behind the needle are Victoria Embankment Gardens, composed of soil from the District Line and from Barking Creek. The *TS Queen Mary* is a former Scottish west coast and Clyde cruising boat.

Between the Strand and the river is the 1889 Savoy, named after the 13th century Count of Savoy, where superstition requires that a meal booked for 13 results in 14 places being laid, the extra place occupied by a wooden cat, Kaspar, present during the meal. In front is the only street in Britain where vehicles drive on the right. This was to avoid Hansom cab passengers having to step down into puddles. The 1881 Savoy Theatre was built by Richard D'Oyly Carte for Gilbert & Sullivan operas. Hotel, theatre, church and street have various first British uses of electricity and underground cables.

What was to have been the Strand Bridge in 1817 was renamed as Waterloo Bridge and it was painted by Turner and is from where Monet painted a foggy London. Carrying the A301, it was rebuilt in 1942 by Sir Giles Gilbert Scott, mostly with female labour because of wartime restrictions, resulting in its also being called Ladies Bridge. The reinforced concrete beam and slab construction is faced with Portland stone across its five shallow 76m spans but it included explosion chambers which could be used to destroy it in the event of invasion. This is the location which inspired Ray Davies' *Waterloo Sunset* and two *Waterloo Bridge* films have been made. It was where a Bulgarian dissident was stabbed in 1978 with a poisoned umbrella tip. The Northern and Bakerloo lines pass under.

Thames Police Station was taken over by the RNLI, their three lifeboat stations on the Thames being the busiest in Britain. A statue of Brunel regards all. Somerset House of 1776, in Classical style with a Palladian facade, reached to the Thames and was the first London office block built as such, recording births, marriages and deaths until 1973. It is now the Courtauld Institute Gallery with some of the world's best Impressionist, Post Impressionist and Early Renaissance paintings. It has the Gilbert Collection of snuffboxes and miniatures and the Hermitage Rooms have exhibits lent from St Petersburg Hermitage. A statue of George III stands in a 110 x 91m courtyard which has 55 fountains but can become an outdoor ice rink in the winter. Kings College adjoins the site.

Proud remains of the London Chatham & Dover Railway.

On the south bank the 1957 National Film Theatre hosts the London Film Festival. It was joined in 1976 by the Royal National Theatre with the Olivier, Lyttleton and Cottesloe theatres in Modernist reinforced concrete by Sir Denys Lasdun. In front of the theatres and the London Television Centre, source of *The South Bank Show* and *Have I Got News for You*, there is a large secondhand book sale and numerous pavement artists in the summer.

The sloop *HQS Wellington* is the livery hall of the Master Mariners. Behind it are the Inns of Court at Temple, named after the Knights Templar who occupied it from 1160 to 1308, across the Strand from the Royal Courts of Justice. The circular church dating from 1185 is one of four in England, featuring in *The Da Vinci Code* and its film. Another sloop is the First World War *HMS President*, the last remaining decoy Q ship to lure German submarines in the First World War, now an RNVR training ship.

The 67m Oxo Tower on the south bank was converted from a pumping station in the 1930s and was London's second highest commercial building, part of the world's largest meat packing factory. To get round an advertising ban the name was picked out in red stained glass. It now contains shops and a restaurant.

Confusingly, the City of London is just 2.7km^2 – a square mile – at the heart of the metropolis, beginning with Blackfriars, named after the Dominican monks who settled in 1279. Blackfriars Bridge of 1769 had semi elliptical arches, much criticized but then much copied. It was called William Pitt Bridge but the public rejected the name. It was rebuilt in 1869 by Joseph Cubitt with five cast iron arches spaced to match those of the adjacent railway bridge for ease of navigation, with red polished Aberdeen granite pulpit shaped cutwaters and sculptures of birds and plants. The A201 passes over and the Fleet emerges from beneath it. It was under the bridge that Italian banker Robert Calvi was found hanged in 1982, allegedly by the Mafia, with $14,000 and five bricks in his pockets. This is the start of swan upping, which continues upstream to Henley to mark the birds belonging to the Queen and the livery companies.

The 1864 railway bridge would not support modern trains but the red Romanesque Doric columns are being used to support a new platform. The Blackfriars or Alexandria Railway Bridge was rebuilt in 1886 by Sir J Wolfe Barry and H M Brunel with five wrought iron rib arches and column spacings to match the earlier bridge. Thameslink trains run over and Blackfriars station has been extended, the first to reach across the Thames, enclosed in a glass and steel shell. The magnificent insignia of the London, Chatham & Dover Railway remains at the southern end.

The Albion flourmill, established by Boulton and Watt as London's first factory and one of the earliest powered by steam, burned out in 1803 and may have been the inspiration for the dark satanic mills in *Jerusalem*, Blake living in Lambeth. The *Daily Express* is now produced here. The Bankside Gallery is the home of the Royal Watercolour Society and the Royal Society for Painter-Printmakers. King's Reach runs past Blackfriars Pier, behind which is the Mermaid Theatre of 1956 in a Victorian warehouse on the site of the Puddle Dock, where Chaucer was born in 1343.

Ludgate Hill was the site of the Temple of Mars and has been a cathedral site since 604. A bonfire outside the old Norman St Paul's in 1521 was used to burn heretical works, mostly books by Martin Luther. The current St Paul's cathedral is the fifth on the site and follows the destruction of its predecessor in the Great Fire of 1666 and the first since the establishment of the Church of England. Built in Portland stone from 1675 to 1710 by Sir Christopher Wren, it is the only cathedral designed and built by a single architect. Based on St Peter's at the Vatican, it is the only major English cathedral in Renaissance style and the dome is the world's third largest. The Whispering Gallery, which allows a whisper to be heard 30m away, was not intentional. The cathedral is 111m high and 157m long with the largest crypt in western Europe. Great Paul is the largest swinging bell in Europe and the 17m spiral geometrical unsupported staircase is one of the widest ever built. Choirstalls were carved by Grinling Gibbons. The Trophy Room has a 5.5m model of Wren's original design of 1674. The library has one of the three remaining copies of William Tyndale's *New Testament* and a model of Wellington's 5.5m funeral carriage. It has been used for other major national funerals, including those of Nelson (in a tomb made for Wolsey) and Churchill, and celebrations including the wedding of Charles and Diana in 1981, watched on television by 750,000,000 people. It has also been used to film *The Madness of King George* and *Lawrence of Arabia*. It was bombed in 1940/1 and water pumped from the subsoil has resulted in settlement which has required remedial action.

Blackfriars Bridge with St Paul's Cathedral, Tower 42, the Gherkin and other distinctive buildings.

London takes its name from the Celtic Llyn-din, river place, or from Lugh, the god of light. The City occupies a Roman site settled by Claudius in 50 although Geoffrey of Monmouth's *Historia Regum Britanniae* of 1136 claimed it had been founded by Brutus in the 12th century BC. It was destroyed by Boudicca and the Iceni in 60 AD. The following year reference was made to Londinium in Tacitus' *Annals*, becoming the capital in the 1st century, the largest city in Britain and the sixth largest in the Roman Empire. The Roman wall from about 190–210 lasted until Stuart times. The Danes occupied it in 871. It became Edward the Confessor's English capital in 1045. In the 12th century Richard of Devizes said 'if you do not wish to dwell with evildoers, do not live in London'. Dick Whittington was Lord Mayor three times between 1397 and 1420. The Bank of England was founded here in 1694. Sir Arthur Conan Doyle, in his *A Study in Scarlet* of 1888, wrote of London as 'that great cesspit into which all loungers and idlers of the Empire are irresistibly drained'.

It was hit in 1914 Zeppelin raids and heavily bombed in the Blitz in 1940, flattening 66ha. It is served by the world's largest urban passenger transport system.

Richard Jeffries' *After London* considers how it becomes a poisonous swamp inhabited by cruel dwarfs.

Crossing the river next to the City of London School with suspension cables partly below deck level is the Millennium Footbridge of 2000, closed for a long period while its notorious wobble was addressed. Its natural frequency was close to walking speed so people tended to walk in time with it, causing it to resonate. Passive damping had to be added to bring it under control.

It leads to Bankside power station, designed by Sir Giles Gilbert Scott to be an acceptable neighbour to St Paul's and used from 1963 to 1981. The 99m chimneys were deliberately kept lower than the dome of St Paul's. At 3.4ha it was the first large power station to be designed specifically for oil fired boilers, the oil being supplied by river. Since being retired it has become the Tate Modern with the UK's largest exhibition of modern art including work by Picasso, Warhol and Dalí. Large exhibits are placed in the 152m long by 35m high turbine hall where they can be handled by the overhead travelling crane.

The Provost of Southwark's residence faces across the river to the wrong cathedral. Wren lived in Cardinal Cap Alley during construction of St Paul's.

Shakespeare's Globe Theatre is a 1997 replica, the 1599 original having burned down in 1613 and its replacement pulled down in 1642 by the Puritans. The current building has the first thatched roof in central London since the Great Fire. The world's largest Shakespeare exhibition is on the site of a 16th century bear baiting ring. Bear Gardens are where the Hope Theatre staged bear baiting and plays in Elizabeth I's reign and is where Jonson's *Bartholomew Fair* was premièred. Dr Francis Moore began *Old Moore's Almanack* here in 1697, the UK's longest running annual.

Southwark is named from suthring weorc, marsh bridgehead, and Queenhithe Stairs were founded over a millennium ago.

The five span Southwark Bridge of 1921 by Basil Mott replaced Rennie's three span bridge which had had a 73m centre span, the longest ever in cast iron, which featured in *Little Dorrit*.

There were 17 frost fairs on the Thames here between 1281 and 1814, particularly after 1564 when the river was broader and shallower, the flow slowed by London Bridge. The greatest was in 1683/4 when the river froze for two months, the 280mm thick ice rising and falling with the tide.

Next to the *Financial Times* building is the 1999

Vinopolis – City of Wine. They face across to the 1411 Guildhall on the site of a Roman amphitheatre, hence the curved roads around it. It was restored in 1953 with the 2.8m giants Gog and Magog and the statue of a snarling dog on the roof.

The pleasure craft *Marchioness* sank here in 1989 with 51 dead after being in collision with the dredger *Bowbelle*. Lifeboats were stationed on the Thames as a result.

Cannon Street station was built by Sir J Hawkshaw on the site of the Roman governor's palace. The 1866 walls and towers containing water tanks for the hydraulic lifts were retained when it was rebuilt in the 1960s, the huge arched roof having been destroyed in the Blitz. Hawkshaw built Cannon Street Railway Bridge at the same time, using cast iron cylinders as fluted Doric columns with Doric capitals. Much of the decoration was removed in 1983 when the bridge was strengthened.

The Anchor Inn was managed for a year by Dr Johnson. It was owned by Henry Thrale, who also owned the Anchor Brewery, the largest in the world at that time. The Clink Prison Museum is on the site of Clink Prison, burned down in 1780 by the Gordon Rioters but the reference to being in the clink remaining as a colloquialism for prisons in general. Close are the remains of Winchester Palace with its rose window in the Great Hall, the residence of the Bishops of Winchester from 1109 to 1626.

St Mary Overie's Dock contains the *Golden Hinde* replica of Drake's galleon which has traced the 1579 route which claimed California. The site of a Roman villa was used for a convent for St Swithun in 606, becoming the church of St Saviour & St Mary Overie. The present building, from 1220 to 1420, is one of the finest Gothic buildings in London, its architecture second only to that of Westminster Abbey. It incorporates part of the Norman church and has a 1275 oak knight effigy, a three tier stone altar screen given by the Bishop of Winchester in 1520, a statue of William Shakespeare, whose brother, Edward, is buried in the chancel, and a chapel for American university founder John Harvard. The Lady Chapel was demolished about 1830 to allow a better London Bridge approach. The church was partly rebuilt in 1890, becoming Southwark Cathedral in 1905. Harvard University was founded on the inheritance of the Queen's Head coaching inn in Southwark.

Across behind the Swan Pier is the

225

Fishmongers' Hall, rebuilt in Greek Revival style in 1835 by Henry Roberts, one of the best of the livery company halls.

The lowest fording point of the Thames was improved in 50 AD by Claudius by the addition of a bridge, since which time the land has subsided by 4.6m. In 1014 the Saxon Ethelred the Unready pulled down the bridge by tying his boats to it, leading to the nursery rhyme *London Bridge is Falling Down*. The most significant of London's

bridges was the 276m long Norman bridge of 1176–1209, its 19 arches with houses, shops and a chapel to St Thomas à Becket on top, constricting the river so that there were 2m falls below it down into the Pool of London. The shops funded the upkeep, a precursor to the airport shopping mall. For 540 years it was the only bridge across the river in London and was used to display the heads of criminals, including those of William Wallace and Sir Thomas More. An earlier fire at the northern end had left a break so that the bridge with its houses up to eight storeys high was not affected by the Great Fire of 1666. In 1749 its 6m width was the site of the first recorded traffic jam, lasting several hours as a result of people attending the rehearsal of the première of Handel's *Music for the Royal Fireworks* in Green Park. Driving on the left was instituted over the bridge. Rennie's five arched bridge of 1831 was sold to the Americans and now crosses Lake Havasu

although it is said that they thought they had bought the rather more distinctive Tower Bridge. The current London Bridge of 1972 is a 260m three span cantilever concrete box girder with a suspended span, carrying the A3 and walkways heated in cold weather. There is a 5.5m tide rise underneath and there can be a standing wave to add to those of the ferries. Any sturgeon caught downstream of here belong to the Mayor.

In 1850 the Austrian General Haynau visited the adjacent brewery but was attacked by draymen for his treatment of Italian and Hungarian revolutionaries two years earlier.

The 310m 72 storey Shard of Glass will be the tallest building in the EU in 2012 and will be the world's first skyscraper to have its core built from the top down. The Northern Line passes under here.

In 1715 actor Thomas Doggett celebrated the defeat of the First Jacobite Rebellion with a race. Doggett's Coat & Badge Race to Chelsea for six single sculls still provides the winner with an orange coat and silver badge.

Daniel Defoe's *A Journal of the Plague Year* describes the 1665 bubonic plague which killed 70,000 people.

The following year the Great Fire of London rid the city of plague by destroying 13,200 houses and 84 churches, burning for four days and clearing 1.7km² but killing less than a score of people. A consequence was that it allowed architects to create some grand schemes on the land cleared. The fire started in a bakery in Pudding Lane. The 61m Doric column Monument with a golden globe and flames at the top is the tallest isolated stone column in the world, its height giving the distance from its base to the start of the fire.

Behind are a number of striking modern office buildings. Tower 42 was the NatWest Tower, its plan in the shape of their logo. At 200m high it was the tallest building in Britain when built in 1981. It includes the City of London Club, badly damaged in 1993 by an IRA bomb. The 2004 Swiss Re Building by Sir Norman Foster is better known as the Gherkin from its distinctively patterned glass shell. Sir Richard Rogers' 1986 Lloyds Building houses the world's biggest insurance market, developed from a coffee house in the 1680s and containing the *Lutine* bell of 1799, rung to announce news, and the Nelson Room and a museum of Roman and medieval finds. The 48 storey Leadenhall Building or Cheese Grater is 225m high, leaning out of view from St Paul's, for opening by Sir Richard Rogers in 2011. Planned or under construction are the 24 storey Can of Ham, the Helter Skelter or Pinnacle on Bishopgate, the Heron Tower and the Walkie Talkie on Fenchurch Street. Adelaide House in Chicago style was built in the 1920s as the first non classical office block, the first in London to have a steel frame, the first with central ventilation, telephones and electricity connections at every level, the tallest building in London at 45m and with a golf course on the roof.

Between London Bridge Hospital and Guy's Hospital with its 1725 entrance is London Bridge station, built in 1849 and restored in the 1970s after Second World War damage. The London Dungeon is a museum of medieval horror.

Beyond London Bridge City Pier is the Hays Galleria shopping arcade in the former Hays Wharf or the Larder of 1857, receiving Indian tea brought by clippers and where food cold storage originated, especially for dairy products from New Zealand. *The Navigators* is an 18m kinetic sculpture by David Kemp. It was the Great Fire of Tooley Street in 1861 which resulted in the formation of the London Fire Brigade. Winston Churchill's Britain at War Exhibition features plenty more fires with the Second World War Blitz and the Home Front.

Custom House is the fifth on a site used since 870. Chaucer worked here but a depressed Cowper was unable to drown himself as the tide was out when he came. The current building was built in 1817 but the riverside facade collapsed in 1825 because of inadequate foundations. It was heavily bombed during the Second World War and partially rebuilt in 1966 with a 353m facade. It includes the Long Room, 58 x 20m.

In 1700 London was handling 69% of Britain's exports and 80% of imports. It was the world's greatest port in the 19th century but suffered the 1889 strike for the Docker's Tanner, the hourly wage. By the 1920s it had the world's largest enclosed docks and still handles 54,000,000t of products per year.

Billingsgate Market, named after the imaginary British King Belin, occupied a Roman wharf and Saxon quay, handling mostly grain and coal until 1699, when it changed to fish. Its building of 1877 has mansard roofs and pavilions with dolphin weathervanes. Workers here included George Orwell and the Kray twins. It was converted to offices in 1982.

Moored permanently as a museum is *HMS Belfast*, Britain's largest Second World War cruiser at 11,500t and the only one surviving in Europe. She is a light cruiser, the last battleship in action in European waters,

HMS Belfast *with Tower Bridge beyond.*

her 150mm guns with 23km range being used against the *Scharnhorst* in 1943 and commenced the firing in the 1945 Normandy Landings. The 1938 ship had three cats and the Russians gave a terrified reindeer which had to be put down. She was retired here in 1971.

The skewed glass globe is the energy efficient 10 storey City Hall of 2002 by Sir Norman Foster as the headquarters of the Greater London Authority. It overlooks Potters Field where Roman pottery has been found.

Tower Millennium Pier was where Mark Wallington start his *Boogie up the River.*

All Hallows by the Tower, dating from 675, has tessellated Roman pavement of about 45 AD, pre Conquest relics, a Saxon crypt, brasses of 1389–1651 and a font cover by Grinling Gibbons showing cupids stealing grapes. It was bombed in 1941 and rebuilt in 1958 with the city's first tower since Wren's time.

The Tower of London was built for William the Conqueror to frighten Londoners. Only one of its four towers is round, its spiral staircase built to give righthanded swordsmen the advantage when defending it, a concept followed elsewhere. The 27m high White Tower is the only Norman part remaining, the finest of all hall keeps and the first English building with latrines. Begun in 1078 by Gundolph, its 3.7–4.6m thick walls were extended from three storeys to four and it was whitewashed in 1241 to make it more intimidating. It has distinctive roofs, an octagonal wall tower of about 1200, a 1270s barbican, 22 towers and two gatehouses by Edward I. St John's chapel has excellent Norman architecture in the keep. It has been a royal palace with all monarchs resident until James I. It has also been a prison, an armoury, a treasury, a mint, an observatory, a record office, a zoo, a merchant bank and, primarily, the most important piece of military architecture in England. There are two curtain walls and a 1270s moat which was filled in the 19th century by Wellington. Towers include the Beauchamp Tower, the Wakefield Tower, which holds the Crown Jewels, and the Bloody Tower, named after the princes murdered in 1483, where Sir Walter Raleigh was imprisoned for 13 years before being executed and where Sir Thomas More was imprisoned. Flambard, the Bishop of Durham, was the first prisoner to escape, using a rope to descend 20m from the White Tower after getting the guards drunk, but Griffin fell to his death in Henry III's reign when his rope broke. Charles of Orleans lived here for 25 years after Agincourt until ransomed. Wyatt and Guy Fawkes were imprisoned in the Little Ease dungeon. Maud, the daughter of Baron Fitzwaller, was imprisoned until her death for resisting the advances of King John. Henry VIII married Anne Boleyn here and she and Catherine Howard were beheaded here. Queen Elizabeth

The Traitor's Gate entrance to the Tower of London.

was imprisoned and Clarence drowned here and the Earl of Essex, Thomas Cromwell and the Duke of Monmouth died here. The last executions were of Lords Lovat, Kilmarnock and Balmerino after the 1745 rebellion. The last prisoners were the Cato Street Conspirators of 1820. The white shape of Lady Jane Grey's ghost has appeared on February 12th, the anniversary of her execution in 1554. Other ghosts include those of a bear, Anne Boleyn and the 1541 execution of the non compliant Countess of Salisbury.

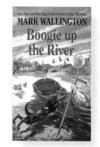

Henry III had three leopards sent by Emperor Frederick in allusion to the royal arms. Visiting the lions resulted in the term to lionize. In the 14th century it cost six times as much to keep a lion as a human prisoner. Most conspicuous of the residents are the Yeoman Warders or Beefeaters in their red uniforms. There are six ravens, the departure of which would presage the downfall of the monarchy so their wings are clipped to ensure they stay. Each night the Ceremony of the Keys is undertaken at 10pm with royal salutes for state events.

Traitors' Gate was the execution site although Londoners and Becket's ghost objected to its construction in 1280, collapsing several times during building, perhaps helped by the mud on which it is founded. It opens onto the river. A change of mood was attempted in 1934 when 1,500 barge loads of sand were tipped to create a beach but this was closed in 1971 because of pollution.

The chapel of St Peter ad Vincula has the graves of Anne Boleyn, Katherine Howard, Protector Somerset, Thomas Seymour, Lady Jane Grey and Sir Thomas More. Protection includes a row of 2.7kg cannons captured from the French at Waterloo. The Tower was used for filming *Johnny English* and *Elizabeth.*

Tower Subway under the river, 400m long and 2.1m in diameter, was the first tunnel in Britain with a cast iron lining and with the world's first underground tube railway. It contained a 12 seater bus hauled by cable from 1870 until Tower Bridge opened in 1894 but now contains cable ducts.

The bridge was built by Sir John Wolfe-Barry and Henry Brunel. Its 1,000t lifting bascules are opened some 900 times per year, interrupting traffic on the A100, a loaded double decker bus having to leap the gap in 1952 as the bridge started to open. A 61m clear channel is left between the four stone towers with their Victorian Gothic detailing. There has been riverbed scouring near the towers. The 40m high walkway was closed in 1910 because of suicides, thieves and prostitutes but is now open again. The side spans of the 240m long structure are suspended. In 1974 it was converted from hydraulic to electrical control but control of mice is still undertaken by two resident cats. An exhibition includes the original steam engines. It was used for filming *Johnny English* and *Between the Lines.*

The girl and dolphin statue with fountain is another by David Wynne near St Katharine Pier. St Katharine Yacht Haven occupies the dock built in 1828 by Telford after 1,200 people had been displaced. The Blitz damaged 10ha badly and the dock closed in 1968. It is now a World Trade

Wynne's Girl & Dolphin statue.

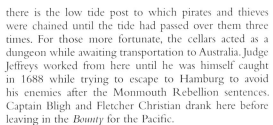

St Katherine Yacht Haven.

Sundial statue in front of Butlers Wharf.

there is the low tide post to which pirates and thieves were chained until the tide had passed over them three times. For those more fortunate, the cellars acted as a dungeon while awaiting transportation to Australia. Judge Jeffreys worked from here until he was himself caught in 1688 while trying to escape to Hamburg to avoid his enemies after the Monmouth Rebellion sentences. Captain Bligh and Fletcher Christian drank here before leaving in the *Bounty* for the Pacific.

Cherry Garden Pier is where Turner painted one of his best pictures, *The Fighting Téméraire*, as she arrived to be broken up. More recent sculptures take the form of statues of seated MP Dr Salter, his daughter, Joyce, and her cat. This was the site of Edward II's moated manor, hence the King's Stairs. The Angel, from 1682 or earlier, was visited by Pepys and Captain Cook. Whistler and Turner sketched Rotherhithe from a balcony which is haunted by the ghost of Judge Jeffreys, who had watched Wapping beach executions from here.

The Mayflower public house is near the point from which the *Mayflower* sailed in 1620 and may sell British and American stamps. It may contain timbers from the *Mayflower*, which was left alongside to rot. St Mary's church has a plaque to the master, Christopher Jones, and incorporates Roman bricks, ships' mast pillars and an altar of wood taken from the *Téméraire*. **Bermondsey** is believed to have escaped some Blitz bombing because Hitler intended to use a block of flats here as his headquarters in London.

The East London Line passes under the river in the Brunels' Thames Tunnel, the world's first successful tunnel under a commercial waterway. There had been two previous failures under the lower Thames, including one which was five sixths complete, using Cornish mining techniques. Marc Brunel invented the tunnelling shield and experimented with reinforced concrete but there were problems and the project nearly bankrupted him. There were two major breaches, one of which swept son Isambard away and badly injured him. Six workers were less fortunate. When the tunnel was half complete a mirror was installed across the bore and a fundraising dinner held in it. Even after this there were two more breaches. The 370m foot tunnel was completed in 1843 after 18 years, becoming a railway tunnel in 1869. As London's most important civil engineering heritage structure it was hastily given Grade II listing in 1995 to prevent a reinforcing shotcrete lining being sprayed onto it. It remains visible as part of the line which was extended in 2010. The 1842 engine house at the southern end is an Ancient Monument, accompanied by a Brunel museum.

The Prospect of Whitby of 1523 is probably the oldest public house on the river in London, named after the *Prospect* which was often moored here. It was used by Pepys, Dickens, Whistler, Turner, Judge Jeffreys,

Centre with the notable Ivory House and two halves of a footbridge designed to withdraw into recesses for access. The Historic Ship Collection is housed here including the North Sea steam herring drifter *Lydia Eva*, the steam tug *Challenge*, the Thames barges *Lady Daphne* and *Cambria*, the Nore light vessel and the replica of *Grand Turk*, used by ITV for filming *Hornblower*. A large sundial sculpture overlooks the river and Hermitage Memorial Gardens have a peace dove sculpture to those killed in the Blitz. The water contains bass, whiting, eels and shrimps.

Butlers Wharf, the largest warehouse complex on the Thames in 1873, was used as studios by David Hockney and David Gentleman and for filming *The French Lieutenant's Woman*, *Dr Who* and *A Fish Called Wanda*. Courage had a brewery here from 1789 to 1981. Spillers dog biscuits and Peak-Frean biscuits, including Garibaldis, were established here. The Design Museum is the world's first for mass produced consumer goods.

St Saviour's Dock was the mouth of the River Neckinger, named after the Devil's neckcloth, the rope used for hanging pirates. It was also referred to as the Venice of Drains and the Capital of Cholera, an area used in *Oliver Twist*.

Wapping was badly bombed during the Second World War. The Town of Ramsgate, one of the oldest public houses in Britain, was the site of Execution Dock. Still

The Prospect of Whitby squeezed between modern buildings.

smugglers and thieves and was also known as the Devil's Tavern. It has been claimed as an alternative site for Execution Dock.

Cupola vents on each side of the river serve the Rotherhithe Tunnel, taking the A101 under the river. Built in 1908, 3,000 people were moved to make way for it. Of its 1.5km length, 1.1km are lined with cast iron. The tunnel features in Iain Sinclair's *Downriver*.

Tobacco Dock is now a shopping centre with two full size replica 19th century sailing ships. Its Tobacco Warehouse was a vast bonded warehouse of 1814 with an internal structure like a forest. Large bascule bridges served London Docks, now closed. Shadwell Basin has become a watersports centre. Coal was supplied over its wall to Wapping pumping station, a Grade II structure which operated from 1892 to 1977 with a 1,900m^3 underground reservoir.

Stepney is from the Old English Stybba's hyth. Ratcliff, its river frontage, is from where Sir Hugh Willoughby left in 1553 to seek a Northeast Passage, to be followed in 1576 by Martin Frobisher looking for a Northwest Passage. A closer channel is that into Limehouse Marina in Limehouse Basin, feeding the Regent's Canal and Limehouse Cut. The name is from the limekilns from the 14th century, used to burn Kent chalk for lime. The area was also called Chinatown from the large Chinese population in the 18th century. The lock only works on the higher part of the tide. The Narrow, run by Gordon Ramsey, was the dockmaster's house and the Grapes of 1583, where Dickens was made to sing to customers as a child, probably inspired his Six Jolly Porters in *Our Mutual Friend*. Booty's Bar & Restaurant is in a former engineering shop. The Limehouse Declaration, setting up the Social Democratic Party, followed a meeting of four former Labour Ministers in Narrow Street.

Rotherhithe, from rethra hythe, sailors' haven, was a market garden village. Michael Caine and Max Bygraves were born here. It was the site of the YHA's flagship 320 bed youth hostel, opened in 1991 but now sold.

Bull Head Dock Wharf at the former Bellamy's Wharf handles aggregates but used to break up ships, including the *Téméraire*. For a century from 1883 Globe Wharf Rice Mill imported all of London's rice. Rotherhithe Heritage Museum in the 1930 Lavender Pumphouse covers beachcombing, dockers' tools and the 1982 Lavender Pond Nature Reserve at Lavender Wharf. A warehouse was used for filming *Little Dorrit*. Between Canada Wharf Museum and Nelson Dock Museum are Horn Stairs at Cuckold's Point, named after a horned ducking stool used until the 1750s.

Dunbar Wharf was the embarkation point for the first voluntary emigrants to Australia. Limekiln Wharf had Limehouse Pottery, the first English factory making soft paste porcelain. David Lean, Sir Ian McKellan and Steven Berkoff have been more recent local residents. The Italianate St Paul's Presbyterian church is now a performing arts centre

Formerly the Isle of Ducks or Stepney Marsh, the Isle of Dogs has had its name for centuries. It may have been because Henry VIII had kennels built here or it may have been for dogs barking for their master, a nobleman drowned while hunting on his wedding night. Millwall takes its name from dykes drained by windmills. It did not become an island, however, until 1805 when the Isle of Dogs Canal was used to cut off the river loop, something which had been suggested for centuries but was not as successful as might have been hoped.

A former spice warehouse houses the Museum of Docklands, which features history and archaeology.

At Poplar London's Docklands have become the world's largest office development, equivalent to a seventh of London's office space, grouped around Canary Wharf which served the Canaries. The 244m high 50 storey One Canada Square of 1991 was the highest building in Britain. Based on a Chicago tower, it used a new method of slipforming the central core because of the high density of the reinforcement. It was badly damaged in a 1993 IRA bomb attack. Beneath is a large shopping mall. It was used for filming *Love Actually* and *Johnny English*.

Next to Canary Wharf Pier are West India Docks. Built in 1802 by Jessop and Rennie, they were the first of London's enclosed docks, the country's greatest civil engineering structures, covering 22ha. They handled products from the West Indies, especially sugar and molasses, but they have seen no commercial traffic since 1980. They have London's finest Grade I warehouses, dating from 1825. Watermen in the fog could tell where they were on Limehouse Reach by the smells from the warehouses.

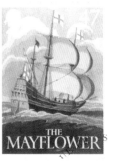

Canary Wharf with One Canada Square, built as the tallest building in Britain.

There was an exodus of Fleet Street newspaper publishers to Docklands. With them is the 12,000 seat London Arena, opened in 1989 on the site of the Olsen Line shed. The 15ha Millwall Docks, the country's leading grain docks, were opened in 1868 to handle Baltic grain. Dock activity peaked in 1964, to be superseded by Tilbury.

Randall's Shipyard was the second largest in London but John Randall committed suicide in 1803 by jumping out of the Nelson Dockhouse window.

The Grand Surrey Canal of 1807 was to serve Mitcham but only reached Camberwell. It was converted to Surrey Docks, the world's largest importers of Scandinavian timber. The wharves were destroyed in 1940 bombing, Surrey Water being what remains. Surrey Quays is the name now used by one of London's largest shopping areas. The Croydon Canal was planned to go to Croydon.

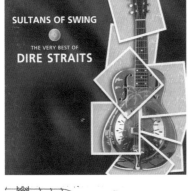

Greenland Dock of 1699 was named after the whaling, built ships and had tanks to extract sperm whale blubber oil. It has now become Surrey Docks Watersports Centre. By Greenland Pier is South Dock Marina and the remains of a slipway at Burrel's Wharf used for building Brunel's *PSS Great Eastern*.

The ragstone tower of St Nicholas' church was used as a shipping mark and collected bodies found in Greenwich Reach of the river. It was also used for the burial of playwright Christopher Marlowe in 1593 after he died nearby in mysterious circumstances.

Deptford was a fishing village until Henry VIII created a royal dockyard here in 1513, quickly becoming England's leading dockyard. Trinity House started here the following year and Deptford Strand was the Royal Victualling Yard from 1858 to 1961 with rum warehouses at the front. Pepys had an office here in the 17th century and another local diarist was John Evelyn. Here is Britain's only statue of a Russian spy. Peter the Great realized that Russia needed to catch up with Western technology so he worked incognito in the dockyard as a carpenter in order to learn about shipbuilding.

Deptford Power Station of 1889 was the world's largest and was sited here as generating at 10kV was considered to be too dangerous for central London, this high tension not being used anywhere else in the world. Coal was delivered by river.

Deptford Creek, the deep ford at the mouth of the Ravensbourne, is where Francis Drake was knighted on the *Golden Hinde* by Elizabeth I in 1581, having become the first Englishman to sail round the world, a journey begun from here in 1577. Howard of Effingham set out from here to challenge the Armada in 1588. Britain's first yacht, the *Katherine* of 1661, was raced by Charles II against his brother James' *Anne* in the world's first yacht race from here to Gravesend. Cook left here in 1768 in the *Endeavour* to chart Australia, with a subsequent last voyage from here in the *Resolution*. Further up the creek, the London to Greewich Railway of 1836 had a 5km viaduct here and was the first railway company to issue season tickets. This is where the first artificial fertilizer was made, where Dire Straits were formed, and Deptford has a significant Buddhist population.

The Deptford–Plumstead Marshes have chalk near the surface but polluted water from the river has entered the aquifer because of overpumping. **Greenwich**, a dry hill in alluvial marshes, is named from Grenvic, town at a green, and was a fishing community. For Victorian MPs the summer recess began here on Whit Sunday with a Whitebait Dinner in the 1837 Trafalgar Tavern, the Opposition having a separate venue. Herrings and sprats were caught, fried and eaten within the hour. Dickens made reference in *Our Mutual Friend* and Tissot painted the river frontage.

Greenwich Market was chartered in 1700. The Docklands Light Railway passes under the river near Greenwich Pier and cupolas on the banks are linked by the Greenwich foot tunnel, 1.1km long and 3.9m in diameter, built in 1902 by Alexander Binnie for dock workers.

This is the starting point for barge driving races and where two notable sailing craft stand out of the water. *Gypsy Moth IV* is the 16m ketch used by Sir Francis Chichester in 1966/7 at the age of 66 to undertake the first solo round the world voyage. The *Cutty Sark* is the world's only remaining tea clipper, the world's fastest sailing ship in the 1880s. Built in Scotland in 1869, she is 65m long with 11m beam and is 44m high. Her three masts support 18km of rigging and 3,000m^2 of canvas. She has been here since 1954 and will be raised 3m to allow the public underneath as part of the restoration work following a serious fire in 2007. She contains the world's largest collection of painted figureheads.

The Old Royal Observatory was built on the hill at Greenwich for Charles II and includes Flamsteed House of 1675, built by Wren and named after the first Astronomer Royal. Passing through the building is the Prime Meridian, accepted by the French in place of Paris in 1884 in return for Britain's metrication, a deal still to be fully honoured by the British. A red timeball on the roof drops at 1pm GMT, many of the world's ships of the day passing it on the water. Inside is an astronomical and timekeeping museum, the 710mm refracting Great Equatorial Telescope of 1893, the UK's largest, and a camera obscura. There is also a Peter Harrison Planetarium and his timepieces. Before he designed his clocks there was no method of timekeeping at sea and so no method of determining longitude, essential for accurate navigation.

The Royal Greenwich Park, laid out by Le Nôtre in 1433 for Charles II, is London's oldest royal park, its 73ha having red and fallow deer, chestnut trees, woods, gardens and a statue of General Wolfe, is the start of the London Marathon for runners and 2012 Olympic equestrian site.

The white Queen's House of 1616–35 by Inigo Jones for Anne of Denmark was the first Palladian building and remains one of the finest. The Great Hall is a 12m cube which may be the model for America's White House. This is where Sir Walter Raleigh spread his cloak over a puddle for Elizabeth I and where she signed the death warrant for Mary, Queen of Scots. A recent addition has been Neptune Court with the world's largest unsupported glass roof. The Tudor Palace of Placentia was where Henry VIII was born in 1491 and he married both Catherine

of Aragon and Anne of Cleves. His daughters, Mary and Elizabeth I, were born here and Edward VI died here in 1553. In 1598 historian John Stow recorded Henry going from Greenwich to Shooter's Hill in 1515 to meet Robin Hood and 200 of his archers, an uncharacteristic slip, these normally reckoned to have been active in the 13th century.

The Royal Hospital for Seamen was built in two parts on the site of the Palace of Placentia to leave a clear view from the Queen's House. With Baroque Doric and Corinthian architecture by Wren, Hawksmoor and Sir John Vanbrugh, it was used for patients from 1705 to 1869. There is a Discover Greenwich centre in the Pepys Building and the Meantime Brewery exhibition on brewing in Greenwich and London in the hospital's former brewery. The neo Grecian chapel was rebuilt in 1789 by James Athenian Stuart with a Samuel Green organ and a Wedgwood ceiling after a fire in 1779. The Painted Hall of 1696–1704 is in the Officer's Mess with the ceiling painting *Triumph of Peace & Liberty* which took Sir James Thornhill 19 years to paint. At 32 x 15m it is the largest in the world. This is one of the finest banqueting rooms in Europe, where Nelson's body lay in state in 1806. The venue was used in filming *The Madness of King George*, *Neverland* and *Four Weddings and a Funeral*.

The Old Royal Naval College, set up by Charles II to rival Versailles, is a Grade I Ancient Monument. In 1957 it hosted Britain's first son et lumière. The college moved to Cranwell and Shrivenham in 1997 and was replaced by the Maritime Campus of the 1890 University of Greenwich and the 1872 Trinity College of Music. The National Maritime Museum, founded in 1933, is the world's largest, covering the Tudors and Cook, Nelson with his bullet pierced jacket from Cape Trafalgar, the Royal and Merchant Navies and the Caird Library, the world's largest marine library with 100,000 books from the 15th century onwards. However, the small boat collection has been moved to Falmouth.

St Alfege church of 1714 by Hawksmoor is on the site of a church where St Alfege, Archbishop of Canterbury, was murdered by the Danes in 1012. Irish pirate Grace O'Malley, Grannuille, was pardoned here by Elizabeth I. General Wolfe and composer Thomas Tallis are buried inside.

A 1906 power station, built to serve trams and supplied with coal by river, is still in use. It had an early steel framed building and a pair of 55m octagonal chimneys. An additional pair of chimneys were restricted to the same height as the site lies almost on the Meridian.

Enderby's Wharf had a ropeworks from 1834. The Enderby brothers found Enderby Land and Green Island during Antarctic whaling expeditions. They made the first transatlantic telegraph cable in 1866, the 8,000km cable being carried to Sheerness by hulk to load into the *Great Eastern*. The first attempt failed, the cable being lost after 1,600km, but the second time the cable was laid from Valentia to Newfoundland.

Cubitt Town, at the start of Blackwall Reach, includes the 1977 Mudchute City Farm and riding stables, the largest urban farm in Europe with cows, pigs, sheep, llamas, chickens and ducks, sited on spoil excavated from Millwall Docks.

A blue lifting bridge crosses the entrance to West India Dock. Coldharbour has 19th century houses and the Gun with a secret spiral staircase and smuggler hideout.

Since 2005 a black cube has housed Reuters, the world's largest supplier of international news. Three ships left Blackwall in 1606 to set up the first permanent colony in North America at Jamestown, leading to English becoming the world's first language. Virginia's first tobacco plantation owner returned to live in Blackwall with his wife, the Indian princess Pocahontas.

The A102 is taken under the river in the two Blackwall Tunnels. When the first tunnel was built in 1897 it was

the world's deepest below water. A 3m layer of clay was tipped on the riverbed to prevent blowout while working in compressed air. A second tunnel was added in 1967 with a vent shaft on Blackwall Point. This had to be incorporated into the Millennium Dome or O2 by Sir Richard Rogers. The world's largest millennium building, the 23,000 seat arena is the world's largest single roofed structure and largest dome although it now has streets of buildings inside. A dozen steel masts and 70km of high strength steel cables support 100,000m² of PTFE coated GRP. It is served by North Greenwich Station, the world's largest underground station. The chase in *The World is Not Enough* was filmed from Westminster, ending up on top of

Greenwich's Old Royal Naval College.

the dome. More filming relates to its use as a venue for the 2012 Olympic gymnastics and basketball. It is accompanied by the David Beckham Academy on what was the site of Europe's largest gasworks. Off the point is a piece of art made up of many L and T shaped pieces of metal.

Next to a power station is Blackwall Yard which built 260 ships between 1612 and 1842 before turning to North Sea oil fabrication work. Trinity Buoy Wharf made buoys and lights for the whole country from 1803 to 1988 and is where Michael Faraday experimented with electric lighting for lighthouses, the site having London's only lighthouse. The wharf is now used by artists who accompany a historic boilermaker's works, a chain store and polygonal brickwork.

Between the wharf and Canning Town is Bow Creek, the mouth of the River Lea, at the start of Bugsby's Reach. The Thames Ironworks built *HMS Warrior* in 1860. She was the first fully ironclad battleship, the largest and longest, and, as the fastest (with steam and sail) and most heavily armed (with 44 guns), immediately made every other warship in the world out of date. She was also the first naval ship to carry washing machines for the crew.

Shelducks occupy an area which is increasingly industrial. In 1917 an explosion of 50t of TNT at the Brunner Mond works killed 73, injured hundreds and flattened the area. Off the Anchor & Hope in Woolwich Reach there had been a collision three years earlier between the liner *Corinthian* and the steamer *Oriole*, which sank, although everyone was rescued.

An interesting segment of ship by the O2.

The O2, built for the new millennium.

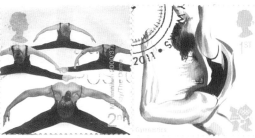

Silvertown was named after the Samuel Winkworth Silver Rubber Works of the 1850s, now accompanied by the Greenwich Yacht Club.

Thames Barrier Park adjoins the 523m wide Thames Barrier of 1981, the world's second largest moveable flood defence. Rotating up from the bed are 3,700t gates spanning 61m gaps. The southern and three northern gaps are closed to navigation, use of the others being controlled by green arrows and red crosses. Flows run out for six hours and forty minutes and in for five hours and forty minutes and there may be eddies beyond the barrier. There has been talk of closing the barrier most of the time to create a calm lake upstream, which would allow passage through only when the tide makes a level. A

The Thames Barrier with one of the gates raised.

The Woolwich Free Ferry.

visitor centre explains the workings. Flood defences were raised upstream in the 1970s and 23km of bank were raised downstream.

The sugar refinery with two chimneys is the world's largest. Its sale in 2010 to American Sugar Refining was the end of an era for Tate & Lyle as they withdrew from the industry in which they had long played the leading role.

Woolwich Ferry has operated since the 13th century and now joins the A205 South Circular with the A406 North Circular. The current vehicle terminals were built in 1966 and use is free. Adjacent is the Woolwich Foot Tunnel, 500m long and 3.9m in diameter. Hand dug, it is lined with cast iron.

North Woolwich Old Station Museum is in an 1850s Italianate Victorian station of the Great Eastern Railway and includes their oldest surviving steam engine. The maze is a copy of the fiendish Chevening House design.

Woolwich was a dry hill in alluvial marshes. It was the site of the Royal Naval Dockyards from 1513 to 1869, the 1784 Superintendant's House with clocktower and the 61m high brick chimney of the 1844 Steam Factory remaining. Prison hulks were moored here until 1857. It was as recently as 1975 that it opened Britain's first McDonald's restaurant, 130 years after Britain's first permanent building society, the Woolwich, opened in a local public house.

The Docklands Light Railway passes under the river and a Crossrail branch to Abbey Wood is also to do so.

Thamesmead is partly built on the site of the Royal Arsenal, in use from 1671 to 1967 and with 18 listed buildings, accompanied by the Royal Victoria Gardens and Royal Arsenal Gardens. Greenwich Heritage Centre is in a 1720 building which became the Royal Military Academy in 1741, the Royal Laboratory in 1806 and an officers' mess in the 20th century. It accompanies the Royal Military Museum – Firepower! In 1886 workers formed what was to become Arsenal Football Club. Their Royal Artillery Band of 1762 remains as Britain's oldest.

Slips lead down to Gallions Reach and disused lighters protect the bank.

A lock leads to the Royal Docks, the world's largest area of enclosed docks, closed to commercial shipping in 1981. The Royal Victoria Dock of 1855 was the first in Britain with hydraulic lock gates, the first built for large steamships and the first with quayside rail links, having been built speculatively by railway contractors Peto, Brassey & Betts, the excavated spoil being used for Battersea Park. Built alongside was Spillers Millennium Mill of the 1930s, one of the largest mill buildings in London. The dock is now a watersports centre accompanied by ExCeL, London's biggest exhibition centre at over 40ha, home to the London Boat Show. The Royal Albert Dock followed in 1880, 2km long with 5km of quayside, the world's largest purpose built dock, the first London dock to be lit electrically. It was bombed heavily during the Second World War, now being used for the London Docklands Regatta and having the University of East London on the north side. King George V Dock completed the trio in 1921, 12m deep and having taken the 35,000t *Mauretania*. The finger of land between the final two docks was used in 1987 as the runway for London City Airport, which uses short take off and landing aircraft, dispensing with tickets.

Beckton sewage works, begun in the 1860s by Joseph Bazalgette, are the largest in Europe. With Crossness, they have Europe's largest sewage sludge incineration plants and the UK's first large desalination plant was opened in 2010. The works were named after Simon Adam Beck, governor of the Chartered Gas Light & Coke Company who had a 1.2m diameter gas main to the City in 1870 from the world's largest gasworks, covering 1.6km^2. It was superseded in 1969 by North Sea gas, used for filming *Brannigan*, *For Your Eyes Only*, *Empire of the Sun* and

Full Metal Jacket and is now the site of Gallions Reach Retail Park. Jetty piers remain where they received coal delivered direct from northeast England. One gasholder held 230,000m³, one of the largest in the UK, and its 55m guide frame was of mild steel, one of the first to use this material.

The worst inland disaster occurred here in 1878 when the *PS Princess Alice* was cut in half by the collier *Bywell Castle*. The 600 deaths from 700 who ended up in the water were accelerated by the putrid state of the water. Outcomes were that the sewage was to be treated rather than just emptied into the river and that ships were to have watertight bulkheads, to have enough lifebelts and to keep to the starboard side of the river.

A light on a 9m red metal framework marks Margaret Ness or Tripcock Point with a pillbox near. Opposite is the 61m high barrier on Barking Creek, protecting the mouth of the River Roding, which had been home to the world's largest fishing fleet in the 19th century. Creekmouth Open Space has been created by removing protective sheet piling and replacing it with a tidal inlet, a sloping surface and a hill with seats to view the river and the mud, where common reed, sea clubrush and avocets might be seen.

There is a slip at Thamesmead and three shelters in the form of upended boats. Large mooring buoys are present. Grey tower blocks provided the setting for filming *A Clockwork Orange*.

Barking Reach passes the former settlement of the Anglo-Saxon Berecings. **Barking** power station was located for coal delivery and, in 1925, was the largest in Britain built as a complete station. Scrap metal is heaped up on the quayside.

Cross Ness is marked by a light on a 12m red metal framework, leading to Halfway Reach. Crossness sewage works has a beam engine house of 1865 containing four James Watt engines which were the world's largest rotating beam engines, 1.2m in diameter with 2.7m stroke, surrounded by ornate cast iron screens. *Prince Consort* has been restored and the others are to follow in what is sometimes called Crossness Cathedral because of its lavish appearance, Victorian engineering at its best. The site was so remote that it required a schoolmaster and a sewing mistress for the staff. Bubbler boats are moored, ready to rush to any point on the river where the injection of air is needed to improve oxygen levels for fish.

Flows run out to 6km/h and in to 5km/h. In 2006 a 6m 4.5t northern bottlenose whale reached here.

Dagenham is named from the Old English Dacca's village. The Thunderer Jetty handles oils while aggregates go to the ARC jetty. Two turbines of the 2004 Dagenham Wind Farm stand by the 2km² location which Ford have occupied since 1929, their car factory on 22,000 concrete piles on the site of a decade long breach in the river wall from 1707 which then became a refuse site, the worst of several breaches. It was repaired by Captain John Perry, using an earth dam with a clay core and interlocking piling near Dagenham dock site and the Ro-Ro berth. It was Europe's largest car plant, producing 11,000,000 vehicles to 2002 before concentrating on diesel engines. One employee at the works was Sandie Shaw, the first Briton to win the Eurovision Song Contest in 1967 with *Puppet on a String* and bare feet.

The Thames formerly flowed between Romford and Upminster to the Blackwater estuary and was a tributary of the Rhine until glaciation so it should be no surprise if the river tries to return to this route.

Riverside is the UK's largest incinerator, built on a former borax site next to a power station. It burns 585,000t of refuse per year, producing 66MW. Delivery by barge could save 100,000 lorry movements per year and it should be the first such plant to reach 27% efficiency.

Frog Island is at the end of Rainham Creek, the dammed Ingrebourne. One of the factories is that of Tilda Rice, who first brought Basmati rice to Europe in the 1970s. **Rainham** Marshes had extensive rifle ranges but are now a 3.4km² RSPB reserve, good for waders and ruffs in the winter. A refuse terminal on Erith Reach is supplied by lighter with material for a tip in the Wennington Marshes.

Coldharbour Point has a light on another 12m red metal framework, followed by industrial premises. Erith Rands is a boardsailing area. **Erith** is another dry hill founded among alluvial marshes. An ancient tower marks the church of St John the Baptist which may contain Roman stones and has Saxon arches and a Norman chancel where the barons met the commissioners of King John after the signing of *Magna Carta*. A large Cory coal depot in the 1880s was used to try out the Butler Petro Cycle, the first car built in Britain. Callendars Cables were world leading producers and also laid the cross Channel PLUTO pipeline which supplied fuel for the D-Day landings. Locals included Denis Thatcher and comedian Linda Smith.

The remains of a mammoth found in **Aveley** Marshes is now in London's Natural History Museum. Much of the marshland to Mar Dyke is restricted by rifle ranges.

Crayford Ness, at the start of Long Reach, is marked by a 23m grey metal framework radar tower. Beyond it, the River Darent, Dartford Creek or the former Dartford & Crayford Navigation joins through a barrier before **Dartford** Marshes, a sewage works and Littlebrook power station. There is a measured distance for shipping, which becomes increasingly large with commercial jetties. **Purfleet**, another dry hill amongst alluvial marshes, has Tunnel Cement and was the site of the lunatic asylum in *Dracula*. Purfleet Heritage & Military Centre is located in the Royal Gunpowder Magazine of the 1760s, moved here after an explosion in Woolwich, which tested and issued gunpowder to the army and navy and shot down a Zeppelin in 1916. The Royal Hotel was noted for its whitebait suppers, the future Edward VII coming in disguise for them.

Dracula

The 215m Littlebrook power station chimney is England's third highest. Conical structures beside the river are ventilation towers for the 1963 Dartford

The Queen Elizabeth II Bridge.

233

Stone Ness light with Grays beyond.

Container cranes lined up at Tilbury.

Distance
77km from Teddington
to Thames Haven

OS 1:50,000 Sheets
176 West London
177 East London
178 Thames Estuary

Admiralty Charts
1186 R Thames
– Canvey Island to
Tilbury (1:12,500)
2151 R Thames
– Tilbury to Margaret
Ness (1:12,500)
2484 R Thames
– Hole Haven to
London Bridge
(1:25,000). Thames
Tidal Barrier
(1:5,000)
3319 R Thames
– Tower Bridge
to Teddington
(1:12,500)
3337 R Thames
– Margaret Ness to
Tower Bridge. Barking
Creek (1:6,250).
Thames Tidal Barrier
(1:5,000)

Tidal Constants
Teddington Lock:
HW Dover +0340
Richmond Lock:
HW Dover +0340,
LW Dover +0600
Chiswick:
HW Dover +0330,
LW Dover +0510
(continued opposite)

Tunnel which, with the 1980 bore, now takes the northbound A282. Since 1991 the Queen Elizabeth II Bridge has carried the four southbound lanes of what is the main route from northern Britain to the Continent. Because of the inadequacy of the toll booths and the refusal to lift the barriers in times of congestion it is usual to see traffic queueing over the 2.8km long bridge and sometimes for tens of kilometres before it. This is the last bridge over the Thames, its 450m main span suspended from 137m masts and giving 54m clearance. When built it was the longest cable stayed bridge in Europe. By it is the Van Ommeran Tank Terminal with LPG tankers and Thames Europort with Ro-Ro berths.

West Thurrock Marshes end at Stone Ness, on the opposite side of the river from Stone. The ness is marked by a light on a 13m red framework tower with a wind generator and is backed by a long and colourful wall, the grafitti of which must have consumed large quantities of gloss paint. The 13th century St Mary at Stone church has long been the Lantern of Kent, acting as a navigation mark defining where the river becomes the estuary.

Ingress Abbey, rebuilt in the 1830s with London Bridge stone, is sited between **Greenhithe** and **Swanscombe**

with its cement works and has provided moorings at times for the training ship *HMS Worcester* and the *Cutty Sark*. Sir John Franklin left here in 1845 to find the Northwest Passage but did not return. Water ebbs for six hours and thirty minutes and floods for six hours every tide.

The HS1 rail link passes under St Clement's or Fiddler's Reach to Ebbsfleet station. Passing high overhead from a power station are powerlines which respond to radar as a ship on a collision course, even when avoiding action is taken. The 190m pylons supporting them are the highest in Britain. A ferry crossed to take pilgrims to Becket's shrine at Canterbury with the little stone and flint banded 15th century church of St Clement on the northern bank, using a Saxon site and incorporating part of a round Norman church. This was restored by giant neighbours Proctor & Gamble and was used for the funeral in filming *Four Weddings and a Funeral*.

Upstream of Broadness, marked by a light on a 13m red metal framework tower, there can be a small race on the ebb and the stream sets northwards onto Black Shelf. After low water there is an eddy above Broadness.

Grays has chemical and petroleum jetties. As another dry hill in the alluvial marshes, it developed on brickworks and cement with a dozen chalkpits, in which rare plants are found. Since 1991 it has had the Lakeside Shopping Centre, the largest retail site in Europe with over 300 stores, 32 places to eat and a seven screen cinema. Thurrock Museum has maritime and prehistoric, Romano-British and Saxon history and archaeology and there is a Thameside Theatre. The church of SS Peter & Paul has a memorial to a schoolmaster and boys who drowned when the training ship *Goliath* was destroyed by fire in 1876. She was replaced by the *TS Exmouth* accommodating 600 and training many poor London boys for careers at sea until 1939.

Swanscombe Marshes, which produced in the 1930s the skull of the palaeolithic Swanscombe Man (now thought to be female), face Northfleet Hope Container Terminal where the ingoing flow is weak on the east side. Slack is at an hour and forty minutes after Dover high water. The Port of **Tilbury** has been in use since 1866 and handles timber, cement, scrap metal and animal and refrigerated food with Europe's largest bulk grain terminal opened in 1969 and is now the main importer of newsprint. It is entered through the largest lock in England, 305 x 34m with a retractable flood gate 34m x 18m high, strangely angled upstream rather than for ships approaching from downstream. As a little light relief it was used for filming *Indiana Jones & the Last Crusade* and *Batman Begins*. A 60MW power station is to be built here, using biomass and incineration. Tilbury Ness takes its name from the Old English Tila's stronghold.

Ferry gliding across from Gravesend.

Behind the cement works and power station at **Northfleet** is St Botolph's church, the tower of which was built as a stronghold against pirates and thieves but this did not prevent the rood screen from being mutilated by the Puritans.

Gravesend Reach was the busiest in the world, including a passenger ferry across to Tilbury. This is where river pilots are replaced by coastal ones and the significance of the name is that anyone dying east of here had to be buried at sea. Customs & Excise and the Port of London Authority health office are both sited here on what was another dry hill amongst the alluvial marshes. Thames sailing barge regattas run from and to here.

Rosherville pleasure gardens are set in an old chalk quarry with crags, a maze and a tea garden. St George's church of 1617 with its Georgian spire has the burial place of Pocahontas, the first North American to be buried in Britain, after she died in a boat off the town. There is a statue to her and another to General Gordon, who lived here for six years from 1865 and reorganized the defences. The Clarendon Royal Hotel was the stately home of Lord Clarendon while the 15th century Three Daws Riverside Inn was used for smuggling and pressgangs.

The 1834 Grade II Town Pier by William Tierney Clark had an original piledriving method and is the world's oldest cast iron pier still in use. The Royal Terrace Pier was added a decade later to replace a temporary structure built by residents and used the novel method of having 1.8m diameter cast iron tubes sunk as cofferdams to prepare the foundations. The Victorian clocktower was inspired by Westminster.

The oldest building in **Gravesend** dates from 1322 and is occupied by the Milton Chantry Heritage Centre. It was founded in 1290 by the Earl of Pembroke as a hospital and subsequently became the chapel of a leper hospital, a tavern and then the New Tavern Fort from 1780 to the 20th century. It has underground magazines, gun emplacements with the world's only remaining 150mm breach guns and an exhibition of Second World War bombardment. General Gordon was stationed here.

The London International Cruise Terminal at Tilbury has a floating jetty attached by a line of riveted rising arms. The first West Indian immigrant ship disembarked here in 1948. The interesting Worlds End public house has old photographs of liners and other ships. The *Ross Revenge* may be seen moored in this area, home of Radio Caroline.

Henry VIII's Tilbury Fort of 1539 is star shaped with two or even three moats on some sides. Near here Elizabeth I made her 1588 eve of the Armada speech about having the body of a weak and feeble woman but the heart of a king of England. Following an attack up the river in

The entrance to Tilbury Fort.

1667 by the Dutch it was extended in the French style from 1672 by Charles II with an ornate arched watergate of 1682. It had a large gunpowder store and, with the fort at Gravesend, provided crossfire over the river. It served as a prison for thousands of Jacobite prisoners after Culloden in 1745 but a surprisingly violent incident in 1776 was a cricket match between Essex and Kent which left three dead. The guns were improved in the 1870s and in 1902, used to shoot down a First World War Zeppelin. The fort was used until 1950 and remains the largest and best example of 17th century military engineering in Britain. The anti aircraft guns on the embankment can be tried. The 1GW Tilbury B power station separates the fort from West and East Tibury Marshes.

The Saxon Shore Way footpath runs from Gravesend to Hastings and includes Saxon protective banks here. The disused Thames & Medway Canal follows at first and could be restored to Higham as part of the Albion Wharf scheme. In practice, the canal offered little advantage over travelling by estuary. The Ship & Lobster had tunnels for smugglers and was visited by Dickens. There are rifle ranges on Denton Marsh and on Shorne Marshes where the Shornmead Fort was built in the 1860s by General Gordon as a backup for Coalhouse and Cliffe forts, attempts to demolish it since having failed.

There are lighter hulks and six covering groynes on the north bank with green light beacons at their ends. Beyond Coalhouse Point is Coalhouse Fort, the best Victorian armoured casemate fort in southeast England, constructed in the 1860s by Gordon to protect against the French and including the Thameside Aviation Museum with artillery and military vehicles. A secret Second World War radar tower rusts close by. St Cedd set up a 7th century minster, later joined by a Norman church of which the Dutch destroyed the tower in 1667.

Higham Bight has strong flows out, draining Higham Marshes and Higham Creek. On the other side of Cliffe Fort is Cliffe Creek and pillboxes guard the river. It also had the Brennan Torpedo Station of 1890, Louis Brennan's guided missile system being the first in the world, the torpedo steered by two wires, rather like flying a kite. In front of Cliffe Marshes the Lower Hope Pools are good for saltmarsh plants and breeding and wintering birds, as foxes have noticed. Ducks and waders increase from here. The Thames estuary has up to 130,000 birds including 30,000 knots, 29,000 dunlin, 20,000 Brent geese, 12,000 oystercatchers, 5,100 bartailed godwits, 2,700 redshanks and ringed and grey plovers which the RSPB claimed were threatened with permanent damage by industry, port expansion, waste disposal, land reclaim, dredging, bait digging and sea level fluctuation, amongst which they seem to have thrived so far.

There was a crossing between Higham and East Tilbury in Roman times, the Romans defending the ridge between East Tilbury and Mucking, where they had a pottery and where there was later an Anglo-Saxon settlement. Flows out are weak on the west side but they are weak on the east side although there are strong flows off Thames Haven.

Mucking explosives anchorage is off Mucking Marshes. Mucking Refuse Jetty with its travelling crane receives 20% of London's waste to supply Britain's largest landfill site, one of the biggest in Europe. The hill is made entirely of refuse and became a country park in 2010. Mucking Flats are a boardsailing area.

The north side of Sea Reach has the fairway with refineries and flarestacks at Thames Haven where there are 5.6km of tanker berths. P&O are building the London Gateway Port on the former Shellhaven refinery site, closed in 1999. Covering 6km², it will take the world's largest container ships. The south shore is a different world with the mud of Blythe Sands backed by a retaining wall and marshes. Between, the river ebbs and floods to 6km/h as it heads directly to the North Sea.

Barnes Bridge:
HW Dover +0320,
LW Dover +0500
Hammersmith Bridge:
HW Dover +0320,
LW Dover +0440
Putney:
HW Dover +0310,
LW Dover +0420
Chelsea Bridge:
HW Dover +0300,
LW Dover +0340
Westminster Bridge:
HW Dover +0250,
LW Dover +0310
London Bridge:
Dover +0240
Greenland Entrance:
HW Dover +0240,
LW Dover +0230
Greenwich Pier:
HW Dover +0240,
LW Dover +0220
India/Milwall Dock:
HW Dover + 0230,
LW Dover +0220
Gallions Point:
HW Dover +0220,
LW Dover +0210
Crossness:
HW Dover +0220,
LW Dover +0200
Coldharbour Light:
HW Dover +0210,
LW Dover +0200
Stoneness Light:
HW Dover +0200,
LW Dover +0150
Tilbury:
HW Dover +0150,
LW Dover +0140
Cliffe Creek:
Dover +0140
Thames Haven:
HW Dover +0140,
LW Dover +0130

Sea Area
Thames

Ranges
Wennington and Shorne Marshes rifle ranges

Rescue
Inshore lifeboats:
Teddington, Chiswick, Tower, Gravesend
All weather lifeboat:
Sheerness
Hovercraft:
Southend-on-Sea

Connections
Grand Union Canal – see CoB p40
Regent's Canal – see CoB p86

235

55 River Medway

Stories, battles and long journeys

For, now De Ruyter's topsails
Off naked Chatham show,
We dare not meet him with our fleet –
And this the Dutchmen know!
Rudyard Kipling

Rising at Turners Hill, the Medway flows northeast to the Thames estuary, separating the Men of Kent on the east side from the Kentishmen on the west. It is tidal from Allington Lock, which works from fifty minutes before Dover high water to four hours ten minutes after Dover high water for those passing through the lock. For small craft wishing to portage, the steps at the downstream end are in a dangerous state and there is no safe place to relaunch until below the first bridge at Aylesford, 2km away.

This is the route used by Geoff Hunter in 1970 in his pioneering circumnavigation of Britain south of the Caledonian Canal using a very unstable plywood Angmagssalik kayak which had never been on the water before he set off.

Opposite the lock is the Cobtree Museum of Kent Life, including an oasthouse, tools and machinery. Trees line the banks, sycamores, willows and ashes, while giant hogweed grows downstream of the M20 bridge. Reeds edge most of the river to the M2. Clumps of dead wood and pieces of branch come up and down the river with the fast flows. Mallards, cormorants and kingfishers give a varied mix of birdlife.

Forstal is passed at the back of industrial buildings while the railway follows the left bank to Strood. Aylesford, however, has some notable construction. It has always been a strategic site. In 43 AD the English under Caractacus failed to stop the Romans here at the Battle of the Medway. Hengist, Horsa and the Jutes defeated the Britons here in 455 although Horsa was killed. The Saxons crossed the river here after their defeat by Offa. Alfred the Great defeated the Danes in 893 and in 1016 Cnut and the Danes escaped across the river after being defeated by Ironside. The ford is now crossed by the finest medieval bridge in southeast England in 14th century ragstone with five pointed arches and an elliptical main arch of 1824 replacing two earlier ones. At 91m long, it no longer carries vehicles.

The dangerous launching steps below Allington Lock.

The medieval Aylesford bridge.

The village has brick and ragstone cottages with Tudor almshouses. Beyond the Chequers the church of SS Peter & Paul has a Norman tower, otherwise it is 14th century with Roman tiles embedded. It had a cage partly below the graveyard, used to hold miscreants until they could be taken to court, bricked up in 1870 but rediscovered in 1975 when the wall started to collapse.

The Friars, dating from 1242, was the first British Carmelite friary. It has notable 14th century cloisters and a 15th century Pilgrims' Hall and gatehouse. The monks had a pottery which remains in use. It was given to Sir Thomas Wyatt at the Dissolution and bought back in 1949. An open air shrine can hold 5,000 pilgrims and smaller shrines have Adam Kossowski ceramic panels.

Industrial premises back onto the river between **Ditton** and New Hythe, the smart Aylesford Newsprint and some less presentable paper recycling buildings. Coots and swans potter as powerlines cross and gravel pits are passed with an arm leading down from a Roman villa site.

Horseshoe Reach is a meander which has almost closed back on itself between Burham Court and **Snodland**, reaching out to the derelict Norman church of St Mary with its 15th century tower. Churches on each side of the river would have been used at the crossing here, the most difficult one on the Pilgrims' Way from Canterbury to Winchester, not a crossing to be attempted today, noxious mud covering the low tide ford on greensand.

An air of dereliction is increased by unusual bank reinforcement in the form of Braithwaite steel tank panels and a pillbox. Herring gulls, herons, Canada geese and lapwings are found around Halling and Wouldham despite the presence of a water skiing area. Powerlines pass each side of a cement works, sited to use mud from the river and chalk, white gashes having become increasingly conspicuous on the dip slope of the North Downs beyond.

North Halling and Cuxton bring Elmhaven and Cuxton Marinas while old limekilns face across to Wouldham Marshes.

Ahead are a set of striking viaducts. The first carries the HS1 Channel Tunnel rail link from St Pancras to Paris and Brussels. At 1.3km long, its 152m centre span is the longest high speed rail span in Europe. The other two, the Medway Bridges, carry the M2 and also the South Downs Way long distance footpath, the first with a 150m main span. At 1km long including approach viaducts and with 30m clearance over the river, its beams were the longest in the world to be built by the cantilever method, up to 41m long.

Port Medway Marina is on the right bank although it may not be obvious that the navigation channel lies to the left of both lines of moored boats. Further up the hill is Fort Borstal which, in 1902, became the first of a series of juvenile reform centres.

Great crested grebes explore off Temple Marsh at **Strood** and a pillbox provides protection. Becket had his own way of responding to Royalists who cut the tail off his horse as he passed. He warned that their offspring would be born with tails, said to have happened.

The Centenary Walk – Rochester follows Tower Reach, overlooked by modern housing blocks and facing across to Strood's Temple Manor, a 1240 hostel for the Knights Templar with 17th century extensions and a vaulted undercroft.

Rochester was Durobruae, stronghold bridges, to the Celts, Dubroviae to the Romans and Dullborough and Cloisterham to Dickens, who lived from the age of five in Chatham, where his father was in the Naval Pay Office, and who featured it extensively in his books.

The Roman walls enclosed 9ha and sections remain, together with parts of the medieval walls, overshadowed by Rochester Castle. The castle was begun by Bishop Gundulph in 1087 on a Roman fort site as one of the earliest masonry castles. Its 34m keep, added in 1126 by William de Corbeuil, Archbishop of Canterbury, was the tallest in England when built with walls 3.7m thick, some of the finest Norman architecture in England. It has battlements, dungeons and a large scale model of the area in the 14th century. It was besieged for two months in 1215 by King John, resisting the stone throwing machines although he finally got entry by setting fire to timbers with the fat of 40 pigs, undermining the southwest tower. Its replacement tower of 1226 is round to deflect missiles, in contrast with the other three towers which are

Part of the Friars at Aylesford.

Cement works and one of the prominent chalk scars at Halling.

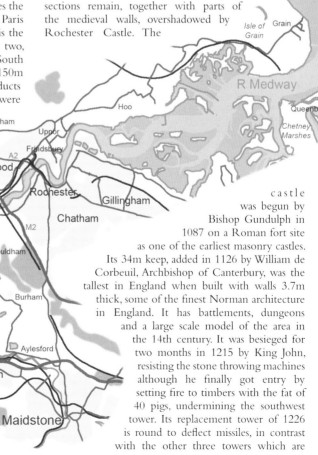

A Eurostar train crosses the Medway Bridges, which also carry the M2. Rochester Castle and cathedral are visible in the distance.

Rochester Castle and the town walls.

Galleon windvane on the Guildhall.

Rochester Cathedral and part of the rare bean tree.

as a freestanding building. The cathedral has the largest collection of medieval wall paintings, memorials of past military campaigns, a 1535 *Bible*, a monument to Dickens who used it in *The Pickwick Papers* and had it central to *The Mystery of Edwin Drood*, a west portal with the only surviving English doorway featuring elongated figures, a 14th century sculpture of Bishop John de Sheppy, which is rare for having most of its original colours, and the tomb of St William of Perth, murdered in 1201 while on pilgrimage to the Holy Land, an important place of pilgrimage itself with various miracles taking place. Cloister Garth is unusual for joining the chancel rather than the nave. Prior's Gate is the most complete set of surviving monastic gates. Henry VIII used the Priory when passing. However, his divorce was opposed by Bishop Fisher, resulting in Fisher's creation as a cardinal by the Pope and his beheading in the Tower of London in 1535. The graveyard has a rare old catalpa or American Indian bean tree. Minor Cannon Row was used in *The Mystery of Edwin Drood*. The Vines were laid out as a public park in 1880, again featuring in *The Mystery of Edwin Drood* and *The Pickwick Papers*. One of the plane trees felled by the 1987 storm has been carved as a monk.

St Nicholas' church was built in 1423 by townspeople barred from the cathedral after a quarrel with the monks. It was rebuilt in 1624. Dickens probably used the name from the Dorrett family memorial for *Little Doritt*.

A large proportion of the buildings in the high street were used by Dickens or carry shop names which imply a link. The Royal Victoria & Bull Hotel was used in *The Pickwick Papers* and *Great Expectations*, the prefix being added after Princess Victoria stayed in 1836. The 1687 Guildhall is one of Kent's best 17th century civic buildings, in red brick with a 1780 sailing ship weathervane above the former market place. It has a museum with 23 charters which form one of the best collections in the country, Victoriana, the conditions in a reconstructed

square. It is where Henry VIII first met Anne of Cleves and was used in *The Pickwick Papers* and *Household Words*.

Rochester has had a cathedral since 604, the second oldest in Britain, surviving many Viking raids. The present building dates from 1080, partially overlapping the site of its predecessor, with Norman and Gothic architecture and a medieval crypt. Gundulph's Tower was built in 1108

Napoleonic prison hulk and fine plaster ceilings which were a gift by local MP Admiral Sir Cloudsley Shovell. It was where Pip was apprenticed in *Great Expectations*. The Old Corn Exchange, also given by Sir Cloudsley Shovell in 1706, featured in *The Uncommercial Traveller* and *The Seven Poor Travellers* and became the Princes Hall. The Watts Charity gave free lodgings to six poor travellers and played an important part in *The Seven Poor Travellers*. The magnificent Elizabethan brick Eastgate House of 1590, home of the Charles Dickens Centre, was used in *The Pickwick Papers* and *The Mystery of Edwin Drood*, being laid out to show scenes from the books. *Great Expectations* and *The Mystery of Edwin Drood* also used Mr Pumblechook's house, opposite, which has in the garden Dicken's writing chalet, moved from Higham. La Providence is a set of 19th century houses acting as a hospital for those of Huguenot descent. Charles II stayed at Restoration House on his return from exile in 1660, Miss Havisham's Satis House in *Great Expectations*, the Latin name given by her in memory of Elizabeth I's mood when running out of patience with the entertainment of Richard Watts while visiting another house in 1573. Draper's Museum of Bygones has period shops. There is an annual Rochester Dickens Summer Festival and Rochester Dickensian Christmas while the Sweeps Festival, dating from at least 1735, includes Morris dancing. Some of *The Canterbury Tales* TV series was filmed here.

The high street is the Roman Watling Street and formed the A2, the main route to the Continent, until 1980. Rochester Bridge had 11 spans in the 18th century. The westbound carriageway crosses on an 1856 bridge, the first to have piers built under compressed air, since modified with a swing section at the western end although this was fixed in 1914. The other carriageway is on a 1970 box girder bridge on former railway bridge piers. The railway now crosses an 1858 plate girder bridge, the river's last bridge. The Bridge Chapel of 1387 was restored in 1937, the board room of the 1398 Bridge Wardens trust, who maintain the bridges independently of public funding. The Mayor of Rochester holds the annual Admiral's Court afloat in a barge, making laws regulating fishing for oysters and floating fish.

Thames barges used to shoot the bridges by dropping their masts briefly. Flows in Bridge Reach run to 5km/h past Medway Bridge Marina and there are eddies and tide rips off Jane's Creek.

At Frindsbury, where a submarine sits below the church, the railway turns into a tunnel built by William Tierney Clark in 1824 for the Thames & Medway Canal. It was the second longest canal tunnel in Britain at 3.6km and had the largest bore, 10.7m high by 8.1m wide. In 1830 it

Eastgate House, as described by Dickens.

was opened out in the middle to provide a passing place. Briefly it was shared by trains running on a platform over the towpath and part of the water before the barges were removed altogether, most of the canal being lost although restoration is being undertaken at the Gravesend end.

By Limehouse Reach between Gashouse Point and Chatham Ness on reclaimed land is the Port of Rochester, including a container terminal. Chatham Reach flows out to 2km/h and in to 1km/h.

Chatham takes its name from the British Celtic cet ham, forest village. The Chatham Naval Dockyard was started in 1547 by Henry VIII and was used until 1984, now being the World Naval Base on a 32ha site with 47 Ancient Monuments and a range of museums.

Fort Amherst of 1756 was extended in 1803–11 by convicts to a 5.7ha site with redoubts and tunnels used during the Napoleonic period to protect the docks from landward attack. On Great Lines hill, it is Britain's finest and most complete Georgian fortress and has a Second World War Home Front exhibition.

Near the Command public house is the Medway Heritage Centre in an old church, covering the tidal river. The Old Brook Pumping Station is an Ancient Monument, formerly used for Chatham's main drainage, with two Campbell diesel engines, the press used for

A submarine lies below the chalk cliff at Frindsbury at the end of the tunnel from Higham.

Shipyard buildings line the river at Chatham.

Kingswear Castle *with historic ships and covered docks beyond.*

the *Rochester Gazette* until 1868 and models of Medway windmills.

Henry VIII moved all Portsmouth's ships here in 1550 to face the Dutch and it was the best dockyard in the country in the 17th century, described in *The Pickwick Papers*. It built many of the major ships, including *HMS Victory*, launched in 1765, the navy's first major iron ship, the *Téméraire*, the battleship with the largest spars, *Achilles*, and submarines. In the 18th century it was the largest employer of civilians in southeast England. It was where Drake first went to sea at the age of 12 or 13, having lived on a boat in Chatham since the age of 8, his father

being vicar of Upchurch, and it was where Elizabeth I ordered the *Golden Hind* to be laid up in 1580 after a three year circumnavigation of the globe. Local ships' pilot Will Adams landed in Japan by accident in the 17th century and founded the Japanese navy. Nelson sailed from here at 12 in 1771 and Hawkins also sailed from Chatham.

Later there were 60 prison hulks, including the *Brunswick* with 500 convicts. More recent construction in 1944 was of sections of Mulberry Harbour.

Sailing from here is the 1924 *Kingswear Castle*, the last working coalfired paddle steamer. Chatham has the world's most complete dockyard of sail. Basins contain Britain's last Second World War destroyer, *HMS Cavalier* of 1944, the 1962 GRP and alloy submarine *Ocelot* and the last Victorian sloop, *Gannet* of 1878 with sail and steam options. There are 17 lifeboats, the 1758 warship construction exhibition in Wooden Walls, the 18th century ropeworks in one of the longest brick buildings in Europe at 346m, founded in 1618 and still commercial, the dockyard steam railway, the Kent Police Museum, a working foundry and Chatham Dockyard Historical Society which includes the Royal Navy. Of the five large covered slipways, only number 7 of 1855 remains, 21m high with a corrugated galvanized iron roof, a new product at the time, on wrought iron trusses and purlins mounted on cast iron lattice beams, designed by Royal Engineer G T Greene. Other facilities include the Dockside Outlet Centre and the Nelson Brewing Company. It has been used for filming *Diamonds are Forever* and *The World is not Enough*.

The Medway Tunnel provides a last crossing between Chatham Reach and Upnor Reach at Upper Upnor.

The turreted 1559 Upnor Castle of Elizabeth I was badly maintained and failed to prevent the most ignominious attack on the navy. In 1667 De Ruyter led the Dutch with English crewmen to tow away the English flagship, *Royal Charles*, from the dockyard and burn several others. Following this it was downgraded to a magazine for gunpowder and arms. Serif lettering on the adjacent wall still tells ships not to anchor in front of it.

Upnor Castle failed to defend Chatham against the Dutch.

Capturing the spirit of sailing at St Mary's Island.

A retaining wall of lighters at Hoo Ness.

Hoo Salt Marsh has a railway round the outside, the corner at Hoo Ness with a retaining wall of barges two high. Flows in **Gillingham** Reach run to 4km/h each way, out from an hour and forty minutes after Dover high water. On the south side of the reach is Bull Nose between the locks at the eastern entrance to Chatham Naval Dockyard, followed by Medway Pier Marine, Gillingham Marina and Whitton Marine. Another notable kayak circumnavigation, the first of Britain and Ireland in one go, left from Gillingham Strand in 1976, described by Bill Taylor in *Commitment and Open Crossings.*

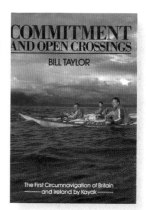

The School of Military Engineering jetty at Lower Upnor is located in front of the Ship Inn, the Pier Hotel and Upnor Sailing Club. Named after the *Arethusa* sail training ship, which used to be moored here, is the Arethusa Venture watersports centre. The Saxon Shore Way footpath runs to the north of Short Reach past Beacon Hill with its aerial and the Medway Yacht Club. Flows run out from an hour and twenty minutes after Dover high water and in from four hours forty minutes before Dover high water to 4km/h, rough with a fresh wind.

St Mary's Island is well anchored to the shore and new housing runs from Finsborough Ness to a modern sculpture of a man and a woman sheeting sails.

Hoo Marina, the Hundred of Hoo Sailing Club and perhaps a couple of moored lightships occupy West Hoo Creek. The estuary widens out considerably and becomes dotted with islands. These are frequently marshy, divided by creeks and surrounded by extensive mudflats so that it is hard to tell what is land and what is not. Many waders use the saltings. What land there is will often be London clay.

Hoo Fort with a vertical wall around it acting as a dry moat.

241

Kingsnorth power station faces Darnet Fort, the twin to Hoo Fort.

Gillingham Marshes, Cinque Port Marshes, Copperhouse Marshes and Nor Marsh curve round to South Yantlet Creek. On the east end of Hoo Salt Marsh is Hoo Fort, a derelict 19th century circular Napoleonic defence with a layout like a dry moat around it, sloping on the outside but with a vertical stone wall on the inside. To the north and east a number of large boats have been abandoned on Hoo Flats next to the island. Far to the east the Swale Bridge can be seen rising in a high arc to the Isle of Sheppey.

On the far side of Pinup Reach is Darnet Fort, the twin to Hoo Fort. Outgoing flows set strongly from Darnett Ness to Slede Ooze and Oakham Ness but are weak on the south side of Long Reach. On the other hand, incoming flows set strongly from Oakham Ness to Bishop Ooze but are weak on the north side. A jetty runs out to the centre of Long Reach to receive coal for the 2GW Kingsnorth power station, scene of demonstrations by environmental protesters objecting to the use of coal. Oakham Ness Jetty receives oil for the power station. Europe's largest LNG terminal is sited here and a fifth of the UK's gas supply is landed here. The estuary has up to 54,000 birds including 23,000 dunlins, 5,900 shelducks, 4,800 grey plovers, 4,200 redshanks, oystercatchers, terns, egrets, Brent geese, pintails and ringed plovers. In 1992 the RSPB said it was the most threatened UK estuary with permanent damage likely from port expansion, marina development, land reclaim, spoil disposal, recreation, bait digging and pollution. Seals also use it.

Outgoing flows set diagonally across Kethole Reach from Oakham Ness to Sharp Ness and Burntwick Island, the incoming flow setting from Sharp Ness towards Bee Ness Jetty and East Hoo Creek. In Saltpan Reach the flow out from ten minutes before Dover high water to 3km/h sets towards Elphinstone Point, especially with southwesterly winds, while incoming flows are to 2km/h along the south side of the channel but weak on the north side. On Sharpness Shelf is the wreck of the 15,000t *HMS Bulwark*, subject to a massive explosion while loading coal. The blast killed 700 people, one of the worst naval accidents ever.

The terminal of the former refinery on the walled Isle of Grain is now the Thamesport container terminal. Ingoing streams run strongly from Horseshoe Point to Stangate Creek. Chetney Marshes, Deadmans Island and Queenborough Spit lead to the West Swale.

Sheerness takes its name from the Old English scie ness, bright headland, but the Blue Town area at the northern end is because so many of the houses were decorated with Royal Navy paint. The naval dockyard was founded here in 1665 by Pepys although much was added by Rennie in 1812. It had the only naval barracks in England, housing 1,000 men. An 1860 iron framed boat store, 64m x 41m x 16m high, reaching for four storeys, was the first multistorey iron framed building and, thus, the precursor to the skyscraper. It was unbraced but had stiff joints for stability.

The fortress was burned by the Dutch in 1667. In 1797 the Nore mutiny led to better living conditions for sailors. It was at Sheerness that Nelson's body was landed after Trafalgar. Much of the town is Victorian because a fire of 1827 destroyed earlier buildings.

The Royal Navy left in 1960 and the port now handles containers, refrigerated products and timber. It imports cars and also has a Ro-Ro vehicle ferry service to Vlissingen.

A white light every 7 seconds at Garrison Point indicates the movement of a vessel over 130m long between Darnett Ness and the Thames estuary.

The 244m chimney of the Grain power station is the prominent landmark for the whole of this part of the Thames estuary. Much smaller is the Grain Tower, a Martello Tower off the village of Grain, the name of which comes from the Old English groen, sand or gravel.

Northwesterly to northerly winds raise the water level with ingoing flows, especially with storm surges. The opposite winds lower outgoing water levels and can cause a stand to four hours ten minutes before Dover high water. Rain increases the ebb and reduces flood flows. The outgoing stream sets northeastwards, westerly to southwesterly winds adding turbulence. The ingoing stream sets west to follow the Grain shore. A weak outgoing stream on the southeast side of the Isle of Grain begins at twenty to fifty minutes after Dover high water. There can be a slack from five hours forty minutes after Dover high water to five hours forty minutes before the next Dover high water and with neaps there can also be a slack from fifty minutes after Dover high water to two hours tenty minutes after Dover high water. Eddies can form to 2km/h downstream of Garrison Point on both flows.

A tug uses its fire cannons off Sheerness.

The Grain Tower defends the mouth of the Medway. Southend lies across the Thames estuary.

56 River Great Stour

The route to visit or conquer Britain

By God's grace aware of their prevision
I sent my letters on another day,
Had fair crossing, found at Sandwich
Broc, Warenne, and the Sheriff of Kent,
Those who had sworn to have my head from me
Only John, the Dean of Salisbury,
Fearing for the King's name, warning against treason,
Made them hold their hands. So for the time
We were unmolested.

T S Eliot

Rising at Lenham, the River Great Stour or Kentish Stour flows northeast to Pegwell Bay and was used to bring in the stone to build Canterbury Cathedral. In 1592 it was made into a navigation from Canterbury but soon silted up. Exactly two centuries later there was a proposal for a cut from Canterbury to below Fordwich, getting round some of the problems in the higher reaches, and in 1800 it was suggested as a branch of an Eastern Rother to Medway canal. In 1811 there was the Act for the Canterbury Navigation to St Nicholas Bay but this was undermined by share speculators and by the building of the Canterbury & Whitstable Railway.

The river is tidal from the A28 at Sturry, a Roman road. The village was heavily bombed during the Second World War but retains its 16th century manor and a medieval tithe barn which belong to St Augustine's Abbey. At the tidal limit there are two branches. The eastern one is the mill channel with a sluice, formerly a flash lock. The other channel is unencumbered.

Tides flow for 3 hours and the water is clear and has trout but is weedy. It is also shallow down to the bridge at Fordwich, on which is a notice banning boats from travelling upstream despite the public right of navigation from Canterbury.

Fordwich was a major port for Canterbury at the time of the Conquest and supplied fighting ships for the Sandwich contingent. From 1594 to 1877 there was a weir and a flash lock. There are still a surprising number of small cruisers moored for the size of the river, little more than a stream, and there is a convenient launching platform for small craft.

Britain's smallest community with a town council, 250 people, Fordwich also has England's smallest town hall on the south bank between the George & Dragon and Fordwich Arms. The half timbered building has stocks and a ducking stool for nagging wives. The church is partly Norman and may have the grave of St Augustine. The attractive town has Tudor houses yet is not the parking nightmare of some better known heritage locations.

As far as Upstreet the river is well shaded, particularly by willows, alders, ashes, dog roses and reedmace which shelter insects. Occasionally there is a bench with horns at each end for those content to lean rather than actually sit down.

This part of the valley is dominated by the mining subsidence lakes of the former Chislet colliery although there is little other evidence of mining. Westbere Marshes and the lakes attract mallards, moorhens, coots, geese, great crested grebes, herons, swans, cormorants, Savi's and Cetti's warblers, kingfishers, waders, terns, bitterns and rare breeding birds including

The River Great Stour with moorings at Fordwich.

bearded tits. Marsh marigolds are joined in the river by arrowhead and, for a while, algae, difficult to penetrate. A diagonal line of pontoons out from each bank leaves boats to undertake a difficult slalom manoeuvre, an arrangement perhaps intended to catch weed or debris.

Beyond Hersden, which is as near as most of the valley gets to an industrial feel and where the Charing Cross to Ramsgate railway arrives alongside intermittently to Sarre, the Stour Valley Walk joins the bank to beyond Grove Ferry. It passes around two sides of the Stodmarsh National Nature Reserve, the largest freshwater marshland in Kent, covering 3.6km^2. Throughout the year there are garganey, teal, gadwall, shoveler, pochard, tufted duck, water rail, bearded reedling, willow tit and redpoll with grasshopper, sedge and reed warblers in the summer and wigeon, hen harrier, snipe and water pipit in the winter plus water rats and grass snakes.

Groups of moorings are met at Upstreet and at Grove Ferry, where the chain ferry was replaced in 1962 by a bridge. Smuggling on the river continued into the 20th century. It helped smugglers to escape if the ferry was on the

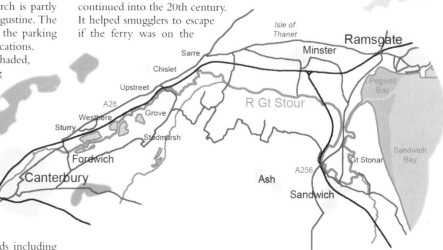

The medieval town hall at Fordwich.

Fordwich's church and the Fordwich Arms.

Stadmarsh's strange slalom course.

wrong side when customs arrived. Ferrymen were said to have been well tipped. Lavender oil used to be distilled from the crop grown here.

The river now becomes more open, the banks lined with reeds. Cuckoos and pheasants might be heard and blue dragonflies encountered.

The River Wantsum arrives through a sluice. In historical times it was a broad arm of the sea, cutting off the Isle of Thanet. Navigability of the channel has been allowed to deteriorate significantly even since the mid 20th century, when there used to be a canoe race around Thanet, and it has even been claimed that the navigation right has been lost as a result.

Sarre was formerly a Cinque Port. The Sarre Wall runs parallel to the River Stour. The Crown Inn was Cherry Brandy House at what was the main crossing point of the Wantsum Channel to the island. Cherry brandy can still be sampled there. Above is the Edwardian Sarre Windmill, the only windmill working commercially in Kent, accompanied by a steam engine and an animal farm.

The Saxon Shore Way footpath arrives with the Little Stour or Seaton Navigation, a double boom across it. The 10km navigation from Seaton was made without parliamentary authority to provide an alternative route to Canterbury.

There are extensive moorings at Plucks Gutter and then the Somerset Maugham Boat House. Ahead lie **Ash** Level and the **Minster** Marshes, used for grazing and serenaded by the skylark. Overhead powerlines are conspicuous and run roughly above the Abbot's Wall.

Minster Abbey, run by Benedictine nuns, is one of England's oldest inhabited buildings. It was founded

Coal mining has left various lakes including this one adjoining the river at Westbere.

in 670 by Domna Eva, the great granddaughter of St Ethelbert, and was the first women's monastery. In 1027 the site was granted by Cnut to St Augustine's Abbey and it now has a 1027 Saxon wing and a 12th century Norman wing.

Reeds obscure views from the river but angling platforms are chopped out of them at regular intervals on this section.

The Ramsgate–Dover railway crosses in front of the disused Richborough power station of 1963. On the river bank are two tall masts and a wind turbine of an early design with a large cap. The power station and its three cooling towers are also on the bank of the river. It was used for filming *Son of Rambow* and the *Full Metal Challenge* series.

The 18th century Stonar Cut is an expected channel, less than 200m long but cutting off a 10km loop in the river. Surprisingly, there is no navigation channel. A boom crosses the cut at the upstream end and the sluices were moved to the downstream end when the A256 was dualled in 2008. Flows run out strongly from two hours after Dover high water and in from four hours fifty minutes before Dover high water. When the sluices are open a red flag is flown 600m upstream and boats are warned not to pass.

In Roman times the Wantsum Channel was nearly 2km wide and the coast of Sandwich Bay was 3km further inland, explaining the layout of some features on the Stour's great loop. Richborough Castle, the Roman port of Rutupiae, was important as the beginning of Watling Street and even for its oysters. It was where Claudius

landed in 43. There was a marble monument to celebrate the conquest of Britain. The foundations remain of a 25m high triumphal arch, erected in 85. Although pulled down in the 3rd century, it could have been the inspiration for

The short waterfront at Sandwich.

Sandwich's old bridge.

the Statue of Liberty. The castle became a watch or light tower, guarded the Wantsum Channel against the Saxons in the 1st century and was rebuilt in 285 as the first Saxon Shore fort. With ramparts by Aulus Plautus, it is one of the best examples with more than two flint walls remaining, vast ditches, a pagan temple inside and the grave of a Roman officer. The 2nd Legion were stationed here in about 300 although it was later captured and burnt down by the Danes and the materials used in local building. There is a museum of Roman relics, the remains of an early Christian church and an amphitheatre.

The A256 crosses on a high bridge. The Monk's Wall, White Mill Rural Heritage Centre with its 18th century smock mill and Gazen Salts Nature Reserve & Sports Field surround the river but all that is seen is the brown water sweeping between high muddy banks where even the reeds seem to have difficulty keeping their grip.

Considering its historical importance, **Sandwich** is remarkably small. It was built on a coastal sandbank and was first mentioned in 661. It was granted to the monks of Christchurch by Edgar, Ethelred the Unready and Cnut, whose charter was for land as far inland as an axe could be thrown from a vessel afloat at high water.

One of the first Danish attacks on England took place at Bloody Point in 851 when Athelstan and Ealhhere defeated a Danish fleet off Sandwich. King Alfred captured 16 ships off the mouth of the Stour but was beaten by a much larger Danish force before reaching the safety of the harbour. The Danes arrived under Olaf in 991 and occupied Sandwich in 1006, King Swein of Denmark first landed here in 1009 and Cnut landed some hostages here five years later and mutilated them before sailing for Denmark. Twenty five Viking ships plundered the town in 1048 and Tostig occupied it in 1066, the Danes being beaten back a couple of years later.

Sandwich was granted to Odo, the bishop of Bayeux and half brother of William the Conqueror, but in 1072 he was accused of holding church land, lost a major case and saw Sandwich returned to the Christchurch monks. It had large herring catches, sending 40,000 to Christchurch in 1086.

It was an original Cinque Port, was the headquarters for the country's navy for centuries and was the main continental ferry port until Tudor times. In the early 13th century it was sacked by the French. The Battle of Sandwich in 1217 took place in Sandwich Bay with the French led by the English traitor Eustace the Monk, who turned his ship invisible by magic. Regardless, Stephen Crabbe of Sandwich was able to find and board Eustace's boat and cut off his head to make the ship visible again. The Cinque Ports fleet of 16 beat 80 French ships by throwing pots of powdered quicklime to blind French crews. Eustace's head was paraded. A hospital was founded on the battle spoils and is still named St Bartholomew's after the day of the battle. Children race for a Bartholomew Bun on August 24th. It was the century in which the wool trade was established through the port. In 1457, 4,000 Frenchmen from Honfleur invaded, killed the mayor and others and largely destroyed the town, since when the mayor of Sandwich has worn a black robe. A daily evening curfew bell is still rung.

On misty nights a Roman might be seen fighting a Saxon on the shore. During the Second World War soldiers on defence watch saw a cohort of ghostly Romans march into the sea.

The walled town has the 1384 Fisher Gate on the quay, the 1539 Barbican Gate, a former blockhouse with twin conical turreted towers, the 14/15th century St Clement's church, the Guildhall with medieval silver maces and

Cinque Port history, 17th century housing after Dutch wool traders settled, the Salutation house of the early 20th century by Sir Edwin Lutyens in gardens by Gertrude Jekyll, the Precinct Toy Collection, the Fisherman's Wharf Restaurant and the Bell Hotel. There was a drawbridge from 1755 until 1893, becoming the Barbican swing bridge with a toll until the 1970s. A riverbus offers a different viewpoint to the public.

The reeds are left behind as the river winds round an industrial estate and timber is traded.

To the east as the North Stream enters are the Royal St George's and Prince's golf links, the former featuring as Royal St Mark's in *Goldfinger* and having hosted the British Open.

Beyond a lake is Great Stonar which was built on the end of a shingle spit and was known as Eastanore to the Romans and Lunden wic or London landing to the Saxons. Another spit grew northwards and sand dunes developed. Chemical works are located on the banks but there are lapwings, curlews, egrets, oystercatchers, blackheaded, blackbacked and herring gulls and shelducks. Seals haul out on the sand.

Richborough Port was used during the First World War for troops and arms going to France and in the Second World War for building sections of Mulberry Harbour. The wharf is no longer commercial.

The estuary of the River Stour has flows outwards from two hours after Dover high water and inwards from four hours fifty minutes before Dover high water. The banks fall away to Shell Ness where there are fish traps, beacons and a wreck, opening up Pegwell Bay Country Park, a nature reserve with a wildfowl and wader roost and drying mud and sand flats. Ebbsfleet, at the back of Pegwell Bay, is where Jutland chieftains Hengist and Horsa landed in 449 with the Saxons and a banner showing a prancing white horse, now the badge of Kent. St Augustine landed in 597, celebrating his first mass in the presence of King Ethelbert. The Spanish Armada had also intended to land here. There are two golf courses. Along the north side of the bay are a former hovercraft terminal slipway and white chalk cliffs leading to Ramsgate.

The shallow channel winds out between small floats and skeleton fixed marks.

The outer mark for the Great Stour, Ramsgate's cliffs beyond.

Distance
34km from Sturry to Pegwell Bay

OS 1:50,000 Sheets
179 Canterbury & East Kent

Admiralty Charts
323 Dover Strait – Eastern Part (1:75,000)
1827 Harbours on SE Coast of England. Pegwell Bay & R Stour (1:12,500)
1828 Dover to N Foreland (1:37,500)

Tidal Constants
Grove Ferry:
HW Dover +0240
Richborough:
HW Dover +0020,
LW Dover +0030

Sea Area
Thames

Rescue
Inshore lifeboat:
Ramsgate
All weather lifeboat:
Ramsgate

57 River Ouse (East Sussex)

Influencing English, French and American democracy

Or south where windy Piddinghoe's
  Beguilded dolphin veers,
And red beside wide-bankèd Ouse
  Lie down our Sussex steers.
Rudyard Kipling

Rising near Lower Beeding on the edge of St Leonard's Forest and the Weald, the River Ouse flows southwards across East Sussex, as it has done as a dip slope river since before the chalk covering was eroded away. It was a navigation from Lindfield from 1790, the remains of locks still being in place, and Rennie suggested it as a branch of the London to Portsmouth canal scheme.

The river was called the Middewinde above Lewes but now the whole river takes its name of Ouse from Lewes. It is slow and brown, weedy in summer. An area of AONB leads down to Heritage Coast.

Anglers are present, especially at Barcombe Mills, the tidal limit, where sea trout can use fish passes to get above the complex of weirs. In Victorian times there were three mills working and there is a water abstraction point when flows exceed 210l/s. A Roman road from London crossed the river here, doing so twice more at Upper Wellingham. The former Uckfield to Lewes railway also followed the river closely and could do again as a section has been restored at Isfield as the Lavender Line.

Trying to approach Barcombe Mills from the southeast faces the motorist with a no entry sign and then further road signs if this is ignored. It may be better to park on the northwest side of the river on the more major road and use the narrow steps which descend at all four corners of the bridge.

The river twists between reeds and low hanging willows and is crossed by a pipe bridge. There are occasional ashes and oaks on the high banks and splashes of purple loosestrife and Himalayan balsam. Mallards, swans and herons are present and buzzards circle. Barcombe, with its Norman church, stands back from the river. Between Upper Wellingham and Hamsey there are several oxbow lakes where meanders have been cut off.

At Hamsey the river is crossed by a second pipe bridge, accompanied by a pillbox and a brick hut with a distinct list. The natural course of the river goes left over an unpleasant weir below high tide at the start of a large meander. The left side of the weir is a lifting metal plate with metal V upstands along its lip. The right side, only used when the river is high, is a series of concrete

The Hamsey pipe bridge and listing hut.

walls with deep troughs between them, a dangerous design. A straight 1km cut leads to the right between the abutments of a former railway bridge. The railway crossed the island one way and powerlines cross at right angles. A medieval church on the hill in the middle of the loop has traces of 15th century paintings. A large barn conversion overlooks the cut at Hamseyplace Farm. Water flows fast, shallow and narrow through this section, which includes the remains of Hamsey Lock, no longer obvious. There are slight rapids under the road bridge before bamboos close in, barely leaving enough room to force a passage through. Kingfishers and coots appreciate the closed in cut section.

The two channels meet again and the Burgess Hill–Lewes railway is pushed close alongside below the chalk upstand of the South Downs. These days the most dramatic activity is parachuting but in 1264 the Battle of Lewes took place on Mount Harry where Simon de Montfort beat Henry III, the royal troops being driven across the river where some of them drowned. This was the birthplace of the English Parliament as the subsequent body formed had representatives of the boroughs and shires as well as the barons and church.

The Saxon borough of **Lewes** guarded the river valley from its position on the Middle and Upper Chalk. It is 'in the most romantic situation I ever saw' according to Defoe, who noted enormous trees which were allowed to grow to full size because of the difficulty of getting them to shipyards. Indeed, transport was difficult not only for trees. He noted a lady going to church in a coach drawn by six oxen because of the state

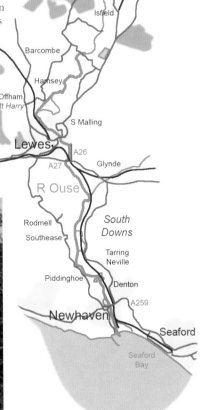

In the upper reaches of the tidal section near Barcombe.

The Hamsey weir. High flows also cover the nearer section.

The narrow artificial cut below Hamseyplace Farm.

The river squeezes the railway against Offham Hill.

Harveys brewery in Lewes.

of the roads. In Georgian times it became a fashionable holiday resort.

Approach to Lewes, county town of East Sussex, is past the backs of industrial units and a Tesco supermarket with the inevitable trolleys in the river. On the east bank is Harvey's brewery, the oldest brewery in Sussex, founded in 1790 and rebuilt in 1881 with a Victorian Gothic tower from which the odours of brewing emanate with an easterly wind. Steam driven vehicles are on show. The Tom Paine seasonal ale is named after the Lewes exciseman who later wrote *The Rights of Man* and who lived in the 15th century Old Bull from 1768 to 1774, influencing both the French and American Revolutions. Bonfire night sees the largest celebrations in the country as many Lewes Protestants were burnt under the Catholic Mary Tudor. Elaborate period costume is used, including throwing a blazing barrel of tar into the river, the quenching relating back to Celtic symbolism of winter overcoming summer. In 2008 the town issued its own pound tokens, only able to be used for local produce and services. Lewes Guitar Festival takes place in the summer.

Architecture includes Tudor and Georgian around a network of Saxon lanes, the town having had a Saxon mint. William de Warren, William the Conqueror's son in law, administered the Rape of Lewes and built the Norman castle in 1077. Its walls are 9.1m thick at the base and still 1.2m thick at the top. There is an oval bailey, a flint knapped shell keep with semi octagonal wall towers

on the west motte and the remains of another on the east motte, the castle being unusual in having two mottes. The 14th century Barbican House Museum, Museum of Sussex Archaeology and Lewes Living History model bring the town's past to the public.

The Sussex Folk Museum is located in the 16th century Anne of Cleves House, one of the finest Tudor buildings in England, part of Henry VIII's divorce settlement although she never lived here. It has 14th century cellars, 17th and 18th century furnishings, Sussex pottery, Wealden ironwork and a Tudor kitchen with a marble topped table on which the knights who slew Becket in 1170 had twice placed their arms, only to have it throw them on the floor each time. A herb garden has been recreated with the remains of the 1077 Cluniac Southover Priory of St Pancras, destroyed by Henry VIII. Nearby is 16th century Southover Grange with its fine timber fireplace, the house where diarist John Evelyn was brought up.

St Michael's church with beautiful stained glass has a 13th century round tower, one of only three in Sussex, all by the Ouse. The early 19th century Calvinistic Jireh Chapel may be the largest surviving example of a timber framed meeting house. Not forgetting the people, in 1822 William Cobbett found the girls remarkably pretty and the men good looking as well.

The Riverside Centre sells local cheeses, meat, fish and flowers.

The disadvantages of a riverside location were shown by bad flooding in 1960 and again in 2000 although the town's sewerage scheme has been improved. A pipeline runs along the bed of the river on the west side through the centre of the town, visible when the tide drops. By now there is seaweed in the river. Rowing takes place on the river and it is also used by sailing craft able to take the ground.

To the east is Malling Hill with a field system, a long barrow, tumuli and an obelisk which is almost above the

A pipe is placed at the side of the riverbed in Lewes.

1970s tunnel taking the A26 through behind the chalk cliff. The Snowdrop Inn is named after the only English avalanche which, in 1836, damaged several cottages and killed eight people.

From here the river has levées and has been designed to carry 170m³/s, often with parallel drainage channels outside. The 400m cut at Southerham is the work of William Jessop in the late 18th century, perhaps a narrowboat present but seeming strangely out of place.

The Lewes to Seaford railway crosses and follows and the A27 also passes over. Powerlines cross twice at the ends of the marshy Brooks area and then follow to Newhaven. Anti scour stakes are driven into the banks, later to be reinforced with timbering. Herring gulls

The site of England's only avalanche.

The South Downs rise ahead.

The Glynde Reach joins under the railway.

appear in flocks with rather fewer blackheaded gulls, cormorants and egrets.

Mount Caburn has a 1.4ha Iron Age camp on top as the high land pulls back towards Glynde. After 100 BC a bank and ditch were added, then grain storage pits inside the ramparts with a new bank and ditch being constructed at the time of the Roman invasion. It is one of the finest remaining sites for chalk plants, including the rare wild rose, and is popular with hang gliders.

The Glynde Reach joins from the east. In 1791 there was a proposal to use it for a canal to Selmerston and to Horsebridge and Hellingly on the River Cuckmere.

A rubbish tip in a former quarry is conspicuous but should be restored and landscaped in due course.

Rodmell has a Norman church and the weatherboarded Monk's House, home of Virginia Woolf from 1919. She drowned herself in the river in 1941 after filling her pockets with stones, her body being found at Itford Bridge, a high swing bridge at Southease which carries the South Downs Way. A 10km/h speed limit is imposed on craft although the flow itself must be of this order here with a good ebb running.

Southease has the 12th century Saxon church of St

Piddinghoe with its unusual Norman church.

Itford Bridge, a swing bridge carrying the South Downs Way path.

249

A sculpted cormorant in the docks at Newhaven.

carrying the A259 which replaced one of 1865 also carrying a railway.

Red lights indicate downstream travel and green lights upstream, green flashing lights being for vessels swinging. Traffic signals must be obeyed and permission to proceed requested of Newhaven Radio Port Control by VHF or telephone. The centre of all the activity is the car ferry service to Dieppe with 1,400 sailings per year including high speed ferries. The service began in 1847 with paddle steamers, giving a route from London to Paris 140km shorter than via Dover.

The lifeboat is moored opposite, above the 320 berth Newhaven Marina in Sleeper's Hole. The marina is below the Hope Inn, blocked out by a forest of apartments built around the marina. There was also a substantial Roman building in Newhaven.

Until 1579 the river flowed to **Seaford** but a storm blocked the mouth, resulting in a new discharge point, hence the new haven and its promenade. The old channel leads to tide mills.

The cross-Channel car ferry terminal and the Newhaven lifeboat.

Distance
22km from Barcombe to the English Channel

OS 1:50,000 Sheets
198 Brighton & Lewes

Admiralty Charts
536 Beachy Head to Dungeness (1:75,000)
1652 Selsey Bill to Beachy Head (1:75,000)
2154 Newhaven Harbour (1:5,000)

Tidal Constants
Barcombe House:
HW Dover +0050,
LW Dover +0110
Newhaven:
HW Dover −0010,
LW Same as Dover

Sea Area
Wight

Rescue
Inshore lifeboat:
Brighton
All weather lifeboat:
Newhaven

Peter with 13th century wall paintings and a round tower. In Norman times it had a herring fishery and paid the Lord of Lewes an annual rent of 38,500 herrings.

The 1km Southease Cut by Jessop dates from the late 18th century.

The river turns away from a long barrow and Dean's Farm towards Piddinghoe, a former chalk mining village of flint cottages and a brick kiln where swallows swoop about the river. St John's church has a round Norman tower with a shingled steeple, topped by a gilded sea trout weathervane, referred to by Kipling as dolphin. The 500m John Smeaton cut of 1770 straightened out a meander which still loops round towards Tarring Neville and its chalk quarry as an oxbow lake.

Newhaven is first met at Denton Island, which is only an island at higher stages of the tide. It is on the west bank with small craft jetties while large craft moor on the east side. The industrial estate behind is home to Paradise Park with its Newhaven Miniature Railway, Sussex in Miniature, Living Dinosaur Museum, Planet Earth, minerals, crystals, Caribbean, Oriental, water, seaside and conservatory gardens and mountain, rainforest and one of the country's largest collections of desert plants.

The final bridge over the river is the 1976 swing bridge

The 1860s Newhaven Fort was built for Lord Palmerston as protection against the French and has clifftop gun emplacements and underground tunnels. In 1942 it was used as the base for the Dieppe Raid by 5,000 Canadians and 1,000 British, resulting in 1,000 killed and 2,000 taken prisoner. There were 106 Allied aircraft lost compared with 48 German planes, the highest daily air battle loss of the Second World War, achieving no military progress. The fort was garrisoned until 1956 and is now a scheduled Ancient Monument. On display are 1860s Victorian barrack rooms, underground tunnels, cliff ramparts and big guns. There is a radio mast on Castle Hill above Burrow Head.

Flows run out of the river from an hour after Dover high water and in from five hours forty minutes before Dover high water to 4km/h, the flows weakening northwards. A tide gauge is located on the west side of the entrance. Piers were built in 1735 by John Reynolds, the East Pier having a 12m white metal framework light at its end. The 850m concrete breakwater of 1878 on the west side has a 14m concrete lighthouse tower at its end. The dredged channel passes close to the end of the pier as the river empties into Seaford Bay. Portable craft can be taken out over the sandy beach where steps lead up to parking.

The cliffs and fort site at Newhaven.

250

58 River Adur

A river flowing towards the hills

Shoreham will hold their names in sacred keeping
  And generations yet unborn shall read;
They fought for Freedom, not for glory seeking
  And died for England in her hour of need.

A F W Eade

The tidal limit, heavily overgrown below Shermanbury Place.

Most rivers rise in the hills and flow down onto coastal plains to reach the sea. The River Adur flows from the fields of the Weald southwards across West Sussex and cuts through the South Downs to reach the English Channel. In fact, the river has been following this line as a dip slope stream since the dome of the Weald was higher than the Downs and has seen no reason to change direction as the Weald has been worn away.

The longer western arm is only tidal from Bines Green but the eastern arm, which rises at Ditchling, is tidal from Shermanbury where another stream joins below Shermanbury Place, set in parkland with a medieval church. There is some roadside parking on the A281 between the river bridge and the Bull Inn. A footpath between the Bull and Ewhurst Manor and its moat crosses the river just above its tidal limit.

A levée on the west side at the confluence is to be followed by levées on one or both sides to limit the views all the way to Shoreham, usually with reeds or reedmace along the edges.

The river takes its name from the Celtic dwyr, water, and is slow and brown, winding between fields of grazing cattle and passing through AONB.

The first 100m has reeds right across the river, making passage a fight through the jungle. Nevertheless, moorhens are present.

A triangular inlet on the east bank looks rather like a winding hole. Rennie suggested the river might become a branch of the London to Portsmouth canal.

The A281 crosses the four stone arches of Mock Bridge with a last defiant clump of reeds in the centre nearly the size of one arch. After this the passage is easier although the surface still has plenty of floating vegetation, including arrowhead. Teasels and purple loosestrife grow on the banks. Herons, dragonflies and damselflies add some activity to what is otherwise a very quiet reach, away from the public.

The Downs Link bridleway crosses on a bridge which was part of the Horsham to Shoreham railway.

The next structure is Chates Dam, a board retention weir which is submerged at high water but is difficult to pass at other times as it has deep water above it and steep banks covered with stinging nettles on each side. There is a corresponding dam on the western arm, which joins just downstream.

Conditions seem to suit Canada geese and kingfishers while overwintering wetlands birds also find shelter here. Skylarks fly above the fields which lead across to **Henfield** with its Victorian Perpendicular church. Nearer at hand there is only a windpump on top of the oilseed rape covered banks.

Between another moat and Stretham Manor the river is crossed again by the Downs Link bridleway.

Powerlines cross near Small Dole, framing the view of the South Downs to the east where the Roman road from Hardham to Hassocks used to cross, the rounded chalk hills, beyond, being topped at Truleigh Hill by an array of aerials. To the west, the feature on the ridge is Chanctonbury Ring, a 1.4ha plantation of beeches from

1760 on the site of an Iron Age fort and a Roman temple and smithy.

Although the river is now saline enough for the odd cuttlefish bone to come floating up on the tide, large numbers of swans gather.

The first building in Upper Beeding is the church of about 1300 which belonged to the adjacent Benedictine priory founded by William de Braose. Oddly, Upper Beeding is lower than Lower Beeding and the names may have more to do with status than latitude or altitude.

The river sweeps over stony shallows at low water past the Bridge and the King's Head. To the right is Bramber with St Mary's House, originally built by the Knights Templar, a Grade I timber framed house rebuilt about 1470 with a rare 16th century wall leather, panelled rooms and a unique Elizabethan painted room, an elegant Victorian music room and fine furniture, tapestries, lace, fabrics and a unique window which folds in a dozen sections. It is said to be the best 15th century timber framed house in Sussex, was built by the Bishop of Winchester, was visited in 1585 by Elizabeth I and is a rare surviving monastic inn for the Wardens of the Bridge, the monks of Sele Priory. It has been used for filming *Dr Who*. St Nicholas' church of 1073 was badly damaged when used as a gun emplacement by the Parliamentarians during the Civil War but was subsequently restored in the 18th and 19th centuries. It fared rather better than Bramber Castle, built by William de Braose also in 1073 to protect Steyning but destroyed in 1641 during the Civil War, now being just a single pillar of the keep rising 23m above the ramparts and dry moat.

Steyning was a major Saxon seaport until silting led to its decline after the Norman conquest. The town itself has survived much better with no less than 125 listed buildings, many 15th to 18th century. Most notable is St Andrews' church, built in 1150 of

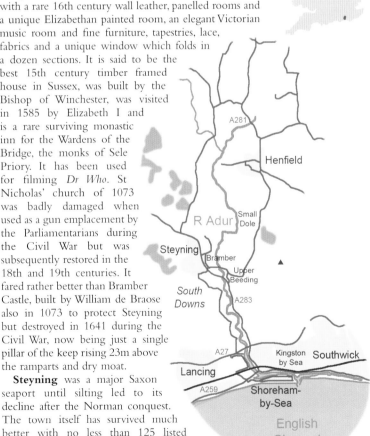

Mock Bridge carrying the A281.

Deep water above and below Chates Dam and nettles beside it.

Section near Henfield.

Bramber Bridge at low water.

Cutting through the Downs past the cement works.

Lancing College chapel.

Caen stone at the point of collapse of the wheelbarrow in which St Cuthman the Shepherd was wheeling his invalid mother from Devon in the 8th century, it not being clear which party was the more grateful. A stranger instructed him to build the church there and, on being asked his name, replied He to whom the temple was being dedicated.

The A283 crosses and follows above the left bank as the chalk Downs rise on each side, cultivation terraces being located on the side of Beeding Hill, possibly since the Iron Age.

The South Downs Way footpath crosses and the dismantled railway line, which used to cross soon after, now proves very popular with cyclists. Prominent is the chimney of the disused cement works although the large quarry is only seen from the south.

The remains of a chapel are inconspicuous above Old Erringham Farm but the chapel of **Lancing** College more than makes up for this. Founded in 1868, it is built in 13th century Gothic style, very French in appearance and dominating this part of the Downs as it stands above the river meanders. At 58m long by 46m high, it has a 10m diameter rose window, one of the largest in England, together with fine tapestries. A Roman temple site seems a more appropriate neighbour than the rifle range to one side.

Blackheaded gulls pick around the sea aster which indicates that the marine environment has taken over. Tide races rush around the columns of the A27 viaduct which sweeps down and over the river. Beyond it is the Grade II Old Shoreham Trestle Bridge, originally built in 1782 for the Duke of Norfolk to carry the south coast road and rebuilt in 1916 to a similar design. At 140m x 3.7m with two widenings for traffic to pass, it is astonishing that it remained as a major part of our road system until replaced by the large new structure upstream in recent decades.

At the left end is the church of St Mary de Haura of 1130, bequeathed to the abbey of Saumur. At the other end is a pillbox which not only protected the bridge but also Shoreham Airport, Britain's oldest licensed airport, which has an Art Deco terminal building, D-Day aviation museum, Second World War blister hanger, Horsa glider, Spitfire and air sea rescue gallery.

Another museum is the Marlipins Museum in a 12th century Norman custom house, later used as a warehouse and courthouse, one of the oldest secular buildings in Europe still in use, with superb nautical paintings and models.

Between the Portsmouth to Brighton railway bridge and the Norfolk Bridge carrying the A259 is the Adur Outdoor Activities Centre on the west bank with eddylines past banks of mussel shells.

Until 500 years ago the River Adur flowed straight out to sea and had the River Arun as a tributary. Shingle pushed the mouth of the Adur eastwards while the Arun broke through to the west in several places.

The harbour has been a port since Roman times and was the largest port on the south coast and a major shipbuilding centre for three centuries from the Norman period. During the First World War it built many concrete barges and the Nab Tower. It was the main port for Normandy before Newhaven took over and the handling of general cargo, aggregates, oil, wine and grain has continued, following the decline of coal to the power station. Notwithstanding the commercial activity, the estuary is an RSPB reserve.

A footbridge with a sliding centre span gives access

from the Kingston by Sea part of Southwick with its Roman villa site, the Crown & Anchor and the Ferry Inn to the resort of Shoreham Beach with its Waterside Inn, part of **Shoreham-by-Sea** on a long peninsula, named after the Old English scora, a steep hill.

Pleasure craft and fishing boats are moored all along and at low tide people with buckets turn over lengths of gutter placed on the mud while lobster pots and floats with black flags are piled up on jetties. Freighters occupy berths nearer the entrance and wharves are piled high with scrap iron or stacked with timber. Modern aerials protrude from the buildings. Opposite the harbour entrance is the Grade II lighthouse of 1848. A red occulting light is visible when shipping movement is imminent and small craft need to keep out of the way.

The Eastern Arm leads through locks to the **Southwick** Canal to Aldrington and Shoreham Power Station, this all being part of the River Adur until the new harbour entrance was established in 1821, a triangular pier being built opposite the entrance in 1826 at Telford's suggestion to help flows and reduce sedimentation. Even so, the harbour silts rapidly following dredging.

The last road access point is inside the harbour entrance on the west side where there are parking and toilets. The coastguard station was built near a Victorian fort of 1857, constructed when a French invasion was expected.

The harbour entrance is protected by a pair of breakwaters and a bar shifts in the entrance after prolonged westerly winds. Flows up to 7km/h at Soldier's Point ease to 4km/h at the entrance.

The river discharges into the English Channel. East of the harbour entrance is a beach used by naturists and surfers. Brighton with its piers and marina and then the chalk cliffs of the Seven Sisters stretch away towards Beachy Head.

Old Shoreham Trestle Bridge, formerly carrying a trunk road.

The 12th century church of St Mary de Haura.

Intense canoeing activity at the Adur Centre in Shoreham.

The opening footbridge across the harbour.

Poling at the harbourmouth.

Distance
20km from Shermanbury to the English Channel

OS 1:50,000 Sheets
198 Brighton & Lewes

Admiralty Charts
1652 Selsey Bill to Beachy Head (1:75,000)
2044 Shoreham Harbour & Approaches. Shoreham Harbour – Western Arm & R Adur (1:5,000). Eastern Arm & Canal (1:5,000). Approaches to Shoreham (1:15,000)

Tidal Constants
Beeding Bridge:
HW Dover +0100
Shoreham:
Same as Dover

Sea Area
Wight

Rescue
Inshore lifeboat:
Shoreham Harbour
All weather lifeboat:
Shoreham Harbour

It's a dangerous place with a ripping stream
Where the ferryman's ghost, or so it would seem,
Straining and heaving on the sturdy oars,
With never a chance to stop or pause,
Was condemned for ever, until the boat sank,
To cross the Arun from bank to bank.

David King

The River Arun rises in St Leonard's Forest between Crawley and Horsham, flowing westwards to Rudgwick before turning south towards the English Channel, staying in West Sussex throughout its length.

The narrow, reedy and rapid flowing channel meets its tidal limit round the next corner from the significantly named Pallingham Quay Farm. At the same point the Wey & Arun Canal joined the river. Two locks stand in

The head of the tidal part of the river at Pallingham. The Wey & Arun Canal joined beyond the willow trees on the right.

Stopham Bridge, a magnificent structure from the 15th century.

the garden of an adjacent house. This far, most of the canal, built in 1790, has not been used as a navigation since 1889 although it is being restored.

A wooded hillside overlooks the river on the west side until Stopham is reached. Here, the realignment to a recent bridge passes behind the White Hart, cutting through sandstone of yellow, brown, orange and blood red. The original bridge is the finest medieval river crossing in Sussex. Built in 1423, it is unchanged except for its centre arch which was enlarged in 1822 to allow craft through.

The line of the Western Rother Navigation, which used to enter on the right soon after, is now barely visible, unlike the River Rother itself which cascades down a stepped weir. The river immediately widens, the trees cease and a new feature appears. Low at first, the South Downs run along the skyline. On the left is the Wyevale Garden Centre with the 260mm gauge standard and narrow gauge trains of the South Downs Light Railway.

After the railway, the river divides round a 900m long island. Only the left channel avoids portaging and it also gives access to **Pulborough**, the first time houses are found grouped together. The Water's Edge has its own mooring inlet while, beyond the bridges, the public hard gives access to the Swan and shops. The second bridge is one of the oldest in Sussex and lies on the route of Stane Street, which ran up onto the Downs at Bignor, perhaps producing some of the wool for which Britain was famed throughout the Roman Empire.

The tide ebbs for 8 hours and floods for 4, the current flowing at 7–11km/h on the ebb. The speed limit is set at 10km/h to Arundel bridge. Seaweed begins to replace the river weed, floating up on the flood.

The scenery is much more open now, raised flood banks replacing the trees while the Downs rise inexorably, dominated by a couple of aerials on Burton Down.

Greatham Bridge has a propped lattice girder main arch, two stone side arches and then a higgledy piggledy line of eight little arches which wander up and down in apparently random fashion. Meanwhile, the old Coldwaltham Cut of the canal once led through a lock and a tunnel.

The sandstone village of Amberley on a sandstone ridge dates from 680 and is claimed to be the prettiest village on the Downs. The church was completed in 1125. The castle, initially built by the bishops of Chichester as a residence, was completed in 1377 and is now a hotel. It is overlooked by the Arun Gap, a chalk cleft carved through the Downs by the river. The railway uses the gap but the A29 rises up Bury Hill, its double white lines visible from the river 3km away.

Opposite Amberley, Bury has a church with a wood shingled broach spire on a flint structure, typical of a number in Sussex. Nearby on the river, the first of the ungainly moorings constructed from scaffolding poles are seen.

Houghton Bridge is another old structure with slits in the stonework. As well as the B2139 it carries the South Downs Way. The nearby community includes the Bridge Inn and a shop selling teas, coffees and ice creams and hiring out rowing boats and caravans to holidaymakers. At the top of the hill is the Amberley Working Museum, an extensive industrial site covering all aspects of chalk extraction from the 1840s to the 1960s for lime production with a foundry, blacksmith and workshops, connected by a narrow gauge railway. Some buildings have been imported. It has a canal area

The rustic Greatham Bridge.

and the last remaining Arun barge, built at Littlehampton in 1948 to carry chalk for bank repair. Also on show are a concrete canoe and a concrete bow firing arrows.

This is one of the few places where the chalk is openly exposed. Normally it is capped by clays, resulting in a thick growth of woodland. The mud on the riverbanks becomes steadily softer and the reach by Burpham, now a backwater because of a new cut to the west of the railway but formerly sufficiently important to have a Saxon fortress with an earthwork across the neck of a promontory, is fringed with an expanse of silt with a very low angle of repose. Lapwing, snipe and shelduck appreciate the peace of this backwater, probably more so than on the nearby wildfowl reserve.

The Black Rabbit was once a port of call for sailing barge crews. Its name is unique to the extent that the landlord once received a letter from South Africa, its only address being two black silhouettes, one of a rabbit and

the other a map of England. The gravel patch just beyond is one of the few mud free areas so far. By the river is the 22ha Arundel Wildfowl & Wetlands Centre with waders and warblers, a tourist centre with a thousand fowl and a swan lake watched by buzzards.

The mud does decrease now. The river becomes pitched with chalk lumps and weed begins to smell of the sea. Larger boats are moored as the river enters **Arundel**.

The major building, visible from some distance back, is the Norman castle. Built by Roger Montgomery, Earl of Shrewsbury, in the late 11th century, it was remodelled in Gothic style between 1791 and 1815. At the turn of the century it was restyled

Arundel is dominated by its castle.

Littlehampton Harbour, a haven for small craft.

Distance
35km from
Pallingham Quay to
the English Channel

OS 1:50,000 Sheets
197 Chichester &
the South Downs

Admiralty Charts
1652 Selsey Bill
to Beachy Head
(1:75,000)
1991 Harbours on
S Coast of England.
Littlehampton
Harbour (1:6,250)

Tidal Constants
Arundel:
HW Dover +0120
Norfolk Wharf:
HW Dover +0010,
LW Dover +0020
Littlehampton
Entrance:
HW same as Dover,
LW Dover −0010

Sea Area
Wight

Rescue
Inshore lifeboat:
Littlehampton
All weather lifeboat:
Selsey

again along the lines of Windsor Castle, a tall motte with two baileys and a shell keep on a motte. It is now the seat of the Duke of Norfolk, who lives in a house in Arundel Park, hosts the Arundel Festival in August and was used for filming *Young Victoria*.

The Roman Catholic cathedral of 1873 by Joseph Hansom dominates the town centre from its high point. In French Gothic styling, it is high with a great west rose window but is cramped in plan and lacks spires or towers. More mundane structures include flint riverside cottages, a black windmill, Arundel Museum & Heritage Centre covering the port of Arundel since the Norman conquest, a Georgian Toy & Military Museum and Georgian and Edwardian houses.

Ravens are joined by flocks of swans. The banks are covered with flexible mattress and then concrete slab revetment. The speed limit increases to 12km/h. If the tide has been used to best advantage the view will be limited.

The railway bridge at Ford is heavily timbered against ship impact but little else is to be seen until just after Ford Prison, an open prison with a riot in 2011. The river bends to give a last view of the Downs to the east of Arundel and the former raised beaches at the 30m level. It passes houses and an industrial estate which gives notice of arrival in **Littlehampton**, a fishing town which became a resort. The Little was only added in the 15th century to distinguish it from Northampton and Southampton.

There is a commercial and yachting port on the river. In the Middle Ages it was used for unloading Caen stone for major Sussex buildings. A white over a red flag on a pilot boat indicates a large vessel movement is due. The marina beyond the road bridge offers showers. Opposite, sea dredged aggregates are offloaded into a concrete batching plant. The Arun View Inn and Steam Packet stand each side of a footbridge across the harbour. Moorings have rows of yachts and dinghies, lines clanking against alloy masts. The Balaton Restaurant, Royal Restaurant and Nelson Hotel are included in a solid line of tourist eating places with a flight of steps up to them reserved for the users of small craft. Smart's Amusement Park is a centre for the tourists who flock in from Littlehampton's sandy beaches. Small cuttlefish which may be found in the estuary.

A pumping station feeds a long sea outfall. When the latter was built in the early 1970s four boreholes were put down along its line to sample the seabed. Two hit wartime mines.

The river has speed cameras to impose a 12km/h limit, one boat having been clocked at 63km/h.

A training wall running out from the lighthouse covers at half tide. Beyond the coastguard lookout, the open structure timber breakwater extends on the west side of the harbourmouth to protect shipping. With a westerly wind blowing, dry sand can be blown through it in a veritable sandstorm. The pierhead has a tide gauge. Overfalls form on the bar with winds from force 5 between southeast and southwest against ebbing spring tides. Flows go out from an hour after Dover high water and in from four hours before Dover high water at up to 11km/h, being affected by heavy rain. Flow conditions at the harbourmouth can be quite complex.

To the west of the river are dunes and a golf course.

Pedestals along the riverfront give recipes for cooking local fish.

60 Chichester Channel

Heavily used by Roman galleys and 21st century yachts

Workmen digging a trench in Fishbourne for a water pipe in 1960 began turning up pieces of mosaic. The experts were called in and they uncovered what was to prove the largest Roman domestic building north of the Alps, probably the palace of the local king, Cogidubnus. Built about 75, it was positioned so that galleys could sail right up to the palace, showing that the Fishbourne Channel was much deeper then than today.

One side of the rectangular palace has been excavated, revealing hypercausts and mosaics, now sheltered within a museum. A prominent selection of about 20 early English mosaics are on display, Britain's best in situ collection, made from cubes of chalk and grey limestone, including that of a nymph riding on a dolphin, one of the best mosaics in existence anywhere. Half of the central hedged garden has been restored to the original plan but the other half of the palace lies buried below the A259 and the houses on each side of it, completing the damage inflicted by a fire at the end of the 3rd century.

The Chichester Channel is in the Hampshire Basin where Tertiary beds overlie chalk breached by the sea, this being one of several channels cut by Ice Age rivers. It runs southwest across part of West Sussex, winding enough for the upper reaches to receive shelter from trees which break up the flat landscape and hamper the prevailing headwind. Although there is road access in several places there is no road following the channel so there is no car noise although powered boats are a quite different matter.

Streams at the head of the channel meet in a 200m long millpond occupied by ducks. The road here is residential and parking rather restricted. Launching is best undertaken downstream of the mill from a public footpath passing through the garden of the mill, now converted to dwellings.

As well as the Romans, the Saxons and Danes each used the channel but these days it dries much of the way to Chichester Marina, the better part of 3km. At the channel's head it has black mud and reedbeds with notices proclaiming the area to be a nature reserve belonging to Southern Wildfowlers & Wetlands Management

A model of the head of the channel as it was in about 75.

Association. Here their targets rear themselves. Mallards, shelducks and swans are out on the water.

Back to the left is the slender spire of Chichester Cathedral, built about 1091. The channel's main tributary is the River Lavant which rises on the Downs at Singleton. Although only a small stream, it does have its moments and has caused considerable flooding in Chichester. On its bank is a sewage works which serves Chichester but does nothing to prevent silting. Perhaps it helps Apuldram Roses where 300 varieties are raised on the east of the channel.

Chichester Harbour is one of the most popular and sheltered harbours on the south coast with more than 3,000 pleasure craft moored in the summer. It has over 10,000 craft exceeding 3m long. The first of the moorings come at Dell Quay, the port of Chichester, the seventh largest British port in the 14th century and still with over a hundred sailing ships in the 19th century. There is a slipway next to the 18th century Crown & Anchor. There are charges for taking motor vehicles onto Chichester Harbour Conservancy hards but not for hand carried launches.

The nymph and dolphin, possibly the world's finest mosaic.

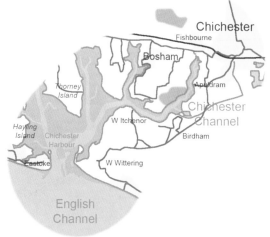

The head of the channel today at high water. The mill is the white building.

Dell Quay's jetty at mid tide.

The twisted oaks of Oldpark Wood collapse onto the gravel.

Oldpark Wood has mostly stunted oaks spread with primroses, violets and broom in the spring and the occasional bird box. The oaks spill over onto the shingle and mud shoreline where sea aster grows between the grotesque shapes. Shoreline saltings are used by oystercatchers, whitefronted geese and curlews while cormorants spread themselves one to each porthand marker post, the conical starboard ones lacking the comfortable flat tops but the light beacons at the end having depth gauges for yachtsmen.

After Copperas Point the channel widens into Chichester Lake, at the back of which is Chichester Marina, one of the biggest in Europe with moorings for 1,000 yachts.

Reaching most of the way back to Birdham is Birdham Pool, the former millpond beside the wooden 1768 tidemill building. These two non tidal reaches of water flank the Chichester Canal which runs from Chichester to Salterns Lock. It is now rather overgrown but with houseboats. It formerly linked with the River Arun and the line continued down the Chichester Channel and up the Thorney Channel towards Portsmouth to complete an inland link from London. Opened in 1823, it was not to prove a commercial success.

Craft from canvas kayaks to old wooden sailing craft on the shore before Longmore Point retain a traditional atmosphere amongst all the modern boats on the water. Houses at **Bosham** Hoe are individually designed with a feeling of affluence. This is not a place for mass housing but somewhere to reside gracefully, looking at the trots of yachts moored in Itchenor Reach.

West Itchenor, named after Saxon chieftain Icca after the Romans left, is important as the location of the Chichester harbourmaster's office, near which is another tidegauge. Sightseeing trip boats run from here and a passenger ferry crosses in summer to a lane beside the Bosham Channel leading to Bosham. In the early 19th century coal was transferred into lighters at Itchenor for carriage up to Dell Quay before being loaded into road wagons for Chichester, a labour intensive and inefficient procedure. Rather earlier, Charles II kept a yacht here to house former mistresses. The four 17th century cottages, extended as the sailing club in Itchenor, were used by the services for planning the D-Day landings. Shipbuilding has gone on over the centuries, including one ship carrying 44 cannons. The village's church dates from the 12th century.

A blackthorn hedge pulls back at Chalkdock Point to leave saltings dissected by shallow channels which are only suitable for exploring by kayaks or by blackheaded gulls.

Opposite, broken piles and islands run from Cobnor Point most of the way across the mouth of the Thorney Channel to Pilsey Island, passing Roman Transit. The piles form an unforgiving slalom course at the height of the tidal flow. Bell Hose is said to contain the church bell from Bosham, dropped by the Vikings in a fight with Itchenor men after a raid. Southbourne, at the head of the Thorney Channel, is backed by the South Downs. What is inaccessible for boats is ideal for birds, Chichester Harbour being one of the best sites on the south coast for Brent geese and other wildfowl and waders plus saltmarsh plants. It is an AONB and noted wildlife reserve with 80km of shoreline around 70km^2 of water, mostly draining. Pilsey Island is an RSPB bird reserve with landing restricted to the beach on the east side from April to October inclusive.

Thorney Island is not quite an island but access has been difficult in the past because of the airfield, now disused. The Transport Research Laboratory chose a shore site on the end to erect frames to expose numerous steel tiles with various paint finishes to the rigours of the salt laden atmosphere.

East Head light beacon has another tide gauge. Roman Landing in Snowhill Creek gives access to West Wittering and a sheltered approach to the car park at the end although the creek should not be used any more than necessary because of the sensitive nature of the environment. The Spit is a 45ha sand and shingle finger with dunes and slack on which are marram grass, plant and marine life and more waders. The banks are subject to great change and there is risk of the sea breaking through and cutting off East Head. An annual sandcastle contest has been banned by conservationists.

At quiet times it is possible to cut the corner but with springs at mid ebb against an onshore wind the area over the Winner bank, stretching most of the way to the Hayling Island shore, is one foaming mass of white. This is the most exposed of the three harbour entrances on this part of the coast and the break can reach right across, being dangerous with a southerly wind against a strong ebb. Conditions are quietest from three hours before local high water to an hour after high water. Flows are outgoing for five hours twenty minutes to 12km/h and ingoing for seven hours twenty minutes to 5km/h. The Winner dries at low water. The deep water channel creeps down the western edge of the entrance from the Emsworth Channel past Black and Sandy Point. The latter is the home of Hayling Island Sailing Club with the country's largest fleet of International Canoes.

Black Point was used for Sir William Treloar's Home for Crippled Children, now dismantled, because it had the highest average sunshine of anywhere in England.

The RNLI have an inshore lifeboat here, located directly opposite the Winner, at one time competing against a privately owned RIB which was beating them to casualties.

The circuit of Hayling Island is the course for the

Bosham Hoe, seen from West Itchenor past lines of moorings.

Round Hayling Marathon, Britain's largest windsurfing event, although an onshore wind can make the area between Eastoke Point and West Wittering seem a strong contender for the title, this being one of the best surfing spots on the south coast, very popular with windsurfers.

Groynes start at the base of East Head and continue right along the shore of Bracklesham Bay. Two cardinal marks out on the East Pole Sands locate wrecks used as targets. East Pole Sands can dry out for a considerable distance, as can West Pole Sands on the other side of the harbourmouth and over which large standing waves can develop at the inshore end at Eastoke Point near high water.

West Wittering is marked by the spire of its 11th century church and is where the Rolls Royce design team were moved when their leader contracted cancer. A signal fire basket on a pole indicates that the car park has been reached.

The hard in front of the harbourmaster's office at West Itchenor.

Snowhill Creek with East Head to the left at mid tide. The creek has a rich fauna and flora despite its unexciting appearance.

Distance
11km from Fishbourne to Bracklesham Bay

OS 1:50,000 Sheets
197 Chichester & the South Downs

Admiralty Charts
2037 Eastern Approaches to Solent (1:25,000)
2045 Outer Approaches to Solent (1:75,000)
3418 Langstone & Chichester Harbours (1:20,000)

Tidal Constants
Dell Quay:
HW Dover +0030
Itchenor:
HW Dover +0020,
LW Dover +0040
Chichester Harbour Entrance:
HW Dover +0020,
LW Dover +0040

Sea Area
Wight

Rescue
Inshore lifeboat:
Hayling Island
All weather lifeboat:
Selsey

61 Portsmouth Harbour

Two millennia of naval defence

Whose corpse by pondrous irons wrung
High up on Blockhouse Beach was hung,
And long to every tempest swung?
Why truly, Jack the Painter.
Anon

An unexpected aspect of the Wallington River.

Few places can give so many changes of environment in a couple of hours on the water.

The Wallington River rises near Denmead and becomes tidal at Wallington, once the site of a ford and now a more recent packhorse bridge across to the Cob & Pen. A Sainsbury's store on the edge of an industrial estate has grabbed the bulk of the parking space in the area.

Above the bridge the river flows between brick walls, to one of which someone has attached a sign showing a shark with the warning that surfing is at one's own risk. The tide needs to be in for there to be any depth of water otherwise there will be only minor flow over a gravel bed. Launching is not easy but is possible for portable craft on the west bank south of the bridge.

The Vikings seem to have got the tides right and attacked Wallington regularly. To prevent an attack repetition during Napoleonic times Fort Wallington was built in a loop of the river as the west end of a line of forts running along Ports Down. Away from the other bank is the shopping centre with the Henry Court Millennium Project. Henry Court was an 18th century resident who pioneered the iron refining process. This is the largest exhibition of sculptural ironwork in Britain, featuring modern iron sculptures by 11 blacksmiths from across Europe.

At first there is a narrow river, little more than a stream, overhung with trees, but this soon opens out with the A32 on the right, a road which will run parallel to the water to Gosport. First, though, it meets the A27 in front of the Roundabout Inn, the roundabout being over the

The old packhorse bridge at Wallington at low water.

river. The first bridge is low but the second is lower with no air gap left at high water. As the tide drops, a culvert to the left of the main span gives a little more headroom through a long and gloomy corrugated tube. The alternative is to portage across a major roundabout where small trees limit visibility. Also crossing the roundabout is the Portchester Road Viaduct carrying the Cosham to Fareham railway. Railway viaducts are relatively rare in Hampshire but this example

from 1848 is Grade II. In red brick with stone capping, it has 16 9m semicircular arches plus an 11m span with an extreme 34° skew dog toothed arch through which one side of the roundabout passes.

Leaving the Delme Arms behind, Fareham Lake opens out as a wooded tidal creek, a few boats moored and a delightful spot with the tide in although it drains to leave mud banks at low tide. Swans, pout, bass and pollock are amongst the wildlife. The ebb is from fifty minutes after Dover high water to five hours twenty minutes after Dover high water followed by a three hour slack.

Cams Hall and a golf course are sited in a large loop in the river while there is a playground opposite, backing onto Quay Street Viaduct, a similar railway viaduct to the previous one but this time with only ten arches. **Fareham** Town Quay begins with a gravel wharf near the Castle in the Air public house, perhaps a reference to Fort Fareham which stands back from the next reach.

The centre of the dormitory town of Fareham, Old English for fern meadow, is further to the west. Here are many moored yachts and a waterfront of older buildings behind a prominent wharf building now used by a yacht business, next door to which the 2nd Fareham Sea Scouts have their headquarters.

The channel turns south again and passes a sludge loading jetty serving a sewage works. Powerlines cross at Power Station Bend, forming a prominent landmark.

Running west to east, Heavy Reach is more exposed to the prevailing wind than others in the area but orange windsocks at a helipad on the south side give an immediate indication of wind strength if it isn't obvious. Cormorants and blackbacked gulls also take to the air as the channel further widens into Cams Lake.

The pier at Foxbury Point is MoD, as are most of the piers along this shore. The inside of Wicor Bend is a Royal Navy Armament Depot and notice is given that it is patrolled by armed sentries. Cranes stand on Bedenham Pier, from which craft are required to keep 12m away. It handles not only explosives but also material with nuclear labels.

The chalk anticline of Ports Down is prominent to the north, topped by the pillar of Nelson's Monument, to the west of which is Fort Nelson and to the east Fort Southwick, used with Fort Widley to control D-Day operations, just before a very conspicuous chalk scar. These forts form part of a line built by Lord Palmerston in the 1860s along the top of the Downs to counter the threat of a French invasion. They were equipped to fire very substantial iron balls, the better part of a metre across, presumably the length of Portsmouth Harbour, some 8km. A sunny day with deep blue storm clouds inland over the Downs makes the area magic.

The Kings Way footpath follows the shoreline to the east where, facing Portchester Lake, **Portchester** Castle stands on the point. The site was used by the Romans in the 3rd century. Their walls, enclosing 3.6ha, are 5.5m high and up to 3m thick, the most complete Roman walls remaining in northern Europe, located at the western end of their Saxon Shore defences. Various kings were involved in the construction of the later castle, particularly Henry II, and a tall, square, Norman keep still stands in the southwest corner. Edward III assembled 15,000 men here to sail to Crecy and Henry V rallied his troops here in 1415 before Agincourt, commandeering ships which formed the first Royal Navy. Richard II converted the inner castle to a palace. In the 18th century it was used as a prisoner of war camp for 4,000 Frenchmen.

Portchester Road Viaduct. The Wallington River flows under the bridge on the right, here with little clearance near the top of the tide.

Portsmouth Harbour forms part of the Dockyard Port of **Portsmouth** and is becoming an international maritime heritage area. Generally, the northern end of Portsmouth Harbour is quiet with large areas of mudflats at low tide, expanses which are largely the preserve of cormorants and other seabirds. It has shellfish and in the winter there are 15,000 wildfowl, including 2,900 Brent geese, which the RSPB said were threatened with permanent damage from marina development, recreational pressure and land reclaim although they seem happy enough with the vast amount of activity in the harbour at present. Trots of yachts are so extensive that it is not possible to see the line of the channel to the harbour mouth. The harbour largely drains, leaving salt marshes, but in February 1895 the whole of the harbour surface froze. In Fareham Lake the ebb runs for four and a half hours from local high water with a three hour slack before a four hour flood.

Naval cannons from Tipner have been found at low water around Pewit Island, opposite which is Frater Lake

which drains. Spider Lake and Bombketch Lake are major channels through the marshes. To the south of Frater Lake is Fort Elson, the northern end of the Gosport Advanced Line, five forts built by Palmerston to defend Portsmouth dockyard on the west against Napoleon III. First of these to be built in the 1850s was Fort Brockhurst which has a circular keep approached across a wide moat and a large central parade ground, protected by 19 heavy guns with eight more on each flank, the weight of gunpower being exceptional for the time. It houses the Gosport Aviation Heritage Museum.

Together with the yachts moored in the harbour may be large naval vessels.

The shore is built up from Hardway and the Jolly Roger public house lacks the gravity of the various piers, Sultan Landing, Vosper's Jetty, Shell Pier and South Jetty plus assorted wrecks. Priddy's Hard at Hardway was a Royal Navy armament depot with a 1770 powder magazine but has become the Explosion! museum tracing navy firepower from gunpowder to Exocet. For

Traditional buildings along the Town Quay at Fareham.

Bedenham Pier, around which the Royal Navy have a 12m exclusion zone.

Ports Down with its prominent chalk scar. Portchester Castle is visible to the right of the picture.

years the frigate *Foudroyant* was moored here to give holidays to youngsters. Built in Bombay in 1817, she is the oldest warship afloat and is now in Hartlepool under her original name, *HMS Trincomalee*. Herons and oystercatchers search these waters.

An opening footbridge connects with a 3km Millennium Promenade to the submarine museum and carries pedestrians and a road train. Weevil Lake, the outer part of Forton Lake, can be entered from the east at the top of the tide by small craft but larger boats need to enter south of Burrow Island, covered with a surprising number of trees in the middle of this built environment,

unofficially called Rat Island and formerly housing Fort James. The Royal Navy Victualling Yard of 1827, one of only three in Britain, has been redeveloped as the Royal Clarence Yard with waterside bars and restaurants. Boatyards and marinas here and in Cold Harbour occupy the shorelines, intersected by the long curve of a fuel jetty which was used for Royal Fleet Auxiliary refuelling tankers. Near the far end is the Oakleaf Brewing Company. Beyond Gosport Marina the Castle Tavern is built on the site of Fort Charles, constructed in the 17th century for Charles II. A stainless steel and glass clock gives the time and tide state.

Priddy's Hard at Hardway, buildings which have stored the munitions for many major naval actions over the years.

HMS Invincible, the first of a brace of aircraft carriers berthed alongside HMS Victory.

Portsea Island converges from the east with Tipner ranges and Whale Island naval gunnery establishment and an observatory. To the south of Fountain Lake lie 3km of naval frontage packed with all kinds of destroyers, frigates, anti submarine ships and aircraft carriers. Here is the Grey Funnel Line in all its glory, lined up for the naval enthusiast to appreciate.

Tucked in at the head of Fountain Lake is the Continental ferry port, opened in 1976 with sailings to Cherbourg, Le Havre, St Malo, Caen, Bilbao and Santander, the second busiest UK passenger port to Dover.

flagship at Trafalgar in 1805 and carried 850 crew and 104 guns. She weighs 3,500t and measures 69m x 16m. Afloat until 1922, she is now in the world's oldest dry dock and restored to her 1805 period to show what life was like aboard under Nelson.

The International Festival of the Sea, the UK's largest ever maritime festival, and the Times Clipper race are events which have been featured here.

The Royal Navy Museum, opened in 1930, hosts *HMS Warrior*. Charles II's state barge, which carried Nelson's coffin in 1806, is present and another important exhibit is W L Wyllie's panorama of the Battle of Trafalgar.

A regular passenger ferry crosses the harbour to Gosport. Until the

The world's longest serving ship, HMS Victory.

Navy Days take place in August. Portsmouth is Britain's premier naval base and the port from which Gulliver was said to have set out in his final journey. An aircraft carrier might be seen towering over ornate cast iron structures onshore. The harbour can be quite choppy with waves reflecting off the ships and landings are strictly limited.

The *Mary Rose* was launched in Portsmouth in 1511 under Henry VIII's instructions, his favourite ship. The 700t carrack carried 415 crew and 91 guns, the first ship able to fire broadsides with guns between decks. In July 1545 she sank with vice admiral Sir George Carew and up to 700 men 2km off Southsea Castle during a French attack when her gun ports dipped below the water. She was preserved in the Solent silts until her dramatic raising in 1982 to become the centrepiece of the *Mary Rose* Museum. She has revealed a time capsule of English life with 23,000 items including the only English shawm, possibly the world's oldest, all but one of the Tudor arrows in existence and wooden combs complete with nits.

The world's longest serving ship and possibly its most famous is the flagship of the Commander in Chief at Portsmouth, *HMS Victory*. Built in 1765, she was Nelson's

project was shelved it had been planned to take the South Hampshire Rapid Transit scheme under the harbour entrance to **Gosport**, Old English for goose market, where the A32 and B3333 both end. Falklands Gardens by the Gosport ferry terminal have a fountain and pair of mosaics, protected by a raised seawall. A 40m Time Space light clock and 17m high sundial have been opened on the front and a Millennium Pier gives fine views of the harbour to those on foot. The high street market is the biggest on the south coast. It was from here that Dee Caffari set off to be the first woman to circumnavigate the globe solo againt the relentless winds in the Southern Ocean. The Jacobean Holy Trinity church of 1696 has an 1887 campanile belltower and an 18th century organ

The Portsmouth waterfront with the masts of HMS Victory *on the left and* HMS Warrior *on the right.*

HMS Warrior *outclassed all other warships when launched.*

Captain the Honourable Edward Legge RN unopposed as their MP in 1747 and then discovering he had died in the West Indies nearly three months earlier. In 1787 *HMS Sirius* took the first settlers from here to Australia and Portsmouth also developed to suit the needs of the New World. Old Portsmouth teemed with ale houses, brothels, sailors, press gangs, narrow lanes and pretty houses. Although 65,000 buildings were destroyed during the war a number of half timbered and other old houses remain amongst the new structures, especially in Old Portsmouth. The Lively Lady Bar and Still & West Country House form part of an attractive harbourside group. HMS Vernon, next to them, was the underwater weapons and mine defence school. Point is dominated by the Round Tower, a first attempt at fortification in 1481. From 1540 to 1912 it was joined to another on the west side of the harbourmouth by a chain with 1.2m links, tightened by a capstan to close the harbour off when necessary. These days there is a magnetic measurement range across the entrance. The tower is adjoined by the 18 gun battery of 1494, the Sally Port, the site of King James' Gate and the Square Tower also of 1494 with its bust of Charles I.

St Thomas' church, marked by its cupola, was founded as a priory in 1180, became a cathedral in 1927 and began to be enlarged in 1930, a job completed in 1991 following interruption by the war.

The northern end of Portsmouth Harbour with Gosport on the left and Portsmouth on the right with HMS Warrior.

which was used by Handel. The 1795 vicarage was used by the Royal Engineers as their headquarters during the Napoleonic War.

Gunwharf Quays are a major development of shopping and leisure facilities and a point for starting maritime events such as yacht races, sited on what was the Royal Navy's main ordnance store. The 170m Spinnaker Tower, the tallest publicly accessible structure in the UK, attempts to embody the spirit of sailing in Portsmouth, more recreational than military, but has been seen by some as a hypodermic needle. Its opening was marred when the mayor became trapped in the external lift and had to be rescued by abseilers. It has viewing platforms from which the whole of the harbour is visible.

Isle of Wight ferries leave from the Camber, the old commercial port at the end of the A3. A 12th century settlement received its charter from Richard I in 1194 when he built the first dock here as a Crusades embarkation point. In 1495 Henry VIII added Europe's first dry dock and there has been steady development since so Portsmouth is now Britain's premier naval base. Portsmouth had the unfortunate experience of electing

The entrance to Haslar Lake, the seaward end of Alverstoke Lake, is marked by a green lightship now used as a clubhouse. There is a fixed wave screen, 700 berth Haslar Marina and Hornet Sailing Club in the former HMS Hornet which was a base for motor torpedo boats and fast patrol boats. A strong southeasterly eddy operates at all times except at three hours forty minutes before Dover high water and winds also eddy round Fort Blockhouse. Indeed, on stormy nights might be heard the chains and bones of James Aitken, the anti monarchist Jack the Painter who set fire to the ropehouse in 1776 and was hanged from a mast and gibbetted from the point for many years.

HMS Vernon, next to them, faces across to HMS Dolphin, the old Fort Blockhouse which became a submarine depot and is now the Royal Navy Submarine Museum, exhibits including the Second World War A Class submarine *HMS Alliance* berthed at Haslar Jetty and *HM Submarine No 1 (Holland 1)*, the Royal Navy's first submarine, recovered from the sea bed where she had lain for 69 years.

The harbour entrance can get very congested, especially in the summer, and is defined as a Narrow Channel for

The original harbour at Portsmouth with Southsea beyond. Palmerston's forts can be seen between Portsea and the Isle of Wight.

Mural on the Bridge Tavern in the Camber.

the purposes of the International Regulations for Preventing Collisions at Sea, regulations which include a ban on the use of whistles. Any combination of flags including a red one with a white diagonal indicates a large vessel movement. The fairway may not be used by craft under 20m in length, which are obliged to use the Small Boat Channel on the west side of the entrance unless they have arranged exemption in advance with the Queen's Harbour Master, who accepts that for some craft it may be safer to take a stepping stones route on the east side, stopping between ferry berths as necessary, rather than having to cross the fairway twice to use the Small Boat Channel. Small craft may only leave the Small Boat Channel at its ends or from its west side and only craft under 20m in length may use the Inner Swashway which passes northwest of the drying Hamilton Bank.

Portsmouth Harbour's benefits of a narrow deep water entrance leading to a large sheltered basin have long been recognized. The 200m wide entrance drains 39km^2 of water, produces strong eddies when tidal flows are fast and may have standing waves, especially with southeasterly winds against a strong ebb. Large ship movements may take place at all times on neap tides but on spring tides are more likely on the first three to four hours of the flood and the first, second and fifth hours of the ebb including low water slack. Tidal flows begin earlier and are stronger here than further north. The ebb begins fifty minutes after Dover high water,

A statue recalling those who emigrated from Portsmouth.

Point's Spice Island Inn and Still & West Country Hotel.

The Round Tower at Point with the Spinnaker Tower beyond.

A former lightship, now a clubhouse on the Gosport waterfront.

Gosport with the Isle of Wight on the far side of the Solent.

reaching 9km/h three hours and twenty minutes after Dover high water. The flood begins five hours and forty minutes before Dover high water, reaches 2km/h an hour later, eases to 1km/h a further hour on and increases to 6km/h an hour before Dover high water, flows begin in a northwest–southeast direction. Winds are erratic at the entrance. The tide streams in Spithead flood west and ebb east and tides over the west part of Horse & Dean Sand are confused and irregular.

Prominent in Spithead are the Spitbank Fort and other forts positioned over towards the Isle of Wight plus vessels of all sizes, the larger ones passing anticlockwise round the island.

Hovercraft operate between Ryde and the Clarence Pier, the latter dominated by the Super Loop and other aerial rides of the funfair which the pier became in the 1960s, rebuilt after being bombed in 1941.

Near the red brick Haslar Royal Naval Hospital, where patients can be landed from Haslar Lake at any state of the tide, is the Admiralty's Experimental Establishment which has a 160m x 6.1m x 2.1m tank for testing paraffin wax models of ship hulls towed from a carriage over the canal. Robert Edmund Froud tested over 250,000 models here but it was William Froud who devised the Froud Number which is a defining characteristic of all boat hulls.

Razor wire has surrounded many establishments to keep people out but now it is to keep them in as a prison is passed.

All along this section of coast outside the harbour there is a sloping stone seawall. In calm conditions it is possible to land at a set of stone steps just before Fort Monckton at Clayhall where there are toilets and large car park, otherwise it will be necessary to continue until the seawall ends or take out inside the harbour entrance.

Distance
10km from Wallington
to Spithead

OS 1:50,000 Sheets
196 The Solent
& Isle of Wight

Admiralty Charts
2036 Solent &
Southampton Water
(1:25,000)
2037 Eastern
Approaches to Solent
(1:25,000)
2045 Outer
Approaches to Solent
(1:75,000)
2625 Approaches to
Portsmouth (1:7,500)
2628 Portsmouth
Harbour – Northern
Part (1:5,000)
2629 Portsmouth
Harbour – Southern
Part (1:5,000)
2631 Portsmouth
Harbour (1:7,500).
Fareham Lake
(1:7,500)

Tidal Constants
Portsmouth:
Dover +0020

Sea Area
Wight

Rescue
Inshore lifeboat:
Portsmouth
All weather lifeboat:
Bembridge

62 Southampton Water

From the great transatlantic liners to the Schneider Trophy races

Southampton's wise sons found their river so large,
Tho' 'twould carry a Ship, 'twould not carry a barge.
But soon this defect their sage noddles supply'd,
For they cut a snug ditch to run close by its side.
Like the man who, contriving a hole through his wall
To admit his two cats, the one great, t'other small,
Where a great hole was made for great puss to pass through,
Had a little hole cut for his little cat, too.

James Henry Pye

The River Test rises at Overton and flows southwards across Hampshire as a clear chalk stream. The longest tidal branch is the one on the east side at Hillyfields, the tidal limit being where the Test Way footpath crosses, leading towards a water treatment works at Testwood above the tidal limit on that arm, the works drawing much water for the refinery and power station at Fawley and being sited to suit angling interests. There is a complex double high water then a fast ebb.

Some of the braiding results from the Andover–Romsey–Redbridge Canal or Salisbury & Southampton Canal which was on the east side, the 7km Redbridge–Northam section to run next to the estuary although the scheme was abandoned during construction.

Notices around the footbridge say that there is an SSSI

The rapid below the bridge at the tidal limit of the River Test.

The 11th century Eling tide mill on Bartley Water.

and that boating and swimming (but not walking) are forbidden, this being repeated on the bridge for boats coming upstream. In fact, launching downstream below the footbridge would be difficult. It is easier where the river comes closest to the Salisbury to Redbridge railway which follows the river.

The River Test reserve is sited around the river as it flows under low hanging willows, becoming walled in by reedbed and saltmarsh with flower meadows hidden beyond as the occasional gravel rapids are left behind. Anglers are present. Swans may include a black swan and there are shelducks, moorhens, kingfishers, Canada geese and herring gulls to give an estuarine mix, other airborne wildlife including large dragonflies and huge swarms of tiny black flies.

The left bank moves from Hampshire to Southampton. Just above Redbridge some half dozen channels of all sizes converge through the reeds. An almost illegible notice facing boats coming upstream says there is no access, apparently because the birds are being shot. The two extremes of attitude towards wildlife are met within a kilometre of each other, both claiming superiority over other interests.

The final three bridges over the river cross in succession at Totton, a stone arched bridge now just leading to the Anchor, a high arched bridge carrying the A35 and a low structure taking the Weymouth–Basingstoke railway over. Egrets might be seen around them on the mud. This bridge site has been chosen because the river then widens significantly into the Redbridge Channel, wide enough for a water skiing area from March to October, powerlines being the last crossing. The fact that Southampton Water is a ria becomes more obvious, becoming flooded after the last Ice Age.

The right bank retains its largely undeveloped feel as it reaches round to the mouth of Bartley Water which discharges through Eling tide mill. There was a mill there in 1086, restored in 1980 and producing flour with two wheels. There is 1.8m head at the high water and it runs for 4 hours. An integral part of the mill is the 76 x 16m wide causeway which stands 2.7m above low water, the causeway noted as needing repair in 1418. The mill houses the Totton & Eling Heritage Centre and has another Anchor inn just downstream, this one from the 15th century.

Although the river is much wider, it froze from Redbridge to Calshot in 1684 and again in 1895. Wrecks are left in place at first. However, the east side is about to change dramatically after Redbridge Wharf with its yellow painted hand crane. In 1936 the largest ever land reclaim in Britain was completed, 1.6km^2 at Millbrook. **Southampton** is still the UK's 5th busiest port, handling over 7% of UK trade, some 42,000,000t per year. It begins with Southampton Container Terminal, the UK's second largest, which can take the largest vessels. A ship over 150m long with three vertical red lights or a black cylinder, sometimes preceded by a Southampton Harbour patrol launch, has a moving exclusion zone around it, 1km ahead and 100m to each side, much of which is a blind spot from the wheel. A tide gauge at the start of the Bury Reach swinging ground may be obscured by moored ships and the array of container cranes.

The sewage works by Bury Creek now have an adjacent incineration plant.

The river kicks left and widens again before shellfish beds off Marchwood with a dome shaped incinerator and a military port. The widening permits another swinging ground in front of Southampton Car Terminal. In the corner is the King George V drydock, 366 x 41m with a 7.6m thick concrete floor able to take 100,000t liners. The River Test Quay is constructed with 146 14m² concrete monoliths. Western Docks handle bulk cement, fertilizer, animal feed, vegetables, fruit and bulk wine. In 1842 Outer Dock was one of the first to have passenger rail access.

The Romans established Clausentum on the River Itchen in 50 AD. The Angles later were present and the Saxons had a mint. The Danes plundered the town in 842. A statue of Sir Bevis commemorates his slaying of the giant Ascapart who was terrorizing the local countryside and now is said to be buried in the Bevis Mound tumulus. William the Conqueror used it as his port for Normandy and it became prosperous from 1070 with Norman city walls and the Norman Bargate as one of the finest town gates in the UK. Richard the Lionheart sailed from here in 1189 on the 3rd Crusade and Henry V sailed from here for Agincourt in 1415.

St Michael's church, founded about 1070, retains its Norman tower and arches. The timber framed medieval Merchant's House of about 1290 is one of the best surviving examples in England, having avoided the destruction of much of the town by the French in 1338. The 14th century Guildhall has a local history exhibition while the Southampton Maritime Museum is in the 14th century Wool House where prisoners of war were housed in the 18th and 19th centuries, exhibits including a 7.9m model of the *Queen Mary*, a 6.7m model of the *Capetown Castle*, an Empress steam engine, paddle steamers, yachting and the 1934 world speed record breaking *Miss Britain III*. By 1450 it was the third most important port in the country.

The port declined in the 16th century when Henry VIII prohibited it from exporting wool. In 1620 the Pilgrim Fathers embarked from here in the *Mayflower* and *Speedwell*, recalled by a memorial column, but others were to come to what was a resort until 1815. Thackeray wrote part of *Pendennis* while staying at the Dolphin Hotel.

The 15th century God's House Tower contains the Museum of Archaeology while the timber framed 16th century Tudor House Museum & Garden has an Elizabethan secret garden and Victorian displays.

In 1852 steam Post Office ships from Southampton replaced the Falmouth packets and the great transatlantic liners were also based here from 1911. The following year it was the departure point for the world's largest, fastest and newest ship, the unsinkable *Titanic*, using coal and crew members from six other ships during a coal strike and narrowly avoiding being damaged in port by the *New York*, adrift after breaking free of her moorings. In 1898 Morgan Robertson had published *Futility*, a novel which told a story of the *Titan*, very similar to that of the *Titanic* disaster in many details. A passenger on the *Titanic* was author William Thomas Stead, who had previously written a story about a ship which sank with too few lifeboats and another story about a boat which sank after hitting an iceberg, the rescue being conducted by Capt E J Smith of the White Star Line, who was to be the captain of the *Titanic*. An Irish stoker claimed to have left the sailing after watching a black cat carrying her kittens off the ship at Southampton.

The city was badly bombed during the Second World War but embarked over 3,000,000 troops in 1944, especially for Normandy. Forty years later it was the embarkation point for the Falklands Task Force.

It is the largest of Associated British Ports' 22 ports, and includes the Mayflower Cruise Terminal. Cunard and P&O Cruises have it as their home port for such liners as the *Oriana* and *Orcadia*. Even those who do not sail here descend on Mayflower Park each autumn in great numbers for the Southampton Boat Show, the largest in-water boat show in the country, to watch the start of

The start of Southampton Container Terminal.

Marchwood's futuristic incinerator.

the Volvo Ocean Race every four years or even to try the concrete walled maze.

R J Mitchell and the Spitfire story are also well exhibited.

The Town Quay, off which there is another swinging ground, has high speed ferries to the Isle of Wight and a passenger ferry across to Hythe. Jet skis and speedboats race up and down to add to the confusion.

Blackbacked gulls, terns and cormorants may be present. Proposals to develop Dibden Bay as a further container handling area were thwarted by the requirement that birds now take precedence. If plans are eventually

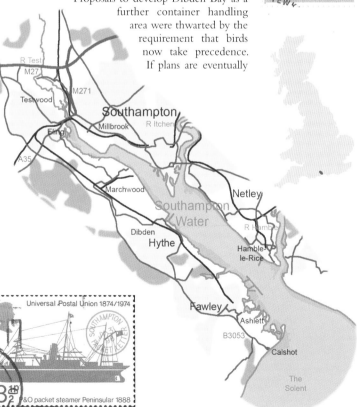

269

Former Cunard liner Queen Elizabeth 2 and container ship at the Test/Itchen confluence.

successful this stretch of water will be used by container ships up to 350m long. Most of this traffic will be ship to ship so there will be a corresponding increase in smaller vessels, the number of containers handled at Southampton more than tripling.

The Test and the Itchen converge to form Southampton Water. The valley is in Tertiary rocks with the overlying chalk breached. The valley was drowned as the sea rose but it was not glaciated so it does not need dredging to remove silt.

The new hybrid common cordgrass, which reclaims land rapidly, spread round the coast from here in 1870, assisted by some deliberate planting.

Ocean Village, with its marina, faces across the Itchen to Woolston and Weston brings Southampton to an end before Hampshire returns.

On the southwest side **Hythe** also begins with a marina village. In the 1930s and 1940s the village built flying boats and it had a US base. The 610mm gauge electric Hythe Pier Railway of 1881 runs along the 640m pier served by the Southampton passenger ferry, a tide gauge being located on the end of the pier.

A hovercraft testing area fronts **Netley**, which begins with a conspicuous castle converted to a Tudor house near the ruin of a 1239 Gothic abbey. At the other end of the village is a heritage centre and the Netley Great

Ashlett Creek leads down from the Jolly Sailor past a large tidemill.

Dome with the Royal Victoria Country Park, formerly the Royal Victoria Military Hospital built in 1856 for the Crimean War and demolished exactly a century later.

Heavy piles with smart rubber extrusion fenders front the jetties of Union Carbide, International Synthetic Rubber and Monsanto on the right shore. A double measured distance in front of them leads down to Cadland Creek, barely noticed against the backdrop of **Fawley** oil refinery with its tanks, chemical plant and flare stacks. It is supplied by the Esso Marine Terminal which has 1.4km of jetty, able to take partly laden VLCCs to 60,000t. Other craft must stay at least 137m from the jetty face because of fire risk, an industrial scale version of not using mobile phones on petrol station forecourts.

BP's Hamble Terminal opposite can take tankers to 110,000t. Hamble-le-Rice has buildings from the 17th century and an earthwork overlooking Hamble Spit, visible at low water beside the River Hamble, a major yachting centre with a vast fortune in yachts berthed, including the Royal Yacht Club, the base for Chay Blyth's 1970 first east–west solo nonstop global circumnavigation.

The College of Naval Studies stands on the east side of the Hamble and overlooks the confluence where King Alfred is thought to have beaten the Danes in the 9th century.

This part of Southampton Water is subject to considerable gusts when wind of any strength is from the northwest. The flood runs for three and a half hours and the ebb for nine, affected in a complex pattern by heavy rain and southwesterly winds in addition to the double high waters north of Calshot.

The Danes held the ash tree to be sacred and planted one wherever they camped, hence Ashlett Creek on the opposite side of Southampton Water, leading up to a tidemill and the Jolly Sailor. Fawley church, to the west, is partly Norman and was one of four spared by William Rufus when he was extending the New Forest. Its treble bell dates from 1603.

Fawley power station, with its 198m chimney, has a seasonal water skiing area along its front. A tunnel and a cave in Sprat's Down Woods used by smugglers show other activities which have taken place in the area. Much of the rest of the coast on this side of Southampton Water is designated as a nature reserve.

A final flurry of activity is located around the spit at Calshot, beginning with the lifeboat station and the distinctive coastguard tower although there is no longer a Calshot Spit light vessel. One of these, in wood, is now the headquarters of the Royal Northumberland Yacht Club in Blyth harbour. The coastguard lookout point and radar scanner are on top of a tall column. For years a large Princess flying boat was moored off this point. It is a strategic site. Cerdic's Saxon army landed near here and fought the British at Fawley. Henry VIII built the Tudor Calshot Castle in 1540 with stone from Beaulieu Abbey to defend Southampton and it has been a base for the Royal Navy and Royal Air Force in the 20th century. It was used until 1956 and has been restored as it was before the First World War with bunks and uniforms on display, a barrack room and the Schneider Trophy races.

Calshot Activities Centre has a vast climbing wall, a dry ski slope, a banked cycle track used by national team members and a large fleet of boats, all housed in the three hangars of the most complete seaplane and flyingboat base in the UK, possibly in the world, in use from 1913 to 1961. It includes Britain's second oldest seaplane hangar. It was the site of the first Royal Naval Air Station in the UK as well as being the site of coastal artillery and anti aircraft guns. Another hangar is the Schneider Trophy hangar. By the 1920s it carried out nearly all the maritime air training. Lawrence of Arabia was based here from 1929 to 1931, the period of the Schneider Trophy races which took place round a triangular course over the Solent and

Fawley power station.

were to lead to Britain's retaining the Schneider Trophy after winning it three times in succession, in the process doing the preparatory work for the Spitfire which was to be of major importance during the Second World War. A more recent battle won here has been the prevention of councillors from clearing the listed buildings to make way for housing development in this AONB with its prime views over the Solent and across to the Isle of Wight. The accommodation blocks were used by refugees from Tristan da Cunha when volcanic eruption threatened their island in the south Atlantic.

The sheer size of some craft is brought home by seeing one towering above and beyond each end of the main hangar at Calshot. Tankers, container ships, liners and car ferries all use this water, together with many yachts. The most important craft to spot are the passenger launches between Southampton and Cowes as these are quite small but travel very fast.

Calshot Spit is not the piece of land which runs northeast then north, but the underwater feature which is growing and which runs southeast then southwest from its end, throwing up testing water conditions to the south of the outdoor centre. Large vessels are required not to create excessive wash which could endanger those on the beach, where sea kale thrives.

Landing within the outdoor centre requires permission but there are beach landings to the southwest. There is parking around the end of the B3053 where beach huts line what an old notice proclaims to be a private beach but which is clearly used by the public. A hut on the beach sells refreshments.

Calshot coastguard tower.

Distance
18km from Hillyfields to the Solent

OS 1:50,000 Sheets
196 The Solent & Isle of Wight

Admiralty Charts
2022 Harbours & Anchorages in E Solent Area. Entrance to R Hamble (1:5,000). Ashlett Creek (1:5,000) 2036 Solent & Southampton Water (1:25,000) 2038 Southampton Water & Approaches (1:15,000) 2041 Port of Southampton (1:10,000) 2045 Outer Approaches to Solent (1:75,000)

Tidal Constants
Redbridge: HW Dover −0020, LW Dover −0010 Southampton: Dover Warsash: HW Dover +0010, LW Same as Dover Calshot Castle: HW Dover +0020, LW Same as Dover

Sea Area
Wight

Rescue
Inshore lifeboat: Calshot All weather lifeboat: Calshot

63 Poole Harbour

BP for oil and Scouts

Then did the Quick pursue the Dead
By crystal Froom that crinkles there;
And still the viewless quire ahead
  Voiced the old holy air.
Thomas Hardy

The River Frome or South River rises at Evershot and flows eastwards across Dorset, following the bottom of a syncline. Formerly, it continued to Spithead but the lower river has been drowned out as far up as Poole Harbour.

Wareham, Hardy's Anglebury on the River Froom or Var, was occupied by the early Britons and then the Romans, who had a pottery kiln here. It was an important Saxon port with a large rectangular fortress, bank and ditch and a mint, their street plan remaining. There were formerly marshes far up the valley but the river silted up. The Danes made it their headquarters in 866, left it a decade later after razing it and then attacked it four times over the next century. In 1016 it was taken by Cnut. The Roundheads captured it in the Civil War. The Bloody Bank section of the Town Walls is where Judge Jefferies had executions in 1685 after the failed Monmouth Rebellion. There are over 200 buildings of architectural or historical interest. The Georgian main street's buildings date from 1762 onwards. The museum has Lawrence of Arabia memorabilia and the Saxon St Martin's church has an effigy of him. Lady St Mary church has magnificent stained glass and the marble coffin of Edward the Martyr, murdered in Corfe in 978. The Rex is the only cinema still lit by gas. On the evening of November 4th, strangely dressed members of the Norman Court Leet visit many public houses, sample the ale and meat, weigh the bread and check the flues for blockages as the town has had serious fires.

Wareham quay at the top of a spring tide.

The river is tidal from at least the B3075 bridge, which is on the line of a former causeway to Stoborough. Canoes and rowing boats can be hired above the bridge. The quay, faced by the Quay Inn and Old Granary, is used for the 700 year old charter market and is the departure

Redclyffe Yacht Club on the River Frome.

The red cliff itself.

The final reach of the River Frome with the Isle of Purbeck beyond.

point for a passenger ferry to Poole in the summer. It is a popular area, as is the riverside grass on the opposite side of the river, and parking can be difficult. For launching small craft there is a footpath and steps down to the river on the east side of the Old Granary, perhaps quieter for unloading before parking a little further to the northeast.

The priory was built beyond the church, together with other desirable residences. The river quickly acquires its character of being lined by reeds and used by mallards and swans, with almost continuous moorings. There are some less obvious salmon holes.

Beyond Redclyffe Yacht Club the river is deflected by a red cliff, untypical of the area. The river winds round Ridge to Ridge Wharf Yacht Centre with berths for over 160 boats at the end of what was a railway to carry clay away to Furzebrook.

Otters, water voles, lapwings, kingfishers and redshanks use the reedbeds and saltmarsh. The final reach down to Swineham Point gives extensive views to the Isle of Purbeck. Small craft may be able to head northeast through the shallows between the two parts of Gigger's Island, on which landing is prohibited above the high water mark, there being only silt below this level. Larger craft need to go north to the mouth of the Piddle, Puddle, Trent or North River to reach the Wareham Channel, the fairway being marked by stakes.

Poole Harbour is one of those claimed to be the world's second largest natural harbour, with 167km of shoreline and mooring for over 5,000 yachts. It is big enough to be exposed to the weather, resulting in some rough conditions. Like the river, it is heavily used, sailing regatta courses often being laid out, and the inshore lifeboat can be kept busy. There is a double high water, the first being higher on springs and the second on neaps. The water is near to high water for six to seven hours and then there is a fast ebb, affected by pressure and wind direction.

It was used by Cnut as an anchorage to conquer Wessex in 1015. By the 18th century it had more trade with the New World than any other British port.

Initially there is soft mud or quags which can be dangerous but then sand over clay and gravel, exposed in creeks at low water. Sometimes there are dolphins. It has 36,000 waterfowl including 2,600 shelducks, 1,000 blacktailed godwits, cormorants, Brent and Canada geese, grebes, oystercatchers and egrets. In 1992 the RSPB said they were under threat of permanent damage from land reclaim, marinas and recreational pressure. More immediate danger came in 1963 when the harbour started to freeze over and some were frozen into the ice.

Arne, with the Arne Toy Museum and a tumulus, is on top of a hill beyond sections of white cliff and pine trees but cannot be reached as the RSPB do not allow landing on the sandy beach. A nature reserve contains Dorset heath, marsh gentians, smooth snakes, sand lizards, nightjars, Dartford warblers and 22 species of dragonfly.

Behind Wood Bar Looe runs the conspicuous Weymouth to Basingstoke railway towards an even more conspicuous caravan park above Rockley Sands. The Rockley Channel drains Lytchett Bay and Rockley Point has a watersports centre for youngsters. Small dinghies and water skiing proliferate.

At Lake there is a marina and a Royal Marines base but it is a block of

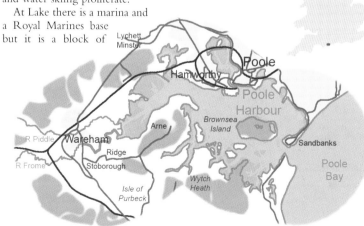

Pine trees hide Arne on its hill.

Conspicuous apartments at Lake.

white apartments which catch the eye, especially in the afternoon sun.

There is a clay pit before Gold Point, around which the sandy shore is backed by trees. The Wych Channel drains marshland in the harbour beyond Patchins Point. Wytch Farm is the sixth largest oilfield in the UK and the largest onshore field in western Europe, operated by BP. Poole Harbour being AONB and Heritage Coast, much effort has had to go into screening the activity and there is very little to be seen from the harbour. In Roman times the channel had a saltworks.

Long Island was the hideout of 14th century privateer and pirate Arripey, probably christened Harry Paye, and is where he looted captured French and Spanish ships. Landing is prohibited above high water, as on Round Island, to which it is joined by marsh.

The built up part of the harbour is around its northern side. **Poole**, Hardy's Havenpool, was a 1st century Celtic settlement. In the 16th century it imported wine, fruit and canvas. It was involved in Newfoundland trading and fishing, especially salted cod, and exported oysters and large pearls. Smuggling and privateering were leading forms of trade in the 19th century. The mayor is Admiral of the Port of Poole and has to beat the bounds every three years, including visiting the floating marks. Lower **Hamworthy** has a marina and Holes Bay is drained by a channel which passes the RNLI's headquarters.

Fitzworth Point, surrounded by fragments of marshy island, has oyster beds, marked by yellow and white buoys.

Landing is forbidden on Green Island above high water. Formerly Helen's Island, it has Roman remains and is where the monks of Milton Abbey built a chapel to St Helen in the Middle Ages, linked to the mainland by a causeway although there is now a deep hole on that line. Covering 8ha and 15m high, it is hidden by trees and rhododendrons. Its Kimmeridge shale may have been worked two millennia ago for utensils, ornaments and tombstones.

With similar vegetation and landing prohibited above high water without permission, Furzey Island is 9m high and covers 13ha. It has red squirrels, wallabies and the most northerly oil wells in this area. South Deep emerges from south of these two islands and drains Brand's Bay.

Brownsea Island is the largest and most prominent island in the harbour, 2km^2 of Bagshot beds over London clay. There has been a resident community since 500 BC. Cnut destroyed the 12th century chapel of St Andrew, built by the monks of Cerne Abbey. Copperas and alum were extracted in the 16th and 17th centuries.

In 1722 it was bought by William Benson, who planted 10,000 trees and rare plants but was declared insane in 1741, claimed to practise black magic and to have sacrificed a servant girl to Satan. Fishermen often heard screams and saw ghostly lights in the woods.

Colonel William Petrie Waugh was advised by his

Brownsea Island from the west.

The southwest corner of Brownsea Island.

amateur geologist wife, Mary, that there was china clay on the beach so he bought the island in 1852 and built Maryland village at the western end. However, the clay was low grade, only good enough for smoking pipes and drainpipes, and he disappeared as he could not afford to repay his loan. Many pieces of glazed fragment remain on the shore and some have been used to fill protective gabions.

Tobacco baron Charles Van Raalte bought it in 1901 and held parties which were attended by royalty and by Marconi, who met his future wife at one. He also introduced the peacocks which are particularly noisy in May.

A memorial stone marks where Robert Baden-Powell held the first Scout camp on the south shore in 1907. Based on skills used in the Boer War, it developed into a worldwide movement. There is still an annual Scout and Guide camp here.

There had been up to 300 residents on the island. Mary Bonham-Christie bought it in 1925 and ordered everyone off, fire breaking out and destroying 90% of the vegetation as the last ones left. There is now a fire tower. The National Trust took ownership in 1962.

There are pinewoods, heather and daffodils, sitka deer, rabbits, pygmy shrews, one of two significant locations remaining in the south of England for red squirrels, seven bat species, a ternenry, the second largest British heronry, wildfowl, winter waders and mosquitoes. Gulls nest in the woods and on heath in the southwest corner.

Blood Alley Lake, marked by stakes, takes its name from a confrontation between Poole smugglers and revenue men.

The island is open to the public between Easter and September, subject to a landing fee. Most of the 60,000 visitors per year arrive by passenger ferry from Sandbanks to the east end of the island, where the buildings are found. The 1548 mock Gothic Branksea Castle was built by Henry VIII. Sir Augustus Foster, the owner in 1845, slit his own throat in the castle. In the Civil War it was held by the Roundheads. A bad fire gutted it and destroyed some important paintings in 1896 when it was owned by MP Kenneth Balfour. It later became a holiday centre for the John Lewis partnership. The 1853 church was by Colonel Waugh. In the Second World War it was a base for refugees and a decoy for Poole.

The Main Channel passes to the north of the island and can be rough at the entrance, any natural turbulence from the fast flow being enhanced by the washes of a stream of yachts, powerboats, RIBs, jetskis and occasional

Branksea Castle guards the entrance to Poole Harbour.

catamaran vehicle ferries to Cherbourg, Guernsey, Jersey and St Malo. Flows out are from an hour and a half before Dover high water to 8km/h and in from six hours and ten minutes after Dover high water to 6km/h with strong rips on the north side of the entrance with both flows. Adding to the confusion is the vehicle chain ferry crossing between Sandbanks and South Haven Point.

Sandbanks, which has grown from the north, has the fourth highest property prices anywhere in the world. In the 2000s, £3,000,000 was paid for a bungalow to be knocked down to obtain its garden for building.

Beyond the Haven Hotel is Poole Bay with steep waves in southerly to easterly force 5 to 6 winds. There are rock groynes on the north side of the entrance and parking off the B3369. The south side of the entrance behind Shell Bay is composed of parallel ridges which are formed eastwards, dunes with heather, bog myrtle, adders, grass and smooth snakes, slow worms and common and sand lizards. This is the end of the Southwest Coast Path, Britain's longest at 1,014km and probably the most popular long distance path. There is parking on the minor road south from South Haven Point but not on the section between the ferry and the roundabout, which is only for ferry traffic queues, so approach is better made from the west.

Distance
15km from Wareham to Poole Bay

OS 1:50,000 Sheets
195 Bournemouth & Purbeck

Admiralty Charts
2035 Western Approaches to Solent (1:25,000)
2172 Harbours & Anchorages on S Coast of England. R Stour (1:7,500)
2175 Poole Bay (1:20,000)
2611 Poole Harbour & Approaches (1:12,500). Wareham (1:12,500)
2615 Bill of Portland to Needles (1:75,000)

Tidal Constants
Wareham:
HW Dover +0030,
LW Dover +0110
Poole Town Quay:
Same as Dover
Pottery Pier:
HW Dover +0020,
LW Dover +0010
Poole Harbour Entrance:
Dover −0030

Sea Area
Wight

Rescue
Inshore lifeboat: Poole
All weather lifeboat: Poole

The chain ferry waits at Sandbanks.

64 The Fleet

Europe's largest lagoon and Britain's largest artificial harbour

Blow wind, rise storm
Ship ashore before morn
J Meade Falkner

The Fleet, also known as the Little Sea, is Europe's largest lagoon, running southeast along the Dorset coast for 13km along what Hardy called the Waddon Vale and enclosed by Chesil Beach. Brackish and tidal throughout, it has been a nature reserve since at least 1393 and is an SSSI and Ramsar site of international importance.

At the northwest end is Abbotsbury, a village of yellow brown oolite, the houses originally thatched with reeds from the Fleet although the thatching has now been replaced by slate because of the rapid spread of fires along the thatched terraces. Lighter coloured stones in the houses have been taken from St Peter's Benedictine abbey, founded in 1026 on land given by Cnut to his steward, Orc. The abbey was dissolved in 1539, the village being given to Sir Guy Strangeways four years later by Henry VIII and being owned by the family ever since.

The 14th century St Catherine's Chapel on Chapel Hill has an elaborately vaulted stone roof, rare in England. It may have been built as a landmark for sailors and its survival was perhaps due to its use as a tower for a maritime fire beacon.

The 14th century tithe barn is one of the largest thatched barns in the world at 84 x 9.4m yet, when built, it was twice as long and had stone slates. It has slit windows and was used for storing reeds for thatching the village.

The small beach at Langton Herring after the turn of the tide.

Today it houses the Croker collection of agricultural exhibits, a farmworker's kitchen, dairy, gamekeeper, reaper, vet, blacksmith, carts and wagons, hedging and ditching and shepherding exhibits.

St Nicholas' church has a 12th century statue of the abbot, a drawing of the abbey, a fine plaster ceiling of 1638 with the Strangeways coat of arms and a pulpit pockmarked by musket shot since 1644 when the village was taken by the Parliamentarians in the Civil War.

A 17th century dovecote has over 600 doves and rare poultry.

The hillside above the head of the Fleet was terraced by monks in the Middle Ages and strip lychets were used until the 1805 Enclosure Act. Subsequent village activities included smuggling and wrecking.

Several of the village houses were built by the Earl of Ilchester in 1858. The village received a conservation award in 1975 and these days it is a retirement village for the affluent.

May 13th is Garland Day when two garlands are carried round the village, one sometimes being cast into the sea, thought to be a survival of sea god worship.

The 8ha Abbotsbury Gardens were founded in 1765 as the castle gardens. They are subtropical, the shingle absorbing the sun's heat and Chesil Beach providing shelter so that there are enormous exotic trees, shrubs and flowers, azaleas, ancient camellias, rhododendrons, 8ha of woodland and formal gardens, 18th century walled gardens of the former Abbotsbury Castle, Victorian garden, New Zealand garden, an aviary, peacocks and rare pheasants and there is still room for some cow parsley and a swan maze. They were used in filming *Harry Potter & the Deathly Hallows*.

Abbotsbury Swannery has developed from a colony reared in the 11th century by the monks for food. This is now a breeding ground for 600 swans and other wildfowl, one of the only places in Britain where swans breed communally. The swans are unable to be territorial so

Duck punt on the beach at Langton Herring.

they do not have the aggression of river swans. Swanherds provide nesting sites and materials and the swans feed on eel grass. The West Fleet is good for winter wildfowl and there may be a thousand swans present in the winter. Founded in the 17th century was the country's oldest working duck decoy. There are also water voles and a reedbed naturalists' walk.

The first 4km of the relatively freshwater West Fleet may only be used by paddlers taking part in the biannual swan roundup. Otherwise it is necessary to launch from the small beach at the end of the track down from Langton Herring. The boats lined up on the beach include some duck punts. The South West Coast Path, which has made a detour round the banned section of water, returns to the shore at the widest point on the West Fleet where there is a line of signs across the water forbidding boats from going any further west when coming from the sea.

The drowned landscape has no cliffs on the Jurassic beds on the north side so they have probably never been exposed to sea waves. The sea has risen 60m relative to the land since the Ice Age, when the coastline was 16km further south. Chesil Beach is still moving slowly northwards. The 13km of graded pebbles of flint, quartzite and limestone, including some chert and jasper, form part of a 29km sweep of shingle around Lyme Bay and is the most fascinating shingle structure in Britain and possibly the longest in Europe. The beach gets higher (to 13m) and wider (to 180m) towards its eastern end, the depth of shingle increasing from 11m to 15m in this direction and the size of the pebbles being carefully graded from

The western end has grebe, pochard, tufted duck, pintail, teal and shoveler. There is a coastguard hut on the north side of the beach opposite Langton Herring. Froth floats amongst the posts and pipes which stick out of the Fleet at random.

On the Dorset Downs to the north can be seen the Hardy Monument beyond Portesham. It was erected in 1844 to Vice Admiral Sir Thomas Masterman Hardy, flag captain of the *Victory* at Trafalgar in 1805, who lived at Portesham and who is popularly remembered in Nelson's dying words 'Kiss me, Hardy.'

The most conspicuous building in Langton Herring is the church tower although the village also boasts a 16th century public house. The story might have been different as the village was selected as a nuclear power station site.

On the far side of Gore Cove is the Moonfleet Manor

The old coastguard hut at the foot of Chesil Beach.

The Moonfleet Manor Hotel as it is today, the setting for J Meade Faulkner's smuggling yarn.

pea size at Bridport to fist size at Chesilton, so precisely that fishermen lost in the fog can tell their location from the size of stones on the beach. Below water level the stones are graded in the opposite direction. Some of the stones have been recovered from Maiden Castle where they were used in slings. Blue clay lies below the shingle some 0.9–1.2m above low water springs. Cans or hollows on the inside of the beach are where water has seeped through and washed the bank away.

Occasionally, the beach is overtopped by storms after strong southwesterly winds. In 1795 seven ships under Rear Admiral Sir Hugh Christian on their way to the West Indies were lost here with 200 men and women. In 1824 the West Indiamen *Carvalho* and *Colville* were lost with all hands in the storm which carried the 95t sloop *Ebenezer* into the Fleet on a wave. A ship was left on top of the beach in 1853.

The Fleet was used in the Second World War for testing Barnes Wallis' bouncing bomb which was used by the Lancaster bombers of 617 Squadron on raids against the Mohne and Eder dams in the Ruhr.

Chesil Beach forms part of the West Dorset Heritage Coast but is closed to walkers for half the year. It has a diverse range of bird and animal life. Three species of tern breed on the shingle bank, being a protected breeding site for the little tern. There is plenty of sea kale, together with the rare sea pea and shrubby seablite. Cormorants mix with herons, shelducks and blackbacked gulls while skylarks fly above the gorse on the mainland.

Hotel and country club. Built in 1603 as Fleet House, it played a central role in *Moonfleet*, J Meade Faulkner's smuggling tale of 1898 which the author named after the Mohune family.

A missile range was established to the east of the hotel at Fleet. Below Sea Barn Farm there is a pillbox guarding the shoreline at Park Wall. There is a ruined church at East Fleet, destroyed by a storm in 1824. Chickerell Hive, between Butter Street Cove and Big Lake, faces the section of Chesil Bank known as the Rudge, which used to be a route for unloading seine net fishing boats.

Launching at high water is

The army's small boat exercise area.

Notwithstanding all the noise of gunfire, a large caravan site is located close by.

A race with standing waves builds up through the narrowest part of the channel and the beach steepens to 1 in 80 at Foxhole Point. The army use this as an

The Ferry Bridge at Small Mouth with the Isle of Portland rising beyond.

advantageous not only for the race through the narrows but also because much of the East Fleet drains. The eastern end has a winter population of 10,000 wigeon, 2,700 Brent geese, red breasted mergansers, goldeneyes and great northern and red throated divers.

Red flags and lookout points on Chesil Beach opposite Charlestown at Tidmoor Point mark the limits of the danger area from the firing range which operates from the camp on the north side but is a danger even on the open sea. Lookouts watch out to sea but may not look behind them as usually they do not expect to see boats passing on the Fleet. The range is heavily used.

exercise area for inflatable and rigid craft and have two large slipway areas on the north side, separated by a control tower.

The channel opens out to form a nature reserve with bulrushes and teasels on the north side and fishing boats moored near huts on Chesil Beach. A prominent aerial above Wyke Regis is not as close as it appears.

Beyond another pillbox is the Abbotsbury Oyster Farm with lobster hatchery, licensed shellfish bar and glass bottomed boat, the *Fleet Observer*, so that customers can view the seabed without having to look over the side. The Ferrybridge Inn overlooks the swift currents as divers and windsurfers go about their sports. Sailboard Alley is used for Portland Speed Week in mid October and is best viewed from the safety of land. Ferry Bridge carries the A354 at Small Mouth or the New Channel, a breach in the Weymouth–Portland bank of limestone shingle. The first bridge was built in 1836. In 1979 the road sank in a storm. Formerly a railway also crossed to serve the naval depot of Portland Harbour, this being an entrance to the Dockyard Port.

The Isle of Portland consists mostly of Portland Stone, so beloved of architects for public buildings. Portland takes its name from Porta, a Saxon pirate who seized the island in 501. To the poet and novelist Thomas Hardy it was the Isle of Slingers while he was working in Weymouth, or Budmouth Regis as he called it, for architect G R Crickmay, and was probably engaged to Tryphena Sparks at the time. Weymouth was the setting for some of the

Chesil Beach and Ferry Bridge at Small Mouth.

The Isle of Portland seen across Portland Harbour from Sandsfoot.

Sandsfoot Castle, the North Ship Channel entrance and the Purbeck chalk cliffs around Lulworth.

1967 film of his book *Far from the Madding Crowd*.

Portland Harbour is Britain's largest artificial harbour, the second largest man-made harbour in the world and, in the 19th century, one of the greatest civil engineering projects undertaken in England, being 4km across. It has been naval since the Crimean War until the recent decision to pull out the Royal Navy from HMS Osprey. The port could be reopened to the Royal Navy, who left in 1995, as it is said that the next generation of aircraft carriers will be too deep for any UK port, something which might have seemed a basic design criterion. The former naval base and dockyard are currently a commercial port. The west side is protected by land and the east side by breakwaters, on which landing is forbidden without a licence. The harbour was constructed in 1847 on a Saxon stronghold by convicts awaiting transportation to Australia. In 1893 the two northern breakwaters were added to give protection against torpedo attacks. The breakwaters are of Portland Stone, up to 7t per block, tipped from trucks on a temporary railway built along the top. Sections of Mulberry Harbour, used for D-Day landings, can be seen on the southern side of Portland Harbour. Older defences come at Sandsfoot Castle, built in 1593 as one of Henry VIII's line of forts to protect the south coast. It stands on 15–18m cliffs, adjacent to the Western Ledges at the opposite end from Castle Cove with its sailing club and slipway. The harbour will host the 2012 Olympic sailing regatta from the new sailing centre built on part of the site of the search and rescue helicopter base on the south side of the harbour. Moorings for leisure craft are placed across the northern end of the harbour. The harbour was the site of a 20th century prison ship at the southern end to supplement overcrowded jails, recalling prison hulks of the 19th century.

The harbour entrances have semicircular walls faced with granite above water level. Notices require craft to keep 30m from these. Flows through the gaps reach 2km/h and there are eddies off the ends of the breakwaters. Regulations require craft not to enter the ship channels and to keep clear of naval squadrons, whose arrival was indicated for the North Ship Channel by a particular flag flying from the *northern* arm of the flagstaff at the East Ship Channel 1.5km away. A torpedo firing point operates eastwards from the North-eastern Breakwater when orange flags fly but operates in an easterly direction so that entering the North Ship Channel avoids any conflicts.

Flows in Weymouth Bay are anticlockwise to 1km/h although there may be a barely perceptible flow for two hours from five hours ten minutes before Dover high water.

Weymouth and Portland were at their busiest during the Second World War when they despatched 600,000 men and 140,000 vehicles in a year. In June 1944 they were two of the main departure points for the Normandy landings with embarkation for Omaha Beach.

One of Weymouth harbour's breakwaters was built in 1903 to deflect waves rebounding off the northern breakwater of Portland Harbour. Overlooking it is the Nothe, 15m high with a fort built in 1860–72 to defend Portland Harbour against the threat of Napoleonic invasion. The fort has been restored with the Museum of Coastal Defence and has the only operational coastal defence searchlight in the country, displays of 40mm anti aircraft and other guns, weapons, Mk VIII torpedo, underground magazines, equipment, garrison life of Victorian and Second World War soldiers, Ferret Scout Car and other military vehicles and paddle steamers, a children's assault course, gardens and picnic area, together with a See Where They Embarked exhibition. The occasional booms of tanks firing on the Lulworth Ranges in the distance add to the atmosphere.

It was used by the BBC for filming *Beau Geste* and *Knockback*. The Nothe has band concerts and the Nothe Gardens with picnic tables, barbecue facilities, a floodlit waterfall and Newton's Cove, which now has a new promenade and seawall as part of a scheme to stop housing and a DEFRA laboratory slipping into the sea as Nothe Clay slides over Nothe Grits, a scheme which was difficult because the contractor could only reach it from the beach at low tide. The Mixon, an underwater ridge, runs out towards a degaussing range after the Port of Weymouth gives way to Portland Port control.

An 11km/h speed limit restricts boat movements into Rodwell, observed by a lookout point above the beach and oystercatchers on the breakwater. In the distance are the chalk cliffs around Lulworth. It is possible to land on the small beach although parking is difficult at the best of times and this area does attract tourists, being one of the warmest and driest areas in the country. The nearest legal parking area is the car park for Brewer's Quay and the old part of **Weymouth**. Brewer's Quay has a narrow street close roofed over to form the old buildings into a shopping arcade, all tastefully done.

Weymouth Museum of Local History features paddle steamers, cross Channel ships, shipwrecks, fishing, George III's bathing machine of 1789, an 18th century fire engine, wartime relics, a Larret mackerel boat, an Armada treasure chest, a Roman pavement, coffin and skeleton and paintings by Hogarth and others. Deep Sea Adventure includes the *Titanic* and underwater exploration.

Trailable craft can take out at the northern end of Weymouth Bay.

Fort Nothe protects the approach to Portland Harbour.

Distance
17km from Abbotsbury to Rodwell

OS 1:50,000 Sheets
194 Dorchester & Weymouth

Admiralty Charts
2172 Harbours & Anchorages on S Coast of England.
Weymouth Harbour (1:5,000)
2255 Approaches to Portland & Weymouth (1:20,000)
2268 Portland Harbour (1:10,000)
2610 Bill of Portland to Anvil Pt (1:40,000)
2615 Bill of Portland to Needles (1:75,000)
3315 Berry Head to Bill of Portland (1:75,000)

Tidal Constants
Portland:
HW Dover −0440

Sea Area
Portland

Range
Chickerell firing range

Rescue
Inshore lifeboat:
Weymouth
All weather lifeboat:
Weymouth

65 River Exe

Clearing Exeter's blockages

Once those bells, those Exeter bells
Called her to praise and pray
By pink, acacia-shaded walls
Several times a day
To Wulfric's altar and riddel posts
While the choir sang Stanford in A.
John Betjeman

The River Exe rises on Exmoor just 8km from the Bristol Channel but, perversely, flows south to the English Channel.

It becomes tidal at Countess Wear, built around Henry III's time by Isabella de Fortibus, Countess of Devon, with a 9m gap for shipping. In 1284 the gap was blocked by the Earl of Devon to prevent ships reaching Exeter, requiring them to offload at Topsham and pay duty to himself. In 1563, having removed the blockage but not having recovered a satisfactory navigation channel, the merchants of Exeter bypassed the problem with the Exeter Canal, the oldest locked canal in the country.

Another bypass goes over the top, the old Exeter bypass, Britain's most notorious summer traffic bottleneck until the coming of the M5 which passes over the next bridge. The bypass bridge has strong eddies and standing waves downstream at certain states of the tide.

The small channels on the lefthand bank on either side of the bridge were the site of a shipbuilding yard in the 18th century. Vessels of up to 600t were built and launched here. As the river was unsuitable for conventional launchings a system evolved whereby ships were raised on floating casks, chained to kegs and towed out to deeper waters. Present day boatyards exist further downstream.

There was also a glassworks here in the 18th century, using coal mined from a spot on the present university campus.

A sewage works between the two bridges produces disconcerting upwellings of effluent from the river bed. In this area moorings commence.

Two reed covered islands have such birds as the avocet and landing is not permitted.

Topsham is steeped in maritime and local shipbuilding history, dating back to Roman times. It sent more ships to catch cod off Newfoundland than any other port did. Many of the houses surrounding the Passage Inn are of Dutch styling, having been built from bricks carried as ballast by ships returning from the Low Countries. A passenger ferry operates across the river towards Exminster. From the church steps beside the public slipway there are splendid panoramic views across the Haldon Hills and estuary.

Out on the estuary, the deep water channel meanders between mud banks which gradually give way to sand. The Turf Inn, designed by James Green, marks the southern end of the Exeter Canal with its curved wooden lock gates. When first finished, the canal stopped just

The River Exe at Countess Wear.

The end of the Exeter Canal at Turf.

Powderham's other castle.

Red cliffs at Lympstone.

below Countess Wear but was later extended to the present point.

Automatic gunfire is heard from ranges at barracks in Exton.

Peters Tower on the shore at Lympstone is a clocktower in polychrome brick, reminiscent of St Mark's in Venice, built in 1885 by Liverpool merchant William Peters as a memorial to his wife, Mary Jane.

Starcross Yacht Club at Powderham is the oldest active British yacht club, having had its first regatta in 1772.

Powderham Castle stands in its deer park. Although most of it was built in 1760–1860, some dates back to 1390 and it has been owned by the Courtenay family for the whole of this period and is still owned by the Earl of Devon. It has much family history and treasures by West Country craftsmen, marble fireplaces, Stuart and Regency furniture and French china, together with a Captain Bligh exhibition and an annual historical vehicle gathering in July. At the top of the park stands a tower which looks much more like a castle should. Further back, the Haldon Belvedere tower can be seen, built in memory of General Lawrence Stringer, known in his day as the Father of the Indian Army.

The harbour at Lympstone nestles between two red sandstone outcrops. Beyond them A la Ronde can be seen, a strange 16 sided house of 1795 around an octagonal hall, based on the church of San Vitale in Ravenna, with a Regency eggshell gallery and collections based on pastimes and hobbies of the period including sand and seaweed collages and paper silhouettes. It was built for two spinsters on their return from a grand tour of Europe.

Starcross has a tower and accompanying building in Italianate style. One of Brunel's biggest failures, this is the only remaining pumping station of the ten which powered his atmospheric railway between Exeter and Totnes. Trains were pulled by pistons drawn along a tube by a vacuum but the scheme failed because of leaking valves and rodent damage to the leather seals. Like with his *Great Eastern*, this was an occasion when Brunel was ahead of his time.

Nearby fencing incorporates rail from his broad gauge railway.

A passenger ferry runs across to Exmouth, past flocks of wading birds and banks of mussels. **Exmouth** is one of the oldest seaside resorts in England. Despite its sandy beach and its safe bathing, it does have a substantial seawall to face winter storms and there is a dangerous area where the water swirls out past Pole Sands, the intertidal part of Dawlish Warren. The Point was the normal landing place for raiders, including the Celts and Romans. It was burned by the Danes under King Sweyn in 1001. One of the principal Devon ports by 1199, it sent 10 ships and 190 men to Calais for Edward III. It was Royalist in the Civil War, was a busy port in the early 16th century and was used as a base by Sir Walter Raleigh. In the 17–19th centuries it was subject to attacks by Algerian and Tunisian pirates. The resort use began in 1720 with largescale development from 1792.

Coastal ships enter the small harbour under a lifting bridge in an area surrounded by shanty huts. Further on these are replaced by beach huts. *Caroline Finch*, the Exmouth lifeboat, is moored off the Point. The Beach and Deer Leap cater for tourists.

The Maer has various amusements for children and the largest 00 gauge model railway complex in the world. The 4ha Maer nature reserve has 400 flowering plant species.

The River Exe ebbs to 8km/h and floods to 7km/h in the channels when banks are uncovered. The sea breaks across the entrance in southerly or southwesterly gales and sandbanks move. Pole Sand spit reaches nearly to Orcombe Point while the spit of Dawlish Warren reaches nearly to Exmouth and has a 2km^2 nature reserve, a low spit running from Warren Point, now half the width it was in the 18th century. It is noted for 180 bird species including blacktailed godwits, greenshanks, curlews, sandpipers and winter migrants, amongst them Brent geese with up to 20,000 birds at a time present. Plants include the sand crocus, which only opens in April when the sun is shining. There are a wind generator and a golf course.

Surf may be found off Dawlish Warren with easterly winds. There are chalets and a visitor centre at the root of the spit, used as a sandy resort with go karts and a safe beach for children. There is parking nearby but it is busy in the summer.

Distance
12km from Countess
Wear to Exmouth

OS 1:50,000 Sheets
192 Exeter
& Sidmouth

Admiralty Charts
2290 R Exe &
Approaches inc Exeter
Canal (1:12,500).
Exmouth Dock
(1:2,500)
3315 Berry Head
to Bill of Portland
(1:75,000)

Tidal Constants
Topsham:
HW Dover −0440
Starcross:
HW Dover −0440
Exmouth Dock:
HW Dover −0450,
LW Dover −0500
Exmouth
Approaches:
HW Dover −0500,
LW Dover −0530

Sea Area
Portland

Rescue
Inshore lifeboat:
Exmouth
All weather lifeboat:
Exmouth

Exmouth, seen from Dawlish Warren.

66 River Dart

Heart of oak

River Dart, Oh River of Dart!
Every year thou claimest a heart.
Anon

Totnes Castle just visible from the River Hems.

The name means the river where oaks grow and there are plenty of them around the valley which was recently drowned by submergence. Steep wooded crags rise above what is one of England's most beautiful rivers flowing through the South Hams AONB to a Heritage Coast.

Like the River Taw, the East Dart, the longest of its headwaters, rises on Hangingstone Hill on Dartmoor but flows southeast across Devon to Start Bay.

The River Dart leads out of Totnes.

An excursion boat ascends the heavily wooded river.

The longest tidal arm is the River Hems, officially tidal from the railway bridge above Totnes although flows can go higher towards the sewage works. The Paddington to Penzance railway had tight curves and steep gradients to the northeast, difficult for the underpowered heavy engines of the day, so Brunel built the line for atmospheric operation. The system was abandoned after a few months, the pumping station at Totnes then being used as a creamery.

On the other side of the main line is the terminus of what is now the South Devon Railway or Primrose Line from Buckfastleigh, possessing the only surviving broad gauge engine.

The brook is narrow and twisty with shingle rapids at the railway bridge, lined with reeds and Michaelmas daisies and with willow trees which don't quite block it with their branches. Mats of dead reeds float up and down with the fast flow while the kingfisher feels at home. There is a low pipe across and a disused accommodation bridge which does not leave much headroom at the top of the tide.

The River Dart itself is much wider, tidal from above the railway where the tidal flows are interrupted by a large weir with a fish ladder down its left side and a diagonal concrete rib down the other, reminiscent of the large weirs on the Exe above Exeter.

Totnes had Saxon origins and parts of the Saxon walls remain. Two bridges cross the river, the A381 and the lowest bridge on the Dart, the 1828 three arched town centre bridge with the foundations of a 13th century bridge alongside and a rapid at low water. The town grew rich on the cloth trade. The 14th century castle with its shell keep by Iudhael has an oval bailey on a tall Norman motte, one of the best surviving early Norman motte and bailey castles, compromised only by having cottages built in the moat. The 15th century church of St Mary has a 37m sandstone tower, one of the last 60 remaining medieval stone pulpits and a Beer stone rood screen which is one of the best in England. Totnes Museum is housed in a fine restored Elizabethan merchant's house of 1575 featuring a Tudor herb garden, history, archaeology and 19th century computer pioneer Babbage, who went to school in the town. The 1553 guildhall, formerly the refectory of a Benedictine priory, has a prison cell, stocks and mantrap and the Tudor Butterwalk on granite columns overhangs the street. Leech Wells supplied a leper hospital. Totnes has long had a reputation for alternative lifestyles so natural medicines, spiritual healing and other smells and bells products are conspicuous in the shops. During the summer, local people can be seen in Tudor costumes on Tuesdays. A monument recalls that a local resident was William Wills, who took part in the first south–north crossing of Australia. The Brutus Stone is where a Trojan or Roman garrison leader is said to have stood after landing to give the town's name in English verse, later capturing local giants Gog and Magog to guard his palace in London. More plausible are Defoe's reminiscences of 3.0–3.7m tides, salmon taken from a fish trap at the Victorian Town Mill with the help of a dog and a school of pilchards being driven up to Totnes by porpoises. There are still salmon but seals are more likely to be the mammals.

The river can flow to 13km/h but there are moorings in the river. Moorhens, mallards and swans are resident. Opposite the popular Steam Packet Inn is the Steamer Quay, from where a passenger ferry runs to Dartmouth in the summer. There are steps up to a car park, toilets and a

Stoke Gabriel on a dammed inlet.

large playground galleon for those who want to play boats without getting wet.

Many of the buildings date from the Middle Ages, when it was one of England's most flourishing ports because of tin and wool exports. There are a number of new buildings on the riverbank above Baltic Wharf but the town still takes ships to 750t, importing Russian and Scandinavian timber at high water although the tide ebbs to reveal much soft mud. It was here that the ill fated *Team Phillips* catamaran was built.

Home Reach begins straight like an aquatic avenue with seats, picnic tables and regularly spaced trees. There are cormorants, egrets, Canada geese and buzzards, patches of floating scum showing where the tide has lifted flotsam off the mudbanks. Fleet Mill Reach and Sharpham Reach take the river into deep valley with high wooded sides. Only the mudbanks prevent it from looking like a scaled up equivalent of the best reach on the Thames at Cliveden. Among the trees is Sharpham Wood heronry. On top is Sharpham House, built in 1770 by Sir Robert Taylor, surrounded by its garden and 5.7ha of Sharpham Vineyard, also a source of cheese.

Gas bubbles up profusely from the covered silt. Beyond Ham Point, Ham Reach receives Hackney Creek and there is a wreck before Ashprington Point. Duncannon Reach leads to Stoke Point, opposite which is Bow Creek. Parties of customers in large Voyageur canoes tour the estuary from Tuckenhay and are often seen on this part of the river as they view the stunning scenery. At Mill Point a creek leads down from Stoke Gabriel, its upper part dammed as a millpond. The 15th century church accompanies a 13th century tower and an enormous yew tree which is over a millennium old. An ancient custom in the village is the orchard wassail in January.

Pighole Point has tree branches hanging down the low red rock cliffs towards a shoreline of wrack, explored by herring and blackbacked gulls and oystercatchers. Opposite is Dittisham Mill Creek.

The Devonian volcanic lavas which have directed the course of the river since Totnes now give way to softer slates but the scenery does not let up. There are some well placed waterside houses as the river widens out and it can give heavy seas with rough weather although that does not prevent its use for extensive moorings. Waddeton shellfisheries are by Galmpton Creek which was used for building highly respected Brixham trawlers, being 1.7km from Tor Bay by land although rather further by water.

Dittisham, its church with a Norman font and carved pulpit, is noted for its plums and cider. A small passenger ferry, well dressed with bunting to make it more conspicuous, crosses to Greenway Quay.

Towards Vipers Quay is the Anchor Stone in the river, to which unfaithful wives were tied.

Greenway House was the birthplace of Sir Humphrey Gilbert who claimed Newfoundland in 1583 for Elizabeth I. It may have been here that a servant tried to extinguish his half brother, Sir Walter Raleigh, who was indulging in the unknown activity of smoking a pipe of tobacco. Until 1976 it was the home of Agatha Christie, the world's best selling fiction author, who had her summerhouse with semi hardy plants and wild flowers beneath.

At the back the Paignton & Dartmouth Railway emerges from a tunnel and passes over Greenway Viaduct before completing its journey to Kingswear along the left bank of the river. Opened in 1864 by the GWR, it was

Idyllic isolated waterside setting opposite Dittisham.

Below the Paignton & Dartmouth Steam Railway at Maypool.

used by Christie for Hercule Poirot's investigations in *Dead Man's Folly* and *The ABC Murders*.

A boatyard and a marina are located at Higher Noss Point but the 1980s plans to expand it to a 8.9ha port came to nothing. Opposite is Old Mill Creek. The area is

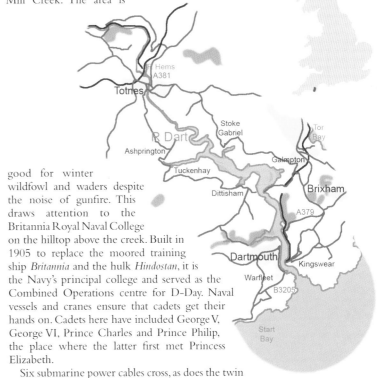

good for winter wildfowl and waders despite the noise of gunfire. This draws attention to the Britannia Royal Naval College on the hilltop above the creek. Built in 1905 to replace the moored training ship *Britannia* and the hulk *Hindostan*, it is the Navy's principal college and served as the Combined Operations centre for D-Day. Naval vessels and cranes ensure that cadets get their hands on. Cadets here have included George V, George VI, Prince Charles and Prince Philip, the place where the latter first met Princess Elizabeth.

Six submarine power cables cross, as does the twin

A steam train approaches Kingswear past extensive moorings.

wire cable Higher Ferry for the A379. Rennie originally proposed a suspension bridge but this was opposed by a landowner so he built his first chain ferry, the Floating Bridge according to the name of a local public house.

There are extensive moorings on the river, the enclosed Boat Float lagoon in the centre of **Dartmouth** and a marina at Kingswear with the Resnova floating inn. One of the busiest recreational sailing ports on the south coast with the Royal Dart Yacht Club and the Dartmouth Yacht Club, it is also a fishing port. It was used by the Normans and was to be one of the nation's chief ports. Richard the Lionheart departed from here for his Second and Third Crusades during the 12th century, at which time Dartmouth was importing claret. It was handling the Bordeaux wine trade in the 14th century, when St Saviour's church was built with its fine rood screen, painting of the *Widow's Son*, two iron beasts guarding the Tree of Life and an ancient manual fire engine. Dartmouth quay was built in the 1580s. Nine ships were sent to fight the Armada and the first captured Spanish galleon was returned here. The Pilgrim Fathers visited in 1620 to have repairs undertaken on the *Mayflower* and *Speedwell*. Dartmouth Museum, in the 17th century

Butterwalk, is located in a merchant's house of the 1630s, where Charles II held court in 1671 while stormbound. On columns over a trading area, it is one of the finest examples of Devon architecture and contains historic and maritime objects, pictures and photographs, more than 150 ship models and material on Drake, Raleigh and Gilbert, who were visitors.

Local ironmonger Thomas Newcomen invented the atmospheric steam engine. A 1711 model is believed to be the world's oldest example, having been used in a Dudley coalmine at first and then in a pumping station to feed the Coventry Canal at Hawkesbury Junction before being returned here in 1963. The 560mm diameter vertical condensing cylinder has a 3.7m rocker beam with chains leading over a quadrant at each end, working at one stroke every 5 seconds and pumping 95l per stroke.

In 1944, 485 vessels gathered here for D-Day. Naomi James undertook the first solo circumnavigation by a woman round Cape Horn from here in 1977/8.

There is a Dartmouth Music Festival, a carnival in June, Dartmouth Regatta in August and a fishing festival in September. The Royal Castle Hotel and the Station Restaurant (with no associated railway on this side of the river) are just two places of refreshment near the Boat Float.

Bayards Cove is the oldest part of town, used for filming *Kidnapped* and the BBC's *Onedin Line*, while *The French Lieutenant's Woman* was partly filmed at Kingswear, now gaining increasingly bright colourwashed houses, reminiscent of Tobermory. Another vehicle ferry connects parts of the B3205 and the Southwest Coast Path across the river.

The small Bearscove Castle was an artillery fort built in 1529 for Henry VIII to protect against Breton raids.

Beyond Warfleet Cove is One Gun Point, where the original riverbed now lies 25m below the surface at low water. A fortalice was built in the 14th century by Hawley, who inspired Chaucer's Shipman in *The Canterbury Tales*. Dartmouth merchants used its ruins to build Dartmouth Castle in 1481–93, its walls 2m thick, one of the first designed to withstand cannon impact. Kingswear Castle

The inner harbour at Dartmouth.

The Britannia Royal Naval College overlooks Dartmouth.

A mermaid seated beside steps at One Gun Point.

was built opposite in 1502 and the river could be closed by a 230m chain between the two, supported on six barges, the attachment ring still present at Kingswear Castle. St Petroc's church was attached in 1641 but the castle was not an ideal neighbour, changing hands twice in the Civil War which quickly followed. The Royal Artillery used to practise firing across the river to Kingswear. Dartmouth Castle had Victorian gun battery positions added and there was a Second World War blockhouse.

White coastguard cottages stand above the lookout point and the start line for yacht races as they prepare to head out into Start Bay with Inner Froward Point to the east above Newfoundland Cove and Combe Point to the southwest with Start Point far beyond.

Many of Kingswear's houses are now colourwashed.

Distance
17km from Totnes to Start Bay

OS 1:50,000 Sheets
202 Torbay &
South Dartmoor

Admiralty Charts
1634 Salcombe to Brixham (1:25,000)
2253 Dartmouth Harbour (1:6,250).
R Dart – to Blackness Pt (1:6,250). R Dart – Blackness Pt to Totnes (1:12,500)
3315 Berry Head to Bill of Portland (1:75,000)

Tidal Constants
Totnes:
HW Dover −0510,
LW Dover −0450
Greenway Quay:
HW Dover −0500,
LW Dover −0520
Dartmouth:
HW Dover −0520,
LW Dover −0540

Sea Area
Plymouth

Rescue
Inshore lifeboat: Dart
All weather lifeboat:
Salcombe

Dartmouth Castle with St Petroc's church.

67 River Tamar

The border between Cornwall and England

Drake he's in his hammock till the great Armadas come,
(Capten, art tha sleepin' there below?),
Slung atween the round shot, listenin' for the drum,
An' dreamin' arl the time o' Plymouth Hoe.
Call him on the deep sea, call him up the Sound,
Call him when ye sail to meet the foe;
Where the old trade's plyin' an' the old flag flyin'
They shall find him ware an' wakin', as they found him long ago!
Sir Henry Newbolt

Named after the goddess Tamara, the River Tamar rises at West Youlstone, just 5km from Marsland Mouth on the north coast. It flows south as the border between Cornwall and Devon to the English Channel although there are some Cornish who would still prefer to see it as the border between Celtic Cornwall and Saxon England. It is in danger of having its headwaters captured by the River Bude, which has already acquired the River Strat from the Tamar.

It is tidal from Weir Head at Gunnislake although any approach has to be from below. The weir is vertical onto a rock apron, nearly 2m high and stretching the full width of the river to create a dangerous enclosed stopper. There are two fish ladders, one with concrete bars across

The weir at the tidal limit at Gunnislake.

Morwell Wood on its high cliff.

the ends and the other with mesh bolted across the top, preventing it from being used as a chute. There are notices banning landing on either bank or on the island below the weir. Small weir steps appear when the tide drops, the one on the right still passable by small craft.

The upper valley is AONB and it is Special Protection Area to Hooe and the banks to Saltash with Special Area of Conservation elsewhere. A drowned valley, it has much mud as the tide drops. There are salmon and sea and freshwater trout. Much of the upper tidal river has high banks, covered with deciduous trees.

Gunnislake was the centre of a copper, tin and arsenic mining area. A disused lock was part of the Tamar Manure Navigation, to which there is access but no parking in the vicinity.

Cormorants, herons and kingfishers are present. The river appears to meander excessively but in these upper reaches it is much restrained by high land. Morwell Rocks form a 60m cliff, at the foot of which the river makes a sharp turn. The view from Morwell Wood at the top was popular with Victorians.

Morwellham Quay was claimed to be the 'greatest copper port in Queen Victoria's Empire' by 1868 and was the busiest inland port in Devon and Cornwall during the 19th century, accepting craft to 200t, the 1908 ketch *Garlandstone* of 150t, formerly at Porthmadog, helping to give some idea of scale. This was also the port for Tavistock. The George & Charlotte Copper Mine was founded a millennium ago by monks. Blanchdown Woods had the richest copper deposits in Europe. The site is now one of the most popular tourist attractions in the southwest, run by Victorian costumed staff and including wharves, a railway, mine wagons, a waterwheel, limekilns, manganese ore crushing stones, a chapel, a 60ha farm and a wildlife reserve. A 72m high inclined plane, the highest in southern England, linked the quay to the Devon Great Consols Mine at Blanchdown and the Tavistock Canal built by French prisoners of war. There is a power station and a tramway follows the riverbank into a mineshaft. Maddacleave Wood has a ruined quay which served limekilns. A mine chimney high on the ridge can be seen to lean significantly to the southeast when viewed from the southern side of this great river loop. After a sunken ship, which looks as if it might have been part of a film set, another chimney has an appearance of having been struck by lightning, its top split. Mine spoil is heaped on the bank and covered by greenery but an old stone building has been partially restored with modern styling to create an interesting architectural design.

The bank is reedy and clumps of reed float in the muddy water, which comes up with a fast flood. There are mallards but jays almost seem to be the commonest birds. Buttspill Mine produced lead and fluorspar and there was a ferry crossing here from Saxon times to the 1950s.

Calstock has a private floating jetty, leading up to the

Tamar Inn, a galleon climbing frame and a civic centre with a painting of the foreshore in 1900 on the end wall. The Calstock area has some of Cornwall's finest hill scenery but also had much commerce with 17 mines plus papermills, brickworks, tileworks, brewery, tannery, foundry, ropeworks, shipbuilders, granite quarries and cherry and other fruit growing. Copper was discovered in the 1770s, giving great prosperity until late in the 19th century. The Devon Great Consols Mine, started in 1845, was the richest coppermine in Europe in the two decades from 1850, employing 1,000 men and sending the copper to south Wales. Arsenic followed in the 1880s with over half the world's production, enough stored to poison the world's entire population. In the 19th century an alternate day stopping service to Devonport was run on the river with rivalry between the providers which ended up in court after a case of ramming in 1866. In 1774 there was a plan to build a Tamar Canal to Bude but it would have been 145km long to cover 45km as the crow flies. Instead, the dramatic structure of historic interest is the railway viaduct across the river. Built 1907, it was one of the earliest uses of precast concrete block construction, its dozen 18m span arches 33m above the ground. The Gunnislake to St Budeaux railway has difficulty following the contours. Trains creep down the hill from Bere Alston to the viaduct at low speed with their brakes applied for the greater part of the 2km. It bypasses the inclined plane serving the quay so the port went into decline although Calstock Boatyard is still active. Straight ahead is the 18th century Prospect Tower.

Cothele House, meaning wood on the estuary, was built from 1485 to 1627 in grey granite and slate with a timber ceiling in the great hall, one of the best examples of an early Tudor manor house and one of the least altered houses in England, not even having electric light. Owned by the Edgcumbe family for six centuries, it has tapestries, needlework, original furniture, armour, a medieval domed dovecote, a Victorian summerhouse, 19th century gardens, an Italian garden, a daffodil meadow garden, a deep valley, a stewpond, magnolias and acers. The chapel was built in 1483 by Sir Richard Edgcumbe in thanks for his escape. Being in league against the Crown, he was chased down the bank by Crown agents, threw his cap in the water and was thought to have drowned. The house has been used for filming *Twelfth Night* and the Travis video *Why Does it Always Rain on Me?*

Cothele Quay has 18/19th century buildings, an art and craft gallery, an 18th century watermill, a large cider press, wheelwright, blacksmith and carpentry workshops, old tools, limekilns and a slipway. An outstation of the National Maritime Museum, it also has the 17m ketch rigged *Shamrock* of 1899, the last Tamar sailing barge.

The disused North Hooe Mine extracted silver and

The ketch Garlandstone and mine trucks at Morwellham.

lead from 1290, employing 200 men and seven steam engines in 1852.

The largest loop on the river progresses it 400m in 4km. Halton Quay was one of the busiest on the river and the limekilns were the most impressive, in use until 1916. A chapel was established in an old coal store.

The mausoleum on Mount Ararat contains the atheist Sir James Tillie, who died in 1712, and was placed sitting in a chair fully dressed and with pipes, tobacco and liquor on the table in front of him, since being transferred to a coffin. The 18th century Gothic Pentillie Castle was built for him and Pentillie Quay used to offer refreshments to passing passengers although it is less welcoming these days.

An indication of the flood tide's importance being greater than that of the ebb is that the channels of tributary streams across the mud all point upstream as they join. Herring gulls and egrets take them as they come.

There are many moorings on the river as it straightens out. Hole's Hole had limekilns and served the mines and fruit and flower trades. Weir Quay took vessels to 400t and served silver and lead mines from 1290 with 18 furnaces smelting ore in the 19th century. Buzzards now nest here.

Cleave also had limekilns. Near overhead powerlines a chimney marks the site of the prosperous South Tamar silver and lead mine, abandoned in 1856 after the river broke through, fortunately on a Sunday evening so nobody was drowned. Between Clamoak Quay and Thorn Point

Filming an Edwardian Farm *episode at Morwellham Quay, using the boat* Idler *from Cothele.*

A mine chimney with a distinct list in Maddacleave Wood.

Calstock wall paiting showing the foreshore in 1900.

Calstock's dramatic railway viaduct.

Shamrock moored off Cothele House.

hoisting a red flag. In the 1830s Cargreen had a boatyard and a steam bone crushing mill but its glasshouses are now conspicuous.

Beyond another set of powerlines Weir Point faces the River Tavy confluence. The Danes sailed up the Tavy in the 10th century to burn Tavistock. Now the long Tavy Bridge carries the railway over the river and then, beyond Warleigh Point, another carries it over Tamerton Lake, opposite Kingsmill Lake.

Landulph had a ship fleet in the 15th century and was the port for pilgrims in the southwest wanting to go to Santiago de Compostella. The village was hit by the Black Death. The church contains the tomb of Theodore Paleologus, descended from the Christian emperors of Constantinople, who died at Clifton in 1636 but who had suffered very little decomposition when the tomb was opened 150 years later. A land reclamation project in the village failed financially and the relevant area reverted to the river.

Beyond Skinham Point is a golf course. The east bank has an industrial estate and then the Ernesettle Armaments Depot with an old battery site behind and a couple of large ribbed domes in the centre. There is a 50m exclusion zone around all naval establishments and moored craft, even when there is nothing to indicate ownership unless perhaps a notice too small to be read from 50m away. A red flag indicates that there are munitions aboard. This is a water skiing area and there can also be surf here up to 1m high.

The left bank becomes Plymouth just before the two famous bridges are reached. The first, replacing a ferry which had operated since the 13th century, is the Tamar suspension bridge carrying the A38 Devon Expressway. With a total length of 642m, it has a central span of 335m which was the longest central span of any suspension bridge in the country when built in 1961. It has a Warren truss deck and, in 1999, became the world's first major suspension bridge to be widened and strengthened simultaneously.

Faced with providing a railway crossing, Brunel considered a steam train ferry, a suspension bridge and a wooden viaduct but the Admiralty demanded more clearance. Finally he built the Royal Albert Bridge, also

are the marshes of Egypt Bay, Liphill Lake, Newpark Lake and Lodge Lake.

From Thorn Point causeway a ferry ran to Cargreen, Cornish for seal rock, summoned by

The Tamar and Saltash Bridges.

known as the Saltash Bridge, to carry the Penzance to Paddington railway. A clever design perhaps developed from a bridge design for St Petersburg, it has elliptical wrought iron arches 5.1m wide x 3.8m deep and also suspension using chains, half of which were originally made for the Clifton suspension bridge in Bristol. The thrust from the arches is counterbalanced by the tension in the suspension chains so that there are no anchorage requirements at the ends, where the bridge runs onto 17 tall masonry arches, and the line of the suspension wrought iron bar chains reflects the line of the arches. The central pier was built using one of the world's first compressed air caissons, the 300t Great Cylinder, Brunel's experience of compressed air work having been gained when he helped his father build the world's first tunnel with compressed air under the Thames at Wapping. It is out of line, giving a 2° dogleg in the centre of the bridge, which also bends with the heat of the day as the sun always heats the same side of the tubes. The two main spans are each 139m long and the total length 335m, giving 30m clearance for the single track bridge. It was built from 1847 to 1859, by which time Brunel was seriously ill. Unable to attend the opening, he inspected the bridge a few days later from his sick bed, towed by an engine across the bridge on a wagon.

Saltash is said to be the oldest borough in Cornwall. In the 12th and 13th centuries it exported tin and was the most important port between Dartmouth and Fowey. It has a 17th century guildhall and steep streets which lead down to the river. There are several prominent buildings on the bank, the Boatman, the Union Inn (painted with a historical mural on the end and a full size Union flag on the front) and the Livewire Youth Project (with a small mural of Brunel on the side and a full size painting on the front of Saltash in 1912). Oystercatchers, common gulls and swans wait to be fed by visitors. The railway crosses Coombe Bay on a viaduct and turns up the Lynher River.

The east bank is continuously built up from Riverside. Beyond Kinterbury Creek, Bull Point, the start of **Devonport** naval base, projects into the channel and the river becomes known as the Hamoaze until the Narrows.

Warships dock in Weston Mill Lake and along the riverfront with enclosed docks behind. The Royal Dockyard was founded in 1691 and is home to half the Royal Navy's submarines and ships, the largest naval base in western Europe although now somewhat reduced and privately run. The Covered Slip of 1763 is the nation's oldest covered slipway. Quays run for 6km with 15 drydocks and 25 berths covering 2.6km². The docks handle aircraft carriers, cruisers, destroyers and nuclear submarines with many boats built here.

The west shore is less regular. Wilcove Lake, beyond Looking Glass, has a road awash at high water. An oil jetty runs out to the fairway from Yonderbury Point with its tanks. Thanckes Lake fronts **Torpoint** with its vehicle ferries. The main crossing point to Cornwall until 1961, it still forms an important link on the A374 and is still free of charge. The ferry began in 1791 with James Rendel introducing the chain ferry in 1835, 5t weights tensioning the chains in order to handle the fast current.

St John's Lake drains to leave extensive tidal marshes and saltings, popular with waders and wildfowl including wintering avocets. HMS Raleigh and a range are located on the northern edge but the attempt to build a 2GW coal fired power station there was unsuccessful.

A public slip is hidden in Mutton Cove at the start of the Mayflower International Marina. Luxury Princess cruisers are built beyond the jetty to which a passenger ferry runs from Cremyll and they tend to be moored along the front of the marina for final adjustments. The Royal William Victualling Yard has many industrial buildings from the 1830s but is being redeveloped for leisure use. At

The unmissable Union Inn. The adjacent Livewire arts centre has a painting of Saltash in about 1912. Each has murals of the local history.

Submarines moored at Devonport.

the end of the site is Devil's Point where Drake is said to have sold his soul to the Devil in return for wind to drive the Spaniards away. It is claimed he whittled a stick on a cliff, each flake turning into an armed ship on hitting the water. Arthur Conan Doyle worked close by as a doctor. The peninsula ends with Western King Point, beyond which are an old tower and a silo.

Beyond the entrance to Millbrook Lake and Empacombe with its windpump is Cremyll with the Edgcumbe Arms in a prime position to watch all the activity. Wilderness Point has to have a blockhouse and battery, firing onto the Narrows where currents run to 6km/h across to Devil's Point.

At the back of Barn Pool is Mount Edgcumbe Country Park. The Tudor Mount Edgcumbe House was built in 1547 by Adrian Gilbert Scott and would have become the residence of Don Alonso Perez do Guzman, Duke of Sidona, if the Armada had been successful. It was a Royalist garrison in the Civil War but the serious damage was done in 1941 when it was incendiary bombed, being restored in 1960. The earliest landscaped park in Cornwall, it has some of Britain's best Grade I gardens in 3.5km² of deer park, including French, Italian, American, New Zealand and Jubilee gardens, the national camellia collection, daffodils, chestnut trees, an orangery, Milton's Temple, a ruined folly and a shell grotto. It was used for filming *Twelfth Night*.

From the Bridge at Raveness Point a ridge runs out to Drake's or St Nicholas' Island. It is a diving area but also popular for naval exercises involving inflatables and landing craft. The island has a medieval prison, Tudor, Stuart and both World Wars' fortifications, tunnels, store rooms, an oubliette, an aerial and the only sandy beach in Plymouth Sound. It is where Sir Francis Drake stopped after the first English world circumnavigation to check the political situation before making his formal landing and it is where Cromwell's General Lambert was imprisoned for many years.

Across the Drake Channel, the deep water approach to the Tamar, is **Plymouth**, from the

Mutton Cove, the Mayflower International Marina and the Royal William Victualling Yard.

Distance
30km from
Gunnislake to
Cawsand Bay

OS 1:50,000 Sheets
201 Plymouth
& Launceston

Admiralty Charts
30 Plymouth Sound
& Approaches to
Hamoaze (1:12,500)
871 Rs Tamar, Lynher
& Tavy (1:12,500).
R Tamar – Cargreen
to Calstock
(1:12,500). Calstock
to Gunnislake
(1:20,000)
1267 Falmouth to
Plymouth (1:75,000)
1613 Eddystone
Rocks to Berry Head
(1:75,000)
1900 Whitsand Bay
to Yealm Head inc
Plymouth Sound
(1:25,000)
1901 Smeaton Pass &
Narrows (1:5,000)
1902 Hamoaze
to Ernesettle Pier
(1:5,000)

Tidal Constants
Weir Head:
HW Dover −0500
Cothele Quay:
HW Dover −0530,
LW Dover −0500
Cargreen:
HW Dover −0540,
LW Dover −0520
Saltash: Dover −0540
Plymouth:
Dover −0540

Sea Area
Plymouth

Rescue
Inshore lifeboat:
Plymouth
All weather lifeboat:
Plymouth

Old English plym tun, plum tree village. It is now the largest city in Devon, primarily built of grey limestone, and is the most famous port in seafaring history. Fleets were assembled here in 1294–7 against the French although the Bretons returned and burnt it in 1402. It was chartered in 1439. It was from here, one of the chief ports of Elizabeth I, that Drake defeated the Armada in 1588 after finishing his game of bowls on the Hoe, meaning high ground, and leading to the landing of a six figure sum in Spanish plunder in the 1590s.

Drake is claimed to be sleeping and will rise again in England's hour of need when his drum is beaten. Drake's drum went round the world with him and is now in Buckfast Abbey. It growled when Napoleon was brought to Devon after Waterloo on his way to St Helena, it was heard at the start of the First World War, it was heard on board the *Ark Royal* when the Germans surrendered at Scapa Flow in 1918 and it was heard during the retreat from Dunkirk during the Second World War.

Plymouth was the last port of call for the Pilgrim Fathers, who abandoned the *Speedwell* here as unseaworthy. It was the destination in 1919 for the US Navy/Curtiss flying boat which undertook the first transatlantic flight from New York via the Azores. It was also the startline for transatlantic races and the legendary 1968/9 Golden Globe, the world's first round the world race, won by Robin Knox-Johnston after Bernard Moitessier abandoned the lead to sail off to Tahiti and second placed Donald Crowhurst committed suicide.

In 1646 the town supported Parliament and held out against the Siege of Plymouth so Charles II sited the Royal Citadel to control the town. Built from 1665 with 6.1m thick walls, it is now the home of 29 Commando Royal Artillery.

Smeaton's Tower was preassembled in Millbay in 1756, an original shape based upon the trunk of an oak tree, before being moved out to the Eddystone Rocks. The Portland stone blocks were faced in granite, dovetailed and joined with Smeaton's quick drying lime and pozzolana mortar. When the rock foundations on which

it was built became unsafe in 1884 it was brought back and erected on the Hoe as a monument.

Millbay Docks were designed by Brunel in 1856, now partly infilled but the departure point for vehicle ferries to Roscoff and Santander.

The dockyard made Plymouth the target for particularly heavy bombing in 1940/1, tens of thousands of bombs hitting 22,000 houses, 40 churches and 20 schools. The redesign, with Armada Way as the central thoroughfare, solved the congestion problems but it is felt that the postwar architecture is now overdue for replacing with buildings having a bit more character.

Viscountess Astor became the first woman MP, representing the city in 1919. It was the birthplace of Scott of the Antarctic and explorers from here have founded 40 other Plymouths around the world. Those sailing from here have included William and Sir John Hawkins, James Cook, Sir Humphrey Gilbert, Charles Darwin, Raleigh, Bligh and, in 1968, Sir Francis Chichester for the first solo circumnavigation of the world.

The Devonian limestone headland offers one of the finest promenades in Europe, apparently the canoodling capital, passing a statue of Drake, an RAF memorial and a dome for visitors. *Wycliffe* was filmed here.

At the other end of what is also a fishing port is Cattewater, the estuary of the River Plym, contained by Mount Batten Point with its breakwater and tower.

The fairway heads across to the northeastern corner of the sound and then cuts across to the Western Channel, used by oil tankers, cargo ships, yachts taking part in international races and warships, smaller boats being cleared from in front of nuclear submarines, submarines sometimes towing sonar equipment as much as 1.5km behind.

Picklecombe Fort has been converted to apartments with their own marina and views over Cawsand Bay and out to the breakwater. Plymouth Breakwater provides defence against the weather and enemy shipping. Built in 1812–40 by Rennie, it contains 3,600,000t of stone on a reef and is 1.6km long. Limestone and granite blocks weighing up to 7t are dovetailed. In 60m of water, the top has no protective wall but its summit is 600mm above high water, 12m across the top with mass blocks on the forward slope. There is a granite refuge and beacon at the east end, a fort in the centre and a granite lighthouse at the west end. It does what it needs to do and no more.

Plymouth Sound and its breakwater.

68 Lynher River

A quiet backwater with important influences

The estuary is called the St Germans or Lynher River yet St Germans is not on the River Lynher. It is on the tributary with the longer tidal flow, the River Tiddy, which runs southeast across Cornwall to the River Tamar, some of it through AONB. The river is a Special Protection Area to Erth Hill, as are the shores to Jupiter Point, and the rest is Special Area of Conservation, including much low tide mud.

The River Tiddy is tidal from a minor road bridge at Tideford but this is surrounded by private gardens and even approach from downstream involves passing several trees which have fallen across the river. It begins narrow and twists through overhanging long grass and sedges, accompanied by moorhens, mallards, pheasants and buzzards, initially with the A38 close by. There was a time when lime was shipped from here to Plymouth. The river makes successive attempts to breach a steep wooded hill on the southwest side without success.

The first significant change is at St Germans with Port Eliot House on the site of a priory. The ornamental garden was laid out in 1792 by Humphrey Repton, including diverting the river round the lawn. The home is still occupied by the Eliots. The Augustinian priory and cathedral church of Cornwall were built in about 1066 on the 926 site of a Saxon cathedral and feature twin towers, a huge west door with one of the best Norman doorways in existence and a Burne Jones and William Morris east window. This is the largest parish in Cornwall, the seat of the bishops of Cornwall from 926 to 1043. The name may come from Germanus, bishop of Auxerre.

Above St Germans occasional outcrops of clay are left.

One chair has a carving of Dando, a 14th century priest from the priory who went hunting with friends one Sunday morning instead of attending to his worship. The hunt was successful so he called for a drink and was handed an ornamented horn by a stranger on a fiery black horse, who then stole his game. Dando said he would go to Hell to recover it. The stranger agreed, threw him across his horse and rode off with his hounds, all heading into the river and disappearing with a hiss of flames and steam.

There are 16th century galleried almshouses close by.

Brunel had eight standard designs for railway bridges but took the Penzance to Paddington railway across the river on a high viaduct which was not to one of those designs.

St Germans Quay is controlled by Quay Sailing Club, who do not allow vehicle access. In the 19th century it

The railway viaduct at St Germans.

Looking from Sheviock Wood to St Germans Quay.

Erth Hill is a prominent feature of the estuary.

exported tin, copper and lead, importing coal, timber and limestone. There are limekilns close by. In 1777 and in 1800 there were plans for a link with the proposed Liskeard & Looe Union Canal.

An owl sanctuary is sited between Polbathic Lake and Sconner Lake, the latter opposite the junction with the River Lynher, which joins from the north. Marshes have oystercatchers, shelducks, swans, waders and wildfowl including avocets.

The grandest stretch of trees is Sheviock Wood, recorded in *Domesday* and having sheltered smugglers. The trees reach to the wrack covered shoreline. Above is an earthwork. There was a ford across the river to Erth Barton but there is no longer any sign of that.

Deer run over Erth Hill, a great rounded hump which rises from Redshank Point and looks less forbidding for being farmed.

Wacker Lake, behind Warren Point, formerly had a tide mill, a tramway and a cable incline from the quay which was built to receive Gunnislake granite to build Scraesdon and Tregantle Forts for Palmerston to defend Devonport. It became a railway to carry supplies and 230mm shells to Tregantle, used until 1904 with a locomotive shed by the quay and the incline visible next to the road.

Beyond Tredown Lake is Black Rock where a slip is used to launch small boats.

Antony's church was rededicated in 1269, enlarged in 1420 and has a full length brass of 1429 to Lady Margery Arundell. Another memorial is on the hillside above Clift.

The 16th century Ince Castle was the first brick house in Cornwall, with a shell house, magnolias and camellias. Its notable location is on a small headland overlooking Wivelscombe Lake. Further up the inlet is Wivelscombe

with a monument. Shillingham Manor, with its ancient chapel, overlooks Shillingham Point.

Cormorants, egrets and herons ignore warships anchored in the river. There used to be a ferry to Antony Passage and a tide mill although its four wheels have now gone. At the head of Forder Lake are the ruins of Trematon Castle, owned by the Earldom then the Duchy of Cornwall since 1275. Forder produced blue elvan roadstone.

Jupiter Point is in the hands of HMS Raleigh, their wide slip handling a range of small military craft. It is approached past Antony House. The house site has been used since the 15th century and is where Richard Carew wrote his *Survey of Cornwall* in 1602, the Carew Pole family still being resident after five centuries. The current Queen Anne mansion was built in 1711–21 in grey Pentewan stone with original panelling, fine 18th century furniture, family portraits by Sir John Reynolds (including the one of Rachel Carew which inspired Daphne du Maurier's *My Cousin Rachel*), excellent books, tapestries, needlework, china and a garden by Repton with an 18th century dovecote and the national day lilies collection. It was used for filming *Alice in Wonderland*. Adjacent is the Woodland Garden with a 1784 bath house, magnolias, rhododendrons, acers, azaleas and the national collection of *Camellia japonica*.

Above Wearde Quay is the cottage of Mary Newman, the first wife of Sir Francis Drake, a rare small 15th century medieval house with Armada roses. Opposite is Carew Point at the end of the Carew domain. Ahead is the Hamoaze with naval vessels of all sizes anchored and, on the far side, Bull Point.

The Lynher River is surprisingly inaccessible, such that Saltash is perhaps the best place to launch to be free of problems of mud and private property.

Distance
12km from Tideford to the River Tamar

OS 1:50,000 Sheets
201 Plymouth & Launceston

Admiralty Charts
*871 Rs Tamar, Lynher & Tavy (1:12,500).
R Lynher (1:20,000)
1267 Falmouth to Plymouth (1:75,000)
1613 Eddystone Rocks to Berry Head (1:75,000)
1902 Hamoaze to Ernesettle Pier (1:5,000)*

Tidal Constants
*St Germans:
HW Dover −0540,
LW Dover −0520
Jupiter Point:
HW Dover −0530,
LW Dover −0540
Saltash: Dover −0540*

Sea Area
Plymouth

Rescue
*Inshore lifeboat:
Plymouth
All weather lifeboat:
Plymouth*

Trematon Castle looks down over a railway viaduct to Antony Passage.

HMS Raleigh at Jupiter Point.

69 River Fowey

Calling the shots in Cornish tin and sailing

O the Harbour of Fowey
Is a beautiful spot,
And it's there I enjowey
To sail in a yot;
Or to race in a yacht
Round a mark or a buoy –
Such a beautiful spacht
Is the Harbour of Fuoy!

Sir Arthur Quiller-Couch

From between Maiden Tor and Buttern Hill on High Moor the River Fowey flows southwest across Cornwall to the English Channel. In a drowned valley, it is all AONB to a Heritage Coast.

It is tidal from the A390 at **Lostwithiel** although most boats are launched from the one way system below the old bridge carrying the B3268 because of the shallow gravel rapids and the access difficulties further up. The Norman Great Bridge of Lostwithiel was first mentioned in 1280. In 1437 the western five pointed arches of the present bridge were built and were nearly blown up in 1644. Four more arches were added in the 18th century to better accommodate a channel which had been dug to the east to form an island above the bridge in the 16th century. An Ancient Monument, it is 3.5 to 4.5m wide between the parapets, with no footway but pedestrian refuges above the cutwaters. In 2010 it was at risk of collapse during floods.

Lostwithiel was the capital of Cornwall in the 13th century, a stannary town, the second most important south coast town to Southampton and still a great port in the 16th century. It continued to administer the Cornish tin industry until 1752. The administrative centre was the Old Duchy Palace of about 1280, sacked and burned by the Parliamentarians in 1644. The 14th century church of St Bartholomew, the patron saint of tinners, has lean to aisles and a clerestory, unusual in Cornwall, but was used for stabling horses in 1644. A museum and the Guildhall are of interest.

There are limekilns by the former quay opposite the Cornwall Railway's disused carriage and wagon works. The Paddington to Penzance railway, which has followed the valley from Doublebois, now crosses and moves away although the line to Fowey has mostly been retained

The Great Bridge of Lostwithiel, in existence by 1280.

for china clay traffic and follows the right bank closely. A slipway by the railway bridge helps boats too big to carry.

By 1400 the river had become silted up by tin mining tailings and there is extensive mud at low tide to Golant. However, it remains an exceptionally popular river for touring canoes with clear water over the mud.

Across Madderly and Shirehall Moors the river is edged by alders, sedges, Michaelmas daisies and reeds and shared with swans, moorhens, kingfishers, mallards and blackbacked and herring gulls.

Beyond powerlines is Lantyan which Béroul had as the palace of King Mark. Queen Iseult is supposed to have met Tristan below by the river. St Winnow is perhaps the most beautiful spot on the river. The Perpendicular church, important in the Middle Ages and with a peal of six bells, is on the riverbank and the church was used for filming *Poldark*. Sir Arthur Quiller-Couch used to row his family up for services. The hamlet developed the St Neots slate trade as Lostwithiel declined and there is a museum.

Beyond Lantyan Wood is Woodgate Pill on the right while the River Lerryn joins on the left after St Winnow Point, smothered by Great Wood and used as the French River Odet in filming *Poldark*. Overlooking these confluences is Penquite where Italian

St Winnow is difficult to reach with the tide out because of mud.

Penquite quay, small but ornate.

The railway embankment forms a harbour wall for Golant.

freedom fighter Giuseppe Garibaldi was hosted in 1864 by Colonel Peard, Garibaldi's Englishman. A ruined boathouse on the shore is where Edward VII is rumoured to have taken part in Bacchanalian revels with Frank Parkyn of Penquite, a china clay magnate, supporting evidence coming from the king's name carved in the stone on the jetty wall.

Cliff Pill has a ford at low water. In 1644, during the Civil War, opposing armies faced each other from opposite ends.

As the railway was built along the edge of the river its embankment cut off some of the existing water, especially at Golant where a narrow enclosed harbour has been formed for small craft able to get under the railway bridge. Large craft have to moor in the estuary. In return, Golant no longer has public transport.

St Sampson's church is late medieval, possibly on the site of a 6th century monastery or the cell of St Sampson. There is a holy well by the porch. Béroul has Iseult hearing mass here. The village has the Fishermans Arms, boatbuilders, a cider press, apples, brambles and bracken and cormorants, herons and egrets.

There is salmon fishing from Penpoll Creek to Mixtow. Bodmin Creek, at the foot of Colvithick Wood with its chestnut trees, was named because it was used by Bodmin merchants. The mills have now become recording studios which are reached by boat.

Moorings in Wiseman's Reach are quiet but that changes after Wiseman's Point. Mixtow Reach has the English China Clay jetties with conveyors loading 1,000t/h, lines of railway wagons alongside and ships to 17,000t, too big for Par. There is often a white dust cloud and the hillside has had to be pinned as it is slipping. Mixtow Pill is too short to get away from the industry and care has to be taken here because of the movement of these large commercial vessels.

Bodinnick has colourwashed cottages, an old chapel and a vehicle ferry, 19th century plans to build a suspension bridge having come to nothing. Ferryside

Interesting architecture on the waterfront at Golant.

Large commercial vessels come to load china clay at Mixtow.

The car ferry crosses from Bodinnick to Fowey.

was the first house in which Daphne Du Maurier lived on her own, when she was 20, originally bought by her Hampstead parents as a holiday house.

In the Middle Ages **Fowey** was one of the most important ports in Britain. It sent 47 ships and 770 Fowey Gallants to help the Siege of Calais in 1346. Raids were made on the French coast in the 14th and 15th centuries by Fowey Gallants, a name which sounds not unlike Golant. Piracy raids were made on Channel shipping in the 15th century, especially by the Mixtow family. The French retaliated with a raid in 1457, burning much of the town, repulsed by Elizabeth Treffry of Place, who ran low on ammunition so she had the lead from the roof melted and poured over the French. Edward IV was forced to bring the piracy under control by confiscating ships from Fowey. The port was not spared the Civil War, a fisherman being killed in 1644 by a gunman who shot at Charles I and missed.

There are many 16th century and Georgian houses. On the front are the Old Quay House Hotel, Galleon Inn and King of Prussia and a museum covers the export of china clay, shipwrights' tools and schooner models. It is one of the finest sailing centres in Britain with Fowey Royal Regatta in August, when a giant pasty plays a significant role.

There is a monument to Q, Sir Arthur Quiller-Couch, who lived by the Esplanade and wrote of Fowey as Troy Town.

St Fimbarrus church is of 14th century origin, built of Polrudden stone with the second highest tower in

The quay at Fowey.

Cornwall, acting as a mark. It has a seascape window in the tower and is where Kenneth Graham was married. He described the town and banks in *The Wind in the Willows* after a trip up to Golant and Q described them in *Memories & Opinions*. Daphne du Maurier lived at Menabilly, to the southwest of Fowey, a house which was central to *The King's General* and *Rebecca*, and she described the *Merry Fortune*'s theft from Fowey in *Frenchman's Creek*. In May there is a ten day Daphne du Maurier Festival of arts and literature.

Polruan, in its sheltered position, is older than Fowey.

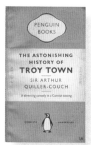

Beyond Pont Pill a passenger ferry crosses to Polruan, Q's Penpoodle, which is probably older than Fowey and had pirates. Slades Yard boatbuilding, now Tom's, was the basis of du Maurier's *The Loving Spirit*. The village is closed to visiting road traffic from 10am to 6pm.

In the 14th century, blockhouses held a chain across the estuary following a Spanish attack, the grooves of the chain still visible in the rocks. The small St Catherine's Castle of 1540 was by Henry VIII but the gun platform below it was used during the Second World War. Beyond the lighthouse on St Catherine's Point is Coombe Haven with a large wheel as wreckage. The Rashleigh mausoleum on the hilltop is probably on the site of St Catherine's chapel.

On the east side of the estuary mouth is Headland Garden, semitropical despite having to survive southwesterly gales. St Saviour's Point has the remains of St Saviour's chapel, which acted as a navigation mark.

In the distance are seen Gribbin Head with its square red and white column mark, Dodman Point and Black Head.

Distance
10km from Lostwithiel to the English Channel

OS 1:50,000 Sheets
200 Newquay & Bodmin
204 Truro & Falmouth

Admiralty Charts
31 Harbours on S Coast of Cornwall. Fowey Harbour (1:6,250). R Fowey – Mixtow to Lostwithiel (1:15,000)
148 Dodman Pt to Looe Bay (1:30,000)
1267 Falmouth to Plymouth (1:75,000)

Tidal Constants
Lostwithiel: HW Dover –0540
Fowey: Dover –0530

Sea Area
Plymouth

Rescue
Inshore lifeboat: Fowey
All weather lifeboat: Fowey

Polruan's blockhouse was linked by chain to another at Fowey to close the estuary.

70 Carrick Roads

England's first port of call

In King Marc's palace at the valley-head
All seemed in happiness: Isolt the Queen
And Marc the King were lovers newly wed;
Brangwen, the maiden, watched them with soft eyes;
Tristan would pluck his harp-strings till they pled
To all hearts there, and April flourisht green.
Men said, 'Our kingdom becomes Paradise'
John Masefield

Carrick Roads and their feeders empty south across Cornwall to Falmouth Bay, all AONB to Heritage Coast. The highest tidal point is at Tresillian on the Tresillian River where it is crossed by the A390. It dries out, to a degree, to leave very soft mud although there are some low tide gravel rapids at first. The drowned coastline is extensively wooded to Feock. The manor of Moresk estate was the largest wooded estate in Cornwall at the time of the *Domesday Book* and part remains of the 12th century poet Béroul's forest of Morais, where Tristan and Iseult hid.

Maltings at Tresillian were supplied by boat and the river was busy with ketches, schooners and barges until the 1930s, handling roadstone, coal and timber, since when the river has silted significantly. There used to be an elegant carriageway on each side, a route still following the east bank to Merther Lane although the west bank has only the A390 until it turns away at Pencalenick, to leave the rest of the estuary largely free of roads.

Posts mark shoals, around which the murky water flows, fish waiting in the shallows. Swans, Muscovy ducks, oystercatchers, egrets, cormorants, shelducks, herring gulls and curlews give a catholic mix of birdlife while the banks have some Michaelmas daisies as well as reeds.

There is access at high water at St Clement although parking is very limited. The slate faced church lychgate has an upper storey which was the school, a church porch with stocks with room for three, astonishing for such a small hamlet, and a churchyard with a Saxon cross.

There is a tumulus on the hillside and lichen on the trees draws attention to the pure air. A 19th century barn is near the site of Moresk Castle, which was destroyed in the 12th century. On top of the hill is Park Farm where 18th century solicitor Charles Warrick invented a hand cranked paddle which he used on a boat to get to Truro, the precursor to paddle steamer paddles.

Malpas, Norman French for treacherous crossing, had an ancient ford. It was mentioned three times by Béroul, including when Iseult returned to her husband, King Mark, at Blanchland, Kea, carried by her lover, Tristan, who was disguised as a leper. It had been prearranged that he would fall so that she could swear that she had never lain with anyone except Mark and the leper. Variations of the story have also been told in Sir Thomas Malory's *Le Morte D'Arthur*, Matthew Arnold's *Tristram & Iseult*, Swinburne's *Tristram of Lyonesse*, Wagner's *Tristan & Isolde*, Arthur Quiller-Couch's *Castle Dor* and John Masefield's *Minnie Maylow's Story*.

Passenger ferries were introduced, operated in the 1800s by Jane Davies, better known as Jenny Mopus. In 1804 she recovered mail stolen from Lord Falmouth and captured the thieves. She had always claimed that it was women and pigs that gave her the most problems.

Malpas had shipbuilding to 180t and caught oysters until these became affected by copper waste. Victoria Point was named after a visit by the Royal Yacht in 1846. Daphne du Maurier spent a night of her honeymoon moored here.

At Malpas Point the Truro River is joined. Calenick Creek is choked with mine spoil but Mopus Reach of the Truro River has extensive moorings and is used by small coasters. There is a heronry.

Below St Michael Penkevil are Parson's Creek and Maggoty Bank, perhaps meaning favourite rather than the larvae. Church Creek is below Old Kea, noted for its Kea plums. St Kea's 15th century church tower ruin with a Norman font is on the site of a 5th century Celtic monastery founded by the Irish St Kea.

The A390 bridge at the Tresillian River's tidal limit.

The hamlet of St Clement on the Tresillian River.

Below Tregothnan a deer park slopes down to an exquisitely sited boathouse just before the Truro River joins the River Fal. The east bank becomes Roseland, ros being Cornish for moor or promontory.

This reach of the river is remarkable for the size and number of merchant ships to 15,000t mothballed here. Tolverne Cottage was used for smuggling. It was requisitioned by the Americans during the Second World War and used for D-Day embarkation, including building a concrete road to the river and a pier two thirds of the way across. Today teas are served at this cottage in which General Eisenhower stayed and where memorabilia is displayed with the American flag flying in the garden. A passenger ferry calls in between Truro and Falmouth. The irony can be the German flag flying on a huge freighter moored in the river directly in front.

Malpas at the end of the Tresillian River.

The Truro River has extensive moorings at first.

Cowlands Creek is a distortion of Kew-nans, ravine, and Lamouth Creek is from valley of pigs. Below a settlement and a fort is Roundwood Quay, built in 350 BC to export tin and copper and able to take a 300t ship, later used for shipbuilding.

King Harry Ferry was named after Henry VI but Henry VIII was claimed to have swum his horse across in order to impress Anne Boleyn. Said to be Britain's loveliest crossing, it was operated by a rowed boat until 1887 and was on the main coastal road from Penzance to London. Today it is a chain guided vehicle ferry. Bark from the surrounding oak coppice was sent to the tannery in Grampound.

The sheltered environment encourages families onto the water.

Trelissik stands in a 10ha garden in 2.4km² of parkland, the 1820s landscaping by Ralph-Allen Daniell for Guinea-a-Minute Gilbert, who made his fortune from tin and copper mining. The gardens are noted for camellias, rhododendrons, photinias, azaleas, magnolias, over 130 species of hydrangea, particularly good spring blossoms, tree ferns, old Cornish varieties in an apple orchard and beeches and oakwood. The house is an 18th century pillared mansion, mentioned in *Poldark*. The Georgian stable block has an art and craft gallery with over 2,000 pieces in the Spode Copeland china collection. The 19th century Old Lodge is in neo Greek style with columns while the Victorian New Lodge of about 1860 has round chimneys. The water tower with its spire is like a lighthouse with a room on each floor.

Channels Creek and Tolcarne Creek precede Turnaware Point, from where many Americans left for D-Day. Between 15 and 40 oyster boats sail from the Turnaware

Bar between the beginning of October and the end of March, the last working sailing fleet in Europe. Most of the northern half of Carrick Roads contains oyster beds in water less than 2m deep at low water and these may only be dredged under sail. Many of the early oyster dredgers were built in Pill Creek where the quay was constructed in 1765 for the mines but this is now obstructed with barriers, chains and private notices.

At Pill Point the River Fal opens out into Carrick Roads, 26km² of clear water with 110km of shoreline. It can be rough, especially with the wind against the tide, but is still a popular venue for regattas. The east side has water skiing, again adding to the chop of this busy estuary with boats of all types going in all directions.

Loe Beach, which exported tin in the 19th century, has a Perpendicular church while Feock has its church with a separate tower.

Waterside buildings below the deer park at Tregothnan.

A number of large commercial vessels are mothballed on the River Fal at Tolverne.

Tolverne Cottage now serves teas in the summer.

King Harry Ferry, claimed to be the country's most scenic.

The spit of Restronguet Point reaches two thirds of the way across Restronguet Creek, resulting in deeper water off Restronguet Passage and Weir Point than further up the Carnon River of which this is the estuary.

Quays by Mylor Pool at the mouth of Mylor Creek were established by the Admiralty in the 19th century, loading stores during the Napoleonic and Crimean Wars and used during the Second World War by the Free French Résistance and by the Americans for fitting out landing craft. Mylor Churchtown used to build warships. The medieval church is sited where St Mylor was said to have been martyred in 411 and has a fine Norman doorway with a serpent and a notable Celtic cross.

A granite pillar on Penarrow Point divides Truro and Falmouth harbours, matched by another on Messack Point. This was a compromise by Queen Anne after Charles II moved the boundary from Black Rock to the confluence of the Fal and the Truro River as punishment for Truro's siding with Parliament in the Civil War.

St Just Creek, which feeds into St Just Pool, has a

boatyard and rooks and was used by Nelson. In the 18th century there were plans for a naval dockyard but St Just in Roseland lost out to Devonport. Plans in the early 20th century for an Atlantic liner terminal failed because of poor road and rail connections. As a result, the church of 1261 remains in one of the most beautiful settings in England. It has a rare double piscina, a Cornish cross, a holy well and a sloping churchyard with a riot of plants, bamboo, Chilean fire bushes, giant rhubarb, subtropical plants, weeping willows, monkey puzzles and palms, the granite headstones with their verses scattered amongst them. One complains that the physicians 'acted wrong'. The lower lychgate has a granite cattle grid. Travel writer H V Morton visited in 1927 and noted the vicarage gate propped open with a couple of cannon balls. It is even said that Christ came here as a boy with tin merchant Joseph of Arimathia.

Beyond a water tower is St Mawes Bank with eelgrass, anemones, molluscs, hermit crabs and the only beds of maerl, calcified seaweed, in southern England, deposits of which have been dredged for fertilizer.

Trefusis Point was the scene of a major disaster, 200 dying when the transport ship *Queen* was wrecked in 1814 after a voyage from Spain. The Penryn River contains the King's Road and the Inner Harbour with naval facilities and an old observatory tower. A new attraction is the National Maritime Museum Cornwall with the National Small Boat Collection and the only underwater tidal zone window in Europe. A major shareholder for the project has been local drummer Roger Taylor of Queen.

Carrick Roads are the world's third largest natural harbour and the first or last port for transatlantic shipping so it was one of the busiest ports outside London. Robin Knox-Johnston completed the first west–east solo nonstop circumnavigation from here in the *Sunday Times* Golden Globe Race, Ellen MacArthur returned here from her record breaking solo circumnavigation and Sean Morley returned here in 2004 after circumnavigating all the inhabited islands in Great Britain and Ireland solo by sea kayak in one season.

A port since Tudor times, **Falmouth** had shipbuilding and was a planned town, although the name did not exist until Charles II decreed it in 1660 for the villages of Penny-Come-Quick and Smithike, issuing a charter the following year. The church of King Charles the Martyr was built in 1665 with 18th century additions and was paid for by Sir Peter Killigrew, one of the family who developed the port. Between 1688 and 1852 Falmouth was the headquarters of up to 40 Post Office packet ships, 200t brigantines sailing to Spain, Portugal, the East and West Indies and North and South America.

Carrick Roads, looking towards Falmouth from Turnaware Point.

Trade was lost to the navy in Devonport and to steam vessels from Southampton after 1851, a monument recording 150 years of the packets. There were also tea clippers and windjammers. In the 1880s there were 25 foreign consuls based here. It has repaired large ships, especially oil tankers. A 1903 dock extension saw one of the earliest uses of encased reinforced concrete piles. The Queen Elizabeth Dock can take vessels to 90,000t.

Falmouth has 18th and 19th century buildings, including the Regency Classic Custom House of 1815, perhaps better known than the Regency Queen's Pipe which was used to burn contraband tobacco. The Greenbank Hotel on the front is where *The Wind in the Willows* was developed. Falmouth Arts Centre features other arts of the region. Falmouth Week takes place in August and there is an oyster festival in October, Falmouth being a fishing port landing oysters, scallops and whitefish. It developed the Falmouth Quay punt with a square transom and deep keel. The railway did not arrive until 1863, by which time the packet ships had already been lost, but there is now also a road train for holidaymakers.

A passenger ferry crosses to **St Mawes**, a fishing village, one of Britain's finest yachting centres and one of the venues claimed to have the warmest climate in Britain. The harbour is on the Percuil River and amongst the early visitors were the Romans, who traded for tin. Sailing and gig racing take place, the oldest gig still racing being *Newquay*, built in St Mawes in 1812 when it was a base for Fal pilots.

The most conspicuous feature, deliberately, on Castle Point is the Tudor St Mawes Castle, small with a central tower and three semicircular bastions. Completed in 1543 for protection against the French, it is the best preserved of Henry VIII's castles. In the Civil War it surrendered to Cromwell's General Fairfax without firing a shot because he attacked from landward and all its guns faced the water. It was expanded up to the Second World War, is now surrounded by rock plants and tropical shrubs and was used as the Breton Fort Baton in filming *Poldark*.

Opposite is a matching castle. Pendennis Castle of 1540 was built on an Iron Age fort site, the last in a line of castles for Henry VIII. The 16th century keep was given a new defence wall round the outside in 1598 for Elizabeth I. It hosted the future Charles II in 1646, the year in which it held out under 70 year old Jack-for-the-King Arundell for five months against Cromwell, being the last mainland garrison except Raglan to surrender. It has a Tudor gundeck, underground magazines, a First World War guardhouse, a half moon big gun battery which was used until 1946 and it still fires a noon gun in July and August. A Tudor blockhouse, the Dennis Fort or Little Dennis, was dismantled in 1654.

Pendennis Point has an aerial, a windsock and a helipad. There were plans for a Fal barrage but the current still flows unhindered at up to 3km/h. At low water the bed of the original river is 34m below the surface.

There has been a mark on Black Rock since the 16th century. A Mr Trefusis of Trefusis rowed his wife out to the rock for a picnic then abandoned her there, a fishing smack picking her off just as the tide covered the rock.

St Anthony Head has a Georgian 19m lighthouse of 1834, used in *Fraggle Rock*. Because of the difficulty of land access it was built from precut granite blocks. Added in 1895 was St Anthony Battery. A dry moat, 150mm Second World War gun battery, officers' quarters, kittiwakes and shags remain.

Beyond Zone Point is Falmouth Bay with Manacle Point in the distance.

St Mawes·Castle on the east side of the entrance.

The blockhouse on Pendennis Point with Pendennis Castle above.

Distance
16km from Tresillian to Falmouth Bay

OS 1:50,000 Sheets
204 Truro
& Falmouth

Admiralty Charts
18 Falmouth Inner Harbour, inc Penryn (1:5,000)
32 Falmouth to Truro (1:12,500). Tresillian R (1:20,000)
154 Approaches to Falmouth (1:35,000)
777 Land's End to Falmouth (1:75,000)
1267 Falmouth to Plymouth (1:75,000)

Tidal Constants
Truro:
HW Dover −0600
St Mawes:
HW Dover −0610,
LW Dover −0550
Falmouth:
Dover −0600

Sea Area
Plymouth

Rescue
Inshore lifeboat:
Falmouth
All weather lifeboat:
Falmouth

Index